Public Administration and Information Technology

Volume 13

Series Editor
Christopher G. Reddick, San Antonio, USA

For further volumes:
http://www.springer.com/series/10796

Bogdan Pătruţ • Monica Pătruţ
Editors

Social Media in Politics

Case Studies on the Political Power of Social Media

Springer

Editors
Bogdan Pătruţ
Monica Pătruţ
Vasile Alecsandri University of Bacau
Bacau
Romania

ISBN 978-3-319-35579-5 ISBN 978-3-319-04666-2 (eBook)
DOI 10.1007/978-3-319-04666-2
Springer Cham Heidelberg New York Dordrecht London

Softcover reprint of the hardcover 1st edition 2014

Printed on acid-free paper

Springer is part of Springer Science+Business Media (www.springer.com)

Foreword

Web Social Media, Politics, and Civism

Ever since O'Reilly used the expression *web 2.0* in a 2005 conference, amplified attention has been paid to it in many aspects of society, organizations, and individuals. First conceptions on Web social media followed the cyber optimism that characterized the studies about the Internet in the 1990s. Studies emphasized the power of the technology and its capacity to overcome physical, economic, political, social, and individual obstacles (Curran et al. 2012).

Web social media have become an integral part of contemporary society and discourse. Arguments stated that they support the human need for social interaction, using Web-based technologies to transform broadcast media monologues (one to many) into social media dialogues (many to many).

There are Web social media solutions to just about every need, and they are designed to be disseminated through social interaction; they were created using highly accessible and scalable publishing techniques. Web social media support a sort of knowledge and information "democratization," transforming people from content consumers into content producers, or "*producers*".

In the digital context, the individuals can be active, and they can produce and manipulate contents in an easy and quick way. Consequently, they stop being dependent on info-communication hierarchy, assuming the control over the contents that interest them. As producers of online contents, the active participants become, consequently, leaders of opinion and creators of noise and buzz, that is, of word of mouth.

The possibility of the user to contribute to web-content development, rate, collaboration, and distribution, as well as to customize Web applications, defines "participative web" and user empowerment. For instance, the effective participation of common Web users gives place to user-generated content (or user-created content), that is, to content made publicly available over the Web, created outside professional routines and practices, using a variable amount of creativity, and shared among Internet users at an increasing speed thanks to broadband availability.

Users that generate content are motivated by factors that include peer interrelation, the pursuit of fame, notoriety, and self-expression. As a consequence, the Web can be seen as an open platform, enriching diversity of opinion and the free flow of information that otherwise would not be available to citizens.

In sum, social media tools can take various forms (more or less sophisticated) and fulfill various needs, which may have existed previously or may not. Nevertheless, the use of the expression "social media" is nowadays associated to Web technology due to its following main characteristics: social media tools are generally available to anyone at little or no cost; they are tools that enable anyone (even private individuals) to publish or access information—audience fragmentation; they have the capability to reach small or large audiences; they are user-friendly, i.e., anyone can operate the means of production; they are real time, i.e., they are capable of virtually instantaneous responses and only the participants determine any delay in response; they exhibit liquidity, i.e., social media can be altered almost instantaneously by comments or editing.

Yet, it is important to stress that the produced content has been for own consumption, since Web social media users have been more keen to create popular culture-oriented and everyday life-oriented content. As such, *producers'* content production has been mostly part of a context of consumption (Jönsson and Örnebring 2011).

Optimism around Web social media must be moderate. Since this optimism surrounds the potential of the technology, dazzling the role played by human beings with motivations, pre-concepts, beliefs, and economic and cultural idiosyncrasies. After all, it is the human prerogative to choose whether to use the technology and to decide how to use it. Additionally, economic access constraints and unequal control of the Internet (e.g., in *less democratic* countries such as Saudi Arabia or China) may undermine the "Technologies of Freedom" conception (Pool 1983).

While being recognized as bringing forth the need to inform about everything with transparency and at the right moment, the Internet primarily contributes to the availability of a number of extended horizontal channels of communication and an immense volume of information, which can be turned into knowledge and lead to enhanced freedom of choice, consequently transforming informed consumers into more demanding patrons. Nevertheless, and as noted by James Curran, the Internet did not give birth to a new economy or to a new kind of politics. The advantaged (large companies and political elites) tend to be the most active, and the imbalance is reproduced in online activism (Curran et al. 2012, pp. 13–14).

As a communication technology, the Internet has also been used in political campaigns to spread messages and contribute to inform and engage voters. However, "the use of digital network technologies to shape public policy is generally met with incredulity by most politicians, public servants, and citizens" (Chadwick 2009, p. 12). Public interest in politics can be limited (political disaffection) and the online realm can be envisaged as a place to "have fun" and "to pass the time" (Curran et al. 2012, p. 14).

The relation between Web and Politics has been studied by several authors, to name a few: Wilhelm (2000), Norris (2001), Bennett and Entman (2001), Lax

(2004), Shane (2004), Hindman (2007), Dahlgren (2007, 2009, 2013), Mossberger et al. (2008), Coleman and Blumler (2009) who tried to state the importance and limitations of these instruments to deepen the relation between citizens and political actors.

The main concerns of the researchers were citizens' information, their participation and engagement in political life and debate, and the communication between political actors and citizens. While in early researches, some optimism could be found and the Web was presented as a tool that would motivate and deepen the relationship between citizens and politicians, later ones focused attention upon the loss of control over information, the lack of citizens' interest in general politics, and the remaining inequalities of access (to Web and to political information).

Nevertheless, and according to Phillips and Young (2009), success in politics is now highly influenced by the online activities of political institutions. On this platform, they can exchange views on the latest political developments or hot topics, inviting the public and citizens to comment and adhere to their political programs (Phillips and Young 2009, p. 88). As a potential way of escaping the "top-down" politics of mass democracy in which political parties make policies with low-level participation or citizens' involvement, the Web provides means for high differentiation of political information and ideas and (at least) theoretical possibilities of participation and high level of involvement in negotiations and feedback between leaders and followers. However, a significant limitation to this online involvement is the lack of interest of the electors (Lax 2004, p. 226). Even if they have access to Internet, that does not mean that they will spend time engaging in political debate, because most people simply do not bother.

As a whole, it is our belief that the Internet has not fundamentally changed the nature of political action (Hindman 2008). It only provides tools that empower people to have a more direct, constant, and personal participation in the formal political process—if they want to. Besides, as Nielsen (2010) also realized, "mundane Internet tools" (such as *Facebook*, *Twitter*, and *e-mail*) are more deeply integrated into mobilizing practices in political campaigns than emerging and specialized ones, since its ubiquity attests to their importance.

In the same vein of Web social media and politics, the academia has also been paying attention to the use of social media in civic engagement and grassroots movements. All over the world, social media have served as platform for spreading word for riots organization, agency, and participation, sometimes with large consequences in the political and social life of countries (e.g., Arab Spring, Occupy Wall Street, and Anonymous). Traditional media give voice to these movements, but the kick-off steps and their activity are continuous and organized on Web social media. Following Curran's thoughts, "the Internet is a very effective mode of communication between activists," linking them together, facilitating interaction, and mobilizing them to a place in a short notice (Curran et al. 2012, pp. 14–15).

Still, and like in political engagement, inequalities can be pointed regarding levels of participation and involvement (Shirky 2008) in social movements. In Portugal, for example, Sebastião and Elias (2012) have realized that young people adhere to *slacktivism*, preferring to press the *like* button to any other action (share, subscribe, production, offline participation) on *Facebook* involving civic practices (political or social protest, solidarity, online petitioning).

The interaction between technology and society is complex, and the latter exerts a greater influence on the former than the other way around. After all, technology is a tool created by man to help him live in society. Consequently, when researching Web social media, the cultural and the human are elements that cannot be undermined.

It is undeniable, though, that the Internet, and particularly, Web social media, have energized and strengthened activism, allowing activists to group together by providing channels of communication and tools for quick exchange of ideas, group creation, and protest assemblies arrangements. Moreover, this is catching conventional media's, academia's, and politicians' attention: but does the technology strengthen it enough to secure real change in democracy?

Social Media in Politics intends to shed light on this question presenting chapters with original research about the use of social media in political campaigns, electoral marketing, riots, and social revolution. By giving voice to research cases from Belgium, Czech Republic, Egypt, India, Indonesia, Israel, Italy, Romania, Slovenia, South Africa, Turkey, and the USA, it presents a significant contribution for a global understanding of how cultural settings and the human factor influence the use of technology in political and civic domains.

With this purpose in mind, the book is structured into three parts. The first part is an introductory one that explores some issues regarding the politics and social media connection, as well as some methodological models. Andrea Calderaro, from the European University Institute, sustains that contextual factors must be taken into consideration in explaining the unequal use of the Internet in politics. His study focuses on the unequal presence of political parties online across the political systems of 190 countries. In the second chapter, Leocadia Díaz Romero (University of Murcia) introduces contemporary social movements and their Web use in their activities, especially the importance of the Web in civic engagement. This chapter also explores the possible creation of a global civic society and the complementary use of traditional and new media for activism.

The characterization and theoretical approach to social movements are developed in the third chapter, with examples from nine countries provided by Amaro La Rosa, from the Universidad Femenina del Sagrado Corazón (Lima).

In Chap. 4, Bogdan Pătruţ and Ioan-Lucian Popa explain the use of graph theory for political discourse analysis with the assistance of the *Political Analyst* software. This technique is particularly helpful if we consider the importance of political speech and its effect in public engagement and political interest. The identification of shared and distinct values in political discourse may be crucial to understand the influence of politics in one's life.

The first part ends with a chapter about the use of *Twitter* in the Italian political election of 2013. Guido Di Fraia and Maria Carlotta Missaglia (Università IULM, Milano) have tried to understand the concrete use of the new media and how politicians actually manage them by analyzing a sample of 41 Italian politicians from the main electoral lists.

The second part presents how social media can be used in electoral marketing at three levels: local elections, general/parliamentary elections, and presidential elections. This is the most extensive part of this volume due to the need to empathize differences from cultures and countries, such as Belgium (Evelien D'heer, Ghent University), Indonesia (Nyarwi Ahmad, Bournemouth University and Universitas Gadjah Mada Yogyakarta & Ioan-Lucian Popa, Vasile Alecsandri University of Bacau, Romania), Italy (Francesca Musiani, Georgetown University and MINES ParisTech), Slovenia (Tomaž Deželan, Igor Vobič, and Alem Maksuti, University of Ljubljana), Turkey (Günseli Bayraktutan, Mutlu Binark, Tuğrul Çomu, Burak Doğu, Gözde Đslamoğlu, and Aslı Telli Aydemir), the USA (Porismita Borah, Washington State University), the Czech Republic (Václav Štětka, Alena Macková and Marta Fialová), and Romania (Monica Pătruţ, Vasile Alecsandri University of Bacău), and also to understand if there are variances in the use of social media at local and national political levels. The political institutions may have common-ground principles, but their organization and actors, and their proximity with voters, are determinant to the ways in which social media are used, and the studies presented in this part are critical for the understanding of *Twitter* and *Facebook* usage differences and obstacles.

Finally, the third part debates the use of social media in mobilizing people for riots and revolutions. Examples from Egypt (Joanna Kulesza, University of Lodz), Turkey (Kamil Demirhan, Hacettepe University), South Africa (Admire Mare, Rhodes University), Israel (David Levin and Sigal Barak-Brandes, Media School, The College of Management), and India (Dr. Swati Bute, AMITY University) are presented and analyzed. In spite of the focus on social media use in civic participation, studies in this part also emphasize ethical concerns, censorship, and human rights violations. Thus, in the final chapter, David Mathew (University of Bedfordshire) presents social media as cyber tools and virtual weapons focusing the similarities of the effects of psychoanalysis and the more insidious traits of social media use in politics and activism.

Lisbon, Portugal Sónia Pedro Sebastião

References

Bennett, W. L., & Entman, R. M. (Eds.). (2001). *Mediated politics. Communication in the future of democracy*. New York: Cambridge University Press.

Chadwick, A. (2006). *Internet politics: States, citizens, and new communication technologies*. Oxford: Oxford University Press.

Chadwick, A. (2009). Web 2.0: New challenges for the study of E-Democracy in an era of informational exuberance. *I/S: A Journal of Law and Policy for the Information Society*, *5*(1), 10–41.

Coleman, S., & Blumler, J. G. (2009). *The internet and democratic citizenship: Theory, practice and policy*. New York: Cambridge University Press.

Curran, J., Fenton, N., & Freedman, D. (2012). *Misunderstanding the internet*. London/New York: Routledge.
Dahlgren, P. (Ed.). (2007). *Young citizens and new media: Learning for democratic participation*. New York: Routledge.
Dahlgren, P. (2009). *Media and political engagement. Citizens, communication and democracy*. New York: Cambridge University Press.
Dahlgren, P. (2013). *The political web: Online civic cultures and participation*. Basingstoke: Palgrave Macmillan.
Hindman, M. (2008). *The myth of digital democracy*. Princeton, NJ: Princeton University Press.
Jönsson, A. M., & Örnebring, H. (2011). User generated content ant the news: Empowered citizens or interactive illusion? *Journalism Practice*, *5*(2), 127–144.
Khang, H., Ki, E.-J., & Ye, L. (2012). Social media research in Advertising, communication, marketing, and public relations, 1997–2010. *Journalism and Mass Communication Quaterly*, *89*(2), 279–298.
Lax, S. (2004). The internet and democracy. In D. Gauntlett, & R. Horsley (Eds.), *Web studies* (2 ed., pp. 217–229). London: Arnold Publications.
Mossberger, K., Tolbert, C. J., & McNeal, R. S. (2008). *Digital citizenship: The internet, society, and participation*. Cambridge: MIT Press.
Nielsen, R. K. (2010). Mundane internet tools, mobilizing practices, and the coproduction of citizenship in political campaigns. *New Media and Society*, *13*(5), 755–771.
Norris, P. (2001). *Digital divide. Civic engagement, information poverty, and the internet worldwide*. New York: Cambridge University Press.
Phillips, D., & Young, P. (2009). *Online public relations: A practical guide to developing an online strategy in the world of social media*. London: Kogan Page.
Pool, I. d. (1983). *Technologies of freedom: On free speech in an electronic age*. Cambridge, MA: Harvard University Press.
Sebastião, S. P., & Elias, A. C. (2012). O ativismo like: As redes sociais e a mobilização de causas. *Sociedade e Cultura Revista de Pesquisas e Debates em Ciências Sociais*, *15*(1), 61–70.
Shane, P. (Ed.). (2004). *Democracy online: The prospects for political renewal through the internet*. New York: Routledge.
Shirky, C. (2008). *Here comes everybody: The power of organizing without organization*. Westminster: Penguin Press, HC.
Wilhelm, A. G. (2000). *Democracy in the digital age: Challenges to political life in cyberspace*. New York: Routledge.

Preface

The book will try to answer questions such as the following:

- Is there a relation between social media and politics?
- How can politicians use social media for their electoral marketing?
- How can social networks be used in order to mobilize people for riots or for a social revolution in a country?

Thus, the book is structured into three parts. The first part is an introductory one, where some issues regarding the politics and social media connection are dealt with. An example of an Italian political election is considered. Another chapter deals with the use of graph theory techniques to develop software and tools for politicians in order to improve their online campaigns.

Part II presents how social media can be used in electoral marketing. This part is structured into three parts that correspond to the level of the elections: local elections, general/parliamentary elections, and presidential elections.

In fact, these chapters will discuss how Twitter, Facebook, or blogging can be used in electoral campaigns.

For example, a chapter will focus on the use of Twitter during the 2012 local elections in Belgium. Another chapter deals with the use of social media in Indonesia, with a case study concerning the 2012 gubernatorial elections of the Special Region of Jakarta.

The examples of social media used in general elections are from Italy (2013), Slovenia (2011), and Turkey (2011). For example, the participation and success of Movimento 5 Stelle in the 2013 Italian parliamentary elections is presented.

The last section of Part II presents different aspects of social media usage in presidential elections. Two chapters discuss Facebook use in the 2012 United States presidential campaign, and another chapter details the use of social media as a means for a virtual referendum.

Part III debates the usage of Twitter and other Web 2.0 tools in mobilizing people for different riots or revolutions: a chapter is about the recent riots in Istanbul and other chapter talks about different protests in South Africa and other countries in the region.

One chapter in this part focuses on social media censorship vs. state responsibility for human rights violations, with a case study on Egypt.

Another chapter presents Gabriel Tarde's model and online protests in the eyes of Jewish-Israeli teenage girls. The last chapter presents the role of social media in four cases of mobilization via social media in India.

The book is addressed to Ph.D. candidates, researchers in social media and in political science, researchers in applied mathematics, politicians, candidates for local elections, and specialists in political marketing.

Bacau, Romania

Monica Pătruţ
Bogdan Pătruţ

Contents

Acknowledgments

We would like to thank all the authors of this book for their innovative contribution. In addition, we wish to express our special gratitude to our collaborators, namely:

- Gabriela Grosseck (West University of Timisoara), Carmen Holotescu ("Politehnica" University of Timisoara), and Virgil Stoica ("Alexandru Ioan Cuza" University of Iasi), for their thorough scientific review of the entire manuscript.
- Ioan-Lucian Popa ("Vasile Alecsandri" University of Bacau) and Nadia-Nicoleta Morăraşu ("Vasile Alecsandri" University of Bacau), for their accurate linguistic assistance and professionalism in proofreading the manuscript.
- Barbara Fess (Springer), Sylvia Schneider (Springer) and Venkatachalam Anand (SPI Global), for supporting our endeavour from the initial idea to the final product, providing us constructive moral and technical advice.

Part I
The Political Power of Social Media

Chapter 1
Internet Politics Beyond the Digital Divide

A Comparative Perspective on Political Parties Online Across Political Systems

Andrea Calderaro

Abstract The Digital Divide has been considered key to understanding the relation between Internet and politics. However, today the use of the Internet is following a normalization trend and new country contextual factors must be taken into consideration in explaining the unequal use of the Internet in politics. This study focuses on the unequal presence of political parties online across political systems. By combining multiple sources, this study explores the relation between the unequal online presence of political parties in 190 countries, and country-contextual factors, including level of Digital Divide, and economic and democratic indicators. Here, the empirical findings resize the relation of causality between the Digital Divide and the use of the Internet for politics. They highlight that democratic status, among various other country-contextual specificities, is the strongest contextual factor in determining the unequal use of the Internet in politics for political parties.

Keywords Internet and international politics • Digital divide • Democracy • Comparativism in internet studies • Political systems

1.1 Introduction

Since the advent of the Internet, great attention has been paid on how political parties would benefit from being present on the Internet. Gibson and Ward (2009) identify three main lines of research in the field: first, the intra-party arena, referring to the use of the Internet by political parties to facilitate communication amongst its members; second, the inter-party arena, referring to how political parties use the Internet to compete with each other in campaigning; and third, the systemic-arena, referring to how political parties reorganise themselves so as to seize the new

A. Calderaro (✉)
European University Institute, Via dei Roccettini, 9, Fiesole Firenze 50013, Italy
e-mail: Andrea.Calderaro@EUI.eu

B. Pătruţ and M. Pătruţ (eds.), *Social Media in Politics*, Public Administration and Information Technology 13, DOI 10.1007/978-3-319-04666-2_1,

opportunities offered by the Internet. However, research in the field neglects a comparative analysis of the use of the Internet from political parties across countries and political systems. This was justified by global inequalities in using the internet. However, the fact that today the Internet is far more used, allows us to extend our analysis and attempt a worldwide comparative analysis.

Here, I address this issue by first exploring the worldwide distribution of political parties on the World Wide Web. Second, I explore whether their unequal distribution may be explained by the Digital Divide and by other local conditions, such as the democratic and economic status of each country.

1.2 Virtual Political Parties

Scholars have paid attention to how the Internet might facilitate better communication between politicians and citizens. In contrast with this expectation however, research has noted that Internet remains mainly used as a one-way flow of information: from politicians to the public (Johson 2003; Levin 2003; Ward et al. 2003). In this way, the Internet has been employed just like a traditional media (Castells and Sey 2004). Coleman (2005) has also questioned the quality of the information, arguing that in some cases while it may be good quality it is not easily accessible. Scholars also argued that the Internet would have a positive impact on mobilizing voters, though we are yet to have empirical evidence on this (Castells and Sey 2004). Ward et al. (2003) point out that in the UK only 38 % of political party web sites offer visitors the opportunity to become members online. In the opinion of other scholars, politicians do not make the most of the Internet to interact with citizens (Ward et al. 2003; Levin 2003). Ward et al. (2003) highlight that less than a third of UK political parties websites allow interactions. Even when politicians try to interact with citizens by opening forums, the experiments are questionable (Ward et al. 2003).

All this initial research in the field brought us to conclude that the general enthusiasm on the Internet as a useful tool for politicians, political parties and political campaigns, has not yet been founded with evidence of more inclusive and participatory politics. So far, research concludes that the websites of official political parties have not provided the opportunities expected of the Internet.

At the same time, today, more recent research on other aspects of the Internet provides host of counter arguments. The advent of the Web 2.0, for instance, has been lauded as a great opportunity to energize political participation by enabling easy interaction between political parties and voters. This is also confirmed in those cases when websites provide political opportunities, such as those designed with social network tools. Evidence can be found in the case of the last American Presidential election. By framing the concept of "cyber party", Margetts (2006) explores how ICTs offer the opportunity to expand political parties at the grass roots level. Thanks to Web 2.0 tools, political parties may encourage the direct involvement of people in their activities, such as in contributing to parties' campaigns with money, signing petitions, or even participating in consultations on policy issues.

To summarize, Chadwick (2006) singles out three key-points of the debate about how the use of the Internet may influence the political party landscape:

Internet increases (1) party competition. Marginalized new parties and non-party political movements may benefit from the Internet to raise their visibility. In many cases, minor political groups suffer from being small. With the Internet as a cheap medium, as well as more accessible than other communication technologies, they can compete with richer parties at a similar level of visibility. The Internet allows minor political parties to reach potential supporters similarly to main parties. The effect of this situation is an increase of pluralism, enabling citizens to better identify with specific claims motivating their political engagement. This may have the consequence of increasing voter turnout. Older media, such as the printed press and the television, still have great power in providing information and making advertising campaigns. However, their form of communication is not as rich and fragmented, as is that of the Internet. The Internet allows the spreading of larger amounts of information permitting people to examine political issues according to their own interest and needs. They are better able to form their own opinions, and thus are more likely to take part in political debates. The democratization of the Internet for making and receiving information is more likely to have an impact in a general framework of democracy.

Still according to Chadwick (2006), the Internet may also (2) diffuse power among citizens, increasing grassroots control over political leaders and candidates. The network structure of the Internet facilitates continued relations between candidates and their supporters who have then more power in controlling their leaders. This interaction can help politicians refine their political programs responding to the demands and expectations of supporters expressed with the Internet. At the same time, parties are able to coordinate their supporters more easily and quickly to mobilize them for instance in key moments of campaigning and fundraising. This is more likely to motivate people to be politically engaged and support their candidates more actively.

In spite of these new trends, Chadwick (2006) identifies the third key-point, also summarized by Morris (1999) in his normalization thesis, and defined by a few others (Davis 1999; Margolis and Resnick 2000; Resnick 1998), as (3) institutional adaptations. This argues that, in shifting the form of doing politics to the Internet, political institutions regulate the Internet's innovative potentials by reproducing the same trends as in off-line politics. While during the 1990s the Internet was the space hosting a proliferation of political websites whose visibility was not linked to the wealth of politics, today conditions have changed. Larger political parties and their candidates are now able to make their Internet communication techniques more effective. More incisive websites and talented staff are likely to work for the wealthiest political parties. They will also have better resources to increase their ability to converge media strategies, integrating television and Internet campaigns into one online and off-line form of communication. Party competition risks being weakened by this, where the Internet is reduced to merely another space in which the already existing political inequalities in off-line politics are perpetuated.

Beyond party competition and the electoral landscape, parties also use the Internet for internal purposes. Analysis in this regard focuses mainly on how the Internet facilitates communication and coordination among local branches and headquarters, and in-groups. Scholars interested in the use of the Internet by political parties started their earliest research focusing on the use of the Internet for internal purposes. Smith and Webster had already highlighted in 1995 that the three main UK political parties were using ICTs to develop their internal communication since the early 1980s (Smith and Webster 1995). Ward et al. (2003) also confirmed this scenario in a later research on the UK party landscape. However, despite this early interest in the topic, scholars developed a limited scope of research. Empirical findings confirm that political parties use the Internet to develop internal communication with emails and the WWW. But, scholars also argue that this use is limited. Critics point out that the Internet has been used mainly to facilitate coordination among elites, rather than connection with members (Gibson and Ward 2009). According to Gibson and Ward (2009), we may expect that the spreading of Web 2.0 tools may change this scenario, though further research needs to be conducted to test this.

Today, it is still difficult to conclude that politicians and political parties make the most of the Internet. It is also difficult to generalize findings on how political parties use the Internet. The use of the Internet is fragmented and we are still experimenting how to include the Internet in political processes. In some cases, the Internet changes faster than our capacity to provide empirical findings on its effects. However, in the framework of the network society, the question is not only how political parties use the Internet, but rather whether they do at all. Given that using the Internet for campaigning is increasingly common especially in Western liberal democracies, political parties that are not on the WWW risk being excluded from political competition. In other words, the Internet could improve pluralistic competition if those parties with less resource could learn to use the Internet as effectively as their more well-off counterparts. The opposite scenario, of not being online, could be fatal to these poorer parties. Hence, a digital political parties divide, at least in Western liberal democracies, could have a serious impact on the wealth of party competition.

The question that now remains open here is: what can explain the unequal presences of political parties online worldwide? Is the Digital Divide determinant to describe the use of the Internet by political parties? In the relation between Internet and politics, how does the political scenario influence the unequal use of the Internet?

Here, I address these questions by, first, mapping the worldwide distribution of political parties online. Second, I explore the reasons for their unequal presence on the Internet.

1.3 Mapping Political Parties Online

So far, most of research on the presence of political parties on the WWW has been focused on the national level. Attention has been paid to the use of the WWW by political parties in the USA (Druckman et al. 2009), and, in Europe such as, for instance, in the UK (Gibson et al. 2005), and in Italy (Vaccari 2008). However, research in this field lacks a cross-national perspective of analysis. As I said earlier, we rely on only a few examples in the literature. With this study, I explore the distribution of political parties on the Internet from a worldwide perspective. I compare the presence of political parties online from 190 countries. I then contextualize the use by political parties of the WWW, by relating their presence online with the level of Digital Divide, economic and political factors.

In most cases, analysis at the national level explores whether and how political parties are online, by investigating the instruments that political parties include on their web pages. From a comparative perspective of analysis, Howard's (2010) study is pioneering in exploring the quality and the purpose of political parties' websites across Islamic countries. However, the study that I conduct here includes more than 3,000 political parties from 190 countries worldwide. The great size of these comparative data does not allow us to enrich this exploration with data on the quality and the efficiency of websites. Future research should address qualitatively the global characteristics of websites. In this study, we are however interested in exploring the unequal presence of political parties online and its causes.

1.3.1 European Political Parties on the WWW

One of the first comparative studies on political parties online was run at the European level by Trechsel et al. (2003). Here, authors compared the presence of parliaments and political parties online across all 25 European member countries. The authors included in their analysis only those political parties that had more than 3 % of seats at the election of the European Parliament in 1999. The report explored a total of 144 political parties.

Given that political parties included in the analysis gained a relevant amount of seats in the parliament, all political parties explored in the report were relevant in their countries of origin. The report does not focus then on whether political parties are online. Rather, the research question was clustered around how political parties use their websites. In order to address this investigation, the authors created an index aggregating six evaluating indicators: information provision, bilateral interactivity, multilateral activity, user-friendliness, presence of networking tools, and political parties' mobilisation potential.

Empirical findings highlighted a significant variation of the use of websites from political parties across European countries. However, in most of the European countries, political parties did not use forms or other tools to interact with website visitors. Trechsel et al. (2003) concluded that political parties used websites mainly to circulate information about their activities and claims, as a mono-directional channel of communication. The authors also explored the causes of the variation in use of the Internet. Empirical findings led authors to reject the hypothesis that the Digital Divide and economic factors are determinant. Neither the nature of the party system and the colour of political parties affect the quality of websites. The report found no relations of causality to explain the variation in the use of the WWW by political parties across European countries. However, the analysis is updated to 2003 and refers to European countries with very similar political systems. We must expect that a different scenario rise by extending our analysis to the global level. This will allow us to compare political parties across different political systems and checking whether and how political parties behaviour online differ accordingly.

1.3.2 Worldwide Perspective of Political Parties on the WWW

Norris (2001) conducted one of the first analyses on political parties online from a worldwide perspective. By using data updated to June 2000, the author highlighted that North America was the continent with the highest amount of political parties online. These were about 41 parties per country. The United States was the country with most political parties online (67 parties online). In Western European countries, an average of 24 political parties were online. In South America, the Middle East, and Africa, less than 5 political parties had a website. By comparing these data with those referring to the unequal distribution of internet users, Norris (2001) highlighted that the distribution of political parties online by countries is similar to the map of the Digital Divide. Political parties were more online in countries with a low level of Digital Divide. However, even if it appeared that the unequal distribution of political parties on the WWW followed the same worldwide inequalities in accessing the Internet, Norris (2001) also noted that there were too many exceptional cases providing a different picture. Further explanations were then required. By comparing the trend of the distribution of political parties online with other data, she confirmed that the Digital Divide was the strongest predictor to explain the unequal distribution of political parties online, though the economic and democratic status of each country also played a role in this regard. Political parties were 18 times more likely to have a website in richer countries than in poorer ones, and they were six times more likely to be online in countries with established democracies than in autocratic regimes.[1] Norris (2001) concluded that established democracies were more likely to have political parties online. In autocratic countries, where the political landscape is characterized by a one-party

[1] Norris defines democratic and autocratic regimes according to the level of democratization measured by the Freedom House Rate (1999).

regime, party competition is restricted and hence the proliferation of political parties online seriously hampered.

Norris's analysis (2001) refers to a scenario quite different from today's scenario. Ten years ago, the Internet was a new tool in most of the countries worldwide. The Digital Divide was at its first stages of normalization, and its size was determinant for the use of the Internet in all fields, including its use in the political domain. Conclusions provided by Norris (2001) about the impact of the Digital Divide on the distribution of political parties online matched with the arguments largely debated in this field at the time. These argue that the Digital Divide is the most determinant obstacle to influence politics via the Internet. However, here I criticize this conclusion, arguing that given the new scenario in which the Internet is more accessible, we have to look at other explanations. According to updated data (Internet World Stats 2011), today the size of the Digital Divide has changed. By following a normalization trend, the Digital Divide in terms of distribution of internet users is narrower compared to that of 10 years ago. Despite the continued serious concentration of owners of Internet domain names in a few countries, it has become easier to open a website today, thanks to the rapid spread of know-how. I then expect that the Digital Divide plays a minor role in explaining the unequal distribution of political parties online pictured below. Rather, I argue that the unequal distribution of parties online is determined by other national factors. In the domain of politics, I argue that political factors play a more relevant explanatory role. I expect that the distribution of political parties online is determined more by the democratic status of countries, rather than the Digital Divide and economic factors.

In order to test this expectation, I first map the worldwide distribution of political parties online today. I then explore how this data is understood in relation to the Digital Divide, and to the political and economic status of each country.

1.4 The Study

1.4.1 Methodological Framework

1.4.1.1 Digital Political Parties

The World Internet Access Report (WIA Report)[2] provides data on the unequal distribution of political parties on the WWW. In this study, I use data from 2008. The WIA Report's research team uses the CIA World Fact Book to collect the list of political parties from each country. The WIA Report then crosschecks the list with information available on Wikipedia. In order to discover how many of these

[2] http://www.wiareport.org.

political parties are online, the WIA Report uses the search engine Google. By combining these sources, the WIA report's research team checks the presence of each political party on the WWW.

WIA Report's research team includes in its dataset political parties that propose candidates for elections. It also defines "joke parties" as political parties that do not take part in elections. However, in the case of countries where political parties are illegal, the WIA Report also includes political parties without a proper party institution in the data set, referred to as "joke parties".[3] In countries with autocratic regimes, "joke parties" are then included in the dataset. The WIA Report's research team points out that in countries with weak democracy, party competition is also weak. "Joke parties" may then play an important role of expressing dissidence, thereby participating in the political debate of the country (Howard 2010).

Data are also categorized according to the "development status" of the country. In the WIA report, each country is labelled as "developed" or "developing" according to the categorization made by the CIA World Fact Book, which includes market-oriented economies of states members of the Organization for the Economic and Commerce Development (OECD). Just like for the United Nations Statistical Office, the designations "developed" and "developing" are intended here purely for "statistical convenience"[4] and do not express a "judgement about the stage reached by a particular country or area in the development process".[5]

1.4.1.2 Explaining the Causes

Once the unequal distribution of political parties on the WWW worldwide has been explored, I investigate the causes of this unequal distribution by running a multivariate regression. The ratio between online and offline political parties is the dependent variable here. I use as independent variables: the Digital Divide indicator (Internet Users), the economic status (PPP GDP xCapita), and the democratic indicator (Polity IV). By running a multivariate regression of Political Parties on the WWW on Internet Users, Democracy, and Economy, I then explore how these country contextual specificities determine the presence of political parties online.

1.4.1.3 Digital Divide

Before measuring the Digital Divide in reference to the distribution of internet users, we must first clarify what an internet user is. There is no agreement on this point. Various agencies have their own definitions. The International Telecommu-

[3] www.wiareport.org/index.php/57/political-parties-online-in-the-muslim-world.

[4] unstats.un.org/unsd/methods/m49/m49.htm.

[5] *Ibidem.*

nications Union (ITU),[6] for instance, defines as internet user someone above 2 years of age who accesses the Internet at least once every 30 days. The US Department of Commerce,[7] meanwhile, defines an internet user anyone above 3 years of age "currently using" the Internet. For this study, I look to the Internet World Stats[8] for both my definition of internet user and as a main source of data. Internet World Stats considers an internet user "anyone currently in capacity to use the Internet" (Internet World Stats 2010). With this definition, Internet World Stats includes in their statistics a person who has both privately or publicly available access to an Internet connection point, and who, at the same time, has a basic knowledge of the use of the Internet. Referring to this definition, in countries where there is a broad use of public Internet points, such as public libraries or Internet cafés, data include internet users who share the same internet connection. This implies that, in these cases, the number of internet users is bigger than internet access subscribers and telephone lines available in each country. Internet World Stats gathers data by combining two main sources: the International Telecommunications Union (ITU) and Nielsen/NetRatings.[9] The first is an international organization focusing on telecommunications. Today it is part of the United Nations (UN). Nielsen/NetRatings is a private company measuring Internet audience via surveys (Internet World Stats 2010).

1.4.1.4 Economic

Thus far, I have argued how the Global Divide is related to existing economic inequalities. In order to test this expectation I explore whether any relationship exists between the distribution of the Internet population worldwide and the economic factors facing each country. I use the Purchasing Power Parity Gross Domestic Product per capita (PPP GDP xCapita) to represent economic factors. The United Nations Development Programme (UNDP)[10] publishes these data annually in the Human Development Report (HDR).[11] I use data published in 2007. I place this data in relation to the population of online Internet users. This regression demonstrates whether access to information technologies is still related to economic factors.

[6] http://www.itu.int.

[7] http://www.commerce.gov.

[8] http://www.internetworldstats.org.

[9] http://www.nielsen-netratings.com.

[10] http://www.undp.org.

[11] hdr.undp.org.

1.4.1.5 Political

Given my focus on the relation of Internet and politics, I explore whether political factors also affect the distribution of the population accessing the Internet worldwide. The Polity IV Project[12] provides data on the political status of each country. In the political science framework, this is currently considered the most accurate data set for measuring political aspects worldwide (Treier and Jackman 2008). I use the indicator POLITY as my reference for the democratic condition of the countries compared in this study. This measures the democratic status within a range from −10, as the most autocratic state, to 10, as the most democratic state. This index is calculated from the combination of several indicators: (a) competitiveness of the selection process of the countries' chief executive, (b) the openness of this selection process, (c) to what extent the system of rules enables control by the chief executive's decision-making authority, (d) how competitive political participation is, and (e) to what extent rules govern political participation.

1.4.2 Digital Political Parties Divide

The map below (Fig. 1.1) shows the relationship between the total number of political parties for each country, and the total amount of parties with a website. The Web Party Penetration (WPP) is the indicator here. We calculate this by normalizing the number of political parties online with the total amount of political parties in each country. The map below shows the WPP for each country.

Figure 1.1 shows that in 20[13] countries all political parties (100 %) have a website. Italy follows, where 97 % of political parties are on the WWW, and Greece with 95 %. In contrast, in 22[14] countries no political party is present online.

1.4.3 Political Parties on the WWW: Over the Time

I already mentioned that scholars commonly highlight that the Internet plays an important role in increasing competition among parties. Yet, the Internet has also evolved, potentially increasing its impact. If all of these considerations are true, I expect that, today, compared with data a decade old, the number of political parties

[12] http://www.cidcm.umd.edu/polity.

[13] These are: Switzerland, United States, Canada, Japan, Denmark, Norway, Slovenja, Hungary, Belgium, Cyprus, Finland, Ireland, Luxembourg, Maldives, Malta, Saudi Arabia, Barbados, Equador, Colombia.

[14] These are: Azerbaijan, Brunei Darussalam, Burkina Faso, Central Africa, Comoros, Congo, Ghana, Indonesia, Iran, Kazakhstan, Kiribati, Korea North, Laos, Niger, Oman, Papua New Guinea, Qatar, Samoa, Solomon Island, Swaziland, Turkmenistan, United Arab Emirates.

Fig. 1.1 Percentage of worldwide political parties on the WWW. Ratio of *online/total, %*. (*Source*: *WIA Report, University of Washington, January 2008*)

on the WWW should have increased as dramatically as the use and development of the Internet.

The graph above (Fig. 1.2) provides a snapshot of the trend on the presence of political parties on the WWW over 7 years. It shows that, from 2000 to 2007, there has been a significant increase of political parties on the WWW. Looking at the "development status" category, we see a serious difference between "developed" and "developing" countries. The graph shows that political parties in "developing" countries are more likely to be online. However, the WIA Report (2008) points out that this is likely to be improved over time. It is important to highlight that many improvements have been introduced in collecting these data since 2005. In the past, "joke political parties" were included in the data set. In 2007, the WIA Report research team decided to include into its analysis only political parties that propose candidates for elections. "Joke parties" are then excluded by this last analysis. However, this decision did not affect countries where political parties are illegal. In these cases, the WIA Report research team decided to keep including "joke parties" in the data set.

Finally, we are able to test the expectations proposed at the beginning of this study: does the Digital Divide affect the unequal presence of political parties online? Alternatively, are other contextual factors such as the political and economic status of a country more important?

1.4.4 Causes

I ran a multivariate regression in order to address this question. The presence of political parties worldwide on the WWW (Web Parties on the Web) is the dependent variable here. I use the Digital Divide indicator for 2007 (amount of Internet Users), democratic indicator (Polity IV), and economic status (PPP GDPxCapita). I

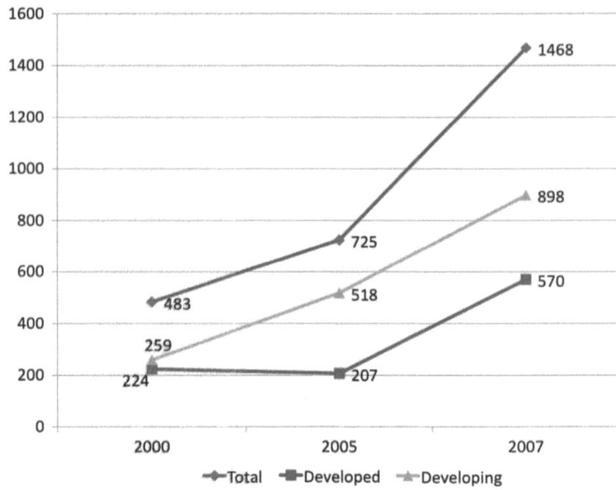

Fig. 1.2 Timeline worldwide perspective of political parties on the WWW, $N = 190$. (*Source*: *WIA Report 2008, University of Washington, January 2008*)

do not use the normalized values of internet users (Internet Penetration Rate—IPR) because this is already correlated to the value of the democratic status of the country. By including this variable in the regression, we would violate the exogeneity assumption typical of standard regression analysis.

The resulting regression (Table 1.1) provides interesting evidence with resulting estimates that are highly significant. The amount of the Internet population, political, and economic factors combined explain 36 % of the variation in the worldwide presence on the Internet of political parties. An F test of joint significance indicates that the model has strong explanatory power compared to an intercept-only model. The model also shows that the level of the Digital Divide, measured with the amount of internet users per country, is less significant than other indicators.[15]

The coefficient estimates (B) imply that the variation of 1 unit in Polity IV, measuring the Level of Democracy, implies a change of almost 1 percentage point (0.96) in Political Parties on the WWW. Increasing the number of Internet Users by one million raises the percentage of Parties on the WWW by 0.156. Increasing PPP GDP xCapita by 1,000 dollars, which is roughly the difference in PPP GDP xCapita of a country leads to a change of 0.001 percentage points in Political Parties on the WWW.

In conclusion, the direct effect of democratic status on the presence of political parties on the WWW is stronger than the direct effect of the dimension of the Digital Divide measured by the number of internet users. However, the Digital Divide is, in turn, strongly affected by democratic and political variables. The evidence clearly shows that democratic and economic conditions are the most important determinants of the use of the Internet for political purposes by political parties.

[15] I tested for multilinearity correlation among the independent variables. None of them is correlated beyond the 0.5.

Table 1.1 OLS regression of political parties online on internet users, democracy, and economy

	Political parties online (ratio)
Internet users (× million)	0.156*
	(0.093)
Level of democracy (polity)	0.965**
	(0.355)
Economy	0.001***
(PPP GDP xCapita)	(0.000)
Constant	27.67
	(3.049)
N	190
R-squared	0.365

***$p < 0.01$; ** $p < 0.05$; *$p < 0.1$ (one-tailed test)—Standard errors in parentheses

Source: Internet Users (Internet World Stats, November 2007); PPP GDP xCapita (UNDP, 2007); Polity (Polity IV Project, 2007)

1.5 Conclusion

This study explored the unequal presence of political parties on the Internet across countries. I have, first, explored how politics may benefit from the use of the Internet in the framework of party competition. I have also highlighted that research in this field still lacks a comparative perspective. Despite the difficulty of measuring how political parties use the WWW in over 190 countries, I pointed out that, given the increased centrality of the Internet in the framework of politics, the unequal presence of political parties on the WWW may reduce the plurality of the political landscape of a country. This is why, in the second part of this study, I explored the unequal distribution of political parties on the WWW worldwide. I have then investigated in which country contextual factors, such as the level of the Digital Divide, the economic and the democratic status, are more significant for explaining how political parties are unequally present online worldwide.

Empirical findings led us to conclude that the Digital Divide is not the most determining factor explaining the unequal presence of political parties online. By running a regression on the ratio of political parties on the WWW and those off-line, on national conditions such as the level of the Digital Divide, and the economic and the democratic status, I provided empirical evidence in this regard. As I expected, all contextual specificities influence the use of the Internet by political parties. However, the Digital Divide is the least significant factor. Economic and democratic factors in each country matter more from the unequal presence of political parties online. This empirical evidence led us to conclude that political parties use the Internet mainly depending on the political framework in which they are active.

A high level of democracy implies a political life characterized by party pluralism and political competition. This last is one of the variables measured by the Polity IV index. Within this framework, being online for political parties is important for competing in party competition systems. This helps us understand why, in countries with high levels of democracy, political parties are more likely to be online. A low level of democracy implies a limited role of party competition in national political life, making parties less likely to be active in campaigning online.

To conclude, the use of the Internet is spreading across countries and diverse political systems. We must not expect that the Internet will be equally used to practice politics across countries. Rather, the use of the Internet to practice politics adapts to the context in which it is used. This is why we must extend our research in the field by further addressing comparative approaches, and including other contextual factors in our analysis. This study shows that the use of the Internet for political parties is determined more by the specificities of country's political systems, than by conventional understandings of the Digital Divide.

Acknowledgment Special thanks go to the World Information Access Project for the data on online political parties here explored.

References

Castells, M., & Sey, A. (2004). The internet and the political process. In M. Castells (Ed.), *The network society: A cross-cultural perspective* (pp. 363–381). Northampton, MA: Edward Elgar Publication.

Chadwick, A. (2006). *Internet politics: States, citizens, and new communication technologies.* New York, NY: Oxford University Press.

Coleman, S. (2005). New mediation and direct representation: Reconceptualizing representation in the digital age. *New Media Society, 7*(2), 177–198.

Davis, R. (1999). *The web of politics: The internet's impact on the American political system.* Oxford: Oxford University Press.

Druckman, J. N., Kifer, M. J., & Parking, M. (2009). Campaign communications in U.S. congressional elections. *American Political Science Review, 103*(03), 343–366.

Gibson, R. K., Lusoli, W., & Ward, S. J. (2005). Online participation in the UK: Testing a "contextualised" model of internet effects. *British Journal of Politics & International Relations, 7*, 561–583.

Gibson, R. K., & Ward, S. J. (2009). Parties in the digital age—a review. *Representation, 45*(1), 87.

Howard, P. N. (2010). *The digital origins of dictatorship and democracy: Information technology and political Islam.* New York, NY: Oxford University Press.

Internet World Stats (2011). Internet usage statistics. The internet big picture. Available at: http://www.internetworldstats.com/stats.htm. Accessed Nov 10 2011

Johson, D. G. (2003). Reflections on campaign politics, the internet and ethics. In *The civic web: Online politics on democratic values.* Lanham, MD: Rowman and Littlefield.

Levin, P., (2003). On line campaigning and the public interest. In *The civic web: Online politics on democratic values* (pp. 47–62). Lanham, MD: Rowman and Littlefield.

Margetts, H. (2006). The cyber party. In R. S. Katz & W. Crotty (Eds.), *Handbook of party politics* (pp. 528–535). London: Sage.

Margolis, M., & Resnick, D. (2000). *Politics as usual: The cyberspace 'revolution'.* Thousand Oak, CA: Sage.

Morris, D. (1999). *Vote.com: How big-money lobbyists and the media are losing their influence.* Los Angeles, CA: Renaissance Books.

Norris, P. (2001). *Digital divide: Civic engagement, information poverty, and the internet world-wide*. New York, NY: Cambridge University Press.
Resnick, D. (1998). Politics on the internet: The normalization of cyberspace. In C. Toulouse & T. W. Luke (Eds.), *The politics of cyberspace: A new political science reader*. New York, NY: Routledge.
Smith, C. F. & Webster, C., (1995). Information technology in political parties. In political studies association annual conference. University of York.
Trechsel, A. H. et al. (2003). Evaluation of the use of new technologies in order to facilitate democracy in Europe, W.P., STOA 116 EN.
Treier, S., & Jackman, S. (2008). Democracy as a latent variable. *American Journal of Political Science, 52*(1), 201–217.
Vaccari, C. (2008). Research note: Italian Parties' websites in the 2006 elections. *European Journal of Communication, 23*(1), 69–77.
Ward, S. J., Gibson, R. K., & Lusoli, W. (2003). Online participation and mobilisation in Britain: Hype, hope and reality. *Parliament Affairs, 56*(4), 652–668.

Chapter 2
On the Web and Contemporary Social Movements

An Introduction

Leocadia Díaz Romero

Abstract The environmental movement in the 1990s marks the beginning of a new era for civic engagement. In the aftermath of the financial crisis, revolts opposing austerity measures and cuts on social policies offer the current version of civic action. Social movements have evolved towards global action or global activism. We witness the trans-nationalization of activist networks. Using information and communication technologies as basic tools, social movements have promoted cooperation, found supporters and organized demonstrations and protests worldwide. New technologies—the Internet, mobile phones and tablets—have showed its capacity to strengthen civic society and consolidate democracy around the world. Scholars have described new forms of democracy rooted in citizen participation (deliberative democracy, associative democracy), also enhanced with online mechanisms. Civic engagement and activism have adapted to virtual societies, maximizing their organizational linkages and networking skills. They represent these emerging participatory channels and have contributed to shaping contemporary forms of political participation.

Keywords Civic engagement • Contemporary social movements • Online activism • Participatory democracy • Virtual public sphere • Hybrid media system

2.1 Mobilization in the Digital Age

New technologies—Internet, mobile phones, tablets—have the capacity to strengthen civic society and consolidate democracy around the world. Civic engagement and activism have adapted to virtual societies maximizing their

L.D. Romero (✉)
University of Murcia, Espinardo, Murcia, Spain

Columbia University, New York, NY, USA
e-mail: leocadia.diaz@um.es

B. Pătruţ and M. Pătruţ (eds.), *Social Media in Politics*, Public Administration and Information Technology 13, DOI 10.1007/978-3-319-04666-2_2,

organizational linkages and networking skills in an attempt, on the one hand, to consolidate democracy in Western civilization; on the other hand, to promote transition processes in autocratic systems.

One of the most innovative effects of digital, transnational activism has been the revitalization of direct, global democracy, which is now closely related to the subject of e-democracy. Rheingold (2002), Grossman (1996) and Negroponte (1996) anticipated a future landscape of citizens engaged in politics through online activities.

Definitely, the interactive capacities of new technologies have enhanced citizen participation and deliberation creating a sort of *virtual agora* or *digital public sphere* where digital citizens discuss worldwide issues of mutual interest. In this discursive space, public opinion is formed and exerts influence on political action.

This introductory chapter aspires to provide with some sort of reasoning and analysis on the way activism has evolved in the last decades, the role new technologies are playing at this respect, the controversial side of IT, the emergence of new forms of democracy associated with citizen participation, consociationalism, and deliberation. These preliminary lines will help the reader get the most of the empirical analysis and particular observation of transnational protest and global activism which comes right after.

Once this has been said, our first reflection deals with Global Activism in the digital age. What is Global or Transnational Activism?

The notion of Global Activism is an intrinsic feature and effect of a globalized world and can evoke two main ideas. On the one hand, it can allude to the rise of social movements and protests which have taken place in different countries and even continents in the last decade, and recently after the austerity measures leading to the financial crisis. On the other hand, it can refer to activists coordinated action—on many occasions through information and communication technologies—which determines events taking place, sometimes simultaneously, around the world, pursuing the same cause.

In order to comprehend this concept, it is convenient to elucidate what the *digital revolution* is, as Global Activism is strongly associated with digital tools and with new media.

The *digital revolution* has generally been referred to as the *third industrial revolution* and implies the change from analog mechanical and electronic technology to digital technology, which has occurred since the 1980s throughout to present day. The *digital revolution* is both a manifestation and result of the emergence of information, communication technologies and, thus, inaugurates the *information age*. This revolution entails mass production and widespread use of digital logic circuits, and its derived technologies– i.e., the computer, digital cellular phone, fax machine. The important technological, social, economic and political consequences brought about explain its revolution-like nature. The *information society* represents the natural environment of this phenomenon.

The term *information society* became popular in 1980 through the work of Japanese sociologist Yoneji Masuda, *The Information Society as Post-Industrial*

Society. Masuda recalls on the notion of *post-industrial society*, which had been previously coined by Alain Touraine.

As continuation of the industrial society, in the *post-industrial society* information is a decisive factor of economic activity. Certainly, the *pre-industrial society* depends essentially on commodities; the *industrial society* is organized around the use of energy to produce goods; in the *post-industrial society* information—the creation, distribution, use, integration and manipulation—and information technology (IT) are the key elements of the productivity model. Therefore, technologies of information and communication represent the catalyst forces, which have pushed forward and enabled changes in politics, in the structure of society and in work organization. Moreover, people's capacity to get to know global events and react instantaneously through online communication has transformed the international society in a *global village* (McLuhan 1962). This "revolution" has marked a new age: the *information age*.

Together with the expression post-industrial society, the information society is frequently compared or identified with the following concepts: post-fordism, super-industrial society, post-modern society, knowledge society, Information Revolution, Liquid modernity, digital society or network society, among others.

On the whole, new technologies are not only a typical feature of the information society, but also a necessary condition or prerequisite for this society to exist and evolve. Nevertheless, their nature is not "democratic" as information and communication technologies have become another element of stratification among people and countries (the *digital divide*).

Finally, the use of information and communication technologies and strategies has played a major role in political participation, civic engagement, and governance processes in this new century. As a matter of fact, contemporary trends on democracy study the use of CIT to enhance citizen participation in democratic processes: E-democracy, E-governance, online politics (Bannister and Connolly 2012).

2.2 Contemporary Activism

Global activism finds its roots in traditional forms of protest and social movements. The elements, which are new and define the quintessence of contemporary activism, are the complex organization together with the implementation of information and communication strategies (Bennett: in Cyberactivism 2004). It seems convenient to examine its origins and initial forms of action in order to grasp the way it has evolved.

2.2.1 Traditional Activism. Origins and Evolution

It has originally crystallized in the *classic* manifestations of political participation: voting, party affiliation and associations. At this respect, Verba, Nie and Kim qualify voting, campaigning, community organizations and individual outreach activities, as basic forms of political participation. The Pew Charitable Trusts (2006) exemplifies the various forms civic engagement can take: individual volunteerism, organizational involvement, electoral participation, efforts to directly address an issue, work with others in a community, solve a problem, and interact with the institutions of representative democracy.

Traditional activism has evolved throughout history and expressed through demonstrations, consumer boycotts, signing petitions. Protest and mobilization are "later" forms of civic compromise. The literature of the early years drew a clear distinction between conventional modes of political participation and protest. The most recent form of this evolutionary transforming process is digital activism or global or transnational activism.

2.2.1.1 Protest and Social Movements

A protest group is by definition collective action of individuals aimed at achieving a set of common goals through influencing the decisions of a target. A social movement is a form of protest group that has, on the one hand, some degree of formal organization; on the other hand, a higher number of members. As a result, the more members a protest group has, the closest it gets to the concept of social movement (Opp 2009). Scholars maintain that most definitions of social movement contain the following elements: the goals or objectives to accomplish, the organizational dimension, a degree of temporal continuity, development of institutional activity—"lobbying", political and extra institutional, i.e., demonstrations (Snow and Oliver 1995).

A rigorous study of social protests, such as petitions, demonstrations, consumer-boycotts, highlights the sharp significance they attained in the 1980s and how nowadays they represent an important mechanism of political mobilization. Barnes and Kaase describe five criteria to identify protest activism: signing petitions, attending legal demonstrations, exercise the right to go on strike and occupy factories or buildings (Barnes and Kaase 1979).

Pacific protest has been widely accepted as a form of political expression aiming at reforming laws, influencing political processes, revisiting patterns of social behavior. We can find its roots in Ghandi's philosophy and testimony, or in the American Civil Rights Movement (1950–1970).

In post-industrial societies, protests occur not only among students and younger generations, but also reach middle-aged segments of population—professional people with a university degree.

2.2.2 Activism in the Twenty-First Century

The environmental movement in the 1990s marks the start of a new era for civic engagement. It was associated with mass demonstrations and protests coinciding with the summits or *fora* where world leaders discussed, negotiated, and reached agreements on "green" issues. We can bring into account global protests and demonstrations against the World Trade Organization ministerial meeting in Seattle (1999), or similar actions denouncing the war in Iraq.

More recently, the "Arab Spring", "Indignados" in Madrid, "Occupy Wall Street" in New York and the U.S.A., "Movimento Cinque Stelle" in Italy and other revolts opposing austerity measures and cuts on social policies, offer the current version of civic action.

Although each of these movements responds to particular causes and presents distinct features, some common, unifying elements can be distinguished.

First of all, most of these groups are convinced that global corporations and transnational economic regimes have eluded government policies and regulations concerning labor, environment, human rights, etc., shaping a political stage, beyond normal legislative, electoral, and regulatory processes, that Beck (2000) calls sub-politics.

Moreover, they all use New Technologies, the Internet, in various ways to achieve goals. The formulas *digital politics*, *Internet politics* and *digital activism* express this trend, which exemplifies in electronic voting, digital campaigns, chat-rooms, or virtual mobilization through Facebook and Twitter (i.e.: hence the name Twitter Revolutions).

Certainly, the new tools of social media have reinvented social activism (Gladwell 2010). In his Foreword to "*Cyberprotest: New Media, Citizens and Social Movements*", Peter Daulgren reveals the key aspect of digital activism when he alludes to the implications that ICTs, information and communication technologies, have for various forms of social movements in the twenty-first century (Daulgren: in Joyce 2010).

As a matter of fact, the Internet reduces organizational and coordination costs (Pickerill 2003). Not only digital tools benefit newer, resource-poor organizations; but also older, more conventional, better-funded political organizations. For the former, the Internet amplifies and reduces the cost of pre-existing communication routine; for the latter, the Internet presence is powerful (Norris 2001). This sort of "equalizing" or "balancing" character of the Internet among different type of organizations is of great concern.

New studies remark how the use of ICTs by activists or less formal actors has multiplied its influence and impact on political parties (Grofman, Trechsel and Franklin 2014).

Considering activism in a wide sense, the formula **digital activism** refers to contemporary forms of political participation strongly anchored in tools and mechanisms provided by the Internet—new social media. While traditional forms of civic engagement have lost force, new modes of participation have emerged and flowered since the 1970s. Public concern for the environment and subsequent action in favor are good examples of this new wave of social movements, transnational policy networks, Internet, or digital activism. In short, civic compromise is not dead. It has transformed itself in terms of the *who*—the agents or collective organizations, *what*—the range of strategies implemented and *where*—the focused targets or goals (Inglehart 1977).

Digital Activism converges with Global activism when opponents around the globe share a common goal and coordinate themselves in order to achieve it using Internet dynamics (Arquilla and Ronfeldt 2001; Gerlach 2001; Lichbach and Almeida 2001; Rheingold 2002). The "Internet dynamics" amplify and economize communication in political organizations (Agre 2002).

In an effort to summarize some of the features of activism in the twenty-first century, the scale or dimension of transnational activism is global and to a great deal the goal, too. It presents as well networked complexity, openness to diverse political identities, and capacity to sacrifice ideological integration for pragmatic political gain (Bennett 2003a, b). Finally, the Internet, social networks are indispensable to accomplish mutual targets, considering that members or supporters of these social movements might find themselves on different continents. For example, in terms of time and tactics, when they convoke protests simultaneously around the world.

2.3 The Other Side of Transnational Activism

Since the beginning of the chapter, the potential benefits of new technologies for political participation in its various forms have been outlined. Nonetheless, among scholars, there are some who reason out "the average positive effect is small in size" (Boulianne 2009). Therefore, certain drawbacks have been identified and we need to reflect on them to draw conclusions and form a whole picture of the question.

What does networked complexity mean? I take the formula used by Bennett to cast light on the challenges related to new technologies in comparison with traditional forms of activism.

Thus, it is necessary to explore the nature of the links created by virtual tools among Internet users. This issue directly appeals to the character of digital culture: it deals with affection, emotion, feeling, in and off the cyberspace. The central concern is to what extent the personal bonds that have emerged, developed and have been conveyed through the net can result in effective activism.

Certainly, new media facilitate activism and even in a more diverse, rich way allowing for all sorts of individual choices. At this respect, Wellman describes "networked individualism" as the ease of establishing personal links that enable people to join more diverse and more numerous political communities than they would ordinarily join in the material world (Wellman 2000).

However, platforms such as Facebook and Twitter, based on connections with people who have rarely met in person, are said to generate **weak ties**. Although some scholars stress the cohesive powers of weak ties (Granovetter 1973), some others argue that social networks' linkages are not likely to result in high-risk activism (Gladwell) by themselves without being completed with traditional activism.

What's more, some unavoidable consequences of weak ties have to do with the fact that this sort of online, loosely linked structures lack hierarchy, ideology, is weak too and decision-making procedures vague or unclear. All in all, hierarchy, ideology and decision-making are said to be indispensable elements for high-risk activism.

In addition, it has been pointed out that web-activism or Internet politics have little likelihood to reach the apathetic or uninterested. They exercise influence among those already engaged in political affairs in the same way traditional forms of political communication—newspapers, radio, TV-do.

Finally, it is convenient to keep in mind that new media are not available to all citizens (digital divide), which would make online mechanisms fully ineffective for this category of the population.

All in all, I recall Bauman's brilliant line of reasoning on liquid modernity and on the frailty of human bonds as a metaphor to depict the fragile nature of digital ties and the "liquid" affection originated. I doubt that online tools can be effective by themselves without conventional ways of mobilization. At this point of my research, the use of new technologies of information and communication has had great impact, but together with classic activism. The potential these channels have for social change will work out to complement and enhance traditional forms of civic engagement.

2.4 A Virtual Public Sphere: A Global Civic Society?

What are the digital tools relevant to activists? These tools are essentially computers and mobile phones. Computers enable to connect to all Internet applications. On the contrary, simple mobile phones allow only texting and calling. Yet, the eruption of smart phones and tablets has enlarged the potential and capacity of mobile phones making them more similar to computers and, thus, vital for social change (Joyce 2010).

Joss Hands emphasizes on mobile devices. He shows the importance of "speed" –of communication, decision-making, and tactical shifts—in the context of mobilization and direct action. In this respect, he recognizes that the introduction of mobile communications –either a simple mobile phone, a more sophisticated 'smart-phone', or other networked mobile computing devices—has had a major impact for the faster coordination and organization of this kind of activities, which he describes as 'mobilezation'.

Regarding the notion of public sphere, the key elements, according to the classic configuration, are the existence of communicative spaces in society where ideas circulate, debate is generated, and public opinion is formed. The communicative actors who exchange views and have discussion are citizens and power holders. Mass media, and now new media, are essential to the creation and development of any public sphere, physical and virtual. The publics, which integrate this sphere, participate in discursive interactional processes (Habermas, Dewey). Thus, “dialogical” interaction among individuals is the central feature. Certainly, the situation where people are exposed to media but do not engage in talks or dialog with each other cannot result in a public sphere. Yet, the media are as well ineludible, as the discursive processes occur through them: citizens have an encounter with the media and interpret reality, reflect about the issues presented; then, they interact with others –in person and/or online, in small or larger conversations or chats.

The theory of the public sphere refines and adds complexity when it is described as digital, virtual, considering the role played by the Internet in the dialogical processes. Moreover, scholars have referred to multiple public spheres, to counter public spheres (cf. Fenton and Downey 2003; Asen and Brouwer 2001) and even to a global civic society. To sum up, there is not a single public sphere, but multiple spaces for political debate. And citizens from all over the world can shape these public spaces.

The discursive processes originating in and nurturing the public space are necessary to deliberative democracy. In other words, deliberative democracy cannot start out without the reality of a public space, where today converge old and new media. Yet the communicative spaces do not entail or guarantee democracy *per se*. As a matter of fact, the discussion, the debate, the exchange of arguments, views and reasons should result in ulterior, subsequent actions taken by the power holders. If there is a gap, deliberative processes are not effective and citizen participation in public issues—participatory democracy—fails (Bennett and Entman 2001).

Indeed, digital technologies offer new forms of horizontal and vertical communication that promote civic engagement and deliberative democracy (Norris 2001). Internet has meant a revolution for democracy as well, due to its global dimension and its immediate effects in real time. Certainly, the “web” offers unexpected opportunities in the areas of information, communication, and political mobilization around the globe, in addition to the well-known electronic voting. Moreover, Internet dynamics are ideal for new social movements that have used this tool to publicize ideas and proposals, to gather supporters around the world, or to galvanize transnational strategies by establishing virtual forums open to all who wish to back up such actions. Through the network, people can become member of pressure groups, join organizations, contribute with funds, receive emails about political issues and make proposals to the authorities, intervene in “online” discussions, circulate electronic petitions, pass on announcements or activities, call for demonstrations.

Castells supports the same line of reasoning in his second volume of the *Information Age Trilogy: the Power of Identity*. He examines the role of social movements and resistance in the network society and chooses the Zapatistas to this purpose, defining them as ‘the first informational guerilla movement’. Castells comes to the conclusion that the use of new technologies—the Internet—allowed the Zapatistas to diffuse information throughout the world instantly, and to develop a network of support groups whose efforts crystallized in a movement of international public opinion.

Not only digital technologies have facilitated mobilization, but they have also stimulated citizen support to global associations. This current trend has gone parallel with the relative fading of party identification and membership (Tarrow 2005).

A global civic society engaged in global causes is taking shape (Keane 2003). This global civic society operates in a virtual public sphere and generates the international public opinion Castell describes. The strengthening of the "public sphere" or civic sphere in these new dimensions—both *cyber* and global—is necessarily related to mass media and new technologies, which foster connections, sharing views, exchanging ideas, arguing and discussion among world citizens.

To sum up, new media contribute to the creation of a *global civic society*, which operates in a *virtual public sphere* or *virtual agora*. Citizen deliberation—expressed through digital tools and social networks—has "enlarged" the 'habermasian' notion of public space. The public sphere is now global and not necessarily limited to the physicality of a space. It can also occur virtually: either based on micro media (e-mail lists) or on middle media Internet channels (blogs, organization sites, e-zines). Some authors stress the capacity of the Internet to create new forms of democratic public spheres and, what's more, to support the already existing ones (Buchstein 1997).

2.5 The "Hybrid Media System"

The world of Politics—political communication, campaigning, mobilization—has gone through major changes as new media have emerged. In an attempt to describe the current state of the media system, we observe 'interactions between old media and new media, and their associated technologies, genres, norms, behaviors and organizations'. This is a "hybrid media system" based upon the principles of adaptation and interdependence among actors (Chadwick 2011). The hybrid media system mirrors a new system of communication integrated by traditional media and new media. The impact this system can have on democracy and civic engagement has increased as new media enhance and expand the potential of conventional media.

Global activism fortifies democratic participation and civic engagement and benefits from this hybrid media system. In a similar line of argumentation, digital activism inserts itself in this dual, hybrid context and profits from it: firstly, because the use of Internet tools and new technologies is inherent to digital activism; secondly, because of the parallel interaction between traditional (old) activism and digital (new) activism.

To sum up, digital activism fortifies democratic participation and civic engagement. It results in greater achievements when it operates on a complementary basis with traditional activism. In other words, the virtual mechanisms facilitate mobilization of individuals but do not drive social change (Keck and Sikkink 1998). The real or physical mobilization—not just online—is needed to promote that end. For instance, the ten thousands protesters that took to the streets in Moldova in the spring of 2009 were brought together through Twitter.

In short, we advocate for this holistic perspective—of new forms and tools together with conventional ones—when approaching democracy, participation and civic engagement in the twenty-first century.

2.6 Representation in Question. The Shift from Government to Governance

Representative democracy has repeatedly been identified with the notion of democracy itself. The essence of representation resides in the celebration of regular, free, fair elections where political parties compete to be in office. The legitimacy of the system is, thus, grounded on parties and elections.

In Western countries, scholars have observed a certain erosion of the representative model: not of democracy itself but of the functioning of representative institutions. Representation has not supervised, restrained and controlled the government effectively (Hirst 2009). This trend does not apply to transitional regimes: they undergo a different path and revolutions have occurred to establish regimes based on electoral democracy, e.g., "the Arab Spring".

Paying special attention to Western countries, the financial crisis that broke out in 2008 and the austerity measures introduced have raised a wave of protests and disenchantment among citizens all over Europe. They are concerned and fear the disintegration of the welfare State, and alert on the increasing poverty income limit.

The current, growing state of disaffection and distrust among citizens has more to do with the poor performance of particular representatives than with a crisis of the representative model. There is a huge "distance" separating the elected from their electors. The latter feel that once the former win the elections, they behave as an elite, as an oligarchy, and do not really pay attention to citizens views, and are not even interested in citizens to be involved in the political process.

Some scholars suggest the convenience to revive political parties while others emphasize the importance acquired by discursive, collaborative processes among citizens and representatives via platforms, networks and associations (deliberative democracy, associative democracy). Deliberative democracy and associative democracy do not intend to replace representative government. On the contrary, they complement and amplify representation with the revitalization of civil society, which takes on a leading role in negotiated governance dynamics, either through deliberative, dialogical processes or consociational practices.

Deliberative democracy presupposes citizens deeply involved in public decision-making and problem solving. Through the implementation of particular techniques and mechanisms, citizens get together to discuss public issues and eventually come to some conclusions or recommendations on what lines of actions should be taken. It is convenient to emphasize that the key actors in this model are not politicians or experts, but the citizens who work actively with the municipalities or other governmental institutions to create synergies to face issues of common interest. Organizations such as the National Coalition for Dialogue and Deliberation (NCDD) and the Canadian Community for Dialogue and Deliberation (C2D2) are good examples of today deliberative practices. Their followers and supporters have grown exponentially in recent years.

According to Carcasson and Sprain, the core principles of deliberation are tough choices, public judgment, democratic governance, inclusiveness and equality. These two scholars also distinguish the particular roles for each actor. Beyond the classic mission of taxpayers, consumers, constituents, or voters, citizens are now vitally involved in public affairs. The government must promote tools for public participation and ultimately nurture citizens' deliberative capacities. The media and the experts assume great responsibilities in engaging citizens and encourage high quality of public discussion.

Regarding **associative democracy**, we need to refer to Paul Hirst and his book *Associative Democracy: New Forms of Economic and Social Governance*, which is rooted in Émile Durkheim's (1957) conception of democracy. Hirst (1994) proposes new theories and formulas to reorganize economic and social governance in Western societies, as liberal democratic capitalism and collectivistic state socialism seemed to have come to a point of stagnation. Hirst denounces that modern representative democracies offer low levels of government accountability to citizens and of public influence on decision-making. He then advocates for the adoption of a new model of democracy, associative democracy, to address these problems. Associative democracy requires (1) devolution of functions of the state to society (except public funding); and (2) democratization of organizations in civil society. The result would be constitutionally ordered democratically self-governing associations, which would receive public funds proportionate to membership and, thus, provide for services like education or healthcare. On the whole, consociational practices would pave the way for the "post-political thrust" from government (control by the state) to governance (regulation, accountability, civil society involvement), which Hirst points out.

To some extent, Hirst's 'doctrine' is encapsulated in the notion of 'big society' elaborated by the UK Conservative Party in its 2010 general election manifesto. The substance of this notion, or the way this big society is formed, lies in taking power away from politicians and attributing it to local people and communities (e.g.: localism and devolution). The transfer of power takes place at the domestic level—e.g., domestic policies. In an article published in 2012 by *The Guardian*, Anne Power, professor of Social Policy at LSE, admits the complementary functions developed by both the state and the civil society and states the convenience to balance the power of each. Prof. Power remarks that the current financial crisis and the austerity measures implemented have had a negative effect for community infrastructures. She finally stresses the leading figure of the citizens and the need as well for intergovernmental cooperation to face transnational challenges.

2.7 Sum Up

New technologies—Internet, mobile phones, tablets—have the capacity to strengthen civic society and consolidate democracy around the world. In postindustrial societies, significant institutions of representative democracy –parliaments, political parties, Government departments—have established web sites where they outline their goals and tasks, put official documents, release updates and announcements. These web pages enhance government transparency and accountability. Regarding political parties, online instruments have contributed to fundraising, to improve management and organization, to diffuse ideas or publicize electoral programs.

Campaigning and voting have substantially benefitted from the whole potential of digital technologies. Indeed, the development of social media and digital marketing strategies in the 2008 Barack Obama campaign has transformed the classic mechanisms of political communication. In the recent 2012 presidential election, both candidates—Barack Obama and Mitt Romney—have laid special emphasis on *cyber* politics.

Electronic voting technology has been improved and become rather popular in the last decade. As a result, countries such as the United Kingdom, Estonia, and Switzerland have implemented this voting system in governmental elections and referenda. E-voting has also been used in Canada municipal elections and primary elections in the United States and France.

In transitional regimes, digital tools have had a gigantic influence in the promotion of democratic change. The use of Twitter in the coordination of different revolutions and protests has resulted in the locution *Twitter Revolution* (Morozov 2011). At this respect, it is convenient to mention civil opposition against fraudulent voting in Moldova (2009), Iranian election protests (2009–2010), and the dissolution of authoritarian regimes in Tunisia (2010–2011) and Egypt (2011).

Activism is evolving towards global action or global activism. We witness to the trans-nationalization of activist networks. Inspired by altruistic solidarity, social movements have promoted cooperation, found supporters and organized demonstrations and protests worldwide. In the aftermath of the financial crisis, thousands of people have gathered against austerity measures and social injustice—from Toronto, New York, Madrid, Athens, Lisbon, London, etc.

Finally, new media and communication technologies, coexisting with traditional ones in a dual arena, have enhanced collective action, nurturing as well deliberation and discursive methods of decision-making (virtual public spheres). The hybrid media system will invigorate political participation, through both representative and participatory channels, and will contribute to the gradual formation of a global civic society engaged in mutual challenges and concerns. Direct democracy is not going to replace representative government, but supplement and extend representation turning representative government into richer representative governance where the presence of civil society will be remarkable.

On the whole, the potential of civic engagement—global activism, e-democracy and again their controversial side—remains largely to be explored and developed throughout the new millennium.

References

General References

Barron, S. (2003). *Technoromantisme*. Paris: L' Harmattan.

Bennett, W. L. (1998). "The Uncivic culture: communication, identity, and the rise of lifestyle politics". Ithiel de Sola Pool Lecture, American Political Science Association, published in P. S. *Political Science and Politics, 31*(4), 41–61.

Carcasson, M., & Sprain, L. (2010). Key aspects of the deliberative democracy movement. *Public Sector Digest.*

Castells, M. (1996). *The information age: Economy, society and culture* (The rise of the network society, Vol. 1). Oxford: Blackwell.

Castells, M. (2004). *The power of identity*. Oxford: Blackwell.

Clough, J. (2012). *Principles of cybercrime*. Cambridge: Cambridge University Press.

Daulgreen, P. (2004). *Cyber protest: New media*. Routledge, NY: Citizens and Social Movements.

Declaration of Principles. (2003, December 12). *World Summit on the Information Society*. Geneva.

Della Porta, D., & Tarrow, S. G. (2005). *Transnational protest and global activism. People, passions, and power*. Lanham, MD: Rowman & Littlefield.

Gerbaudo, P. (2012). *Tweets and the streets: Social media and contemporary activism*. London: Pluto Press.

Hands, J. (2010). *@ is for activism: Dissent, resistance and rebellion in a digital culture*. London: Pluto Press.

Hobsbawm, E. (1973). *The age of revolution: Europe 1789–1848*. London: Weidenfeld & Nicolson. ISBN 0-349-10484-0.

Hoppit, J. (2011). The nation, the state, and the first industrial revolution. *Journal of British Studies, 50*(2), 307–331.

Karatzogianni, A., & Kuntsman, A. (2012). *Digital cultures and the politics of emotion: Feelings, affect and technological change*. London: Palgrave Macmillan.

Karpf, D. (2012). *The MoveOn effect: The unexpected transformation of American political advocacy* (Oxford studies in digital politics). New York, NY: Oxford University Press.

Lucas, R. E. (2002). *Lectures on economic growth* (pp. 109–110). Cambridge, MA: Harvard University Press. ISBN 978-0-674-01601-9.

Macintosh, A., & Coleman, S. (2003). *Promise and problems of e-democracy: Challenges of online citizen engagement*. Paris: OECD.

Masuda, Y. (1980). *The information society as post-industrial society*. Bethesda, MD: World Future Society.

McHale, J. (2004). *Communicating for change*. Lanham, MD: Rowman and Littlefield.

Norden, L. (2006). *The machinery of democracy: Voting system security, accessibility, usability and cost*. New York, NY: The Brennan Center for Justice.

Power, A. (2012, September 13). Is the big society the answer to neighborhood problems? *The Guardian.*

Reitan, R. (2007). *Global activism*. New York, NY: Routledge.

Touraine, A. (1971). *The post-industrial society*. New York, NY: Random House.

Verba, S., Nie, N., & Kim, J. (1978). *Participation and political equality: A seven-nation comparison*. New York, NY: Cambridge University Press.
Wellman, B., Salaff, J., Dimitrova, D., Garton, L., Gulia, M., & Haythornthwaite, C. (1996). Computer networks as social networks. *Annual Review of Sociology, 22*, 213–238.

Cited References

Agre, P. (2002). Real-time politics: The internet and the political process. *The Information Society, 18*, 311–331.
Asen, R., & Brouwer, D. C. (Eds.). (2001). *Counterpublics and the State*. Albany, NY: State University of New York Press.
Arquilla, J., & Ronfeldt, D. (2001). The advent of Netwar (revisited). In J. Arquilla & D. Ronfeldt (Eds.), *Networks and netwars: The future of terror, crime, and militancy* (pp. 1–25). Santa Monica: RAND.
Bannister, F., & Connolly, R. (2012). Forward to the past: Lessons for the future e-government from the story so far. *Information Polity, 17*(3–4), 211–226.
Barnes, S. H., & Kaase, M. (1979). *Political action: Mass participation in five Western democracies*. Thousand Oaks, CA: Sage.
Bauman, Z. (2003). *Liquid love: On the frailty of human bonds*. Oxford: Blackwell.
Beck, U. (2000). *What is globalization?* Cambridge: Polity Press.
Bennett, W. L. (2003a). New media power: The internet and global activism. In N. Couldry & J. Curran (Eds.), *Contesting media power*. New York, NY: Rowman and Littlefield.
Bennett, W. L. (2003b). *News: The politics of illusion* (5th ed.). New York, NY: Longman.
Bennett, L., & Entman, R. (Eds.). (2001). *Mediated politics: Communication in the future of democracy* (pp. 75–95). New York: Cambridge University Press.
Boulianne, S. (2009). Does internet use affect engagement? A meta-analysis of research. *Political Communication, 26*(2), 193–211.
Buchstein, H. (1997). Bytes that bite: The internet and deliberative democracy. *Constellations, 4* (2), 248–263.
Chadwick, A. (2011, August 25). *The hybrid media system*. European Consortium for Political Research General Conference, Reykjavik, Iceland.
Dewey, J. (1927). *The public and its problems*. Athens, OH: Ohio University Press.
Durkheim, É. (1957). *Professional ethics and civic morals*. London: Routledge and Kegan Paul.
Fenton, N., & Downey, J. (2003). *Counter public spheres and global modernity*. http://javnost-thepublic.org/
Gladwell, M. (2010) Small change. *The New Yorker*. http://www.newyorker.com
Granovetter, M. (1973). The strength of weak ties. *The American Journal of Sociology, 78*(6), 1360–1380.
Grofman, B., Trechsel, A. H., & Franklin, M. (Eds.). (2014). *The internet and democracy in global perspective. Voters, candidates, parties, and social movements*. Berlin: Springer.
Grossman, L. (1996). *The electronic republic: Reshaping democracy in the information age*. London: Penguin.
Habermas, J. (1991). *The structural transformation of the public sphere*. Cambridge: The MIT Press.
Hirst, P. (1994). *Associative democracy: New forms of economic and social governance*. Cambridge: Polity Press.
Hirst, P. (2009). Representative democracy and its limits. *The Political Quaterly, 80*, S199–S213.
Inglehart, R. (1977). *The silent revolution: Changing values and political styles among western publics*. Princeton, NJ: Princeton University Press.

Joyce, M. (Ed.). (2010). *Digital activism decoded: The new mechanics of change*. New York, NY: International Debate Education Association.
Keane, J. (2003). *Global civic society?* New York: Cambridge University Press.
Keck, M. E., & Sikkink, K. (1998). *Activists beyond borders: Advocacy networks in international politics*. Ithaca, NY: Cornell University Press.
McLuhan, M. (1962). *The Gutenberg galaxy: The making of typographic man*. Toronto: University of Toronto Press.
Morozov, E. (2011). *The net delusion: The dark side of internet freedom*. Philadelphia, PA: Perseus Books Group.
Negroponte, N. (1996). *Being digital*. London: Hodder & Stoughton.
Norris, P. (2001). *Digital divide. Civic engagement, information poverty, and the internet worldwide*. New York, NY: Cambridge University Press.
Opp, K. (2009). *Theories of political protest and social movements. A multidisciplinary introduction, critique, and synthesis*. Florence, KY: Routledge.
Pickerill, J. (2003). *Cyberprotest: Environmental activism on-line*. Manchester, UK: Manchester University Press.
Rheingold, H. (2002). *Smart Mob: The next social revolution*. Cambridge, MA: Basic Books.
Snow, D. E., & Oliver, P. E. (1995). Social movements and collective behavior: Social psychological dimensions and considerations. In K. S. Cook, G. A. Fine, & J. S. House (Eds.), *Sociological perspectives on social psychology*. Boston: Allyn and Bacon.
Tarrow, S. G. (2005). *The new transnational activism. Cambridge studies in contentious politics*. New York: Cambridge University Press.
The Pew Charitable Trusts. (2006). http://www.pewtrusts.org/
Wellman, B. (2000). Changing connectivity: A future history of Y2.03 K. *Sociological Research Online, 4*. http://www.socresonline.org.uk/4/4/wellman.html

Chapter 3
Social Media and Social Movements Around the World

Lessons and Theoretical Approaches

Amaro La Rosa

Abstract Undoubtedly, the Internet has a multilevel impact on the everyday life of the humankind. In the age of web 2.0, social media have proven to be an essential tool for social movements; to spread their ideas, gain followers and go into action, showing to the world testimonies, pictures, and videos in real time. Using updated research evidence and diverse approaches, this study focuses on the social media role in nine social protests of the twenty-first century that are now part of the history and allowed important conclusions for the scientific and practical understanding of this issue. Social network participation is not isolated from the countries' characteristics and the media. For this reason, social, political, and communicational factors that contextualize these cases are presented, developing some theoretical models.

Keywords Internet and society • Social movements • Social media • Communication research • Politics

3.1 On Social Movements Theory

To place this paper into context, it is very important to present some viewpoints about social movements. First, one of the most quoted viewpoints Della Porta and Diani (1999) has identified four features of social movements:

1. Informal interaction networks;
2. Shared beliefs and solidarity;
3. Collective action;
4. Use of protest.

A. La Rosa (✉)
Universidad Femenina del Sagrado Corazón, Lima, Peru
e-mail: amaro@unife.edu.pe

B. Pătruţ and M. Pătruţ (eds.), *Social Media in Politics*, Public Administration and Information Technology 13, DOI 10.1007/978-3-319-04666-2_3,

Table 3.1 Four approaches: 1965–2010 Jasper (2010)

US	Materialist	Culturalist
Macrosocial	Mobilization or process: Tilly, Obserchall, Mc Carthy, Zaid, Ferrow, Mc Adamn, Tarrow	Programmed society: Touraine, Melucci. Castells
Microsocial	Rational-choice or game theory: Olson, Hechter, Coleman	Pragmatism, cultural-historical activity theory. Feminism queer theory, cultural-strategic or emotional approaches: Cefaï, Emirbayer, Jasper, Krinsky and Barker. Taylor

After having studied several social movements, Gerlach (2001:289–290) developed the SPIN model and assumed that the most common type of organization structure has the following features:

- Segmentary: Integrate many different groups in diverse stages;
- Polycentric: Multiple leaders or centers of influence;
- Networked: Imply a reticulate network with multiple linkages.

From our viewpoint, one problem of traditional sociological studies was their tendency to focus their attention in macrosocial or microsocial phenomena without establishing connections between them. In practical terms, although they involve different levels of analysis they are interdependent part of the same reality. This traditional divergence of focus was used by Jasper (2010) to explain the diverse approaches to social movements formulated from 1965 to 2010 (Table 3.1)

García (2013) makes a very interesting review of the historical development of the theory of social movements. Starting from the description of classical viewpoints upon this issue, he explained the two major theoretical orientations that appeared in the latter half of the twentieth century. In the United States, the resource mobilization and the political process theories assumed one economic-political explanation while the European viewpoints of the New Social movements took the socio-psychological approach. From his viewpoint, the contemporary tendency is to complement both of them in the constructionist approach (Fig. 3.1).

3.2 Communication, Social Media, and Social Movements

Communication technologies and resources are very important tools for social movements as they report about the initiative and influence collective action. Now, in the digital age, social media and mobile phones with access to the Internet are very important resources used for social protests that can start as rapidly as the technology allows, in some cases in a few hours after the first motivational impulse was decided. The application of restrictive governmental practices usually comes late, when the messages are circulating without control in the cyberspace, have been read, and shared around the world by thousands of people on the screens of

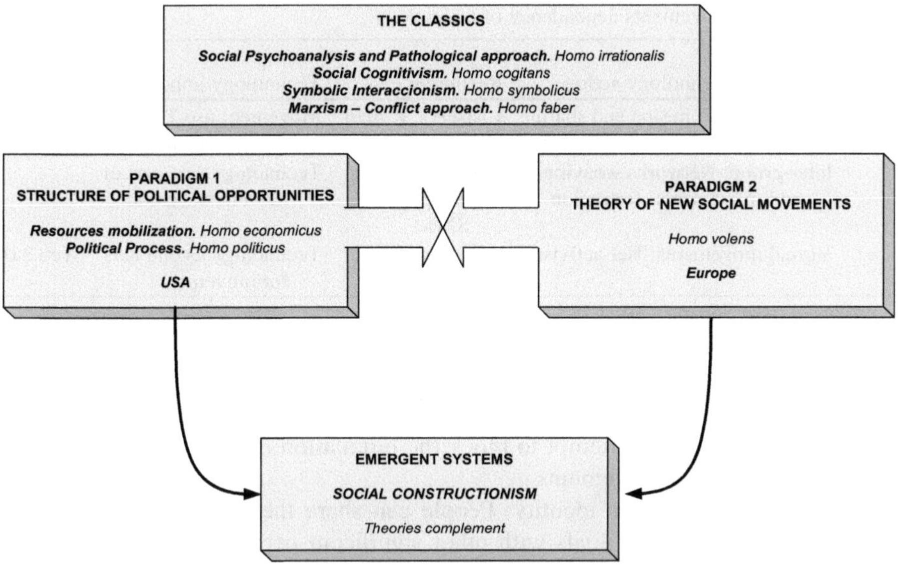

Fig. 3.1 From the classics to the constructionist approach. Reproduced from García (2013:87)

their computers or mobile phones. Some countries have applied restrictions for Internet and social media use, but the people always have made use of the networks to protest. Perhaps some pages, accounts, services, or resources could be hacked or blocked, but the traces of the social movement remains active in many places in the cyberspace and progress.

From Harlow's (2012:229) viewpoint, scholars have two perceptions about the Internet and social movements:

- the Internet facilitates the traditional offline activity giving more resources for activists' repertoire;
- the Internet creates new forms of activism improving social impact.

Sádaba (2012:784) formulates a historical approach considering the levels of dependency between technology and social movements, that we reformulate taking into consideration the evolution of the Internet (Table 3.2).

Garrett (2006) describes three mechanisms that potentially link technology and the social movements' participation: reduction of costs, promotion of collective identity, and creation of community. How can we apply this viewpoint discussing the relationships between social movements and social media?

- Reduction of costs: considering the convergence of telecommunications, the cost to send messages is almost zero, because people could send SMS, SNS, Facebook posts, WhatsApps, videos, podcasts, photos, or tweets from their smart phones that are now multiplatform devices. These messages are directed to their all contacts or followers, with the advantage of the absence of national

Table 3.2 Social movements dependency of technology

Level	Context of technology action	Resources	Technology importance	Internet stage
1	Intra-group: Cohesion and sharing of identity	Listservs, E-mail	Movement use Technology as a tool	Web 1.0
2	Inter-group: Networks weaving and movements' formation	Organizations webpages, SMS	Technology as a part of movement spread	
3	Virtual movements: Net activism	Social media	Technology as one axis for movement	Web 2.0

Reproduced from Sádaba (2012):784

boundaries to obtain high impact in other societies. The costs of participation and engagement of people are drastically reduced in the circumstances when authoritarian regimes attempt to block the circulation of messages that convey the voice of social movements.

- Promotion of collective identity: People can share the same needs, concerns, viewpoints, and social goals with other significant people, in a growing community of thousands of dispersed members building one movement that proves their existence in the collective actions of people identified with the ideals.
- Creation of community: The participation in the virtual actions of diffusion for the social movement reinforces the perception of community and social ties with many people located in different places. Applying *mutatis mutandis* the principles of group dynamics to the virtual community in non-orthodox terms, we can talk about of a cohesion process within the social movement.

Van Laer and Van Aelst (2009:247) assumed that the Internet has changed the action repertoire of social movements in two ways:

1. by facilitating pre-existing actions forms: engaging more people, much easier than other previous resources, in a very short time span;
2. by creating new or adapted tools to motivate activism.

Cohen (1998) identifies some characteristics of social movements that, in our opinion, could be linked with social media:

- capacity to rapid mobilization: the real time of the connection is a guarantee for it;
- vision of an alternative and better existence. The words, pictures, or videos inform about one undesired situation and motivate people to think of the desirable future;
- use of unorthodox strategies to attract public support and confront institutions. The messages are transmitted by the new media that are attractive, interactive, and mobile.

Social movements imply social actors engaged in collective actions. Of course, the behaviors do not always have the same characteristics and do not obtain the same impact on society.

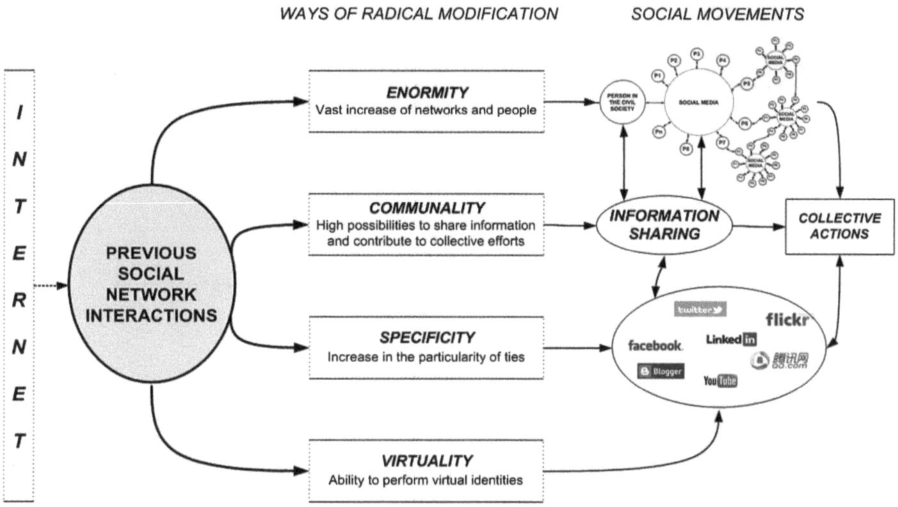

Fig. 3.2 Social media and social movements. Author's elaboration based partially in Christakis and Fowler (2009)

From the perspective of Christakis and Fowler (2009), the Internet modifies in four ways the previous social network interactions: enormity, communality, specificity, and virtuality. Figure 3.2 presents their explanation and our viewpoint of the relationship between social media and social movements.

The increasing connections between people (P1, P2, etc.) and social media allow more possibilities of information sharing and, simultaneously, the improvement of collective actions to pursue common goals.

A consideration of the potential contribution of social media to social movements reinforces the conviction that it supposes different forms of communication, from official to informal and from those used in the closed circle to the public circle, with different conditions and requirements in each case. *The Cocktail Analysis* (2011:40) makes a depiction of these ideas taking into account the most important social media (Fig. 3.3).

After the study of three social movements, the Arab Spring, the Spanish Movement 15-M, and the Orange Revolution in Ukraine, Hintler (2011) concluded that, in all of them, the social media and the SNS (social network sites) played a crucial role of. In the case of the Arab Spring, two protagonists led to the final act of the revolt: civil society and social media (Frangonikolopoulos and Chapsos 2012:10)

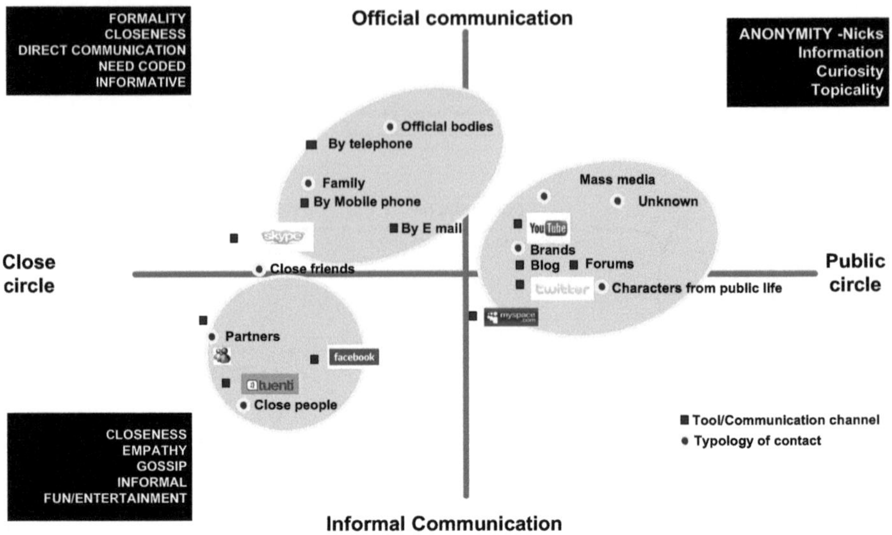

Fig. 3.3 Contacts and communication tools (Reproduced from *The Cocktail Analysis* (2011:40)

3.3 Social Media in Social Movements: Some Cases

Some social movements of the present century that have a very important impact around the world have one common feature: the use of social media as mobilization and diffusion resources. They are presented in chronological order.

In November 2004, activists took to the streets of Ukraine peacefully protesting against the notorious fraud in the second round of elections in which Victor Yanukovych was proclaimed winner. International elections standards were not fulfilled as proven by observers from the Organization for Security and Cooperation in Europe (OSCE). After days of people mobilizations and several rounds of negotiations, a new electoral process was decided by the Central Election Commission and Victor Yuschenko, the massively supported candidate, becomes the winner. Younger people were usually involved in the protests; the majority of people that used mobile phones and Internet resources and were engaged in the 2004 Orange Revolution in Ukraine were 30 years old or were younger (Goldstein 2007).

On January 4, 2008, Oscar Morales, a systems engineer from Barranquilla, created the Facebook group "Un millón de voces contra las FARC" (One million of voices against FARC) to protest on behalf of people kidnapped by the guerrilla. The successful campaign involving social media progressed with an accelerated rhythm in Colombia and became a massive international event that involved traditional media, civic society actions, and private support. Over ten million people in 20 cities of Colombia and other 45 million in many cities around the world had protested in one month since the start of the initiative (Zuluaga 2012), and obtained a high impact in the world's public opinion.

Scenario: Moldova. Date: April 6, 2009. Reason: protest for the reelection of the Communist Party by means of fraudulent parliamentary elections. Thousands of tweets with the hashtag #pman invited people to participate in the protest at Piaţa Marii Adunări Naţionale, the biggest square of the capital city Chişinău. By the use of LiveJounal, Facebook, blogs, E-mails, and SMSs the participation of 15,000 people in the street protests was obtained in a few hours (Cullum 2010). The national level mobilization, named as the *Twitter Revolution* or *the Grape Revolution* followed with disturbances that received international attention almost immediately.

vanNiekerk et al. (2011) depicted the use of ICTs in the Jasmine Revolution in Tunisia that began in December 2010 with protests against the government, unemployment, and corruption. As a result of the magnitude of the protest, one month later the Tunisian President Zine El Abidine Ben Ali resigned and fled the country. Using the information warfare lifecycle model, the study has proven that "offensive weapons" were the social media (especially in the early stages they were used to spread the idea, to coordinate social actions and to show videos of the protest), international mass media (Al Jazeera reported the uprising from the very beginning) and the massive human mobilizations.

Tufekci and Wilson (2012), subsequent to a survey of 1,200 participants in Tahrir Square protests, proved that mobile phones were the most important tool for information about the protests and that, in the social media, more than half of the participants used Facebook for this action. The majority used email for general purposes (Table 3.3).

From the viewpoint of Eltantawy and Wiest (2011:1212), social media technologies represent an important instrumental resource that contributed to the birth and sustainability of the January 25 protests. The resource mobilization theory makes it clear that both the availability of resources and the social actors' efficacy in using them effectively are essential. In the Arab Spring context, mobile phones, and social media were available resources intensively used and the Egyptian people, and especially the younger generation had enough competences to use their digital devices very efficiently.

Storck (2011: 24–25) analyzed tweets, journalistic articles, and academic journals to outline the role of social media in the Egyptian uprising, and identified three trends:

1. social media as organizational tool: the impulse of social media to strengthen online organizations for obtaining quick change;
2. social media as an alternative press and outlet for citizen journalism: social media act as another form of media as diffuser of information, with the supplementary advantage of the virtual interaction;
3. social media as a tool for generating awareness both regionally and internationally. The most important international TV networks discussed the issue for many hours and the newspapers devoted many covers and pages to it.

Table 3.3 Resources of information in Tahrir Square protests

Resource	General use	Communication about protests
Mobile phone	92 %	82 %
Facebook	52 %	51 %
Twitter	16 %	13 %
E-mail	83 %	27 %

Based on Tufekci and Wilson (2012)

Nevertheless, other communicational factors contribute to the promotion of social movements by means of social media. In the case of the Arab Spring, I share the viewpoint of Tufekci and Wilson (2012) who explained that, on the one hand, there are social, political and economic reasons linked with the maintenance of one authoritarian regime and, on the other, that a new system of political communication emerged, which they identified as the "complex ecology of connectivity" operating in close interaction and integrated by:

1. satellite TV channels such as Al Jazeera;
2. Internet resources, especially social media;
3. mobile phone technology:

The nature of these trends is outlined in Fig. 3.4.

Aqueveque (2013) describes the role of the Internet in the young students' social movement in Chile against the educational system that deserved global media coverage in 2011, especially because this country has been viewed for years as a model of development in Latin America (the so-called Chilean miracle). When the local television depicted the actions as terrorism, pictures and videos posted on the Internet and, then, massively distributed showed another reality.

Vicari (2013) used a mixed-method approach and analyzed over 8,000 tweets with hashtag#15ott, related with the Italian protest for global economic changes of 15 October 2011 (part of one transnational movement that took place in over 10,000 cities around the world). The results demonstrated a concentration phenomena: 80 % of the tweets were posted by 44 % of its twitterers and the most active twitterers had also been participants in similar mobilizations.

Not always have the social movements that used social media been successful as proven by the so-called *Green Revolution* of Iran. On June 2009, thousands of protesters walked peacefully in the streets of the major Iranian cities alleging fraud in the presidential elections that the candidate Mahmoud Ahmadinejad had won. The protests that became bloody after police intervention had lasted for months through the use of blogs, Facebook, and Twitter. The main objective failed (El-Nawawy and Khamis 2012).

However, social media resources are also used by governments to alleviate the impact of social movements and manage offline and online relationships. On 14 February 2011, thousands of people protested in the streets of Bahrain against the political and social situation. The regime used social media to overcome the crisis and maintain social control. Diverse types of trolls were used to disqualify dissent messages, the Hareghum Twitter account disclosed information about the

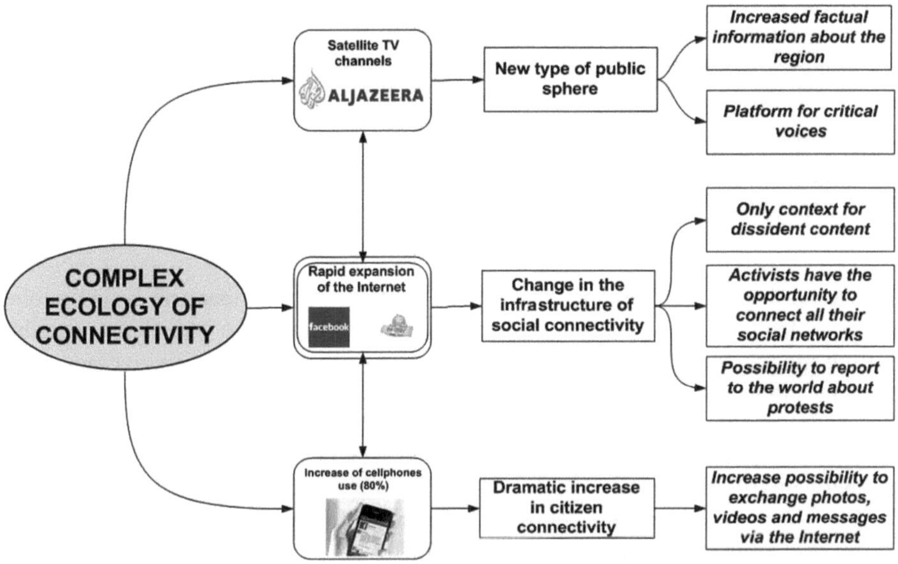

Fig. 3.4 The new complex ecology of connectivity (Based on Tufekci and Wilson 2012)

activists that were stereotyped as traitors provoking shame in the people (Jones 2013).

3.4 Some Lessons Explained from Diverse Theoretical Viewpoints

As a start point for this section, we can ask a question: are the ICTs alone the unique factor to start and make a social movement successful? Of course, we need to consider several factors:

- the prevalent situations that we can label *conditioning factors*;
- the motivational situation that stimulates the reaction of activists that we can term *trigger factor*;
- the specific conditions of society at the moment the mobilization starts;
- the people's perception of the situation.

The psychosocial factors. In this respect, Flam (2005:28) considered the importance of emotional stimulus, and assumed that "at the theoretical level the recognition of anger as an emotion [is] necessary for mobilizing in protest". She distinguished between the ambivalent role of anger in social movements' activism in democratic systems and authoritarian regimes (Table 3.4)

Diffusion of ideas and especially actions are very rapid and in real time through the social media. Oral diffusion contributes to massive adhesion of behaviors in

Table 3.4 Anger in social movements

Type of society	Anger expression	Reason
Democratic	Open	Anger not punished and push change Great number of people enhance protests
Authoritarian	Limited Hope to manage fear	Avoid confrontation with power-holders and harm

Based on Flam (2005)

relatively short time. Viral videos viewed by the people impact on world public opinion. In the web 2.0 era, social media have changed the traditional agenda-setting model. In our opinion, using Toffler's words, prosumers receive and send messages that influence media agenda. Figure 3.5 shows how people, integrated in the social media exchange, share messages with other people but also with the media. In this sense, media agenda and public agenda are now constructed through collective participation via social media.

Let us try to explain our subject matter through the intermediary of the basic features of symbolic interactionist approach.

Social life is a constant process of interaction: in the social media age people are always iterconnected, especially in the case of digital natives.

- As we have explained in another article (La Rosa 2012), there is a feeling of isolation when people do not have temporary possibilities to establish connections with the others. Usually, people could be talking with another but are attentive to the messages that are coming to their mobile phones from the social media, SMS, WhatsApp, or emails.
- Interaction is building and is adjusted on the go: it is not possible to identify in each case the person who begins the chain of transmission of messages or contributes with the diffusion of messages. Everyone builds the interaction and adjusts it to their needs, possibilities, and technological competences.
- Interaction is one symbolic process: all the social movements use symbolic resources to report or motivate the action like: #pman, No more FARC, Indignados, We are all Khaled Said, etc.

The dissonance cognitive theory assumes that people need to have congruence among their concepts. When some stimulus is not in concordance with the others, individuals experiment a state of dissonance, i.e., an aversive motivational state that implies the need to recover the lost congruence. In the case of social movements "social media has helped spread cognitive dissonance connecting opinion leaders and activists to regular citizens, which quickly expanded the network of anti-regime protestors" (Chebib and Sohail 2011:152)

Thinking in terms of the traditional spiral of silence theory of Noelle Neumann, people fear isolation and adopt the viewpoint of the majority of the public opinion. But what about the case of the social movements linked with social media? This theory fails because, in many cases, there are minority groups that disseminate the information using social media and other technological resources and go forward

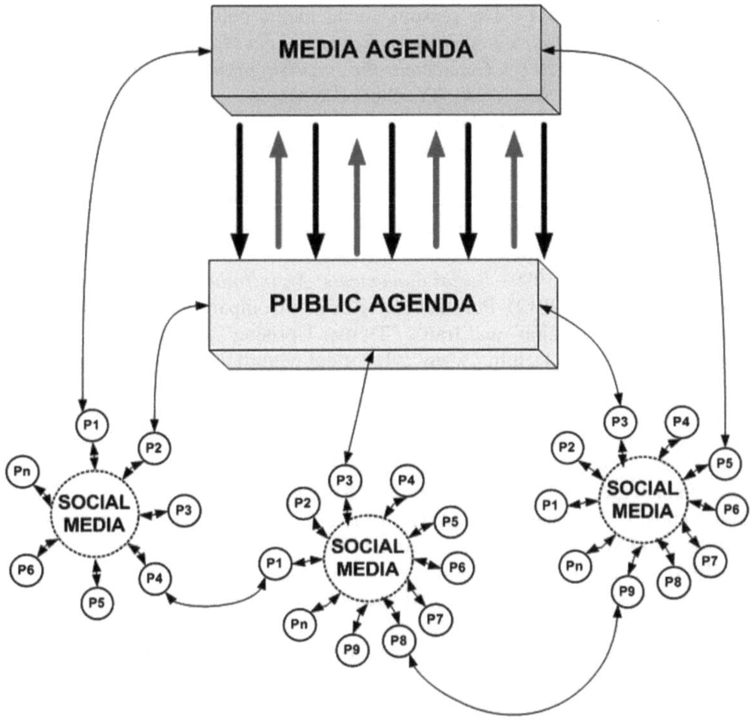

Fig. 3.5 Agenda setting in the web 2.0 era

with their goals which are subsequently adopted by many people who are motivated to support them or take part in collective actions.

Finally, we outline some operative conclusions from our theoretical review:

- social media could activate social movements, but there are other previous social, political and communicational conditions for their emergence;
- the same social media do not always have the same impact in all of the social movements.
- social media allow social movements to use short time spans between planning and implementing the social actions and protests, before actions to prevent or stop them could be launched.

References

Aqueveque R. (2013). Proceedings of the IX Bienal Iberoamericana de Comunicación Santiago de Chile: Universidad de Chile/RAIC.

Chebib, N., & Sohail, R. (2011). The reasons social media contributed to the 2011 Egyptian revolution. *International Journal of Business Research and Management, 2*(3), 139–162.
Christakis, M., & Fowler, J. (2009). *Connected: the surprising power of our social networks and how they shape our lives*. New York, NY: Back Bay Books.
Cohen, R. (1998). Transnational social movements: an assessment. Paper presented to the Transnational Communities Programme seminar held at the School of Geography, University of Oxford, 19 June 1998.
Cullum, B. (2010). Were protests in Moldova a Twitter revolution? Movements.org Posted on June 27. http://www.movements.org/case-study/entry/were-protests-in-moldova-a-twitter-revolution/. Accessed Sept 25 2013.
Della Porta, D., & Diani, D. (1999). *Social movements: An introduction*. Oxford: Blackwell.
El-Nawawy M., Khamis, S. (2012). Political activism 2.0: Comparing the role of social media in Egypt's "Facebook revolution" and Iran's "Twitter Uprising". CyberOrient Oline *Journal of the Virtual Middle East*. 6(1). http://www.cyberorient.net/article.do?articleId=7439. Accessed 15 Sept 2013.
Eltantawy, N., & Wiest, J. (2011). Social media in the Egyptian revolution: Reconsidering resource mobilization theory. *International Journal of Communication, 5*, 1207–1224.
Flam, H. (2005). Emotions' map: A research agenda. In H. Flam & D. King (Eds.), *Emotions and social movements* (pp. 19–40). New York, NY: Routledge.
Frangonikolopoulos, C., & Chapsos, I. (2012). Explaining the role and the impact of the social media in the Arab Spring. *GMJ: Mediterranean Edition, 8*(1), 10–20.
García, E. (2013). Antropología y movimientos sociales: Reflexiones para una etnografía de los movimientos sociales. *Intersticios: Revista Sociológica de Pensamiento Crítico, 7*(1), 83–113.
Garrett, R. (2006). Protest in an information society: A review of literature on social movements and new ICTs. *Information, Communication and Society, 9*(2), 202–224. doi:10.1080.1369118060063.7.3.
Gerlach, L. (2001). The structure of social movements: Environmental activism and its opponents. In J. Arquilla & D. Ronfeldt (Eds.), *Networks and netwars: The future of terror, crime, and militancy* (pp. 289–310). Santa Monica, CA: The Rand Corporation.
Goldstein, J. (2007). The role of digital networked technologies in the Ukrainian Orange Revolution Cambridge: The Berkman Center for Internet & Society, Research Publication No. 2007–14 http://cyber.law.harvard.edu/publications. Accessed 19 Aug 2013.
Harlow, S. (2012). Social media and social movements: Facebook and an online Guatemalan justice movement that moved offline. *New Media Society, 14*(2), 225–243.
Hintler, G. (2011). Dissertation. Brandenburg University of Technology.
Jasper, J. (2010). Social movement theory today: Toward a theory of action? *Sociology Compass, 4* (11), 965–976.
Jones, M. (2013). Social media, surveillance and social control in the Bahrain uprising. *Westminster Papers in Communication and Culture, 9*(2), 71–91.
La Rosa, A. (2012). Usuarios de nuevos medios, comunicación e interacción social. *Comunifé, 12*, 101–113.
Sádaba, I. (2012). Acción colectiva y movimientos sociales en las redes digitales. *Aspectos históricos y metodológicos ARBOR, Ciencia, Pensamiento y cultura, 188*(756), 781–794.
Storck, M. (2011). Dissertation, University of Saint Andrews.
The Cocktail Analysis (2011). Informe de resultados Observatorio Redes Sociales, http://www.slideshare.net/TCAnalysis/tca-observatorio-redes-sociales2011publico
Tufekci, Z., & Wilson, C. (2012). Social media and the decision to participate in political protest: Observations from Tahrir square. *Journal of Communication, 62*, 363–379.
Van Laer, J., & Van Aelst, J. (2009). Cyber-protest and civil society: The Internet and action repertoires of social movements. In Y. Jewkes & Y. Majid (Eds.), *Handbook of Internet crime* (pp. 230–254). Portland: Universia Press.

vanNiekerk, B., Pillay, K., & Maharaj, M. (2011). Analyzing the role of ICTS in the Tunisian and Egyptian unrest from an information warfare perspective. *International Journal of Communication, 5*, 1406–1416.

Vicari, S. (2013). Public reasoning around social contention: A case study of Twitter use in the Italian mobilization for global change. *Current Sociology, 61*(4), 474–490.

Zuluaga, J. (2012). Internet: Nuevas audiencias, nuevos ciudadanos? In J. Bonilla, Cataño, O. Rincón, & J. Zuluaga (Eds.), *De las audiencias contemplativas a los productores conectados* (pp. 241–262). Bogotá: Universidad EAFIT/Pontificia Universidad Javeriana/ Universidad de Los Andes.

Chapter 4
Graph Theory Algorithms for Analysing Political Blogs

The *Political Analyst* Software

Bogdan Pătruţ and Ioan-Lucian Popa

Abstract In this chapter, we show how we developed software for analyzing texts from political blogs. The software is based on solving some problems of graph theory. The premises of our analysis are: we have the corpus of a political blog, as empirical data; the posts on this blog convey economic, political, and socio-cultural values which constitute themselves as key words of the blog; there are interdependences among the key words of a political post; these interdependences can be studied by analyzing the co-occurrence of two key words in the text, within a well defined fragment; established links between values in a political speech have associated positive numbers indicating the "power" of those links; these "powers" are defined according to both the number of co-occurrences of values, and the internal logic of the discourse where they occur, for example in the same category of a blog, or in the same context. In this context, we intend to highlight the dominant values in a post, groups of values based on their links between them, the optimal order in which political values should be set for a more concise speech etc.

4.1 Introduction

In text analysis, we are interested in methods for summarizing a discourse, or methods for extracting relevant information from a blog post. Time and again, extracting relevant data from texts is confronted with complex modeling of data, as presented in Tishby et al. (1999), where the information bottleneck method is described. Also, Chen and Lin (2000) proposed a multilingual summarizer for news posted on the web. They proposed an architecture of a multilingual news summarizer, including monolingual and multilingual clustering, and similarity measure among meaningful units. Their method can be also applied to political

B. Pătruţ (✉) • I.-L. Popa
"Vasile Alecsandri" University of Bacău, 600115 Bacau, Romania
e-mail: bogdan@edusoft.ro; i.l.popa@hotmail.com

B. Pătruţ and M. Pătruţ (eds.), *Social Media in Politics*, Public Administration and Information Technology 13, DOI 10.1007/978-3-319-04666-2_4,

blogs, because the posts of a politician in his/her campaign can be considered as hot news. Chechik and Tishby (2002) invented a method for extracting relevant structures with side information for text data.

START [see Katz et al. (2006)] is a natural language question answering system, which aims at supplying users with "just the right information," instead of merely providing a list of hits. In Pătruţ et al. (2008), a method is described for constructing a question answering system for a text describing a social context, based on some pragmatic particularities of verbs describing actions or feelings that can emerge between two human beings.

In this chapter, we show how, using graph theory, we can extract relevant information from the posts on politicians' blogs. As empirical data, our approach will consider texts that refer to some *values*. i.e. some key terms in the text of a post on a political blog. Certainly, political discourses contain words that can be considered as political, economic, and socio-cultural values. Our content analysis will be based on the graph built on these values.

Having to deal with the graph of such values, we will highlight the following: (a) which is the dominant value in a political blog, or just in a post? (b) which groups of values have ties among them and have no connection with the rest? (c) which is the order in which political values should be set so as to obtain an equivalent although more concise speech compared to the already given one? (d) which are the links between values that form the "core" political speech? (e) how can one get from one value to another by using as few words as possible from the discourse to be analyzed?

4.2 A Brief Terminology of Graph Theory

The *graph theory* is usually used when dealing with social networks, recruitment into political movements, diffusion of information, markets studies, social organizations, and military intelligence. Kitsak et al. (2010) wrote on the influential spreaders in networks. The social networks are related to the main topic of graph theory.

Of course, in social and political sciences, the graphs can be used in various forms, because the graphs can represent all kinds of mathematical structures, used to model pairwise relations between objects from a certain collection. Individuals (as in social networks) can be considered objects and so can words from a text.

A graph is a collection of *nodes* (or vertices) and a collection of *edges* that connect pairs of nodes. In a formal manner, the *graph* means a couple G = (N, E), where *N* is a finite non-empty set of nodes, and *E* is a finite set of edges. Edges are pairs of nodes. If the order of nodes from an edge is important, then the graph is called *directed graph*; otherwise it is called *undirected graph* [see Diestel (2012)] for details).

Subsequently, we will refer only to undirected graphs as they are used by the *Political Analyst* program, developed by us and presented in Sects. 4.5 and 4.6.

Considering the case of a political blog, an example of a graph is the following

$$G = \begin{pmatrix} \{education, gun\ violence, work, jobs, health\ care, health\ insurance, \\ climate\ change\} \\ \{(education, gun\ violence), (education, work), (gun\ violence, work), \\ (work, jobs), (health\ care, health\ insurance)\} \end{pmatrix}.$$

In this graph we can highlight:

- the set of nodes, N = {*education*, *gun violence*, *work*, *jobs*, *health care*, *health insurance*, *climate change*};
- the set of edges, E, given by the following pairs: (*education*, *gun violence*), (*education*, *work*), (*gun violence*, *work*), (*work*, *jobs*), and (*health care*, *health insurance*).

The number of nodes is often denoted by n, and the number of edges by m. In our case, with these notations, we have $n = 7$ and $m = 5$. As you can see, the seven nodes of this graph represent political, economic, and socio-cultural values from the blog of President Barack Obama (http://www.barackobama.com). Of course, the set of edges consists of five links between pairs of such values. These pairs can represent co-occurrences in the same category of the blog, or in the same fragment of the corpus etc.

In order to make working with graphs easier, in practice, researchers use most frequently graphical representations. Thus, nodes are represented by labeled circles or rectangles and edges are represented by straight or curved lines, connecting nodes, two by two (Fig. 4.1).

Neither the placing of the nodes is not important, nor the shape of the edges. It is preferable to use straight lines for edges, and to avoid their intersecting. Of course, what matters is just which the nodes are and which are connected to which.

Two nodes linked by an edge are called *adjacent nodes* or *neighbors*. A sequence of distinctive nodes, adjacent two by two, is called a *path*. For example, *(education, work, jobs)* is a path in the graph in Fig. 4.1. Such a path can represent a path in the discourse of the politician, such "If you have education, you will get a job". But the example is just illustrative, because the paths can represent various situations, depending on how we define the edges in the graph.

A node with only one neighbor is called a *leaf node*. In Fig. 4.1, *jobs*, *health care*, and *health insurance* are leaves. The *degree* of a node is its number of neighbors. Thus, a leaf node has degree 1.

A node which has no neighbors is called an *isolated node*. The node *climate change* is an isolated node.

If in a graph, whichever the two nodes, a path could be found from one to the other, then that graph is called *connected.* It is not the case of the previous graph which is *disconnected.* Any disconnected graph can be decomposed, in a unique way, in a disjoint union of graphs which have no common elements. These (sub) graphs are called *connected components.* Thus if there is no path between the two nodes to link them, then these will belong to two different connected components. In the case of our graph (Fig. 4.1), there are three connected components. The first

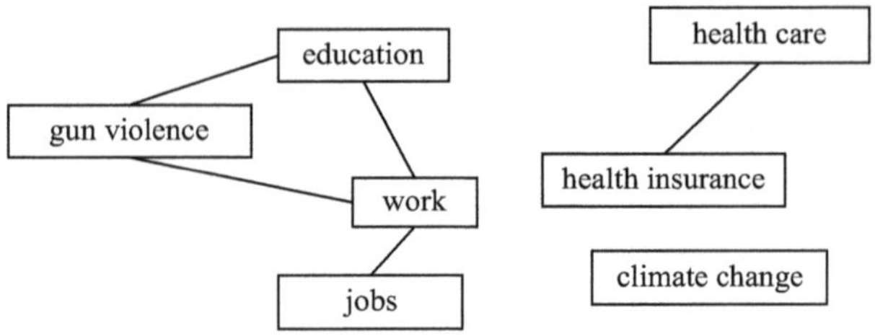

Fig. 4.1 An example of a graph where nodes are the values of the political blog of Barack Obama, and edges are links between them

connected component is provided by the nodes *education, work, gun violence, and job*, the second is provided by the nodes *health care* and *health insurance*, whereas the third is given by the isolated node *climate change*.

When speaking about a connected component, one also means the edges which connect the respective nodes.

A path in which the first and the last node are neighbors is called a *circuit* (*cycle*). For example, the path *(education, work, gun violence)* is a circuit.

A connected graph without circuits is called a *tree*. In Fig. 4.1, the connected components from the right side are trees, but the connected component from the left side is not (it has a circuit).

Using the notions introduced so far, we may mathematically model the problems raised in the introduction of this chapter (Pătruţ et al. 2014).

Thus, (a) determining the dominant value in the political discourse may mean finding the node that has the largest number of neighbors. In the case of the graph in Fig. 4.1, which has three connected components, the dominant value is *work*. If the graph is not connected, as the one in Fig. 4.1, there occurs the problem of finding the dominant values for each of the connected components. However, if the graph is not connected, one may add edges, based on the previous analysis of the represented discourse, until obtaining a connected graph. In this case, the *dominant value* will be the one which has the greatest degree. It has the maximum number of neighbors. Judging in this way, the dominant value is *work* in Fig 4.1.

In problem (b), we must find the groups of values that are interconnected. This would mean determining the connected components of the values' graph. In our example, the answer for (b) has already been given.

For problems (c) and (d), we should present new graph theory notions.

Modeling real problems often requires associating numerical values to edges in a graph. These numbers (real, positive) that are associated to the edges form a *weight* or a *cost function*. Thus, the graph becomes a *weighted graph* (Fletcher et al. 1991).

Some authors use the term *network* for weighted graph (Strang 2005).

Depending on the problem at hand, such weights might represent cost, time, distance etc.

In our case, the weight of an edge between two nodes (political, economic, and socio-cultural values) could be given by the "strength" of the connection existing between two such nodes, in terms of desirability.

Referring to the example of the graph in Fig. 4.1, we associate some weights to the edges and we obtain Fig. 4.2.

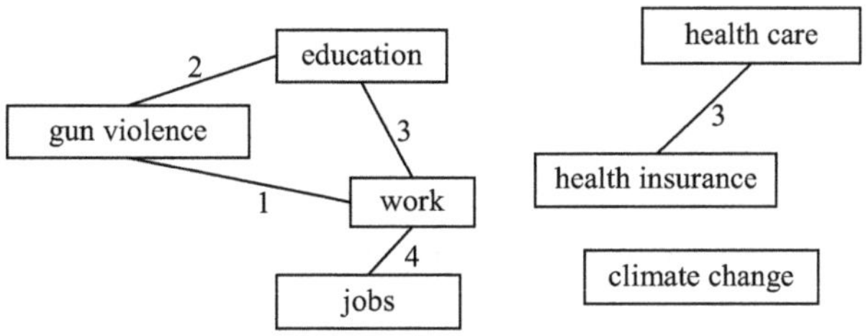

Fig. 4.2 The graph from Fig. 4.1, where edges have costs, the costs representing the power of relationships between values

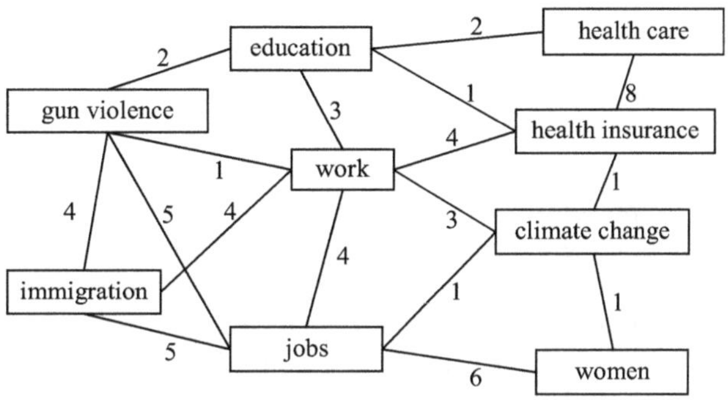

Fig. 4.3 A connected weighted graph, with circuits

The weight/cost may be considered as a desirability, and it may be given either by the number of co-occurrence of those two values in a given context. Also, the weight can be represented by different implications between values in the political discourse of the blogger.

The weights of the edges can be represented by numbers, and also by the thickness of the lines, lines which represent edges of the graph (Fig. 4.3).

Trying to find the dominant value, we can now consider the weights of the edges, too. Adding the weights of the edges connected with a node, we will obtain a value of its "connectivity" with its neighbor. However, this will not reflect the power of that node to dominate. But, in the case of two maximal nodes (with the same degree), we can consider a sum of the weights, in order to sort the maximal nodes by their power to dominate. Thus, the power of a node can be defined as (Pătruţ et al. 2014):

$$P(v) = \sum_{i=1}^{d(v)} w(e_i), \tag{4.1}$$

where $d(v)$ is the degree of the node v, and e_1, e_2, … $e_{d(v)}$ are the edges starting from node v. Thinking in this way, the power of the node *work* in Fig. 4.2 is 8.

Let us consider now the case of the weighted graph from Fig. 4.3.

In Fig.4.3, one can see some circuits containing all nodes. Such a circuit is called a *Hamiltonian circuit* (Livovschi and Georgescu 1986). For a circuit, its cost is defined as the sum of the costs/weights of its component edges.

For the graph in Fig. 4.3, we can consider these two Hamiltonian circuits: (*education, health care, health insurance, climate change, women, jobs, immigration, gun violence, work*), with cost: 2 + 8 + 1 + 1 + 6 + 5 + 1 + 3 = 27 and (*education, gun violence, immigration, work, jobs, women, climate change, health insurance, health care*), with cost: 2 + 4 + 4 + 4 + 6 + 1 + 1 + 8 + 2 = 32.

A classical problem of graphs is to determine the cheapest/shortest Hamiltonian circuit (the *minimum cost Hamiltonian circuit problem*) (Tollis 2012).

The solution to this problem is not unique, because the same Hamiltonian circuit may start from any of the nodes of the graph and the order of the nodes can be considered in both directions.

In a post from a political blog, we can have values in the same category of the blog, or even in the same context of the post. In the latter case, we can consider the links between the values in a post as edges, and the frequency of their co-occurrences as weights of those edges. Then, a Hamiltonian circuit of minimum cost represents an order where values may be presented so as to use the least number of sentences and also to keep the basic ideas of the discourse.

Therefore, the answer to this problem of graph theory provides the answer to our problem of political discourse analysis: (c) which should be the order of presenting political values so as to achieve a political discourse equivalent with the given one but also a much more concise one?

4.3 The Minimum Spanning Tree

Any connected graph with no circuits is called a tree. A (undirected) graph with no cycles is called a *forest*.

The graph in Fig. 4.3 is not a tree, because it has many circuits. Given a connected graph, which has circuits (therefore it is not a tree), we can remove some of the edges, so that circuits are eliminated but connectivity is kept. Thus, we obtain a tree with the same nodes but only some of the edges of the initial graph. Such a tree is called a *spanning tree* of the initial graph. In Fig. 4.4, we have highlighted a partial tree of the graph in Fig. 4.3. The concept of spanning tree is useful in solving problem (d).

If we take into consideration the costs/weights of the edges, we can define the cost of the spanning tree as the sum of the costs of its edges. A key problem is to obtain a *minimum spanning tree* for a given graph. However, in the case of political discourses in political blogs, we are interested in determining a *spanning tree of a maximum cost*. Because the costs of edges can be represented by the "strength" of the connections among the values from the nodes, the problem may be solved in a similar way as the problem of the minimum spanning tree is solved. For these problems, we can use the algorithms of Robert Clay Prim and Vojtěch Jarník (Cormen et al. 2001).

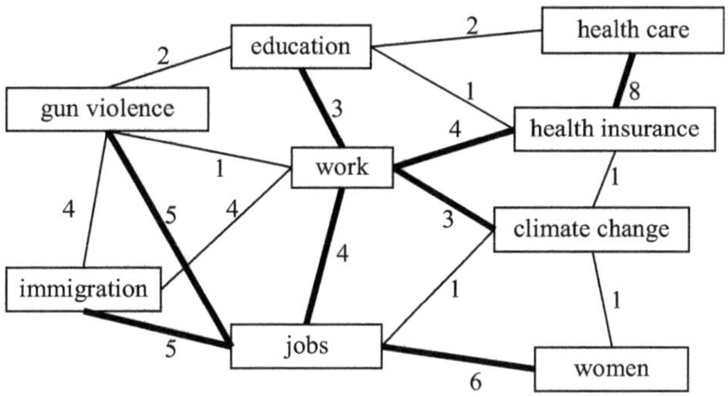

Fig. 4.4 A maximum spanning tree of the graph in Fig. 4.3. Its cost is 32

For the case of our initial graph of political, economic, and socio-cultural values, the partial tree of maximum cost is the one in Fig. 4.8. A tree always has $n - 1$ edges (n being the number of nodes).

After mathematical modeling, such a problem is reduced to a classic problem of graph theory: given $G = (V, E)$ a graph and $w : E \rightarrow R$, $w(e)$ = weight of edge e, determine the spanning tree of G with the minimum weight.

We consider the weight of a tree the sum of the weights of its edges:

$$\mathrm{c(T) = c(e_1) + c(e_2) + \ldots + c(e_{n-1})} \tag{4.2}$$

Thus, the minimum spanning tree T * will have the weight w(T *), where:

$$\mathrm{w(T*) = min\{w(T) \mid T - spanning\ tree\ of\ G\}.} \tag{4.3}$$

In a similar way, the maximal spanning tree T^{**} will have the weight w(T * *), where:

$$\mathrm{w(T*) = max\{w(T) \mid T - spanning\ tree\ of\ G\}.} \tag{4.4}$$

The minimum/maximum spanning tree will have $n - 1$ edges)

This result is done in $n - 1$ steps (Croitoru 1992). There are three well-known algorithms to solve this problem, like Prim-Jarník's algorithm, Kruskal's algorithm, and Prim's algorithm. In Pătruţ et al. (2014) we have presented Prim's algorithm, used by the *Political Analyst* software.

The maximum spanning tree can be computed by negating the weights for each edge and applying the minimum spanning tree algorithm (Pemmaraju and Skiena 2003).

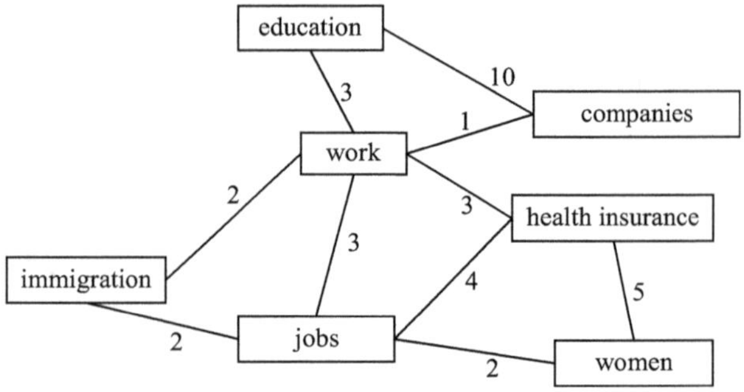

Fig. 4.5 A graph to illustrate the shortest path problem. We have highlighted the path of minimum cost between *education* and *women*

4.4 The Shortest Path Between Two Values

The graph theory may also be useful in determining the optimal sequence of passing from the presentation of one value (political idea) to another by using phrases from the given discourse. Thus, Edsger W. Dijkstra's algorithm determines the path of minimum cost within a graph, starting from a node and reaching another (Dijkstra 1959). The problem which arises is that of establishing a cost function which is representative for problem (e): *how can one get from one value to another by using as few words as possible from the discourse to be analyzed?* (Patrut and Cmeciu 2008).

Now, suppose we consider the cost of an edge as being the minimum distance (in words) between the two values (political keywords), within a post of a political blog. The shortest path problem will provide us the minimum path between one value to another, in terms of costs. This can have various interpretations, like:

- the required order to move from one value to the other, using as few words as possible.
- the least number of intermediary nodes (values) between two given values, if we consider the cost of each edge being 1

Dijkstra's algorithm will provide us with the solution of the shortest path. Considering the graph in Fig. 4.5, *education* as start node and *women* as end node, the shortest path between education and women is *education* → *work* → *jobs* → *women*, with the total cost of 3 + 3 + 2 = 8.

If we consider the costs/weights of the edges representing the "strength" between values, then the problem will change into the longest/maximal path problem and it can be solved in a similar way, using an adapted Dijkstra's algorithm.

The minimum cost Hamiltonian circuit, the minimal/maximal spanning tree, and *the shortest/longest path* are examples of problems of improving the political discourse, provided that they want to express the same political ideas but use fewer words and the same relations among political, economic, or socio-cultural values, as in the initial discourse in a post of a blog. These mathematical

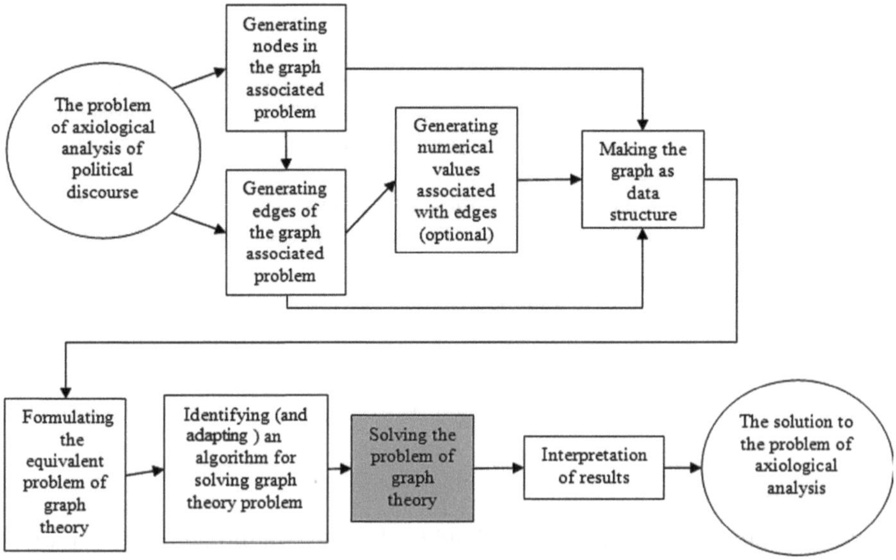

Fig. 4.6 Political speech analysis scheme using graph theory. The computer is responsible only for the grey phase

instruments can be used to achieve a summary or a synthesis of the discourse of some politicians, when it is restricted to a post on a political blog, or in the space of an advertorial, or to some limited time in a video clip on Youtube or other video-sharing web services.

Therefore, solving a problem of political discourse analysis will follow the diagram in Fig. 4.6 (Pătruţ and Patrut 2010).

4.5 Using *Political Analyst* for the Axiological Analysis of the Political Blog of US President, Barack Obama

The program *Political Analyst* has been developed by programmers from the Vasile Alecsandri University of Bacău, Romania, and EduSoft Ltd. (http://www.edusoft.ro/ company). It runs on Windows operating systems, requiring a minimum of 5 MB for installation. You can select between English and Romanian as GUI[1] language. The current version can simultaneously analyze different types of values (political, economic, and socio-cultural) for several parties and their candidates. Although there is a set of predefined values, the user can create his/her own sets of values. Add, delete, select or deselect operations are allowed. Once a value has been added into a set of values, it can also be included in the subsequent analysis.

[1] GUI = Graphical User Interface.

The program allows for the automatic generation of the values' graph and of the connections among them based on the co-occurrence of political key words in fragments of sizes established by the user, based on a personal analysis of the text. Subsequently, the user may insert new edges and associate weights/costs to the edges. The nodes may be moved on the graph's editing area and the edges between these nodes are preserved.

After entering all the data related to the party and its candidate, one can find the frequency of values in the political text. This text can be a post from the blog of a politician.

The most important thing is that the program can create and analyze the graph of values:

- firstly, we must choose the types of the values that will constitute the graph;
- then, the program will automatically generate the graph, with the values as nodes and any edges.

After that:

(a) one can proceed to filling the graph with edges, drawn through *drag and drop* operation, followed by the entrance of the edge's weight (this weight is entered by the researcher on the basis of the discourse) or
(b) the edges may be automatically generated, between co-occurring nodes within a blog post, and the weights are represented by the number of co-occurrences of the two values forming the edge.

In Fig. 4.7, one can see a screen capture from the Political Analyst program, where the thickness of an edge is directly commensurate with its cost.

The generated graphs can be subsequently modified by the researcher. However, generally, the resulted graphs are very complex, so their visual analysis by a human user is difficult to perform. The program *Political Analyst* can generate answers to all the questions specified in the previous sections.

For the graph in Fig. 4.7, we have considered the following parameters:

- as corpus: the posts of the Barack Obama's political blog. between October 2013 and December 2013;
- the edges (and their costs) were determined by the co-occurences in a fragment of 100 characters of the keywords/

Obama's blog is organized into different categories. In fact, each category is a blog. Each category has posts, in reverse chronological order. However, there are some posts, which belong to 2–3 categories.

Obama's blogs/categories are:

- Climate Change Blog
- Gun Violence Prevention Blog
- Health Care Blog
- Immigration Reform Blog
- Jobs & the Economy Blog
- Stand with Women Blog

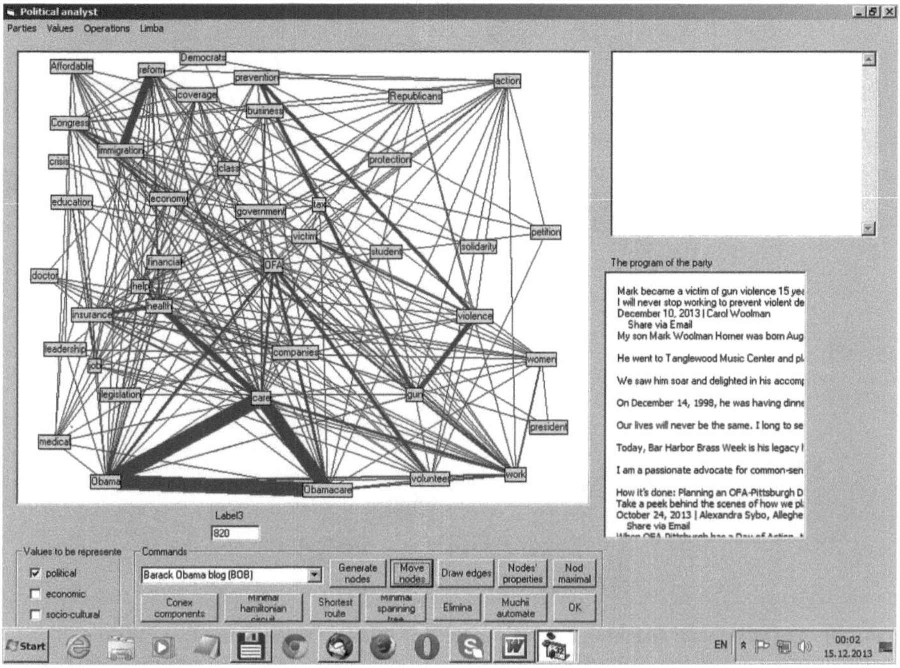

Fig. 4.7 An example of a graph

After reading the blogs, in period October–December 2013, we conclude the following words can be used as keywords or political values of President Obama's political blog:

action, Affordable (Care Act), business, cancer, care, checks, class, company, Congress, contraception, coverage, crisis, daughter, Democrats, doctor, economy, education, financial, friend, government, gun, health, help, hope, immigration, insurance, job, killed, leadership, legislation, leukemia, medical, medicare, Obama, Obamacare, OFA, patient, petition, president, prevention, protection, reform, Republicans, Romney, solidarity, sons, students, tax, victim, violence, volunteer, women, work.

Of course, some words can be found only in singular form, or in plural form, and other words can be found in both form.

Figure 4.8 presents the solution to the problem of the maximum spanning tree for the graph in Fig. 4.7, i.e. the maximum spanning tree for the graph associated to the blog of Barack Obama (http://www.barackobama.com), as it was on December 10, 2013.

This tree contains the edges below, with their respective weights.

action-Congress (7)
Congress-OFA (17)
OFA-volunteer (38)

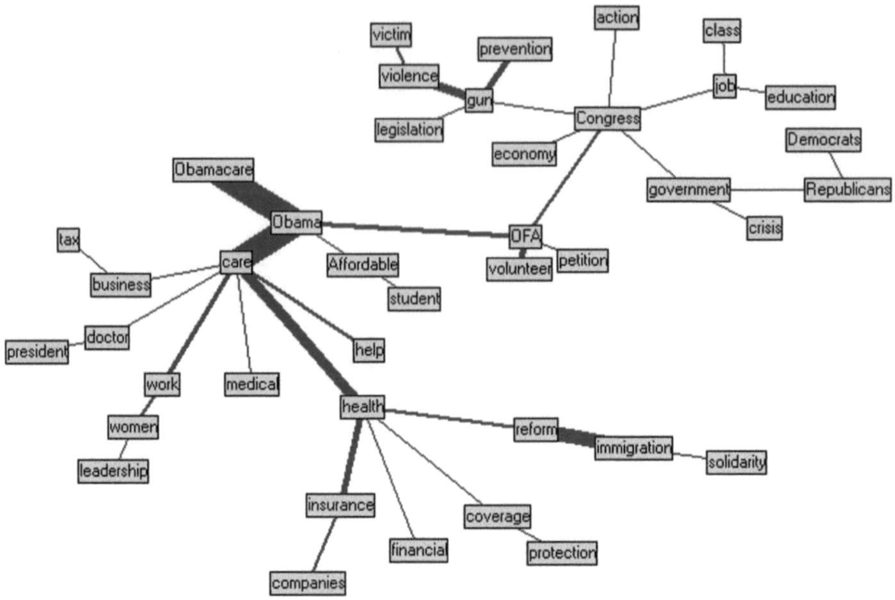

Fig. 4.8 The maximum spanning tree for the blog of Barack Obama (Oct–Dec. 2013)

Obama-OFA (29)
care-Obama (163)
Obama-Obamacare (160)
care-health (62)
health-insurance (39)
care-work (21)
care-help (19)
health-reform (13)
immigration-reform (94)
companies-insurance (12)
women-work (10)
care-medical (9)
coverage-health (8)
Congress-government (7)
Congress-gun (7)
gun-violence (53)
gun-prevention (33)
victim-violence (12)
Affordable-Obama (6)
Congress-job (6)
class-job (5)
government-Republicans (5)
Democrats-Republicans (4)

business-care (3)
Congress-economy (3)
financial-health (3)
gun-legislation (3)
leadership-women (3)
care-doctor (2)
education-job (2)
OFA-petition (2)
Affordable-student (1)
business-tax (1)
coverage-protection (1)
crisis-government (1)
doctor-president (1)
immigration-solidarity (1)

We can notice the importance of the name of the president. His surname, *Obama*, is used like a brand in the president's political blog. In addition, the focus is on his *Obamacare* health care reform.

Another important keyword is OFA, the acronym of the Organizing for Action, a nonprofit social welfare organization and community organizing project in the United States, which advocates for the agenda of the President Barack Obama.

The U.S. Congress and the immigration are other keywords in the President's political blog.

4.6 Conclusions

Political blogs of politicians may sometimes be difficult to analyze manually. Political blogs may contain many posts, with long texts, extending over several pages. Sometimes, the blogs can also be too intricate. Sometimes, politicians use "wooden language" or casual speech. In this latter case, it is difficult to follow and extract the main political ideas or political, socio-cultural, and economic values from their discourse. It is difficult to "decipher" such a political discourse.

Graph analysis can be, in this case, a useful mathematical tool for researchers, and they can easily distinguish the main ideas of political blogs, or they can highlight the topics of interest, and the links among them.

By the mathematical modeling of such problems and by using the *Political Analyst* program, we could highlight aspects of the political blogs that may escape detection during superficial analysis. We conducted a case study for the blog of President Barack Obama, and have highlighted various important aspects of his current political ideas. Our chapter has set up a model that can be used for any political blog or political discourse, in general.

References

Chechik, G., & Tishby, N. (2002). Extracting relevant structures with side information. In *Proceedings of the conference neural information processing systems—NIPS* (pp. 857–864).

Chen, H.-H., & Lin, C.-J. (2000). A multilingual news summarizer. In *Proceedings of the 18th international conference on computational linguistics*. http://nlg.csie.ntu.edu.tw/conference_papers/coling2000b.pdf. Accessed 24 Nov 2012.

Cormen, T. H., Leiserson, C. E., Rivest, E. L., & Stein, C. (2001). *Introduction to algorithms, second edition*. McGraw-Hill: MIT Press. Section 23.2: The algorithms of Kruskal and Prim.

Croitoru, C. (1992). *Tehnici de baza in optimizarea combinatorie*. Iaşi: Editura Universitatea "Alexandru Ioan Cuza".

Diestel, R. (2012). *Graph theory (Graduate Texts in Mathematics)* (4th ed.). Berlin: Springer.

Dijkstra, E. W. (1959). A note on two problems in connexion with graphs. *Numerische Mathematik, 1*, 269–271. doi:10.1007/BF01386390.

Fletcher, P., Hoyle, H., & Patty, C. W. (1991). *Foundations of discrete mathematics*. Boston: PWS-Kent Publishing.

Katz, B., Borchardt, G., & Felshin, S. (2006). Natural language annotations for question answering. In *Proceedings of the 19th international FLAIRS conference (FLAIRS 2006)*. Melbourne Beach, FL.

Kitsak, M., Gallos, L. K., Havlin, S., Liljeros, F., Muchnik, L., Stanley, H. E., et al. (2010). Influential spreaders in networks. *Nature Physics, 6*, 888–893.

Livovschi, L., & Georgescu, H. (1986). *Sinteza şi analiza algoritmilor*. Bucharest: Editura Ştiinţifică şi Pedagogică.

Patrut, M. P., & Cmeciu C. M. (2008). The theory of graphs—a means of decoding political discourses. In *Proceedings of the international conference "Verbal Communication Techniques"*. Tbilisi: Georgian Academy of Educational Sciences.

Pătruţ, B., Furdu, I. M., & Patrut, M. (2008). Bivalent verbs and their pragmatic particularities. In E. Kapetanios, V. Sugumaran, & M. Spiliopoulou (Eds.), *Proceedings of the 13th international conference on applications of natural language to information systems*, NLDB 2008, London, UK, June 24–27. Lecture Notes in Computer Science (Vol. 5039, pp. 327–328), doi: 10.1007/978-3-540-69858-6_33.

Pătruţ, B., & Patrut, M. (2010). *New mathematical methods for analyzing political discourse: Functions and graphs for political speeches*. Saarbrücken: VDM.

Pătruţ, B., Pătruţ, M., & Cmeciu, C. (2014). Using graph theory software for political discourse analysis. In A. M. Solo (Ed.), *Political campaigning in the information age* (pp. 1–359). Hershey, PA: IGI Global. doi:10.4018/978-1-4666-6062-5 (in press)

Pemmaraju, S., & Skiena, S. (2003). *Computational discrete mathematics: Combinatorics and graph theory in mathematica*. Cambridge, England: Cambridge University Press.

Strang, G. (2005). *Linear algebra and its applications* (4th ed.). Stamford, CT: Brooks Cole.

Tishby, N., Pereira, F. C, Bialek, W. (1999). The information bottleneck method. In B. Hajek, & R.S. Sreenivas (Eds.), *Proceedings of the 37th annual allerton conference on communication, control and computing* (pp. 368–377). University of Illinois.

Tollis, I. G. (2012). Eulerian and Hamiltonian Path, HY-583 graph algorithms, University of Crete, http://www.csd.uoc.gr/~hy583/papers/ch14.pdf. Accessed 14 Nov 2012.

U.S. President Barack Obama's Political Blog—http://www.barackobama.com/news

Chapter 5
The Use of Twitter In 2013 Italian Political Election

Guido Di Fraia and Maria Carlotta Missaglia

Abstract Since 2011, a considerable number of Italian politicians have started to use social media platforms, particularly Twitter, giving rise to a late Twitter Italian revolution in political communication. A specific research was developed to understand the concrete use of the new media and how politicians actually manage them. The study has analysed a sample of 41 politicians from the main electoral lists from September 2012 until April 27, 2013. Data collected have shown a mainly unidirectional and top-down use of Twitter that reproduces the traditional mass-mediatic logic of political communication.

Keywords Political communication • Italian politics • Twitter • Social media • New media • Electoral campaign • Social tweet • Political election • Mass-mediatization

5.1 The Italian Political Communication Before the Social Media Era

Politics and media have always established relations of mutual influence, representing two of the major subsystems on which complex societies are articulated (Luhmann 1995). To outline the specific forms taken in Italy by such systems as scenario of our research, first, we need to understand their role and their peculiarities within the more general processes faced by the media and political communication in advanced Western countries over the past decades. A process mainly characterised by an epoch-making passage, generically indicated as the transition from the "*solid modernity*" to the "*liquid postmodernity*", and connected

G. Di Fraia (✉)
Università IULM, Milan, Italy
e-mail: Guido.difraia@iulm.it

M.C. Missaglia
Department of Communication, Behaviors and Consumptions, Università IULM, Milan, Italy

B. Pătruţ and M. Pătruţ (eds.), *Social Media in Politics*, Public Administration and Information Technology 13, DOI 10.1007/978-3-319-04666-2_5,

to technological evolution of media, communication paradigms, social and cultural forms. Such a transition, which has also expressed itself through the progressive decline of "big narratives", and therefore of the main ideological systems, has profoundly influenced the forms and practices of politics: giving rise, among other things, to the secularisation of the sense of political affiliation, the crisis of traditional parties and militancy, and the growing lack of interest in politics, especially with young people. Furthermore, the development of mass media, has deeply influenced the forms and languages of political communication, and of politics itself.

To summarise these processes, Mazzoleni (2004) identifies three main phases (Blumler and Kavanagh 1999). The first one refers to the post-war period, when parties were the most important element of politics. They were considered to be the link between the political beliefs of the citizens and the institutions that, at that moment of renewal and rebirth, certainly had a crucial role in the life of the country. Leaders were characterised by strong ideas and values, and little attention was given to their personal image and forms of communication. People felt a strong bond with their chosen political parties. In that period, citizens' political participation expressed itself through militancy in the mass political parties, namely the Italian Communist Party (PCI) and Christian Democracy (DC).

The second phase, starting from the 1960s, corresponds to the period of the affirmation of television as the dominant mass media and the transformation of citizens into "*citizen-spectators*". During the 1960s, 1970s and 1980s (Anania 2012), the influence of mass media culture generated well-known phenomena, such as the progressive personalisation of politics and the transformation of political parties and candidates into products to be promoted by marketing activities. The selection of candidates was no longer exclusively in relation to their competence and knowledge, but also for their image on television. Even more relevant is the large proven capability of mass media to influence the political agenda through the effects of "*agenda building*" and "*agenda setting*".

Television allowed parties to reach a bigger part of the population. Politicians tried to adapt their traditional forms of communication to the television language, realising in time the weight their words had when broadcasted to the Nation.

During the same time, political communication leaned more towards marketing styles; for this reason, it was entrusted to professionals of that industry.

For Italians, television became the principal means to gather general news and to be kept informed about politics. In this phase, some peculiarities of the conspiratorial relationship between the Italian political and media system started to develop.

In its early days, the Italian broadcasting system was state-owned and controlled by the Italian government, mainly led by DC. With the arrival of the second RAI channel in 1961, followed by Rai 3 in 1979, the division of the public television networks amongst the main mass parties (DC, PCI, PSI) was accomplished, leading to the logic of "one channel-one main party".

At this point, a series of new elements characterising the political communication was forming. In Italy, like in the rest of Europe, a strong personalisation and mediatisation of politics took place. New TV formats, such as "*politainment*", a term describing the combination of politics and entertainment, came to life. Since the early 1980s, the political language started to abound in claims and slogans, adopting simpler communication phrases, which were designed to reach out to the voters and connect with their feelings and emotions.

This period is referred to as the new era of "*Political Advertising*" (Jamieson 1992; Trent and Friedenberg 1991) and of "*Image Campaigns*" (Scammell 1998; Thompson 1995). In those years, the concept of political parties was transformed: it was no more a community to which citizens could belong, but only a product that some political consultant (a new profession created during this period) tried to package and sell. The peak of this evolution and the actual realisation of the so-called "*Italian anomaly*" took place in 1994, when Berlusconi entered successfully the political arena.

In the Western World, he was the unique case of a Prime Minister, a person able to influence indirectly the media contents of the public networks, that was in fact the owner of the only other subject that composed the Italian television duopoly. In this specific case, political and media systems were combined in the person of the leader.

Furthermore, during the 1994 campaign, the airtime that the media dedicated to political messages, programs, debates and spots increased, with a total pre-campaign airtime of 14.052 min,[1] demonstrating the transformation of the political campaign into a television and media event.

The last phase that Mazzoleni (2004) identified coincides with the 1990s. Certainly, a fundamental characteristic of that period was the multiplication of media and the fact that the audience started to be a plural-subject: it was no more just an audience, but different audiences with different interests and passions. However, looking back at that moment from today's perspective, it is possible to recognise in those past decades a phase of consolidation and development of the previous characteristics. The television system was changed from broadcasting to narrowcasting, but the communicational model was still one-to-many, and television remained the focal element in the media communication for the Italian scenario.

This slight evolution of the characteristics of that phase, within the period under analysis, suggests the need to theorize a further step: the *"2.0 Era"*, characterized by a new communicational paradigm shift.

Starting from the first decade of the new millennium, a new model was affirmed within the global societies. It was a brand-new paradigm characterized by a reticular-model, where the principal communication system shifted from one-to-many to one-to-one. With the birth and the affirmation of Social Media, this period corresponds to what Castells (2009) has called the era of "mass self communication", in which mediated communication became, for the first time in human history, "*self-generated*" content, "*self-directed*" emission, and "*self-selected*" reception.

[1] The data comes from the Observatory-Archive about political communication of University of Study of Perugia.

This new paradigm has had many effects on the forms and languages of political communication. For the first time, politicians can communicate openly with citizens and electors without the mediation of the journalistic system or of their affiliation party.

In Italy, the adoption of social media was slower than in other European countries, as demonstrated by research developed by the auditing society ISTAT (2009). This study indicated that, during 2009, only 47.3 % of the total Italian population was connected to the Internet.[2]

However, in recent years, the use and adoption of Internet and Social Media from Italian families is still growing at a fast rate. A study done in 2012 shows that 41.30 % of the Italian population has a Facebook profile.[3] Twitter is a small-scale phenomenon, but its use has increased, starting from 10 December 2011, when a new Italian interface was introduced. Today, there are 4 million Twitter users and the number has doubled since last year.

A recent study conducted in 2013 by News-Italia,[4] a think-tank studying changes in forms of consumption, shows some interesting data: while general television remains the primary source of information, national newspapers have lost more than 13 % of relevance, and radio listeners have decreased from 57 % to 47 %. However, web usage has increased by 21 %, as a tool to scout for information. This growth is cutting across all age groups, with the 30–49 year-old one growing the fastest.

It is important to stress the steady change and improvement of Italians' usage of digital technology during this fourth period. Personal computers, the Internet, tablets, and smart phones have become a commodity for Italians, even if they are living in a moment of voluntary austerity.[5] These tools give people a new feeling of power and a new way to express their point of view to the world.

A common observation in this fourth period is the increase in confidence of peer-to-peer relationships, and a tendency to not being passive or uninformed about new products. The new interest about sharing information, feelings, experiences, and reviews of products is steadily growing. In recent years, the peer-to-peer revolution opens the door to new possibilities for consumers and companies. The importance of the increase in social media, and the communication possibilities cannot be overlooked.

So, how do these changes affect politics? Digital media offer new opportunities that partially revive citizens' interests in politics, in a moment in which there is a deeply rooted disaffection with politics. This situation is confirmed by the increasingly high percentage of abstainers and undecided citizens. It coincides with a

---

[2] www.istat.it

[3] CENSIS/USCI, report about communication, 2012.

[4] http://news-italia.org; Osservatorio sulle Nuove Forme di Consumo di Informazione e sulle Trasformazioni dell'Ecosistema Mediale.

[5] This definition was created after the analyses made by the XXI edition of the monitor 3SC, a GPF society research.

brand-new voters' need for changing the political class and for direct participation of citizens that is well represented by the electoral success of the Five Star Movement (M5S) headed by Beppe Grillo and can be summarized with a tweet that was collected during our research: "Politicians wearing a tie can't understand people wearing a sweatshirt"[6] Different variables contribute to the complex relationship between politicians, communication, and the voters; namely the penetration of digital media, the political culture, and the electoral law.

Indeed, the actual electoral law represents another Italian anomaly: it was named "*porcellum*" by the very Member of Parliament who proposed it, and it creates a proportional system with blocked lists where the secretaries of parties decide candidates to be voted by Italians (Bentivegna 2012). In this way, the candidates' communication with the secretaries of the Parties has become more important than the direct communication with the voters, who now do not have the possibility to vote directly for the candidates.

On the other hand, the candidate's chance to obtain more visibility through the media mainstream is often hampered because of the limited resources, which are almost exclusively reserved for the party leaders. Therefore, social media can offer new opportunities to the less prominent candidates and figures of the various parties to obtain more visibility and a more widely known reputation.

The goal of our research was to observe how candidates of different political parties used Twitter for their political communication during the last 2013 Italian elections.

5.2 The International Research

The first researches on the use of Twitter in political communication date back to 2009. At that time, the penetration of the use of Twitter in Europe and the United States was relatively high, while in Italy the tool was still almost unknown.

These researches, mainly conducted using a quantitative and qualitative approach, were focused on the comprehension of the politicians' use practices of the new media, and on the communicational functions activated with voters. Those developed by Jackson and Lilleker in Great Britain (2011), and by Lassen and Brown in USA (2010) are interesting examples of this kind of research.

The data collected in 2009 by different scholars on the diffusion of Twitter among politicians are pretty similar. In England, the percentage of the Members of Parliament having a Twitter account was about 12 % of the total, in Denmark was 10 %, in Holland was 7 % (Hansard Society 2009). In the U.S.A., the percentage recorded on data gathered in 2010, was slightly higher oscillating between 25 % and 30 % (Goldbeck et al. 2010; Lassen and Brown 2010).

---

[6] Facebook Users status on September 21, 2012.

Both the English and the American researches converge on the detected predictive variables. Chi and Yang (2011) demonstrated that politicians more familiar with digital media were also more likely early adopters of the Twitter platform. In particular, they underlined that politicians having a Facebook (Fb) profile tend to open a Twitter page about 6 month before those who did not have an Fb profile (ibidem).

Worthy of note is the fact that, in the U.S.A., the diffusion of Twitter was higher within the Republican Party, whose members are on average older and, of course, more conservative than those of Democratic Party. On the contrary, results obtained in the English research, more similar to the Italian one, showed a higher percentage of early adopters inside progressive and leftist parties. However, although this seems a contradiction, it actually confirms a cross result of many researches, demonstrating how the adoption process of digital media, particularly of Twitter, is not related to few variables but to a complex series of factors, such as: the dimension of the party, the economic resources and, in the U.S.A., the number of the laws promoted by the party and the political composition of the affiliation commission.

From a more qualitative point of view, scholars have mainly focused their attention on the comprehension of how politicians manage this micro blog, within their more general communicative strategy. Using content analyses techniques, Goldbeck et al. (2010) recognise five different functions in the tweet generated by politicians: 1. Direct Communication (tweets containing @ and direct to specific users); 2. Personal Message (emotional tweets); 3. Information; 4. Questing Action; 5. Activities (tweets containing informations about politicians' and institutional activities) 6. Fundraising.

Moreover, different researches that have analysed the communicational model related to the use of Twitter, show how the tools can be utilised as: (a) a means of direct communication to citizens (following the traditional model one-to-many); (b) a medium of relation and bidirectional communication; (c) an useful tool to activate listening processes and to collect issues and themes from people (Chi and Yang's 2010; Jackson and Lilleker 2011).

Researches on Anglophone countries converge in demonstrating that politicians seem to be poorly oriented to use Twitter to generate an effective relationship with voters and activate with citizens a dialogue on political issues.

The use of the medium resulted instead in being oriented by an informational communicational model intended for the re-mediatization of contents of other communicational media, mainly useful for informing citizens about candidates' whereabouts or participation at political events. This kind of use of Twitter is very close to the broadcasting model typical of mass media communication.

5.3 Social Tweet in Italian Political Communication

As many researchers and academics claim [see, for instance, Valeriani (2011)], in Italy, Twitter, even if is still a medium-scale phenomenon (Bracciale 2012; Cosenza 2012), is now the principal Social Media platform used to create conversational flow about political, diplomatic, or journalistic issues.

The first major study about Twitter use in Italian political communication was developed by Antenore (2012). The research analyses 17,000 tweets produced by Italian politics from 31 of January until 27 of February. At the moment of the detection, only 9.70 % of the total number of politicians were using the platform. From the recorded data, it can be inferred that some accounts were very active but others were completely abandoned.

From a socio-demographic point of view, the results demonstrated a slightly higher presence of female profiles, with a superior level of education, and a prevalence of freelancers. As described in other countries (Chi and Yang's 2010), in Italy too the age does not seem strongly correlated to the adoption of Twitter. On the other hand, minor parties with a small visibility, are the major users of the social network. Other interesting data are relative to the "seniority within politics". The presence of Twitter is associated with the 38 % to subjects that are at their first legislature. The longer the political career, the more reduced the presence on the social networks.

The average value of tweets measured for each politician was equal to 185 while the median was 43. Considering this data, Antenore deduced that a small part of the politicians produced about the 80 % of the content. After careful analysis, she claimed that the major parties were the ones that tweeted more. A fact indicating that the cyberspace would move towards a "*normalization*" (Margolis and Resnick 2000) of the use of the medium. However, focusing the analyses on the single active subjects, the results are inverted: the minor parties' representatives are those who tweet more to get a greater visibility than that they can obtain in media mainstream.

To point out the use practises of politicians, a content analysis on a sample of 1400 tweets was conducted, using the categories of Goldbeck et al. (2010) previously quoted. 49 % of tweets were of information type, 13 % were of reporting about participation on the media, 11 % asked for participation of citizens/electors, while 9 % are personal tweets. These tweets are part of the macro-category *Activities* that Antenore adapted to the Italian contest creating the subcategories of *Official Business*, *Location*, and *Media*.

Considering these data it is possible to say that, during 2011, the "Direct communication" (containing @ and addressed to specific person) appeared very limited, while the "Internal Communication" (tweets addressed to other politicians) is totally absent. Then, 6 % represent political activities for the local government, and 4 % the institutional activities.

Another important item of information is that 85 % of the "Informative" tweets contain links to blogs, to Parliamentary, or party sites. This indicates a use of the social media as a press review and underlines how politicians were not interested in being more transparent with the voters through the use of the medium.

To conclude, it is meaningful to notice that only 5 Members of Parliament from a total of 92 used the retweet function, and only 279 tweets of 1400 contained a hashtag, revealing a basic use of the tool and a difficult appropriation of its specific grammar by politicians. Moreover, the communication activated on the medium appeared to be totally unidirectional and poorly addressed to involve or confront voters.

The growing interest in politics and social media in Italy is demonstrated not only by the increase of academic researches, but also by the birth of many web sites and analytic tools trying to explain the new phenomenon of the first social Italian election. The majority of such tools are user-generated. Some of them are similar to news websites; instead, others are instruments for bloggers, journalists, and researchers who can use them to extract useful data. Some examples of the first type are sites such as *Italia2013.me* and *Bachecapolitica.it.*

Italia2013 is a web site of this kind that presents itself with the following quote: "Participate, share, vote" and offers a collection of useful information for the voters: such as informative articles, photos about political events and links to "social events" like a movement on Facebook, or hashtags that become case-history because of their massive use.

The new political Italian environment, characterized by a strong intolerance toward politicians' false promises, has created a new desire of transparency. To respond to the citizens' needs, many sites have been developed about politics, "fact checking", and reliability of politicians' statements. For instance, in Bachecapolitica.it, every user can contribute to verify the truthfulness of what a politician has said: he/she can post a comment, say like or don't like on a post, and he/she can insert a politician's promise. Indeed the site is entirely composed by user generated posts reporting promises made by politicians.

On the other hand, the diffusion of social media marketing has stimulated companies and private subjects to work on these themes to apply them for business and personal promotion. Therefore, in this particular conjuncture, many scientists and analysts start researches aimed to intercept buzz on the Internet and to measure sentiment about the different political lists with the intention to predict electoral results.

For example "Voices from the Blog"[7] has adapted an equation proposed by Hopkins and King (2010) by which it is possible to analyse the "sentiment" of the web on different relevant arguments. Their work is just at the beginning but, with the mix of the mathematic formula and the team of manual analyses, they obtained

[7] *Voices of the Blog* is a scientific project realised and developed by L. Curini, S. M. Iacus and G. Porro. From March 2012 the coordinator is A. Ceron and from January 2013 I. Iasinovschi is a new member of the group. It is a scientific and academic project in collaboration with the University of Milan.

data about last Italian and American election, affected by an error lower than 2 % (Ferrazza 2013).

Another important role in this field of analysis is played by *BlogMeter*, that has developed software for the semantic analysis of the buzz related to political topics in Italian Facebook and Twitter. Specifically for the last election they developed "PolisMeter",[8] a web-based tool where Italians can follow the "social" communications produced during the 2013 political campaign.

5.4 Twitter Uses and Communicational Functions Before and After the 2013 Political Election

We can say that, in Italy, the 2013 political election was the first "Social Media Italian Election"; a phenomenon, even if on a smaller scale, similar to the one won by Obama in 2008 in the USA (Brown 2012). This election represented the starting point of a "Twitter (R) Evolution" in Italian political communication.

However, if it is possible to identify this last election as the first social election, could we say that Italian politicians are really aware of the "social" use of Twitter? Have politicians understood the voters' need for one-to-one communication in the social media age?

To answer these questions, we analysed the activity on Twitter of a sample of Italian political candidates in two defined ranges of time. The first period was the "campaign period", from 25 January 2013 until 26 February 2013; the second one was the "post-election" period from 27 February 2013 until 27 April 2013. During this long-lasting phase, Italy remained without a government and without a President of the Republic.

The party lists chosen for the research were: the Democratic Party (PD), the People of Freedom (PDL), Future and Freedom (FLI), Left Ecology Freedom (SEL), Civic Choice-Monti, Act to Stop the Decline (FiD), Five Star Movement (M5S), CasaPound Italy (CPI), Italian Civil Revolution, and The Union of the Center (UDC). These lists represent the general situation and the big parties, but also a more distinctive situation—the new one that emerged during this election. Indeed M5S, FiD, Civic Choice, and CasaPound represent an alternative dimension of Italian politics and a new possibility for the constituency.

While analysing these two dimensions, it is possible to highlight the complexity of the Italian political environment, recognise new rules, and modus operandi that transform these parties in national case histories.

From these lists we studied, 41 specific candidates were selected by means of two different criteria. For each list, there was the leader and three other exponents chosen if they were among the first three most popular inside the regional electoral

[8] http://www.polismeter.it

lists.[9] The actual sample was, finally, made up of 33 politicians because only the active profiles were considered in the study, and six politicians no longer have a Twitter page.

We analyzed the Twitter profile of each politician selected in two main ways: quantitatively and qualitatively.

For the quantitative part, we observed that the extracted data underlined if the communication was one-to-one or one to many, if the number of tweets per day was reasonable or not, if the grammar of Twitter has been understood or not.

Starting from the quantitative analyses, a strong heterogeneity within the total number of tweets generated by the different candidates was shown. Candidates presented a maximum of 1230 tweets and a minimum of 5 in the first period; and a maximum of 335 and a minimum of zero in the second period. The average for each candidate was about 109 tweets in the first period (with a median of 49) and 30 for the second one (with a median of 30).

Other macroscopic data are the differences between the tweets generated in the campaign and those in the post-election period. Data shows a transition from 3,592 tweets in the first period, to 2,020 tweets in the second one. They decreased by about 44 %. Until now, these data suggest an actual strategic use of the tool. It appears to be mainly finalised to obtain more visibility and a better reputation during the campaign.

In support of this hypothesis, we can consider that some politicians opened their account in the pre-campaign period, while others disappeared from the channel immediately after the election day. Indeed, about nine politicians, including the Senator and ex Prime Minister Mario Monti, stopped tweeting or reduced their Twitter use drastically (for instance Mario Monti tweeted 273 times during the pre-campaign, and only three times in the following period).

A cross result founded in the research was the total absence of shared strategies of Twitter use among members of the same party. Effectively, the variable "party affiliation" did not generate any statistically significant difference in the obtained data. This results is consistent with the possibility offered by Twitter as a "personal medium", which allowed candidates to bypass the traditional logic of mediation carried out by the parties between them, the media, and citizens.

For the qualitative part of research, all the tweets tweeted by the sampled candidates has been collected and 654 of them, extracted from a total of 1,230, were analysed. For each politician, tweets were selected following this sampling pattern: if the tweets were less than fifty, they were all analysed; if they were more, only one tweet out of three has been analysed.

Tweets were studied using different variables: Jakobson's functions of language (Jakobson 1963), the presence of the @ symbol, the presence of the # symbol, issues, and slogans.

[9] In Italy, during political election every district has its own list of political exponents.

Jakobson divided the functions of language into six: the *referential*, the *emotive*, the *conative*, the *poetic*, the *phatic* and the *meta-linguistic* one. The phatic function is the one with which it is possible to activate, maintain or terminate a conversation; this function is connected with the emission channel. The conative is addressed to the recipient. It is useful to express what can be defined as a "call to action". The poetic one is focused on the message: its language is complex, rich, and rhetorical. The meta-linguistic function is completely interested in the construction of the message and in its language features. The referential one is related to the context and is useful when it is necessary to describe actions and behaviours in a specific space and time. The last one is the emotive, which is focused on one's personality, feelings, and desires.

Through the analysis of Jakobson's language functions, the net prevalence of tweets with referential function emerges both in the campaign (50 % of the total) and in the post-campaign phase (40 % of the total). This function is mainly generated by tweets that gave information about candidates' presence on a TV show or at electoral events, or that indicated articles or links connected with their sites or blogs. This practice demonstrates a mainly unidirectional and top-down use of Twitter, finalized to narrate the politicians' agenda and to construct the press review of their activities. The emotive function is the second most present in the messages produced during the two periods. Respectively, they were 30 % and 40 % of the tweets generated. These interesting data leave room for two different ways of interpretation.

First, the considerable weight of emotive tweets can be read as an appropriate use of the medium that users can utilise to communicate with the outside in a non-mediated way, showing their subjectivity and their emotional experiences with openness, and authenticity.

Secondly, it appears as a further testimony to the personalisation process in politics that is also reproduced through Twitter. This consists of a communicational logic of self-centeredness and self-reflection, which penalises against the opportunities that Twitter offers to create an active audience and a direct communication with the voter. The phatic tweets were only generated during the campaign period, and with a very small percentage compared to what we could have expected. Only 7 % of the total tweets were of this type. This percentage, which was reduced to zero in the post-election phase, shows the politicians' low interest in the actual process of communication that Twitter can achieve, and to its ability to directly connect the profile's owner with his/her followers.

In both periods, the conative function was very low within the analysed tweets, and was limited to stimulating the participation to events.

In both periods, the lowest Jakobson's functions embodied in the politicians' tweets were: the poetic (4.40 %) and the meta-linguistic one (0.02 %).

One of the most important items of information we collected was the reduced presence of political issues: only 40 % of the tweets created in the two phases of analysis connected with issues that had a political relevance, and this applies equally to the various parties. Particularly, the economy was the most quoted topic present in 31 % of the tweets, followed by the themes of justice (2 %), welfare

(3 %) and work (2 %). The changes recorded in the percentage of tweets connected with the different themes were minimal in both periods and not significant.

This result, coherent with those resulting from other Italian researches[10] is in line with the styles of the political communication on all media that characterizes Italy. Indeed, they confirm how in the "3P System"—"Policy, Political and Personal Issues"—the Policy area is, in Italy, the most under-represented in political discourse where discussions prevail about skirmishes between parties and about the principal and more mediatised politicians.

In Twitter language, the hashtag (#) identifies a theme that converges all the tweets that contain it. It is useful when creating a flux of conversation that allows debates among users about specific issues. The analysis of the hashtags most used by the studied candidates allowed us to rebuild the themes debated during the election. The study confirms how politicians tend to use the medium in accordance with the self-centeredness typical of the Italian political communication. Self-centeredness is merely transported from the traditional media to Twitter. About the total of 1,899 hashtags collected, only 156 (about 8 %) are correlated to policy issues, 4 % referred to television programmes or other media, 6 % to institutional issues, 10 % to places of significance for the election campaign, and about 63 % (equal to 1,189 hashtags) correlated to the political candidates themselves. Among these, the communicational anomaly of Berlusconi emerges. His hashtags (#berlusconi, #consilvio) are present in a large majority of the messages produced by the account activated by the ex-Premier during the 2013 electoral campaign (@berlusconi2013) and they represent about 37 % of the total hashtags used in the two analysed periods. It is important to indicate that the hashtag #noprodi refers to Romano Prodi (PD), which encompassed 60 messages generated in the post-election period. It is connotative of an oppositional conversation against the election as President of the Republic of the ex-Prime Minister Romano Prodi. Such hashtags accompanied and facilitated the failure of his candidature that negatively influenced the subsequent Italian political affairs.

The textual analysis conducted of the most retweeted tweets during the campaign period offers interesting insights about the virtual conversation between candidates and citizens. Among these retweets, the emotive ones are largely prevalent (they account for 47 % of the most retweeted, compared to 35 % of the total examined tweets). This result shows that, even in political communication, the messages' passionate components are those that easily generate engagement and viral effect. The most retweeted messages are those that, largely expressed in an emotive way, contain critical essays of other politicians (mainly regarding Berlusconi, Grillo, and Bersani). Further evidence of how, even on Twitter, the interest of voter-followers is mainly captured by content relative to clash between leaders and other personal or political issues. To summarize, the logic of the political spectacle, typical of mass media and mainly of television, seemed also be passed through the 140-character social media.

[10] The political debate on Twitter is only 10 % of the total debates (http://polismeter.it/)

The centrality of the leaders in the relationship's dynamics between politicians and followers is also confirmed for M5S. The findings show that despite its characteristics of a political movement that could result in more horizontal and equal relations among members, the most retweeted tweets were exclusively those of the leader Beppe Grillo, while those of the other candidates of the same party generated very little interest.

5.5 The "Mass-Mediatization" of Twitter

The 2013 Italian election marked the arrival of Twitter as a popular communication tool between politicians and citizens. Its use reached a significant level of importance to the point of influencing the general dynamics of political communication.

The research here presented was addressed to investigate the use of Twitter by Italian politicians and candidates and the related communicational functions.

The collected data reconstruct an extremely differentiated and contradictory scenario. On one hand, this environment shows the typical characteristics of every adoption phase of communication technology. During this phase, early adopters, who, by definition, are not yet accustomed to a new medium, tend to reproduce on it the communicational logics and the grammars of previous media.

On the other hand, however, it is possible to identify some features that negatively characterise the Italian political communication by analysing the communicational model and the content of tweets.

It was in that period that candidates became aware of the strategic importance of Twitter as a powerful political tool, as its penetration in Italy increased significantly, particularly within the most advanced segment of society, wherefrom the majority of its users are. Such awareness can be demonstrated by the large number of tweets produced during the pre-election phase and by the fact that many politicians, including Prime Minister Mario Monti, and On. Silvio Berlusconi, opened a Twitter account after the electoral campaign had already started.

Nevertheless, the Italian politicians' awareness did not match their actual knowledge of the medium and therefore their ability to understand its communicational logics. The majority of the politicians, which this study takes into account, used Twitter in a tactical way, mainly centred on focusing attention on their electoral campaign. Indeed, it is not coincidental that a drastic decrease of tweets by politicians occurred in the weeks after the election, with some accounts even becoming idle. Among the communication functions generated by micro-blogging, namely information, relation, and listening of the followers, the candidates analysed by this study have mostly focused on the first one, thus replicating a communication model typical of mass-media. In fact, by analysing the communication functions (Jakobson 1963) on Twitter, it has emerged that the majority of tweets were of the referential type, aimed to give out information to the public rather than to attempt to create relationships, build a dialogue and stimulate feedback from the users, which is exactly what Twitter can help achieve when used properly.

With regards to content, a very small number of tweets discussed policy issues, whereas tweets on political and personal matters were largely prevalent, similarly to what occurred on mainstream media. Emotional tweets, often containing critical or direct attacks against other candidates (particularly on main leaders like Berlusconi, Bersani, or Grillo), were those that obtained the major viral effect and engagement, resulting as the most retweeted.

A textual analysis of such tweets has demonstrated that politicians reproduced on Tweeter pretty much the same traditional communication grammar used in mass media. Elements that allow us to talk about a *mass-mediatization* of Twitter on 2013 Italian elections can be found in the nature of many of those tweets, such as the self-referential quality of the outbound communication. Most of the hashtags used by the sample referred to the politicians themselves, and mostly to the party leaders, creating a reference system in which politicians are, at the same time, objects and subjects of the overall generated discourse. This trend reproduced on Twitter, represents a long-time identified characteristic of the Italian political communication (Mazzoleni 2004).

A second element is the high quantity of tweets generated by some of the already most known politicians. These data confirm the process of *normalisation* of the medium used, as already described by other researches (Margolis and Resnick 2000). Indeed, Tweeter, which could represent a new possibility for smaller party candidates to reach out to citizens and connect with them, seems to be used in a massive way, and with greater efficacy in terms of followership, in particular by already well-known politicians and leaders. In essence, those politicians and parties who are able to mobilise the necessary financial resources to outsource the communication to PR agencies or consultants, according to a typical mass media model.

Finally, an additional element is given by the explicit and strong "orientation towards the mass media" of the content and the release timing of tweets produced by the monitored candidates, orientation, which is recognisable on at least two levels. First, the mainstream media are directly present in a significant number of tweets and hashtags in the form of information concerning, for example, television shows in which the tweeting candidate has participated or will participate. In the analysed tweets, Indeed, the Media System appears to be the true recipient of messages. In fact, it is mainly the mainstream media that candidates (and/or their staff) seem to think when they write their own tweets, not so much to get in touch directly with the citizens, yet rather to attract the attention of the media system and rely on the re-launching effect it is able to ensure. This explains the frequent use of tweets by candidates containing "strong", therefore "easily expendable" content, using the tool to create attention or generate conflict and release previews and statements in order to make sure to get noticed by the media, thus influencing their agenda.

To conclude, it is possible to say that the 2013 Italian election campaign was the first to see Twitter as an important channel of communication, but italian politicians have used improperly this media; more like a mass media rather than a social media. From here our definition of a "mass-mediatizated" use of Twitter. Probably also as a result of this improper use, Twitter has played a very ancillary and peripheral role in the political communication of 2013 election campaign, at least if compared to classic media and, in particular, to television.

References

Anania, F. (2012). *Potere politico e mass media, da Giolitti a Berlusconi*. Roma: Carocci Editore.

Antenore, M. (2012). Soundbite Politics. I parlamentari su Twitter. In S. Bentivengna (Ed.), *Parlamento 2.0. Strategie di comunicazione politica in internet* (pp. 116–131). Milano: FrancoAngeli.

Bentivegna, S. (Ed.). (2012). *Parlamento 2.0, strategia di comunicazione politica in internet*. Milano: Franco Angeli.

Blumler, J. G., & Kavanagh, D. (1999). The third age of political communication: Influences and features. *Political Communication, 16*(3), 209–230.

Bracciale, R. (2012). Il Parlamento italiano alla prova del web: alla ricerca delle affinità elettive. In S. Bentivengna (Ed.), *Parlamento 2.0. Strategie di comunicazione politica in internet* (pp. 186–204). Milano: Franco Angeli.

Brown, G. (2012). *Social media influencing the 2012 political campaigns*. Berglund Center for Internet Studies. http://bcis.pacificu.edu/interface/?p=1131

Castells, M. (2009). *Communication power*. Oxford: Oxford University Press.

Chi, F. & Yang, N. (2010) Twitter in congress: Outreach vs transparency. Social Science Research Network (SSRN), (pp. 1–9), http://ssrn.com/en/abstract=1630943.

Chi, F., & Yang, N. (2011). Twitter adoption in congress. *Review of Network Economics, 10*(1), 1–44.

Cosenza, G. (2012). *Spot Politik, Perché la «casta» non sa comunicare*. Roma-Bari: Editori Laterza.

Ferrazza, F. (2013, February). Questa volta vincono i dati. *Wired*, pp 34–46.

Goldbeck, J., Grimes, J. M., & Rogers, A. (2010). Twitter use by the U.S Congress. *Journal of the American Society for Information Science and Technology, 61*(8), 1612–1621.

Hansard Society (2009). Twitter: Communication tool or pointless vanity, http://www.hansardsociety.org.uk

Hopkins, D. J., & King, G. (2010). A method of automated nonparametric content analysis for social science. *American Journal of Political Science, 54*(1), 229–247.

ISTAT, Istituto nazionale di statistica, "Cittadini e Nuove Tecnologie", dicembre 2009

Jackson, N. A., & Lilleker, D. G. (2011). Microblogging, constituency service and impression management: UK MPs and the use of Twitter. *The Journal of Legislative Studies, 17*(1), 86–105.

Jakobson, R. (1963). *Essais de linguistique générale*. Paris: Minuit.

Jamieson, K. H. (1992). *Dirty politics. Deception, distraction, and democracy*. New York: Lang.

Lassen, D., & Brown, A. R. (2010). Twitter: The electoral connection? *Social Science Computer Review, 28*(4), 1–18.

Luhmann, N. (1995). *Social systems*. Standford: Standford University Press.

Margolis, M., & Resnick, D. (2000). *Politics as Usal: The cyberspace 'Revolution'*. London: Routledge.

Mazzoleni, G. (2004). *La comunicazione politica*. Bologna: Il Mulino.

Scammell, M. (1998). The wisdom of the war room: US campaigning and Americanization. *Media, Culture and Society, 20*(2), 251–275.

Thompson, J. B. (1995). *The media and modernity: A social theory of the media*. Cambridge: Polity Press.

Trent, J. S., & Friedenberg, R. V. (1991). *Political communication campaign*. New York: Praeger.

Valeriani, A. (2011). *Twitter factor, come i nuovi media cambiano la politica internazionale*. Roma-Bari: Editori Laterza.

Part II
Using Social Media in Electoral Marketing

This section will describe how politicians and their staff uses social media for their electoral marketing. Three chapters will deal with the different types of elections in recent 2 years.

A: Social Media in Local Elections
B: Social Media in Parliamentary Elections
C: Social Media in Presidential Elections

Chapter 6
An Intermedia Understanding of the Networked Twitter Ecology

The 2012 Local Elections in Belgium

Evelien D'heer and Pieter Verdegem

Abstract The chapter will focus on the use of Twitter during the 2012 local elections in Belgium. Via a multi-method approach we aim to understand how the Twitter debate links up to mainstream media outlets and how political actors, media actors and citizens interact in this decentralized and interactive Twitter sphere. In doing so, we elaborate on the role of Twitter (as one of the most popular social media platforms) in the agenda setting and building processes between politicians, media and public opinion. Further, we discuss the role of social media, and Twitter in particular, in the rejuvenation of democracy.

6.1 Agenda Setting in a Mediated Democracy

Our research will focus on the election debate, as conducted on Twitter. Based on the platform's technical features, myths and prophecies have been articulated about its transformation power on democracy. Both positive and critical accounts are techno-centric as they fail to take into account the context in which these technologies are embedded (Curran et al. 2012). In this respect, the understanding of the mediated political debate via Twitter will focus on the position of and relation between media or journalists, political actors and citizen-audiences.

Related to the 'blurrification' of what is public and private on social media, monitoring and scrutinizing the political realm becomes more easy (Papacharissi 2009). In reflecting upon political activity in contemporary society, Rosanvallon (2008) refers to 'surveillance' or oversight, reflecting the vigilant citizen and the

E. D'heer (✉)
iMinds–MICT—Ghent University, Research Group for Media and ICT, Department of Communication Sciences, Korte Meer 7-9-11, 9000 Ghent, Belgium
e-mail: Evelien.dheer@ugent.be

P. Verdegem
Research Group for Media and ICT, Department of Communication Sciences, Ghent University, Korte Meer 7-9-11, 9000 Ghent, Belgium

B. Pătruţ and M. Pătruţ (eds.), *Social Media in Politics*, Public Administration and Information Technology 13, DOI 10.1007/978-3-319-04666-2_6,

organization of people as watchdogs. Mass media have traditionally functioned as intermediary system between society and political institutions, but social media enable both citizens and politicians to circumvent the media, and directly influence each other within this networked new media environment (Bruns 2008; Benkler 2006). In addition to the potential to impact agenda setting processes, Twitter carries the promise of more direct forms of democracy (Bruns 2008).

Agenda setting theory, often applied in election campaign research, provides a useful framework to investigate the shifting and dynamic power relationships between these three actors—media, political elites and citizens—each with their own issue agenda (Dearing and Rogers 1996). We recognize that the socio-technological context the agenda setting theory traditionally assumes no longer holds in contemporary society (Chaffee and Metzger 2001; Bennett and Iyengar 2008). The rise and implementation of social media for political purposes potentially challenges the interplay between these agendas and the position of traditional power elites. The shifting dynamics between mainstream media and social media are highly relevant for the functioning of the public sphere and democracy in general.

Political actors can circumvent traditional media and directly address citizen-users, which is convenient during election times when mainstream media focus on party leaders and larger parties (Hermans and Vergeer 2012). At the same time, these mainstream media are still key arenas for political communication (Curran et al. 2012). Their presence in this networked media environment might provide additional possibilities for politicians to access and influence the mass media agenda or endorse and enhance the visibility of particular existing mass media outlets (cf. secondary gatekeeping, Singer 2014). This post-broadcasting era (Prior 2006) fragments and expands the news environment, in which not only citizens, but also politicians can embrace the creativity, interactivity and autonomy that is associated with this decentralized media environment. In reflecting upon the concept of 'networked politics' (Curran et al. 2012: 164), notions of interactivity, participation and autonomy need to be empirically understood.

The focus and set-up of the study is to grasp the broader (i.e. socio-technological) spectrum of Twitter use during this highly intense period of public attention upon the elections, guided by the prominent question to what extent and how Twitter can impact agenda setting processes. We focus on the local and regional elections in Belgium, that nonetheless their distinct local orientation received a lot of attention in national media outlets (Epping et al. 2013). During election times, the importance and influence of media increases, for national as well as local campaigning (Van Aelst 2008). Concerning the use of social media, online means of narrow casting to inform and mobilize—specific groups of—citizens (or vice versa) relate to the local nature and social embeddedness of the elections. Next, in the methodology section, we will elaborate on the collection of Twitter data, the possibilities of the Twitter platform for intermedia connections and user interactions and the analysis of the data.

6.2 Methodology

6.2.1 Context and Data Collection

The case study here concerns the local elections in Belgium, held on the 14th of October 2012. Through the use of the Twitter streaming API, we collected a corpus of 43,447 Twitter messages containing the official hashtag on the local elections (i.e. #vk2012) between the 1st of September and the 21st of October. These messages correspond to 11,658 users participating publicly (i.e. through the use of the hashtag) in the debate. Notwithstanding the substantial number, we make no attempt to generalize this specific userbase to the wider population or the electorate as such. Aside users that represent politicians and/or political parties and media institutes or journalists, it is likely we are dealing with 'political junkies' (Coleman 2003) or in similar vein 'news junkies' (Prior 2006). These people are highly engaged with news, current affairs and politics in particular.

The country under investigation in this study is Belgium. Based on the media models that Hallin and Mancini (2004) distinguish, Belgium represents a democratic corporatist model. Without extensive elaboration upon all its dimensions, it signifies media autonomy and journalistic professionalization, early development of the mass-circulation press and strong public service broadcasting. The electoral context in Belgium is characterized by a multiparty system, whereby parties compete against one another but must work together with each other to form a local coalition. In this chapter, we focus on Flanders, the Dutch speaking part of Belgium, as it has a separate media landscape and usage patterns. When we speak of national media, this reflects Flemish media, as there are no national media for Belgium.

Via the open source tool *yourTwapperkeeper*, Twitter messages containing hashtag #vk2012 are captured and stored in a MySQL database, which allows a flexible approach to subsequent processing. Via the use of Gawk scripts,[1] key metrics are extracted and stored in Excel databases, which are used for further analysis in SPSS and UCINET (Borgatti et al. 2002). In addition to these computational methods for data processing, manual analysis of the data is executed and discussed below.

6.2.2 Data Analysis

Our understanding of the Twitter debate in the broader media ecology is twofold and contains (1) an analysis of the Twitter messages with a focus on inter-linkages

[1] Gawk scripts allow the identification and filtering of data, e.g. hashtags, URL's or '@reply messages'. http://mappingonlinepublics.net/tag/gawk/.

with other media outlets and (2) an analysis of interactions between politicians, media actors and citizens based on a division of the debate into four periods. The first part will focus on particular characteristics of the messages as such, whereas the second part of the study focuses on the senders and receivers of the messages.

6.2.2.1 The Twitter Debate in a Multi-Media Constellation

We would like to point to two conventions that reflect intermedia connections on Twitter (with a particular focus on mainstream media), i.e. hashtags and hyperlinks. Hashtags refer to words or phrases in conjunction with the # sign and refer to particular themes or topics (Bruns 2012). These core #themes and #topics can be brought in comparison with traditional media outlets to look for cross-media correspondence in issues. As a content analysis of mass media outlets is not at stake here, we primarily focus on more 'explicit' references to traditional media outlets. Through the use of hashtags, e.g. referring to television channels or shows, Twitter users re-distribute and discuss its content (Deller 2011). Flemish TV broadcasters facilitate this via the promotion of dedicated hashtags, related to specific programs. In addition to hashtags, the use of hyperlinks allows the user to refer to other sources on the web, including for example the traditional media's online news agenda. Hyperlinking practices have been studies in the context of intermedia agenda setting influences between traditional and newer, emerging media such as blogs (Meraz 2011). Twitter, on the other hand, reflects a networked, time-compressed interface consisting of continuous streams of content between users, creating an ambient, always-on news environment (Elmer 2012; Hermida 2010). In this respect, it presents different and/or additional challenges to the agenda setting process.

6.2.2.2 Interaction Patterns Between Media, Political Actors and Citizens

To allow for one-to-one communication on Twitter, the @ sign is used as a marker of addressivity. Concerning the use of @ signs (i.e. @username), Twitter demarcates 'replies' and 'mentions', whereby the former puts the @ sign at the beginning of the Tweet, whereas 'mentions' do not start the messages with an @ sign. Both conventions predominantly reflect addressivity (Honeycutt and Herring 2009) and were retained for the composition of four different interaction networks. We acknowledge that the hashtag-based approach to collect Twitter messages does not enable us to examine the level of relevant interaction that may take place outside the #hashtag (Bruns 2012).

The division of the Twitter debate into four periods is based on the assumption that each of the different periods represents different dynamics in terms of interaction (or influence) between citizens, media and political actors. The four different time-frames in the debate are the following: the pre-election period (01.09.12–

07.10.12), the prior week (08.10.12–13.10.12), election day (14.10.12) and the post-election period (15.10.12–21.10.12). For each period, we discuss the structural characteristics of conversation via Twitter and the position of the different actor types in these conversation networks via the Social Network Analysis Software UCINET (Borgatti et al. 2002). In order to understand communicative patterns between media actors, political actors and citizens, all actors in the network are manually coded alike. We acknowledge Twitter identity is problematic as it is self-defined and therefore does not always fit traditional categorization schemes (Lewis et al. 2013) or remains obscure; e.g. when no user description is provided. The definition of the actors as politicians and media actors and citizens is based on their username and description, as publicly available, at the time the network analysis was conducted (April 2013).

6.2.3 *Findings*

In correspondence with the methodology, the discussion of the results is divided into two parts, whereby the first part places the debate within the broader media environment. The second part of the results elaborates on the interaction patterns between media actors, political actors and citizens.

6.2.3.1 The Twitter Debate in a Multi-Media Constellation

A Chronological Overview and Understanding of Twitter Traffic

The timeline as shown in Fig. 6.1 is highly similar to other, international studies on Twitter traffic during the elections (Bruns and Burgess 2011; Larsson and Moe 2012). The graph is characterized by a number of spikes, with the election day representing the largest upsurge in messages. The election day takes up more than 50 % of the total number of tweets from the 1st of September until the 21st of October, or a total of 25,803 messages of the 43,447 messages reflecting the total debate. The peak on election day is excluded from Fig. 6.1, to make visible the more modest increases in Twitter traffic that can be related to offline events staged by traditional media.

The first small spike, the 4th of September, is related to the publication of the list numbers in print and audiovisual media. Before the elections, a lottery takes place to define the numbers of the parties on the elections lists. The second peak, the 12th of September, is related to the election day in the Netherlands, whereby the official hashtag (i.e. #vk2012) is used to discuss the results of the election. October the 5th represents the third peak and is related to the publication of a large-scale study on the upcoming elections in the most prominent cities in Flanders (i.e. Antwerp, Bruges, Ghent, Leuven, and Hasselt). The election polls were published in print media (including the main news websites) and were discussed on television as well.

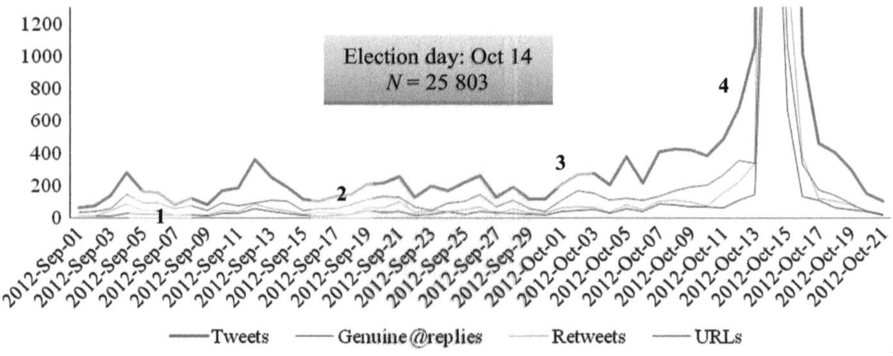

Fig. 6.1 Chronological overview of Twitter use during the 2012 local elections in Flanders

The week before the election day, or the fourth increase in traffic indicated on the graph, is characterized by an increase in media attention for the upcoming elections. Especially the public service broadcaster VRT features multiple dedicated programs on the upcoming elections (Epping et al. 2013). During this final week before the elections, the VRT program 'De Laatste Ronde' (i.e. 'the roundup') reports from five large Flemish municipalities, being Bruges, Leuven, Hasselt, Antwerp, and Ghent. Also, the commercial Flemish broadcaster VTM aired 'Het Ultieme Debat' (i.e. 'the ultimate debate'), containing a final discussion amongst the most prominent candidates. Each of the programs had dedicated hashtags, which allows us to link the increase in Twitter traffic with these televised political debates. Concerning the publication of the list numbers or the election poll that was executed, thematic tags such as #poll or #listnumbers were found.

Considering different traditional media channels, significant (live) television events are often found to relate with spikes in Twitter traffic (Larsson and Moe 2012; Bruns and Burgess 2011). When these shows are watched live, they create a shared viewing experience, allowing real-time and collective comments and discussion which results in upsurges in Twitter traffic.

Hyperlinks as Intermedia Connections

In order to understand potential influences between Twitter and other media platforms, one must get a networked understanding of the Twitter environment. On a total of 43,447 Twitter messages, 9,201 short URLs were found, of which the most prominent are analyzed. These relative frequencies are similar to the amount of links that were found for Twitter traffic during the 2010 Australian Federal elections ('#ausvotes') (Bruns and Burgess 2011). Interconnections with mainstream media and other content point to the fact that the platform does not stand alone but influences and is influenced by other media channels. Table 6.1 shows the most prominent categories of online resources: social media, traditional media, and official political party websites.

Table 6.1 Hyperlinks in #vk2012 tweets

Category	Frequency	%
Social media	4.202	100
Twitter	2.229	53.1
YouTube	607	14.4
Blogs	428	10.2
Instagram	417	9.9
Facebook	270	6.4
Twitpic	160	3.8
Foursquare	91	2.2
Traditional news media	3.112	100
National media	2.535	81.5
Audiovisual media	1.350	43.4
Print media	1.185	38.1
Regional media	577	18.5
Audiovisual media	455	14.6
Print media	122	3.9
Political party websites	620	100

We notice that many URLs refer to other social media, and more specifically Twitter. Taking a closer look at these Twitter links, they almost exclusively refer to photos related to particular user profiles. In addition, platforms such as Twitpic, Instagram, and YouTube were frequently found as well. Generally, we can already say audiovisual material far exceeds more textual sources, whereby we particularly refer to blogs. In this respect, the concept of (intermedia) agenda setting will need to take into account new, creative forms of political communication suggesting affective or social influences in addition to informational ones. As Fenton (2012) points out, social media practices are characterized by affective and social (yet very individual) dimensions of communication.

Concerning references to traditional media, the Twitter platform can be acknowledged as a 'secondary gatekeeper' (Singer 2014). Through the incorporation and secondary circulation of the hyperlinks on Twitter, visibility of existing mainstream media outlets increases. As media actors are also present on the platform, they can employ Twitter as an additional channel to increase the visibility of their media outlets. Taking a closer look at the subcategories, we consider both national and regional news media, as the elections concern municipalities and provinces. Concerning the type of content, a distinction is made between broadcasting television and radio on the one hand and print media, including newspapers and magazines, on the other. Television and radio channels provide audiovisual material on their website, allowing users to distribute but also comment TV content without watching it real-time.

External sources to official political party websites seem take a minor part in the Twitter debate, compared to informal, mediated platforms for political communication (i.e. social and mainstream media).

Although the information is not provided in Table 6.1, we discuss the most prominent mainstream media outlets. The website of the Flemish public service broadcaster VRT is most frequently mentioned within the category of national news media. The website provides video footage on news and current affairs programs of the public service broadcaster. As mentioned above, they invested heavily in coverage of the elections and hold an overall strong position in the audiovisual landscape in Flanders. Concerning print media, Flemish newspapers have a freely accessible news website, in addition to their print version. Here, most references refer to a national quality newspaper, called 'De Standaard', followed by the popular newspaper 'Het Nieuwsblad'. Concerning regional media, we found a great number of URLs of 'Brussel Nieuws', covering the Belgian capital city of Brussels and 'TV Limburg', representing the province of Limburg in Flanders.

Hashtags as Intermedia Connections

As mentioned above, the use of hashtags serves to aggregate and categorize Twitter messages around specific topics and are highly visible and searchable elements of the Twitter architecture. In Table 6.2 below, the most common hashtags (i.e. >20) of a total of 3,304 additional hashtags are listed and categorized.

Explicit references to traditional news platforms are very modest compared to hashtags referring to the parties and municipalities. Here again, we found hashtags that relate to audiovisual and print media. Reference to audiovisual material is far more common compared to print, whereas for the hyperlinks this difference is a lot smaller. The use of hashtags whilst (or after) watching particular programs is common in Flanders as broadcasters indicate dedicated hashtags per program. The public service broadcaster VRT (as a channel, as well as its programs) is mentioned more frequently than its commercial opponent VTM. In addition, to a very limited extent, users refer to print newspaper titles, whereby the most popular titles are identical with the results of the hyperlinks. The low amounts of hashtags to mass media outlets does not imply only so much is tweeted. If users indicate only the hashtag of the program, without the one of the elections (i.e. #vk2012), these messages are excluded from the dataset resulting in an underestimation of the actual amount of tweets.

Concerning the other categories provided in the table, it is mostly political parties than are discussed, except for one politician (Bart De Wever), party leader of the N-VA. While we do not aim to focus on the particular parties/politicians here, we would like to put the use of explicit references to traditional media in relation to other hashtags and acknowledge these topical hashtags as potential expressions of more indirect forms of intermedia congruence. In thinking of hashtags as indicators of the content of particular tweets, they indicate the dominant themes and topics of the Twitter platforms. Although this study does not provide a systematic overview of the parties and municipalities discussed in traditional media during election times, we can compare our results with a Flemish study on media attention for political parties, politicians (and the municipalities they represent) on public service TV (Epping et al. 2013). During the election campaign, starting the 1st of September, attention for the political party N-VA and the Bart De Wever is most

Table 6.2 Additional hashtags in #vk2012 tweets

Category	Frequency	%
Political parties/politicians[a]	2.676	100
Bart De Wever[a] (N-VA)	1.286	48.1
N-VA (Flemish nationalists)	813	30.4
Open Vld (Liberal democrats)	174	6.5
Vlaams Belang (Extreme right-	92	3.4
wing)	90	3.3
Groen (the green party)	87	3.3
sp.a (Social democrats)	79	2.9
CD&V (Christian democrats)	55	2.1
Municipalities	2.513	100
Antwerpen	864	34.4
Kortrijk	578	23.1
Gent	470	18.6
Brussel	382	15.2
Brugge	219	8.7
Traditional news media	921	100
Audiovisual media	869	94.4
Print media	52	5.6

[a]Politician, make the text (N-VA) online.

prominent. In analogy with the results in Table 6.2 above, the public service broadcaster focuses on larger cities, including Antwerp and Ghent. Although the study only represent a part of the traditional mainstream offer, albeit a substantial part, these initial similarities at least allude issue correspondence between traditional media outlets and Twitter.

6.2.3.2 Interaction Patterns Between Media, Political Actors and Citizens

For the second part of the paper, we move our focus from the content of the messages to the senders and receivers of Twitter messages, i.e. interaction structures and flows. Within the field of Twitter research, network studies seem to be emergent (Bruns 2012). This part of the paper is dedicated to a networked understanding of the Twittersphere during election times. As discussed in the methodology, the second part of the study departs from the division of the Twitter debate into four periods, being: the pre-election period (01.09.12–07.10.12), the prior week (08.10.12–13.10.12), election day (14.10.12) and the post-election period (15.10.12–21.10.12). For each period, we discuss interaction via Twitter and the position of media actors, political actors and citizens.

Table 6.3 Number and type of users per period

	Actor types				
	Media (N = 271)	Politicians (N = 425)	Citizens (N = 1393)	Other[a] (N = 92)	Total
The pre-election period	119	295	383	51	848
(01.09.12 to 07.10.12)	(14 %)	(35 %)	(46 %)	(5 %)	(100 %)
The prior week	83	143	234	16	476
(08.10.12 to 13.10.12)	(17 %)	(30 %)	(49 %)	(4 %)	(100 %)
Election day	119	90	585	15	809
(14.10.12)	(15 %)	(11 %)	(72 %)	(2 %)	(100 %)
Post-election period	94	129	530	28	781
(15.10.12 to 21.10.12)	(12 %)	(17 %)	(68 %)	(3 %)	(100 %)

[a]'Other' actors are for example universities or companies. They are less relevant for this study

Network Characteristics of Twitter for Conversational Interaction

We start with an overview of the number of participants in each of the debates. For the four consecutive periods, networks are constructed, based on sender-receiver interactions that make use of addressivity markers or @signs, which allows users to direct a tweet to a specific other user. For each of the periods, the 'main component' or largest group of connected actors was extracted for further analysis.[2] Table 6.3 above provides an overview of the total number of actors in the debate and how many of them are media actors, political actors and citizens. Concerning citizen actors, we labeled 'private individuals' as citizens when no professional affiliation with media or politics was provided by the user. We acknowledge that this categorization has its shortcomings, as for example prominent academics are included as well, although they were regularly staged by traditional media as experts.

In comparing the different periods, we notice the relative number of political actors, media actors and citizens alters. Although citizen users always represent the largest group, this tendency is most salient for the election day and the period thereafter, which is related to a substantial drop in political actors once the elections took place. It seems that politicians mobilize or are mobilized before the elections (i.e. during campaigning times), which indicates their temporal visibility and presence in the debate. If these interactions are instigated by politicians or political parties, it reflects a rather pragmatic use of the platform. A Danish study on the use of social media in election campaigns elaborates on the purposes of using social media in the campaign mix (Skovsgaard and Van Dalen 2013). The study shows

[2]ia the software program for social network analysis UCINET, the main component or largest collection of connected nodes can be extracted for a set of interactions. This reduces the data to feasible amounts for manual analysis without the loss of important data. For example for the first research period, 848 out of 1,173 actors were retained for further analysis, indicating that most of the data is retained.

Table 6.4 Network centralization by period[a]

	Period 1	Period 2	Period 3	Period 4
In-degree centralization	3.96 %	3.46 %	4.39 %	12.49 %
Out-degree centralization	5.22 %	3.02 %	3 %	8.23 %

[a]P1: The pre-election period (01.09.12–07.10.12), P2: The prior week (08.10.12–13.10.12), P3: Election day (14.10.12) and P4: The post-election period (15.10.12–21.10.12)

that Danish candidates indicate two important purposes underlying the use of social media, i.e. (1) making their political views visible and (2) directly communicating with voters. Concerning the latter, the authors point to the fact that interaction or dialogue with citizens might be overrated or otherwise said: *ideal* and *actual* social media practices do not always correspond. In the following section, we will elaborate on interactive uses of Twitter by political actors, as well as media actors and citizens. For this section, we finish with an understanding of the general network in terms of centrality.

Table 6.4 shows to what extent incoming messages (or 'in-degree') or outgoing messages (or 'out-degree') are centered around one or very few actors. The numbers signify low levels of centralization, suggesting interactions that are centered around various actors in the debate. The large size of the networks (476–848 actors) contributes to the very low scores. In addition, the results relate to the low number of interactions (or 'degrees') that take place between the actors. For all the periods, the average number of interactions between network actors (or 'nodes') lies between 1.24 and 1.58 and median scores are 1. This points out a distribution that is strongly skewed to the right, whereby few actors have (very) high amounts of interaction but the most of actors are only related to one other actor in the network. In other words, the strength of the interactions is very low. We do acknowledge that relevant Twitter interactions possibly take place outside the official hashtag on which data collection is based (Bruns 2012) and in this respect an underestimation of the real amount of interactions probably occurred.

Inter-group Conversationality and Reciprocity

The final part of the results provides an overview of the interaction patterns among the different actor types, as demarcated above in Table 6.3: media actors, political actors, and citizens.[3] Aside centralization as a network characteristic, network analysis allows us to look for in-degree (or messages received) and out-degree (or messages sent) centrality per actor. Although the network as such indicates a high level of decentralization, we notice significant differences when we compare

[3] For each period, the category 'other' is left out of the analysis of the interaction patterns. Via UCINET, we extracted network relations between media actors, political actors and citizens.

Table 6.5 Actor type in-degree centrality by period[a]

	Media actors	Political actors	Citizens
Period 1	M = 3.24 (SD = 7.98)	M = 2.60 (SD = 5.61)	M = 0.80 (SD = 1.49)
Period 2	M = 2.57 (SD = 4.44)	M = 2.20 (SD = 4.04)	M = 0.59 (SD = 1.08)
Period 3	M = 2.95 (SD = 6.23)	M = 3.36 (SD = 5.39)	M = 0.85 (SD = 1.49)
Period 4	M = 3.57 (SD = 8.57)	M = 4.16 (SD = 11.41)	M = 0.57 (SD = 1.28)

[a]P1: The pre-election period (01.09.12–07.10.12), P2: The prior week (08.10.12–13.10.12), P3: Election day (14.10.12) and P4: The post-election period (15.10.12–21.10.12)

media and political actors and citizens.[4] These differences were found for the average amount of messages actors received, whereas no significant differences were found concerning the number of messages the actors sent. Table 6.5 above provides the differences in in-degree centrality between the three actor types, showing that media and political actors receive a lot more directed messages than citizen. These results endorse the tendencies that similar Twitter studies indicate, based on the Gephi visualization software, i.e. the central positions of users that '*enjoy privileged positions in their respective professional capacities of journalists, politicians*, etc.' (Larsson and Moe 2012: 740; Bruns and Burgess 2011).

The appropriation of Twitter for conversational interaction reflects two-way exchanges whereby directed messages preferably flow in both directions. Before elaborating on the differences between the actor types, we point out that reciprocity on a network level is very low. In total, 2–4 % of the relations between two actors (or 'dyads') are reciprocal.[5] The discrepancies between the actor types as discussed in Table 6.5 suggest one-way communication going from citizens to established actors, which is further endorses when we look at the reciprocity scores per actor type (see Table 6.6, in italics).

Overall, two-way interaction is mostly established by citizens, as they seek to react to 'established actors' that address them personally. However, when citizen actors address these established actors, politicians and/or media actors show much lower levels of reciprocity. In this respect, similar to research during the 2012 Australian elections (Bruns and Burgess 2011), citizen users tweet '*at* or *about* rather than engaging *with*' established elites. Comparing the different periods, we notice that, on the election day, media actors become highly reciprocal towards politicians compared to the other periods. The timing here suggests that rather than politicians engaging with journalists to influence the mass media agenda, the discussion of the election results and the traditional media channels that report them, is at stake here. In addition, responsiveness of citizen users towards politicians drops after the elections, which might insinuate interactions taking place before the elections occur with the upcoming voting practices in mind.

[4] In UCINET, an Anova analysis was conducted for indegree and outdegree differences between media, political and citizen actors. F-statistics per period: (**1**) 18.63 (2,797), $p < 0.001$, (**2**) 19.31 (2,457), $p < 0.001$, (**3**) 37.55 (2,791), (**4**) 27.37 (2,750), $p < 0.001$.

[5] The exact levels of dyad-based reciprocity per period: (**1**) 3.38 %, (**2**) 2.22 %, (**3**) 4.3 %, (**4**) 1.9 %.

Table 6.6 Reciprocity[a] by period[b]

	M → C	P → C	P → M	C → P	C → M	M → P
Period 1	*12 %*	*12.87 %*	1.11 %	5.31 %	1.79 %	1.12 %
Period 2	*20 %*	*12.9 %*	2.22 %	3.28 %	4.26 %	3.23 %
Period 3	*14.29 %*	*11.54 %*	*14.29 %*	1.84 %	2.57 %	1.96 %
Period 4	*22.22 %*	5.45 %	3.23 %	0.87 %	0.97 %	2.86 %

[a]The percentage of ties going from actor A to B (A → B) that are reciprocated (B → A) (>10 %)
[b]P1: The pre-election period (01.09.12–07.10.12), P2: The prior week (08.10.12–13.10.12), P3: Election day (14.10.12) and P4: The post-election period (15.10.12–21.10.12)

Table 6.7 Network and group level E-I index by period[a]

	Observed (Expected)	Media actors	Political actors	Citizens
Period 3	0.140* (−0.155)	0.596	0.604	−0.157
Period 4	0.430* (−0.079)	0.617	0.661	0.235

[a]P1: The election campaign (01-09-12 to 07-10-12), P2: The pre-election week (08-10-12 to 13-10-12), P3: The election day (14-10-12), P4: The week after the elections (15-10-12 to 21-10-12)
***p < 0.001; **p < 0.01; *p < 0.05

To conclude, network analysis allows us to understand to what extent communication flows *among* the different actor groups or whether each of the actor types tends towards *in*-group communication. Obviously, the size of the subpopulations has consequences for the number of internal versus external ties that can be and are formed. For each of the networks, 'expected E-I values' are calculated given the structure of the networks, which are then compared to the observed E-I values.[6] The higher the values in Table 6.7 above, the more obvious the tendency towards out-group communication.

On the election day (period 3) and the week after the elections (period 4) there is a high tendency towards out-group communication. From the perspective of social media use during election campaigns (i.e. to make visible one's opinions and communicate directly), the periods *before* the elections should have yielded significant results. Direct communication with voters or with journalists to influence the public and media agenda would be the rationale then (Skovsgaard and Van Dalen 2013). The high 'out-group' values for politicians are in conjunction with the higher number of messages political actors receive on the election day and the week after (see Table 6.5). Additional content analysis needs to shed light on the relation between this quantitative upsurge of inter-group communication and the content of the messages.

[6]The E-I index is calculated as following: [number of ties external to the group minus the number of ties that are internal to the group] divided by [the total number of ties]. The values range from −1 (all ties are internal) to +1 (all ties are external).

6.3 Discussion

Based on a two-fold study on Twitter use during election times, we aimed to reveal intermedia and inter-agenda connections. A close reading of the content materials that are shared and the relations between the actors in the debate allows us to put forth some concrete theoretical and methodological insights.

Agenda setting is one of the main perspectives in mass communication and political communication effect research (McCombs 2004). The theory matured to also include shared news agendas among different media, or intermedia agenda setting, as is at stake here. Via the analysis of two Twitter conventions, i.e. hashtags and hyperlinks, we understand Twitter's embeddedness in the broader media ecology. The high number of links to other social media platforms (and audio-visual content), suggests affective and social aspects of the communications are relevant in addition to (or instead of) the emphasis on cognitive aspects of the communication process, notably attention and understanding. Relative to it, Meraz (2011) points to links between agenda setting processes and social influence theories to better understand these networked media environments. Links between mainstream media outlets and the Twitter platform are complicated by the presence of traditional media outlets in it. Although we assessed relations between content and users separately, further studies preferably link the content or conventions of the messages (i.e. hashtags and hyperlinks) with user information.

The network analysis of direct interaction patterns between users provides interesting findings concerning the platform's promises of open and equal interaction flows. Although we did not discuss the content of the messages, research indicated that content with @signs reflects more interactive messages, more likely to activate or influence others (Honeycutt and Herring 2009). In this respect, network theories and measures are relevant in the context of agenda setting research as well. In this particular context of hashtag research, one can exceed the established network of follower and followees, resulting in new connections (Bruns and Burgess 2011). The (possible) connection of otherwise unconnected ties might link up to the high number of weak ties that were found in the network. In addition, the central positions of established elites can be linked to their visibility in other media.

We can conclude that citizen users' position in the network does not represent a shift in traditional power hierarchies and elite domination. Concerning the different periods we demarcated, we notice small differences in in-degree centrality of the actor types and large differences in reciprocity and out-group communication between pre-election and (post-) election periods. These structural differences can be first indicators of different flows of content or influence between the media and political agenda and public opinion. For a more valid and in-depth understanding, we obviously need to take into account the content of the messages as well. In addition, more qualitative methods on the appropriation of '@signs' by Twitter users are at stake here as well. Potential questions for additional validation are: do addressivity markers always reflect interaction or is it contingent on the type of actors to which these messages are addressed? Do people expect responses when they address particular actors or do they just want to make visible what they are writing about a particular actor?

To conclude, we would like to stress the particularity of heightened political periods such as the elections. In addition, the specific characteristics of the election context suggests precaution towards the generalization of the findings to other countries and elections.

References

Benkler, Y. (2006). *The wealth of networks. How social production transforms markets and freedom*. New Haven, CT: Yale University Press.

Bennett, W. L., & Iyengar, S. (2008). A new era of minimal effects? The changing foundations of political communication. *Journal of Communication, 58*, 707–731.

Borgatti, S. P., Everett, M. G., & Freeman, L. C. (2002). *Ucinet for windows: Software for social network analysis*. Harvard, MA: Analytic Technologies.

Bruns, A. (2008). *Blogs, wikipedia, second life and beyond*. New York: Peter Lang.

Bruns, A. (2012). How long is a tweet? Mapping dynamic conversation networks on Twitter using Gawk and Gephi. *Information, Communication & Society, 15*, 1323–1351.

Bruns, A., & Burgess, J. (2011). #Ausvotes: How twitter covered the 2010 Australian federal election. *Communication, Politics and Culture, 4*, 37–56.

Chaffee, S. H., & Metzger, M. J. (2001). The end of mass communication? *Mass Communication and Society, 4*, 365–379.

Coleman, S. (2003). A tale of two hourses: The house of commons, the Big Brother house and the people at home. *Parliamentary Affairs, 56*, 733–758.

Curran, J., Fenton, N., & Freedman, D. (2012). *Misunderstanding the Internet*. New York: Routledge.

Dearing, J. W., & Rogers, E. M. (1996). *Agenda setting*. Thousand Oaks, CA: Sage.

Deller, R. (2011). Twittering on: Audience research and participation using Twitter. *Participations, 8*, 216–245.

Elmer, G. (2012). Live research: Twittering an election debate. *New Media & Society, 15*, 18–30.

Epping, L., De Smedt, J., Walgrave, S., et al. (2013) Gemeenteraadsverkiezingen 2012: Er werd vooral over de N-VA gesproken. Media-aandacht voor politici in de gemeenteraadsverkiezingsprogramma's van 2012 op de VRT. Het Steunpunt Media.

Fenton, N. (2012). The internet and social networking. In J. Curran, N. Fenton, & D. Freedman (Eds.), *Misunderstanding the internet* (pp. 123–148). New York: Routledge.

Hallin, D. C., & Mancini, P. (2004). *Comparing media systems: Three models of media and politics*. Cambridge: Cambridge University Press.

Hermans, L., & Vergeer, M. (2012). Personalization in e-campaigning: A cross-national comparison of personalization strategies used on candidate websites of 17 countries in EP elections 2099. *New Media & Society, 15*, 72–92.

Hermida, A. (2010). Twittering the News: the emergence of ambient journalism. *Journalism Practice, 4*, 297–308.

Honeycutt, C. & Herring, S. C. (2009). *Beyond Microblogging: Conversation and collaboration via Twitter*. Forty-Second Hawai'i International Conference on System Sciences. Los Alamitos, CA.

Larsson, A., & Moe, H. (2012). Studying political microblogging: Twitter users in the 2010 Swedisch election campaign. *New Media & Society, 14*, 729–747.

Lewis, S. C., Zamith, R., & Hermida, A. (2013). Content analysis in an era of big data: A hybrid approach to computational and munual methods. *Journal of Broadcasting & Electronic Media, 57*, 34–52.

McCombs, M. (2004). *Setting the agenda: The mass media and public opinion*. Cambridge: Polity Press.

Meraz, S. (2011). Using time series analysis to measure intermedia agenda setting influence in traditional media and political blog networks. *Journalism and Mass Communication Quarterly, 88*, 176–194.

Papacharissi, Z. (2009). The virtual geographies of social networks: A comparative analysis of Facebook, LinkedIn and ASmallWorld. *New Media & Society, 11*, 199–220.

Prior, M. (2006). *Post-broadcast democracy: How media choice increases inequality in political involvement and polarizes elections*. Cambridge: Cambridge University Press.

Rosanvallon, P. (2008). *Counter-democracy. Politics in an age of distrust*. Cambridge: Cambridge University Press.

Singer, J. B. (2014). User-generated visibility: Secondary gatekeeping in a shared media space. *New Media and Society, 16*(1), 55–73.

Skovsgaard, M., & Van Dalen, A. (2013). Dodging the gatekeepers? Social media in the campaign mix during the 2011 Danish elections. *Information, Communication & Society, 16*(5), 737–756.

Van Aelst, P. (2008). De lokale verkiezingscampagne: tussen huisbezoek en televisiestudio. In J. Buelens, B. Rihoux, & K. Deschouwer (Eds.), *Tussen Kiezer en hoofdkwartier*. Brussel: VUBPRESS.

Chapter 7
The Social Media Usage and the Transformation of Political Marketing and Campaigning of the Emerging Democracy in Indonesia

Case Study of the 2012 Gubernatorial Election of the Special Region of the Capital City Jakarta

Nyarwi Ahmad and Ioan-Lucian Popa

Abstract For nearly one decade, parties, their candidates and electorates across the world have become acquainted with the Internet and social media usage especially during campaigns and elections. Concerning this trend, scholars have investigated the proliferation of the Internet and social media usage in the political sphere. However, little attention has been directed to explore to what extent the proliferation of social media usage have transformed marketization of politics and campaigning of parties and their candidates during direct local elections in the emerging democracy of Indonesia. By using the case study method, in-depth interviews have been conducted to address the campaign volunteers, media relations' managers, political consultants, candidates, and pollsters during the 2012 gubernatorial election in Jakarta. As concerns its contributions, this paper argues that concerning the electoral and media arenas, there has been parallelism between marketization of politics and professionalization of campaigning among parties and their candidates during this election. As a lesson learnt from the marketization and the professionalization of campaigning of Jokowidodo-Basuki Tjahaya Purnama, this paper reveals that the integrative participatory political marketing (IPPM) and the mixed-mediated and online political campaigning (MMOPC) have been successfully utilized due to strong support from voluntary campaigners of outstanding candidates that have creatively combined the axis of the complementary powers of the underground, of the air war and of the online war of marketing and campaigning. As a practical contribution, this chapter identifies the fact that there

---

N. Ahmad (✉)
Bournemouth University, Poole Dorset, UK

Universitas Gadjah Mada Yogyakarta, Yogyakarta, Indonesia
e-mail: nahmad@bournemouth.ac.uk; gloryasia2008@gmail.com

I.-L. Popa
Vasile Alecsandri University of Bacău, Bacău, Romania

B. Pătruţ and M. Pătruţ (eds.), *Social Media in Politics*, Public Administration and Information Technology 13, DOI 10.1007/978-3-319-04666-2_7,

are countries that apply the candidate-centered system rather than party-centered system and have a multi party system (such as Indonesia); once partisanship to parties and their candidates has been reduced with the passing of time, there has been extensive use of the Internet and social media networks sites by candidates, by their campaign teams and by voluntary-campaigners, the IPPM and MMOPC can be used to fortify and buzz of the personal political brand of candidates in the marketing and campaigning for winning elections.

Keywords Social media usage • Transformation • Political marketing and campaigning • The emerging democracy of Indonesia • Case study and the 2012 gubernatorial election of special region of Jakarta

7.1 Introduction

To date, the Internet and social media as tools of marketization and professionalization of campaigning of parties and their candidates have taken their place in democratic countries all over the world. Within the US political context, some of us might have seen the extensive usage of social media that occurred during the 2008 and 2012 US presidential election. During those US presidential elections, Obama's campaign teams, campaign managers, campaign consultants, and campaign volunteers succeeded in using the Internet and social media networks not only for raising campaign donations, but also for mobilizing swing electorates. Meanwhile, within the European political context, some of us might have seen how parties and their candidates have tremendously advanced online professionalization of campaigns during Sarkozy's 2007 presidential campaign, the 2010 UK Elections, and the 2011 Poland Elections.

Modern television broadcasting and the advancement of ICT always carry out changing patterns of political communication and political marketing of parties and their candidates while dealing with structural and cultural changes of political market environments. Since 1960s, when television became strongly involved in the political sphere, there have been changes in the way politicians packaged their political messages and self-presentation to connect with the electorates (Maarek 1995). The rise of television exposure has transformed the mediatisation of politics wherein political marketing and campaigning have shifted from the propaganda age to the media and marketing ages (Wring 2005). As marketization of politics gradually intruded the political sphere, most of the campaigning of the parties and their candidates has been carefully designed and tailored to follow the media logic. Meanwhile, once the post-modern campaigning (Norris 2000), the professional campaigning (Gibson and Römmele 2001), and the hyper-media campaigning gradually arrived in political sphere, there have been increasing numbers of the Internet (from web 1.0 to web 2.0) and social media networks usage by parties, their candidates, and electorates across democratic countries in the world.

Within the context of the emerging democrary of Indonesia, the Internet and the germ of social media usage have contributed to the processes of democratization of politics against the Soeharto authoritarian regime (1966–1998) (see Hill and Sen 2000, 2002; Lim 2003a, b, 2005; Hill 2003). Scholars have investigated the usage of the Internet and social media in Indonesian politics. However, little attention has been focused to reveal how and to what extent the proliferation of the Internet, and social media usage have refashioned political marketing and campaign model of parties and their candidates during the national or local elections.

Meanwhile, once the Indonesian political landscape has changed dramatically since Soeharto's New Order—as indicated by the establishment of a new democratic political system, the mass media system, and the election system—the extensive usage of the Internet and social media networks as political marketing and campaign tools of parties and their candidates have gradually emerged. In regard to the political sphere, the Internet and social media have shifted away from their previous roles as the tool for democratization of politics against authoritarian political regimes to their new prominent role as tools of marketization and professionalization of campaigning of political actors and political organizations. Moreover, during campaigns and elections, parties and their candidates have gradually used the Internet and social media networks as strategic professional campaigning tools in the national election (the parliamentary election and the presidential election) and the local election of head/vice head of the Local Government of Indonesia.[1]

Indeed, to date, most of parties and their candidates that run for national and local elections in Indonesia have strongly recognized that media outlets are very important media for managing the positive impression and for packaging and delivering the contents of political advertising as well as for political debates across various electorate groups. As marketing and campaigning have been strongly implemented using the commercial media outlets and because no rigorous regulations are in use to limit the campaign budgets that are spent on commercial media outlets, campaigning financing of parties and their candidates has been constantly increasing. As a consequence, only the richer candidates or parties would succeed

[1] One of political regulations that were established after the Reform Era is Local Government, which is held under principles of decentralization and local autonomy. By 1999, the Indonesian House of Representatives and the Habibies' Government issued the Law No.22/1999 about Local Government. This regulation imposed two things: (1) changing the principles of the Local Government rules and authorities; and (2) changing the mechanism to elect the head/vice head of the Local Government of Indonesia. This Law dictated that the Indonesian Central Government accept the democratic, autonomy, and decentralization principles of local government, which is led by the head/vice head of Local Government, and that the Local Indonesian House of Representatives/members of local parliament elected them. This election system model was largely criticized by the public because of the non-implementation of the direct system of elections model. After that, by 2004, the Indonesian House of Representative and Megawati's Government had changed the content of that Law and they had laid down the new Law i.e., Law No.32/2004 about The Local Government, which declares that the head/vice head of Local Government should be elected directly by the local voters.

in developing their marketization and professionalization campaigning programs using various commercial media outlets during national and local elections. Otherwise, the rest of the candidates that lacked campaign financing have had to search for alternative strategies of marketization of politics and professionalization of campaigning in order to win elections.

Against this background, this chapter will be specifically directed at investigating how and to what extent the Internet and social media usage have transformed the marketization and professionalization of campaigning of candidates during the direct local elections in Jakarta, Indonesia. In doing so, this chapter will focus on two research questions: (1) to what extent the proliferation of social media usage has stimulated the emergence of the integrated political marketing model (IPPM) and (2) to what extent the mixed-mediated and online political campaigning (MMOPC) have been successfully advanced by Jokowidodo-Basuki Tjahaya Purnama as the winner candidate during the 2012 Gubernatorial Election in Jakarta?

7.2 Political Marketing of the Candidate for Governor/Vice Governor

Some models of marketization and campaigning of parties and their candidates have been in use in democratic countries. In some of those countries where elections are focused on candidates and not parties, political marketing of candidates can be advanced during the presidential elections (Newman 1994). Meanwhile, within the context of democratic countries where elections are focused on parties and not on candidates, the political marketing of parties will dominate.

Under the party-centred system, there are three models of political marketing of parties: the Product-Oriented Party (POP), the Sales-Oriented Party (SOP), and the Market-Oriented Party (MOP) (Lees-Marshment 2001, 2004, 2008; Lees-Marshment and Lilleker 2005). Meanwhile, considering that political marketing as a concept is not similar with market-orientation, some preferred to posit the measurement of attitudes and behaviors of political market-orientation of parties (Ormrod 2005, 2009) and political market-orientation of parties in regard with four kinds of political market arenas that are: (1) the internal party arena; (2) the parliamentary arena; (3) the media arena, and (4) the electoral arena (Stromback 2010).

Meanwhile, as countries have extreme multi-party systems, reduced electorate partisanship to parties, weakness of parties' organization and parties that are very reliant on the political brand of candidates, the marketization of politics and campaigning of candidates will be strongly favored over the marketing and campaigning of parties. In other words, as parties have already lacked political partisanship across groups of electorates, political marketing of candidates seems to be dominant over the political marketing of parties. Within the context of the emerging democracy of Indonesia, there have been parallelisms and complementary functions between political marketing of parties and political marketing of candidates and vice versa during the national and local elections.

Post-Soeharto Indonesia has a multi party system characterized by diversity; as there is less partisanship of electorates towards parties, parties rely much upon the personal branding of candidates, therefore political marketing of candidates has superseded political marketing of parties. However, there have been parallelisms between political marketing and campaigning of candidates and political marketing and campaigning of parties, therefore, the complementary functions of marketization and campaigning commonly exist during national and local elections. Taking into account these conditions, the political marketing concept of candidates (Newman 1994) and political marketing of parties (Lees-Marshment 2001, 2004, 2008; Lees-Marshment and Lilleker 2005) in their relationship with media and electoral arenas (Stromback 2010) will be used as the main conceptual framework to posit new alternative models of marketization of politics and professionalization of campaigning that are the Integrated Participatory Political Marketing (IPPM) and the Mixed-Mediated and Online Political Campaigning (MMOPC) concepts.

7.2.1 The Emergence of Integrated Participatory Political Marketing (IPPM)

As a concept, integrative participatory political marketing (IPPM) can be derived from the two main concepts that are the participatory political communication and the integrated marketing communication (IMC). Theoretically speaking, the idea of political participatory communication stems from a wide rage of existing concepts such as the principle of democracy, communication development, the concept of public participation and political participation. The earlier participatory political communication concept emanates from the participatory democracy theory as suggested by Barber (1984). However, Barber (1984) did not clearly outline and define what exactly the meaning of participatory political communication is. Considering that participatory democracy is inseparable from public participation, (Meijer et al. 2008) then proposed three concepts of public participation in political spheres that include: (1) the policy participation, which means the type of public participation either to support or to criticize government policies; (2) the political participation, which is a type of public participation to direct or to influence the process of political decision-making during the campaign and election and (3) the social participation, which is a type of public participation that is used to increase the social capital of democratic countries.

Other scholars also proposed the concept of participatory communication that originates from political participation, communication development, and campaign communication concepts. As concerns communication development, Tufte and Mefalopulos (2009: 6–7) have outlined four types of participatory communication that are passive participation, participation by consultation, participation by collaboration, and empowerment participation. In terms of campaign communication, participatory political communication has been posited by Lileker and Jackson

(2010a, b) that refer to the participatory/voluntary activities of the electorates to engage in the political campaign activities of parties and candidates either in the unmediated political communication or the mediated political communication, such as the participatory style in the web-campaigning.

Meanwhile, marketing scholars have posited IMC as a concept since the 1990s. Schultz (1993) and Schultz et al. (1993:1–10) have firstly introduced the integrated marketing communication (IMC) as a concept when the decline of mass marketing, the rise of de-massification, and the emergence of empowerment of customers occurred within the global marketing phenomena. According to Schultz and Schultz (2004:9), the development of the IMC has been advanced in regard to three main factors that are: the development and diffusion of digital technology, the increasing emphasis on brands and branding as major competitive differentiating tools, and the increasing focus on multi-nationalization and globalization as marketing spread across the traditional geographic boundaries. Generally speaking, since the 1990s, the IMC has gradually shifted the traditional marketing model based on 4 Ps (Product, Place, Price and Promotion), has advanced the SIVA model (solution, information, value, and access), and then has favoured the development of the IMC model due to changes in the nature of corporate communication and changes in marketing environments (Granati 2012:xv).

Theoretically speaking, IMC as a concept emphasizes the added value of a comprehensive plan that is useful in evaluating the strategic roles of several communications methods (such as the general advertising, direct response, sales promotion, and public relations) and to strengthen the maximum communication impact (Schultz 1993). IMC also refers to the audience-driven business process of strategically managing stakeholders, content, channels, and results of brand communication programs (Kliatchko 2008:140). As a consequence of the fact that marketers started using the IMC, they need to smartly craft the synergy, creation, and integration of communication to direct the process for planning, executing, and monitoring the brand messages, which enable the creation of brand-customer relationships (Ouwersloot and Duncan 2008:14). In this respect, by employing this concept, marketers must decide to what extent each function of IMC will be used by taking into account eight elements that are advertising, sales promotion, direct marketing, publicity and public relations, personal selling, packaging, events and sponsorship, and customer services (Ouwersloot and Duncan 2008:10–11).

The implementations of IMC will rely on three main players (Ouwersloot and Duncan 2008:20–21). First, the companies and the brands behind the marketing communication should have something to sell. Second, the marketing communication agencies have become the strategic partner by offering several marketing and communication services to the targeted customer. In terms of the marketing communication agencies, there are two main categories (Ouwersloot and Duncan 2008:27). First, the full-service agency is the agency that provides all or most of the services needed in its area of IMC specialization. Second, the specialist agency is type of the agency that provides special services in particular area of IMC programs. Third, the media as the channel of communication to deliver the content and product information and its brand that should be directed to several targeted customers.

Beyond the mass-mediated IMC concept, for nearly one decade, the advancement of IMC within online political communication has taken place in line with the extensive usage of the Internet and social media networks in political market arenas. The adaptation of IMC will enhance the strategy of online participatory marketing and campaigning. According to Lilleker et al. (2011), there have been four tendencies of web campaign model: informing, engaging, persuading, and mobilizing and interacting. In this respect, the Internet and social media usage can be generated as a tool for listening, engaging, creating the political message and sharing and integrating values and information in the political market and repeating the political message, political product or mentioning the personal branding of candidates and parties (Adi and Lilleker Darren 2012: 9–12).

As seen from Fig. 7.1, by anchoring the IMC concept as posited by Ouwersloot and Duncan (2008), the IPPM can be seen as a parallel process between the political marketing of parties (Lees-Marshment 2001, 2004, 2008; and Lees-Marshment and Lilleker (2005) on the one hand, and political marketing of candidates (Newman 1994), on the other. In this respect, the integrated marketing communication and political marketing can be set up as “an organizational philosophy, principles and strategy” to develop the professional campaign structures, strategies and tools to address various political market arenas (Stromback 2010). By using those concepts, the political consultants, campaign volunteers, and the mainstream mass media and citizen journalism will be the important partners of the implementation of communication campaign programs. As anchored by the IMC concept, the campaign platforms can be expected to strongly stimulate the participatory/voluntary push marketing and the pull marketing in the electoral market arenas.

Compared with the existing political marketing of parties (Lees-Marshment 2001, 2004, 2008) and political marketing of candidates (Newman 1994), the key advantages of the IPPM as a new model is that the axis of the strategic of political marketing power no longer relies on the parties, candidates and their campaign consultants and marketers *per se*, but also on the voluntary campaigners of candidates that have emerged as powerful actors to generate the pull marketing and push marketing of parties and their candidates during campaign and election.

Moreover, unlike with the previous political marketing models of parties and their candidates which were fully steered by the central organization of parties and campaign organizations of candidates and very relied upon by political consultants, the IPPM had immanent abilities to generate resources of participatory power either from journalists’/senior editors’ communities of the mass media industries or voluntary campaigners. In this respect, more attractive and influential personal political branding of parties and/or their candidates and more participatory campaigning have been generated among volunteers, and increased power of political marketing and campaigning of parties and/or their candidates can be achieved for winning the elections.

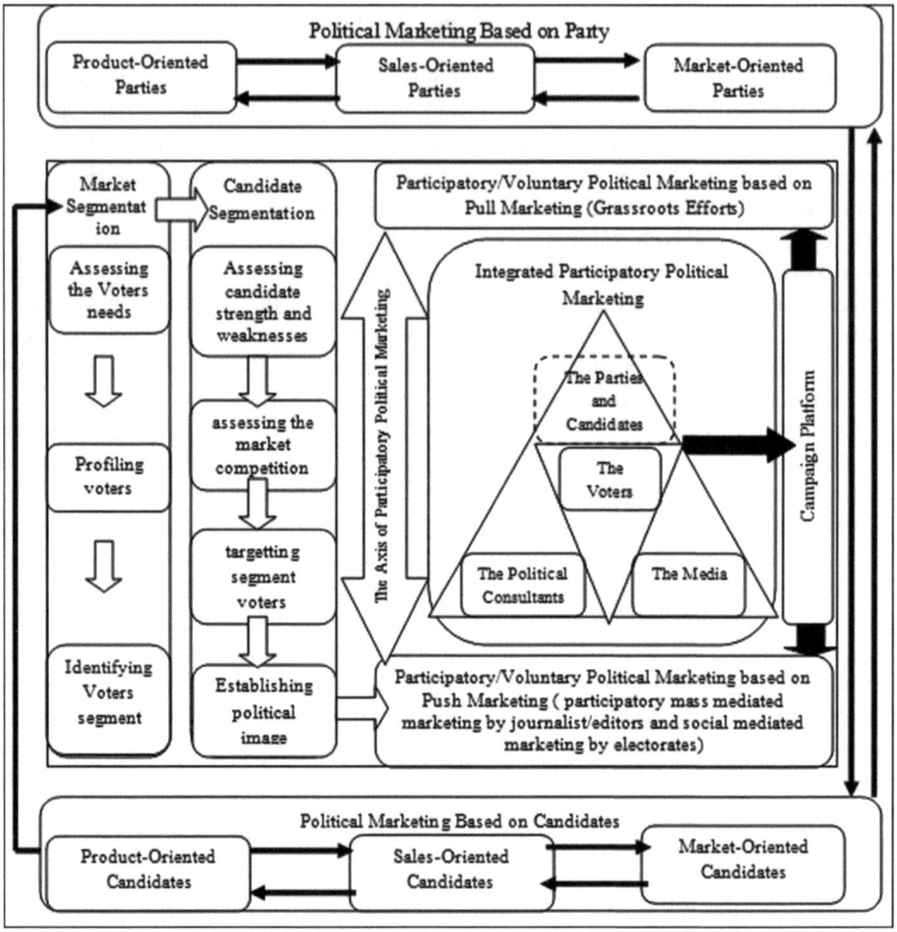

Fig. 7.1 The integrated participatory political marketing (IPPM): a proposed model

7.3 The Rise of the Mixed Mediated and Online Political Campaigning (MMOPC)

Television has remained the prominent medium of political marketing and campaigning. Meanwhile, easier access to the Internet and social media networks has been offered by smartphone technology that is commonly used by parties' leaders, parties' officials, campaign managers of parties, and their candidates as well as electorates. As there have been various types of online interactions using the Internet and social media (Rice and Haythornthwaite 2006), they may have advanced the smart hyper-media campaign during elections.

In regard to mediated and online communications, there are three important aspects that should be considered by parties and their candidates. The first

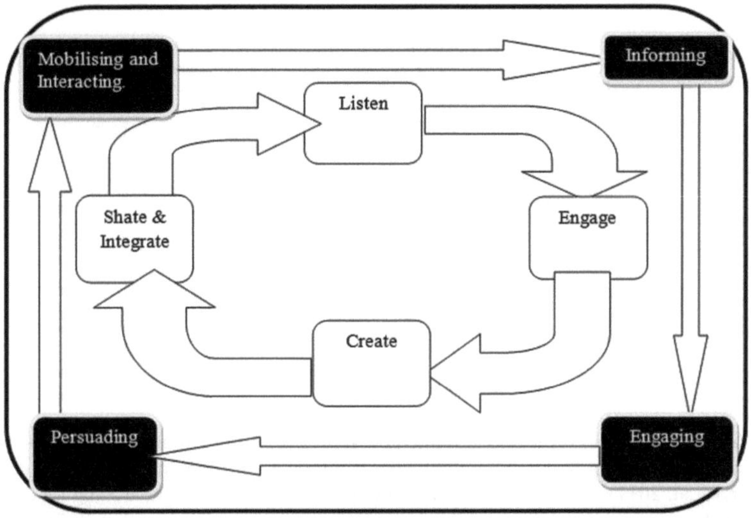

Fig. 7.2 The Pattern of the Internet and Social Media Usage as the Medium or Arena of Political Marketing. Source: Adaptation form: (1) Ana Adi and Darren G. Lilleker (2012). Getting the message out: Social media daily activity plan. The Creative Enterprise Bureau, The Media School, Bournemouth University, UK, July 6, 2012, dan (2) Darren G.Lilleker, (et.al. 2011). Informing, Engaging, Mobilising, or Interacting: Searching for a European model of web campaigning. *European Journal of Communication* September 2011 vol. 26 no. 3 195–213

important issue is how each political party should enable the promotion and delivery of their political product (such as ideas, ideology, policies and candidates personalities) to the public via various mass media. Another issue is how each political candidate has been enabled to deliver his/her policies and image by means of various media outlets. The subsequent issue is how each mass media industry has mediated and constructed positive and negative political news frameworks and political impressions both for political parties and candidates using various types of media outlets (Lees-Marshment and Lilleker 2005).

Once parties, their candidates and electorates, have extensively used the Internet and social media networks there have been various patterns of communication and campaigning that have resulted from them. As outlined by Fig. 7.2, by modifying the proposed-model of the social media usage made by Lilleker et al. (2011) and Adi dan Lilleker (2012: 9–12), the Internet and social media can be generated as a smart tool for listening, engaging, creating the political message, integrating and sharing, persuasion concerning values and information that are presented by parties and their candidates to political market arenas. Moreover, these tools can be used for repeating the political message, buzzing political products, or mentioning the personal branding of candidates and parties as well as mobilizing and interacting across volatile electorates.

Yet, traditional and mediated marketing and campaigning are still being used by parties and their candidates to connect with various groups of voters. However, as

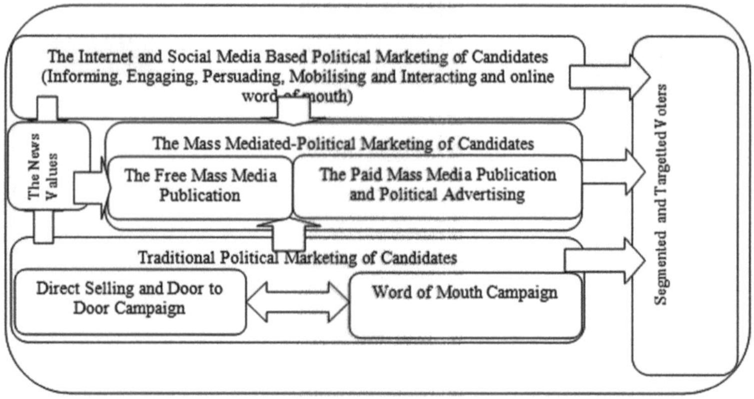

Fig. 7.3 Mixed mediated-political marketing model. Source: Adaptation from: (1) McNair, Brian. 201. An introduction to political communication. Routledge: London and New York; (2) Darren G. Lilleker, (et.al. 2011). Informing, engaging, mobilising or interacting: searching for a European model of web campaigning. European Journal of Communication September 2011 vol. 26 no. 3 195–213

candidates, parties and electorates have successfully used the Internet and social media networks as marketing and campaign tools, the mixed-mediated and online political campaigning (MMOPC) can be implemented as outlined by Fig. 7.3. Based on this campaign model, there are three important campaign elements that complement each others: (1) the online war campaigning of parties and their candidates that is run using the Internet and social media networks; (2) the mediated war campaigning of parties and their candidates, which includes free mass media publication and the paid mass media publication and political advertising and (3) the ground war campaigning of parties and their candidates which includes the direct selling and door-to-door and word-of-mouth campaigning. Theoretically speaking, this model can be established not only by considering the specific conditions of parties and their candidates whether incumbent or non-incumbent, as leaders, challengers, and followers in the political market arena (Butler and Collins 1994:35) *per se*, but also concerning the characteristics, conditions and development of volatile electorates during campaigns and elections.

The subsequent question is how and to what extent this model can be implemented by parties, candidates, consultants, campaign managers, and volunteers. Generally speaking, based on this model, those three campaign elements can be utilized simultaneously, consecutively, and complementary. Once it was implemented, the employment of the direct-selling marketing and campaigning potentially leads to the establishment of the mixed-mediated political marketing and campaigning model of parties and their candidates. Under the conditions of mounting volatile electorates and reduced party partisanship, this method will be more effective to re-engage the voters' trust, loyalties, and sympathies. In this respect, parties and candidates continue the traditional face-to-face direct selling and marketing of their unique personal branding alongside with the mediated and online war of their marketing and campaigning strategy. Because of the complementary functions of these strategies, more and more parties and their candidates succeed in the ground war of marketing and campaigning by using direct selling and the word-of-mouth and they favour the increased use of mediated war the online war for marketing and campaigning and vice versa. The resultant is that more positive personal brand of candidates and or parties' candidates can be crafted in the media and electoral arenas during the series of campaign and election events.

7.4 The Emergence of IPPM and MMOPC During the 2012 Gubernatorial Election of Special Region of Jakarta

7.4.1 The 2012 Gubernatorial Elections of the Special Region of Jakarta

Constituted as the capital city since 1945, Jakarta has become the most strategic city in Indonesia. Even though the decentralization and autonomy policies of the Local Governments have been implemented in the local provinces, regions and municipalities, Jakarta has remained the most important centre of political and economic power. As this city has become the home of the central office government department/agencies, the home of the central offices of the national parties, and location of the headquarters of national and multinational corporations, the gubernatorial elections of Jakarta have become the most interesting political issue in Indonesia.

Meanwhile, compared with other Indonesian provinces, Jakarta exhibits more diverse socio-demographic voter characteristics. It is inhabited by 9,607,787 people (Centre of Indonesian Statistical Agencies 2010), the majority of which are Indonesian educated middle class who have access to various media outlets. Jakarta has the highest concentration of urban professional and middle-class communities in Indonesia. Therefore, the gubernatorial elections of Jakarta have always deserved significant attention among leaders of parties, candidates, as well as among the members of the national and international business communities in Indonesia.

The 2012 gubernatorial elections of Jakarta took place under different conditions as compared with the previous elections that were held in 2007. First, during the 2007 gubernatorial elections of Jakarta, there have been only two candidates that were nominated as governor/vice governor: Fauzi Bowo-Prijanto (nominated by the coalition of the Golkar Party, The Indonesian Struggle Democratic Party, The Nation Awakening Party, National Mandatory Party, and the Democratic Party) as incumbent candidate, and Adang Darajatun-Dhani Irawan (nominated by The Prosperous Justice Party/Partai Keadilan Sejahtera) as challenger candidate. The first direct election was held on August 8, 2007 and was run under Law No.32/2004. At that time, in the first-round election, Fauzi Bowo-Prijanto came out as the winner by getting 57.8 % of the votes. Some Indonesian political consultants and pollsters argued that the key strategic factors that led to Fauzi Bowo's success story of marketing and campaigning during that election was the prominent role of his political consultants and campaign teams. They have successfully lobbied to parties' leaders to form coalitions of parties that led to the nomination of only two gubernatorial candidates.[2]

During the 2012 elections, there were six candidates that ran for office during the first-round of the elections. There were two candidates that entered the second round of the 2012 Gubernatorial Election of Jakarta. In the first round of that election, there were four candidates that had been nominated by parties and coalitions of parties, and there were two non-party candidates. An iron law of political market is that the more candidates compete in the political arena, the more volatile electorates are and create opportunities for each candidate to win the election (Table 7.1).

Second, during the 2012 gubernatorial elections of Jakarta, even though, to some extent, political consultants took upon themselves the task of organizing the campaigns of the parties' candidates, most of them were strongly challenged by the emergence of participatory/voluntary-campaigners that mainly supported Jokowidodo-Basuki Tjahaya Purnama. As seen from Table 7.2, various hired pollsters supervised most of the candidates and political consultants and each candidate had a particular type of relationship with their political consultants. To some degree, however, most of them failed to fully persuade and mobilise the increasingly volatile electorates of Jakarta. Otherwise, only Jokowidodo-Basuki Tjahaya Purnama's hired political consultants and campaign managers succeeded in assembling a large numbers of participatory/voluntary campaigners.

Third, slightly contrasting with previous elections that were mainly driven by party-centred rather than candidate-centred marketing and campaigning, the 2012 gubernatorial elections in Jakarta were characterized by candidate-centred marketing and campaigning wherein the prominent role of personal branding of candidates superseded the political branding of parties. During that election, political branding of candidates had priority over that of parties. In doing so, each candidate tried to develop his personal political branding. In this respect, some of them (Fauzi Bowo-Nahrowi Ramly, Hidayat Nurwahid-Didik Rahbini, and Alex Nurdin-Nono Sampono) shaped up their personal branding based on or in line with their political party brand.

Meanwhile, other candidates, such as Jokowidodo-Basuki Tjahaya Purnama did not believe that their political parties' brand would strengthen their personal political brand. Therefore, they tried to elevate their personal political branding, which is inseparable from that of the parties.[3] Yet, the rest of the non-party

---

[2] See Eriyanto and Sukanta (2007). The Governatorial Election of Jakarta and The Effectiveness of Parties' Coalition (Pilkada DKI Jakarta dan Efektifitas Koalisi). The Monthly Review (Kajian Bulan). The Indonesian Survey Cyrcle (Lingkaran Survey Indonesia). Vol,4. August 2007(Edisi 04-Agustus, 2007), page 1–12. See also Eriyanto (2007). Why Fauzi Bowo Can Be The Winner (Mengapa Fauzi Bowo Menang). The Monthly Review (Kajian Bulan). The Indonesian Survey Cyrcle (Lingkaran Survey Indonesia). Vol,4. August 2007(Edisi 04-Agustus, 2007), page 13–31.

[3] Bimo Nugroho, one of the campaign strategists of Jokowidodo-Basuki Tjahaya Purnama, Personal Interview, September 2012.

Table 7.1 The parties and the candidates during the 2012 gubernatorial elections of the special region of Jakarta

No	The candidates	Background	Parties
1	Fauzi Bowo dan	Fauzi Bowo a.k.a. Foke: the incumbent governor of special region of Jakarta (2004–2012)	Democratic party (Partai Demokrat)
	Nahrowi Rahmli	Nahrowi Ramli: major general (ret) of the Indonesian army	
2	Hendardji Supandji	Hendardji Supanji: retired major general of the Indonesian army	Non-party
	Achmad Riza Patria	Achmad Riza Patria: one of the chairmen of the Great Indonesian Party (Gerindra Party)	
3	Joko Widodo	Joko Widodo: major/head of Municipality of Surakarta, Central Java	Coalition of the Indonesian Struggle Democratic Party (Partai Demokrasi Indonesia Perjuangan/PDIP) and the Great Indonesian Party (Gerindra Party)
	Basuki Tjahaya Purnama	Basuki Tjahaya Purnama/Ahok: the former Head of West Belitung (Belitung Timur), Belitung Province and member of the Indonesian Parliament/the Indonesian House of Representatives (2009–2014) from the Golkar Party	
4	Hidayat Nur Wahid	Hidayat: Lecturer, the former Speaker of the Indonesian People Consultative Assembly (2004–2009) and the former president of the Prosperous Justice Party	Coalition of Prosperous Justice Party (Partai Keadilan Sejahtera/PKS) and National Mandatory Party (Partai Amanat Nasional/PAN)
	Didik J. Rachbini	Didik: Lecturer (Professor), former member of the Indonesian Parliament/the Indonesian House of Representatives, from the National Mandatory Party	
5	Faisal Basri	Faisal: lecturer at the Faculty of Economy and Business, the University of Indonesia, political activist and national media commentator on economy and business issues and one of the founders of the National Mandatory Party)	Non-party
	Biem Benyamin	Biem Benyamin: popular local artist, Jakarta/the local leader of Betawi Communities	
6	Alek Nurdin	Alex Nurdin: the Governor of South Sumatera	The Functional Group of Party (Golkar Party)
	Nono Sampono	Nono Sampono: lieutenant general (ret), of the Indonesian Navy	

Source: The general election commission of the special region of Jakarta, 2012

Table 7.2 The pollsters and political consultants hired by the candidates of the 2012 gubernatorial election of Jakarta

No	Candidates	Political consultants/pollsters
1	Faisal Basri- Biem Benyamin	Mr. Santoso, Personal Professional Consultants, Spin-Doctor and Media Strategist, and Senior Journalist of Radio 68 H Network
2	Hendarman Supanji- Achmad Riza Patria	Unknown Campaign Manager
3	Alek Nurdin—Nono Sampono	The Indonesian Survey Institute (Lembaga Survei Indonesia
4	Hidayat Nur Wahid- Didik J. Rachbini	Furtune PR led by Mrs. Indira Abidin
5	Fauzi Bowo dan Nahrowi Rahmli	Pollsters and Political Consultants of the Indonesian Voices Network (Jaringan Suara Indonesia/JSI) led by Widi Aswidi, and supported by Saiful Mujani Research Consulting (SMRC)
6	Joko Widodo-Basuki Tjahaya Purnama	Cyrus Network (led by Andrinof Chaniago and Hasan Hasbi) and PolMark Indonesia (led by Eep Saifullah Fatah)

candidates tended to generate their personal political branding. However, because of the lack of attractiveness of their personal branding and political products, most of them—especially non-party candidates—failed to improve their personal branding. Generally speaking, only one of the leading candidates, Jokowidodo-Basuki Tjahaya Purnama, successfully generated his personal political brand within electoral and media arenas.

Fourth, compared with the previous election, the political market arenas of the 2012 gubernatorial election of Jakarta showed different characteristics. In this respect, during that election, Jakarta's electorates expected more from non-incumbent candidates rather than the incumbent ones. What were the expectations? Most of the volatile electorates needed that candidates offered them the best solution for several existing social problems of Jakarta, such as: (1) the social economic divide between the rich and the poor; (2) the unresolved problem of public transportation management; (3) poor public service management system of traditional markets; (4) the annual flood disaster; (5) health service for poor people, etc. Indeed, as regards those public demands, each candidate tried to develop his political products based on candidate-centred marketing and campaigning on the one hand, and the party-centred marketing and campaigning on the other. However, because of the lack of political trust of electorates towards parties, only candidates that strongly pursued the candidate-centred marketing and campaigning and had a more attractive personal political branding (such as Jokowidodo-Basuki Tjahaya Purnama) could raise the political engagement of the volatile electorates of Jakarta.[4]

[4] Personal Interview with Ajianto Dwi Nugrono, one of the coordinators of the voluntary campaigner communities of Jokowidodo-Basuki Tjahaya Purnama, September 2012.

Table 7.3 The rate of likeability of the candidates in the 2012 gubernatorial election of Jakarta

The candidates of governor and vice governor	March 2012	May 2012	June 2012
Candidates for governor			
Fauzi Wibowo	79.1 %	73.2 %	81.2 %
Joko Widodo	75.0 %	75.0 %	66.6 %
Faisal Basrie	68.4 %	50.4 %	60.1 %
Hidayat Nurwahid	66.2 %	66.7 %	66.8 %
Hendardji Soepandji	59.8 %	46.1 %	56.2 %
Alex Noerdin	50.7 %	47.4 %	50.5 %
Candidates for vice governor			
Nachrowi Ramli	73.9 %	58.5 %	67.2 %
Nono Sampono	62.0 %	58.0 %	56.1 %
Basuki Thahja Purnama	57.8 %	52.4 %	57.9 %
Biem Benjamin	56.4 %	60.5 %	56.9 %
Ahmad Riza Patria	52.2 %	47.1 %	53.3 %
Didik J Rahbini	51.3 %	44.0 %	57.0 %

Source: the Indonesian survey circle (Lingkaran Survei Indonesia). 2012

Table 7.4 The degree of electability of the candidates for the 2012 gubernatorial elections of Jakarta

The candidates	March 2012	May 2012	June 2012
Alex Noerdin—Nono Sumpono	3.9 %	5.3 %	4.6 %
Faisal Basrie—Biem Benjamin	5.8 %	4.1 %	1.8 %
Fauzi Bowo—Nachrowi Ramli	49.1 %	43.3 %	43.7 %
Hendardji Soepandji—Ahmad Riza Patria	1.2 %	1.1 %	0.5 %
Hidayat Nur Wahid—Didik J Rahbini	8.3 %	7.6 %	5.3 %
Joko Widodo—Basuki Thahja Purnama	14.4 %	20.9 %	14.4 %
Undecided Voters/Floating Mass	17.4 %	17.7 %	29.7 %

Source: The Indonesian Survey Circle (Lingkaran Survei Indonesia). 2012

After the first round of the 2012 elections, according to the series of survey researches of the Indonesian Survey Circle, Fauzi Bowo-Nahrowi Rahmi still retained the top rate of electability among the candidates, by getting 43.7 % of total voters. However, his rate of electability had been decreasing as time went by (by March 2012 at 49.1 %, by May 2012 at 43.3 % and began to slowly increase by June 2012 at 43.7 %). In contrast, Jokowidodo-Basuki Tjahaya Purnama's rate of electability had been rising with the passage of time (from 14.4 % by March 2012, to 20.9 % by May 2012, and then had slowly been declining to 14.4 % by June 2012). The most interesting trend this survey detected is an increase in the huge amount of undecided voters (from 17.4 % by March 2012 and May 2012 to 29.7 % by June 2012).

Generally speaking, as seen from Tables 7.3 and 7.4, unlike the previous gubernatorial elections of Jakarta, one of the most important stumbling blocks for candidates, parties and their hired political consultants during the 2012 Gubernatorial Elections of Jakarta was the increase of volatile electorates. Based on the series of survey researches concerning the first round of elections, most of the Indonesian pollsters forcasted Fauzi Bowo-Nahrowi Ramli as the potential winner candidate. In this respect, even though equipped with a more precise sampling method, most of Indonesian pollsters failed to produce more accurate prediction about the voter preferences due to the huge number of undecided voters. Therefore, the first round of the elections showed different results. Fauzi Bowo-Nahrowi Ramli's strongest competitor, Jokowidodo-Basuki Tjahaya Purnama, came out as the winner by collecting 42.6 % (1,847,157) of the total number of votes, and Fauzi Bowo-Nahrowi Ramli came out second after getting 34.05 % (1,476,648) of the total number of votes.

7.4.2 The IPPM: The Lesson Learnt from Jokowidodo-Basuki Tjahaya Purnama's Political Marketing Strategy

The incumbent candidate, Fauzi Bowo-Nahrowi Ramli seemed very reliant on the political marketing of parties—which is based on the Product-Oriented Party (POP)—during the first round of the elections; then he began to develop the Sales-Oriented Party (SOP) strategy and shifted to the Market-Oriented Party (MOP) strategy during the second round of the elections. Meanwhile, the non-incumbent candidates, Hidayat Nur Wahid-Didik J.Rahbini and Alex Nurdin-Nono Sampono also used the political marketing of parties, but unlike incumbent candidates, they combined the political marketing of parties with the political marketing of candidates. In this respect, Hidayat Nur Wahid-Didik J. Rahbini seemed to employ the Sales-Oriented Party strategy, while Alex Nurdin-Nono Sampono utilized the Product-Oriented Party strategy. Generally speaking, most of the candidates that were very reliant on the political marketing of parties failed to enter the second round of the elections because of the weaknesses of the internal political marketer of their parties' campaign organization, on the one hand, and because of the reduced attractiveness of their personal political branding across electorates.[5] Meanwhile, the non-party candidates, Faisal Basrie-Biem Benyamin and Hedardji Supandji-Achmad Riza were more likely to implement the political marketing of candidates. However, because of lack of strong personal political branding, they failed to enter the second round of the elections (Table 7.5).

Meanwhile, slightly constrasting with the incumbent candidates and the rest of the aformentioned non-incumbent candidates, Jokowidodo-Basuki Tjahaya Purnama seemed to successfully implement smarter political marketing of candidates. Professional communities in Jakarta first endorsed Jokowi's integrated participatory political marketing. Most of them had backgrounds as political activists

[5] Personal interview with the Sunarto Ciptohardjono, one of the general political consultants of the Lingkaran Survey Indonesia/The Indonesian Survey Circle, February, 2013.

Table 7.5 The tendencies in the implementation of the political marketing model of the candidates in the 2012 gubernatorial election of the special region of Jakarta

No	The candidates	Political marketing of parties (PMP)	Political marketing of candidates (PMC)	Integrated participatory political marketing (IPPM)
1	Fauzi Bowo – Nachrowi Ramli	PMP was run from the POP model during the first round of the elections, then switched to the POP model and then adopted the MOP model in the second round of the elections	PMC was run by employing the Sales-Oriented Candidate (SOC) and began to adopt the Market-Oriented Candidate (MOC) during the second round of the elections	No obvious evidence
2	Hendardji Supandji-Achmad Riza	No obvious evidence	PMC was set up by employing the Sales-Oriented Candidate/SOC	No obvious evidence
3	Jokowidodo-Basuki Tjahaya Purnama	PMP was established by developing the Sales-Oriented Party (SOP) and Market-Oriented Party during the first round and second round of the elections	PMC was established by employing the Product Oriented Candidates (POC) and then developing the Sales-Oriented Candidate (SOC) during the first round of the elections	IPPM was smartly designed by developing the integrated participatory political marketing focusing on the candidate during the second round of the elections
4	Hidayat Nur Wahid-Didik J. Rachbini	PMP was developed by employing the Sales-Oriented Party (SOP) and Market-Oriented Party (MOP) during the first round of the elections	No obvious evidence	No obvious evidence
5	Faisal Basrie-Biem Benyamin	No obvious evidence	PMC was advanced by employing the Sales-Oriented Candidate (SOC) and then moved to Market-Oriented-Candidate (MOC) during the first round of the elections	No obvious evidence
6	Alex Nurdin-Nono Sampono	PMP was run by employing Product-Oriented Party (POPO during the first round of the elections	No obvious evidence	No obvious evidence

Note: Outlined by the author and based on the personal interviews with the Campaign Teams of Jokowidodo-Basuki Tjahaya Purnama (Bimo Nugroho, Budi Purnomo and Adjianto Dwi Nugroho, September, 2012, and February, 2013) and the political consultants of the Lingkaran Survei Indonesia/The Indonesian Circle Survey (Arman Salam, Totok Izzul Fatah and Sunarto Ciptohardjono, September 2012 and February, 2013).

against the authoritarian Soeharto New Order regime (1966–1998).[6] These volunteer communities had very eagerly stood for Jokowidodo to be nominated by an Indonesian political party as the candidate for the 2012 Gubernatorial Election of Jakarta. Applying the political marketing of candidates, before the first round of the elections, Jokowidodo-Basuki Tjahaya Purnama had begun to use the Product-Oriented Candidate (POC) strategy. Thus, Jokowidodo introduced himself in the political market arenas as the current Mayor of Surakarta Regency, Central Java and succeeded in developing an outstanding public services management system in his region. In a similar manner with Jokowido's, Basuki Tjahaya Purnama also presented himself to the public as the former successful Head of the West Belitung Regency, Bangka Belitung Province who had promoted some outstanding popular policies—such as providing health services and education services with priority to the underdeveloped areas and health subsidies for poor communities—that were appreciated by his electorate.

As regards increasing volatile electorates of Jakarta, Jokowidodo-Basuki Tjahaya Purnama began to follow the Sales-Oriented Candidates (SOC) strategy. Based on this political marketing strategy, his election staff devised the ground war marketing and campaigning and used the mixed mediated and online political campaigning (MMOPC). Firstly focused on the ground war marketing and campaigning, Jokowi's campaigning products were centred on his success story based on the innovative public service system in the health services, managing the traditional market services, and promoting the automotive-car industries strategy as well as encouraging the development of local vocational schools and creating more opportunities for the creation of new jobs. Moreover, he had begun to utilize the Market-Oriented Candidate (MOC) strategy, before the first round of the elections by adopting marketing intelligence, survey researches, and focus group discussions to adjust his political product in order to meet the voters' expectations, needs, and demands. Based on this strategy, he successfully co-created his personal branding as tailored by the expectations, wants, and needs of the Indonesian urban middle class as the strategic electorates of Jakarta.

Meanwhile, as of the end of April 2012, when the Indonesian Democratic Struggle Party and the Gerindra Party nominated him, he formed his campaign team which was headed by Mr. Boy Bernardi Sadikin—son of the former Governor of Jakarta (1966–1977), General (ret.) Ali Sadikin—and the party-centred political marketing strategy began being implemented.[7] Before the first round of the elections, the political marketing approach of the above-mentioned coalition of parties had been carried out on the basis of the product-oriented parties (POP) strategy, and

---

[6] One of them is Bimo Nugroho who had previously assembled the Professional Communities for Democracy (PCD) [Masyarakat Profesional untuk Demokrasi (MPD)] by April 18, 2012 in order to sign the specific agreement with Jokowi, which endorsed Jokowidodo's candidacy nomination for the 2012 Governor Election of Jakarta. The most importantly, this agreement was based on mutual trust and self-funded campaign strategy (Wisesa, in Nugroho and Nugroho 2012: xi).

[7] Personal Interview with Sunarto Ciptohardjono, one of the general political consultants of the Lingkaran Survey Indonesia/The Indonesian Survey Circle, February, 2013.

then it shifted to the market-oriented party (MOP) strategy. Moreover, before the second round of the elections, they began to advance their political marketing and campaign programs based on the integrated participatory political marketing (IPPM). Jokowi's personal branding attracted hundreds of thousands of voluntary campaigners.

Generally speaking, the IPPM model was developed based on two main objectives: (1) enlarging the positive news frame of free and paid publicity, and (2) accumulating huge political endorsements from the participatory/voluntary campaigner communities of electorates, either by direct and pull marketing *(grassroots efforts)*, and push marketing by using social media. In this respect, the IPPM model was firmly established not only based on political marketing of parties *per se*, but also fully by being supported by the participatory/voluntary political marketing of professional urban communities who had no officially affiliation with any political parties.[8]

The IPPM model of Jokowidodo-Basuki Tjahaya Purnama was developed on the basis of the three steps of political marketing strategy.[9] The first step was implemented based on the traditional/face-to-face participatory political marketing to address various segmented electorates. In this respect, voters mainly came from three main groups: (1) trader communities of the traditional market of Jakarta, and (2) the urban professional communities and young communities of Jakarta; (3) the poorest communities who live in the small sub-region (*Kampoeng*) of Jakarta (Fig. 7.4).

The participatory political campaigning within the framework of the mediated political communication was developed as the second step. To this end, Jokowidodo and his campaign team developed "personal close contact" and organized special informal meetings with the senior editors of political departments of national newspapers, senior producers of private/commercial national television broadcasting companies in Jakarta. The main goals were: (1) establishing personal connections and attachment with them; (2) sharing the ideas about the future of the local government of Jakarta as the capital city of Indonesia; and (3) meeting their expectations towards the new Governor of Jakarta. Finally, to amplify Jokowi's personal branding, his voluntary campaigner communities established the use of participatory political marketing in the online political communication arenas. To do so, Jokowidodo and his campaign teams and voluntary campaigner communities organized the direct informal and formal meetings with various groups of the electorate and buzzed positive branding of Jokowi using the Internet and the social media networks to persuade the volatile electorates of Jakarta.

[8] Ajianto Dwi Nugroho, the Chief of the Political Marketer Manager of Jokowidodo's Volunteers, personal interview, September 2012.

[9] Based on personal interviews with: (1) Bimo Nugrono, one of the Strategic Campaigners of Jokowidodo-Basuki Tjahaya Purnama; (2) Budi Purnomo, the Head of the Media Center and Chief of Media Strategies of Jokowidodo-Basuki Tjahaya Purnama, February, 2013, and (3) Ajianto Dwi Nugroho, the Chief of the Political Marketer Manager of Jokowidodo's Volunteer, personal interview, September 2012).

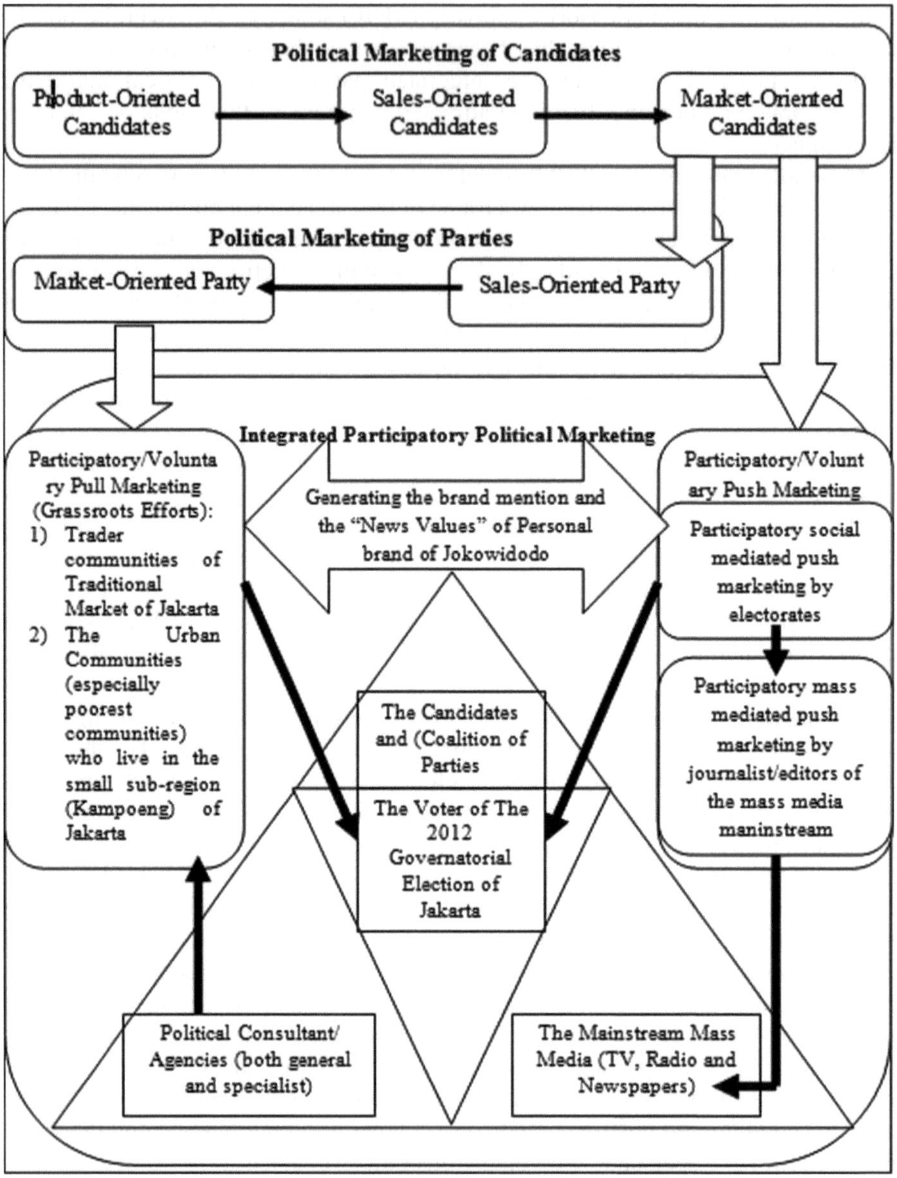

Fig. 7.4 The integrated participatory political marketing (IPPM) model implemented by Jokowidodo-Basuki Tjahaya Purnama during the 2012 Gubernatorial elections of the special region of Jakarta

7.4.3 From "Blusukan" to the Mixed Mediated and Online Political Campaigning (MMOPC): Jokowidodo-Basuki Tjahaya Purnama's Smart Campaign Model

Guided by IPPM, Jokowidodo-Basuki Tjahaya Purnama's campaign teams tried to establish and generate the ground war campaigning using traditional face-to-face direct marketing and campaigning ("blusukan") to enhance the commentary functions of the airwaves war and the online war campaigning. To do so, the three types of political marketing had been used: (1) traditional political marketing which is generated from the direct selling, door-to-door campaign and word of mouth; (2) political marketing and campaigning on the Internet and social media; and (3) the free and paid private/commercial mass media political marketing, especially television broadcasting.

First, the traditional political marketing was used to develop and implement the best-tailored approach using direct selling, door-to-door, and both traditional and online word-of-mouth campaign methods to address the mounting volatile electorates of Jakarta directly and personally. In this respect, Jokowi and his campaign teams, as well as the campaign volunteers, utilized the humanistic communication approach to them. The volatile electorates were mainly made up from two main groups: (1) trader communities of the traditional market of Jakarta, and (2) the urban communities, especially the poorest communities who live in the small sub-region (*Kampoeng*) of Jakarta. This *humanistic campaign approach* of the ground war campaign is called *"blusukan"*.[10] The term *humanistic campaign approach* became a popular issue across commercial media outlets. Taking into account that this *humanistic campaign approach* improved news values across media outlets, most of Jokowi's campaign activities attracted positive news reactions from Indonesian newspapers and commercial television broadcasting.

The other groups of segmented and targeted voters were the young government official staff of the Special Region of Jakarta. Why was this group also important? The main reason was that by addressing the young and idealist bureaucrats of the Special Region of Jakarta, the campaign teams, political consultants, and campaign managers could easily explore the weaknesses of incumbent candidates' leadership (Governor Fauzi Bowo) and to assess the electorates' needs and expectations as regards the new governor. As the qualitative data had already been provided, Jokowidodo's campaign teams, political consultants and campaign managers could adjust their campaign products, styles of packaging and delivering not only

[10] As derived from the generic traditional Javanese language *"blusukan"*; it means campaign activities by candidates and/or campaign teams as well as their campaign volunteers by using humanistic and close personal contact to get the message across to various groups of electorates. This humanistic campaign approach was implemented by using the relationship marketing and campaigning (Henneberg 2002) to establish warm, personal, direct, and informal communication with electorates by going to the venues of their daily professional activities (such as traditional markets or the locations inhabited by the poorest electorates.).

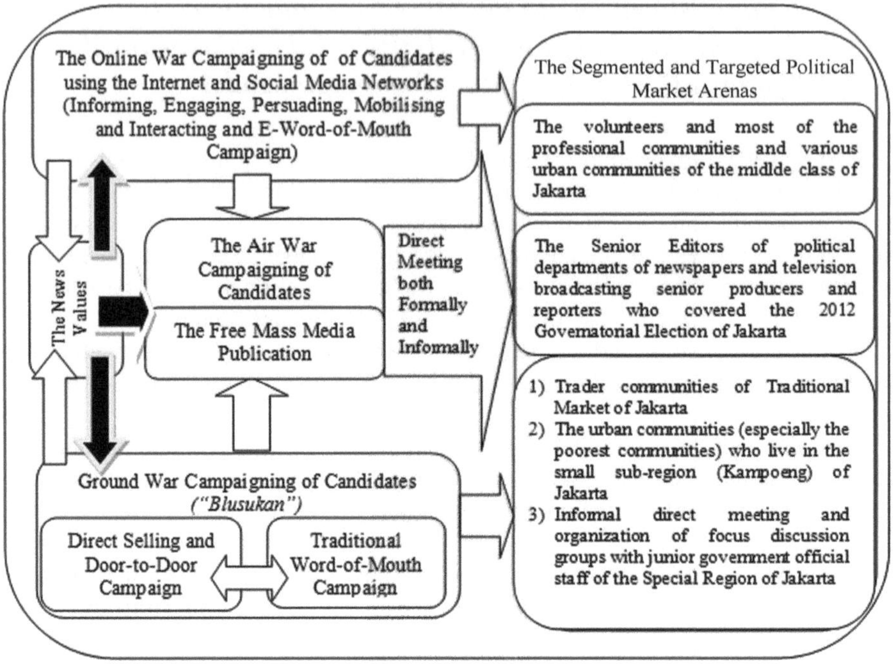

Fig. 7.5 Jokowidodo-Basuki Tjahaya Purnama's Smart Campaign Model: from *"Blusukan"* to mixed mediated and online political campaigning (MMOPC)

in order to meet the demands and expectations of the bureaucrats of the Special Region of Jakarta *per se*, but also to fulfil the expectations, needs and demands of Jakarta' electorates (Fig. 7.5).[11]

The other segmented and targeted political market arenas were the senior editors of the political departments of national newspapers, senior producer of private/commercial national television broadcasting companies in Jakarta. Mr.Budi Purnomo, Jokowidodo's Head of the Media Centre, organized special meetings with senior editors/producers of commercial media outlets with the following agenda: (1) making personal contact with them; (2) sharing ideas about the future of the Local Government of Jakarta as the capital city of Indonesia; (3) absorbing their expectations towards the new Governor of Jakarta; and (4) organizing strategic cooperation to strengthen the positive Jokowi's personal branding. Most interestingly, the agenda was carried out and, even though Jokowidodo did not spend for commercial space in the mass media—because of reduced campaign budgets—he obtained positive media coverage during the campaign and the elections.

The third segmented and targeted political market arena was that of the urban professional communities and the middle class electorates of Jakarta. Thus, a special team of Jokowi's campaign volunteers was organized. This team was

[11] Bimo Nugroho, personal interview, by January 2013.

formed from members of various professional and urban communities that did not want the incumbent candidate (Governor Fauzi Bowo) to be re-elected. As it was supported by hundreds thousands of volunteers, this team vigorously marketed their main political idea, i.e., *"The New Jakarta" (Jakarta Baru).*[12] Guided by the principles of the candidate-centred marketing and campaigning, they tried to market Jokowi's branding as "the hoped for and upcoming leaders of Jakarta" and mobilised hundreds of thousands of anonymous campaign volunteers by extensively using social media features. Once in line with the direct selling and marketing approach, Jokowi's campaign managers imagined and crafted Jokowi's personal brand image as that of an artist and celebrity. Taking into account that in the imagination of the volatile voters of Jakarta their expected leaders should look like idols, by using the journalism techniques of tabloidization, Jokowidodo's personal brand was strongly delineated by his media centre, then re-linked, and re-mentioned by his campaign volunteers using the social media networks.

Massively supported by various social media networks users, this mixed mediated and online political campaign (MMOPC) strategy was successfully advanced by Jokowi's campaign teams, consultants and voluntary campaigners and placed Jokowi's name as the top personal political brand.[13] First, this was done by informing and by engaging political marketing strategies; using the social media, Jokowi and his campaign team extensively used Twitter and Skype for making personal contact with hundreds of thousands of volunteers and swing voters[14] during the first round and second round of the elections.[15] Second, Jokowi's political marketers mobilized and interacted with volatile electorates that were very frequent users of the social media networks. Another strategy that was used by Jokowidodo's political marketers was that of founding the "The Jokowi-Ahok Social Media Volunteers" (JASMEV) by August 2012.[16] As a result, before the

[12] This tagline envisages the future of Jakarta without discrimination, having positive appreciation towards cultural activities, and upholds the idea of plurality and open equality and access for Jakarta's people to achieve their personal and their communities' dream. Ajianto Dwi Nugroho, the Chief of the Political Marketer Manager of Jokowidodo's Volunteers, personal interview, September 2012.

[13] Budi Purnomo, the Head of Jokowi's Media Centre, personal interviews, February 2013.

[14] Jokowidodo's Twitter account (@jokowi_do2) had 193,000 followers. During the campaign and election he responded to all the comments of his followers.

[15] In this respect, Jose Rizal, one of the Indonesian social media network analysts, noted that before the first round, Jokowidodo-Basuki Tjahaya Purnama had been supported by 54.9 % buzz of 900,000 social media users, while Fauzi Bowo-Nahrowi Ramli just got 45.1 % buzz. Meanwhile, before the second round of the 2012 Gubernatorial Elections, by September 2012, the social media mentions of Jokowi's personal brand went up to 26 %, while Fauzi Bowo just obtained 21 %. In this respect, the positive and negative sentiment toward Jokowi's personal brand was 8: 1, while Fauzi Bowo's was only 2: 1. All in all, Jokowododo's personal brand went up in the important social media such as *Twitter, Facebook, Youtube, Google plus, Tumblr, and Yfrog (KOMPAS, 24 September, 2012).*

[16] Jokowi is Jokowidodo's nickname and Ahok is the Basuki Tjahaya Purnama's "Chinese nickname". Jokowi's ethnicity background is Javanese middle class, while Basuki Tjahaya Purnama's ethnicity background is Hokian-Chinese (he was born on Belitung Island, Bangka Belitung Province which is geographically located in the South-East Area of the Sumatra Island).

second round of the elections, they had more than 10,000 volunteers for social media based political marketers,[17] and 562,598 unique users supported Jokowidodo, while only 309,678 unique users supported Fauzi Bowo-Nahrowi Ramli. In the social media networks, there were 1,365,234 unique users who mentioned Jokowidodo's personal brand.[18]

As the mixed-mediated and online political campaigning (MMOPC) had been successfully implemented, Jokowi's personal brand generated more positive brand mentions and attracted more positive news across commercial media outlets. The main factor was that most of Jokowi's campaign events and personal activities championed the "new values" across commercial media outlets. Jokowi' news values met with the logic of mass media coverage. Therefore, Jokowi's political news coverage—in hard news, soft news, or feature programs—benefited from the increasing number of private/commercial television programs. As a result, Jokowi, as the non-incumbent candidate, became "the media-darling" across various commercial media outlets.[19]

As he enjoyed positive coverage in the social media network sites and in the mass media, Jokowi's personal brand attracted the majority of the volatile electorates of Jakarta. In spite of the fact that, before the elections, Fauzi Bowo was predicted as the winner in those elections, after the first round of elections, Jokowido-Basuki Tjahaya Purna was the winner; he was voted by 1,847,157 voters, i.e., 42.60 % of the total number of voters, while Fauzi Bowo-Nahrowi Rahmli came out second as he obtained 1,476,648 votes, i.e., or 34.05 % of the total number voters. As there was no candidate with more than 50 % of the total number of votes in the first round of the elections, the second round was organized.[20] The second round of the elections was held in September 2012. The result surprised the incumbent candidate and most of the Indonesian pollsters and political consultants; Jokowidodo-Basuki Tjahaya Purnama obtained 2,472,130 votes or 53.82 % of the total number of voters, while Fauzi Bowo-Nahrowi Ramli obtained 2,120,815 votes or 46.18 % of the total number of voters, Based on these election results, on September, 29, 2012, the General Election Commission of the Special Region of Jakarta declared Jokowidodo the Governor of Jakarta for 2012–2017 (Table 7.6).

---

[17] http://pilkada.tempo.co/konten-berita/pilkada_dki/2012/09/19/430388/Dalam-Sebulan-Ada-2-Juta-Mention-untuk-Jokowi.

[18] *Akun @Triomacan2000 Jadi Jangkar Pendukung Foke* (@Triomacan 2000 account had become the anchor of Foke' supporters), Rabu, 19 September 2012, dalam http://pilkada.tempo.co/konten-berita/pilkada_dki_serba_serbi/2012/09/19/430415/Akun-Triomacan2000-Jadi-Jangkar-Pendukung-Foke.

[19] Based on personal interwiews with two senior editor/executive producers of Indonesian private/commercial television broadcasting companies: (1) Alvito Deanova Ginting, Senior Editor/Executive Producer of Political News Programme of TV ONE, February 2013; and (2) Pasaoran Simanjutak, Senior Editor/Executive Producer of Political News Programme of Trans 7, February 2013.

[20] Based on Article No.11, paragraph 2, Law No.29/2007 on the Goverment of the Special Region of Jakarta.

Table 7.6 Distribution of voters in the 2012 gubernatorial elections of Jakarta: Jokowidodo-Basuki Tjahaya Purnama vs. Fauzi Bowo-Nahrowi Ramli in the second-round of election

Sub-region of special region of Jakarta	Jokowidodo-Basuki Tjahaya Purnama (total number of voters)	Fauzi Bowo-Nahrowi Ramli (total number of voters)
West Jakarta	577,232	474,298
East Jakarta	695,220	611,366
Central Jakarta	256,529	249,427
North Jakarta	432,714	300,188
South Jakarta	507,257	476,742
The thousand islands of Jakarta REGENCY	3,178	8,794

Source: The General Election Commission of the Special Region of Jakarta 2012

7.5 Conclusions

IPPM and MMOPC use gradually emerged during the 2012 Gubernatorial Elections of Jakarta. Jokowi's campaign teams successfully established the Integrated Political Marketing Model (IPPM) and the mixed-mediated and online political campaigning (MMOPC) while dealing with an increase in the volatile electorates of Jakarta. By using IPPM and MMOPC, the cost of Jokowi's campaign was widely recognized as the cheapest campaign that had ever been run compared with any those of other candidates for governor/vice governor of the Indonesian provinces.[21] Moreover, once IPPM and MMOPC had been successfully established, there had been overwhelming positive coverage and political endorsement that came from the majority of senior editors, senior producers, and reporters of various commercial media outlets due to the high news values of the candidate's personal branding. The main reason is that Jokowi's campaign activities and events tended to meet the mass media logic, and this fact was indicated by increasing rating of various programmes of the television broadcasting companies during first and second round of the elections.[22] In this respect, the IPPM and MMOPC can be considered as a new ideology of political re-connection, wherein decentralized, democratized and equalized participatory marketing and campaigning can be co-created and co-implemented across candidates, parties and electorates.

Indeed, several conditions need to be fulfilled in order to develop the IPPM and MMOPC in the political market arenas. First, they may be established once candidates already have strong political branding and thus they can attract political support and political endorsement from voluntary campaigner communities.

[21] Jokowidodo campaign fund just spend no more than 23 Billion rupiah or equal with around 22.000 $ US (Based on current exchange of first October 2012). Sunarto Cipto Harjono, Senior Political Consultants of The Lingkaran Survei Indonesia/The Indonesian Circle Survey, Personal Interview, January 2013).

[22] Totok Izzul Fatah, Senior Media Strategist Consultants of The Lingkaran Survei Indonesia/The Indonesian Circle Survey, Personal Interview, January 2013).

Second, they may be redeveloped if there is a massive well-informed middle class that will stand for any party and candidates that fulfil their expectations of better leadership and policies of the future government. Third, they may be advanced if there is easier access and networking among candidates, campaign managers, and campaign volunteers based on the interactive-online political marketing and campaigning tools. Fourth, they may be crafted if there is clear differentiation between the ideas of the incumbent officials and the challengers that will strongly polarize the electorates.

To put it briefly, the IPPM can be crafted once marketing and campaigning strategies have been already anchored with IMC and participatory communication concepts and there are parallelisms between the political marketing of candidates and the political marketing of parties and vice versa. Meanwhile, the MMOPC can be advanced when there is stronger personal branding of non-incumbent candidates than that of incumbent candidates and when candidates succeed in influencing the majority of volatile electorates. Theoretically speaking, the lesson learned from this episode of the emerging democracy in Indonesia is that IPPM can be considered as one of the alternative models to complement the existing mainstream model of political marketing of parties (Lees-Marshment 2001, 2004, 2008) and political marketing of candidates (Newman 1994), while MMOPC can be considered as one practical model of professionalized campaign based on the candidate-centred system to complement the existing party-centred of professionalized campaign model (Gibson and Römmele 2001, 2009; Stromback 2009).

In the future, research needs to be advanced by focusing on several directions. First, from the perspective of a more comprehensive mix of quantitative and qualitative methods, research needs to be directed to address both the party-centred and or candidate-centred IPPM and MMOPC by using both subjective and objective quantitative measurements. Second, another research area to be developed by using comparative the conceptual frameworks of IPPM and MMOPC is that of the specific political market arenas as suggested by Stromback (2010) that are the parliamentary, the internal, the mass media, and electoral arenas. Third, as there have been diverse structural factors—political system, government system, media system, and election system, on the one hand—and cultural factors—in relation with the degree modernization and secularization of societies- on the other hand, across the well-established democratic countries and the emerging democracies, research needs to be carefully catered for are revealing the inter-links and relationships between the party-centred and the candidate-centred of IPPM and MMOPC whether within and across those countries. Fourth, taking into account that there have been diverse tendencies of political engagement, political trust, political knowledge, the degree and type of the mass media exposure and the Internet and social media networks use across parties, candidates and electorates, further research needs to be focused on examining how, in which way, and to what extent the IPPM and MOPC can be developed as an ideology of political re-connection to overcome the existing problem of the democratic deficit and declining political engagement that still occur across the democratic countries in the world.

References

Adi, A., & Lilleker Darren, G. (2012). *Getting the message out: Social media daily activity plan*. Bournemouth, UK: The Creative Enterprise Bureau, the Media School, Bournemouth University.

Barber, B. R. (1984). *Strong democracy: Participatory politics for a new age*. Berkeley, CA: California University Press.

Butler, P., & Collins, N. (1994). Political marketing: Structure and process. *European Journal of Marketing, 28*(1), 19–34.

Eriyanto. (2007). Why Fauzi Bowo can be the winner (Mengapa Fauzi Bowo Menang). *The Monthly Review (Kajian Bulan)*. The Indonesian survey cycle (Lingkaran Survey Indonesia). vol. 4. August 2007(Edisi 04-Agustus, 2007), pp. 13–31.

Eriyanto and Sukanta. (2007). The governatorial election of Jakarta and The effectiveness of parties' coalition (pilkada DKI Jakarta dan Efektifitas Koalisi). The Monthly Review (Kajian Bulan). The Indonesian Survey Cyrcle (Lingkaran Survey Indonesia). vol. 4. August 2007 (Edisi 04-Agustus, 2007), pp. 1–12.

Gibson, R., & Römmele, A. (2001). Changing campaign communications: A party-centred theory of professionalized campaigning. *The Harvard International Journal of Press/Politics, 6*, 31.

Gibson, R. K., & Römmele, A. (2009). Measuring the professionalization of political campaigning. *Party Politics, 15*, 265.

Granati, F. (2012). *Integrated marketing communication- back to communication*. London: Amazon.Co.UK, Ltd.

Henneberg, S. C. M. (2002). Understanding political marketing. In N. J. O. Shaughnessy & S. C. M. Henneberg (Eds.), *The idea of political marketing*. London: Praeger Publishers.

Hill, D. T. (2003). Communication for a new democracy: Indonesia's first online elections. *The Pacific Review, 16*(4), 525–547.

Hill, D., & Sen, K. (2000). The internet in Indonesia's new democracy. In P. Ferdinand (Ed.), *The internet, democracy and democratization* (pp. 119–136). London: Frank Cass.

Hill, D., & Sen, K. (2002). Netizens in combat: Conflict on the Internet in Indonesia. *Asian Studies Review, 26*(2), 165–87.

Kliatchko, J. (2008). Revisiting the IMC construct: A revised definition and four pillars. *International Journal of Advertising, 27*(1), 133–160.

Lees-Marshment, J. (2001). *Political marketing and the British political party: The party just begun*. Manchester: Manchester University Press. First Edition.

Lees-Marshment, J. (2004). *The political marketing revolution: Transforming the government of the UK*. London: Routledge Publication.

Lees-Marshment, J. (2008). *Political marketing and British political parties*. Manchester, UK: Manchester University Press. Second Edition.

Lees-Marshment, J., & Lilleker, D. G. (Eds.). (2005). *Political marketing: A comparative perspective*. Manchester, UK: Manchester University Press.

Lileker, D.G., Jackson, N. (2010). Interactivity and branding, public political communication as a marketing tools, in eprints.bournemouth.ac.uk/15074/2/LillJack_-_PSA2010.pdf. Accessed Sept 2012.

Lileker, D.G., Jackson, N. (2010). Towards a more participatory style of election campaigning? The impact of Web 2.0 on the UK 2010 General Election, dalam http://microsites.oii.ox.ac.uk/ipp2010/system/files/IPP2010_Lilleker_Jackson_Paper_0.pdf. Accessed by Sept 2012.

Lilleker, D. G., et al. (2011). Informing, engaging, mobilising or interacting: Searching for a European model of web campaigning. *European Journal of Communication, 26*(3), 195–213.

Lim, M. (2003a) The information terrains and politics: The internet and political power in Indonesia. *Indonesian Journal of Social and Cultural Anthropology, 73*, Jakarta: University of Indonesia.

Lim, M. (2003b). The internet, social networks and reform in Indonesia. In N. Couldry & J. Curran (Eds.), *Contesting media power. Alternative media in a networked world* (pp. 273–288). Oxford: Rowman & Littlefield.

Lim, M. (2005) The internet and political activism in Indonesia. Unpublished PhD Dissertation, the Universiteit Twente, Nedherland.

Maarek, P. (1995). *Political marketing and communication*. London: John Libbey.

Meijer, A., Burger, N., Ebbers, W. (2008) *Citizens4Citizens: Mapping participatory practices on the Internet*. Paper for Politics: Web 2.0: An International Conference, New Political Communication Unit, Department of Politics and International Relations, Royal Holloway, University of London, April 17–18, 2008.

Newman, B. I. (1994). *Marketing of the president: Political marketing as campaign strategy*. London: Sage Publications.

Norris, P. (2000). *A virtuous circle: Political communication in post-industrial societies*. Cambridge: Cambridge University Press.

Nugroho, B., & Nugroho, A. D. (2012). *Jokowi: Politic Tanpa Pencitraan (Jokowi : The Politics Without Image Making)*. Jakarta: PT Gramedia.

Ormrod, R. P. (2005). A conceptual model of political market orientation. *Journal of Non-Profit and Public Sector Marketing, 14*(1/2), 47–65.

Ormrod, R.P. (2009). Understanding political market orientation. Thesis submitted for the degree of Doctor of Philosophy, Institute for Marketing and Statistics, Aarhus School of Business, University of Aarhus, Denmark. January 2009.

Ouwersloot, H., & Duncan, T. (2008). *Integrated marketing communication*. London: The McGraw-Hill Companies. European Edition.

Rice, R. E., & Haythornthwaite, C. (2006). Perspectives on internet use: Access, involvement and interaction. In L. A. Lievrow & S. Livingstone (Eds.), *Handbook of new media: Social shaping and social consequences of ICTS*. London: Sage Publication.

Schultz, D.E. (1993). "Integrated marketing communications: maybe definition is in the point of view." *Marketing News*, January 18, 1993.

Schultz, D. E., & Schultz, H. (2004). *IMC, the next generation: Five steps for delivering value and measuring financial returns*. New York: McGraw-Hill.

Schultz, D. E., Tannenbaum, S. I., & Lauterborn, R. F. (1993). *Integrated marketing communications: Putting it together & making it work*. Chicago: NTC Business Book.

Stromback, J. (2009). Selective professionalisation of political campaigning: A test of the party-centred theory of professionalised campaigning in the context of the 2006 Swedish election. *Political Studies, 57*, 95–116.

Stromback, J. (2010). A framework for comparing political market-orientation. In J. Lees-Marshment, J. Stromback, & C. Rudd (Eds.), *Global political marketing*. London: Taylor & Francis Group.

Tufte, T., & Mefalopulos, P. (2009). *Participatory communication: A practical guide*. Washington, DC: The World Bank.

Wring, D. J. (2005). *The politics of marketing of labour party*. New York, NY: Palgrave Macmillan.

Newspaper/Online News

http://pilkada.tempo.co/konten-berita/pilkada_dki/2012/09/19/430388/Dalam-Sebulan-Ada-2-Juta-Mention-untuk-Jokowi

http://pilkada.tempo.co/konten-berita/pilkada_dki_serba_serbi/2012/09/19/430415/Akun-Triomacan2000-Jadi-Jangkar-Pendukung-Foke

http://www.tempo.co/read/news/2012/08/25/228425465/Sosial-Media-di-Mata-Jokowi

http://www.tempo.co/read/news/2012/09/17/228429899/Siapa-Penentu-Kemenangan-Foke-atau-Jokowi

Laws

Law No.29/2007 About the government of special region of Jakarta.
Law No.32/2004 about the Local Government.
The Government Regulation No.3/2005 (for amendment and substitution of the Law No.32/2004) about the Local Government.

List of In-Depth Interviews

Ajianto Dwi Nugrono, one of the coordinator of the voluntary-campaigner communities of Jokowidodo-Basuki Tjahaya Purnama, 22 September 2012.
Alvito Deanova Ginting, Senior Editors/Executive Producers of Political News Programme of TV ONE, 20 February 2013.
Arman Salam, the Director of the Pollster Firm of Lingkaran Survey Indonesia (the Indonesian Circle Survey). Personal Interview, 23 February 2013.
Bimo Nugroho, one of the Strategic Campaigner of Jokowidodo-Basuki Tjahaya Purnama, Personal Interview, 21 September 2012
Budi, P. (2013). The head of media centre and chief media strategies of Jokowidodo-Basuki Tjahaya Purnama, 26 February, 2013.
Pasaoran, S. (2013). Senior editors/executive producers of political news programme of Trans 7, 25 February 2013.
Sunarto Ciptohardjono, one of the general political consultants of the Lingkaran Survey Indonesia/ The Indonesian Survey Circle, 23 February 2013.

Chapter 8
Avant-garde Digital Movement or "Digital Sublime" Rhetoric?

The *Movimento 5 Stelle* and the 2013 Italian Parliamentary Elections

Francesca Musiani

> *"Are you a* grillino? ***Do you enjoy streaming?"***
> *Italian comedian Maurizio Crozza impersonating a puzzled Giorgio Napolitano, President of the Italian Republic, April 2013.*

Abstract With 25.5 % of voices obtained at the 2013 parliamentary elections in Italy, the *MoVimento 5 Stelle* (M5S or Five Star Movement) has become a central actor of Italian politics. The Movement relies to a large extent on a vision of Internet-driven and -based direct democracy; as such, social media have been the main organizational tools behind its rise of the past few years. At the same time, it is argued that the power of networking, the allegedly egalitarian approach to public debate, and the horizontality of relations typical of social media are not, in fact, the backbone of the Movement, but a primarily discursive device destined to hide the importance of much more "traditional" political instruments of hierarchical authority and opaque management of financial flows, and to legitimize the amateurism of the movement along with its anti-political drive. This chapter provides a portrait of the digital and social "vision" posited by the Movement—its practical, organizational consequences alongside its narrative(s). It aims at showing how the different components of this vision all contribute to the M5S's status of new force to be reckoned with in the Italian political space—not always, and maybe not primarily, for the reasons the Movement itself provides.

Keywords Movement • Italy • Politics • Elections • Social media • Horizontality • Web • Organization • Direct democracy • Rhetoric

---

F. Musiani (✉)
MINES ParisTech, Paris, France

Georgetown University, Washington, DC, USA
e-mail: francesca.musiani@gmail.com

B. Pătruţ and M. Pătruţ (eds.), *Social Media in Politics*, Public Administration and Information Technology 13, DOI 10.1007/978-3-319-04666-2_8,

It was somewhat foreseen, anticipated, and by some, hoped for or deeply feared. But what was certainly unexpected was its order of magnitude. The *MoVimento 5 Stelle* (M5S or Five Star Movement)'s sweep of a spectacular 25.5 % at the recent Italian parliamentary elections of February 24th and 25th, 2013, was doubtlessly even more of a tsunami[1] than the two leading minds behind the Movement, Beppe Grillo and Gianroberto Casaleggio, had envisaged. With an electoral result that made it Italy's most voted party in the Chamber of Deputies and an equal "third force" alongside the traditional left- and right-wing coalitions—the crucial actor in the formation of alliances and coalitions that would eventually lead to a government—the M5S has established itself as the newest, most sought-after fieldwork of Italian sociologists, political scientists and journalists. All of them have attempted to dissect this unprecedented phenomenon, as puzzling as it is rife with problematic consequences and open questions for the close future of Italian politics.

As a long-term Italian expatriate in France and in the United States and a scholar of Internet governance—but somewhat of an "invested outsider" to Italian politics—I am both thrilled and doubtful as I start writing this essay on M5S. Yet, the fact of not having experienced "in the flesh" the Italian electoral campaign of early 2013 likely allows me to develop an external point of view on the manifold "instant studies" on the Movement. There has been a proliferation of such studies in the past few months, and these provide many interesting entry points of reflection into the topic, with a diversity that clearly reflects the variety of interpretations and viewpoints about M5S—not only among its analysts, but among politicians themselves.

One of the main "disorienting forces" deployed by the Movement is, without a doubt, the central role it attributes to the Internet and to digital, social media tools; the quote that opens this chapter is a particularly on-target parody and illustration of the difficulty, by the traditional political establishment, to grasp these mechanisms and the discourses surrounding them. In this quote, the famous Italian comedian Maurizio Crozza, impersonating President Giorgio Napolitano, ironically highlights one of the stand-out features of a true *grillino*[2]: insisting that every political procedure that deserves to be known by citizens should be broadcast live and then archived on the Internet, through video streaming technology. During the March 2013 political consultations aimed at forming a government—a somewhat desperate attempt by the left, despite the "hung parliament" situation that had followed the elections—the M5S imposed live video streaming to every event of this type that concerned representatives of the Movement, much to the other parties' dismay and disarray. These, too, broadcast live for the whole country—and the world—to see.

The Movement relies to a large extent on a vision of Internet-driven and -based direct democracy, and social media have been the main organizational tools behind

[1] Tellingly, Beppe Grillo chose to name "Tsunami Tour" his itinerant political campaign in Italian squares, in the spring of 2013. See his eponymous blog post http://www.beppegrillo.it/2013/01/tsunami_tour.html.

[2] In a way that followers of the Movement consider demeaning, because of the *reductio ad personam* it implies, the press often labels the M5S as *grillini* ("Grillo's people").

its rise of the past few years. At the same time, interesting arguments are being made about the extent to which networked, egalitarian approaches, and the horizontality of relations typical of social media are not, in fact, the backbone of the Movement, but a primarily discursive device destined to hide the importance of much more "traditional" political instruments of hierarchical authority and opaque management of financial flows, and to legitimize the amateurism of the movement along with its anti-political drive. This chapter provides a portrait of the digital and social "vision" posited by the Movement—its practical, organizational consequences alongside its narrative(s)—hoping to show how the different components of this vision all contribute to the M5S's status of new force to be reckoned with in the Italian political space—not always, and maybe not primarily, for the reasons the Movement itself provides.

8.1 M5S, The New Actor in Italian Politics

The *MoVimento 5 Stelle* is doubtlessly *the* new actor on the Italian political scene—the history of which has already, repeatedly shown its originality and peculiar balances in the past—and as such, it has been attracting international and national attention, in particular at the European level. Led by former comedian Beppe Grillo, the Movement has established itself as one of three forces of equal weight in the Italian parliament at the recent elections of February 2013. It has secured over 160 seats in the two Chambers combined, following a process of "direct nomination" of candidates on the Web, and surpassed even the most optimistic anticipations by the Movement's leaders. A clear signal of the M5S's steady rise in the Italian political landscape had taken place in the regional and municipal elections of 2012, making it known that the Movement was successfully proceeding to fill a spot left empty by traditional politics, shaking the foundations of the deeply-entrenched Italian party system and channelling those voices who oppose austerity measures as a remedy for the future's uncertainty.

In the wake of the 2013 electoral results, the M5S has quickly been hailed as one of the most successful examples to date of a movement "grown from the Web" that is able to parallel and even surpass the endeavours of traditional political parties. Even the Net-sceptic Evgeny Morozov has remarked: "There's no shortage of examples of citizen[s] being asked for advice on how to govern or being involved in some minor decision-making but I'm not aware of similar examples when it comes to elections. I suspect the Pirates Parties in Sweden and Germany may have experimented with similar methods, even if not on such a scale" (Morozov 2013). Throughout its rise, the M5S has indeed made the Internet and Web 2.0 applications, social media in particular, one of its main organisational resources as well as one of the core, underlying elements of its vision of what politics is and should be, and its conception of democracy. The central role—in practice and in narrative—of digital information and communication technologies is paralleled by the M5S communities' engagement in a number of in-person collective activities, including meet-ups and "protest days".

As the leader of the Movement, Beppe Grillo is a controversial figure. On one hand, he claims for himself an "inspirational" role, dedicated to rallying bottom-up participation and acting as a spokesman of the Movement's consensus—gathered through his widely-visited *Blog*,[3] that I will come back to later in the chapter. On the other hand, the total practical and financial control that he and the firm of his associate, Gianroberto Casaleggio, exert over the strategic choices of the Movement and the material platform around which it gathers has been deemed as inconsistent with his alleged leadership profile of "peer among peers". Questions have also been raised on the transparency of the Blog's management choices, which would not mirror the transparency requested and fostered by the M5S as a political model.

Grillo's profile is, indeed, very atypical for an Italian political leader, inasmuch as he is neither a "politician by profession" nor an outsider coming from the professions that have, in the past, proposed their services to Italian politics on a temporary basis—from university professors to judges and businessmen. His past as a comedian has fine-tuned his perception of the love–hate relationship between media and politics, and his capacity to use it; he leverages, through these media—prominently, so-called "new media", the Internet first and foremost—the dissatisfaction and lack of trust in the traditional political establishment which has been constantly increasing, in particular during the past few years, further fuelled by the economic crisis. He is, according to Fabio Bordignon and Luigi Ceccarini, "a political entrepreneur who mobilises resources, activating the potential 'protest energy' widespread in a considerable section of public opinion" (2013: 2).

The extent to which the alleged "inspiration" provided by Grillo hides, in fact, a relatively rigid and traditional hierarchy is a matter of on-going scrutiny, alongside the "one is worth one" M5S motto, which implies the centrality of direct consultation, absence of left/right identification, and hailing of professional skills as opposed to "political" skills. Evgeny Morozov points out that "the reasons why we need hierarchies and leaders don't always have to do with communication costs. [The Internet] reduces communication costs. But leaders and hierarchies are needed to produce charisma and to [. . .] sound cohesive and credible when negotiating with other parties, then the Internet hasn't changed anything: charisma and discipline don't emerge from bytes. [. . .S]omeone has to counter the [hostile] blog comments—they don't just go away on their own" (Morozov 2013). However, deliberate attempts, driven by populist and technocratic dreams of leaving politics behind, to escape negative attributes of politics—ideology, bargaining, prevarication and hypocrisy—may only make things worse. For whatever flaws of the current political system, the only alternative in that case may be the replacement of politics with either "managerialism" or populist totalitarianism, as argued by Bernard Crick well before the Movement and the Internet itself (Crick 1962).

[3] Blog di Beppe Grillo, http://www.beppegrillo.it/

8.2 The Web as an Organizational Home

A former "digital luddist"—he used to break a computer into pieces at the end of each of his shows in the early 2000s[4]—Grillo has found a home for his Movement in the World Wide Web. His Blog, *beppegrillo.it*, created in 2005, is the central rallying point around which the political initiatives of the Movement develop. The blog enjoyed immediate success, with *Forbes*, *TIME* and *The Observer* enthusiastically reporting about it in the years immediately following its creation, hailing the platform as one of the world's most influential blogs[5] and its creator as a Web Celeb[6] and a European Hero.[7]

Simultaneously to his blog's spectacular rise in notoriety, Beppe Grillo was touring Italy "in the flesh", recruiting supporters and followers among his fans, making his identities as a stage man and a blogger more and more intertwined. The *beppegrillo.meetup.com* platform was created as a parallel, somewhat independent tool of rallying and organization for the community. His shows were becoming increasingly political, while at the same time, he was preaching anti-politics with colourful and impolite language from the stage, until the climactic "V-day" (abbreviation for Vaffanculo-day, roughly translatable as "F*** Off day"; Ruggiero 2012), a calling for the introduction of a Bill of popular initiative to remove from office members of the Italian Parliament previously tried and convicted for crimes. The V-day is considered to be the first case, in Italian history, of a political demonstration developed and promoted via bottom-up mobilization on the blogosphere and on a number of social networking services (Pepe and Di Gennaro 2009).

To this day, the Web remains the core organisational resource of the Movement, primarily through the Blog and the Meetup platforms, paralleled with an extensive use of social media tools such as Twitter and Facebook. Bordignon and Ceccarini have argued that the global dimension of the Movement is mostly represented by the Blog, while the local dimension is mostly identifiable in the Meetup platform, and the different instances of meetups "in the flesh" that the platform allows to put in place: "[v]isitors to the blog were invited by Grillo to use this platform to organise themselves independently in local activist groups. At a central level, the distinguishing features are great professionalism, the availability of sophisticated technical skills and a strong orientation towards political marketing. At the peripheral level, groups of 'friends of Beppe Grillo' form the backbone of the organisation" (Bordignon and Ceccarini 2013: 11).

---

[4] See for example http://scaccoalweb.dotblog.it/2007/09/grillo-distrugg.html

[5] http://www.guardian.co.uk/technology/2008/mar/09/blogs

[6] http://www.forbes.com/2009/01/29/web-celebrities-internet-technology-webceleb09_0129_top_slide_8.html

[7] BBC News (February 26, 2013). Profile: Beppe Grillo. http://www.bbc.co.uk/news/world-europe-21576869

Web-based applications and tools are understood by the Movement as the facilitators of local-level participation, the instruments enabling mobilisation and monitoring around central, controversial issues and ultimately, an "active" conception of citizenship and citizenry (Tisch 2010), as well as a reconciliation between citizens and institutions by bringing them closer. Reports, articles and critical questions, published on the Web for everyone's perusal, allegedly increase the visibility of the problems that "really matter", and gather citizens around those problems. The Blog itself is the primary venue to exert one's right to active citizenship: it may be likened to a "super-node" among peer nodes in a network, with some coordination functions such as, for example, ensuring the communication between meetups. Damien Lanfrey highlights the M5S's structure as a "meta-organisation", a network of micro-organisations of different sizes, scope, and activities, partially coordinated at the central level, through the blog, and partially autonomous (Lanfrey 2011).

8.3 The Internet and Direct Democracy: A Vision and a Narrative

While the Web was quickly becoming the main organizational tool of M5S, by means of Grillo's blog and a number of word-of-mouth initiatives resting with social networking tools such as Twitter and Facebook, a "digital narrative" was taking shape in the discourse of Grillo and his followers as one of the underlying foundational themes of the Movement—an ideology, a vision and an electoral programme at once. Free and Open source software, broadband connectivity, Internet infrastructure development, peer-to-peer exchange, Creative Commons, even analogies between the M5S and the Norwegian, Icelandic and German Pirate Parties, acquired an increasingly prominent role in Grillo's speeches. In the leader's rhetoric, the Internet became the monitoring tool *par excellence* (Lanfrey 2011), able to maintain the elected accountable and to break into the heavily politically-unbalanced Italian media system, by providing a plurality of alternative voices and the means to spread them, with no need for intermediation.

Most of all, the idea of participatory and direct democracy fostered by Grillo and his followers is construed as having a "natural counterpart" in the Internet. Because of its alleged lack of intermediaries, Web- and application-based tools are the foundations of the user/citizen's "turning into the State". The delegation of decision-making responsibility from voters to elected officials, the cornerstone of representative democracy, supposedly becomes obsolete with the Web. Within a recurrent frame of "each person counts as one", reminiscent of the peer-to-peer paradigm, the role of the citizen becomes one of supervision and surveillance of whoever is in charge—who remains a peer among peers, as s/he was chosen by them. Politicians should be the people's "employees" and their mandate should be temporary—their actions and operations subjected to a continued monitoring process, facilitated by digital and social tools. A practical experiment of direct democracy via the Web was carried out in Fall 2012 for the *primarie*, the M5S internal elections that would prelude to the 2013 parliamentary elections and select candidates for them, and later in the year, by the *quirinarie*, the preliminary selection of candidates to the presidency of the Italian Republic. However, according to the MoVimento's very sources, the experiment was undermined in both cases by limited participation (about 40,000; Valentini 2013), and a number of criticisms, which we will come back to later, were raised about the transparency and consistency of the methodology used for gathering votes.

Beppe Grillo's direct democracy narrative has been varying from an initial desire of "improvement" of existing direct democracy systems, such as referendums and popular initiative bill proposals, to the cancellation of such instruments—which still presuppose a final intervention by the established political class to take into account the will of the people thus expressed. The (so far) final version of direct democracy advocated by Grillo suggests a "replacement" of politics with citizens (Valenza 2013), which entails a number of rules aimed at ensuring that elected officials act as civil servants, not as career politicians. Such requirements include the acceptance of substantial cuts in their deputies' and senators' salaries, the rejection of electoral reimbursements (a usually heated topic in Italian politics), and a strict limitation in the number of parliamentary mandates. Other requirements are more intimately linked to the M5S's reliance and large presence on the Web: direct democracy also means that elected officials should periodically submit themselves to the judgement of the voters on the Web, and ensure that political procedures, where decisions related to citizens are taken, are made as transparent as possible. The extensive use of live video streaming and Web archiving of all kinds of political meetings and consultations is an answer to this requirement.

8.4 Internal (non-)Democracy: From Web Strategists to Logos

If the "directness" and the "peer-to-peer" dynamics—as well as the role of the Internet in the implementation of such dynamics—are emphasized in the M5S's relationship to the external world, the internal organization and governance of the Movement and its digital platforms is more complicated, and has been heavily criticized, on occasions, by M5S affiliates themselves—sometimes with drastic consequences.

As previously mentioned, the M5S has in some respects a decentralised, networked structure, with independent initiatives on a variety of issues being carried out in different local contexts. Yet, the "*Movimento 5 Stelle*" symbol and the *Blog di Beppe Grillo* are managed in an entirely centralized and somewhat opaque way, by Grillo himself and his associate, Gianroberto Casaleggio, a Web strategist. Notwithstanding the proliferation of M5S-related alternative Web platforms, as the "central node of the membership network" (Bordignon and Ceccarini 2013), the Blog is crucial for M5S elected representatives to be widely heard. Based on the Movement's "Non-Statute",[8] its access can be forbidden to members who, according to a non-appealable sanction from Grillo, are deemed to have infringed one or more of the seven rules regulating the Movement. Furthermore, the M5S logo is "registered in the name of Beppe Grillo, the exclusive owner of the rights of use [of the mentioned logo]". With this clause, Grillo is concentrating the set of rights related to the political and electoral use of the Movement's symbol in his hands—as well as the capacity and right to expel members from the M5S. Bordignon and Ceccarini note that, "[i]n this sense, the M5S is dissimilar to the pirate party, which has adopted instruments and practices of liquid democracy, by employing technologies for the decision-making process, such as the *LiquidFeedback* platform" (2013: 12).

The role within the Movement of Casaleggio, the CEO of the marketing and Web strategy consultancy firm Casaleggio Associati, managing the Blog, is also ambiguous. Several M5S activists perceive him as a "shadow figure", with a profile that is a lot more discreet than that of the leader and spokesperson Grillo, but with an influence on the Movement's governance that is perhaps even greater. In May 2012, Casaleggio will end up writing a "self-discharge letter" to the *Corriere della Sera*, one of Italy's most-read newspapers, stating that "For those people asking who is behind Grillo, or talking about a 'shady marketing firm', I would like to point out that I have never been 'behind' Beppe Grillo, but at his side. [. . .] I am the cofounder of this movement" (Casaleggio 2012).

The fragility and shortcomings of the M5S's internal democracy ultimately spill over the boundaries of the Internet and the Web, to be exposed via more traditional media. In April 2012, Giovanni Favia, then a M5S prominent representative, is hosted by journalist Michele Santoro in his programme *Servizio Pubblico*. Off-the-air, he uses strongly negative words to describe Grillo's supremacy over the Movement's political symbols, and the spin doctor, "Small Brother" role played within M5S by Casaleggio. In September 2012, at *primarie* time, the TV programme *Piazzapulita* broadcasts the video containing Favia's frank remarks, exposing his deception, as an activist, for the ways in which Grillo and his guru manage internal expressions of dissent, as well as the governance, management and decision-making of the Movement and its platforms. Together with Federica Salsi (another M5S representative, municipal councillor in Bologna), "guilty" of taking part in another popular TV programme contrary to the Non-Statute's provisions, Favia is expulsed from the Movement, and the decision posted on the Web with great drama and fanfare—and criticisms.[9]

[8] https://s3-eu-west-1.amazonaws.com/materiali-bg/Regolamento-Movimento-5-Stelle.pdf

[9] http://www.ilfattoquotidiano.it/2012/12/12/movimento-5-stelle-grillo-espelle-giovanni-favia-e-federica-salsi/443548/

8.5 The *Imperative Mandate* and Its Dilemma

The model fostered by the M5S proposes that politics be structured around the "imperative mandate", i.e., that the elected representatives should be directly dependent from, and directly accountable to, the voters. However, the political will of the latter is—albeit based on an ongoing feedback system with followers and militants, enacted through the Internet—interpreted by the leader and "guarantor" of the Movement and his thought leader of reference, contested web strategist Gianroberto Casaleggio.

Sociologist Ilvo Diamanti, a long-time careful observer of Italian politics, observes that the full implementation of both of these core features is very difficult to achieve, as they presuppose two very different conceptions of what the Movement is (Diamanti 2013). The "room for interpretation" by leaders that has de facto characterized the Movement's actions as a political entity so far makes it more alike to a party like any other: an organization of politicians, more or less "professionalized", with a common identity and common interests, and vulnerable *vis-a-vis* the temptations and privileges of power. However, the M5S was indeed born as a network, not only because of its digital networking component, but because it was created out of that fabric of groups and committees engaged on themes of common good, environment, public ethics, that are somewhat separated from mainstream politics, populated by mostly young people, operated at the local level on a voluntary basis, and drawing their line of conduct by pragmatic, daily experience.

For this reason, the prompt answer to the leader's call may be difficult to achieve in every occasion—and it may be equally difficult to let the model of direct democracy and the imperative mandate prosper, now that political elections have assimilated the Movement's exponents into the rules and principles of representative democracy. The individuation of the voters' very needs and demands may be difficult to achieve as well, lest the interpretation by the leaders become too cumbersome. Because of the M5S's very lack of ideological cohesion and structure, which has assembled a variety of markedly different citizen profiles under the banner of the "five stars" (public water, environment, sustainable transport, development and connectivity), the allegiance to the leader, necessary to trust his "interpretation", may be equally problematic. Elected people and activists do not answer exclusively or directly to the leader, as they have not been chosen by him but by other activists and followers with whom they have developed a close, independent, often personal relationship. Interviews of M5S militants show how their accountability, allegiance and in turn, their commitment and action, is based on the trust-informed relationship with their peers, rather than with Grillo himself (Corbetta and Gualmini 2013). That of M5S is the dilemma of a political entity oscillating between "traditional" and "personal" parties: it would most likely not exist without Grillo, the proprietor of a trademark, a platform, and a strategy. However, Grillo's "property" does not, or *should* not, extend to the Movement itself; the M5S is no "business-party" with elected representatives as employees,[10]

[10] A metaphor that has often been used for Silvio Berlusconi's Forza Italia.

but a bus on which, at different stops, a heterogeneous group of passengers with different destinations has found its place (Diamanti 2013). Will this bus, with its heterogeneity, be able to maintain its route as it faces the long-standing, albeit creaky, structures of representative politics?

8.6 Technical Obfuscation, Political Uncertainty

Moving beyond the imperative mandate dilemma, criticism of the heavily Web-based M5S model extends to the intrinsic technical uncertainties that arise if the Web is used not only as a "mere" rallying platform, but a true instrument of direct democracy, used to vote candidates in preliminary rounds of election before the final M5S representative goes on to the national, final round. Polemics have arisen, for example, during the *quirinarie*—the preliminary elections for the M5S candidate to the presidency of the Republic. In this occasion, relatively few people voted, and those who voted were not given much information about how their input (and their personal information) was handled (Valentini 2013).

It is argued that the M5S's Web-based direct democracy will end up being an imaginative variation of technocracy, for a number of reasons. First, and perhaps obviously, any individual who controls the technology has the capability to influence the voting process; less obviously, users of the platform are in fact very "profilable[11]", making it easier to identify specific cores of users/militants/voters. Most of these users have very limited technical knowledge of the platform but are, nonetheless, very "digitally active" and willing to get informed online, despite any warning message that may come from their machine; thus, they may be most easily attacked and eventually integrated into a botnet.[12] Once they are part of such a system, they may be exposed to a very sophisticated level of attacks.

Using the "rallying platform" constituted by the Blog as something more—as a true instrument of direct democracy—is certainly a laboratory of experimentation of participatory and emancipatory technologies that have been investigated, studied and tested in the past with very limited practical implementation. While this is hailed as an interesting result in itself (Luna 2013), it is argued, however, that the experiment may be going too far all of a sudden: an important amount of power and control is bestowed upon a technology that may not be sufficiently mature—and, in the process, to its administrators—with the idea that, if need be, a backup plan will

[11] Users that make their tastes, interests, and preferences explicit on the Web; these elements make it easier for third parties to establish their profile, and target them with content they are more likely to follow—content that may be malicious.

[12] A merger of robot and network, a botnet is set of computer programs, connected via the Internet, communicating with one another to perform tasks. While not all botnets are illegal, botnets often include computers whose security defenses have been breached, and whose control is now in the hands of a third party. Computers can be co-opted into a botnet to execute malicious software.

be envisaged later on. Both processes should be monitored, however, as "political history merged with technology".[13]

Second, the closed-source technical platform, managed exclusively by the Casaleggio Associates firm, gives its administrators a complete liberty of action—and the means for implementing a technical obfuscation of such actions. Administrators are not only the staff of the firm, but also the anonymous consultants that are likely helping what is and remains a social media marketing company to propose a direct democracy platform. The opacity of the platform makes it a lot more complicated, as well, for the public to know about—let alone react to—any deliberate attack enacted by any entity that is sufficiently technically savvy to take over the system. There is a lack of transparency in technical and political choices, especially when it comes to electronic voting and selection of candidates. Only long-time associates can access the voting platforms, while the Blog is the only public space where the debate happens in an open way.

The M5S model provides yet one more occasion—and perhaps one of the most interesting so far, in terms of the co-evolution of politics and the Internet—to rethink and challenge the myths surrounding the modes of operation of online platforms and their supposedly intrinsic democratic value. The model, with its qualities and its shortcomings, encourages further scrutiny of what constitutes the "objectivity" and the "neutrality" of algorithms subtending platforms such as Google, Twitter, and Facebook, crucial to the daily lives of our online, socially active selves (Musiani 2013). It suggests, once again, that the "invisible work" subtending the infrastructures and the architectures that make the Internet operational constitutes inherent arrangements of power (DeNardis 2012). Finally, the M5S model may be a laboratory to observe a further incarnation of what Evgeny Morozov describes as a widespread "rhetorical trick" of Internet culture. According to him, the public tends to think about features such as objectivity and neutrality as being consubstantial to networked technologies. "We think (those features) represent 'the Internet' and then we transfer those features to the 'Internet' itself, so that whatever other projects come out from 'the Internet' are essentially believed to have these features. So I'm not surprised that M5S can claim to be totally horizontal, transparent and Internet-driven while exercising few of these features" (Morozov 2013). The ways in which online platforms for political engagement may be "black boxes" in need of further scrutiny, and technical obfuscation may be a proxy for political uncertainty—the impression of participating in the political process without ever getting full assurances that your actions count—are brought to the fore by the M5S experience.

[13] In the words of Claudio Agosti, director of Hermes—Center for Transparency and Digital Human Rights. http://logioshermes.org, on the NEXA mailing list (April 2013).

8.7 Conclusions. Technology and Rhetoric: The M5S Facing Itself

As I am writing this piece, the M5S looks in trouble. After the national elections triumph just a few months ago, the Movement's following has drastically dropped in most cities where the June 2013 municipal elections were held.[14] Internal and external controversies shake the Movement, ranging from Grillo's "iron-fisted" management of dissident voices to the poor performances displayed by some M5S senators and deputies in the first months of life of the new Parliament.[15] Is the M5S destined to a fall as spectacular as its rise has been? Without attempting a prediction that will most likely be obsolete by the time this essay is published, my conclusions try to highlight what, in the unfolding narratives and daily practices of the Movement, makes it an interesting novel actor in the relationship between politics and the Internet—regardless of what its ultimate fate is going to be.

For reasons prompted by, but not limited to, the economic crisis, traditional, mainstream, representative politics are currently undergoing a deep crisis of legitimacy and public trust. The M5S, regardless of its online persona, can be interpreted as a search for answers to this crisis, by providing an innovative party model and suggesting that "other ways" are possible for the relationship between citizens and politics. The drive behind the M5S's spectacular rise in Italy rather than elsewhere, in this moment of history rather than others, probably has more to do with the structural, deep-rooted problems of Italian politics, the magnitude of the challenges to the sustainability of its economy, rather than with "revolutionary" changes prompted by the Internet.

The point where the Internet becomes crucial is the practical "organization of democracy" fostered by the Movement, based on collective action regrouped ad-hoc around specific issues; on "monitoring citizens" with a wealth of online information and instruments at their fingertips; and on liquid democracy instruments that facilitate the gathering of consensus around people and issues, allowing citizens to directly shape candidates, programmes, decisions. These very practical aspects, clearly linked to the use and daily practice of networking technologies, come wrapped in a narrative of *natural* and unavoidable consequences of the Internet "age", "spirit", or Zeitgeist.

However, both these sets of practices and narratives of the Internet as a liberating and inherently democratic force co-exist in a highly problematic way—problematic for the daily operations of the Movement, and for its public image *vis-à-vis* third parties—with an intentionally opaque management of the material devices, platforms, arrangements subtending the organisation of the Movement. These often

---

[14] Huffington Post (May 27, 2013) Comunali 2013, Il Movimento 5 Stelle fa flop alle urne. http://www.huffingtonpost.it/2013/05/27/comunali-2013-il-moviment_n_3342376.html.

[15] E.g. L'Unità (March 4, 2013). Lombardi scivola sull'elogio del fascismo. http://www.unita.it/italia/capogruppo-camera-alzata-mano-fascismo-casapound-mussolini-cinquestelle-meeting-eletti-grillo-m5s-1.486668.

remain hidden behind M5S's very "virtual" persona, fostered and encouraged by its leaders, but are no less present for that—and are ultimately affecting the Movement's very legitimacy. M5S is and remains an entity with a permanent organisation, professional employees, a centralized management of its material infrastructure, and a top-down, highly personalised management whose problematic approach to the control of dissent and criticism is a persistent issue within the Movement.

The recent evolution of M5S from a primarily destructive "call to arms" into a parliamentary force to be reckoned with, entering those very institutions and political processes it allegedly wishes to erase, has made explicit what is the Movement's main challenge in the close future: not to be afraid of its own success, of its connecting, lobbying and rallying instruments. Rather, to build on them, by engaging in a reflection about the M5S's apparently irreconcilable features[16] and the ways in which this peculiar nexus can move forward in a sustainable way.

What's in all this for the Internet and digital social media, as means, facilitators, detonators of another possible way of doing politics? Traditionally reluctant to address all matters "digital" in a more complex and evolved fashion than seeing them as challengers of the status quo, and creators of need for further (legal) reform, Italian politicians appear dumbstruck by the current situation where for the first time, a strong component of the political opposition in the country is not a traditional party but a so-called "digital movement". Bedazzlement has led them to react in one dominant way: diffidence, distance and "enemy-framing". On his side, Grillo has done nothing to reduce this effect; rather, he has amplified it, by choosing to ignore any possible "institutionalization" of the Movement (even after the fragmented electoral result had made it almost mandatory if one wished to obtain any practical result), and radicalizing its anti-political image.

While this retreat into trenches, on both sides, looks like a missed opportunity in several obvious ways, it is a pity for one, perhaps less obvious, reason: that it prevents further practical investigations of the ways in which the M5S may indeed keep its promise of *avant-garde* new politics, facilitated by (if not dependent upon) online digital and social networks. Without an everyday "trial", in the real world, of its undeniably innovative and fascinating model, the Movement will find it increasingly hard to respond to its detractors. And it will find increasingly difficult to contest that the Internet may just be playing, within M5S, a rhetorical role: that of

[16] Bordignon and Ceccarini (2013: 21) summarize them exhaustively and concisely: "the 'rational' elaboration of political proposals with iconoclastic and anti-political impulses; technical competence with charisma; the party understood as a company that sells a product on the political market with the party understood as a consumer advocacy group; the centrality of engagement and discussion with the leader's extreme and uncompromising verbal style and propensity for monologue; the inclusive demands of the grassroots with the (democratic?) centralism of the leader; the insistence on the 'shared' nature of the political organisation with the 'proprietary' mindset that still regulates its functioning; the emphasis on deliberation from the bottom up with the necessity to 'decide'".

great legitimizer of amateurism and anti-politics, wrapped in the emancipatory narrative of the *digital sublime*.

Acknowledgments The members of the Institute for the Study of Diplomacy, School of Foreign Service, Georgetown University, have provided helpful comments on earlier drafts. I am grateful to Patrizia Galletti Musiani for her patient constitution of an impressively complete dossier of Italian press articles on M5S in the spring of 2013.

References

Bordignon, F. & Ceccarini, L. (2013). Five stars and a cricket. Beppe Grillo shakes Italian politics. *South European Society and Politics* (Online publication only). www.tandfonline.com/doi/abs/10.1080/13608746.2013.775720#.Ub8gVYWonXU

Casaleggio, G. (2012). Ho scritto io le regole del MoVimento 5 Stelle. *Il Corriere della Sera*, 30 May 2012. http://www.corriere.it/politica/12_maggio_30/casaleggio-regole-mov-5-stelle_9e8eca9c-aa1a-11e1-8196-b3ccb09a7f99.shtml Accessed 8 Nov 2013.

Corbetta, P., & Gualmini, E. (Eds.). (2013). *Il partito di Grillo*. Bologna: Il Mulino.

Crick, B. (1962). *In defense of politics*. Chicago, IL: University of Chicago Press.

DeNardis, L. (2012). Hidden levers of internet control. An infrastructure-based theory of internet governance. *Information, Communication & Society, 15*(5), 720–728.

Diamanti, I. (2013). Il partito autobus dei Cinque Stelle. *La Repubblica*, 18 March 2013. http://www.repubblica.it/politica/2013/03/18/news/diamanti_cinque_stelle-54795281/ Accessed 8 Nov 2013.

Lanfrey, D. (2011). Il MoVimento dei grillini tra meetup, meta-organizzazione e democrazia del monitoraggio. In L. Mosca & C. Vaccari (Eds.), *Nuovi media, nuova politica? Partecipazione e mobilitazione online da MoveOn al MoVimento 5 Stelle* (pp. 143–166). Milan: Franco Angeli.

Luna, R. (2013). Cambiamo tutto! La rivoluzione degli innovatori. Rome: Laterza.

Morozov, E. (2013). Morozov e la 'retorica Web' del M5S (interview with Raffaella Menichini). La Repubblica, 5 March 2013. http://www.repubblica.it/politica/2013/03/05/news/intervista_morozov-53835572/. Accessed 8 Nov 2013.

Musiani, F. (2013). Governance by algorithms. *Internet Policy Review*, August 2013. http://policyreview.info/articles/analysis/governance-algorithms. Accessed 8 Nov 2013.

Pepe, A. & Di Gennaro, C. (2009). Political protest Italian–style: The blogosphere and mainstream media in the promotion and coverage of Beppe Grillo's V–day. *First Monday*, 14(12). http://www.firstmonday.org/ojs/index.php/fm/article/view/2740/2406. Accessed 8 Nov 2013.

Ruggiero, C. (2012). Forecasting in the politics of spectacle, from Berlusconi to Grillo: The narrative of impolite politics. *Bulletin of Italian Politics*, 4(2): 305–322. http://www.gla.ac.uk/media/media_264086_en.pdf. Accessed 8 Nov 2013.

Tisch, J. (2010). Active citizenship: A new approach to volunteering. *Huffington Post,* 27 April 2010. http://www.huffingtonpost.com/jonathan-tisch/active-citizenship-a-new_b_553417.html. Accessed 8 Nov 2013.

Valentini, G. (2013). La grande illusione della web-democrazia. *La Repubblica*, 13 April 2013. http://giovannitaurasi.wordpress.com/2013/04/13/la-grande-illusione-della-web-democrazia-di-giovanni-valentini-da-la-repubblica-del-13-aprile-2013/. Accessed 8 Nov 2013.

Valenza, D. (2013). Le Mouvement 5 Etoiles en Italie: un parti 'anti-système'? *Nouvelle Europe*, 23 April 2013. http://www.nouvelle-europe.eu/le-mouvement-cinq-etoiles-en-italie-un-parti-anti-systeme. Accessed 8 Nov 2013.

Chapter 9
Twitter Campaigning in the 2011 National Election in Slovenia

Strategy and Application of the Twitter Social Media Outlet in Party Election Campaigns

Tomaž Deželan, Igor Vobič, and Alem Maksuti

Abstract The chapter examines the Twitter campaigning of parliamentary political parties and their influential members during the 2011 preterm national election campaign. We examine the rationales behind the adoption and appropriation of Twitter in the Slovenian political arena. Content analysis of 4,610 Tweets and conducted interviews with campaign managers of seven lists of candidates allowed us to revisit three perennial hypotheses about political communication on the web: the copycat, revolution and normalisation hypotheses. While the examined parties' move into the Twittersphere confirmed the copycat hypothesis, their utilisation of the tool revealed mixed evidence for the revolution vs. normalisation dilemma. Party campaigning did show signs of 'politics as usual', with political powerhouses taking the lead on Twitter as well. However, it also demonstrated a substantial degree of genuine direct political interaction between politicians and citizens.

Keywords Twitter • Slovenia • Election campaign • Copycat theory • Normalisation thesis

T. Deželan (✉)
Department of Political Science, Centre for Political Science Research, University of Ljubljana, Ljubljana, Slovenia
e-mail: tomaz.dezelan@fdv.uni-lj.si

I. Vobič
Department of Communication, Social Communication Research Centre, University of Ljubljana, Ljubljana, Slovenia

A. Maksuti
Faculty of Social Sciences, University of Ljubljana, Ljubljana, Slovenia

B. Pătruţ and M. Pătruţ (eds.), *Social Media in Politics*, Public Administration and Information Technology 13, DOI 10.1007/978-3-319-04666-2_9,

9.1 Introduction

The ongoing economic crisis in Slovenia that emerged in early 2009 rapidly extended into a governmental crisis due to the government's inability to reach a consensus with social partners on much-needed reforms. The online campaigning of various social factors, including the main political stakeholders, played an influential role in the eventual dissolution of the parliament and the call for a pre-term election[1] (Mekina 2011). Web-based tools became the main channel of communication with the public and political adversaries, as it became common practice for government ministers to reflect on the rumours surrounding them, for the opposition to attack certain governmental measures without serious challenge or with fraudulent claims and even for the political 'big guns' to engage in open confrontation with each other via Twitter[2] or Facebook (Košak and Žumer 2012). The fact that all parliamentary[3] political parties except the Democratic Party of Pensioners of Slovenia—something stereotypically expected from a party with such a base—actively utilised the official Twitter account of the party and/or the party leader is an additional indication of the relevance of this outlet.

With an unexpected election campaign on the horizon and the broad perception that big campaign spending is immoral during times of crisis, the political actors reshaped the 'permanent' political communication campaign into a formal short-term election campaign. The extensive focus on the use of web-based tools was primarily grounded on their less capital-intensive nature, accompanied by the wave of enthusiasm regarding the democratic and participatory effect the tools appeared to have during the early stages of the Arab Spring uprising (Bertoncelj 2011; Štefančič 2011). As a result, social networks stepped out of the shadows of the conventional modern campaign strategies Slovenia was used to (see Deželan et al. 2010), introducing certain new qualities that had otherwise not been present (e.g. negative campaigns). In fact, even the traditional media started to report and reflect on the impact of online campaigning as part of their regular campaign activities. An additional drive towards online campaigning in general also fostered the appearance of two influential new political newcomers that deprived the minor political parties of the usual media attention.

The above-mentioned collage of new contextual features demands a revisit of certain key hypotheses about party politicking on the web that relate in one way or another to the modernisation framework of political communication. The first is the copycat theory of party web campaigning (see Gibson and Ward 2000; Newell 2001; Selnow 1998; Gibson et al. 2003), which argues that political parties tend to lack a clear rationale for their activities on the web, particularly when taking initial

[1] E.g. '**@strankaSDS:** Government coalition is occupied with itself and stalls pre-term elections http://t.co/tXxJ17nV 6:50 p.m. Sep 17th, 2011'.

[2] E.g. '**@strankaSDS:** @PGantar During Pahor's government you increased the public debt from 8.2 to 16.4 billion euros (source SURS). You know SURS [Statistical office of Slovenia], right? 10:22 a.m. Sep 22nd, 2011'.

[3] With deputies in the National Assembly of the Republic of Slovenia or the European Parliament.

steps into new territory. Hence, their main rationale for a move into new territory is usually connected with keeping up to pace with political adversaries in order to maintain the appearance of being modern and up-to-date. Since Twitter is a relatively new and politically relevant web-based outlet, imbued with positive normative claims regarding its effects due to the aforementioned events involving Slovenes (e.g. Tomažič 2013), the analysis of the 2011 pre-term election promises to provide us with new insights into the rationales for changes in parties' election campaign strategies. While the 2011 pre-term election was the first Twitter election, notably under the influence of the tool's use in the Obama 2008 campaign (see Solop 2010) and across the globe (e.g. Grant et al. 2010), the observed national election race was also the only appropriate occasion to date for testing this hypothesis.

Secondly, exploration into the conditions leading to election day in early December 2011 compels us to revisit a major theoretical dilemma in the relevant literature—the revolution vs. normalisation hypothesis—which inspired a series of seminal studies on online politicking (e.g. Wright 2012; Strandberg 2008; Baxter et al. 2011; Gibson and Ward 2000; Margolis and Resnick 2000). Although the pre-eminence of this debate has been criticised for its technological determinism (Wright 2012, pp. 248–251), it has proved to be very influential, and the view that online activities reflect offline politics—contrary to expectations of major shifts in the political process and power-relations—progressively began gaining an edge. Nevertheless, the emerging patterns of party use of Web 2.0 outlets, particularly Twitter, in the Slovenian case may shed new light on the validity of these arguments. Our examination into the revolution-normalisation hypothesis is based on the professionalisation/modernisation framework of political campaigning (see Negrine and Lilleker 2002; Norris 2004; Farrell and Webb 2000; Plasser and Plasser 2002; Gibson and Römmele 2008, 2009) that traces changes in the tools and strategies political actors employ to appeal to voters due to major societal changes and increasing de-alignment of the electorate (see Holtz-Bacha 2002).

Our re-examination of these hypotheses in the political communication literature is divided into three parts. The first part explores the theoretical premises of party politicking from the aspect of election campaigns, while the second elaborates on the methods applied in our study. The third part is divided into three separate entities that put forward the intensity of and reasoning behind Twitter usage, the character of Twitter communication in the 2011 national election campaign and the implications of the direct communication modality. We conclude the chapter with a discussion of the impact of Twitter on the political process and thoughts regarding the relevance of new technologies and how they are appropriated.

9.2 Party Politicking Through the Lens of Election Campaigning

It is obvious that technological and communication developments play a central role in the way political actors communicate messages to their voters (Ward et al. 2003, p. 14). Be it a matter of utility or image-selling, the political parties were evidently 'obliged' to step online due to processes of social differentiation and changes in media systems and technology (Holtz-Bacha 2008, p. 657). As is argued by Holtz-Bacha (ibid.), these changes have been influenced by the modernisation of society, and the professionalisation of political communication is an inevitable consequence of that. Whether it is described as professionalisation or modernisation—it also shares some theoretical premises with the Americanization thesis (Kavanagh 1995; Swanson and Mancini 1996) and with globalisation (Scammell 1998)—is a matter of lively debate outside the scope of this chapter (see Holtz-Bacha 2008; Negrine and Lilleker 2002; Gibson and Römmele 2007). However, this perspective encompasses (1) the adoption of new tools and tactics; (2) a shift in the overall style of campaigning to a more capital-intensive, aggressive or attack-oriented and continuous mode; (3) a reorientation in the relationship with the electorate towards a more interactive and individualised engagement; and (4) the restructuring of power relations within the party with an increasing centralisation of power, as well as some resurgence of the local level (Gibson and Römmele 2009).

Political parties differ in their motivation for adoption and utilisation of technological innovations. When looking at the rationales behind the parties' move online, three main reasons prevail. Agranoff (1972, p. 129) claimed that parties may introduce technological innovations when they perceive the job will be done 'cheaper and faster'. Still, the reasons for introduction of technological innovation—particularly the move online—tend to be much more prosaic. Ward et al. (2003, p. 13) identified the symbolic value of adopting new technology as very significant, since parties want to display themselves to their electorate as modern, relevant and up-to-date. Maintaining an image of professionalism is therefore an important drive itself (Gibson and Ward 2000, p. 302); however, this is frequently coupled with peer pressure from other political parties. This reasoning—also known as the copycat approach (see Gibson and Ward 2000; Newell 2001; Selnow 1998; Gibson et al. 2003), the 'me too effect' (Selnow 1998, p. 88) or the domino theory (Gibson and Ward 2000, p. 302; Tops et al. 2000)—has been the most widely defended rationale for parties moving online and highlights the bandwagon effect, in which all political actors fear 'not boarding' with everyone else (Selnow 1998, p. 88). Parties therefore decide instead against giving opponents the edge despite being uncertain of the tangible benefits of moving to the new territory (Gibson et al. 2003, p. 13). Although this hypothesis has been widely confirmed for parties gaining a foothold in cyberspace across different contexts (e.g. Stone 1996; Gibson and Ward 2000; Deželan 2005; Newell 2001; Tops et al. 2000), the jury is still out for parties moving to 2.0. As previous studies put forward the lack of a clear rationale for Slovenian parties gaining a foothold in cyberspace—having no clear idea about its potential (Franz 2003, p. 40), primarily utilising the web's informing function (Oblak and Željan 2007) and failing to present much more than party manifestos and candidate CVs (Deželan et al. 2010)—*we expect that the examination of motivations for the move to Twitter will reflect the same 'me too' reasoning.*

The bandwagon effect came under criticism in the case of the smaller and extremist parties that devised a clear rationale for their appropriation of new technologies. Due to their inferior resource capacity and very limited exposure in traditional media outlets, this type of political actor began to perceive the Internet not just as a mere technological utility but as a 'game-changer' (see Gibson and Ward 2000, p. 302). The manner and intensity of utilising this new technology (in addition to a clearly devised adoption strategy) provide the basis for the equalisation theory (see Baxter et al. 2011; Strandberg 2008; Norris 2003), promoted by 'revolutionaries' (Wright 2012, p. 245) who were also called 'cyber-optimists' (see Margolis and Resnick 2000). This approach symbolises the initial utopian wave of deliberation on the impact of the Internet on the political process. The main aspiration of this wave may be observed under the ambitions for direct democracy (Budge 1996), new opportunities for empowerment (Dertouzos 1997), virtual communities that could help citizens revitalise democracy (Rheingold 2000), a more participatory style of politics with the activation of an increasingly disaffected electorate (see Baxter et al. 2011) and a new platform for political competition among political actors on a more equal basis (Strandberg 2008, p. 224). Hence, the general claim of the utopians was that the move online would challenge existing power structures (Margolis and Resnick 2000, p. 1) and introduce a distinct type of political engagement that sharply differed from traditional activities (Norris 2003, p. 23). Following this rationale *we expect that the smaller and extremist Slovenian political parties, with comparatively modest resources and little appeal for traditional media outlets, perceive Twitter as a potential 'game-changer' and therefore intensify their efforts related to it compared to mainstream political powerhouses.* In addition, *we expect more interactive and individualised engagement with the adoption of new tactics that are not common to the previous TV-dominated one-way-traffic political interaction.*

Contrary to utopian aspirations, a second wave of more sceptical voices of cyber-realists raised growing doubts about the impact the move online might have on the political process. By putting forward a 'politics as usual' assertion, Margolis and Resnick (2000, p. vii) have probably made the strongest case for the normalisation hypothesis by rejecting revolution in the conduct of politics and stressing that the Internet tends to reflect and reinforce the patterns of behaviour of the real world. This 'no-change' scenario simply reflects the politics online as an extension of offline politics (Strandberg 2008, p. 224). According to normalisation theorists, the utopian hopes of a new politics that would spill out of the computer and revitalise citizenship and democracy have been shattered by ordinary politics and commercial activity, which have invaded and captured cyberspace (Margolis and Resnick 2000, p. 2). Building on the libertarian tradition and the Lockean state of nature, the authors argue that the brief revolutionary golden age ceased with rapid state and market regulation (see Wright 2012, p. 247). Hence, a sophisticated political economy increasingly designed and guided by web professionals crowded out the amateurs and hobbyists and began to dominate political, economic, social, and recreational life on the Internet (Margolis and Resnick 2000, p. 4). Despite the accumulated evidence of the validity of this line of thought (see Norris 2003, p. 42), the emergence of Web 2.0 tools—in this case, Twitter—calls for its re-examination. This is primarily the case for the shift in the overall campaign style to continuous and more capital-intensive campaigning led by professionals and centralisation of power—a hallmark of professionalisation (see Norris 2004; Farrell and Webb 2000;

Plasser and Plasser 2002; Gibson and Römmele 2009). Accordingly, *we therefore expect to find Twitter communication to be more or less equally intensive during and outside of the election campaign, of a similar nature*[4] *to conventional (offline) political communication and led by professionals hired or employed by parties and under high scrutiny by the party leadership.* The main purpose of our scrutiny of parties' appropriation of Twitter is therefore (1) to resolve whether and to what extent the existing power positions are mirrored on Twitter and (2) how and to what effect the process of political (campaign) communication changed.

9.3 Methodology

In order to analyse ways of using and applying the Twitter social media outlet in the political parties' overall strategies for the 2011 Slovenian national election, we employed the framework of Golbeck et al. (2010) to analyse the content of microblogs in the political realm. Additionally, we conducted qualitative interviews with campaign team leaders of seven lists of candidates to obtain data indicating their perspectives on social media, find out various ways to give meaning to Twitter usage during the campaign and relate this to larger dynamics of political communication (e.g. Ritchie and Lewis 2003). Employing both methods is congruent with the method mix of seminal studies in the field (Gibson and Ward 2000; Newell 2001; Baxter et al. 2011). In this regard, we used the concurrent triangulation approach, where we collected both quantitative and qualitative data concurrently and compared the two databases to determine if there was convergence, differences or some combination of the two (e.g. Creswell 2009, pp. 384–85).

9.3.1 Quantitative Content Analysis

In addition to news coverage (e.g. de Vreese et al. 2006) and online media releases (e.g. Gibson and Ward 2000), content analysis is also a favourable method for analysing Twitter microblogs, which are extensively used by politicians and public officials (Golbeck et al. 2010; Waters and Williams 2011; Bruns and Stieglitz 2012). Aimed at detecting the latent campaign communication strategy in Slovenia, we prepared a codebook that identified different features of collected tweets as analysed units. Taking into consideration the essentials of campaign communication strategies, the codebook was prepared based on the coding scheme of Golbeck et al. (2010) for providing the internal content of analysed tweets. The codebook was based on additional elaboration of some classified categories in order to distinguish to whom politicians communicated, how they did that (spontaneously,

[4] The nature of communication is analysed on the basis of a framework for the analysis of the content of microblogs. See the following section.

with @ or by a RT (retweet)) and/or what they talked about (#). In this regard, the codebook intertwines indicators of both election campaign communication and Twitter communication:

DC ***(Direct Communication)*****:** A message directed at a specific person or institution identified with the @name convention. DC was divided into five subclasses: DC1, internal communication with members of the party; DC2, external communication with media (DC2a) or journalists (DC2b); DC3, external communication with citizens (DC3a) or opinion makers (DC3b); DC4 internal communication within the institution (ministry); and DC5, communication with oppositional politicians from other parties.

DCC ***(Direct Conflict Communication):*** A message directed at a specific person or institution identified with the @name convention and explicit competitive or opposing communicative action.

DAC ***(Direct Affection Communication):*** A message directed at a specific person or institution identified with the @name convention and explicitly expressed tender attachment.

PM ***(Personal Message)*****:** A message or note with personal expressions. PM was divided into two subclasses: PMI, personal messages with a non-political character; and PMP, messages with a political campaign character.

ACT ***(Activities):*** A message reporting on persons' or institutions' 'offline' campaign activities. This was divided into two subclasses: OB, official and predictable campaign activities; and LA, non-official or unpredicted activities.

INF ***(Information)*****:** A message providing a fact, opinion, or attitude expressed on Twitter.

RA ***(Requesting Action)*****:** A message providing a request to take action—for instance, voting on elections, signing a petition, attending rallies.

FU ***(*****Fundraising)**: A message asking for donations and contributions.

XX ***(Unknown)*****:** A message that cannot be classified—for instance, a single-character post.

LINK: A message that provides a link to other websites that have also been coded—for instance, a link to a personal blog, personal Facebook account, political party website, state or European institution website, news website, YouTube or another social network.

RT ***(Retweet)*****:** A message that provides a repost of tweets posted by others, usually accompanied by the abbreviation 'RT'.

HT ***(Hashtag):*** A message containing a word or a phrase prefixed with the symbol #, a form of metadata tag for grouping similar messages.

EMO ***(Emotional Icon):*** A message containing a verbal emotional expression or a non-verbal one—for instance, an emotional icon such as ☺ or ☹.

Based on positive tests for intra- and inter-coder reliability[5] (Krippendorff 2003; Benoit 2011), tweets were coded by two independent coders in May 2013.

[5] A sample of 100 randomly-selected tweets was coded by two independent coders before the coding process (inter-coder reliability) as well as after the coding process (intra-coder reliability).

With this apparatus, we analysed tweets from official accounts of all former and current parliamentary political parties using Twitter, party leaders involved in social media communication and the most prolific party twitterians[6] during the official 30-day election campaign—4 November to 2 December 2011. Altogether, 4,610 tweets were collected and analysed, from 16 accounts:

six political party accounts (@Zares—811 tweets; @LDSstranka—531; @strankaSD—436; @StrankaSLS—447; @strankaSDS—333; @NovaSlovenija—29);

five party leaders' accounts (@ZaresGregor—375 tweets; @ZoranDELA—198; @KatarinaKresal—171; @JJansaSDS—59; @gregor_virant—15); and

four prolific party twitterians (@zzTurk—671 tweets; @PGantar—259; @matevzfrangez—169; @AlesZalar—76; @Libertarec—30).

9.3.2 *Qualitative Interviews*

The interviews conducted were characterised by three criteria (Flick 2006, p. 161): 'problem centering', that is, the researcher's orientation to a relevant problem (i.e. Twitter usage in political parties' overall strategies for the 2011 Slovenian national elections); 'object orientation', that is, developing or modifying interviews with respect to an object of research (i.e. party specifics in their Twitter adaptations); and 'process orientation', that is, understanding of the object of the research (i.e. normative grounding of political communication and dynamics of its social media negotiations during election campaigning). In interview conversations, we adopted a 'heuristic interviewing' (Legard et al. 2003, p. 140) approach, which emphasises the personal approach of the interviewer and sees the process of interviewing as a collaboration between the researcher and the participant, where both partners share reflections and information.

Thus, the study methodology departed from 'focused' or 'structured' interviews, in which the interviewer strictly follows the interview guide, and adopted what is known as a 'semi-structured' or 'semi-standardised' type of interview. Indeed, the interview guide was organised, but not fixed—we adopted it as a tool for theoretically informed and contextually grounded conversation. The interview conversations appeared as what Hermanns (2004) calls 'an evolving drama' (ibid., 212), in which the interviewer's task is to facilitate this drama to develop. Thus, the conversations were steered by the rather flexible application of the guide and the active involvement of the interviewer.

The inter-coder reliability analysis was performed using Krippendorf's Alpha to determine consistency among and within coders. The inter-coder reliability for two coders for all utilized variables was found to be at least Krippendorf"s Alpha (nominal) = 0.83, while the intra-coder reliability for all utilized variables did not drop below Krippendorf"s Alpha (nominal) = 0.93.

[6] We selected up to one visible party member with at least one thousand followers per political party.

More specifically, we combined three types of questions, each of which was a distinct stimulus used for a particular purpose in a certain stage of the conversation. First, 'open' (Flick 2006, p. 156), 'content-mapping' (Legard et al. 2003, p. 148) or 'non-directive' questions (Lindlof and Taylor 2002, p. 195) were used in order to get the conversation on the topic started; they were answered on the basis of the knowledge the interviewee had at hand (e.g. *'Why does the party use Twitter'?*). Then, the interviewer asked 'theory-driven' (Flick 2006, p. 156) questions based on the literature review and the theoretical framework of the study (e.g. *'What are the basic characteristics of Twitter communication with the citizens'?*). Finally, the third type of questions—'confrontational' questions (Flick 2006, p. 157) or 'content-mining' questions (Legard et al. 2003, p. 150)—responded to the notions the interviewee had presented up to that point in order to critically re-examine them in light of competing alternatives or even contradictions identified through content analysis (e.g. *'How do you explain differences in communication patterns on the party's account and party leader's account'?*).

Between 29 April and 21 May 2013, we conducted interviews with campaign team leaders of seven lists of candidates. We interviewed general secretaries or heads of parties' public relations offices from *Positive Slovenia* (PS), the *Social Democrats* (SD), the *Civic List* (DL), the *Slovenian People's Party* (SLS), *New Slovenia—Christian People's Party* (NSi), *Zares,* and *Liberal Democracy of Slovenia* (LDS). Interviews in this study had an average length of 1 h and were held in quiet public spaces, party offices in the parliament, or party headquarters. Interviews were voice-recorded and later transcribed in full. We were not able to conduct an interview with the campaign team leader of the *Slovenian Democratic Party* (SDS), but only had a short telephone conversation with the head of their public relations office, in which he stated that they had addressed Twitter usage 'several times publicly, in the media' (Jernej Pavlin, personal communication, 7 May 2013). Therefore, in the empirical part of the study, we use party members' statements about Twitter published in media outlets in 2012 and 2013 to explain the data gathered through content analysis. Additionally, we conducted a short interview with an SDS member who asked for anonymity.

9.4 Contextualization and Results

9.4.1 Internet and Social Networks in Slovenia

National statistical office reports that more than 67 % of the general population of Slovenia use the internet at least once a week (SORS 2012). According to the national survey on the use of internet (Vehovar et al. 2011, 4), 60 % of internet users in Slovenia have at least one social network profile. Moreover, the UK Office for National Statistics (2013) ranks Slovenia among countries with the highest proportion of social network users in the EU, which is also indicated by the fact that 92 %

of young Slovenes use social networks. In addition, the majority of Slovenes believe social networks are a modern way of keeping up to date with political affairs and are a reliable source of political information (Eurostat 2012, 48). Accordingly, the use of social networks by politicians is extensive and continually rising. To be precise, during the 2008–2011 parliamentary term, 64 % of MPs had a Facebook account; that percentage rose to 69 % in the present term. Likewise, although less extensive than Facebook, the use of Twitter has increased significantly in the past few years, from 18 % in the 2008–2011 parliamentary term to 46 % in the current one. Twitter is also widespread across the executive branch since 66 % of current governmental ministers and a significant share of ministries and state secretaries have an official Twitter account. Political parties make no exception, as only one out of six current parliamentary political parties do not use Twitter as an official channel for communicating with the public.

9.4.2 Twitter Usage: Intensity and Reasoning

Analysis of interviews with campaign team leaders indicates that 'me too' reasoning was prevalent in political parties' narrative about the adoption of Twitter as a campaign tool. Interviewees stressed that Twitter is 'used by everybody' (Bogdan Biščak, Zares, 10 May 2013), appeared to be an 'indispensable communication tool' (Uroš Jauševec, SD, 21 May 2013) and emerged as 'an important tool for targeted communication' (Jernej Vrtovec, NSi, 10 May 2013). Furthermore, by triangulating interview data with results of the content analysis of tweets, it became evident that Twitter was not only regarded as a significant factor by a large majority of campaign teams, but also an extensively used communication tool in the month before the national election of 2011.

On the one hand, as Table 9.1 shows, not only small parties, but also established ones intensified their Twitter activities during the campaign in comparison to other time periods. Small liberal parties (@LDSstranka and @Zares) and their leaders (@KatarinaKresal and @ZaresGregor) were the most salient examples of intensification. For instance, when interviewed, the general secretary of LDS acknowledged that before the election, their Twitter strategy was clear and fixed: 'We had a precise timeline with topics for each part of the day. In the morning we launched a certain topic, later a YouTube video on the same topic, for example, and then we followed the dynamics on Twitter and tried to respond to them' (Uroš Petohleb, LDS, 15 May 2013). As the content analysis showed, among the established parties, Social Democrats were the most active (@StrankaSD): 'Before the election campaign Twitter usage intensified and became professionalised. We used outsourced staffers as a result of strategic decision-making to use specific slogans, for instance' (Uroš Jauševec, SD, 21 May 2013). There were a few exceptions, though. For instance, the largest conservative party (@strankaSDS) did not substantially change its tweeting practices during the campaign but still remained active in comparison to others (see Table 9.1). This was also the case for the conservative NSi

Table 9.1 Twitter activity in and outside of the official election campaign by individual accounts

Twitter account	Tweets per day (campaign 2011)	Tweets per day (in general)	RT in 2011 campaign (in %)	RT in general (in %)	# in 2011 campaign (in %)	# in general (in %)
@strankaSD	15.10	3.01	29.0	14.0	30.6	0.1
@matevzfrangez	5.83	1.06	7.7	14.0	21.3	0.1
@strankaSDS	11.48	11.08	9.9	30.0	18.9	0.0
@JJansaSDS	2.03	0.94	78.0	52.0	33.9	0.0
@zzTurk	23.14	6.56	6.7	7.0	11.9	0.1
@strankaSLS	15.40	4.02	9.4	14.0	40.7	0.3
@ZoranDELA	6.83	0.61	8.6	7.0	2.0	0.1
@NovaSlovenija	1.00	1.03	0.0	29.0	6.9	0.0
@gregor_virant	0.52	0.53	0.0	1.0	0.0	0.0
@Libertarec	1.03	2.04	0.0	1.0	0.3	0.0
@LDSstranka	18.31	1.05	23.0	19.0	34.7	0.2
@KatarinaKresal	5.90	0.65	21.1	5.0	19.9	0.0
@AlesZalar	2.62	1.08	21.1	5.0	25.0	0.0
@Zares	27.97	1.27	66.0	29.0	19.5	0.0
@ZaresGregor	12.93	4.75	21.6	31.0	9.6	0.1
@Pgantar	8.93	6.26	2.7	4.0	6.2	2.9

(@NovaSlovenija) and liberal DL (@gregor_virant and @Libertarec), which were the least active parties on Twitter (see Table 9.1)—mostly due to a lack of resources, as they stressed: 'During the campaign we were not actively communicating via Twitter. We published a few posts, but this was negligible at that moment. We only had the desire, but the realisation was poor. ... We did not have enough resources' (Igor Bordon, DL, 15 May 2013).

On the other hand, content analysis of tweets indicates that usage of specific elements of Twitter communication, such as retweets (RT) and hashtags (#), increased during the national election campaign in comparison to the usual activities of the analysed Twitter accounts (see Table 9.1). This was particularly evident in the case of hashtag usage in Twitter posts, as 21 % of all published tweets had this metadata tag. This fact signals that political parties and politicians were keen on participating in unmoderated discussions during the campaign, first and foremost in those general ones grouping messages about the national election (#volitve2011) and television debates (#soocenje). Paradoxically, when discussing Twitter trends, interviewees hardly addressed hashtags explicitly and did not understand them as meaningful elements of deliberation or agenda-building.

The only exception was the general secretary of the liberal DL: 'We started using our own keywords in tags. These tags are being used, they are noticed. However, we are not on the level we would like to be' (Igor Bordon, DL, 15 May 2013). Additionally, Table 9.1 shows that retweeting emerged as a significant campaign practice, especially in regard to two accounts: the leader of the SDS (@JJansaSDS, 78 % of all tweets were RTs) and the party account of the liberal Zares (@Zares, 66 % of all tweets were RTs). Otherwise, 24.2 % of all tweets posted the month before the election were retweets. Content analysis also shows that analysed accounts mostly retweeted posts published by party colleagues or by their own party (13.1 % of all tweets), followed by those by citizens (5.6 %), and media and journalists (3.8 %).

Despite acknowledging Twitter as an important campaign tool and the intensified use of this social network, in the month before the national election, interviewees stressed that traditional campaign tools were more important, with the foremost being mass media, in particular television. 'Television is the first' (Igor Bordon, DL, 15 May 2013) and 'television is dominant' (Lejla Kogej, SLS, 29 April 2013) are only two examples emphasising a clear hierarchy; in particular, television debates were regarded as 'crucial' by interviewees (Tanja Sodnik Dodig, PS, 10 May 2013). In this context, interviewees understood Twitter, together with other social networks—for instance, Facebook—as a complementary communication tool central for gaining cross-media momentum. 'The combination of Twitter, Facebook, and television is the winning combination. … This was not so clear in 2011, but it has emerged as such now' (Uroš Jauševec, SD, 21 May 2013).

9.4.3 The Character of Twitter Communication in the 2011 National Election Campaign

During the 2011 pre-term election campaign, the observed political actors' tweets could mainly be placed into two categories: information and direct communication. The former encompassed more than 54 % of all captured tweets and presented the dominant mode of political actors' communication on Twitter (see Fig. 9.1). However, we have to note that in general, official party Twitter accounts reflected much higher shares of tweets classified under information modality than official accounts of party presidents or the most influential twitterians, even when the president's account performed the function of the official party account and when professionals were handling it (e.g. @ZoranDELA). The Twitter communication of smaller and new party presidents therefore reflected a far less traditional informative position (less than one-third) than those of established parties and some of their presidents, which amounted to up to 90 % of all tweets (see Table 9.2).

The informative tweets generally consisted of information about a party's or president's position on various topics that emerged during the election campaign. These positions frequently replicated statements from the party manifesto or provided a more personalised interpretation. The following are examples of these statements:

@Zares: Let's enhance the competitiveness of the economy and let's encourage entrepreneurship. http://t.co/UgPUE1Kl 7:34 a.m. Dec 1st, 2011.[7]

[7] All tweets written in Slovenian language are directly translated.

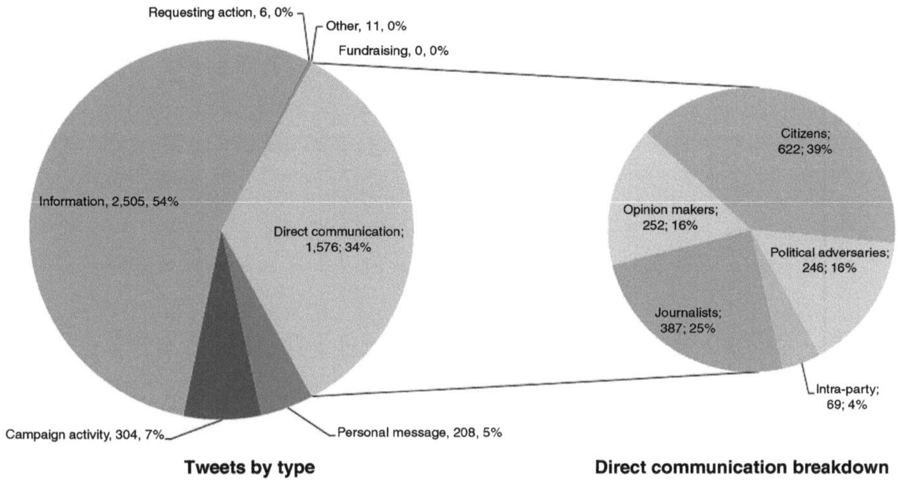

Fig. 9.1 Tweets by type and types of direct communication in the 2011 election campaign

@strankaSDS: SDS Manifesto: 10 + 100 Solution for justice, jobs and development. http://t.co/dDoLnB0X 6:46 p.m. Nov 4th, 2011.

Very infrequently, tweets involved opinions that did not have grounds in certain party programmatic documents or practices:

@AlesZalar: The presumption of innocence should not be an alibi for political irresponsibility in a parliamentary democracy. 6:03 p.m. Nov 20th, 2011.

In 21 % of the cases, these positions, facts, or opinions were substantiated by links to external information sources—most frequently, party, personal, or mass media websites. The latter frequently performed the function of external legitimation (either by including a link or without one) of the party's or individual's position, hence making the claim much more valid and tangible.

@strankaSD: The last public opinion poll from Ninamedia estimates already 14.3 % support. Forward. 9:31 p.m. Dec 2nd, 2011.

@ZaresGregor: Krugman: From Euromess to Eurogeddon http://t.co/CcEe5DeB #evrozona is all over me 2:09 p.m. Nov 7th, 2011.

Barring one obvious exception (@ZaresGregor), informative tweets from party accounts—inherently adopting a more official stance—included higher shares of links in tweets (approximately 4 %), thus reaffirming the legitimation strategy observed earlier.

It could be argued that information tweets performed like press release postings, where key facts and positions were posted as part of the overall strategy to invite followers to visit websites, Facebook accounts, or other information sources, or to react to an issue that arose during the campaign.

@strankaSDS: Janez Janša: One of the key instruments is cutting-down the legal entities' income tax. #odprtiforumtujeinvesticije 9:15 a.m. Nov 26th, 2011.

Informative tweets with hashtags represented one-tenth of all tweets of this modality. In the case of hashtag utilisation in informative tweets, we observe one

Table 9.2 Tweets by type and contained elements by analysed Twitter accounts

		Tweet type										
		Direct communication	Personal message	Activity	Information	Raising awareness	Other	Total	Link	Retweet	Hashtag	Emoticon
@AlesZalar	Count	17	17	6	36	0	0		24	16	19	2
	% within	22.4 %	22.4 %	7.9 %	47.4 %	0.0 %	0.0 %	100.0 %	31.6 %	21.1 %	25.0 %	2.6 %
@gregor_virant	Count	10	1	0	4	0	0		0	0	0	0
	% within	66.7 %	6.7 %	0.0 %	26.7 %	0.0 %	0.0 %	100.0 %	0.0 %	0.0 %	0.0 %	0.0 %
@JJansaSDS	Count	4	6	0	47	1	1		25	46	20	4
	% within	6.8 %	10.2 %	0.0 %	79.7 %	1.7 %	1.7 %	100.0 %	42.4 %	78.0 %	33.9 %	6.8 %
@KatarinaKresal	Count	54	20	28	68	1	0		81	36	34	37
	% within	31.6 %	11.7 %	16.4 %	39.8 %	0.6 %	0.0 %	100.0 %	47.4 %	21.1 %	19.9 %	21.6 %
@LDSstranka	Count	192	21	53	263	1	1		185	122	184	117
	% within	36.2 %	4.0 %	10.0 %	49.5 %	0.2 %	0.2 %	100.0 %	34.8 %	23.0 %	34.7 %	22.0 %
@Libertarec	Count	1	4	0	25	0	0		2	0	1	1
	% within	3.3 %	13.3 %	0.0 %	83.3 %	0.0 %	0.0 %	100.0 %	6.7 %	0.0 %	3.3 %	3.3 %
@matevzfrangez	Count	51	28	11	79	0	0		32	13	36	6
	% within	30.2 %	16.6 %	6.5 %	46.7 %	0.0 %	0.0 %	100.0 %	18.9 %	7.7 %	21.3 %	3.6 %
@NovaSlovenija	Count	0	1	3	25	0	0		5	0	2	1
	% within	0.0 %	3.4 %	10.3 %	86.2 %	0.0 %	0.0 %	100.0 %	17.2 %	0.0 %	6.9 %	3.4 %
@PGantar	Count	212	10	10	25	1	1		21	7	16	67
	% within	81.9 %	3.9 %	3.9 %	9.7 %	0.4 %	0.4 %	100.0 %	8.1 %	2.7 %	6.2 %	25.9 %
@strankaSD	Count	100	1	24	310	0	1		132	127	134	21
	% within	22.9 %	0.2 %	5.5 %	71.1 %	0.0 %	0.2 %	100.0 %	30.1 %	29.0 %	30.6 %	4.8 %
@strankaSDS	Count	6	13	1	311	2	0		125	31	63	3
	% within	1.8 %	3.9 %	0.3 %	93.4 %	0.6 %	0.0 %	100.0 %	37.5 %	9.3 %	18.9 %	0.9 %
@StrankaSLS	Count	90	11	100	245	0	1		212	42	182	136
	% within	20.1 %	2.5 %	22.4 %	54.8 %	0.0 %	0.2 %	100.0 %	47.4 %	9.4 %	40.7 %	30.4 %
@Zares	Count	93	10	27	680	0	1		327	535	158	44
	% within	11.5 %	1.2 %	3.3 %	83.8 %	0.0 %	0.1 %	100.0 %	40.3 %	66.0 %	19.5 %	5.4 %
@ZaresGregor	Count	237	18	2	117	0	1		101	81	36	19
	% within	63.2 %	4.8 %	0.5 %	31.2 %	0.0 %	0.3 %	100.0 %	26.9 %	21.6 %	9.6 %	5.1 %
@ZoranDELA	Count	129	2	27	39	0	1		28	17	4	22
	% within	65.2 %	1.0 %	13.6 %	19.7 %	0.0 %	0.5 %	100.0 %	14.1 %	8.6 %	2.0 %	11.1 %
@zzTurk	Count	380	45	12	231	0	3		131	45	80	36
	% within	56.6 %	6.7 %	1.8 %	34.4 %	0.0 %	0.4 %	100.0 %	19.5 %	6.7 %	11.9 %	5.4 %
Count		1,576	208	304	2,505	6	11		1,431	1,118	969	516
% within all accounts		34.2 %	4.5 %	6.6 %	54.3 %	0.1 %	0.2 %	100.0 %	31.0 %	24.2 %	21.0 %	11.2 %

important detail: established parties that reported clear interest in Twitter as part of their overall strategy and devoted resources to it (@LDSstranka; @strankaSD; @StrankaSLS) clearly used informative tweets with hashtags more frequently (in more than 40 % of informative tweets) and hence tried to influence and shape the debates evolving on Twitter.

@StrankaSLS: Zerjav: Slovenian farmers' problem today is that they cannot sell without middlemen #povecalibomosamooskrbo #soocenje #volitve11 8:22 p.m. Dec 2nd, 2011.

Contrary to expectations and some previous findings on the tweeting of politicians, the second most frequent category of tweets may be subsumed under the direct communication umbrella. More than 34 % of all tweets posted by examined accounts pursue two-way interaction, which is somewhat of a novelty in Slovenian electioneering as well as political communication in general. As this novelty deserves more detailed investigation, we devote a separate section of the paper to the characteristics of direct (campaign) communication on Twitter and its significance. For now, we will just briefly mention that direct communication entailed a much higher degree of personalised communication, since more than half of the tweets with emotional expressions by way of utilising emoticons were classified under this modality.

@StrankaSLS: @jgyorkos Every stand deserves its pic :) especially because we buy good and healthy domestic food. Maybe we've given you an idea for today's lunch :) 10:52 a.m. Nov 26th, 2011.

Overall, 18.2 % of direct communication tweets included these symbols. In addition, barring one exception (@zzTurk), a pattern of users with declining or minor support engaging into more direct communication with their followers is clearly visible (see Table 9.2).

As far as other modalities of tweets are concerned, the general conclusion is that they constitute only a minor slice of the entire pie of tweets (see Fig. 9.1). Tweets about official campaign activities or less formal occasions that formed the overall campaign folklore covered only 7 % of the total and were mostly posted by either very well-versed twitterians (e.g. @KatarinaKresal) or parties with a clear strategy for promoting the event (@StrankaSLS). One example is the following tweet capturing 'unintended' hand-shaking with voters on the street:

@StrankaSLS: Very pleasant and inventive postman stopped me right on the street. RZ [Radovan Žerjav] http://t.co/UhGohDRw 11:56 a.m. Dec 2nd, 2011.

Personal messages additionally emerged as a less frequent modality with only 5 % of all tweets. As expected, the majority of these tweets was posted by accounts personally tweeted by politicians, not their staff (e.g. @AlesZalar). Other modalities such as fundraising and requesting action, thus mobilising the electorate, proved completely insignificant in the Slovenian context (see Fig. 9.1).

9.4.4 Direct Communication: Between Conflict and Affection

As Fig. 9.1 shows, in the month before the national election, parties, their leaders and prolific party twitterians directly communicated with citizens (39 % of all direct communication tweets), media and journalists (25 %), opinion makers (16 %), political adversaries (16 %), and colleagues within the party (4 %). However, analysis of interview data paints a rather different picture of the perceived significance of Twitter. Campaign team leaders hardly mentioned the importance of direct communication with citizens or potential voters. A synthesis of their answers reveals that their priorities lay in their relations with media and journalists, whereas other Twitter users were mostly not differentiated according to their role in the political processes. In this context, two extremes can be identified: there are parties that did 'not pay much attention' to whom they directly communicated with (Bogdan Biščak, Zares, 10 May 2013), while some set a clear hierarchy in direct communication practices, reflecting their campaign strategies: 'For political parties primary communication should foremost be with journalists, followed by opinion makers and also their internal community (Uroš Petohleb, LDS, 15 May, 2013).

Furthermore, interviewees emphasised that direct communication was straightforward and expressive, portraying the Twitter communication environment as highly interactive. For instance, the general secretary of the Social Democrats acknowledged the unpredictability and liveliness of Twitter: 'The complexities of communication and user demands are growing. It is no good if you ignore the users. If they are really rude and indecent, then it is of course a matter of decency and criteria whether you react or not' (Uroš Jauševec, SD, 21 May, 2013). Content analysis indicates that direct communication of politicians with other actors in political processes was articulated between affection and conflict, modestly tipping in favour of the latter (see Table 9.3). Analytics show that a significant portion of all direct communication effectively conveyed thoughts or feelings: 41.9 % of direct communication was conflicting and 25 % expressed affection.

Explicit competitive or opposing communicative action on the accounts of political parties, their leaders and prolific party twitterians mostly involved journalists—more than one-third of the cases (34.2 %). This mode of direct communication is even more intriguing, since 30 % of all direct communication involving journalists—the group for whom Twitter was mostly introduced—emerged as conflictive. Regardless of the political parties' ideological leaning, examples of direct conflict communication are traceable with a variety of different discursive elements:

@strankaSDS: @TjasaSlokar Ms. editor, when are you going to publish those facts we sent you 4 h ago and you intentionally left them out in #24ur? 7:58 p.m. Nov 25th, 2011.

@PGantar: @KatjaSeruga24ur are you also going to confront kitties, hamsters, puppies and parrots #soocenje 11:42 p.m. Nov 24th, 2011.

Table 9.3 Conflict and affection between politicians and various groups in direct communication

		Intra-party	Journalists	Political adversaries	Citizens	Opinion makers	Total DC
Conflict	Count	7	116	86	82	48	339
	% within DC	2.1 %	34.2 %	25.4 %	24.2 %	14.2 %	100 %
	% within group	10.3 %	30.0 %	35.0 %	13.2 %	19.0 %	41.9 %
Affection	Count	11	33	21	78	33	176
	% within DC	6.3 %	18.8 %	11.9 %	44.3 %	18.8 %	100 %
	% within group	16.2 %	8.5 %	8.5 %	12.5 %	13.1 %	25.0 %

However, affection was also traceable in 8.5 % of cases in direct communication with journalists and represented one-fifth of all tweets containing direct communication affection. The following examples address public gatherings where politicians and journalists met:

@JJansaSDS: @RadioOgnjisce Congratulations for an excellent concert for the 20th anniversary of Slovenian independence. Homeland received a marvellous present. 10:14 p.m. Nov 20th, 2011.

@KatarinaKresal: @SamoTrtnik @a_kocjan It was very nice, lots of youth, some journalists, even the mayor came by. 3:43 p.m. Nov 16th, 2011.

In this context, interviewees speak of a 'give and take relationship' with journalists (Bogdan Biščak, Zares, 10 May, 2013): for instance, 'We are all—some more and some less—professional. Everybody makes mistakes, everybody has their own interests. In all that you need to know how to act and try to do the best' (Lejla Kogej, SLS, 29 April, 2013).

Direct communication with opinion makers—that is, public figures outside of politics or society in general and Twitter users with more than 1,000 followers—is articulated somewhere between conflict and affection: 19 % of all direct communication with opinion makers was conflictive and 13.1 % expressed affection. Additionally, a significant portion of all tweets identified as direct communication effectively conveying thought or feeling happened between political accounts and opinion makers: 14.2 % conflictive and 18.8 % affectionate. In this sense, interviewees stressed that Twitter was an important tool for 'influencing opinion makers with weak predispositions' (Uroš Petohleb, LDS, 15 May 2013) and 'indirect effects on opinion makers' (Lejla Kogej, SLS, 29 April, 2013). Also in this context, direct communication with other citizens—the most numerous category of tweets involving direct communication—explicitly expressed tender affection in 12.5 % of cases (although this represented 44.3 % of all affectionate direct communication tweets!) and conflict (13.2 %), the latter being mostly reduced to brief communication instances such as the following two:

@ZoranDELA: @stanejersic @had Distinguished Mr. Jeršič. You are slowly losing your contact with reality. 9:45 a.m. Nov 11th, 2011.

@LDSstranka: @time_child Aha, you see us in the next government. Great!:) We think we performed well in the government and therefore remained part of it till the end. 10:40 a.m. Dec 1st, 2011.

When it comes to politicians directly communicating with other politicians, there seems to be a clear division among intra-party actors and political adversaries in terms of conflict or affection in direct communication. There were only few examples of expressive direct communication among accounts of the same party, while in the case of political adversaries, such communication was more common. It represented a substantial amount of all direct exchanges among accounts of different parties, with conflict being dominant at 35 % presence and affection at 8.5 %. The following examples show that prolific twitterians of the conservative SDS addressed political adversaries conflictingly as well as with affection:

@zzturk: @PGantar And how are you going to achieve that as an non-parliamentary party? Should I be afraid? 7:38 p.m. Dec 2nd, 2011.

@zzturk: @krejecl Here you go. We've got another thing in common. :) 7:44 p.m. Nov 29th, 2011.

9.5 Discussion

An examination of the political parties' move into the Twittersphere could be well summed up with an old Slovenian proverb: 'The bear changes fur, but not its coat'. To be precise, political parties rightfully sensed the need to introduce a new tool into their political communication arsenal, but with shallow motives and dubious intentions. The move was nothing close to revolutionising the political process in the ossified Slovenian 'ivory-tower' politics, but a consequence of peer pressure, societal advancement and electoral pragmatism—after all, parties are in their pure essence nothing more than organisations competing for votes. The 'me too' reasoning was therefore omnipresent among political parties, either in the fear of being left behind or as a consequence of keeping up appearances in front of the electorate. In that sense, the move to Twitter does not differ much from the move online in the early years of this millennium: when everyone else was proficient in the use of the Internet, only the parties were still shuffling along. This rationale was valid even for parties that struggled in the offline battle for voters and the attention of the main media outlets.

However, the scenario is not as grim as one would imagine. Despite the initial Potemkin-like strategies devised only to impress voters, this tool that political actors were compelled to use was slowly being moulded into an indispensable one for targeted communication. As such, political actors employed it substantially during the 2011 election campaign, particularly smaller actors with minor or declining electoral support. This converges with the utopian view that this tool could provide a Lockean state of nature, free of offline chains, which consequently drives minor actors to use the potential 'game-changer' in their struggle against political powerhouses.

Indeed, some minor parties did invest meaningful attention in this outlet in their overall strategy; however, offline capabilities began to haunt the Twittersphere as well. They mainly did so on two accounts. Firstly, the resources available (financial or human) enabled them to set a clear and intensive strategy and, under the high scrutiny of party leadership, implement it according to plan. Either hired or internally available personnel executed planned Twitter activities on a daily basis, something minor political actors in the Slovenian political arena are unable to cope with. This is also evidenced by more sophisticated use of metadata tags and retweet options to shape discussions or externally legitimise standpoints and actions. The most dominant political parties even do this as part of their 'permanent' campaign, with very little variation in intensity within and outside the official campaign. Secondly, however, the appropriation of the tool made even more 'politics as usual'. The dominant information modality shaped the message on Twitter according to political communicators' conventional practice, as part of a one-way process from the actor to the recipient. In addition, the tool was utilised as a proxy for television, the Shangri-La of Slovenian spin-doctors, therefore significantly stripping it of its potential in the case of many major parties.

Nevertheless, Twitter did emerge as an importer of certain novelties into Slovenian political process. This is primarily so in terms of the insertion of a considerable amount of direct communication into the campaign process. Despite information proving to be the dominant modality of posts, the direct communication between politicians and various groups appears to be the most far-reaching consequence of Twitter introduction. Despite our expectation that this would be in favour of communication with specialised publics, such as journalists and opinion makers, in order to shape the media agenda—as was accentuated also by the parties themselves—the dominant group politicians communicated with were citizens. To be precise, this portion of affectionate and conflictive tweets introduced a rare chance for citizens to engage in unmediated conversation with politicians and was, potentially, the basis for true political discussion.

9.6 Conclusion

The Slovenian experience with Twitter in the 2011 election campaign may be subsumed under the well-known thesis that it is never about the actual impact of technology upon politics (see Wright 2012: 246); it is always the case of how technology is designed, exploited and adopted by actors in specific social and political contexts. The Slovenian case shows that Twitter offered a platform, and the stakeholders in the political process tailored it according to their needs and capabilities. There are several patterns of Twitter use that we can observe. The first is the complementary vs. supplementary use of social networks. Certain political actors talk to different publics via Twitter and Facebook and assign different functions to the two while others straightforwardly multiply the core strategy originating from their utilization of the internet (website) in general. Secondly, there is a clear bifurcation in terms of Twitter account personalization since several political parties opted for personalized official Twitter accounts, leaving the party leader to tweet on the party's behalf. Thirdly, this may be done by an individual or collective production of tweets. To be precise, certain party strategies entailed professionalized teams that posted tweets in a well-thought-out manner, while others tweeted without any clear strategy (sometimes this work was even carried out by their personal assistants). Fourthly, political actors contrasted in terms of the nature of their communication on Twitter. While a lot of them still retained the old information provision form known from the use of websites and dull press releases, some of them engaged in an entirely different nature of communication—they began to interact and engage in meaningful political conversations with citizens, opinion makers, and journalists.

It is primarily the composition of each actor's patterns that offers new and potentially far-reaching changes. However, in the case of Twitter, all far-reaching patterns touch upon direct communication; one of those is between the politicians' and the journalists' utilization of the tool. For them, be it a matter of cooperation or adversity, the tool provided a valuable instant contact point to immediately inform about or respond to issues that arise with the speed of light during the election campaign. The other overlap is between citizens and politicians. Although politicians rarely follow anyone other than journalists, opinion makers and fellow politicians on Twitter, the dominant mode of politicians' direct communication is with citizens. While this could be a case of 'preaching and listening to the converted', we should not disregard the potential for genuine democratisation of the political process. However, the social media environment, with its omnipresent and always-on stream of information and interpretation, additionally blurs boundaries between intimate and public discourses as well as personal and institutional relations between journalists and politicians. These dynamics indicate that at least to a certain extent, social processes and relations are getting minced into small, almost personalized communication spaces where traditional societal roles and power relations are minimized. If articulations between journalism and political communication do not respond to the trend of fragmentation of the public sphere accordingly and fail to contribute to the common communication bases for citizens, democracy's troubles might deepen.

Is this enough to be classified as a revolution? No, probably not. However, at the same time, we have to ask ourselves whether we are putting the bar too high. The value and relative worth of the democratization seen in the 2011 election should not be underestimated.

References

Agranoff, R. (Ed.). (1972). *The new style in election campaigns*. Boston: Holbrook Press.

Baxter, G., Marcella, R., & Varfis, E. (2011). The use of the internet by political parties and candidates in Scotland during the 2010 UK general election campaign. *Aslib Proceedings, 63* (5), 464–483.

Benoit, W. L. (2011). Content analysis in political communication. In E. P. Bucy & R. L. Holbert (Eds.), *The sourcebook for political communication research: methods, measures, and analytical techniques* (pp. 268–279). New York: Routledge.

Bertoncelj, T. (2011). Omejevanje svobode. Mladina 23 September 2011. Available via Mladina. http://www.mladina.si/105795/. Accessed 25 May 2013

Bruns, A., & Stieglitz, S. (2012). Quantitative approaches to comparing communication patterns on Twitter. *Journal of Technology and Human Resources, 30*(3–4), 160–185.

Budge, I. (1996). *The new challenge of direct democracy*. Cambridge, MA: Polity Press.

Creswell, J. (2009). *Research design: Qualitative, quantitative, and mixed methods approaches* (3rd ed.). London: Sage.

De Vreese, C. H., Banducci, S. A., Semetko, H. A., & Boomgaarden, H. G. (2006). The news coverage of the 2004 European parliamentary election campaign in 25 countries. *European Union Politics, 7*(4), 477–504.

Dertouzos, M. L. (1997). *What will be: How the new world of information will change our lives*. San Francisco, CA: HarperEdge.

Deželan, T. (2005). Predvolilna kampanja, volilna udelezba in izid volitev: analiza vpliva predvolilne kampanje na problem nizke volilne udelezbe na volitvah v EP. In S. Kustec Lipicer (Ed.), *Politološki vidiki volilne kampanje* (pp. 147–166). Ljubljana: FDV.

Deželan, T., Krašovec, A., & Kovačič, M. (2010). Volilna kampanja po slovensko. In S. Kustec Lipicer (Ed.), *Politične vsebine in volilna kampanja: slovenska izkušnja z volitev v Evropski parlament 2009* (pp. 53–70). Ljubljana: FDV.

Eurostat (2012). Media use in the European Union. Report November 2012. Available via http://ec.europa.eu/public_opinion/archives/eb/eb78/eb78_media_en.pdf. Accessed 29 Aug 2013.

Farrell, D. M., & Webb, P. (2000). Political parties as campaign organizations. In D. J. Rassell & M. P. Wattenberg (Eds.), *Parties without partisans* (pp. 102–128). Oxford: Oxford University Press.

Flick, U. (2006). *An introduction to qualitative research*. London: Sage.

Franz, D. (2003). Digitalna demokracija in politična kultura na primeru Slovenije. *Časopis za kritiko znanosti, 30*(21), 34–53.

Gibson, R., Nixon, P., & Ward, S. (Eds.). (2003). *Political parties and the internet net gain?* London: Routledge.

Gibson, R., & Römmele, A. (2007). Political communication. In D. Caramani (Ed.), *Comparative politics* (pp. 473–492). Oxford: Oxford University Press.

Gibson, R., & Römmele, A. (2008). Political communication. In D. Caramani (Ed.), *Comparative politics* (pp. 473–492). Oxford: Oxford University Press.

Gibson, R., & Römmele, A. (2009). Mesauring the professionalization of political campaigning. *Party Politics, 15*(3), 265–293.

Gibson, R., & Ward, S. (2000). A proposed methodology for studying the function and effectiveness of party and candidate web sites. *Social Science Computer Review, 18*(3), 301–319.

Golbeck, J., Grimes, J. M., & Rogers, A. (2010). Twitter use by the U.S. Congress. *Journal of the American Society for Information Science and Technology, 61*(8), 1612–1621.

Grant, W. J., Moon, B., & Grant, J. B. (2010). Digital dialogue? Australian Politicians' use of the Social network tool Twitter. *Australian Journal of Political Science, 45*(4), 579–604.

Hermanns, H. (2004). Interviewing as an activity. In U. Flick, V. E. Kardorff, & I. Steinke (Eds.), *Companion to qualitative research* (pp. 203–208). London: Sage.

Holtz-Bacha, C. (2002). The end of old certainties: Changes in the triangle of media, political system, and electorate and their consequences. *Ethical Perspectives, 9*(4), 222–229.

Holtz-Bacha, C. (2008). Professionalization. In L. L. Kaid & C. Holtz-Bacha (Eds.), *Encyclopedia of political communication* (pp. 656–657). Los Angeles, CA: Sage.

Kavanagh, D. (1995). *Election campaigning: The new marketing of politics*. Oxford and Cambridge, MA: Blackwell.

Košak, K., & Žumer, J. (2012). Njihova govorica. Mladina. Available via Mladina. http://www.mladina.si/115464/. Accessed 25 May 2013.

Krippendorff, K. H. (2003). *Content analysis: An introduction to its methodology*. Thousand oaks, CA: Sage Publications.

Legard, R., Keegan, J., & Ward, K. (2003). In-depth interviews. In J. Ritche & J. Lewis (Eds.), *Qualitative research practice: A guide for social sciences students and researchers* (pp. 138–169). London: Sage.

Lindlof, T. R., & Taylor, B. C. (2002). *Qualitative communication research methods* (2nd ed.). London: Sage.

Margolis, M., & Resnick, D. (2000). *Politics as usual: The cyberspace 'revolution'*. Thousand oaks: Sage.

Mekina, B. (2011). Lažna alternativa. Mladina. Available via Mladina. http://www.mladina.si/54328/lazna-alternativa/. Accessed 25 May 2013.

Negrine, R. M., & Lilleker, D. G. (2002). The professionalization of political communication: Continuities and change in media practices. *European Journal of Communication, 17*(3), 305–323.

Newell, J. L. (2001). Italian political parties on the web. *The Harvard International Journal of Press/Politics, 6*(4), 60–87.

Norris, P. (2003). Preaching to the converted? Pluralism, participation and party websites. *Party Politics, 9*(1), 21–45.

Norris, P. (2004). *The evolution of election campaigns: eroding political engagement?* Paper for the conference on Political Communications in the 21st Century, St Margaret's College, University of Otago, New Zealand.

Oblak, T., & Željan, K. (2007). Slovenian online campaigning during the 2004 European parliament election: struggling between self-promotion and mobilization. In R. K. Kluver, N. W. Jankowski, K. A. Foot, & S. M. Schneider (Eds.), *The Internet and national elections: a comparative study of web campaigning* (pp. 60–76). London: Routledge.

Plasser, F., & Plasser, G. (2002). *Global political campaigning: a worldwide analysis of campaign professionals and their practices*. Westoprt: Praeger.

Rheingold, H. (2000). *The virtual community: homesteading on the electronic frontier* (Rev. ed.). Cambridge, MA: The MIT Press.

Ritchie, J., & Lewis, J. (2003). *Qualitative research practice*. London: Sage.

Scammell, S. (1998). The wisdom of the war room: US campaigning and Americanization Media. *Culture and Society, 20*(2), 251–275.

Selnow, G. W. (1998). *Electronic whistle-stops: The impact of the Internet on American politics*. Westport, CT: Praeger.

Solop, F. (2010). RT @Barack Obama we just made history. Twitter and the 2008 Presidential election. In J. A. Hendricks & J. R. Denton (Eds.), *Communicator-in-chief. How Barack Obama used new media technology to win the white house* (pp. 37–49). Lanham: Rowman & Littlefield Publishers, Inc.

SORS. (2012). Usage of information-communication technologies in households and by individuals, Slovenia, 2012—final data, Statistical Office of the Republic of Slovenia. http://www.stat.si/eng/novica_prikazi.aspx?id=5037 Accessed 30 Aug 2013.

Štefančič, M. (2011). Revolucija! Mladina. Available via Mladina. http://www.mladina.si/53094/revolucija/. Accessed 25 May 2013.

Stone, B. (1996). Politics'96. *Internet world, 7*(11), 44–50.

Strandberg, K. (2008). Online electoral competition in different settings—a comparative meta-analysis of the research on party websites and online electoral competition. *Party Politics, 14* (2), 223–244.

Swanson, D. L., & Mancini, P. (Eds.). (1996). *Politics, media, and modern democracy: An international study of innovations in electoral campaign and their consequences*. Westport: Praeger.

Tomažič, A. (2013). Moč družbenih omrežij. Available via Pogledi. http://www.pogledi.si/druzba/moc-druzbenih-omrezij. Accessed 29 May 2013.

Tops, P. W., Voerman, G., & Boogers, M. (2000). Political websites during the 1998 parliamentary elections in The Netherlands. In J. Hoff, I. Horrocks, & P. W. Tops (Eds.), *Democratic governance and new technology* (pp. 88–100). London: Routledge.

UK Office for National Statistics. (2013). Social networking: The UK as a leader in Europe, UK, New South Wales. http://www.ons.gov.uk/ons/rel/rdit2/internet-access—households-and-individuals/social-networking–the-uk-as-a-leader-in-europe/sty-social-networking-2012.html. Accessed 30 Aug 2013.

Vehovar, V., Jerman Kuželički, A., & Lebar, L. (2011). Socialna omrežja 2011 (#94). Available via http://www.ris.org/uploadi/editor/1307495011poroilo_spletneskupnosti.pdf. Accessed 29 Aug 2013.

Ward, S., Gibson, R., & Nixon, P. (2003). *Parties and the internet: New gain?* London: Routledge.

Waters, D. W., & Williams, J. M. (2011). Squawking, tweeting, cooing, and hooting: Analyzing the communication patterns of government agencies on Twitter. *Journal of Public Affairs, 11* (4), 353–363.

Wright, S. (2012). Politics as usual? Revolution, normalization and a new agenda for online deliberation. *New Media & Society, 14*(2), 244–261.

Chapter 10
The Use of Facebook by Political Parties and Leaders in the 2011 Turkish General Elections

Quantitative and Qualitative Content Analysis

Günseli Bayraktutan, Mutlu Binark, Tuğrul Çomu, Burak Doğu, Gözde İslamoğlu, and Aslı Telli Aydemir

Abstract This paper, mainly accepting that web 2.0 has a contribution to the development of citizenship culture, examines the uses of Facebook by Turkish political parties and their leaders during the 2011 Turkish General Elections. By examining the relationship through the discursive practices of social media interface, this study reveals the possible converting effects of those practices of political parties by the usage of social media in the process of political communication. During the study, 9 Facebook accounts have been recorded for 3 months and analyzed by means of the quantitative and qualitative content analysis technique. Qualities of the accounts, such as customizations, information shared on the accounts, and the numbers of posts, have been examined for each account; topics,

This study is a part of the project called "Examination of Social Media Environments in Terms of Political Communication Practices: The Use of Facebook and Twitter by Political Parties and their Leaders in the 2011 Turkish General Elections", funded by The Scientific and Technological Research Council of Turkey (TÜBİTAK), November 2011–November 2012 (Project Number: 111K263).

G. Bayraktutan (✉)
Faculty of Communication, Başkent University, Ankara, Turkey
e-mail: bayrakt@baskent.edu.tr

M. Binark
Faculty of Communication, Hacettepe Universitiy, Ankara, Turkey
e-mail: mbinark@gmail.com

T. Çomu (✉)
Faculty of Communication, Ankara University, Ankara, Turkey
e-mail: tugrul.comu@gmail.com

B. Doğu
Faculty of Communication, İzmir Ekonomi University, İzmir, Turkey

G. İslamoğlu
Faculty of Communication, Kocaeli University, Kocaeli, Turkey

A. Telli Aydemir
Faculty of Communication, İstanbul Şehir University, Istanbul, Turkey

B. Pătruţ and M. Pătruţ (eds.), *Social Media in Politics*, Public Administration and Information Technology 13, DOI 10.1007/978-3-319-04666-2_10,

themes, styles, linguistic practices etc. have been examined for each post. Hence, this paper focuses on the opportunities offered by web 2.0 that have been used for election campaigning in Turkey, the mutual and interactive communication between the party and/or the candidate and the voters forming during the campaigning period, and the qualities of the online communications between the candidate and his/her competitors throughout the analysis of Facebook usage by both the party and the leaders.

10.1 Introduction

Social media, which play an important role in the development of civic citizenship due to the manifestation of speech-act activism in the digital public space, has become, in our days, an increasingly visible area in the evaluation and assessment of political developments. It is one of the main means used by political parties and leaders for expressing, reinforcing and spreading political preferences. Due to its multi-layered structure, the usage of social media for political communication leads to results and experiences that differ from one another. To be able to define the "successful" and "effective" use of the social media as a means of political communication, it is necessary to understand the specific conditions that fashion the experiences and results pertaining to the use of the social media, and to investigate how the features of these new media environments are utilized by both the followers and the account holders on the social media.

However, the role of social media in political communication is not free of its relation with the Internet. Therefore, while treating social media as part of political communication processes, the use of the Internet for political purposes should be briefly examined. In the study of Davis et al. (2009), the role of the Internet in the US election campaigns is analyzed in three periods, the *first* is discovery, the *second* is maturity and the *third* is post-maturity. The use of the Internet in the discovery period started with the operations carried out by George H. W. Bush and Bill Clinton in 1992 election campaigns. In the first years, the main purposes of using the Internet involved exchanging e-mails and being present on computerized information systems, but by 1998, several candidates and parties had already opened websites. During the discovery period, which continued up to 2000, the Internet was used in order to exhibit the informational content which was not updated so often. The maturity period marked by the interaction function started with the launch of political campaign websites improved with advanced features. It can be put forth that the ideas which were put into practice through the websites of that period have laid the foundations of the social media practices in today's world. The support of the Internet to the election campaigns in the maturity period can be categorised into four groups: *campaign activities*, *communication*, *mobilization*, *source creation*. Campaign activities can be associated with data collection and distribution of election materials; communication can involve giving an advertisement, reaching certain communities and collecting e-mail addresses; motivation may be connected to the involvement of electors in the election process more; and source creation can be linked to the strategies targeting to generate income out of several sources in little amounts. The post-maturity period corresponds to the period when election campaigns spread to the Internet as a whole instead of being limited to the corporate websites. The fact that the websites do not suffice to reach electors triggers the process during which two types of political communication come into the play: *media-controlled online communication tools* under third parties' thumb are the information transmission channels that reach more electors compared to news websites or campaign websites such as blogs. *User-controlled online communication tools*, however, involve social networks including Facebook and Twitter. Thus, the category to which social media belong is constituted by user-controlled online communication tools.

It can be said that the first time Turkish political parties prepared websites was in 2002 early general elections (Aktaş 2004; Öksüz and Turan-Yıldız 2004), and social media practices were first apparent in the 2009 local elections. In the 2009 local elections, it was observed that the youth branches of political parties intensively used social networks like Facebook for the purposes of explaining the party policy and announcing their activities, and some mayor candidates preferred to address their electors on their Facebook accounts. The study of Toprak et al. (2009) revealed that there were more than 500 groups which were launched in the name of the Adalet ve Kalkınma Partisi (AKP) (Justice and Development Party in English) and appeared in the search results on Facebook by the summer of 2009. In the light of this, it was foreseen that political parties and their leaders would use social media more in the 2011 General Elections. In reality, both political parties and deputy candidates used social media a lot more in the 2011 General Elections compared to the previous elections. The fact that Turkey ranks the fourth in the world in terms of Facebook use has lead many political parties to open and set up hundreds of pages and groups on this interface. Twitter also became widespread in Turkey as of 2009–2010, and many young members of the parliament with high digital literacy levels in particular have gained thousands of followers on their Twitter accounts. It was observed that political party leaders began to use Twitter actively especially during election periods. Thus, the transition to web 2.0 from web 1.0 during political communication campaigns in Turkey was completed. This study describes how the leaders and members of these parties defined democracy, explained the meaning of democratic participation, produced and disseminated their own ideological positions and values and interacted with citizens by using their official accounts on Facebook during the elections. Within this perspective, we seek answers to the following questions: how and to what extent did political parties and their leaders use Facebook during the 2011 General Elections? What were the differences and similarities in the practices involved in the use of Facebook? How do the interaction and participation in the social media, as well as features such as the production of user-generated content, affect the political communication process and the discursive practices of the political party leaders?

10.2 Method

In this study, the accounts of political parties (or their representatives) on the social media in question were followed, their posts/sharings were examined from a thematic perspective, and they were put to quantitative and qualitative content analysis. Orhan Gökçe states that the objective of content analysis is "to analyse the texts produced and designed for public use" (2006: 20).

According to Paul Skalski, the points to be considered in content analysis within interactive media are content creation, content search, content archive and content coding. During the coding process, the code should absolutely be tested and put to a reliability test. Just like in empirical researches, "code" is the most fundamental unit in Internet research, too (Jensen 2011: 52). Gökçe points out that if the search categories are clearly formulated and properly adapted to the problem and content, the search can be productive (2006: 57). Christopher Weare and Wan-Ying Lin underline the importance of sampling unit, capturing and context unit in a content analysis to be carried out on web interface (2000: 272–292). It is especially demanding to code a material on web. It requires archiving as well as a high storage capacity. In this research, archiving and capturing are particularly emphasized.

In qualitative content analysis, the frequency of the use of certain themes, subjects and phenomena is examined (Mayring 2011: 116). Mayring states that qualitative and quantitative content analyses do not oppose each other, but on the contrary, they support each other. He adds that "classical quantitative research is a preliminary research for qualitative research..." (2011: 149). In this research, quantitative and qualitative content analyses are used in a way to complement each other.

At this point, we should explain how the sampling was taken out from the research population. In this research, "sampling for the purpose" as mentioned in the article entitled "Content Analysis in Political Communication" by William L. Benoit was used (2011: 272). Therefore, the official accounts of political parties, leaders and the members of their central boards of directors that gained the right to form a group in the Türkiye Büyük Millet Meclisi (TBMM) (in English, Grand National Assembly of Turkey) according to the results of 12 June 2011 General Elections were captured in pdf format[1] by using a web interface (we reached the web pages through an internet browser without using a special application). The sampling consisted of the official accounts reached between April 1st, 2011 and June 30th, 2011. We accessed the accounts shown in Table 10.1 respectively.

The restrictions we encountered while creating a database in the sampling result from the fact that the account owners might have deleted some of their posts on Facebook. The official Facebook accounts of political parties and leaders were

[1] It is recommended to use the "print screen", "save as file" or "convert to file" features in capturing social media from the web (Skalski 2012). For Facebook accounts, the PDF converters doPDF and CutePDF Writer were used, whereas PDF was used in storing Twitter accounts. Separate files were created for each political party and candidate.

Table 10.1 Turkish and English names of the parties and the accounts

Account	Account name in english	Party	Party name in english
Recep Tayyip Erdoğan	[Person]	AKP	Justice and Development Party
AK Parti'yi Seviyoruz	We Love AK Party	AKP	Justice and Development Party
Cumhuriyet Halk Partisi	Republican People's Party	CHP	Republican People's Party
Kemal Kılıçdaroğlu	[Person]	CHP	Republican People's Party
Sakin Güç	Calm Power	CHP	Republican People's Party
SesVerTürkiye	SpeakUpTurkey	MHP	National Movement Party
BDP BARIŞ VE DEMOKRASİ PARTİSİ	BDP PEACE AND DEMOCRACY PARTY	BDP	Peace and Democracy Party
A. Levent Tüzel	[Person]	Independent	Labour, Democracy and Freedom Block
Ertuğrul Kürkçü	[Person]	Independent	Labour, Democracy and Freedom Block

captured. However, if there was no official account owned by the party or political leader, the accounts which had more than 1,000,000 "likes" and looked like an official account and where there was a continuous flow were captured. After Facebook launched its page account application, opening a page account became more widespread than opening a group account. As there was no active group account created for political parties and leaders, we did not include group accounts in the sampling.

10.3 Facebook Experience by Political Parties and Leaders in the 2011 General Elections: Quantitative and Qualitative Content Analysis

This research involves sample units from four political parties which joined the 2011 General Elections in Turkey: Adalet ve Kalkınma Partisi (AKP), (Justice and Development Party) Cumhuriyet Halk Partisi (CHP) (Republican People's Party), Milliyetçi Hareket Partisi (MHP) (National Movement Party) and Emek, Demokrasi ve Özgürlük Bloku (EDOB) (Labour, Democracy and Freedom Block).

In this research, we followed the official Facebook accounts of the leaders of these four political parties (and/or other real persons representing the parties in question on social networks), their members of the central boards of directors as well as the deputy candidates who are media professionals (e.g. journalists,

Table 10.2 The Facebook accounts followed and captured

Party	Account	Facebook address (URL)
AKP	Recep Tayyip Erdoğan	http://www.facebook.com/RecepTayyipErdogan
AKP	AK Parti'yi Seviyoruz	http://www.facebook.com/AkPartiyiSeviyoruz
CHP	Cumhuriyet Halk Partisi	http://www.facebook.com/herkesicinCHP
CHP	Kemal Kılıçdaroğlu	http://www.facebook.com/K.Kilicdaroglu
CHP	Sakin Güç	http://www.facebook.com/sakingucuz
MHP	SesVerTürkiye	http://www.facebook.com/svturkiye
BDP	BDP BARIŞ VE DEMOKRASİ PARTİSİ	http://www.facebook.com/BDPMERKEZ
Independent	A. Levent Tüzel	http://www.facebook.com/abdullahleventtuzel
Independent	Ertuğrul Kürkçü	http://www.facebook.com/ertugrulkurkcu

columnists, etc.). Data from 9 Facebook accounts were captured in the study. The details of the accounts in question can be seen in Table 10.2.[2]

We need to provide brief information about the parties whose Facebook accounts we examined in the 2011 General Elections. **AKP**[3] was founded in 2002. The leader, Recep Tayyip Erdoğan was elected as the founding president by the founders' committee. Defining its ideology within the frame of conservative democracy, AKP came to power alone in all the general elections (2002, 2007 and 2011) and Recep Tayyip Erdoğan took charge of the premiership. He has been serving as Turkish Prime Minister since 2002. **CHP**[4] was founded by Mustafa Kemal Atatürk in 1923. The ideology of CHP is formed with regard to the principles of Kemalism and social democracy. CHP, also known as the party which has established the republic, was in power alone for 23 years until 1946 when the first general elections were held in Turkey. Today CHP is the main opposition party in the parliament. Its current president Kemal Kılıçdaroğlu has been on duty since 2010 as the 7th chairman of the party. The period beginning with the Millet Partisi (MP) (in English, Nation Party) and continuing with the Cumhuriyet Köylü Millet Partisi (CKMP) (in English, Republican Villagers National Party) represents the prehistory of **MHP**.[5] The party participated in 1969 general elections with its leader Alparslan Türkeş. Devlet Bahçeli was elected

[2] The official Facebook accounts owned by the political parties were taken into account in the selection of Facebook accounts. If the parties had no Facebook accounts, the pages liked by more than 500,000 people were included in the sampling. Among independent candidates, the ones with web pages liked by more than 8,000 people were included in the sampling. The accounts we captured cover both "Personal accounts (profiles)" and Page Accounts (previously known as Fan Page), but we could find no data available for analysis in the personal accounts. Thus, the analysis was purely based on the data retrieved from "page accounts".

[3] Official website: http://www.akparti.org.tr/english [Accessed 25 November 2012].

[4] Official website: http://www.chp.org.tr/en [Accessed 25 November 2012].

[5] Official website: http://www.mhp.org.tr [Accessed 25 November 2012].

as the second leader after the demise of Türkeş and he is currently in office. Positioning itself within the framework of Turkish nationalism and Islam, MHP has had a significant role in the politics of Turkey since its foundation. The new Kurdish political movement, which began with the Halkın Emek Partisi (HEP) (in English, People's Labour Party) in 1990, is now represented by Barış ve Demokrasi Partisi (BDP) (in English, the Peace and Democracy Party). **BDP** was founded in 2008 in preparation for the possibility of closure of the Demokratik Toplum Partisi (DTP) (in English, the Democratic Society Party) and actually took over its place when it was closed by the Constitutional Court in 2009.[6] Unlike in other parties, the co-presidential system is applied in BDP instead of the general presidency. The co-presidents of the party are Gültan Kışanak and Selahattin Demirtaş. BDP did not join the 2011 General Elections but supported the independent candidates that were reunited under the roof of the **EDÖB** (Labor, Democracy and Freedom Block). EDÖB has a very important place in the new Kurdish political movement. Within this block, 65 people from 41 cities announced their candidature. Supporting its independent candidates, BDP used the following slogans: "Democratic Republic", "Freedom and Democracy for Democratic Autonomy". In the meantime, independent candidates A. Levent Tüzel and Ertuğrul Kürkçü entered the election as the candidates of EDÖB.

The table below shows the number of "likes" as of February 18th, 2012 on the accounts included in our analysis (Table 10.3). The accounts with the highest number of likes were owned by Kemal Kılıçdaroğlu (1,397,220 "likes") and Recep Tayyip Erdoğan (1,258,412 "likes"). It should be noted that neither of these accounts were official accounts of political parties. They were both opened in the name of their leaders.

It is observed that all of the pages included in the analysis, except for the one owned by A. Levent Tüzel, were managed by a social media expert, which is ordinary when it comes to the Facebook pages that represent the entire party. However, it is interesting that the accounts owned by the leaders, who are individuals, were also managed by social media experts.

The only user who did not provide any link address (URL) under the profile information of the accounts covered in the analysis was A. Levent Tüzel. All of the remaining accounts had a link to a Facebook page or to other website. As to the content position of the link addresses provided, it is seen that the page of CHP, "Calm Power" (original account name in Turkish: Sakin Güç) and the page of MHP, "Speak up, Turkey" (original account name in Turkish: SesVerTürkiye) are both available on and off Facebook. The links provided by other account owners were related to content outside Facebook; such addresses were mainly the official website addresses of the political party or the user him/herself. Table 10.4 shows the link addresses provided by the accounts.

An examination of the link addresses to websites other than the parties' official websites shows that the accounts of CHP, SesVerTürkiye and Ertuğrul Kürkçü

[6] Official website: http://bdp.org.tr [Accessed 25 November 2012].

Table 10.3 Number of "likes"

Party	Account	Account management	Number of likes
AKP	Recep Tayyip Erdoğan	by a social media expert	1.258.412
AKP	AK Parti'yi Seviyoruz	by a social media expert	548.920
CHP	Cumhuriyet Halk Partisi	by a social media expert	19.593
CHP	Kemal Kılıçdaroğlu	by a social media expert	1.397.220
CHP	Sakin Güç	by a social media expert	43.169
MHP	SesVerTürkiye	by a social media expert	62.953
BDP	BDP BARIŞ VE DEMOKRASİ PARTİSİ	by a social media expert	113.707
Independent	A. Levent Tüzel	by himself	8.375
Independent	Ertuğrul Kürkçü	by a social media expert	25.006

Table 10.4 Link addresses

Party	Account	Link address shared[a]
AKP	Recep Tayyip Erdoğan	http://www.rte.gen.tr
AKP	AK Parti'yi Seviyoruz	http://akpartiyiseviyoruz.blogspot.com
CHP	Cumhuriyet Halk Partisi	https://twitter.com/herkesicinCHP http://www.chp.org.tr
CHP	Kemal Kılıçdaroğlu	http://www.kemalkilicdaroglu.com
CHP	Sakin Güç	www.facebook.com/sakinguc www.facebook.com/sakingucuz http://www.facebook.com/K.Kilicdaroglu http://www.chp.org.tr
MHP	SesVerTürkiye	http://www.sesverturkiye.com.tr http://www.twitter.com/sesverturkiye http://www.facebook.com/svturkiye http://www.youtube.com/svturkiye http://www.mhp.org.tr http://www.sesverturkiye.com.tr
BDP	BDP BARIŞ VE DEMOKRASİ PARTİSİ	http://bdpblog.wordpress.com
Independent	A. Levent Tüzel	NONE
Independent	Ertuğrul Kürkçü	http://twitter.com/#!/ekurkcu http://www.ertugrulkurkcu.org

[a]Quoted directly from the Facebook interface

Table 10.5 The features of profile visuals

		Profile visuals		
Party	Account	Represented by	Use of background[a]	Use of logo
AKP	Recep Tayyip Erdoğan	Himself	None	None
AKP	AK Parti'yi Seviyoruz	Recep Tayyip Erdoğan	None	None
CHP	Cumhuriyet Halk Partisi	Party Logo	Not Coded	Existing
CHP	Kemal Kılıçdaroğlu	Himself (With other people)	Existing	Existing
CHP	Sakin Güç	Kemal Kılıçdaroğlu	None	Existing
MHP	SesVerTürkiye	Devlet Bahçeli	None	Existing
BDP	BDP BARIŞ VE DEMOKRASİ PARTİSİ	Party Logo	Not coded	Existing
Independent	A. Levent Tüzel	Himself (With other people)	Existing	None
Independent	Ertuğrul Kürkçü	Himself	Existing	None

[a]The term "background" refers to a photograph which was taken when the candidate was in a meeting or was giving a speech giving an idea about the candidate's place

provided a link to their Twitter accounts; SesVerTürkiye provided a link to YouTube and BDP provided a link to Wordpress, which is a blog application.

The only account which provided content/information in a language other than Turkish was the account of BDP. The account information was provided in Kurdish and English as well as in Turkish.

Table 10.5 shows the features in the profile visuals of the accounts.

The representations in the profile visuals show that the accounts connected to the party (Sakin Güç, We love AK Party—original name in Turkish: AK Partiyi Seviyoruz-, SesVerTürkiye) used the visuals of leaders. BDP Barış ve Demokrasi Partisi and Cumhuriyet Halk Partisi used just the party logo in their accounts. As to the representation of individuals in profile visuals, it was seen that Kemal Kılıçdaroğlu and A. Levent Tüzel preferred to be represented with other people. An examination of the use of party logo reveals that CHP, MHP and BDP used party logos. A. Levent Tüzel and Ertuğrul Kürkçü, however, preferred not to use party logos in their accounts, a standard procedure for independent candidates. However, it is interesting that AKP did not use the party logo in its profile visuals, while all other political parties did.

The accounts of Cumhuriyet Halk Partisi, Sakin Güç, BDP Barış ve Demokrasi Partisi, and Ertuğrul Kürkçü were all mentioned to be "official accounts" (Table 10.6). Yet, there is no information about whether the accounts of AK Parti'yi Seviyoruz, Kemal Kılıçdaroğlu Ses Ver Türkiye, and A. Levent Tüzel were official. Some of the accounts (Recep Tayyip Erdoğan, AK Parti'yi Seviyoruz, Kemal Kılıçdaroğlu and Ses Ver Türkiye) shared certain rules for the prospective users. Cumhuriyet Halk Partisi, Sakin Güç, BDP Barış ve Demokrasi Partisi, A. Levent Tüzel and Ertuğrul Kürkçü, however, preferred not to set any "page rule".

Table 10.6 Page type and rules

Party	Account	Official page	Page rules
AKP	Recep Tayyip Erdoğan	No	Yes
AKP	AK Parti'yi Seviyoruz	No	Yes
CHP	Cumhuriyet Halk Partisi	Yes	No
CHP	Kemal Kılıçdaroğlu	No	Yes
CHP	Sakin Güç	Yes	No
MHP	SesVerTürkiye	No	Yes
BDP	BDP BARIŞ VE DEMOKRASİ PARTİSİ	Yes	No
Independent	A. Levent Tüzel	No	No
Independent	Ertuğrul Kürkçü	Yes	No

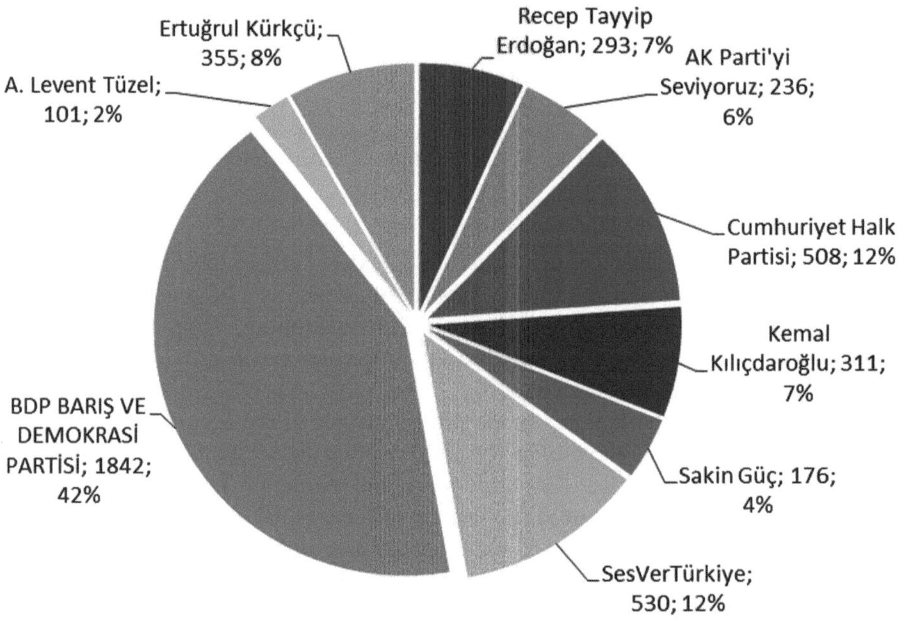

Fig. 10.1 Sampling—number of posts sent

The number and distribution of posts sent by the accounts analysed within this research during the sampling period (April 1st, 2011–June 30th, 2011) can be seen below (Fig. 10.1):

Among the accounts analysed in the sample, BDP, with 1,842 posts, is the party which used Facebook more intensively than the others. The numbers of posts sent by the other accounts are respectively as follows: Recep Tayyip Erdoğan—293, AK Parti'yi Seviyoruz—236, Cumhuriyet Halk Partisi—508, Kemal Kılıçdaroğlu—311, Sakin Güç—176, Ses Ver Türkiye—530, A. Levent Tüzel—101, and Ertuğrul Kürkçü—355. Among the accounts related to CHP, the official account named

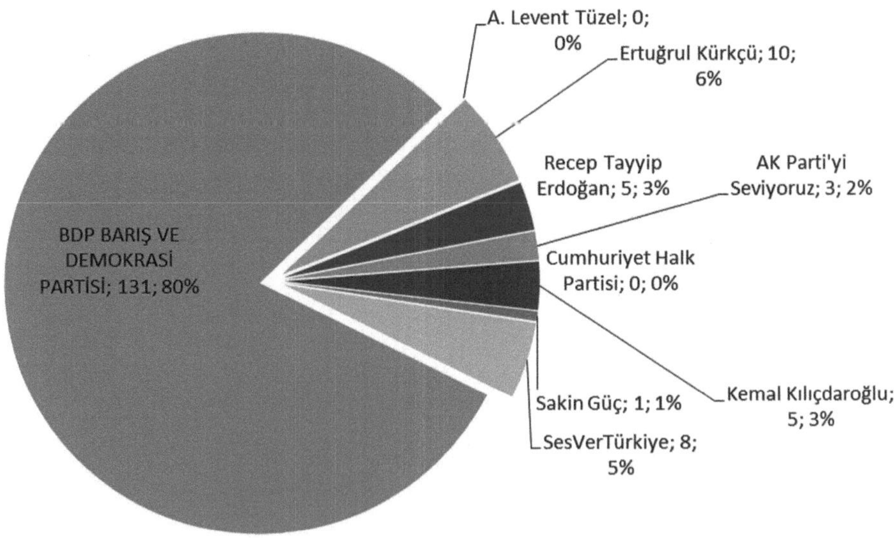

Fig. 10.2 Number of posts sent on June 12th

"Cumhuriyet Halk Partisi" used Facebook more intensively than the others did. The number of posts sent by this account is much higher than the other CHP accounts.

Figure 10.2 shows the posts sent on June 12th, the Election Day. The posts sent on the Election Day are of great importance because in Turkey the conventional media are banned from publishing or broadcasting anything related to the elections until the end of voting. However, there is no such ban on social media.

Since the frequency of posts changes, the daily post number in each account is divided by the total post number within the sample and converted to percentage.

The outlook of AKP posts on daily basis can be seen in Fig. 10.3.

An examination of the frequency of posts sent by AKP accounts shows that, during the election week, the number of posts sent by the accounts of Recep Tayyip Erdoğan and AK Parti'yi Seviyoruz exceeded the average number of posts sent by these accounts. It is seen that the number of posts sent by the account of Recep Tayyip Erdoğan is higher on the following days; April 22nd; May 1st, 18th, 15th, 19th and 30th; June 7th, 8th and 11th. The number of posts sent by AK Parti'yi Seviyoruz increased on the following days: April 5th; May 25th and 30th; June 5th, 6th, 7th, 8th, 9, 10th and 26th. No posts were sent by the account of Recep Tayyip Erdoğan on April 6th, May 3rd and June 18th. The account of AK Parti'yi Seviyoruz did not send any posts on April 21st and 29th; May 10th; June 14th, 15th and 29th.

Figure 10.4 shows the daily number of posts sent by CHP accounts.

An examination of the frequency of posts sent by CHP accounts show that the accounts of Cumhuriyet Halk Partisi and Sakin Güç were used much more frequently towards the end of May. The frequency of the posts sent by these accounts is at its peak between May 31st and June 12th. The account of Kemal Kılıçdaroğlu

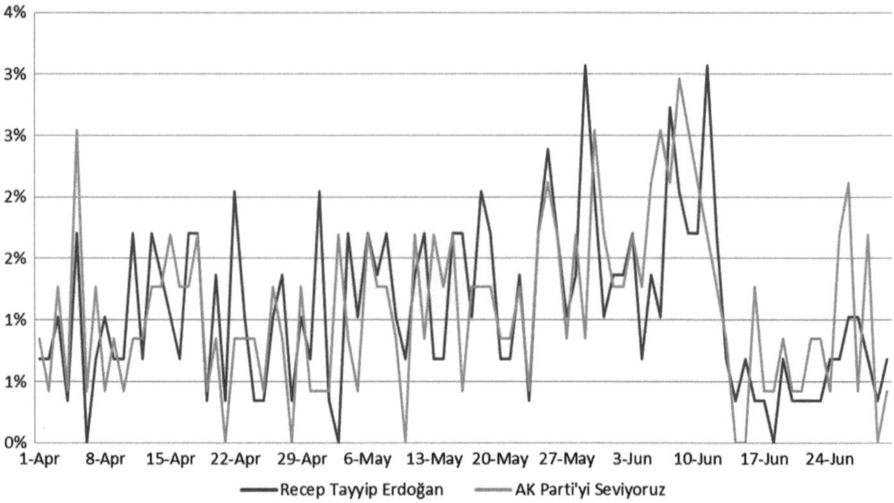

Fig. 10.3 AKP accounts daily post rates

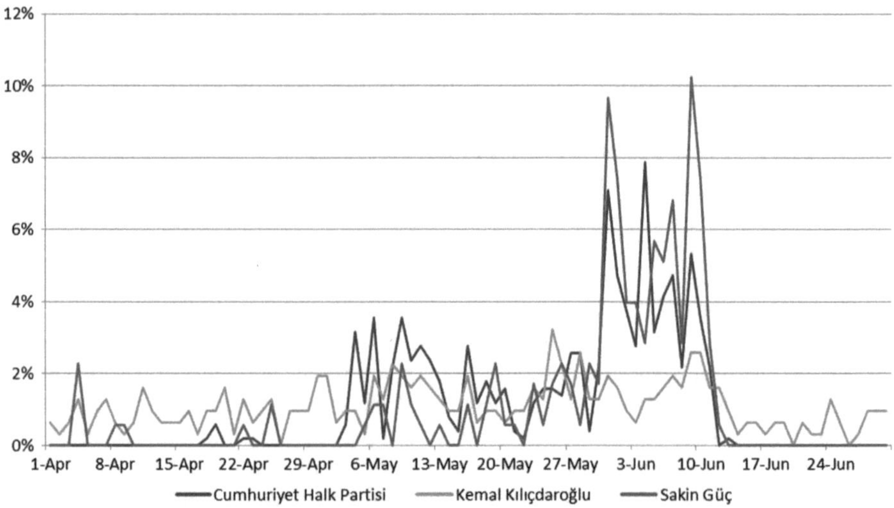

Fig. 10.4 CHP accounts daily post rates

is, however, used in a more stable way. Some posts are circulated over this account nearly every day. It is seen that during some days no posts are sent by the accounts of Sakin Güç and Cumhuriyet Halk Partisi in April and after June 12th.

The daily post rates of MHP and BDP accounts are shown in Fig. 10.5.

It is observed that there is a rather fluctuating trend in the SesVerTürkiye account representing MHP in the sample. On some days, there are no posts, but on some others, very many posts are circulated one after another. BDP Barış ve Demokrasi

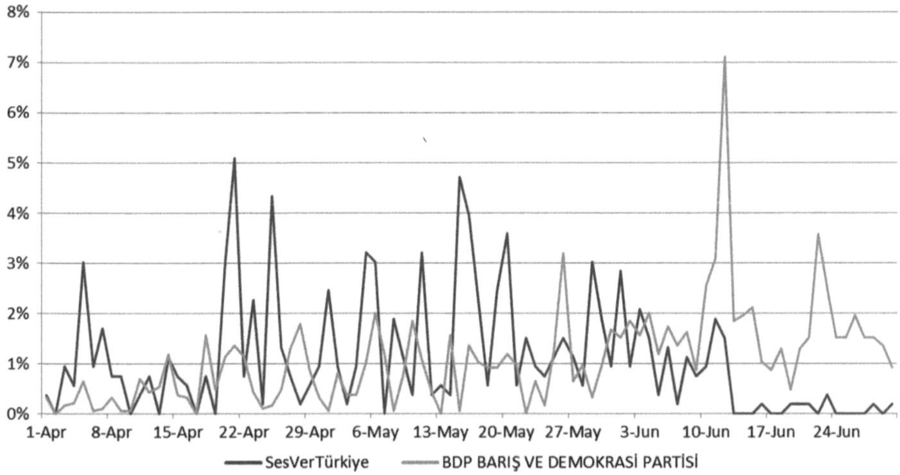

Fig. 10.5 MHP and BDP accounts daily post rates

Partisi, however, used its account quite frequently. There are only a few days when no post is sent by the account of Barış ve Demokrasi Partisi. The day when BDP used the account the most frequently is June 12th, 2011, the Election Day. The accounts are used a lot more on May 26th, June 10th, 11th, 15th, 22nd and 23rd compared to other days.

Figure 10.6 shows the daily practices of the independent candidates.

There are many days when A. Levent Tüzel did not send any posts. It is also observed that during some days lots of posts were consecutively circulated by the same account. May 31st, 2011 is the day when the account is used the most. There are no posts sent by the account of Ertuğrul Kürkçü on April 2nd, 4th, 8th and May 3rd and 6th. On other days, there is at least one post sent by Ertuğrul Kürkçü. Therefore, it can be said that this account is used in a stable way. This account is used the most on June 2nd, 2011. The account is used a lot also on June 12th, the Election Day and June 11th, the day before the election.

Below is the use of visual aids in the accounts (Fig. 10.7).

Visual aids in Facebook posts are used the most by the account of BDP Barış Ve Demokrasi Partisi with a ratio of 17.26 % (3,128). BDP is followed by AK Parti'yi Seviyoruz with a ratio of 14.41 % (34) and Sakin Güç with a ratio of 14.20 % (25). Another account where visuals are used on a large scale is the account of Kemal Kılıçdaroğlu. 12.54 % of the posts in this account (39) covered visuals. The proportion of the posts which covered visuals and are sent by the account of Recep Tayyip Erdoğan is, however, 6.48 % (19). The use of visuals in other accounts included in the sampling is below 5 %. The proportions of the posts with visuals sent by these accounts are as follows: Ertuğrul Kürkçü—3.38 % (12), A. Levent Tüzel—2.97 % (3), Cumhuriyet Halk Partisi—2.56 % (13) and SesVerTürkiye owned by MHP 1.70 % (9).

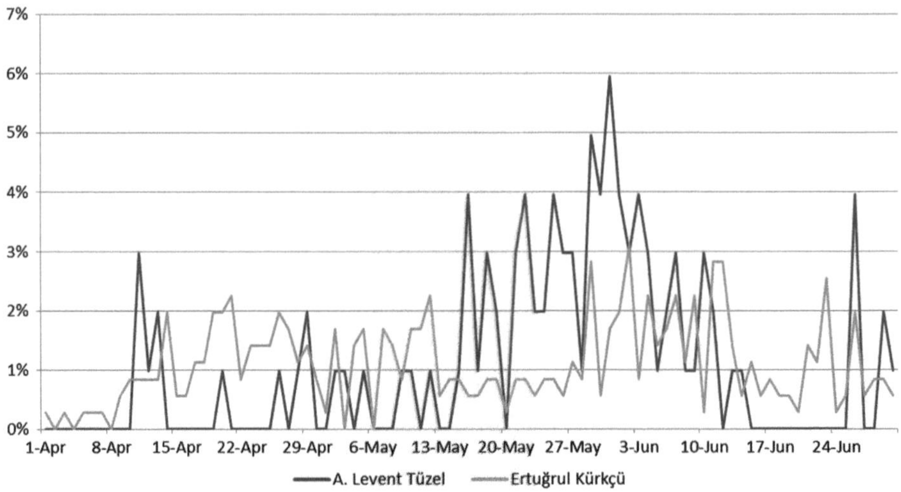

Fig. 10.6 Daily post rates of the accounts owned by independent candidates

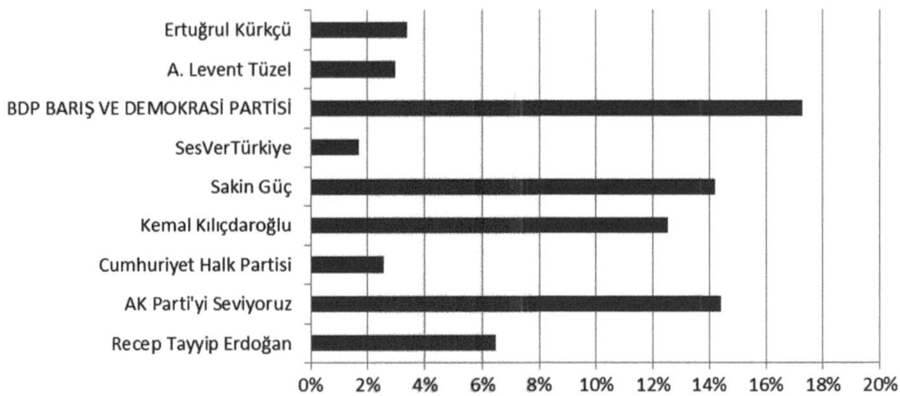

Fig. 10.7 Use of visual aids in the posts

It is detected that the content circulated by the accounts in question are specifically produced for Facebook (Fig. 10.8).

The ratio of contents specially produced for Facebook is clearly high in all accounts except the accounts of Cumhuriyet Halk Partisi owned by CHP and SesVerTürkiye owned by MHP. The numbers of the content specially produced for Facebook are as follows: Recep Tayyip Erdoğan—247, AK Parti'yi Seviyoruz—210, Cumhuriyet Halk Partisi—48, Kemal Kılıçdaroğlu—239, Sakin Güç—149, SesVerTürkiye—217, BDP Barış ve Demokrasi Partisi—1,757, A. Levent Tüzel—70 and Ertuğrul Kürkçü—327. 455 of the contents (89.57 %) in the account of Cumhuriyet Halk Partisi are shared on Facebook over Twitter. 13 contents from the account of Recep Tayyip Erdoğan and 1 content from the

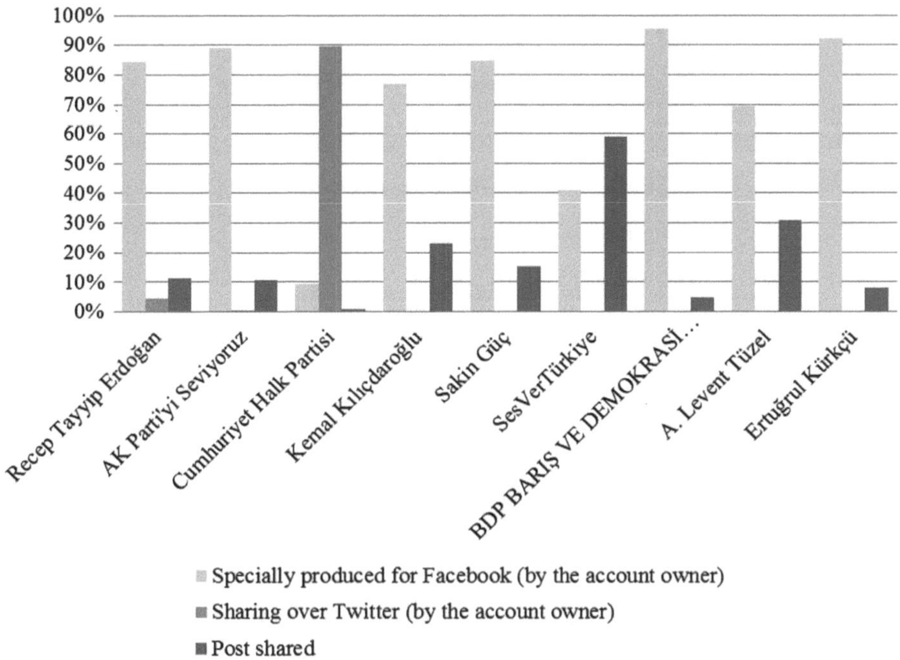

Fig. 10.8 Source of post

account of AK Parti'yi Seviyoruz are forwarded to Facebook in the same manner. The other accounts do not cover any contents shared on Facebook through Twitter. An examination of the posts sent by the accounts reveals that some part of the content circulated by all accounts consists of the posts shared. The post shared refers to the content that is shared and thus re-circulated by a Facebook user (over his/her account) within the Facebook network or another position on the Internet. The account that used this method the most is the account of SesVerTürkiye with 313 posts. The numbers of posts shared by the accounts are as follows: A. Levent Tüzel Facebook—31, Kemal Kılıçdaroğlu—72, Sakin Güç—27, Recep Tayyip Erdoğan—33 and AK Parti'yi Seviyoruz—25. The posts shared by other accounts are below 10 % of all the contents. The numbers of posts shared by these accounts are as follows: Cumhuriyet Halk Partisi—5, BDP Barış ve Demokrasi Partisi—85, and Ertuğrul Kürkçü—28.

Figure 10.9 shows the themes of the posts sent from Facebook accounts.

The theme "his/her own party" is present in most of the posts. This theme is preferred by A. Levent Tüzel the most with a ratio of 98.02 % (99). He is followed by Ertuğrul Kürkçü with a ratio of 92.68 % (329) and Kemal Kılıçdaroğlu with a ratio of 91.32 % (284). The ratios of the posts covering "his/her own party" theme as per the other accounts in the sampling are as follows: SesVerTürkiye 85.28 % (452), BDP Barış ve Demokrasi Partisi 82.52 % (1,520), Cumhuriyet Halk Partisi

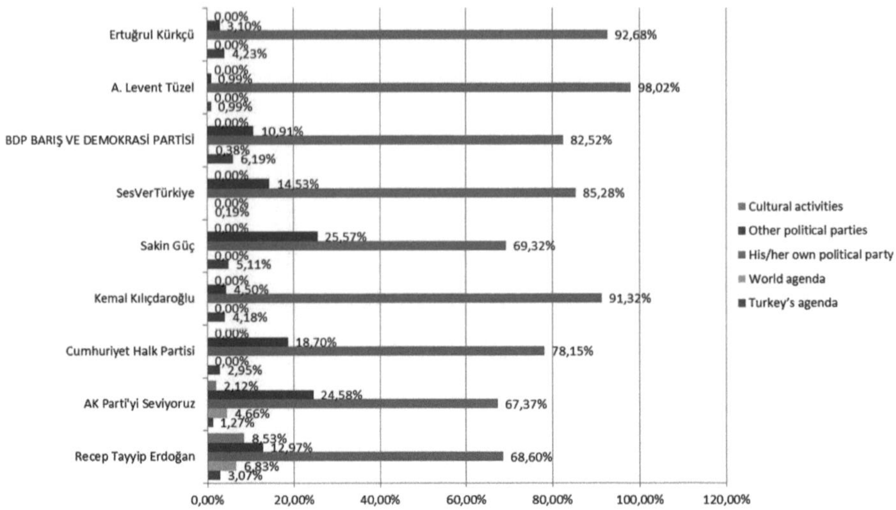

Fig. 10.9 Themes of posts

78.15 % (397), Sakin Güç 69.32 % (122), Recep Tayyip Erdoğan 68.60 % (201), and AK Parti'yi Seviyoruz 67.37 % (159).

The second most preferred theme in Facebook posts is "other political parties". The account which preferred this theme the most is Sakin Güç with a ratio of 25.57 % (45). It is followed by AK Parti'yi Seviyoruz with a ratio of 24.58 % (58). The account with the lowest number of the theme "other political parties" is that of A. Levent Tüzel with a ratio of 0.99 % (1). The distribution of the theme "other political parties" as per the accounts is as follows: Cumhuriyet Halk Partisi—18.70 % (95), SesVerTürkiye—14.53 % (77), Recep Tayyip Erdoğan—12.97 % (38), BDP Barış ve Demokrasi Partisi—10.91 % (201), Kemal Kılıçdaroğlu—4.50 % (14), and Ertuğrul Kürkçü—3.10 % (11).

The other themes used in Facebook accounts are "Turkey's agenda", "World Agenda" and "Cultural Activities". The theme "World Agenda" is used by 6.83 % (20) in the account of Recep Tayyip Erdoğan, (20), by 4.66 % (11) in the account of AK Parti'yi Seviyoruz and by 0.38 % (7) in the account of BDP Barış ve Demokrasi Partisi. The other accounts did not cover any contents related to the theme "World Agenda". It is seen that the theme "Cultural Activities" is used only in two accounts, which are the accounts of Recep Tayyip Erdoğan by 8.53 % (25) and AK Parti'yi Seviyoruz by 2.12 % (5).

It is observed that there are other types of links in Facebook posts (Fig. 10.10).

A great majority or the posts sent by the accounts of BDP Barış ve Demokrasi Partisi and A. Levent Tüzel did not cover any link address and were specifically written for Facebook. The number of such posts is 1287 (69.87 %) in the account of BDP Barış ve Demokrasi Partisi and 62 (61.39 %) in the account of A. Levent Tüzel. The numbers of Facebook posts without any link addresses are as follows: Recep Tayyip Erdoğan—59, AK Parti'yi Seviyoruz—58, Cumhuriyet Halk

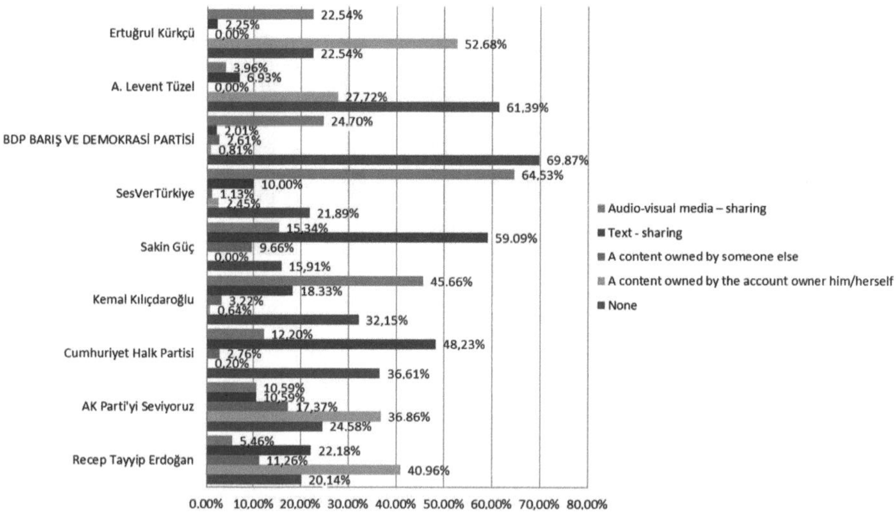

Fig. 10.10 Use of links within posts

Partisi—186, Kemal Kılıçdaroğlu—28, Sakin Güç—28, SesVerTürkiye—116 and Ertuğrul Kürkçü—80. In most of the posts sent by the accounts of Recep Tayyip Erdoğan and Ertuğrul Kürkçü, a link address to a Facebook content that belongs to the account owner was shared. The numbers of posts with such a link address are as follows: Recep Tayyip Erdoğan—120 (40.96 %), Ertuğrul Kürkçü—187 (52.68 %), AK Parti'yi Seviyoruz—87, Cumhuriyet Halk Partisi—1, Kemal Kılıçdaroğlu-2, SesVerTürkiye -13, BDP Barış ve Demokrasi Partisi—15 and A. Levent Tüzel—28. The account of Sakin Güç did not include any link address to a Facebook content that belongs to the account owner. The number of link addresses to a Facebook account owned by someone else is low in all accounts, and A. Levent Tüzel and Ertuğrul Kürkçü did not share such a link address at all. The account with the highest number of link addresses to a Facebook content owned by another user is AK Parti'yi Seviyoruz with 41 posts (17.37 %). Although BDP account seems to take the lead with 48 posts including a link to another content, such posts constitute 2.61 % of their posts. The numbers of posts with a link address to a Facebook content owned by another user are as follows: Recep Tayyip Erdoğan—33, Cumhuriyet Halk Partisi—14, Kemal Kılıçdaroğlu—10, Sakin Güç—17, SesVerTürkiye—6. Recirculation of a Facebook post belonging to the account owner or another user through other posts is significant in that discourse and expressions created on Facebook can, thus, be spread to a higher number of users. At this point, the posts sent by another person's Facebook account may make up the opinion of candidates, supporters and electors.

An examination of the sharings of the web-content apart from the Facebook posts reveals that there are two types of content, which are web-based text and audio-visual media. Under both groups are the digital copies of the traditional media productions and user-derived contents. The sharing of web-based content

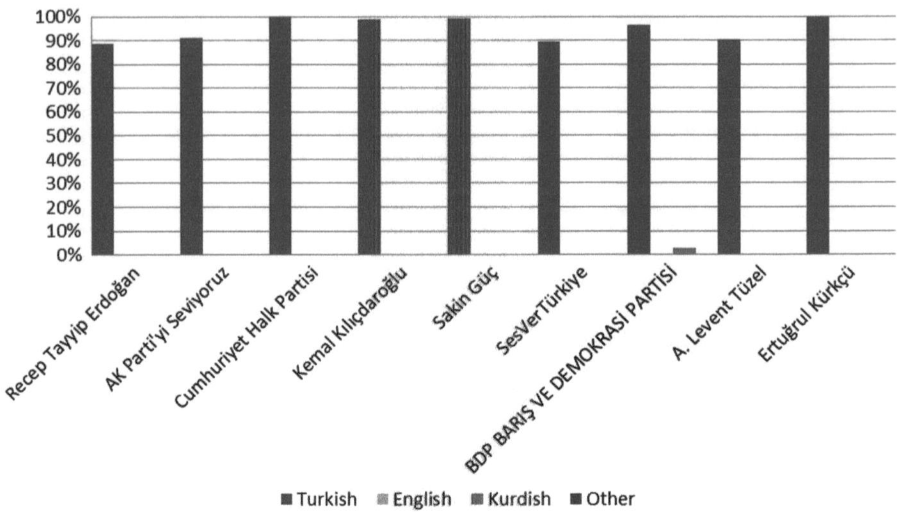

Fig. 10.11 Language of the post

such as blog articles or the news on news websites is seen in the account of Sakin Güç the most with a ratio of 59.09 % (104), which is followed by the Cumhuriyet Halk Partisi with a ratio of 48.23 % (245). The number of the web-based content on Facebook recirculated by other accounts on Facebook are as follows: Recep Tayyip Erdoğan—65, AK Parti'yi Seviyoruz—25, Kemal Kılıçdaroğlu—57, SesVerTürkiye—53, BDP Barış ve Demokrasi Partisi—37, A. Levent Tüzel—7 and Ertuğrul Kürkçü—8. The sharing of audio-visual web content such as videos is seen the most in SesVerTürkiye account with a ratio of 64.53 % (342), followed by Kemal Kılıçdaroğlu account with a ratio of 45.66 % (142). The highest sharing in number belongs to BDP Barış ve Demokrasi Partisi with 455 posts (24.70 %). The numbers of the posts including audio-visual content are as follows: Recep Tayyip Erdoğan—16, AK Parti'yi Seviyoruz—25, Cumhuriyet Halk Partisi-62, Sakin Güç—27, A. Levent Tüzel—4 and Ertuğrul Kürkçü—80.

An examination of the language used in the Facebook accounts within our sampling shows that nearly all of the posts are in Turkish (Fig. 10.11).

260 posts in the account of Recep Tayyip Erdoğan, 215 posts in the account of AK Parti'yi Seviyoruz, 508 posts in the account of Cumhuriyet Halk Partisi, 307 posts in the account of Kemal Kılıçdaroğlu, 175 posts in the account of Sakin Güç, 474 posts in the account of SesVerTürkiye, 1,777 posts in the account of BDP Barış ve Demokrasi Partisi, 91 posts in the account of A. Levent Tüzel and 354 posts in the account of Ertuğrul Kürkçü are in Turkish. A language other than Turkish is very rarely used in the posts. 1 post is in English in the account of Recep Tayyip Erdoğan. BDP Barış ve Demokrasi Partisi sent 5 posts in English in addition to 47 posts sent in Kurdish. The posts which are not composed as a text but appeared as a result of the activities on the interface can be displayed in other languages

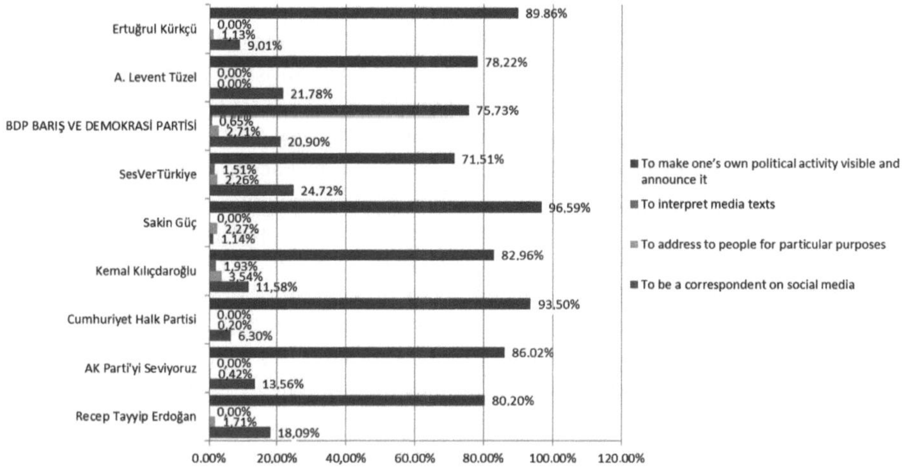

Fig. 10.12 Purposes of sending posts

supported by the interface. Such posts (e.g. the posts signalling that a photo is added to the album) are not coded in any language.

An examination of the purposes of sending posts through the Facebook accounts in our sampling shows that the most common purpose is to "make one's own political activity visible and announce it" (Fig. 10.12).

The graphic shows that the usage ratios of Facebook posts for the purpose of "making one's own political activity visible and announcing it" as per the accounts as follows: Sakin Güç—96.59 % (170), Cumhuriyet Halk Partisi—93.50 % (475), Ertuğrul Kürkçü—89.86 % (319), AK Parti'yi Seviyoruz—86.02 % (203), Kemal Kılıçdaroğlu—82.96 % (258), Recep Tayyip Erdoğan—80.20 % (235), A. Levent Tüzel—78.22 % (79), BDP Barış ve Demokrasi Partisi—75.73 % (1,395) and SesVerTürkiye- 71.51 % (379).

The account which used Facebook posts for the purpose of "being a correspondent on social media" the most is SesVerTürkiye with a ratio of 24.72 % (131), followed by the account of A. Levent Tüzel 21.78 % (22) and BDP Barış ve Demokrasi Partisi with a ratio of 20.90 % (385). The purpose of being a correspondent on social media is below 20 % in other accounts. The ratios of posts sent for the purpose of being a correspondent on social media are as follows: Recep Tayyip Erdoğan—18.09 % (53), AK Parti'yi Seviyoruz—13.56 % (32), Kemal Kılıçdaroğlu—11.58 % (36), Ertuğrul Kürkçü—9.01 % (32) and Cumhuriyet Halk Partisi—6.30 % (32). The lowest ratio in this category belongs to the account of Sakin Güç, which is 1.14 % (2).

In the accounts apart from that of A. Levent Tüzel, we detected posts serving the purpose of "addressing to people for particular purposes". This purpose is most visible in the account of Kemal Kılıçdaroğlu. 3.54 % (11) of the posts in this account covered a special address to people. The ratio of posts with a special address to people varies from 0.20 % to 2.27 %.

Different from other accounts in our sampling, the accounts of Kemal Kılıçdaroğlu, SesVerTürkiye and BDP Barış ve Demokrasi Partisi shared posts for the purpose of "interpreting media texts". The ratios of posts sent for this purpose are as follows: Kemal Kılıçdaroğlu—1.93 % (6), SesVerTürkiye—1.51 % (8) and Barış ve Demokrasi Partisi—0.65 % (12).

An examination of the target group of the posts on Facebook accounts reveals that the target group is mainly composed by "general electors".

The number of posts targeting the general voters as per the accounts are as follows: Recep Tayyip Erdoğan—273, AK Parti'yi Seviyoruz—215, Cumhuriyet Halk Partisi—495, Kemal Kılıçdaroğlu—284, Sakin Güç—175, SesVerTürkiye—464, BDP Barış ve Demokrasi Partisi—1,553, A. Levent Tüzel—77 and Ertuğrul Kürkçü—330. In all accounts included in the sampling, the second target group of the posts is the party's own electors, though the number of posts may vary. The numbers of posts targeting the party's own electors are as follows: Recep Tayyip Erdoğan—4, AK Parti'yi Seviyoruz—4, Cumhuriyet Halk Partisi—9, Kemal Kılıçdaroğlu—23, Sakin Güç—1, SesVerTürkiye—66, BDP Barış ve Demokrasi Partisi—258, A. Levent Tüzel—24 and Ertuğrul Kürkçü—25. There are posts targeting "other electors", too: Recep Tayyip Erdoğan—11, AK Parti'yi Seviyoruz—10, Kemal Kılıçdaroğlu—2 and BDP Barış ve Demokrasi Partisi—15. An examination of other categories shows that only in the account of AK Parti'yi Seviyoruz, there is 1 post targeting the "party members and delegates". The accounts targeting international public opinion and organisations and the number of posts aimed at them are as follows: Recep Tayyip Erdoğan—5, AK Parti'yi Seviyoruz—6, Cumhuriyet Halk Partisi—14, BDP Barış ve Demokrasi Partisi—14. In the accounts of Cumhuriyet Halk Partisi 3 and BDP Barış ve Demokrasi Partisi 2, some posts are also targeting individuals with whom there is a private conversation.

An examination of words and word groups used in the posts shows that the posts sent by the accounts of Recep Tayyip Erdoğan, AK Parti'yi Seviyoruz, BDP Barış ve Demokrasi Partisi and Ertuğrul Kürkçü mainly cover connotations (Fig. 10.13). The words are used with their connotations in 62 posts sent by the account of Recep Tayyip Erdoğan, 91 posts sent by the account of AK Parti'yi Seviyoruz, 194 posts sent by the account of BDP Barış ve Demokrasi Partisi and 83 posts sent by the account of Ertuğrul Kürkçü. The number of idioms used in the posts of Recep Tayyip Erdoğan is equal to the number of posts with connotations. In that account, idioms are frequently used. The numbers of posts covering idioms as per the accounts are as follows: Cumhuriyet Halk Partisi—160, Kemal Kılıçdaroğlu—79, Sakin Güç—68, SesVerTürkiye—76, BDP Barış ve Demokrasi Partisi—175 and Ertuğrul Kürkçü—30. In these accounts, idioms constitute the most frequently used words and word groups. In the account of AK Parti'yi Seviyoruz, there are 50 posts with idioms constituting one third of the most frequently used word group in this account. The second most frequently used word group in the account of AK Parti'yi Seviyoruz is metonymy, with 52 posts in this category. The numbers of posts with metonymy as per the accounts are as follows: Recep Tayyip Erdoğan—41, Cumhuriyet Halk Partisi—61, Kemal Kılıçdaroğlu—4, Sakin Güç—3,

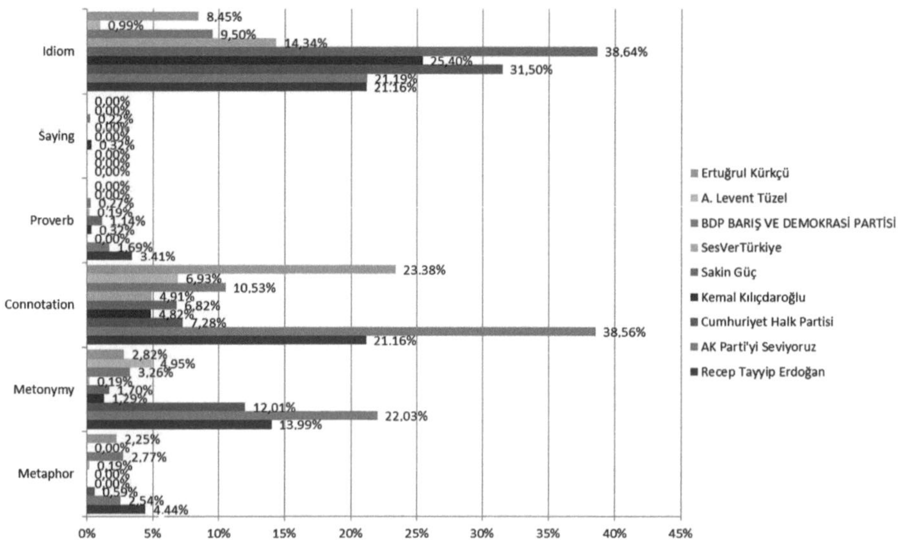

Fig. 10.13 Words and word groups in the posts

SesVerTürkiye—1, BDP Barış ve Demokrasi Partisi—60, A. Levent Tüzel—5 and Ertuğrul Kürkçü—10. The use of metaphors in the posts is as follows: Recep Tayyip Erdoğan—13 posts, AK Parti'yi Seviyoruz—6 posts, SesVerTürkiye—1 post, BDP Barış ve Demokrasi Partisi—51 posts and Ertuğrul Kürkçü—8 posts. The use of proverbs in the posts is low. 10 posts in Recep Tayyip Erdoğan's account, 4 posts in AK Parti'yi Seviyoruz account, 1 post in Kemal Kılıçdaroğlu's account, 2 posts in Sakin Güç account, 1 post in SesVerTürkiye account and 5 posts in BDP Barış ve Demokrasi Partisi account contain proverbs. An examination of sayings in the posts shows that Kemal Kılıçdaroğlu used a saying in 1 post and BDP Barış ve Demokrasi Partisi used a saying in 4 posts.

The style of the posts is coded as reproach, mockery, teasing, despising, extolling, praising, provocation and settlement. All options available for each post are marked in the coding table (Fig. 10.14).

The analysis revealed that the most preferred style in the posts is "praising". The numbers of posts including "praising" as per the accounts are as follows: Recep Tayyip Erdoğan—208, AK Parti'yi Seviyoruz—149, Cumhuriyet Halk Partisi—345, Kemal Kılıçdaroğlu—232, Sakin Güç—107, SesVerTürkiye—273, BDP Barış ve Demokrasi Partisi—1,085, A. Levent Tüzel—99 and Ertuğrul Kürkçü—235. With the exception of the account of SesVerTürkiye, the second most preferred style in posts is teasing. The numbers of posts including "teasing" as per the accounts are as follows: Recep Tayyip Erdoğan—82, AK Parti'yi Seviyoruz—89, Cumhuriyet Halk Partisi—166, Kemal Kılıçdaroğlu—77, Sakin Güç 65, BDP Barış ve Demokrasi Partisi—516, A. Levent Tüzel—2 and Ertuğrul Kürkçü—87. The second most frequently used style in the account of SesVerTürkiye is provocation with a ratio of 27.92 % (148). Provocation is followed by teasing with a ratio of

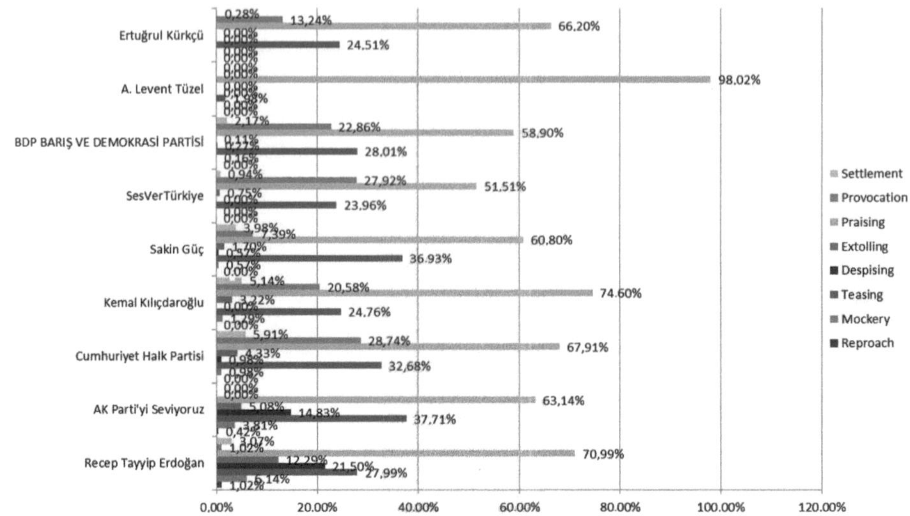

Fig. 10.14 Style of posts

23.96 % (127). The third most preferred style in the accounts of Recep Tayyip Erdoğan and AK Parti'yi Seviyoruz is "despising" with a ratio of respectively 21.50 % (63) and 14.83 % (35). "Provocation" is the third most preferred style in the accounts of Cumhuriyet Halk Partisi—28.74 % (146), Kemal Kılıçdaroğlu—20.58 % (64), Sakin Güç—7.39 % (13), BDP Barış ve Demokrasi Partisi—22.86 % (421) and Ertuğrul Kürkçü—13.24 % (47). The other posts which gave place to despising are the accounts of Cumhuriyet Halk Partisi (5 posts), BDP Barış ve Demokrasi Partisi (5 posts), Sakin Güç (1 post). The accounts which gave place to "extolling" are the accounts of Recep Tayyip Erdoğan (36 posts), AK Parti'yi Seviyoruz (12 posts), Cumhuriyet Halk Partisi (22 posts), Kemal Kılıçdaroğlu (10 posts), Sakin Güç (3 posts), SesVerTürkiye (4 posts) and BDP Barış ve Demokrasi Partisi (2 posts).

The numbers of posts giving place to "settlement" as per the accounts are as follows: Recep Tayyip Erdoğan—9, Cumhuriyet Halk Partisi—30, Kemal Kılıçdaroğlu—16, Sakin Güç—7, SesVerTürkiye—5, BDP Barış ve Demokrasi Partisi—40 and Ertuğrul Kürkçü—1. The numbers of posts giving place to "mockery" as per the accounts are as follows: Recep Tayyip Erdoğan—18, AK Parti'yi Seviyoruz—9, Cumhuriyet Halk Partisi—5, Kemal Kılıçdaroğlu—1 and BDP Barış ve Demokrasi Partisi—3. Although the number of posts giving place to reproach is low, 3 posts sent from the account of Recep Tayyip Erdoğan and 1 post sent from the account of AK Parti'yi Seviyoruz were marked by reproach as a style.

The most widely used subject in the posts is "his/her own party" (Fig. 10.15). It is observed that the same title is applicable to the posts of independent candidates, as well. The title of "his/her own party" refers to the independent candidates' own campaign activities.

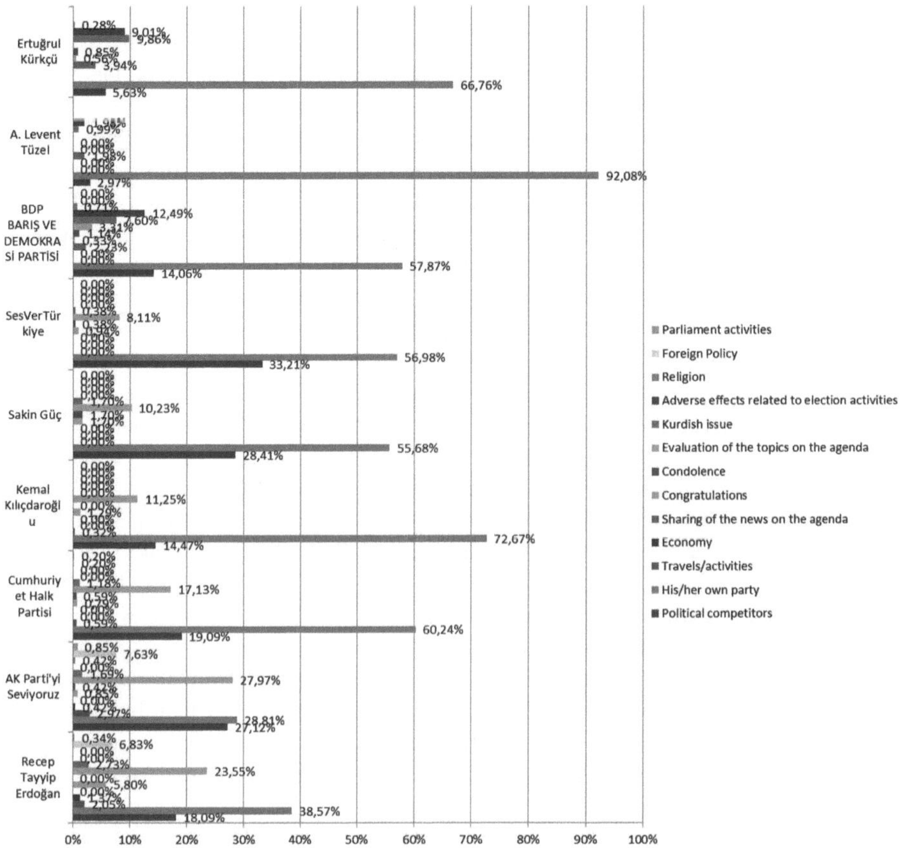

Fig. 10.15 Subject of the post

The numbers of posts giving place to the subject of "his/her own party" as per the accounts are as follows: A. Levent Tüzel—93, Kemal Kılıçdaroğlu—226, Ertuğrul Kürkçü—237, Cumhuriyet Halk Partisi—306, BDP Barış ve Demokrasi Partisi—1,066, SesVerTürkiye—302, Sakin Güç—98, Recep Tayyip Erdoğan—113 and AK Parti'yi Seviyoruz—68. The second most widely used subject in the accounts of Recep Tayyip Erdoğan (69) and AK Parti'yi Seviyoruz (66) is the "evaluation of the topics on the agenda". The third most widely used subject in these accounts is "political competitors". 53 posts sent from the account of Recep Tayyip Erdoğan and 64 posts sent from the account of AK Parti'yi Seviyoruz are marked by the subject of "political competitors". The posts coded under the subject of "political competitors" constituted the second most widely used subject in the sharings of the following accounts: Cumhuriyet Halk Partisi (97), Kemal Kılıçdaroğlu (45), Sakin Güç (50), SesVerTürkiye (176), BDP Barış ve Demokrasi Partisi (256) and A. Levent Tüzel (3). The second most widely used subject in the account of Ertuğrul Kürkçü is the Kurdish problem with 35 posts. It is followed by "adverse effects related to election activities" (32). The fourth most widely used subject in this account is "political competitors" (20). The subject of "adverse effects related to campaign activities" can be seen in the accounts of BDP Barış ve Demokrasi Partisi (230) and A. Levent Tüzel (2) in addition to the account of Ertuğrul Kürkçü, while the other accounts examined within this research did not give place to this subject. The subject of "adverse effects related to campaign activities" constituted the third most widely used subject in the posts of BDP Barış ve Demokrasi Partisi. The subject of "evaluation of the subjects on the agenda" was the third most widely used subject in the accounts of Cumhuriyet Halk Partisi (87), Kemal Kılıçdaroğlu (35), Sakin Güç (18) and SesVerTürkiye (43). 61 posts sent from the account of BDP Barış ve Demokrasi Partisi gave place to the subject of "evaluation of the subjects on the agenda", which constituted the fourth most widely used subject in the posts of this account. The posts coded under "Kurdish issue" can be seen in all accounts except for the account of Kemal Kılıçdaroğlu, though not so high in number. The account that gave place to this subject the most is the account of BDP Barış ve Demokrasi Partisi with 140 posts. The numbers of posts which covered this subject are as follows as per the accounts: Recep Tayyip Erdoğan—8, AK Parti'yi Seviyoruz—4, Cumhuriyet Halk Partisi—6, Sakin Güç—3, SesVerTürkiye—2 and A. Levent Tüzel—1.

The accounts which shared posts related to the parliament activities are Recep Tayyip Erdoğan (1), AK Parti'yi Seviyoruz (2) and Cumhuriyet Halk Partisi (1). The posts covering the subject of foreign policy were sent from the accounts of Recep Tayyip Erdoğan (20), AK Parti'yi Seviyoruz (18) and Cumhuriyet Halk Partisi (1). Other accounts did not use this subject at all. The accounts which gave place to the subject of religion and the number of posts are as follows: BDP Barış ve Demokrasi Partisi—13, AK Parti'yi Seviyoruz—1, Ertuğrul Kürkçü—1. All accounts, excluding that of A. Levent Tüzel, gave place to the subjects of congratulation and condolence, though not so much. The number of posts with the subject of applause are as follows: Recep Tayyip Erdoğan—17, AK Parti'yi Seviyoruz—2, Cumhuriyet Halk Partisi—4, Kemal Kılıçdaroğlu—4, Sakin Güç—3, SesVerTürkiye—5, BDP Barış ve Demokrasi Partisi—6 and Ertuğrul Kürkçü—2. The numbers of posts with the subject of condolence are as follows: AK Parti'yi Seviyoruz—1, Cumhuriyet Halk Partisi—3, Sakin Güç—3, Ertuğrul Kürkçü -3, SesVerTürkiye—2 and BDP Barış ve Demokrasi Partisi—21. A. Levent Tüzel gave place to neither condolence nor applause. Recep Tayyip Erdoğan and Kemal Kılıçdaroğlu did not give any place to condolence in their posts. The subject of sharing the news on the agenda was present in 41 posts sent by the account of BDP Barış ve Demokrasi Partisi, 2 posts sent by the account of A. Levent Tüzel and 14 posts sent by the account of Ertuğrul Kürkçü. The other accounts did not cover this subject. The subject of economy is seen only in the following accounts: Recep Tayyip Erdoğan (4 posts) and AK Parti'yi Seviyoruz (1 post). The accounts which gave place to travels and activities are as follows: Recep Tayyip Erdoğan (6), AK Parti'yi Seviyoruz (7), Cumhuriyet Halk Partisi (3) and Kemal Kılıçdaroğlu (1).

There are also other subjects that are included in the coding, but they are not covered in the graphic because they are observed only in a few posts. The subjects

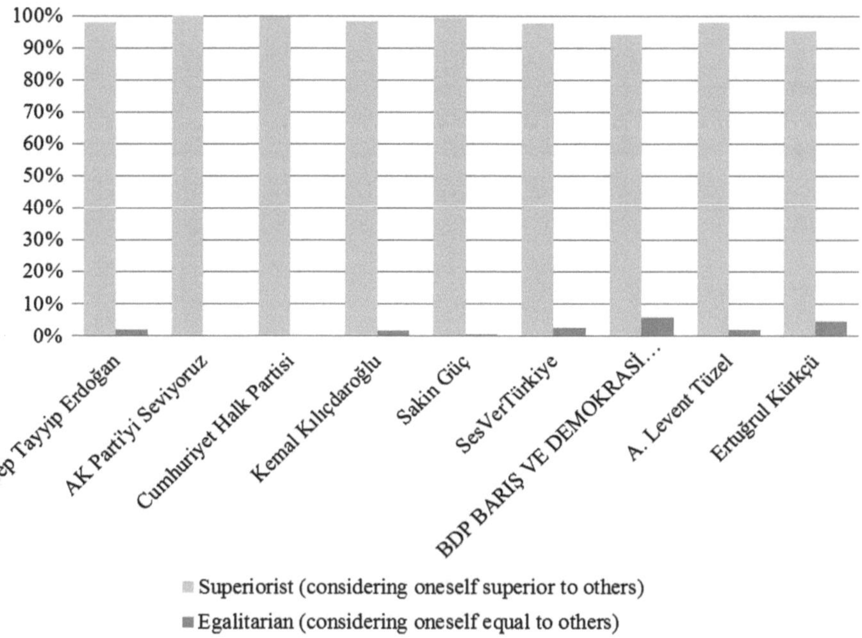

Fig. 10.16 Perspective of the language

in question and the number of posts covering them are as follows: "Use of traditional media for political identity" is present in 2 posts sent by Recep Tayyip Erdoğan and 3 posts sent by BDP Barış ve Demokrasi Partisi. "Opening an institution and activity of the local institution" is present in 7 posts sent by Ertuğrul Kürkçü. "Personal agenda" is present in 1 post of BDP Barış ve Demokrasi Partisi. "Thanks for the election result" is present in 3 posts sent by the account of Ertuğrul Kürkçü. "Sports events" was present in 1 post of Sakin Güç. "Request from the electors" is present in 1 post of Ertuğrul Kürkçü. "Turkish Armed Forces" is present in 2 posts sent by AK Parti'yi Seviyoruz. There are also other subjects which are included in the coding table but are not covered by any posts. These are: "EU-related issues", "Election campaign announcements", "Wishes about the elections", "Local agenda of the polling district" and "Social events".

An examination of the perspective in the language of posts on Facebook accounts has revealed that nearly all of the posts had a "superiorist" perspective, i.e., not "egalitarian" (Fig. 10.16).

The ratios of the Facebook posts written with a superiorist standpoint are as follows per accounts: AK Parti'yi Seviyoruz—100 % (236), Cumhuriyet Halk Partisi—99.61 % (506), Sakin Güç—99.43 % (175), Kemal Kılıçdaroğlu—98.39 % (306), A. Levent Tüzel—98.02 % (99), Recep Tayyip Erdoğan- 97.95 % (287), SesVerTürkiye—97.55 % (517), Ertuğrul Kürkçü—95.21 % (338) and BDP Barış ve Demokrasi Partisi—94.25 % (1,736). The accounts, excluding those of AK Parti'yi Seviyoruz, shared some posts with an egalitarian standpoint, though not so

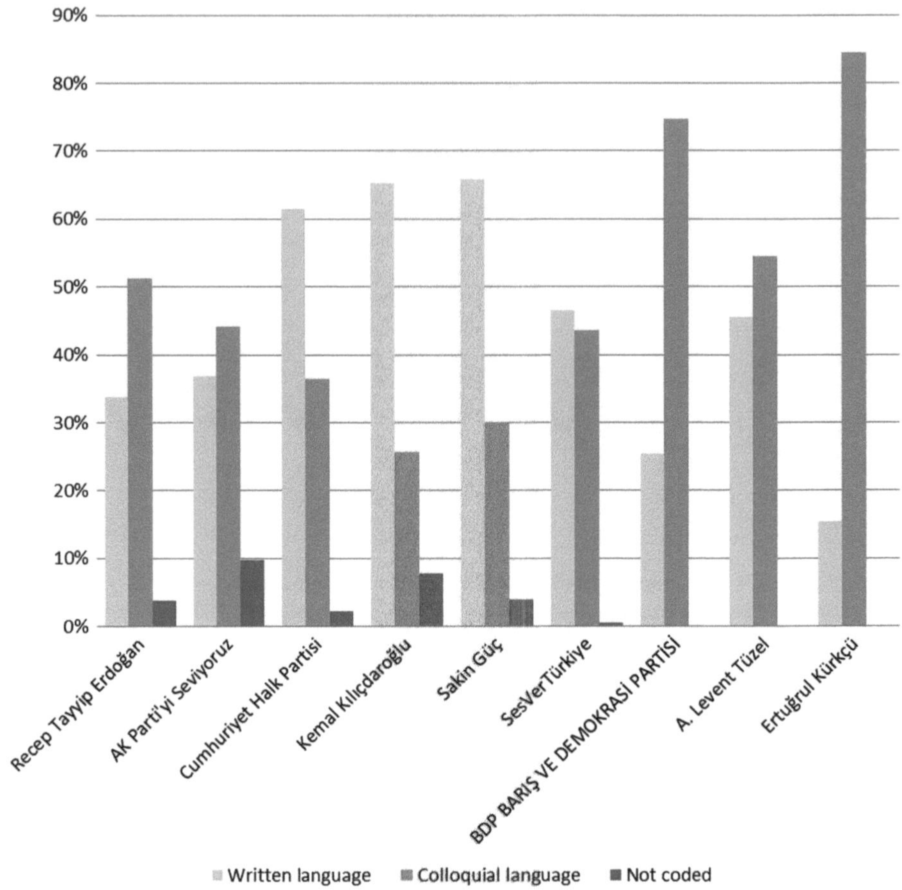

Fig. 10.17 Register of language

many. The account which adopted the egalitarian standpoint the most is BDP Barış ve Demokrasi Partisi with a ratio of 5.75 % (106 posts). The account which adopted the egalitarian standpoint the least is the Cumhuriyet Halk Partisi with a ratio of 0.39 % (2). The use of egalitarian language is as follows in other accounts: Ertuğrul Kürkçü—4.79 % (17), SesVerTürkiye—2.45 % (13), Recep Tayyip Erdoğan—2.05 % (6), A. Levent Tüzel—1.98 % (2), Kemal Kılıçdaroğlu—1.61 % (5) and Sakin Güç—0.57 % (1).

An examination of the register of language used in the posts shows that Ertuğrul Kürkçü usually preferred the colloquial language (Fig. 10.17).

The ratio of colloquial language used in the posts of Ertuğrul Kürkçü is 84.51 % (300), while the ratio of written language in the same account is 15.49 % (55). From this perspective, it can be said that the account which used the written language the least is Ertuğrul Kürkçü. The second account with a high ratio of colloquial language is the account of BDP Barış ve Demokrasi Partisi (74.65 %) with 1,375

Table 10.7 The most frequently repeated words as per the accounts

Word	The number of accounts where the word is repeated	The account	Number of repetition
Seçim (Election)	7	BDP Barış ve Demokrasi Partisi	201
		Ertuğrul Kürkçü	52
		Cumhuriyet Halk Partisi	25
		SesVerTürkiye	22
		Kemal Kılıçdaroğlu	19
		Sakin Güç	11
		A. Levent Tüzel	10
Türkiye (Turkey)	6	Kemal Kılıçdaroğlu	80
		AK Parti'yi Seviyoruz	40
		SesVerTürkiye	38
		Recep Tayyip Erdoğan	37
		Cumhuriyet Halk Partisi	24
		Sakin Güç	17
Genel (General)	6	Cumhuriyet Halk Partisi	107
		Kemal Kılıçdaroğlu	34
		SesVerTürkiye	33
		Recep Tayyip Erdoğan	27
		AK Parti'yi Seviyoruz	18
		Sakin Güç	9
Demokrasi (Democracy)	5	BDP Barış ve Demokrasi Partisi	512
		Ertuğrul Kürkçü	74
		A. Levent Tüzel	31
		Cumhuriyet Halk Partisi	21
		Sakin Güç	8
CHP	5	Cumhuriyet Halk Partisi	108
		Sakin Güç	58
		Kemal Kılıçdaroğlu	37
		AK Parti'yi Seviyoruz	29
		Recep Tayyip Erdoğan	20
Yeni (New)	5	SesVerTürkiye	77
		Recep Tayyip Erdoğan	47
			40

(continued)

Table 10.7 (continued)

Word	The number of accounts where the word is repeated	The account	Number of repetition
		AK Parti'yi Seviyoruz	
		Kemal Kılıçdaroğlu	30
		A. Levent Tüzel	23
İstanbul (Istanbul)	4	Cumhuriyet Halk Partisi	21
		AK Parti'yi Seviyoruz	18
		Sakin Güç	13
		A. Levent Tüzel	7
Kendi (Own)	3	BDP Barış ve Demokrasi Partisi	258
		SesVerTürkiye	38
		AK Parti'yi Seviyoruz	18
Özgürlük (Freedom)	3	BDP Barış ve Demokrasi Partisi	159
		Ertuğrul Kürkçü	89
		A. Levent Tüzel	29
Milletvekili (Deputy)	3	BDP Barış ve Demokrasi Partisi	230
		Ertuğrul Kürkçü	34
		A. Levent Tüzel	6
Kürt (Kurdish)	3	BDP Barış ve Demokrasi Partisi	201
		Ertuğrul Kürkçü	38
		A. Levent Tüzel	5
Kemal	3	Kemal Kılıçdaroğlu	144
		Cumhuriyet Halk Partisi	53
		Sakin Güç	31
Emek (Labour)	3	BDP Barış ve Demokrasi Partisi	108
		Ertuğrul Kürkçü	61
		A. Levent Tüzel	27
Kılıçdaroğlu	3	Kemal Kılıçdaroğlu	110
		Cumhuriyet Halk Partisi	51
		Sakin Güç	18
AKP	3	BDP Barış ve Demokrasi Partisi	151
		Sakin Güç	13
		SesVerTürkiye	13
Blok(u) (Block)	3	BDP Barış ve Demokrasi Partisi	112
		Ertuğrul Kürkçü	56
		A. Levent Tüzel	8

(continued)

Table 10.7 (continued)

Word	The number of accounts where the word is repeated	The account	Number of repetition
Bağımsız (Independent)	3	BDP Barış ve Demokrasi Partisi	127
		Ertuğrul Kürkçü	31
		A. Levent Tüzel	7
Oy (Vote)	3	BDP Barış ve Demokrasi Partisi	104
		Cumhuriyet Halk Partisi	25
		Sakin Güç	8
Biz (We)	3	AK Parti'yi Seviyoruz	52
		Recep Tayyip Erdoğan	51
		Ertuğrul Kürkçü	31
Recep	3	Recep Tayyip Erdoğan	69
		AK Parti'yi Seviyoruz	21
		Kemal Kılıçdaroğlu	18
Erdoğan	3	Recep Tayyip Erdoğan	60
		AK Parti'yi Seviyoruz	22
		Sakin Güç	9
Halk (Public)	3	Cumhuriyet Halk Partisi	51
		A. Levent Tüzel	16
		Sakin Güç	13
Barış (Peace)	2	BDP Barış ve Demokrasi Partisi	377
		Ertuğrul Kürkçü	36
Saat (Hour)	2	BDP Barış ve Demokrasi Partisi	117
		SesVerTürkiye	12
Ak[a] (Clean)	2	AK Parti'yi Seviyoruz	59
		Recep Tayyip Erdoğan	53
Tayyip	2	Recep Tayyip Erdoğan	72
		AK Parti'yi Seviyoruz	20
Mayıs (May the month)	2	SesVerTürkiye	38
		A. Levent Tüzel	22

(continued)

Table 10.7 (continued)

Word	The number of accounts where the word is repeated	The account	Number of repetition
Bin (Thousand)	2	Recep Tayyip Erdoğan	34
		AK Parti'yi Seviyoruz	23
Rahat (Comfortable)	2	Cumhuriyet Halk Partisi	35
		Sakin Güç	22
Haziran (June)	2	Ertuğrul Kürkçü	32
		SesVerTürkiye	23
Parti (Party)	2	Recep Tayyip Erdoğan	34
		AK Parti'yi Seviyoruz	20
Nefes (Breath)	2	Cumhuriyet Halk Partisi	31
		Sakin Güç	18
2011	2	SesVerTürkiye	41
		A. Levent Tüzel	5
Bizim (Our)	2	Recep Tayyip Erdoğan	27
		AK Parti'yi Seviyoruz	19
O (He/She/It)	2	Recep Tayyip Erdoğan	25
		AK Parti'yi Seviyoruz	21
Halkın (The public's)	2	Cumhuriyet Halk Partisi	28
		Sakin Güç	16
Karşı (Against/Opposing)	2	Cumhuriyet Halk Partisi	21
		Ertuğrul Kürkçü	20
Herkes (Everybody)	2	Cumhuriyet Halk Partisi	26
		Sakin Güç	14
Sandık[ğa] ([to the] ballot box)	2	Cumhuriyet Halk Partisi	24
		Sakin Güç	14
Büyük (Big)	2	AK Parti'yi Seviyoruz	21
		Sakin Güç	12
Gücünü (His/her/its power)	2	Cumhuriyet Halk Partisi	20
		Sakin Güç	11
Devlet (State)	2	SesVerTürkiye	16
		Sakin Güç	9

(continued)

Table 10.7 (continued)

Word	The number of accounts where the word is repeated	The account	Number of repetition
12	2	SesVerTürkiye	12
		Sakin Güç	9

[a]A homonymic word meaning "clean" or the shortened form of AKP

posts. The ratio of written language in this account is 25.35 % (467). The Facebook account with the highest ratio of written language is that of Sakin Güç (65.91 %) with 116 posts. Sakin Güç is followed by Kemal Kılıçdaroğlu with a ratio of 65.27 % (203) and Cumhuriyet Halk Partisi with a ratio of 61.42 % (312 posts).

The ratios of colloquial language and written language are very close to each other in the account of SesVerTürkiye. 43.58 % (231) of the posts sent from this account are typed with colloquial language, while 46.60 % (247) of the posts are typed in written language.

The register of language in the other 3 accounts examined in this research is as follows: colloquial language in the account of Recep Tayyip Erdoğan with a ratio of 51.19 % (150 posts), written language in the account of Recep Tayyip Erdoğan with a ratio of 33.79 % (99 posts); colloquial language in the account of AK Parti'yi Seviyoruz with a ratio of 44.07 % (104 posts), written language in the account of AK Parti'yi Seviyoruz with a ratio of 36.86 % (87 posts); colloquial language in the account of A. Levent Tüzel with a ratio of 54.46 % (55 posts), written language in the account of AK Parti'yi Seviyoruz with a ratio of 45.54 % (46 posts).

The most frequently repeated 25 words in each account are examined in this research. Table 10.7 shows the list of the most frequently repeated words in different accounts.

While calculating the number of repeated words, we looked at each recurring word. Then, we omitted the words such as prepositions and conjunctions that are meaningless when used alone and finally detected the 25 words that were repeated the most.

An examination of the use of these words revealed that the words "Kemal" and "Kılıçdaroğlu" are used only by the CHP accounts, but they are used several times. The word "Tayyip", which is a part of the name Recep Tayyip Erdoğan is used a lot only by the accounts of AKP. The words "Recep" and "Erdoğan" are, however, used a lot in two accounts representing CHP in addition to the accounts of AKP. It is observed that the names of other parties are not mentioned a lot in the posts of AKP accounts, whereas the posts of CHP accounts frequently gave place to words referring to Recep Tayyip Erdoğan, the leader of AKP.

It is interesting that the two accounts representing AKP as well as 3 accounts representing CHP used the word CHP more than the others did. BDP Barış ve Demokrasi Partisi, Sakin Güç, SesVerTürkiye accounts frequently gave place to the word "AKP". Yet, in AKP posts, the words "Ak" and "Party" (not AKP) ranked among the most frequently used words.

The word "Kurdish" is used the most by the accounts of BDP Barış ve Demokrasi Partisi, Ertuğrul Kürkçü and A. Levent Tüzel, who entered the elections as the independent candidates of EDÖB. The word "Kurdish" is not used a lot in the accounts of AKP, CHP and MHP.

10.4 Commentary

The research revealed that the political parties, which invested in web 1.0 technology and used it efficiently in a period when web proved to be a political communication tool, developed relatively successful applications and strategies in their social media experience. Especially AKP, which is one of the first parties to invest in web 1.0, has applied successful strategies on social media. The social media practices of the political parties in the 2011 General Elections showed that social media constitute a "new power" for all political parties.

It was observed that all of the political parties whose Facebook accounts are examined within this research have a common objective: to make announcements and explanations. In this regard, the social media opportunities that the politicians can enjoy and frequently have recourse to can be listed as follows:

- to present their political parties, leaders and discourses;
- to continuously update such information;
- to inform the electors about the activities through a regular information flow;
- to compile/observe electors' opinions about certain topics;
- to provide support and find audience for the offline activities of the political parties and leaders.

The main purpose of using posts on Facebook is to "make the political activity visible and to announce it". With the exception of Sakin Güç, the second most widespread purpose of using posts is "to be a social media correspondent" with a ratio of 20 %. BDP and MHP cannot find a place to spread their discourse on mainstream media, which forces them to turn to Facebook for sharing their own agenda. Several research studies have revealed that the Turkish mainstream media are going through an evolution in favour of AKP and they do not share the discourse of opponent parties (Kurban and Sözeri 2012, 2013; Çaylı and Depeli 2012). Therefore, it would not be wrong to say that social media accounts will increasingly be used by other political parties and social movements. For instance, the deputies of BDP and MHP are currently using their Twitter accounts for citizen journalism practices and posting hashtags intended for supporting the ideology of their own parties. Twitter accounts are often integrated into the Facebook page of the parties.

A brief evaluation of the parties in this research shows that BDP is the party that used Facebook more than the others did. The share of BDP Barış ve Demokrasi Partisi in all the accounts examined is more than 40 %. It is followed by MHP, with a share of 12 %. The total share of two different AKP accounts included in the sampling is more or less the same. The total share of three accounts representing

CHP is 23 %. The share of the account of Ertuğrul Kürkçü is 8 %. Given that, it can be said that BDP, which looks disorganised in the political milieu, is more cohesive on Facebook than other parties are.

Compared to other parties, AKP and CHP arouse much more interest with their leaders. The accounts with the highest number of "likes" are the accounts opened in the name of "Kemal Kılıçdaroğlu" and "Recep Tayyip Erdoğan". These two unofficial pages have fewer sharings but more "likes" than others. Thus, it can be stated that they draw attention because they represent political leaders.

It is also observed that the number of posts sent on Facebook is higher than the number of posts shared through Twitter.[7] This difference can be explained by the fact that, technically, Facebook overlaps with multi-media content better than Twitter does. As Facebook posts cover visuals, they need to be analyzed separately. The accounts that shared visuals the most are BDP Barış ve Demokrasi Partisi, AK Parti'yi Seviyoruz, Sakin Güç and Kemal Kılıçdaroğlu. The use of visuals in the accounts of MHP and BDP is relatively lower. On the other hand, it should be noted that Twitter accounts are usually operated by the users themselves, whereas Facebook accounts are managed by the social media experts of the parties and leaders.

On Facebook, all accounts except for those of AKP and "A. Levent Tüzel" used logos and shared links to various addresses. It is also seen that AKP and MHP did not use backgrounds images/decorations on their Facebook accounts, while independent candidates did. It is observed that CHP did not have a coherent approach to its accounts. None of the pages examined on Facebook were opened as official accounts. Despite this, certain rules were set and elements of political representation were shared on these pages.

Regarding Facebook, there is one more point to be considered: the source of posts. The contents circulated on Facebook were mainly produced especially for Facebook. There are two exceptions to this use: Cumhuriyet Halk Partisi and SesVerTürkiye. In the former, the content was forwarded from Twitter to Facebook, whereas in the latter prevailed other types of online sharings. The difference in the use of links is associated with the quality of the material shared on the media. For instance, conversations and texts were more prominent on Twitter, while links to other contents came to the forefront on Facebook. Besides, the fact that Facebook is a multilateral medium makes it more available for sharing links within itself.

The continuity of the political campaigns' run on social media is significant. It is important that the people or groups working in this field are members, or at least sympathisers of the party, so that there is no interruption or any other similar problem. When a professional group leads the political communication campaign

[7] In this research, the Twitter accounts of the political parties and leaders were also captured and examined during the sampling period. For the analysis of Twitter usage see Bayraktutan et al. (2014), "Siyasal İletişim Sürecinde Sosyal Medya ve Türkiye'de 2011 Genel Seçimlerinde Twitter Kullanımı", in Bilig, 68, 59–96 (Online edition: http://www.yesevi.edu.tr/yayinlar/index.php?action=show_article&bilig_id=57&article_id=923).

of a political party, it means that there is a contract between the party and the professional group and, at the end of contract period, this communication channel will be closed. It is necessary that the number of followers on social media should be kept and not decreased. The followers should be channelled to new political campaigns. While the Facebook accounts of AKP and MHP were managed by social media experts, CHP hired a professional firm. BDP, however, preferred volunteers to manage its social media accounts. The social media accounts of a party should be managed by the party itself. The policies and discourses of the party should be supported and circulated by the official account of the party or various accounts of its voters of sympathisers. The need for this was detected as a result of the elaboration of the social media practices in the 2011 General Elections.

Political leaders should take into consideration the fact that the social media users in Turkey are mainly young people. Therefore, leaders should revise their social media strategies according to the features of this target group. Political parties should take advantage of the opportunity of the way young people carry out interpersonal communication. From the perspective of political actors, the phenomenon of interpersonal communication, as mentioned by Castells, has a hidden power in terms of creating an army of volunteers in the election campaign. The army of volunteers proves that social media play the role of a controlled online communication tool in the political communication process. It would not be wrong to say that political parties will continue to use social media more interactively by promoting user-generated content production. Such features of new media will help to involve personal mass communication in political communication processes.

Finally, social media practices of Turkish political parties and leaders are unilateral and do not support interaction. In fact, unilateral communication conflicts with the spirit of web 2.0. At this point, it is possible to say that BDP has such a network management, that it can interact with its voters and make it possible for voters/users to produce content. We share the opinion that the real political language and structure in Turkey should be changed so that the accounts of political parties allow the participation of citizens and citizens can interact with political parties and the political language can be evolved into a negotiant democracy (Young 1998: 176). Following the viewpoint of Lincoln Dahlberg (2001: 615–633), we can say that the language that political actors use on social media should help them be sincere, honest, frank, well-intentioned, self-reflective and allow them to listen to various political opinions and develop wise arguments and criticism. Self-reflection, in this context, means that political actors can criticize their own opinions, values, and arguments when confronted with new and different arguments. It is only in this way that social media can contribute to the development of democracy and civic citizenship, by providing eager citizens with a public platform where they can have a direct say in the political discussion.

References

Aktaş, H. (2004). *Bir Siyasal İletişim Aracı Olarak İnternet*. Konya: Tablet Kitabevi.

Benoit, W. L. (2011). Content analysis in political communication. In E. P. Bucy & R. L. Holbert (Eds.), *The sourcebook for political communication research: methods, measures, and analytical techniques* (pp. 268–279). New York: Routledge.

Çaylı, E., & Depeli, G. (2012). *İfade Özgürlüğünün On Yılı: 2001–2011*. İstanbul: BİA.

Dahlberg, L. (2001). The internet and democratic discourse, information. *Communication and Society, 4*(4), 615–633.

Davis, R., Baumgartner, J. C., Francia, P. L., & Morris, J. S. (2009). The internet in U.S. election campaigns. In A. Chadwick & P. N. Howard (Eds.), *Routledge handbook of internet politics*. New York: Routledge.

Gökçe, O. (2006). *İçerik Analizi: Kuramsal ve Pratik Bilgiler*. Ankara: Siyasal Kitabevi.

Jensen, K. B. (2011). New media, old methods—internet methodologies and the online/offline divide. In M. Consalvo & C. Ess (Eds.), *The handbook of internet studies* (pp. 43–58). Malden: Wiley-Blackwell.

Kurban, D., & Sözeri, C. (2012). *İktidar Çarkında Medya*. İstanbul: TESEV Raporu.

Kurban, D., & Sözeri, C. (2013). *Türkiye'de Özgür ve Bağımsız Bir Basın İçin Siyasa Önerileri*. TESEV Demokratikleşme Programı Medya Raporları Serisi, 4.

Mayring, P. (2011). *Nitel Sosyal Araştırmaya Giriş: Nitel Düşünce İçin Bir Rehber*. Turkish edition. (A. Gümüş & S. M. Durgun, Trans.). Ankara: BilgeSu.

Öksüz O., & Turan-Yıldız, E. (2004). *Siyasal İletişimde İnternet Kullanımı: Türkiye ve ABD'deki Siyasal Partilerin Web Sitelerinin Karşılaştırmalı Analizi*. 2nd International Symposium: Communication in the Millenium, İstanbul.

Skalski, P. (2012). *Content analysis of interactive media*. http://academic.csuohio.edu/kneuendorf/c63309/Interactive09.ppt [Accessed 5 April 2012].

Toprak, A., Yıldırım, A., Aygül, E., Binark, M., Börekçi, S., & Çomu, T. (2009). *Toplumsal Paylaşım Ağı Facebook- Görülüyorum Öyleyse Varım!* İstanbul: Kalkedon Yayınları.

Weare, C., & Lin, W. Y. (2000). Content analysis of the world wide web. *Social Science Computer Review, 18*(3), 273–292.

Young, I. M. (1998). İletişim ve Öteki: Müzakereci Demokrasinin Ötesinde. In S. Benhabib (Ed.), *Demokrasi ve Farklılık-Siyasal Düzenin Sınırlarının Tartışmaya Açılması* (pp. 174–196). İstanbul: Dünya Yerel Yönetim ve Demokrasi Akademisi Yayını (WALD).

References

Chapter 11
Facebook Use in the 2012 USA Presidential Campaign

Obama vs. Romney

Porismita Borah

Abstract Politicians and political groups have quickly realized the potential of social networking sites as campaign tools. Although scholars have begun examining the political impact of social networking sites, more research should explore the use of these sites for political purposes. The present study uses content analysis of both the 2012 Presidential candidate's official Facebook pages to understand how politicians use social networking sites to reach out to voters. Currently, President Barack Obama's Facebook page has 35 million users, while Mitt Romney's has 11 million users. Employing concepts from the political campaigns literature, the study examines how each candidate used campaign tools in Facebook. The duration of the study was September 3rd (Labor Day) to November 6th, 2012 (the day of the election). The present study found that both candidates used several similar strategies in reaching out to their fans. Both the candidates' most common purpose for the posts was to promote their candidacy. However, in case of attack and contrast posts, Romney used the strategies more frequently. Overall, Romney led a more aggressive campaign on Facebook, using negative strategies and fear appeal.

Keywords Political campaigns • Facebook • Barack Obama • Mitt Romney • Elections 2012

11.1 Introduction

One of the prominent trends in the online world in recent years is the boom in the use of social networking sites. Facebook now has over 1.6 billion members from around the globe (Facebook 2013). Nearly three-fourths of the electorate is now online, with over 65 % of adults using social media to share and discuss information

P. Borah (✉)
Edward R. Murrow College of Communication, Washington State University, Pullman, WA, USA
e-mail: porismita@gmail.com

B. Pătruţ and M. Pătruţ (eds.), *Social Media in Politics*, Public Administration and Information Technology 13, DOI 10.1007/978-3-319-04666-2_11,

(Madden and Zickuhr 2011). During the 2010 mid-term election cycle, 53 % of adults reported using the Internet for political purposes, while 22 % adults particularly used social media platforms such as Facebook to receive campaigns or find election information (Smith 2011). As Americans have started using these sites for political information and to share their political views online, "politicians and political groups on both ends of the ideological spectrum have begun using them to organize and communicate with their supporters and the public at large" (Smith 2011, p. 3).

Of course, social networking sites were not initially considered as political tools. However, politicians and political groups have quickly realized the potential of these sites. Obama's utilization of social networking in the 2008 election is often used as an example to demonstrate the success of reaching his audience, particularly the youth (Dalton 2009; Nagourney 2008). Johnson (2012) examined Twitter feeds of 2012 Presidential candidate Mitt Romney to examine the rhetorical situation of the campaign. The author found that Romney used Twitter to build his credibility, attempted to connect to his audience, and explained reasoning for his policies. Romney used "Twitter bites to create a firsthand, immediate experience for the audience that takes out the middleman—the media... Romney reminded readers of the situation while also guiding his readers to his specific policy plans and stances on social issues" (Johnson 2012, p. 63).

Although scholars have begun examining the political impact of social networking sites (Williams and Gulati 2013; Zhang et al. 2010; Hong and Nadler 2012; Johnson 2012), more research should explore the use of these sites for political purposes. The present study uses content analysis of both the 2012 Presidential candidates' official Facebook pages to understand how politicians use social networking sites to reach out to voters. Currently, President Barack Obama's Facebook page has 35 million users, while Mitt Romney's has 11 million users. Employing concepts from the political campaigns literature, the study examines how each candidate used campaign tools in Facebook. The duration of the study was September 3rd (Labor Day) to November 6th, 2012 (the day of the election).

11.2 Political Use of Social Networking Sites

Using the theory of diffusion of innovations, Williams and Gulati (2013) examined the use of Facebook and Twitter in the 2006 and 2008 elections to the US House of Representatives. Their findings show that Facebook adoption diffused rapidly. Several variables such as money, level of education, and higher adoption rates by competitors explained both adoption of this new technology and implementation. Compared to 2006, the authors found that by 2008 the majority of both Democratic and Republican candidates had a presence on Facebook. About 72 % had a 'Politicians' page, which they regularly updated.

In the 2012 Presidential elections, both President Obama and Presidential candidate Mitt Romney used social networking sites to reach their audience.

Johnson (2012) studied Romney's use of Twitter during the time leading to the elections. Findings show that Romney attempted to build his credibility, expressed his reasoning, and connected emotionally with the audience.

Examining Twitter discussions of the seven republican candidates running for the 2011 Presidential nominations, Mejova et al. (2013) show the political sentiments expressed in the site. They found that the posts were largely negative rhetoric made up of sarcasm and humor. McClelland (2012) studied how politicians used big data from social networking sites to influence voters. In the case of President Obama, the author writes, "the Obama campaign understood how to find distinct patterns in vast amounts of unstructured data. It knew which districts to target and which ones to ignore" (p. 16). The author also explains how these political campaigns learned to raise money by targeting potential donors.

Hence, political use of social networking sites has been well established. Increasingly the mainstream media have recognized the importance of social networking sites for political use. Winslow (2012) examines how major broadcast networks streamed their primetime coverage to multiple platforms during the election season. For example, CNN had a partnership with Facebook, providing Election Night data and analysis of the activity on its widely used social media platform. NBC worked with Crimson Hexagon, and analyzed Twitter, Facebook, blogs, and other social media activity; and ABC used Yahoo and other providers.

Prior research has thus shown that politicians and political parties are using social networking sites for political use. However, few scholars have examined the strategies used in these posts to reach their audience. To understand the kind of appeals politicians use in these sites to reach out to their audience, the present study asks the following questions:

RQ1: What is the primary purpose of the post?
RQ2: What is the primary focus of the post?
RQ3: Does the post contain an emotional appeal?
RQ4: Does the post appeal to the audience to take an action?
RQ5: What is the main issue of the post?
RQ6: Does the post use any images, videos or mainstream media links?
RQ7: Is there a difference between the two candidates in their use of Facebook?

11.3 Methods

A content analysis was conducted to answer the research questions. The unit of analysis was each post in the Facebook pages of President Barack Obama and Presidential candidate Mitt Romney. Coders accessed the posts by logging into Facebook. They coded each post between September 3rd (Labor Day) to November 6th, 2012 (Election Day).

11.3.1 Coding

The primary variables coded were for the purpose of the post, focus of the post, emotional appeal of the post, appeal to the audience to take specific action, issue of the post and the use of video, images, and mainstream media links in the post. The purpose of the post included three categories: to promote a specific candidate, attack a candidate, and contrast the candidates. The focus of the post had two categories: personal characteristics of either candidate, and policy matters. Emotional appeal of the post included six primary emotions such as fear, enthusiasm, anger, pride, humor, and sadness. The next variable examined if the post appealed to the audience to take some specific action. The categories included register to vote, volunteer your time, and donate money.

The issues of the post was categorized into economic policy, social issues, environment issues, social welfare issues, foreign policy issues, and other. Economic Policy included Taxes, Deficit/Budget/Debt, Government Spending, Recession/Economic Stimulus, Minimum Wage, Employment/Jobs, Poverty, Globalization, Housing, and Economy (generic reference). Social Issues included Abortion, Gay Rights, Affirmative Action, Gun Control, Race Relations, and Civil Rights. Environmental issues covered Environment (generic reference), Global Climate Change, and Energy Policy. Within Social Welfare issues, Education, Health Care, Social Security, Women's Health and Welfare were included. Foreign Policy included Military (generic reference), Foreign Policy (generic reference), Veterans, Foreign Aid, Middle East, Afghanistan, Iraq, Israel, and Iran. The other category was used to include any issue that was not captured in this list.

11.3.2 Inter-Coder Reliability

Two coders were trained to use the coding instrument. A random sample of 10 % articles was used to calculate inter-coder reliability. Reliability was calculated by using Cohen's Kappa. The resulting score was 0.90 or higher on all measures. Individual scores of all measures are reported in Table 11.1.

11.4 Results

A total of 83 posts were analyzed from both Barack Obama's and Mitt Romney's Facebook pages. The duration of analysis was between September 3rd, 2012 to November 6th, 2012. Barack Obama had a total of 23 posts while Mitt Romney posted 59 times during this time period.

Examining the purpose of the post for Barack Obama's page shows that the incumbent President primarily used the space to promote himself or important

Table 11.1 Reliability results for the variables used in this study

Variable	Reliability score[a]
Purpose	1.00
Focus	0.89
Emotional appeal	0.90
Specific action	0.83
Issue	0.79
Multi-media use	1.00

[a]Cohen's Kappa

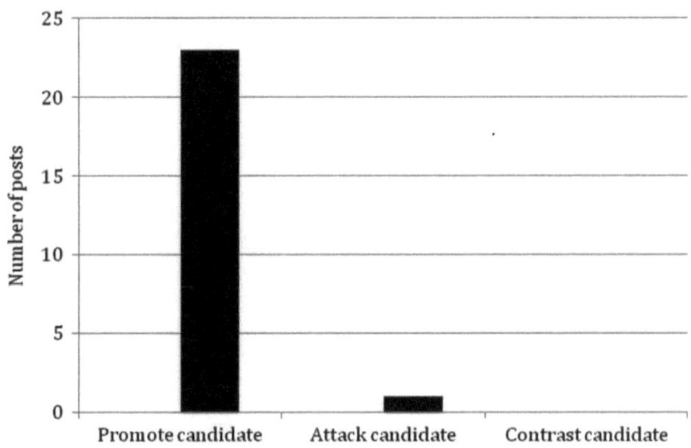

Fig. 11.1 Purpose of posts: Barack Obama

events (Fig. 11.1). Of the total 24 posts, Obama used 23 posts (97 %) for promoting, only one post (3 %) to attack his opponent, and none to contrast between the two candidates. Romney used 45 posts (76 %) to promote himself, 11 posts (19 %) to attack his opponent and 3 posts (5 %) to contrast the candidates (Fig. 11.2).

The next variable was focus of the post, which had three categories: personal characteristic, policy matters, and other. Eight of Obama's posts (33 %) focused on policy matters. There was no post of personal characteristic, while 16 posts (66 %) were coded as other (Fig. 11.3). These posts mainly promoted events or urged people to vote. In the case of focus of the post, Romney's page was very similar to Obama's. Romney used 17 posts (29 %) for policy matters, while 44 posts were coded as other (Fig. 11.4). These posts were mainly used to promote events, urging fans to vote or promote the mobile application.

The posts were also coded for their emotional appeal. The categories were fear, enthusiasm, anger, pride, humor, sadness, and other. Obama's posts consisted of 19 (79 %) showing enthusiasm, two posts (8.3 %) showing pride and three posts (12.5 %) showing humor. There were no posts coded in the categories of fear, anger, and sadness. Romney's posts showed similar enthusiasm with a total of 36 posts (61 %). There were three posts that showed pride (Fig. 11.5). The big difference from Obama's posts was Romney's use of fear. Romney used 20 posts (34 %) to discuss the problems that America will face if Obama is reelected. Romney's page did not have any posts showing anger, humor, and sadness (Fig. 11.6).

Fig. 11.2 Purpose of posts: Mitt Romney

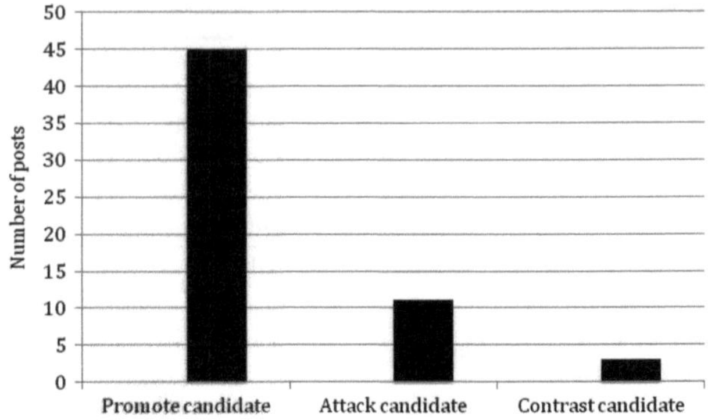

Fig. 11.3 Focus of posts: Barack Obama

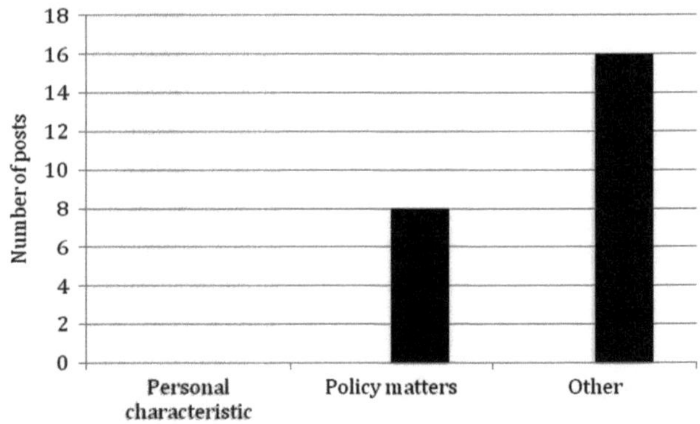

Fig. 11.4 Focus of posts: Mitt Romney

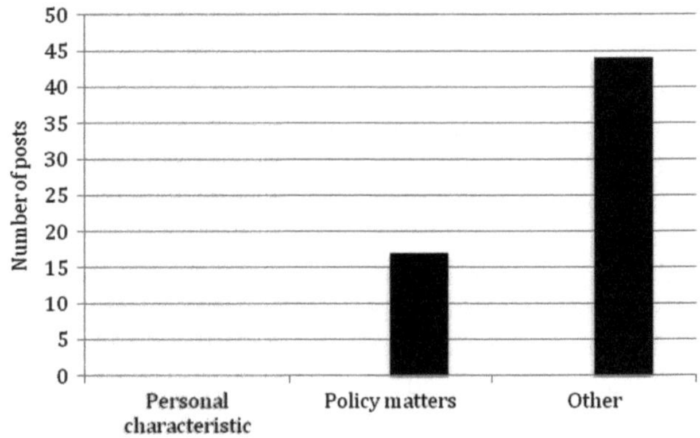

The next variable coded was appeal for specific action. Obama's campaign employed 7 posts (30.4 %) to urge the audience to vote, 2 posts (8.6 %) to volunteer their time, and 5 posts (21.7 %) to donate money (Fig. 11.7). Similarly, Romney's campaign used 27 posts (45.7 %) to encourage his fans to vote, 6 posts (10.1 %) to volunteer their time, and 17 posts (28.8 %) to donate money (Fig. 11.8).

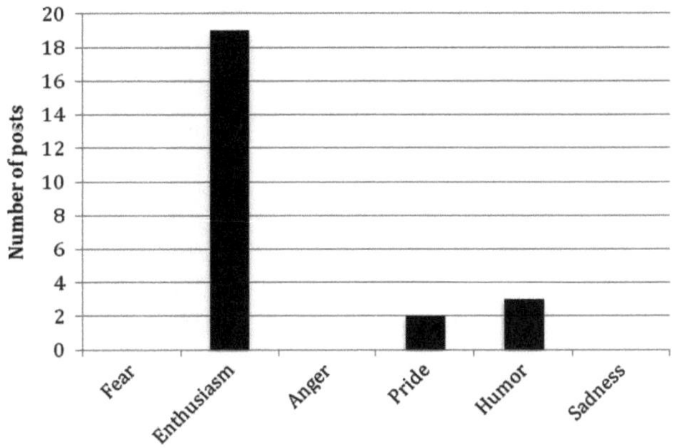

Fig. 11.5 Emotional appeal of posts: Barack Obama

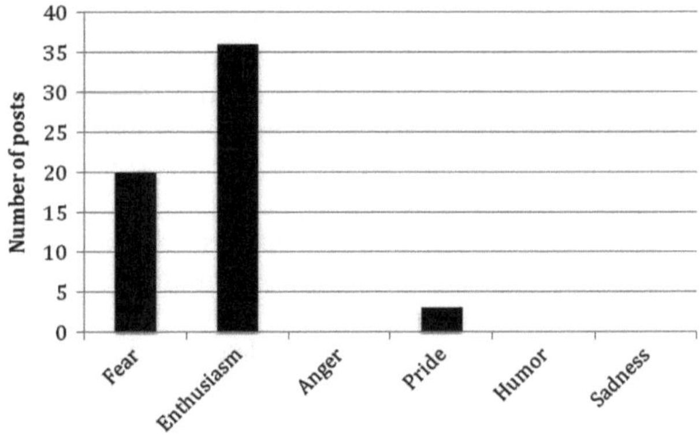

Fig. 11.6 Emotional appeal of posts: Mitt Romney

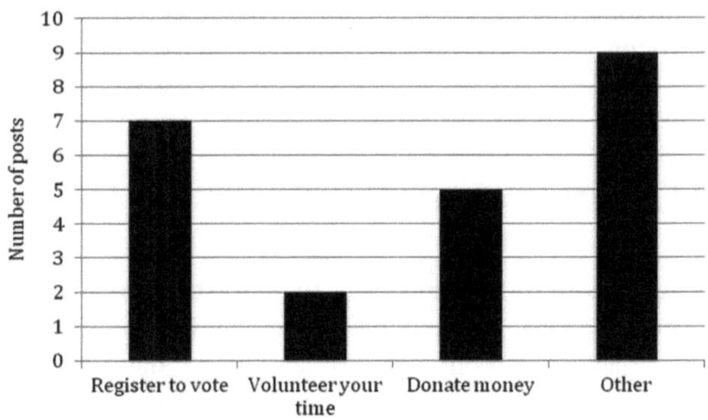

Fig. 11.7 Appeal for specific action: Barack Obama

Another variable coded was the issue of the posts. Four (16.6 %) of Obama's posts discussed economic policies, one (4 %) post about environmental policies, and one (4 %) about social welfare. There were no posts about foreign policy and social issues (Fig. 11.9). Romney's posts were dominated by economic policies

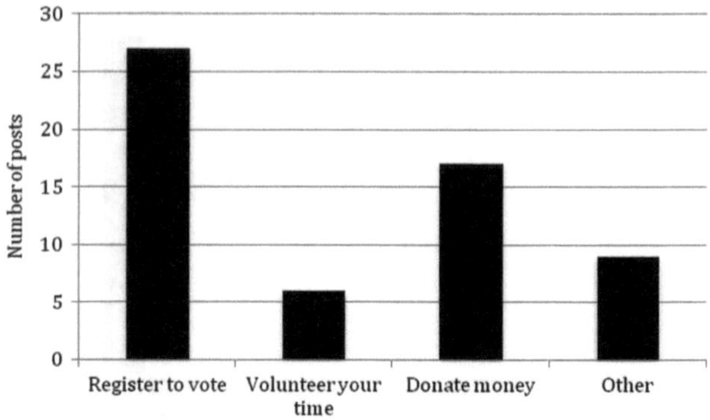

Fig. 11.8 Appeal for specific action: Mitt Romney

with 14 (23.7 %) posts, followed by two (3 %) posts about social welfare and one (1.6 %) post about environmental issues. Similar to Obama, his campaign also did not discuss social and foreign policy issues (Fig. 11.10).

The final variable examined the multi-media use by the two candidates. Obama's page consisted of 15 (62.5 %) images, 9 (37 %) videos and 4 (16.6 %) links (Fig. 11.11). Romney (Fig. 11.12) used 52 (88 %) images, followed by 14 (23.7 %) and 7 (11.8 %).

Besides examining the Facebook posts on both the candidate's pages, chi-square tests were conducted to examine the differences between Barack Obama and Mitt Romney's use of Facebook. There were several variables that showed significant differences between the two candidates. Within the purpose of the post, attacking the opponent showed a significant difference (chi-square = 10.54, $p < .01$). The next variable that demonstrated differences was emotional appeal. Enthusiasm (chi-square = 11.23, $p < .01$), fear (chi-square = 15.33, $p < .001$), and humor (chi-square = 12.11, $p < .001$). The other variables did not show any significant differences between the two candidates.

11.5 Discussions

The purpose of this study was to understand how Barack Obama and Mitt Romney used Facebook to reach their audience. Before the implications of the findings are discussed, a few limitations should be mentioned. The study examined only Facebook, comparing other social media use such as Twitter and Youtube would be useful to generalize the findings. The duration of the content analysis was from September 3rd (Labor day) to November 6th (Election Day). Although this is the time for majority of the election campaign action, a longer time period could help understand the strategies used by the campaigns better. Despite some of these shortcomings, the present study helped in understanding the strategies used by the Obama and Romney campaigns on Facebook.

Fig. 11.9 Issue of posts: Barack Obama

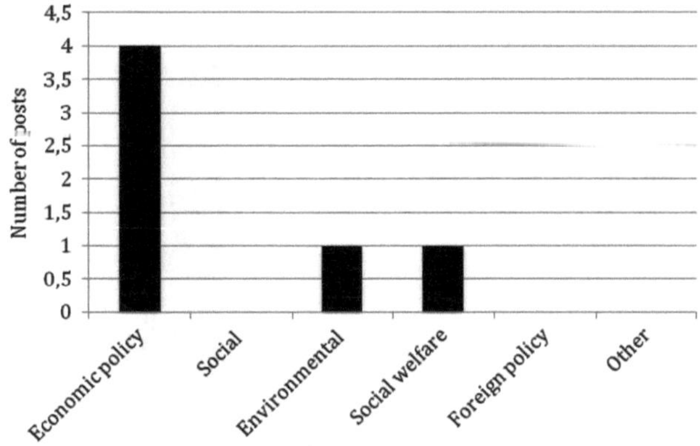

Fig. 11.10 Issue of posts: Mitt Romney

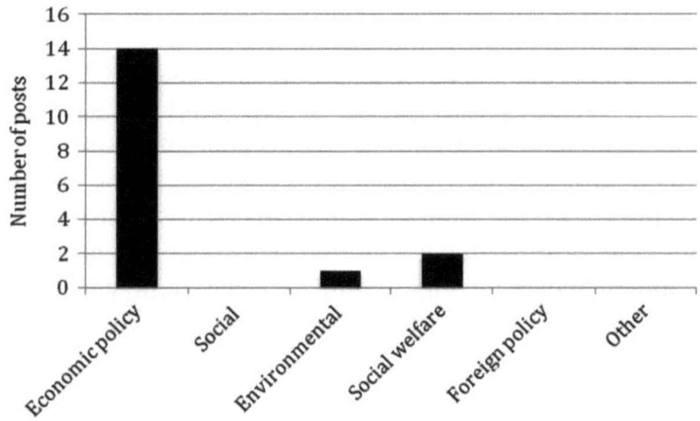

Fig. 11.11 Multi-media use in posts: Barack Obama

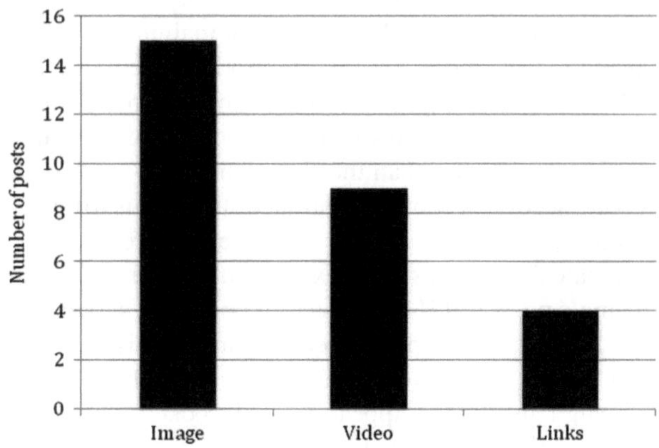

Even though social media were mostly known for connecting with friends and networking, recently there has been a lot of attention paid to the political use of social media. Political campaigns have successfully used social media to reach their audience. However, not much research has been done on understanding the kind of

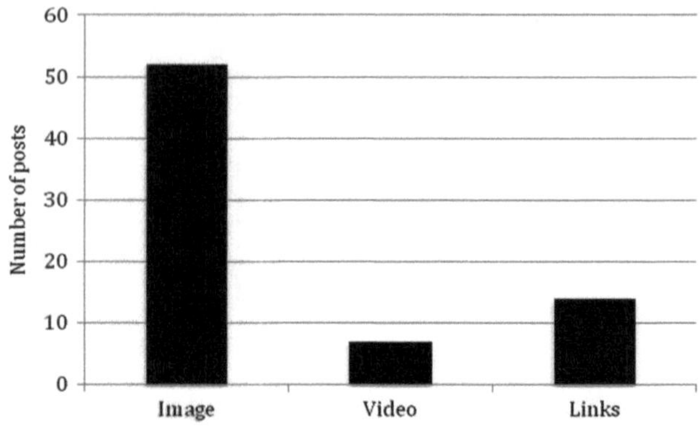

Fig. 11.12 Multi-media use in posts: Mitt Romney

strategies that are most commonly used by politicians. The 2012 US Presidential elections was a unique opportunity to explore these strategies.

The present study found that both candidates used several similar strategies in reaching out to their fans. Both the candidates' most common purpose for the posts was to promote their candidacy. However, in the case of attack and contrast posts, Romney used the strategies more frequently. During the study period, Obama used only one post to attack Romney. This post was about the 47 % comment made by Romney, where Obama's campaign shared the video of Romney speaking about his opinion about 47 % of the country who will never vote for him. On the other hand, Romney's campaign used several posts to attack Obama. 19 % of Romney's posts attacked Obama and talked about why he is not the right candidate for the country. In 5 % of the posts, Romney's campaign also highlighted the contrasts between the two candidates. Examining just the purpose of the posts demonstrates that the strategy employed by Romney's campaign was more aggressive than Obama's. Obama's was more casual, promoting events, sharing campaign images, and highlighting the importance of voting. Romney's campaign also used the same strategies, but they also attacked Obama's policies, and highlighted why Romney's policies were better than the President's.

The second variable examined the focus of the posts, and generally both candidates used very similar strategies. However, the differences between the two candidates' strategies were explicit in the use of emotional appeal. The majority of Obama's posts (79 %) consisted of posts that showed enthusiasm about the upcoming elections and various events related to his campaign. Obama's campaign also used humor (12.5 %) to reach their audience. While 34 % of Mitt Romney's campaign used fear appeal in their posts. These posts mostly highlighted the problems the country will face if Obama is re-elected. Unlike Obama, Romney's campaign did not use any humor appeal in the posts. In the case of appeal for specific action, issue of the post, and multi-media use, both candidates mostly used the same strategies. Overall, Romney led a more aggressive campaign on Facebook, using negative strategies and fear appeal. Quantitatively too, Romney's campaign posted (59 times) far more often than Obama's (23 times) during the study.

The present study is a preliminary examination of the social media uses of two candidates in 2012 US Presidential elections. Findings demonstrate similarities and important differences in the strategies used by the two campaigns. Future studies should explore social media other than Facebook in election campaign.

References

Dalton, R. J. (2009). *The good citizen: How a younger generation is reshaping American politics*. Washington, DC: CQ Press.

Facebook, (2013). Retrieved from https://www.facebook.com/

Hong, S., & Nadler, D. (2012). Which candidates do the public discuss online in an election campaign? The use of social media by 2012 presidential candidates and its impact on candidate salience. *Government Information Quarterly, 29*(4), 455–461.

Johnson, J. (2012). Twitter bites and romney: Examining the rhetorical situation of the 2012 presidential election in 140 characters. *Journal of Contemporary Rhetoric, 2*(3/4), 54–64.

Madden, M., & Zickuhr, K. (2011). 65% of online adults use social networking sites. Pew Research Center. Retrieved from http://www.pewinternet.org/Reports/2011/Social-Networking-Sites/Overview.aspx

McClelland, S. (2012). News analysis/blogosphere intermedia's best of the web. *Intermedia*, 40(5), 16–17.

Mejova, Y., Srinivasan, P., & Boynton, B. (2013). *GOP primary season on Twitter: "Popular" political sentiment in social media*. Paper presented at WSDM, Rome, Italy.

Nagourney, A. (2008, November 3). The '08 campaign: Sea change for politics as we know it. The New York Times. Retrieved March 3 from nytimes.com.

Smith, A. (2011, January 27). Social media and politics in 2010 campaign. Pew Research Center. Retrieved from http://www.pewinternet.org/Press-Releases/2011/Politics-and-Social-Media.aspx

Williams, C., & Gulati, G. (2013). Social networks in political campaigns: Facebook and the congressional elections of 2006 and 2008. *New Media and Society, 15*(1), 52–71.

Winslow, G. (2012, November 5). In Election Tech, the battleground goes digital networks look to more closely integrate on-air with online and mobile coverage. *Broadcasting and Cable*.

Zhang, W., Johnson, T. J., Seltzer, T., & Bichard, S. L. (2010). The revolution will be networked: The influence of social networking sites on political attitudes and behavior. *Social Science Computer Review, 28*(1), 75–92.

Chapter 12
Tweet of Hope

Social Media's Impact on Young Adults' Political Participation in the Obama 2008 and 2012 Presidential Elections

Theresa Renee White and Theresia Anderson

Abstract The idea of creating a community of political supporters is not a new concept (Vaccari 2008). However, the way in which the Obama campaign used social media to mobilize a historically difficult group (Rice et al. *Social Science Computer Review, 31*(3), 257–279, 2012), as well as the size of the resulting social media communities, was a new concept during the 2008 and 2012 presidential campaigns. Previous online campaigns had failed to effectively mobilize young adults, due to the political campaigners unsuccessfully translating the existing campaign formula, which focused more on older adult voters from the real world, rather than voters who frequently interact in the virtual realm (Vaccari 2008; Haynes and Pitts *Symposium,* 53–58, 2009). During the 2008 presidential campaign, Barack Obama's team improved upon the strategies of the previous Internet mobilization campaigns, by placing great emphasis on social media (Godsall 2010; Bronstein *Online Information Review, 37*(2), 173–192, 2012). His online campaign deviated from the disciplined and traditionally structured format of previous Internet campaigns (Johnson and Perlmutter *Mass Communication and Society, 13* 554–559, 2010), encouraged the formation of online coteries among users (Bronstein *Online Information Review, 37*(2), 173–192, 2012), and facilitated civic political involvement (Fernandes et al. *Mass Communication and Society, 13*, 653–675, 2010). Obama re-built a sense of community assumed to have been previously lost (Jefferson-Jenkins, as cited in Dudash and Harris *American Behavioral Scientist, 55*(4), 469–478, 2011), and created a link between the lives of young adults and the election (*American Behavioral Scientist, 55*(4), 469–478, 2011).

T.R. White (✉)
Pan African Studies Department, California State University, 18111 Nordhoff, Santa Susana 217, Northridge, CA 91330, USA
e-mail: Theresa.white@csun.edu

T. Anderson
California State University, Northridge, USA

B. Pătruţ and M. Pătruţ (eds.), *Social Media in Politics*, Public Administration and Information Technology 13, DOI 10.1007/978-3-319-04666-2_12,

Keywords Social media • President Barack Obama • Political campaign • Presidential election • Young adults

12.1 Introduction

In 1960, Democratic Senator John F. Kennedy commanded the stage of the nation's first televised presidential debate against, then Vice President, Richard Nixon. At that point in history, 88 % of American households had televisions, enabling an estimated 74 million viewers to tune into this monumental political campaign (Webley 2010). According to political analysts, Kennedy successfully secured the presidency in 1961, primarily due to his effective campaign use of new mass media and his appeal to young adults (Webley 2010). Forty-eight years later, Barack Hussein Obama not only became the first African-American Presidential candidate, but, following in the path of President Kennedy, he was also the first to use a new form of mass media—social media—as a political campaign platform.

This paper suggests that President Barack Obama effectively utilized multiple social media platforms in 2008 and 2012, to politically target the young adult age group (18–29 year olds) as a way to connect with them on a personal level, and to mobilize them to become active participants in the political process. As a result of Obama's primarily virtual campaign, relatable slogans and videos, young voters developed internet social media communities using Facebook, Twitter and YouTube, which influenced more participants in this age demographic to increase political efficacy, and to become politically mobilized through community activism. This approach was instrumental in the success of Obama's 2008 election and 2012 re-election.

12.2 Internet Media Use in Political Campaigns

In recent years, the Internet has become a significant factor and political tool in presidential campaigns (Hayes 2009), much increased since its initial use in the 1992 presidential election (Bronstein 2012). The Internet proved to offer a broad scope of political possibilities, such as participating in forums, organizing electronic petitions, and researching political information (Bakker and de Vreese 2011). In 2004, presidential candidate Howard Dean is noted for pioneering the framework for the Internet's use by integrating the use of web-blogging (Johnson and Perlmutter 2010) along with e-mails and static Web sites as a political organization tool (Hayes 2009). Obama later cites Dean's Internet organization model as attributing to the framework for his successful social networking campaign. The 2004 presidential election exhibited the Internet's potential for raising campaign funds (Haynes and Pitts 2009; McGarth 2011), financially balancing "the people" against large special interest groups and political action committees (McGarth 2011), displaying endorsements (Kaid and Postelnicu 2005), and mobilizing political electorate support. In addition, Internet campaigns were found to be more effective at communicating a candidate's political message and image to the electorate (Kaid and Postelnicu 2005).

While television remains the public's main source of political information, the Internet has been found to be the preferred alternative source (Kaid and Postelnicu 2005; Haynes and Pitts 2009). Pinkleton and Austin (2004) found traditional media such as television and newspapers failed to connect with, and motivate young voters. Additionally, it has increased levels of political apathy (Edwards 2000) and political disengagement. Bakker and de Vreese (2011), however, emphasized that while political apathy has been cited in previous research as a reason for young adults' political disengagement, they asserted that this population may be less "attracted" to traditional forms of political engagement. Other researchers discovered Internet political communication to have a positive increase in efficacy (Kaid and Postelnicu 2005), election knowledge (Hayes 2009; Kushin and Yamamoto 2010), and participation (Bakker and de Vreese 2011) in young adult populations. The Internet, which was found to be the leading source of information for young adults, (Pew Research Center 2008, 2013), was documented as appealing to young voters' increased levels of individualism (Edwards 2000), further motivating political participation and engagement (Pinkleton and Austin 2004; Kaid and Postelnicu 2005). Political participation here is defined as political party membership and voting turnout (Bakker and de Vreese 2011).

Bakker and de Vreese (2011) found political participation levels to increase among the young adult population, when low levels of voter input and low cost were required. This model was practiced during the 2008 presidential election with the introduction of social networking site campaigns, in addition to traditional Web site campaigns (Hayes 2009). The main social networking sites (SNS) used during the 2008 election were Facebook, MySpace, and YouTube, with a micro-blogging site, called Twitter, which developed as a significant social network later during the 2012 election. The information relayed on these sites was defined as social media.

Social network sites are defined as "Web-based services, which allow individuals to articulate a list of other users with whom they share a connection, view and traverse their list of connections and those made by others within the system, and construct a public or semi-public profile with a bounded system" (Ellison 2007 as cited by Hayes 2009). Eighty three percent of young adults, aged 18–29, report using SNS (Pew Research Center 2013), and state that it has become a part of their daily lives (Hayes 2009). Facebook, the more popular social networking platform, allows users to gather information from group and individual profiles (Weaver and Morrison 2008), real-time interaction with established friends through "wall" posts (Hayes 2009), status updates, and instant messages. MySpace, which launched in 2003, was used for discovering new trends, campaign issues, and organizations (Hayes 2009). YouTube, an online video-sharing network, allowed for users to interact by sharing personal and popular culture videos, browse and comment on uploaded videos, and display videos on their personal Web sites (Weaver and Morrison 2008), such as Facebook and MySpace. Twitter, a newer micro-blogging style SNS, allowed for users to "follow" other users, celebrities, and organizations. "Following" allows users to stay updated with various information, candidate's stances on political issues, and personal opinions, displayed in 250 words or less, while interacting with other users by "liking", commenting, and sharing "tweets" on personal Web sites noted above.

The interactive SNS environment created a platform for candidates to reach and mobilize young supporters, increase communication venues where people gain a sense of personal interaction with candidates (Westling 2007; as cited in Bronstein 2012), which enabled discussions and political interaction with friends and family while online (Hayes 2009). Fernandes et al. (2010) suggested that open political interchange facilitated on SNS encouraged civil engagement in young adults, and promoted political information-seeking behavior (Hayes 2009). In addition, authors suggested that the use of SNS might have decreased political apathy by increasing political participation, while lowering the traditional barriers to political communication and participation, through instant connection and sharing with peers (Edwards 2000; Pinkleton and Austin 2004; Hayes 2009; Kushin and Yamamoto 2010).

12.3 Social Media Communities and Young Adult Political Involvement

Depending on traditional foundations, including social class, ethnicity, and political distinction (Komaromi and Scott 2011), community has been contextually defined in numerous ways. Derived from the Latin root communis, community, in the simplest definition, is defined as a unified body of individuals ("Merriam-Webster," 2013). Frank Beck (2001) expands on this definition by adding that community is a group of people sharing common territory, culture, and set, with the most important aspect being member interaction and the promotion of this inter action. Cohen (1985) supports Beck's standing, but asserts that a community need not exist in the physical sense, but rather symbolically, or virtually, such as presented in the context of SNS. These social media communities are ultimately defined by symbolical boundaries within the minds of the community members (Cohen 1985). These online communities are suggested as being allotted more interaction and collaboration between and among users (Komaromi and Scott 2011), while still allowing the community members to develop a sense of identity (Cohen 1985), due to not being limited by geographical boundaries. Godin (2008) asserts that these non-geographically bound communities, to be centered on a standard set of social relations, are connected to one another, connected to a leader, and or connected to an idea.

Online social media communities during the most recent presidential elections centered on the candidates' ideas and political agendas. These post-modern campaigns were found to successfully create a community where young voters felt a sense of ownership within their respective political organizations, while candidates had the ability to communicate online with their political communities with the purpose of mobilizing young voters (Vaccari 2008). Previous online campaigns had failed to mobilize young adults effectively, because of political campaigners unsuccessfully translating the existing formula, which focused more on older adult voters from the real world, rather than those that frequently dwell in the virtual realm (Vaccari 2008; Haynes and Pitts 2009). Additionally, Fernandes et al. (2010) found that, when online communities are formed with the goal of supporting a political candidate, the focus on the political process becomes important to the collective. Moreover, Godsall (2010) affirms that social media allowed for users to engage in "passive persuasion", such as updating their Facebook status with personal political insight and opinions to influence their peers, rather than "active persuasion," which Godsall defines as associating with "exposing themselves to potential social complexities and pitfalls" (2010). This point asserts that the ability to influence peers as a byproduct of normal everyday practices for young adults, allowed for these social media communities to flourish.

Simply joining a social media community made it easier to communicate with other individuals with similar political interests (Rice et al. 2012) and expose themselves to the enthusiasm surrounding the political party and candidate (Fernandes et al. 2010; Bronstein 2012). When young adults "friended" a political candidate or party, they were exposed to party specific political information and received unsolicited invitations for additional information (Rice et al. 2012), including YouTube videos created by individual users, as well as campaign-generated videos. The inclusion of user-generated content created a "personal" connection between more young adults than had been previously possible with the use of only traditional media (Vaccari 2008; Godsall 2010).

12.4 Obama's Social Media Community

The idea of creating a community of political supporters is not a new concept (Vaccari 2008). However, the way in which the Obama campaign used social media to mobilize a historically difficult group (Rice et al. 2012), and the size of the resulting social media communities, was new. McGarth's (2011) research suggests that the size of Obama's social media campaign increased the excitement and amount of youth contributions. Many young adults were influenced by new technology, such as smartphones, which enabled them to view community-created media while communicating views and opinions, on the move. Additional research suggests that Obama's general popularity and the significance of electing him (the first African American) President may have increased his campaign's popularity on social networking sites, while equally engaging young adults to gather their political information online to communicate their opinions (Haynes and Pitts 2009; Kushin and Yamamoto 2010). The resulting mobilizations lead to the creation of a "community of the campaign" (Godsall 2010). Moreover, online conversations, interwoven with offline political participation activities with like-minded peers, allude to the fact that the online community became a real community outside of the social network realm (Fernandes et al. 2010).

During the 2008 presidential campaign, Barack Obama's team improved upon the strategies of the previous Internet mobilization campaigns, by placing great emphasis on social media (Godsall 2010; Bronstein 2012). His online campaign deviated from the disciplined and traditionally structured format of previous Internet campaigns (Johnson and Perlmutter 2010), encouraged the formation of online coteries among users (Bronstein 2012), and facilitated civic political involvement (Fernandes et al. 2010). By way of social media, Obama's campaign team was able to mobilize large groups of young adults, who politically identified as Independents (Johnson and Perlmutter 2010), to start the pro-Obama supporter websites, and increase youth supporter turnout offline (McGarth 2011). Previous research suggests that this turnout was made possible by Obama's heavy emphasis on relevant issues that were viewed as important to the young adult population, such as the Iraq war, funding higher education, lowering loan interest rates, and healthcare (Bronstein 2012). Obama re-built a sense of community assumed to have been previously lost (Jefferson-Jenkins, as cited in Dudash and Harris 2011), and created a link between the lives of young adults and the election (Dudash and Harris 2011).

Arguably, Obama's campaign rhetoric, offline and online, could be seen as the main influence as to how he increased young adult involvement and support. By way of analyzing several of Obama's speeches, Jenkins and Cos (2010) argued that the candidate offered Americans a message of hope through various modes of persuasion. They noted that Obama was able to recognize and reach the alienated, diverse young adult population. His message generated common knowledge, expressed individualism and built communities (Jenkins and Cos 2010). Through specific word choice of inclusive language such as "we", "us", and "together", Jenkins and Cos's research supported the way in which Obama was able to bind together communities, offering hope and change for all people to enjoy (Jenkins and Cos 2010). Some authors define Obama's rhetoric choice as revolutionary, which may have added enthusiasm and appeal to younger generations, connecting Obama's image to popular activists including Abraham Lincoln, Martin Luther King, Jr., and John F. Kennedy (Jenkins and Cos 2010).

Through an open discussion with young first time voters, Dudash and Harris (2011) found that young adults felt Obama reached out to them through his effective and "catchy" slogans such as "Change" and "Yes We Can", which they, in turn, proclaimed as a reason for their choice of becoming politically engaged and contributing to social media communities. By way of joining political social networking groups, young adults felt a part of the larger community (Dudash and Harris 2011). Likewise, Hart and Lind (2010) defined Obama's rhetoric as possessing a Rorschach aspect in that Americans saw what they wanted to interpret. This open for translation style arguably "attracted" the support and minds of young adult voters (Hart and Lind 2010) by appealing to their group diversity. Furthermore, Obama's tone and style was found to be grounded and highly focused, in comparison to the opposing candidates such as McCain (and Romney), whose style was perceived as partisan and highly embellished (Hart and Lind 2010; Dudash and Harris 2011).

12.4.1 Obama vs. McCain

During the primaries in 2007 and 2008, Obama and McCain's political campaigns both launched political Web sites, "MyBarackObama.com" and "McCainspace" respectively (Hayes 2009). These websites were noted as both being highly interactive and linked to social networking sites. McCain's campaign used less streaming videos and social media tools (Haynes and Pitts 2009), in comparison with Obama's campaign, which heavily used SNS and social media to present his issues and stances to young adults in particular (Dudash and Harris 2011). Comparatively, Obama's supporters were noted as being "louder" and could have been more influential than McCain's (Dudash and Harris 2011). This could have been a result of Obama's heavy social media usage, which has connected young adults, and increased their political efficacy through social media community motivation.

Moreover, McCain's supporters were found less likely to visit his campaign Web site and social networking sites (Haynes and Pitts 2009). McCain's supporters were older adults, a group that his campaign found to be highly focused on and favored (Haynes and Pitts 2009). Research on McCain's overall political campaign found it to lack the ability to speak to issues concerning young voters, and failed to offer them a hopeful vision for their future (Greenberg 2009). Pro-Obama social networking sites had more site activity and were found to appeal to both young adult voters and their use of social technology (Fernandes et al. 2010). Additionally, Obama's campaign, in comparison to McCain's, was viewed as "personal" and "modern" (Greenberg 2009).

12.4.2 Obama vs. Romney

In 2012, Mitt Romney and incumbent Barack Obama campaigned for the Presidency of the United States. Following Obama's successful mobilization of young voters during the primary campaign, the Republican Party invested more into the area of social networking and the use of social media. This time, social media campaigning was noted as being "more controlled" than previous indicators, in the sense that the excitement surrounding the Obama campaign had slightly declined (Bronstein 2012). There was excitement, however, generated around this election due to the "closeness" of the election results. The catch phrase, "Tight race with high stakes," was noted by researchers, arguing that this concept inspired young adult political involvement through social media (Fernandes et al. 2010).

During Obama's run for re-election, his campaign team revamped the SNS and social media strategy that had assisted in his winning the 2008 election. Similar to his original social networking campaign, Obama implored the use of persuasive language, which was based upon elements of ethical, emotional, logical appeal (Bronstein 2012). Obama's social media content was believed to heavily emphasize topics concerning young adults, such as affordable higher education (Bronstein

2012). Additionally, Obama's social media message was found to significantly place emphasis upon his wife and daughters, who he mentioned as inspiring him to work harder towards making the world a better place (Bronstein 2012). One significant difference during this cycle was the increased interaction between Obama and his supporters when he "liked" supportive posts and social media platforms related to voting and donations, rather than political issues (Bronstein 2012).

Comparatively, Romney's SNS described his character as an accomplished businessman and politician (Bronstein 2012). Romney's social media message stressed his heavily business oriented agenda, which highlighted the economy, higher wages for middle-class Americans, and an increase in job production (Bronstein 2012). While Romney also addressed the young voter, his focus pertained more to increasing American economic affairs over supporting education (Bronstein 2012). Furthermore, Romney's campaign attempted to make up for past Republican mistakes by following Obama's example and connecting to young voters through "personal" interactions on platforms such as Facebook (Bronstein 2012). His strategy eventually proved to be unsuccessful.

12.5 Gender and Minority Group Participation in 2008 and 2012

During the 2008 Presidential election, there was a significant increase in political engagement among young African-Americans and women, ages 18–29 (Godsay and Kirby 2010). Additionally a significant gender gap was observed, with young women being more politically engaged than young men, 55 % to 47 %, respectively (Godsay and Kirby 2010). However, previous research noted that young women have constantly been more politically involved than young men since the legal voting age was lowered to 18 in 1972 (Godsay and Kirby 2010). Consistent with the overall gender voting trend, young African-American and Latina women voter turnout was significantly higher than young African-American and Latino men, 64 % and 44 % to 52 % and 38 %, respectively (Godsay and Kirby 2010). Additionally, young African-American women had a higher percentage of political engagement than young white women (56 %) for the first time (Godsay and Kirby 2010; "Voter Turnout Among Young Women and Men", Center for Information and Research on Civic Learning and Engagement [CIRCLE] 2013).

McGarth (2011) suggested that the significant increase of political engagement among young African-Americans and Latinos in 2008 was due to Obama's successful campaign use of new technologies and social media platforms. African-Americans and Latinos were found to heavily use social media as their main source of sharing and gathering political information (Smith 2010). In particular, previous research concluded that mobile cellular phones were the most significant political engagement tools, particularly among African-Americans, due to the high usage of cell phones by minority populations (Smith 2010; McGarth 2011). Each social media platform has a mobile application feature, which allowed young adults to engage politically, as well as share and gather political information about the campaign and the candidates from any location, at any time.

During Obama's 2012 re-election campaign, young political participation fell to 45 %, a six-point decline from 51 % in 2008 ("The Youth Vote In 2012", CIRCLE 2013). The gender gap remained relatively the same with 48.6 % of young women voting compared to only 41.5 % of young men ("Voter Turnout Among Young Women and Men", CIRCLE 2013). Young African-American political participation (53.7 %) remained higher than the average for overall young Americans, but fell 4.5 points from their previous record high voting percentage (58.2 %) in 2008 ("Voter Turnout Among Young Women and Men", CIRCLE 2013). Young African-American women continue to have the highest voter turnout rate in 2012 at 60.1 %, although the percentage declined by 4 points since 2008 ("Voter Turnout Among Young Women and Men", CIRCLE 2013). Consistent with 2008, the young African-American women voting percentage remained higher than that of young white women (48.7 %) ("Voter Turnout Among Young Women and Men", CIRCLE 2013). Young African-American men's political participation remained high at 46.4 %, 3 points higher than young white men, but still down from 2008 ("Voter Turnout Among Young Women and Men", CIRCLE 2013). Young Latinos political participation also sharply declined to 36.9 % ("Voter Turnout Among Young Women and Men", CIRCLE 2013).

12.6 Effect on Young Adult Political Involvement

Forty-six million young adults (18–29) are eligible to vote, and they account for 21 % of America's eligible voting population ("The Youth Vote In 2012", CIRCLE 2013). During the 2008 presidential election, 52 % of eligible young adults voted, reflecting the highest percentage of voters from this population since 1972 (Godsay and Kirby 2010), when 18 became the legal voting age in America. Prior to 1996, young adult voter turnout was found to have been relatively consistent around 50 %, with a gradual decrease following the 1996 presidential election ("Young voters in the 2012 presidential election", CIRCLE 2012). According to a Center for Information and Research on Civic Learning and Engagement (CIRCLE) exit poll, 48 % of young voters stated being "excited" if Obama won the 2008 presidential election. There was a considerable amount of excitement surrounding the historic election, motivating young adults to want to be a part of history by engaging politically (Dudash and Harris 2011).

In 2012, there was a decline of enthusiasm for President Obama, with only 50 % of eligible young adults voting during the presidential election, although young voters still preferred him to Romney—60 % to 36 % respectively ("Young voters in the 2012 presidential election", CIRCLE, 2012). Young adults felt that Obama was better equipped to handle the federal deficit, the economy, the international crisis, and healthcare more efficiently than Mitt Romney ("Young voters in the 2012 presidential election", CIRCLE 2012). This could be due to the growing increase of ethnic and racial diversity of the young adult population in America, and young adults perceiving the Republican Party as "increasingly white" (Edwards 2000). Young adults were found to be more liberal on a variety of issues, with 64 % supporting a pathway to citizenship, 66 % supporting legalizing same-sex marriage, and 53 % willing to expand healthcare laws ("Young voters in the 2012 presidential election", CIRCLE 2012). This suggests that young adults are more inclined to be politically involved if there is a connection with the candidate and party, if the candidate generates high levels of excitement, and if issues pertaining to their demographic are addressed. Additionally, young adults viewed Obama's campaign as personal and modern due to his use of social media (Edwards 2000).

Moreover, CIRCLE research surveys found that registered young adults were more likely to vote if they felt prepared to vote by having enough information, if they were contacted by the campaign prior to voting, and if the medium used connected to them ("The Youth Vote In 2012", CIRCLE 2013). During the 2008 and 2012 presidential elections, social networking sites and social media were highly used to connect to young adults, who were found to be attracted to social media due to contribution opportunities that were presented to them (Fernandes et al. 2010). Likewise, research linked passive mobilization on SNS platforms to increase young adult political participation (Godsall 2010). Rice et al. (2012) further supported the idea that online political engagement of any form leads to further online contributions, although the researchers asserted that participation by young adults may fail to translate to greater offline political engagement.

References

Bakker, T. P., & de Vreese, C. H. (2011). Good news for the future? Young people, Internet use, and political participation [Electronic version]. *Communication Research, 38*(4), 451–470. doi:10.1177.009365021038.7.8.

Beck, F. D. (2001). Introduction to the special section, "struggles in building community". *Sociological Inquiry, 71*(4), 455–457.

Bronstein, J. (2012). Like me! Analyzing the 2012 presidential candidates Facebook pages. *Online Information Review, 37*(2), 173–192. doi:10.1108/OIR-01-2013-0002.

Center for Information and Research on Civic Learning and Engagement [CIRCLE]. (2013, July 17). Youth voting quick facts. In *CIRCLE Fact Sheet*. Retrieved August 11, 2013

CIRCLE. (2012, November 13). Young voters in the 2012 presidential election. In *CIRCLE: Fact Sheet*. Retrieved August 13, 2013.

CIRCLE. (2013, May). Voter turnout among young women and men in the 2012 presidential election. In *CIRCLE Fact Sheet*. Retrieved September 12, 2013.

Cohen, A. P. (1985). *Symbolic construction of community* (pp. 70–99). n.p.: Ellis Horwood & Tavistock.

Dudash, E. A., & Harris, S. (2011). New kids on the block: My first time in a political community. *American Behavioral Scientist, 55*(4), 469–478. doi:10.1177.000276421139.0.4.

Edwards, C. (2000). Out to rock the vote. *Insight on the News, 16*(39), 16.

Fernandes, J., Giurcanu, M., Bowers, K. W., & Neely, J. C. (2010). The writing on the wall: a content analysis of college students' facebook groups for the 2008 presidential election. *Mass Communication and Society, 13*, 653–675. doi:10.1080.15205436.2010.516865.
Godin, S. (2008). *Tribes: We need you to lead us*. London: Portfolio, Penguin Group (USA).
Godsall, D. (2010). *Violet is hopeful for change. Social media and Barack Obama's 2008 U.S Presidential election campaign*. n.p.: ProQuest, UMI Dissertations Publishing.
Godsay, S., & Kirby, E. (2010, October). Voter turnout among young women and men in the 2008 presidential election. In CIRCLE: The Center for Information & Research on Civic Learning & Engagement. Retrieved August 13, 2013.
Greenberg, A. (2009). A generation apart: young voters and the 2008 presidential election. *The Hedgehog Review, 11*(1), 74. Retrieved from General OneFile.
Hart, R. P., & Lind, C. J. (2010). Words and their ways in campaign '08. *American Behavioral Scientist, 54*(4), 355–381. doi:10.1177.000276421038.7.2.
Hayes, R.A. (2009). New media, new politics: political learning efficacy and the examination of uses of social network sites for political engagement (Doctoral dissertation, UMI Dissertations Publishing, Ann Arbor). Retrieved August 5, 2013, from ProQuest (304952463).
Haynes, A.A., & Pitts, B. (2009, January). Making an impression: new media in the 2008 presidential nomination [Electronic version]. *Symposium*, 53–58. doi:10.1017/S1049096509090052
Jenkins, K. B., & Cos, G. (2010). A time for change and a candidate's voice: pragmatism and the rhetoric of inclusion in Barack Obama's 2008 presidential campaign. *American Behavioral Scientist, 54*(3), 184–202. doi:10.1177.000276421038.7.6.
Johnson, T. J., & Perlmutter, D. D. (2010). Introduction: the facebook election. *Mass Communication and Society, 13*, 554–559. doi:10.1080.15205436.2010.517490.
Kaid, L. L., & Postelnicu, M. (2005). Political advertising in the 2004 election. *American Behavioral Scientist, 49*(2), 265–278. doi:10.1177.000276420527.4.1.
Komaromi, K., & Scott, EG (2011). Using social media to build community. *Competition Forum, 9*(2), 325–333. Retrieved July 16, 2013, from ProQuest.
Kushin, M. J., & Yamamoto, M. (2010). Did social media really matter? College students' use of online media and political decision making in the 2008 election. *Mass Communication and Society, 13*, 608–630. doi:10.1080.15205436.2010.516863.
McGarth, M. (2011). Technology, media, and political participation. *National Civic Review, 100*, 41–44. doi:10.1002/ncr.20075.
Pew Research Center. (2008, January 11). Internet's broader role in campaign 2008. In *Pew Research: Center for the People and the Press*. Retrieved August 11, 2013.
Pew Research Center. (2013, February 14). The demographics of social media users—2012. In *Pew Research Center*. Retrieved August 13, 2013.
Pinkleton, B. E., & Austin, E. W. (2004). Media perception and public affairs apathy in the politically inexperienced. *Mass Communication & Society, 7*(3), 319–337. Retrieved August 12, 2013.
Rice, L. L., Moffett, K. W., & Madupalli, R. (2012). Campaign-related social networking and the political participation of college students. *Social Science Computer Review, 31*(3), 257–279. doi:10.1177.089443931245.4.4.
Smith, A. (2010, September 17). Technology trends among people of color. In *Pew Internet*. Retrieved September 11, 2013.
Vaccari, C. (2008). From the air to the ground: The internet in the 2004 US presidential campaign. *New Media Society, 10*(4), 647–665. doi:10.1177/1461444808093735.
Weaver, A. C., & Morrison, B. B. (2008). Social networking [electronic version]. *Computer, 97–100*.
Webley, K. (2010, September 23). How the Nixon-Kennedy debate changed the world [Electronic version]. *TIME*.

Chapter 13
A Winding Road from "Likes" to Votes

The Role of Social Media in the 2013 Czech Presidential Elections

Václav Štětka, Alena Macková, and Marta Fialová

Abstract This case study analyzes the use of social media in the campaign for the historically first direct presidential elections in the Czech Republic in January 2013. Following a brief outline of the political context and outcomes of the elections, this study explores and compares the strategies of campaign communication of the nine presidential candidates on the social networking sites Facebook and Twitter. Apart from mapping the dynamics of the campaign and the responsiveness of Facebook and Twitter users, we have used content analysis to examine basic formal characteristics of over 1,000 messages posted on Facebook in the course of the campaign by the candidates and their teams. Additionally, this chapter also examines more closely the place of social media in the campaign of Karel Schwarzenberg, the eventual runner-up of the presidential race, whose team distanced all other candidates in both the extent as the level of sophistication of communication carried via the social networking sites. Overall, the presidential elections have revealed both the potential as well as limits of electoral mobilization through social networks, while at the same time it has demonstrated the continuing importance of more traditional means of campaign communication in the Czech Republic.

Keywords Social media • Election campaign • Czech Republic • Online mobilization • Political marketing

---

V. Štětka (✉)
Charles University in Prague, Institute of Communication Studies and Journalism, Prague, Czech Republic
e-mail: stetka@fsv.cuni.cz

A. Macková • M. Fialová
Masaryk University, Brno, Czech Republic

B. Pătruţ and M. Pătruţ (eds.), *Social Media in Politics*, Public Administration and Information Technology 13, DOI 10.1007/978-3-319-04666-2_13,

13.1 Introduction

The first direct presidential elections in the history of the Czech Republic were held in January 2013. 61 % of the electorate took part in the first round, which was nearly the same number as in the 2010 parliamentary elections (62.6 %). The direct elections not only broadened the range of acts by which the Czech citizens can influence politics and participate in public life, but they also brought a new challenge for the election campaign communication. The rise in the use of political marketing and the general shift in professionalization of political communication arrived in the Czech Republic a little later than in most Western European countries or in the U.S. A clear landmark in the development of election campaigns was the 2006 parliamentary elections, during which some Czech political parties resorted to PR agencies and began to develop a more long-term strategy in their communication (Matušková 2009). However, the direct presidential elections differed in many respects from parliamentary elections, and these differences were also reflected in the character of the campaign. First and foremost, these elections were focused on individual candidates instead of political parties. The second difference concerned the way of financing the campaign, with the candidates being obliged to transparent accounting and having the maximum size of the budget for their campaign determined by law. Last but not least, it was a political opportunity for a number of independent candidates, who were able to run for the presidential office without the support of a political party and often with limited resources for the campaign.

These novelties in the format of the elections, opening up new opportunities for campaign management, had naturally a significant impact on the transformation of campaign communication. As in the parliamentary elections, the presidential candidates tried to make use of the broad range of traditional media channels in order to address potential voters. The classical mass communication strategies were however also supplemented by online communication instruments and platforms, since a considerable part of the election campaign also took place on online social networking sites, very much for the first time in the Czech political history. In a sense, the 2013 presidential elections thus became a testing ground for the exploitation of this new type of communication media in political communication in the Czech Republic.

13.2 Theoretical Background

The rapid spread of the new media and communication technologies over the course of the last decade and their gradual adoption by political actors has significantly affected the character of public sphere in which democratic politics is played out, and has presented new opportunities and challenges for political communication. Especially with regards to election campaigns, the arrival of the social networking sites (SNS) and other Web 2.0 applications (see O'Reilly 2005) has enabled political actors to directly approach, interact with, get feedback from and mobilize voters, bypassing thereby editorial control of the traditional news media organizations (Zittel 2004) and significantly cutting down on campaign costs (Gueorguieva 2008). Ever since the remarkable success of the 2008 Barack Obama campaign, one of the first ones to ever utilize social media (Lilleker and Jackson 2010; Fernandes et al. 2010; Cogburn and Espinoza-Vasquez 2011), social networking sites have been increasingly used by the political parties as well as individual politicians and integrated into election campaigns across the Western world (Jungherr 2012; Strandberg 2013; Gibson 2013;). In Europe, several countries have recently experienced the phenomenon of "cyberparties" (Gibson 2013), the rise of new political parties or movements which have generated electoral support mainly or almost entirely from new media, including the Polish party Ruch Palikota (currently the most followed Polish party on Facebook), Slovak party Freedom and Solidarity (whose success in the 2010 elections was largely driven by its new media campaign) or the Pirate Party of Germany ("Piraten"), succeeding between 2009 and 2012 in several regional elections.

Apart from the already mentioned advantages, one of the main benefits of the use of SNSs in campaign communication is arguably their suitability for targeting specific voting groups (Strandberg 2013; Baumgartner and Morris 2010), and also the ability to start a viral campaign which can spread out to reach even those voters who are not SNS users (Greyes 2011). Summarizing the "direct" and "indirect" effects of social media on campaign communication, Kim Strandberg notes that:

> "On the one hand, it [the social media] serves as an affordable and versatile direct link to various types of voter segments, as well as an efficient fundraising and organizing tool.
>
> On the other hand, it could provide campaigns with added leverage through the traditional media and 'word-of-mouth' effects" (Strandberg 2013: 4).

The interactive nature of social media, while offering the politicians new ways of reaching and mobilizing the electorate, has at the same time opened space for more direct participation of citizens on the electoral process, and for their more active engagement in democratic politics in general (Kirk and Schill 2011; Effing et al. 2011). Even though the claims about the democratic potential of online technologies have frequently been made from the onset of the internet (Poster 1995; Norris 2001), which has been seen as a space for political participation that twenty-first century liberal democracies were sorely lacking, the explosion of social media in the recent years has rejuvenated these hopes, particularly with respect to the potential of mobilization of young people who are the most extensive users of social media (Junco 2013).

13.3 Aim and Methodology of the Study

While the role of social media in both political communication and participation of voters has been examined by an increasing number of nation-based case studies as well as cross-national comparative analyses across Europe (e.g. Elmer 2012; Larsson and Hallvard 2012, 2013; Gustafsson 2012; Jungherr 2012; Graham et al. 2013; Strandberg 2013), this research area has so far been rather neglected by an academic enquiry in the Czech Republic, arguably owing to the fact that new media of all sorts have been used in the previous Czech election campaigns only as a marginal tool (Macková et al. 2013). This chapter attempts to expand the rather sparse scholarship on the adoption of social networking sites in political communication and political marketing in the Czech Republic, and add to the ever growing body of international research on the use of social media in electoral marketing by means of a case study of the 2013 Czech presidential election campaign. The principal aim of this study, therefore, was to examine the extent of adoption of social networking sites by the nine presidential candidates, and compare their formal characteristics as well as their success in mobilizing social networks users. Given the novelty of the topic in the political context of the Czech Republic, the research was designed as descriptive, focusing on mapping of the main similarities and differences between individual candidates in their ways of use of the two particular social networking sites, Facebook and Twitter, during the campaign.

With around 3.8 million registered Czech user accounts, Facebook is by far the most popular social networking site in the Czech Republic, as indeed in many other countries around the world.[1] Twitter, which is widely popular network abroad, and increasingly more used for political communication, is much less widespread in the Czech Republic—in spring 2013 it had only about 150,000 users,[2] which resulted in the fact that its exploitation in the presidential campaign turned out to have been rather marginal when compared to Facebook. Therefore, we decided to monitor Twitter only for the basic features (dynamics of the number of tweets and followers), while for the exploration of communication on Facebook we also used content analysis, identifying selected formal characteristics of the posts (types of messages and candidates' statements).[3]

The data were gathered during the 51 days preceding the first round of the elections, resulting in a total of 1,197 unique contributions on Facebook[4] and

[1] According to http://www.socialbakers.com/facebook-statistics/czech-republic, retrieved 20 August 2013.

[2] According to Klaboseni.cz (http://www.klaboseni.cz), retrieved 12 March 2013.

[3] The formal characteristics of the posts on Facebook were coded by two coders; the intercoder reliability, calculated on a pilot sample of 100 posts, was between 0.89 and 0.97 (Cohen's kappa).

[4] The Facebook data for the first round of the elections come from the period between 23 November 2012 (official announcement of the candidates) and 12 January 2013 (the second day of the first round). For the second round, the data cover the period between 13 January 2013 and 26 January 2013. In both cases, the data were collected after midnight of the second election day.

607 on Twitter.[5] The second round followed after 2 weeks, during which the accounts of the two remaining candidates were monitored. The quantitative part of the analysis was supplemented by qualitative observations focusing on the establishment of other online groups and events related to the campaign, particularly in relation to the campaign of the eventual runner-up Karel Schwarzenberg, and also on the mutual resonance of the online and offline campaign communication.

13.4 The Course and Results of the Elections

Until 2013, the head of the state used to be elected indirectly, by the vote of the Parliament. Candidates for the elections used to be nominated by deputies (groups of representatives from the Upper or Lower Chamber of the Parliament). In direct elections, candidates could be proposed not only by members of Parliament, but also by citizens, once their application was endorsed by at least 10 senators (in the Upper House), 20 deputies (in the Lower House) or 50,000 citizens of the Czech Republic.[6] For these first direct presidential elections, 20 candidates applied in early November 2012 but more than half of them were excluded by the Ministry of Interior for not having met the requirement of collecting the necessary number of signatures.

In the end, the election contest included nine legally registered candidates. The MPs of the ruling Civic Democratic Party (ODS) endorsed the Vice Chairman of the Senate, Přemysl Sobotka. The coalition partner of ODS, the second strongest right-wing party in the country, TOP 09 (Tradition, Responsibility and Prosperity) nominated the Minister of Foreign Affairs and chairman of TOP 09, Karel Schwarzenberg. The Senator and Prague Council deputy Jiří Dienstbier (Czech Social Democratic Party) did gather a sufficient number of signatures from his fellow citizens but in the end entered the election on the basis of his nomination by 27 senators. The other candidates for the Czech presidency included the former Prime Minister and chairman of the Social Democrats, Miloš Zeman; the former Prime Minister and Vice-President of the European Bank for Development and Recovery Jan Fischer; the European Parliament member and ex-Minister of Health Zuzana Roithová (Christian Democratic Union-Czechoslovak People's Party); the ex-European Parliament member and chairperson of the Sovereignty Party Jana

---

[5] The beginning of the data collection on Twitter was delayed by 3 days due to the ambiguity in the official accounts of the candidates (from 27 November 2012 to 12 January 2013, the second round from 13 to 26 January 2013).

[6] The direct election of the President was officially legislated by the Constitution act no. 71/2012. Additionally the procedural regulation no. 275/2102 was adopted, about the election of the president of the republic, which among other things defined the details of the proposal of candidates. Both acts became effective in October 2012, when the date of first round of the election (January 2013) was proclaimed by the chairman of the Senate.

Bobošíková; the former Senator Taťana Fischerová, as well as the composer and painter Vladimír Franz. The last candidate, differing from the rest not only in his ostentatious distancing from party politics but also in his alternative appearance—Franz is a devotee of body art and his body is 90 % tatooed—told the media that he decided to accept the candidature in response to the initiative born on Facebook.[7]

The interval between the official announcement of the confirmed candidates (23 November 2012) and the first round of elections (11 and 12 January 2013) did not leave much leeway for the efforts of the election teams and candidates' supporters. In the public service media, the Czech Television and the Czech Radio, the election campaign was officially opened as late as 26 December and terminated on 9 January 2013. In this period, each candidate was given space in these media for his or her presentation in the form of election spots. The nominees thus had little time left for the campaign. Moreover, this time included the Christmas holidays, which normally tend to considerably subdue political communication. This situation contributed to a sizable increase in the intensity of the campaign only in the last 2 weeks before the elections.

The biggest favorite in the pre-election polls had for a long time been Jan Fischer, who was overtaken only as late as by the end of December by Miloš Zeman, who in the end won the first round of the elections (see Graph 13.1). The second round was quite surprisingly not reached by the widely favored pair (Fischer and Dienstbier) but instead by the then-Foreign Minister Karel Schwarzenberg, a 73-year old aristocrat who spent most of his life in Austria and who, at the beginning of the campaign, was given minimal chance by the polling agencies.

Although the presidential campaign did not last very long, it greatly affected the Czech society and clearly split the public opinion. Especially around Schwarzenberg, a group of enthusiastic supporters became active, particularly (but not only) on social networking sites which played a major role in his campaign (as will be demonstrated further in this chapter). On the other hand, Zeman gathered supporters mainly through his appearances in pre-election television discussions and by exploitation of other, more traditional channels of communication, like outdoor billboards. In the end, not even the open support by the majority of social networks users and by the mostly right-wing press (with three main dailies explicitly endorsing the chairman of TOP 09) could help Karel Schwarzenberg to victory, and Miloš Zeman took the second round with a fairly decisive margin of nearly 10 %, having gained 2,717,405 votes (54.8 %).

---

[7] See http://www.guardian.co.uk/world/2013/jan/09/vladimir-franz-tattooed-czech-elections, retrieved 02 June 2013.

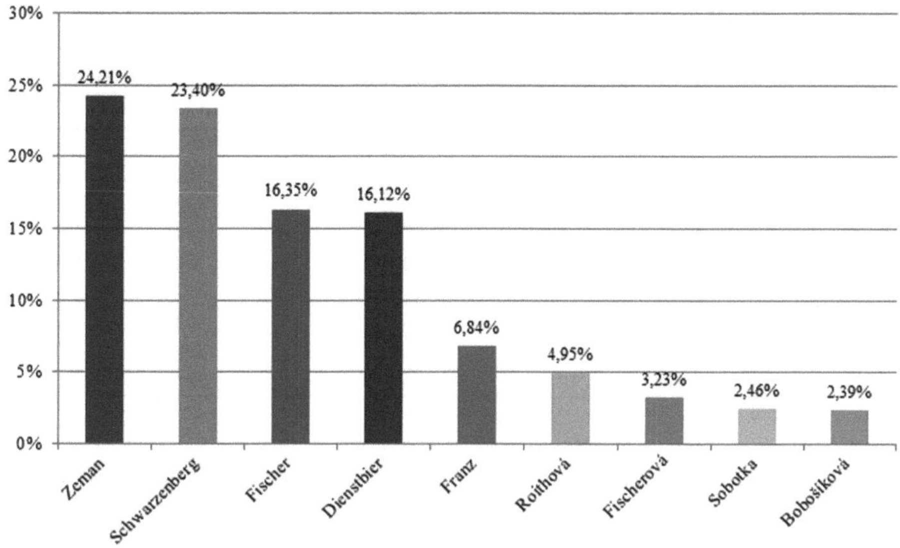

Graph 13.1 Results of the first round of the 2013 Czech presidential elections (% of votes). Source: Czech Statistical Office and authors

13.5 Presidential Elections on Social Networks: A Basic Overview

Aside from their own websites,[8] all candidates—with just one exception—used both Facebook and Twitter for online communication with the electorate. However, many of them established their online profiles only for the purposes of the presidential campaign, without having previously been users of social networking sites. Among the exceptions were Schwarzenberg (with already existing profiles on both Twitter and Facebook), Sobotka, Bobošíková, as well as Dienstbier, all of whom had managed their profiles or pages on Facebook in a more or less active way before the start of the presidential campaign. The remaining candidates were therefore slightly disadvantaged by the necessity of having to develop the base of their followers virtually "from scratch", a task arguably difficult to achieve within the limited period of the campaign, which was apparent especially on Twitter. As it is clear from the data (see Table 13.1), some of the candidates used Twitter in the campaign only marginally (often in the form of merely copying of their Facebook contributions)[9] or they gave up on using it completely.

[8] Zuzana Roithová did not use Twitter in her election campaign.

[9] For example, Táňa Fischerová had these two channels interlinked, which explains the fact that she was nominally the most "active" candidate on Twitter, generating 304 tweets during the campaign period (more than 50 % of all of the candidates' tweets). The second highest number of tweets (which was however the highest number of *original* tweets) was posted by Karel

Table 13.1 The dynamics of the number of fans on Facebook and audience on Twitter in the campaign

	Number of Facebook fans			Number of followers on Twitter		
Candidate	23/11 2012	12/1 2013	Increase	27/11 2012	12/1 2013	Increase
Bobošíková	1,300	**1,955**	655	13	**59**	46
Dienstbier	1,560	**3,862**	2,302	172	**364**	192
Fischer	7,125	**10,226**	3,101	105	**130**	25
Fischerová	3,069	**7,749**	4,680	137	**214**	77
Franz	42,089	**65,723**	23,634	697	**780**	83
Roithová	1,186	**3,005**	1,819	–	–	–
Sobotka	5,526	**12,970**	7,444	555	**692**	137
Schwarzenberg	35,021	**95,726**	60,705	2,497	**5,550**	3,053
Zeman	4,915	**15,654**	10,739	26	**59**	33

Source: Authors

Another fact which made the use of Twitter in the campaign more challenging was the number of fake accounts which emerged during the campaign. While some of them were rather satirical (the most successful was the fake account of Karel Schwarzenberg, @schwarzenbergk),[10] others were more easily interchangeable with the official accounts launched by the candidates' teams. Communication on these accounts was usually less formal and therefore very popular. Of all the candidates, only Schwarzenberg succeeded in attracting a significant number of users on Twitter, as he managed to gather more than 8,000 followers by the second round of elections, a historically unique achievement on the Czech Twitter (and in particular among political profiles). At the same time, Schwarzenberg's team made a great effort adjusting the communication on this network to this specific communication environment.[11]

As already mentioned, the penetration of Twitter is rather underdeveloped in the Czech Republic, so it comes as little surprise that Facebook became the dominant social networking site for campaign communication in the 2013 presidential election. Despite its promising potential (based on the number of users), the intensity of Facebook use by the candidates differed greatly, with some of them clearly not paying too much attention to this new communication platform. Facebook became an important tool particularly for the so-called civic candidates, particularly Franz and Fischerová, who did not enter the elections based on the support of large political parties but who were nominated directly by the citizens and presented

Schwarzenberg (165), with the third place belonging to Jana Bobošíková (88). The fourth-highest number was 22 (Dienstbier), indicating the remaining six candidates did not really take Twitter seriously as a platform for mobilization of voters.

[10] This fake account was followed by more than 20,000 users (http://www.socialbakers.com/twitter/schwarzenbergk, retrieved 15 June 2013).

[11] In one case, when commenting upon a television discussion of the candidates, Schwarzenberg's team went so far in the assessment of the political opponents that after many aggravated responses by other users, the contributions were erased and the team was forced to apologise for them.

Table 13.2 The number and success of contributions by presidential candidates on Facebook

	Number of posts	Average number of daily posts	Likes (average per post)	Comments (average per post)	Share (average per post)
Bobošíková	97	**1.9**	29.4	13.8	5.7
Dienstbier	100	**2.0**	44.7	9.4	11.9
Fischer	77	**1.5**	187.6	141.8	18.03
Fischerová	285	**5.6**	74.8	11.7	41.5
Franz	182	**3.6**	637.1	84.3	113.3
Roithová	40	**0.8**	85.6	11.3	32.4
Sobotka	63	**1.2**	90.1	39.8	10
Schwarzenberg	141	**2.8**	1280.1	165.1	298.5
Zeman	64	**1.3**	424.8	168.2	72.8
Schwarzenberg—second round	96	**6.9**	3964.2	723.2	1056.5
Zeman—second round	53	**3.8**	1978.0	760.8	727.7
Total	1,197				

Source: Authors

themselves as non-political candidates. Most of these candidates also had low-budget campaigns, largely based on the work of volunteers, within which Facebook often served as a tool for mobilization of citizens and for coordination of their commitment.

> "A wonderful wave of creativity is rising. People themselves produce printed matter, visuals, texts and various materials in support of Táňa Fischerová. A proof of this may be another nice version of a pin, which has reached us today." (Facebook of Fischerová, 19 Dec 2012)

> "Billboards are not needed, active people will do!" (Facebook of Fischerová, 30 Dec 2012)

In case of two civic candidates, Fischerová and Franz, the intensity of communication was visibly higher than in case of most others—with the notable exception of Karel Schwarzenberg, who succeeded in winning by far the most "likes". Because of such a wide base of followers, their contributions were also the most shared ones of all the candidates (Table 13.2).

A notable mobilization of followers, as measured by the dynamics of their growth (and other activities connected with the increasing number of fans) was observable during the campaign on the profiles of Schwarzenberg, Franz, and finally (between the first and second round) of Miloš Zeman as well. Franz succeeded in mobilizing his followers considerably in the autumn months, during the period of collection of signatures (necessary for his nomination), but later his activity declined and during Christmas holidays his profile became silent for 2 weeks. Just like many other candidates, he was not very successful in restarting the mobilization wave at the beginning of January.[12] On the other hand, an

[12] Although the team of Fischerová was most active on this network, the mobilisation was lower than in case of the second civic candidate, Vladimír Franz (Table 13.1).

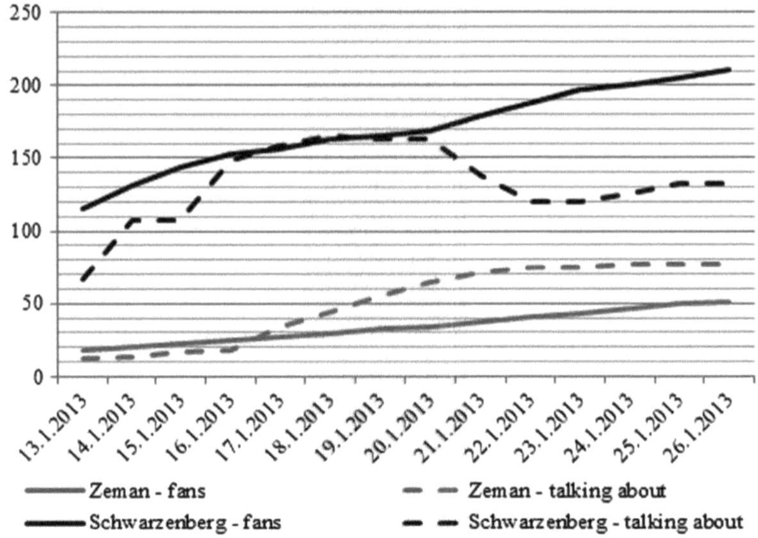

Graph 13.2 Development of the number of fans and "talking about" on Facebook before the second round of elections (in thousands). Source: Authors

enormous wave of support arose after the New Year's Day in favor of Karel Schwarzenberg. While before the first round, there was an increase of more than 60,000 followers on Facebook, in the 2 weeks between the first and second rounds another 166,000 was added (see Graph 13.2), which was naturally reflected in the increased activities on his Facebook page. A surprisingly low activity on Facebook was displayed by the long-time favoured candidate Fischer, who launched his campaign a little earlier than the rest of the candidates and soon exhausted his potential for mobilization. This candidate was also harmed by becoming the target of several negative campaigns and of more or less open attacks by his political opponents. Criticism was turned especially to Fischer's previous membership in the Communist Party, and this information was also heavily disseminated via social networks.

Before the second round, the two remaining candidates made a greater effort at mobilizing online support. After his victory in the first round—albeit a very tight one—Zeman's team increased the targeting of the Facebook users, although the majority of his voters in the first round (mainly elderly people and citizens living in small towns and villages) hardly represented typical users of social networks. Given this situation, the challenge for Zeman's team was clearly how to win the support of voters for other candidates from the first round, and particularly the younger ranks. In an attempt to address this part of the electorate, Miloš Zeman's team set up a special Facebook page "We are also young but we vote for Miloš", directly aimed against the wave of support for Schwarzenberg by the young people before the first round. As shown in Graph 13.2, this strategy was probably successful, at least partially, given the increased number of his fans on Facebook as well as the number of the so-called "talking about",[13] measuring activities of Facebook users connected in some way to particular profile.

What can these statistics tell us about the campaign before the second round? Of interest may be the fact that while the number of Schwarzenberg followers continued to grow, the statistics "talking about" began to drop sharply around the middle of the campaign before the second round, following a rising wave of criticism of Schwarzenberg by Zeman's supporters.[14]

Zeman's partial success on Facebook is also documented by the poll conducted by the polling agency Median during the second round of elections, showing that the differences in composition of voters for the two candidates slightly dropped when compared to the first round. Thus, Zeman managed to address 16 % of the voters in the youngest age category, as compared to 27 % who voted for Schwarzenberg. No less interesting may be the data on the voters' Internet use, which was part of the same survey. 23 % of Zeman's voters used the Internet daily (and 18 % were daily users of Facebook and other social networks), while among Schwarzenberg's voters, 33 % were daily Internet users and 30 % daily Facebook users. These figures show that the wave of support of Schwarzenberg before the first round may not have been so easily transferable and its impact could possibly be smaller than initially predicted. While the course of the election campaign and the results of the first round created a widely shared idea about the mass support of Schwarzenberg by the young voters, the survey revealed that 58 % of the voters aged 18–29 declared, on Election Day, they would abstain from voting, which was arguably a blow to Schwarzenberg's changes in the run.[15]

13.6 The Content of Facebook Campaign: Supremacy of Meta-Communication

Since the use of social media for political communication is not yet widespread in the Czech Republic, the social networks channels of each candidate were mostly set up directly for the presidential campaign, as demonstrated by the names of the Facebook pages and profiles (e.g. "Zeman for the Prague Castle" or "President Táňa

[13] "Talking about" is the number of people on Facebook who have engaged with certain FB page during the last 7 days. It measures all activities connected to the particular profile (sharing, mentions, comments, etc.), not just the number of "fans".

[14] A wave of criticism, displaying features of a negative campaign, focused on the issue of Schwarzenberg's wife being allegedly "unsuitable" for the post of the First Lady because of her poor Czech and the Nazi past of her father, as well as on Schwarzenberg's opinions regarding the violent expulsion of the Sudeten Germans in 1945, which he was heavily critical of, alluding it to war crimes. Zeman, on the other hand, endorsed this act, much in line with the still-dominant, nationalistic interpretation of the Czech post-war history.

[15] See http://www.median.cz/docs/Median_PREZIDENT_II_KOLO_determinanty_vysledku.pdf, retrieved 14 June 2013.

Fischerová") as well as by the content of the communication, the vast majority of which was oriented towards the presidential campaign only. The narrowing down of the content to the matters of the campaign was probably also related to the relatively weak position of the president within the Czech political system. According to the Constitution, the Czech president has no significant powers (even though both previous Czech presidents, Václav Havel and Václav Klaus, often managed to extend their powers beyond the scope of the Constitution) and so the candidates themselves faced the problem of a relative shortage of issues to be communicated to the citizens. The themes of the campaign were often produced artificially and the candidates were obliged to publish their opinions and comments even on topics that do not belong within the scope of competences of the presidential office. To a large degree, the live television discussions became the main "producers" of themes for the campaign, especially between the first and second rounds of elections.

What were the main features of the communication facilitated by candidates' teams on Facebook? As already hinted, the vast majority of candidates were focused in their Facebook communication on the actual course of the campaign (see Table 13.3). A surprisingly small amount of communication was devoted to emphasizing the personality of the candidate him/herself; relatively more attention to the presentations of the candidates' political opinions and statements was paid by the teams of Schwarzenberg, Zeman, Fischer and Sobotka. In the case of the civic candidates, Fischerová and Franz, expressions of political opinions were almost entirely absent, a fact which was indeed much criticized by their opponents, especially in Franz's case who largely based his communication strategy on his controversial image (the tattooed face and body).[16] This certainly helped him in attracting the attention of international media that treated him as a sort of curiosity:

> "Vladimir Franz, an opera composer and painter, is tattooed from head to toe, his face a warrior-like mix of blue, green and red. He's also running in a surprising third place ahead of this week's Czech presidential elections." (*The Guardian*,9 Jan 2013)[17]

> "This is the most interesting presidential candidate ever." (*Huffington Post*)[18]

Looking at the content of candidates' statements in greater detail (Table 13.4), we can see that on average, only 19 % of them were devoted to political causes, problems or topical events (value "Issue"); a much greater portion (68 %) was taken by comments regarding the course of their own campaign.

---

[16] More often than other candidates, Franz shared pictures on Facebook. They made up a quarter of all his contributions (as opposed to the average of 17 % in case of the rest of other candidates), and the vast majority of them depicted his face and body.

[17] See http://www.theguardian.com/world/2013/jan/09/vladimir-franz-tattooed-czech-elections , retrieved 12 January 2013.

[18] See http://videos.huffingtonpost.com/world/this-is-the-most-interesting-presidential-candidate-ever-517478350, retrieved 14 January 2013.

Table 13.3 Content of contributions by presidential candidates on Facebook (%)

Candidate	Candidate's statements	Promotion and campaign	Information	Others
Bobošíková	32.0	34.0	34.0	–
Dienstbier	21.2	42.4	35.4	1.0
Fischer	40.3	42.9	11.7	5.2
Fischerová	12.6	66.3	18.6	2.5
Franz	15.9	47.3	31.9	4.9
Roithová	22.5	62.5	15.0	–
Sobotka	44.4	41.3	12.7	1.6
Schwarzenberg	38.3	48.9	9.2	3.5
Zeman	25.0	59.4	14.1	1.6
Schwarzenberg—second round	18.9	71.7	7.5	1.9
Zeman—second round	42.7	52.1	3.1	2.1
Total	22.6	52.6	19.3	2.6
N	306	629	231	31

Source: Authors

Table 13.4 Types of statements by presidential candidates on Facebook (%)

Candidate	Issue	Campaign	Others
Bobošíková	6.5	77.4	16.1
Dienstbier	33.3	61.9	4.8
Fischer	25.8	61.3	12.9
Fischerová	13.9	83.3	2.8
Franz	10.3	82.8	6.9
Roithová	44.4	44.4	11.1
Sobotka	7.4	63.0	29.6
Schwarzenberg	7.1	78.6	14.3
Zeman	18.8	62.5	18.8
Total	18.6	68.4	13.0
N	57	209	40

Source: Authors

Thus, in general, this online social network primarily served as a platform for informing about the campaign; in other words, it was mainly filled with "meta-communication". The candidates' opinions or information about their personality as themes of communication were kept rather in the background, while contributions of a more private character were entirely absent. Arguably, Facebook was not even used as a tool for developing a long-term relationship with the followers, which was perhaps due to the relatively short duration of the pre-election campaigns. Online communication was based more on efforts at fast mobilization and at informing citizens about the ongoing campaign (by pointing out topical events, activities, interviews in the media, etc.) For the civic candidates, Facebook was clearly a very important tool of communication as well as of coordination of their campaign volunteers, which was of major importance especially in the initial phase of the campaign, when the volunteers collected signatures in support of their candidature and tried to engage the citizens.

13.7 Endorsements by Celebrities

Although the support of politicians by celebrities has already occurred in the Czech Republic, it was the 2013 presidential elections that have really brought forward the trend of celebritization of politics. In the Czech presidential elections, both types of celebritization mentioned by John Street (2004) could be identified. The first is the type classified by Street as "celebrity politicians", i.e. well-known people trying to assert their own political interest through the elections. An example of such celebrity in the Czech elections was one of the civic candidates, the composer Vladimír Franz, or a Czech of Japanese origin, Tomio Okamura, who after the check of the petition sheets was found just below the 50,000 signatures needed for nomination. The second type of celebritization according to Street, that is, the exploitation of the qualities of the celebrities for the campaign, was much more frequent. The statements of many celebrities became a significant feature of the presidential campaign. While in the Parliamentary elections the phenomenon of personal endorsement has so far not been very common in the Czech Republic, the presidential campaign brought onto the web pages and Facebook accounts a large number of well-known persons expressing their support for this or that candidate.

Many famous people from the domains of culture, politics or science made known their preferences for the candidates, who then used this support in their official campaigns—either directly in TV advertisements (election spots) or indirectly, in communications on online social networks. The latter strategy was particularly strongly adopted by Schwarzenberg and Dienstbier. Nearly one third of the Facebook contributions categorized as promotion in our analysis (see Table 13.3) was actually a statement of support by well- (or sometimes less-) known public personalities.

Of all the candidates, Schwarzenberg enjoyed the widest endorsement by celebrities coming from politics, culture, and science, very much from the moment when he first announced the launch of his campaign in September 2012. On his official communication channels, short quotes by the celebrities giving reasons for preferring him were frequently posted:

> "Why do I want to vote for Karel Schwarzenberg? Because he is an aristocrat. Not because he has a coat of arms but because he has an aristocratic spirit." Jiří Menzel, film director (Facebook of Karel Schwarzenberg, 13 Dec 2012)

> "I cannot see anyone else among the candidates who is able to develop the legacy of Václav Havel in his presidential office but Karel Schwarzenberg." Michal Prokop, musician (Facebook of Karel Schwarzenberg, 16 Dec 2012)

The endorsement by individual musicians and popular music bands was widely promoted by Schwarzenberg's election team on social networks even in the early phases of the campaign, especially with regard to the so-called "Nights with Karel", public events which took the form of concerts by the supporting bands and musicians, and which were aimed primarily at the youngest voters. An important role in the first but especially in the second round of the campaign was also played by the stylization of Schwarzenberg as a successor of the particular style of presidency attributed to the first Czech president, Václav Havel. In the final phase of his campaign, his team often referred to their long-term friendship, as well as to Schwarzenberg's contacts with the dissidents. Miloš Zeman, on the contrary, was often presented as the successor of the (infamous) political style of the 1990s, directly linked to the outgoing president Václav Klaus.

13.8 Karel Schwarzenberg: An Aristocrat Ruling the Facebook

As already mentioned, the unexpected success of Karel Schwarzenberg in the first round of the presidential elections became almost a sensation, especially given the polls showing the voters' support for him in single digits until late December. However, in 2 weeks his team succeeded in stepping up the campaign, which started later than in the case of the other candidates (a mere 4 months before the elections). Although Schwarzenberg was the only one to already have some base of followers on Twitter and Facebook before the elections, in these 4 months he managed to multiply this base several times (Table 13.2 and Graph 13.2).

In spite of being the oldest candidate (73 years of age) and deliberately pursuing a very conservative image (perhaps most notably symbolized by his bowtie or his somewhat archaic Czech), Schwarzenberg managed to win the hearts of the largest part of the young electorate. This was certainly helped by the fact that apart from the more conservative line of his campaign, emphasizing his overall amicable, humorous but very level-headed personality which clearly distanced him from the other candidates, his election team led a "punk-tinged" campaign targeting young voters and voters from big cities.[19] The visuals disseminated mainly through the outdoor campaign—posters, leaflets, stickers or badges (Fig. 13.1)—with Schwarzenberg with a pink hair typical of the punk subculture and with the slogan "Karel for PreSIDent" bore a clear reference to Sid Vicious from the Sex Pistols (Eibl, Gregor and Macková 2013).[20] These visuals mainly served for promotion of many events linked to the campaign. Apart from the events called "Let's have a beer with Karel", which were launched already in the 2010 parliamentary elections, his election team organized a series of concerts "A Night with Karel", held in regional towns and widely promoted on Facebook. It can be therefore claimed that he succeeded in interlinking the online and offline campaigns, which could be seen

[19] For more information about the style of his campaign which caught an eye of international media see an article in *The New York Times* of 24 Jan. 2013: http://www.nytimes.com/2013/01/25/world/europe/czech-prince-schwarzenberg-runs-a-punk-campaign.html?_r=2& last accessed 26 August 2013.

[20] The consistent use of Karel Schwarzenberg's first name only was yet another strategy in the campaign that aimed at bringing him closer to the young people, sending a message that despite of his aristocratic family origin he is a very informal and youth-spirited man.

Fig. 13.1 An example of a visual used in the campaign of Karel Schwarzenberg. Source: VolimKarla.cz

for example in the rapid spreading of the badges both throughout Facebook profiles as well as in their physical form.

A strong potential for viral dissemination on online social nets was also exhibited in many video programmes produced by his election team or his promoters from the ranks of well-known public personalities, as discussed above. These videos, usually emphasizing humor, which was an essentially part of Schwarzenberg's campaign, became widely popular already before the official election spots were made public.

A significant role in the rise of the enormous wave of support on online social networks for Schwarzenberg was played by the followers themselves, who took an active part in the mass spreading of campaign-related events (e.g. "I'm going to the elections and voting for Karel") or information about the campaign and the elections (e.g. the video "World Politician", featuring an endorsement to Schwarzenberg by one of the country's most popular young singers on 10 January 2013, became one of the most shared online contributions in the elections).

13.9 Social Networks as Catalysts of the Polarization of Society

The candidates for the office of the Czech president used online social networks in a limited way, and the number of their followers—with the exception of Schwarzenberg and Franz—was measured in thousands, rather than tens of thousands. Still, there was a notable activation of the social networks users in general, beyond the group of fans and followers of the candidates themselves. People used social media to express and spread support for their favorite candidate or expressed their antipathy towards their rivals. Unsurprisingly, Facebook became the centre of this communication buzz. There was some mobilization on Twitter as well but due to the lesser number of its users who formed a rather homogenous opinion group (displaying an overwhelming support for Schwarzenberg), there were fewer conflicts of opinion on Twitter than on Facebook.

A major part of those activities on social networks which were not managed by the candidates' election teams but rather fuelled by the enthusiasm of the citizens was the use of political satire. The citizens produced various memes and viral videos, founded a range of groups and Facebook pages filled with praise or calumny, or launched entire web pages. Much of this satire was turned against Miloš Zeman, especially after the first round of the elections, and this trend has continued even after him entering the presidential office, with the main theme of most of the jokes being Zeman's openly positive attitude to alcohol and smoking.

Schwarzenberg was not saved from becoming a target of jokes either, a large part of which was focusing on his frequent dosing off during the Parliament sessions, as well as on his often inaudible pronunciation. These two qualities became the focus of parody pictures and many jokes.[21] However, as Baumgartner (2007) has argued (based on his analysis of satirical clips of the JibJab group), the effects of political satire on citizens can differ based on the kind of humor used in the satirical materials. While the kind of satire which is very critical in its substance may radicalize already existing opinions about the candidate (which seems to fit the case of jokes on Miloš Zeman), the use of kind-hearted humor does not necessary lead to an increase in antipathies towards politicians but, according to Baumgartner, has often a reverse effect, which is exactly what might have happened with the rather amiable (and certainly not malicious) jokes about Schwarzenberg.

The public circulation of political satire, disseminated mainly (although not exclusively) through social media, undoubtedly contributed to the strong polarization of the Czech society especially before the second round of the elections. Interestingly, the candidates themselves waged no negative campaign on social networks; the polarization was probably caused and reinforced simply by the activity of the citizens and self-organized online groups.[22] As for the actual sources of polarization, we can first identify the activities connected with the production of videos and their diffusion through social media. A specific group of activists tried to persuade citizens to think carefully whether to give their vote to those candidates who they believed had little chance of reaching the second round. Another such group tried to prevent the two most-favoured candidates ahead of the elections, Zeman and Fischer, from reaching the second round (this was the aim of the initiative "How to get rid of Zeman and Fischer?"). These attempts were met with many reactions on social networks. Many citizens or groups even demanded

[21] And yet Karel Schwarzenberg managed to turn this criticism in his favour. He entered the 2010 parliamentary elections with the slogan "When they talk rubbish, I sleep". He used the same strategy in the 2013 presidential elections, when his outdoor campaign used the slogan "From time to time you may not understand what I say but my opinions are clear.

[22] This phenomenon—the rise of homogeneous opinion groups that can easily become radicalized—is often seen as a possible weak spot of the new media (see e.g. Stromer-Galley 2003).

that the less favoured candidates should resign; there were new initiatives for the election of some candidates or rejecting the election of others, either launching special web pages (e.g. LepsiPrezident.cz [BetterPresident.cz]), or establishing Facebook groups, pages, (e.g. "We are also young but we vote for Miloš [Zeman]") or events ("I'm going to the elections and voting for Karel!").

13.10 Concluding Remarks

The 2013 presidential elections were the first serious "test" of the usability of online social networks in the Czech political campaign. Although the Czech politicians have occasionally used online media in election campaigns before, only these January elections fully revealed their potential for mobilization of voters. Based on the outcome of these elections and the reactions of the public as well as many experts it can be argued that social media have proved to be an efficient instrument for mobilization especially of the younger segment of the electorate, plus the voters from cities and larger towns. Without the support of these groups, Karel Schwarzenberg would most probably not have achieved such a great and surprising result in the first round. Without doubt, the presidential elections indicated that, in the future, social networks will play a much more significant role in election campaign communication in the Czech Republic than what we have witnessed so far. Having said that, the ultimate triumph of Miloš Zeman, who in the first round virtually ignored social networks, and even in the second round concentrated primarily on traditional media of political persuasion—especially live television debates and outdoor campaign—pointed out the limitations of campaigns conducted on social networks, in particular because of the relatively low election participation of the voters belonging to the so-called "Facebook generation", which finally cost Karel Schwarzenberg the president's post. In other words, the road from the "likes" on Facebook to the ballot boxes appears to be more complicated and a way less predictable than what online activists or marketing enthusiasts might assume.

Acknowledgment Research for this chapter was conducted as part of the project VITOVIN (CZ.1.07/2.3.00/20.0184), which is financed by the European Social Fund and the Ministry of Education of the Czech Republic.

References

Baumgartner, J. C. (2007). Humor on the next frontier: Youth, online political humor, and the JibJab effect. *Social Science Computer Review, 25*, 319–338.

Baumgartner, J. C., & Morris, J. (2010). MyFaceTube politics: social networking web sites and political engagement of young adults. *Social Science Computer Review, 28*(24), 24–44.

Cogburn, D. L., & Espinoza-Vasquez, F. K. (2011). From networked nominee to networked nation: Examining the impact of Web 2.0 and social media on political participation and civic engagement in the 2008 Obama campaign. *Journal of Political Marketing, 10*(1-2), 189–213.

Effing, R., Hillegersberg, J. van, & Huibers, T. (2011). Social media and political participation: Are Facebook, Twitter and YouTube democratizing our political systems? In E. Tambouris, A. Macintosh, & H. de Bruijn (Eds.), *Electronic Participation* (pp. 25–35). Heidelberg: Springer. Retrieved from http://link.springer.com/chapter/10.1007/978-3-642-23333-3_3.

Eibl, O., Gregor, M., Macková, A. (2013) Kampaně před prezidentskou volbou. In: Šedo, J. (eds) *České prezidentské volby* 2013. Brno: Centrum pro studium demokracie a kultury.

Elmer, G. (2012). Live research: Twittering an election debate. *New Media & Society, 15*(1), 18–30.

Fernandes, J., Giurcanu, M., Bowers, K. W., & Neely, J. C. (2010). The writing on the wall: A content analysis of college students' Facebook groups for the 2008 presidential election. *Mass Communication and Society, 13*(5), 653–675. doi:10.1080.15205436.2010.516865.

Gibson, R. (2013). Party change, social media and the rise of 'citizen-initiated' campaigning. *Party Politics*, published online before printing 1–15, doi:10.1177.135406881247.5.5

Graham, T., Jackson, D., Broersma, M. (2013). New platform, old habits? Candidates' use of Twitter during the 2010 British and Dutch general election campaigns. Paper presented at the ECREA Political Communication Section Conference "New Trends in Political Communication: Evidence, theories, implications, opportunities," 19–20 September 2013, Milan.

Greyes, N. (2011). The untapped potential of social media: A primer for savvy campaigners. *Campaigns and Elections, 300*, 45–47.

Gueorguieva, V. (2008). Voters, Myspace, and Youtube the impact of alternative communication channels on the 2006 election cycle and beyond. *Social Science Computer Review, 26*(3), 288–300.

Gustafsson, N. (2012). The subtle nature of facebook politics: Swedish social network site users and political participation. *New Media & Society, 14*(7), 1111–1127. doi:10.1177.146144481243.5.1.

Junco, R. (2013). Inequalities in Facebook use. *Computers in Human Behavior, 29*(6), 2328–2336. doi:10.1016/j.chb.2013.05.005.

Jungherr, A. (2012). The German federal election of 2009: The challenge of participatory cultures in political campaigns. *Transformative Works and Cultures, 5*(10).

Kirk, R., & Schill, D. (2011). A digital agora: Citizen participation in the 2008 presidential debates. *American Behavioral Scientist, 55*(3), 325–347.

Larsson, A. O., & Hallvard, M. (2012). Studying political microblogging: Twitter users in the 2010 Swedish election campaign. *New Media & Society, 14*(5), 729–747.

Larsson, A. O., & Hallvard, M. (2013). Representation or participation? Twitter use during the 2011 Danish election campaign. *Javnost—The Public, 20*(1), 71–88.

Lilleker, D. G., & Jackson, N. A. (2010). Towards a more participatory style of election campaigning: The impact of Web 2.0 on the UK 2010 general election. *Policy & Internet, 2* (3), 67–96.

Macková, A., Fialová, M., & Štětka, V. (2013). *Nová média jako nástroj politické kampaně v České republice: případová studie krajských a senátních voleb 2012*. Vol: Politologický časopis. 4/2013.

Matušková, A. (2009) *Volby 2006 - Volební strategie a využívání politického marketingu v České republice*. Dissertation, Masaryk University in Brno.

Norris, P. (2001). *Digital divide: Civic engagement, information poverty, and the internet worldwide*. Cambridge: Cambridge University Press.

O'Reilly, T. (2005). What is Web 2.0. Retrieved April 3, 2013, from http://oreilly.com/web2/archive/what-is-web-20.html

Poster, M. (1995). CyberDemocracy: Internet and the public sphere. Retrieved March 31, 2013, from http://www.hnet.uci.edu/mposter/writings/democ.html

Strandberg, K. (2013). A social media revolution or just a case of history repeating itself? The Use of social media in the 2011 finnish parliamentary elections. *New Media & Society*, online. Retrieved March 31, 2013 from http://nms.sagepub.com/content/early/2013/01/13/1461444812470612

Street, J. (2004). Celebrity politicians: Popular culture and political representation. *British Journal of Politics and International Relations, 6*(4), 435–452.

Stromer-Galley, J. (2003) Diversity of political conversation on the internet: Users' perspectives. *Journal of Computer-Mediated Communication, 8*(3), retrieved from http://jcmc.indiana.edu/vol8/issue3/stromergalley.html

Zittel, T. (2004). Political communication and electronic democracy: American exceptionalism or global trend? In F. Esser & B. Pfetsch (Eds.), *Comparing political communication: Theories, cases, and challenges* (pp. 231–250). Cambridge: Cambridge University Press.

Chapter 14
Facebook Dispute Concerning the Presidency

Case Study: Romania, 2012

Monica Pătruţ

Abstract Facebook has proved to be an efficient means of political communication between citizens and politicians. On this virtual stage, political actors display their competence, consolidate their fame, mobilize their volunteers and attack their political opponents, encourage donations and debate some sensitive issues of the society. Citizens have the chance to get informed, to organize and to mobilize themselves for different causes or candidates, to participate in different events or elections campaigns. Our study will analyze the use of Facebook during the campaign for the impeachment referendum (July 29, 2012). The analysis will focus on the posts made both by the pro-Băsescu citizens and by those that are against him. The research questions addressed will focus on: (a) the types of information posted by both opposite groups; (b) the degree in which the Facebook accounts are used for acclaims, attacks, or defenses; (c) the time span during the campaign in which" the dialogue" between the two groups gets more intense; (d) the degree of interactivity between those who post the information and their" friends". The research methods are functional analysis and content analysis. The two opposing groups sent their messages by the use of photographic images, verbal texts and advertising images. They used more attacks than acclaims, and had an intense activity during the middle and the end of the campaign. Their Facebook pages were interactive allowing the posting of appreciations, comments and the distribution of the materials posted.

Keywords Political communication • Social media • Referendum • 2012 • Traian Băsescu

Some of the results presented in this study were also published in Pătruţ M., "Pro şi contra suspendării preşedintelui. Referendum pe Facebook", (For and Against Impeaching the President. Facebook Referendum) in *Sociologia Românească*, *1*, 2013: 29–35.

M. Pătruţ (✉)
Department of Communication, Faculty of Letters, Vasile Alecsandri University of Bacău, Bacau, Romania
e-mail: monicapatrut@yahoo.com

B. Pătruţ and M. Pătruţ (eds.), *Social Media in Politics*, Public Administration and Information Technology 13, DOI 10.1007/978-3-319-04666-2_14,

14.1 Introduction

The referendum on the impeachment of the President of Romania was held on July 29, 2012 and was the consequence of the Parliament vote on July, 6. The president Traian Băsescu went through another impeachment referendum in 2007, in which 74 % of voters chose to keep him in office.

The reasons for the 2012 referendum were the following: usurping the role of the Prime Minister and of the government control; continuous infringement on the citizens' rights and freedom, on the Constitution, on the principle of separation of powers in the State and of the independence of justice; direct pressures on the judges from the Constitutional Court; infringement on the Court's decisions and the abandonment of his role as a mediator in the political and social life. Above all, the President claimed that he would not name a Prime Minister belonging to the Social Liberal Union (USL) although this party had won the parliamentary elections. The President claimed that the USL representatives were interested in controlling the judicial system and he labeled the latest USL actions as attacks upon the State of Law and upon the Romanian democratic institutions (Andrei 2012).

The turnout for the vote on July 29 was 46.24 % out of the 18,292,464 Romanian citizens who had the right to vote. 87.52 % of Romanians were in favour of the impeachment, whereas 11.15 % were against. On August 21, 2012, the Constitutional Court declared the referendum invalid because the quorum was not reached for Băsescu's dismissal (Dinu 2012).

Starting from this situation in the Romanian political context, this article will focus on the way in which the campaign for the 2012 referendum was carried out in the online environment, namely on Facebook, the best-known social network in Romania. After presenting the advantages of using Facebook for political communication, we analyzed the online political stage in order to identify the two opposite points of view (the dismissal versus the non-dismissal of the President), which had thousands of virtual supporters. The functional analysis helped us in quantifying the acclaims, attacks, and defenses of the two groups involved. The content analysis provided the evolution of the Facebook activity of the two groups (the beginning, the middle, and the end of the election campaign), the types of materials posted, and the interactive character of the Facebook pages (the possibility for the visitors to like, to comment and to share).

14.2 The Use of Facebook in Political Communication

The growing number of Facebook users highlights that this stands for a postmodern communicational agora. There is not another online community that can connect the members of an offline community more efficiently than Facebook (Westling 2007). This is also used as a political communication channel in two ways: political actors may send messages to internet-users-citizens who are willing to listen to them and they may receive feedback to their messages.

We consider that Facebook has the following strong points in political communication:

- it allows its members to get informed from an alternative source, to connect, and to organize themselves. The Facebook users can have different political behaviors: from online donations, encouraging their friends to vote, up to posting charts and statistics or to updating their status, thus highlighting different opinions and political attitudes. (Kushin and Yamamoto 2010, p. 612).
- it intensifies the interaction and direct communication between community members and political actors. Within the context of young persons' declining interest in political life and of their lack of trust in political parties, Facebook plays an important role in diminishing the distance between voters and politicians, the public "wall" being the space where some people post questions, answers, positive or negative comments for others. Citizens may turn from passive viewers into active users: they may be invited to take part in debates on the politician's online profile or supporters' page, they may send solutions to the problems mentioned in his/her campaign. Through this type of communication, citizens may be heard by politicians who may provide a better management of his/her image.
- it stimulates the growth of his members' political participation especially during election campaigns. Through interactivity and direct communication, younger members are helped to acquire more political knowledge, to increase their interest in political issues and to become more efficient/competitive in this domain. For example, users may join different political groups, download various applications about candidates and measures implemented by them, express their political opinions starting from their virtual friends' opinions, get involved in taking decisions, or develop different civic competences (Vitak et al. 2011, p. 34). Facebook is the proper space to express one's political vision, this being mentioned on the information section of every member's profile.
- it satisfies the need of belonging to a discussion group or to a community online. People are afraid of loneliness and the belongingness to a group is an important aspect of one's self-image (Zhang et al. 2011, p.734). The (non)political users' concern for the management of their image through Facebook profiles is fully justified. On a personal level, there are some other rewards (social surveillance, entertainment, acknowledgment, emotional support, extension of the friend network) or some psychological rewards (boosting of self-esteem, emotional openness towards others).
- it is the most powerful tool of mobilizing supporters and volunteers, Barack Obama's 2008 election campaign being an example. Obama succeeded in mobilizing almost 6 billion young volunteers to share his message and to convince the undecided that he was the best candidate for president (Toader 2009, pp.182–198). During the 2008 election campaigns, Facebook was a very active social network at the political level: 5.4 billion voters, Facebook

members, clicked on "I voted" on the page dedicated to elections and 1.5 billion users mentioned the name of a candidate on his/her page (O'Neill 2008). Facebook helps in not only attracting and mobilizing a high number of supporters but also in collecting the data about the voters' demographic segmentation and in contacting voters in order to remind them to go to vote.

Facebook facilitates political communication both horizontally, among its members, and vertically, between members and politicians from the real world. Horizontal communication among the network members is stimulated by the fact that these may organize themselves in various thematic groups and may invite others to join them. The common purpose is to discuss upon various political issues, to share messages, images, films, links with others, and to engage as many members as possible in political debates. On the vertical level, communication among politicians should serve not only the purpose of shaping the politicians' image and increasing donations during election campaigns, but especially that of maintaining a permanent dialog with the citizens and of involving the public in the political decision.

Facebook provides politicians with the environment where they may present themselves not only as unique and competitive characters who may resemble or distinguish them from their opponents, but also as "the centre of a created world". Facebook is formed of nodes and each member is a node. For the political actor, it is important to be a central node with as many connections and friends as possible. The greater the number of connections is in the online environment, the higher his social status and importance would be (Dalsgaard 2008). The political actor turned into "the great man" should display his social capital in the online environment, should continuously present the size of his social network that he can mobilize. The great number of friends-supporters may be interpreted as a sign of virtual citizens' support and sympathy and the election campaign may also be won through the quantitative dimension of the social network, Facebook (Dalsgaard 2008).

The candidates to different political positions post information on the social networks to show their competence and to increase their fame, to present themselves as viable alternatives and valuable spokespersons of citizens.

Depending on the incumbent or opponent position they have, politicians will make a virtual plea on Facebook either to continue or to bring a change, they will invite the citizens to get involved in the political process, to present their achievements and projects, to defend their points of view regarding various important social issues, to use statistics as supporting arguments and to address their virtual friends as if they were colleagues (Cozma and Chen 2011). At the same time, they will mobilize their voters and attack their opponents, they will encourage donations and debate upon the problems of the society/community (Sweetser and Lariscy 2008).

14.3 The Use of Facebook in the 2012 Impeachment Referendum

The 2008 parliamentary elections and the 2009 presidential elections were the first temporal contexts when Facebook was used in Romania as an instrument of election communication. It was mainly used to promote the political actor's image and to mobilize supporters (Momoc 2011, p.39). Even if some Romanian politicians joined the virtual world, they interacted less with their online friends. The Romanian members of Parliament prefer to post on their Facebook accounts official impersonal messages, information and images about their activity in the Parliament or within their party, family and travel photos, and rarely do they have direct interaction with their online friends, possible supporters and voters (Boşoteanu 2011, p.50).

In 2011, 85 Romanian MPs had a Facebook account: 32—Social Democratic Party, 25—Liberal-Democratic Party, 19—National Liberal Party, 4—Democratic Union of Hungarians in Romania, 2—National Union for the Progress of Romania. The same year, the three most popular politicians on Facebook were Crin Antonescu—16,210 fans, Elena Udrea—9,000 fans, and Nicolae Robu—5,000 friends (Ciocotişan 2011).

14.3.1 Theoretical and Methodological Framework

The starting point of the election campaign for the 2012 impeachment referendum in Romania was marked by the creation of many Facebook pages, which either supported the President or required his dismissal. For our study, we selected three pages that supported the President (Alături de preşedintele nostru/By the side of our president, Eşti supărat pe Băsescu. De ce?/You are upset with Băsescu. Why?, Flacăra democraţiei/The torch of democracy) and four pages which militated for the dismissal (Flacăra democraţiei 2/The torch of democracy 2, Sătul de Băsescu/Fed up with Băsescu, Ţara arde. Dă Like dacă ai fost dezamăgit de Traian Băsescu/The country is burning. Give a like if you were disappointed with Băsescu, Da, demiterii lui Băsescu!/Yes, for the dismissal of Băsescu (Pătruţ 2013, p. 32)).

In this study, we will use content analysis and functional analysis. Taken from Benoit et al. (1998, p. 234), functional analysis starts from the assumption that nowadays' candidates want to place themselves on as high a scale of preferences as possible, an element that the voters' process of judging values relies upon. Being or not being preferred is achieved through three discursive functions:

- *acclaims* (A1)—positive statements whose purpose is to highlight the candidate's qualities and good deeds;
- *attacks* (A2)—positive statements whose purpose is to emphasize the counter-candidate's weak points;

- *defense* (A3)—statements whose purpose is to reject the attack of the counter-candidate.

These discursive functions may be related to two themes: *politics* (P = actions disposed on a temporal axis: previous achievements—PA, future plans—FP, general goals—GG) and *character* (personal qualities—PQ, leadership skills—LS and ideals/values—IV).

Following the studies by the authors of the functional theory, we know that their analyses upon the American presidential debates that they performed (Benoit et al. 1998), but also in the 2009 Romanian presidential debate (Pătruţ and Cmeciu 2010, p. 61), have confirmed the hypotheses below: (1) in the space dedicated to the candidates' self-presentation, acclamations are more frequent than attacks; (2) in the candidates' self-presentations, the chapter *politics* is better represented than *character*; (3) the representative of the party in power uses acclamations to a wider extent and attacks less than the representatives of the opposition parties; (4) in contrast to the counter-candidates, the candidate of the party in power uses former achievements to acclaim rather than to attack; (5) personal qualities are used to acclaim more frequently than to attack.

The content analysis as a research method allows us to study the communicational processes without interfering with their development (Babbie 2010). We will use the simple sentence or complex sentences as our unit of analysis. We will code the posts to transform them into conceptual categories. The examples below are examples of our coding procedure of the texts posted on the Facebook pages under analysis:

Traian Băsescu: "Ponta is a liar, you can't help it, lying seems to be his second nature"/[Attack, Character, Personal Quality], and Dragnea has absolutely no character [Attack, Character, Personal Qualities]. I would like to say that what USL did is not fair [Defense, Politics, Previous Achievements]. It is not fair to have as main objective to monopolize the state institutions and to place them at the party disposal [Defense, Politics, General Goals]" (http://www.facebook.com/PresedinteleTraianBasescu, 2012).

"I believe that Romanians are honest with their president [Acclaim, Character, Leadership Skills], they will appreciate that alongside with the government, I took responsibilities in the difficult moments Romania went through [Acclaims, Politics, Previous Achievements]" (http://www.facebook.com/PresedinteleTraianBasescu, 2012).

The research questions are the following:

RQ1: What types of materials did the two opposing groups post on Facebook?

RQ2: How much do the groups involved use their Facebook accounts for acclaims, attacks, or defense?

RQ3: When are the greatest numbers of items of information posted on the Facebook (the beginning, middle, or end of the campaign)?

RQ4: Is the communication between the persons who post and their virtual friends interactive?

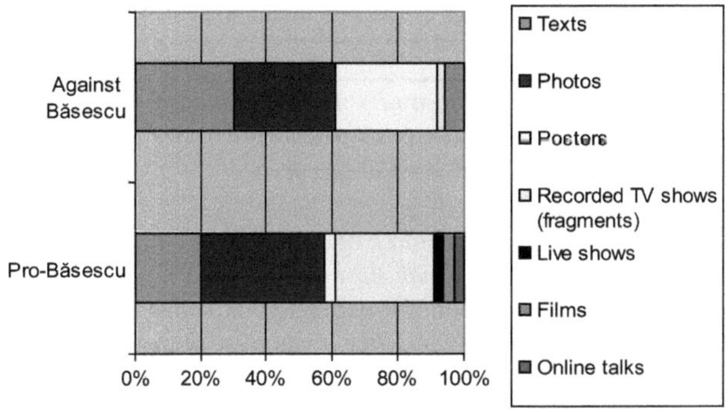

Fig. 14.1 The content of Facebook pages

14.3.2 *Findings*

For RQ1, we coded the Facebook posts between July 7 and 29, 2012. The pages supporting the president had 59 posts, whereas the ones for the president's dismissal had 208 posts. As Fig. 14.1 shows, the materials embedded texts, photos, posters, links to TV shows recorded and uploaded on Youtube or to live shows, short movies, online talks, talks between the candidate and citizens or journalists.

The campaign staff members or the virtual pro-Basescu citizens posted on Facebook 13 texts, 24 campaign photos, 2 posters, 19 fragments from recorded TV shows where the president was present, 2 live TV shows, 2 short movies and 2 online talks. The citizens against Basescu posted 63 attack texts, 64 photos and caricatures, 64 posters, 5 recorded shows, and 12 movies.

RQ 2 focused on the degree in which the Facebook accounts were used for acclaims, attacks, or defenses. Table 14.1 illustrates the findings. As noticed, a more persuasive activity was carried out by the citizens against Basescu, through 124 acclaims and 257 attacks. Many of the acclaims make an appeal to citizens to come to vote in order to stop the president's abuses and to denounce the possible election frauds and, at the same time, they focused on democratic values. The page *Sătul de Băsescu/Fed up with Băsescu* was the most efficient one in promoting this civic involvement. The virtual protesters against the president used a high number of attacks (257). The president is attacked both in what his *politics* and *character* are concerned.

To support the president, his virtual friends used 103 acclaims, 38 attacks, and 27 defenses. The defenses provided more explanations regarding the motives and the actions which provoked the gradual decrease of Traian Basescu's popularity throughout the last 2 or 3 years. The acclaims were used to motivate the reasons for which Basescu should continue as the president of Romania: his previous achievements, his future plans, and his general goals. Some of Basescu's achievements mentioned were the following: the independence of the judicial system, the dismissal of corrupt politicians, the disclosure of the abuses made by the Romanian politicians. At the same time, Basescu is considered honest by his supporters in what concerns the budget cuts. He is also appreciated for having rejected the

Table 14.1 The findings of the functional analysis

	Acclaims	Attacks	Defenses
Alături de preşedintele nostru/*By the side of our president*	76	38	24
Eşti supărat pe Băsescu. De ce?/*You are upset with Băsescu. Why?*	4	0	3
Flacăra democraţiei/*The torch of democracy*	3	0	0
Total 168	103	38	27
Flacăra democraţiei 2/*The torch of democracy 2*	0	32	0
Sătul de Băsescu/*Fed up with Băsescu*	70	133	0
Ţara arde. Dă *Like* dacă ai fost dezamăgit de Traian Băsescu/*The country is burning. Give a like if you were disappointed with Băsescu*	21	38	0
Da, demiterii lui Băsescu !/*Yes, for the dismissal of Băsescu*	33	54	0
Total 381	124	257	0

populist economic policies, which caused the amplification of the country's economic and social crises.

The president's plans for the future mentioned by his virtual friends focused on the independence of the judicial system, the impeachment of the corrupt politicians, the imposition of a unicameral parliament, the decrease of the number of the members of parliament in consequence of the 2009 referendum. The general goals mentioned by the online friends focused on the legitimacy of the elected president, on the credibility he has earned in the relationship with the EU and NATO, and on the guarantee that he is the only viable opponent against the USL monopoly.

Having been a ship captain is a valuable character trait that his Facebook friends often mention. They appreciate his leadership abilities, his character (especially his ability to utter painful truths) and his ideals and values according to which he guides his political views (democracy, state of law, reforms in all fields and the acceptance of the West in detriment of the East.

The other side, the online opponent citizens mention some previous negative actions (the infringement of the Constitution, the cutting of pensions and salaries, the humiliation of many socio-professional categories, the dictatorial imposition of policies and decisions, the destruction of the fleet, the incapacity of debating and negotiating, the protection of corrupt politicians from the Liberal Democratic Party, the infringement of the separation of state powers, bringing the country into a state of indebtedness, the public humiliation of Raed Arafat) and some plans (his rejection of naming a prime minister from the USL alliance, the exploitation of gold reserves at Roşia Montană). The attacks also focused on the lack of his abilities to lead, to have proper values and ideals that may be guiding issues in the Romanian political life.

Both groups (pro and against Basescu) focused their attention more on *Politics* (65 %) than on *Character* (35 %). Within *Politics*, a greater attention was focused on *previous achievements* (59 %), then on *general goals* (26 %) and on *plans for the future* (15 %).

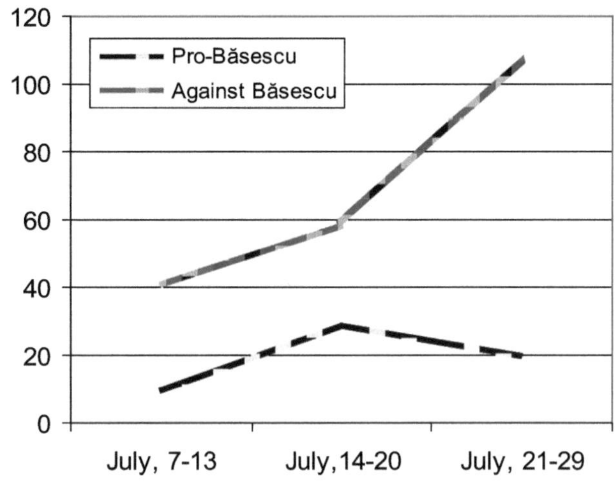

Fig. 14.2 The evolution of the number of posts—beginning, middle, and end of the campaign

To find the answer to RQ3, we divided the election campaign into three periods (beginning, middle, and end) and we analyzed the intensity of postings made by the two groups involved throughout these three periods. As Fig. 14.2 shows, the group against the president had an increasing activity, the climax point being reached in the last 2 days of the campaign. The posts in this period included not only the attacks against the president, but also the mobilizing appeals to vote.

The supporters who were pro-Basescu were less active, the number of their posts decreasing by the middle of the campaign and having a visible decrease after the president encouraged the citizens not to legitimize the *coup d'état* run by USL and not to go to the polls.

Previous research showed that the use of the interactive component of the Internet in political communication provides many advantages: the decrease of political cynicism, opportunities for the public to learn more about politics, the increase of the participation of Internet users in elections, and their involvement in the development of election campaigns.

Despite these strong points, many candidates avoid or postpone an online interaction with the Internet users (Stromer-Galley 2000, pp. 130–132).

In our study, we will quantify the potential of interactivity provided by Facebook in two ways: from user-to-user and from user-to-document (Tedesco 2007, p.1187). Whereas the user-to-user interactivity implies the sharing of various posts of the network members, the user-to-document interactivity focuses on the likes and comments posted by users regarding various available documents. In order to evaluate the degree in which the candidates' posts generated more involvement of the online friends, we compared the number of likes, comments, and shares, on the one hand, and that of the candidate's posts, on the other hand.

RQ4 focused on the interactive character of the Facebook pages. As Fig. 14.3 shows, the three pro-Basescu Facebook pages had 59 posts which received 357,876 likes and 72,605 comments and they had 38,403 shares in the network.

Fig. 14.3 Forms of interactivity—Facebook pages—2012 impeachment referendum

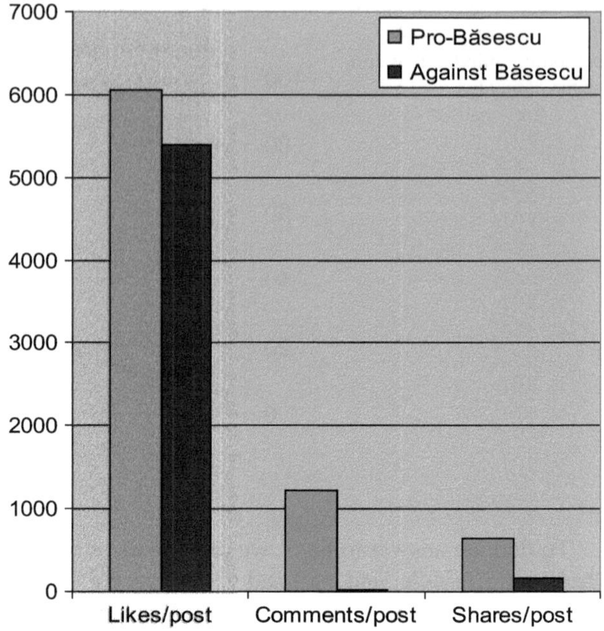

The Facebook pages, which were against the president, had 1,120,694 likes 5,533 comments and 33,817 shares among the online friends.

To evaluate the degree in which the posts of the two groups involved triggered more involvement of the virtual friends, we compared the number of likes, comments, and shares and the number of posts. As Fig. 14.3 shows, although the posts pro-Basescu were fewer than the posts of the opposing group, they were more efficient because they generated a greater number of likes, comments, and shares. In both cases, interactivity involved, first of all, liking, then commenting, and sharing the online materials.

14.4 Conclusions

The 2012 campaign for the referendum for the impeachment of the president of Romania started in the online and offline environments on the same day. It was not only the campaign staff members who started this online campaign, but also regular citizens, the Net Generation representatives (Tapscott 2011), who are more interested in virtual cooperation, interactivity, and content generation. Their meeting place, Facebook—the most popular social network in Romania—turned into a battlefield for the opponents and supporters of the Romanian president. They created Facebook accounts whose names reflected the political situation: *Alături de preşedintele nostru/By the side of our president*, *Eşti supărat pe Băsescu. De ce?/ You are upset with Băsescu. Why?*, *Flacăra democraţiei/The torch of democracy*) and four pages which militated for the dismissal (*Flacăra democraţiei 2/The torch of democracy 2*, *Sătul de Băsescu/Fed up with Băsescu*, *Ţara arde. Dă Like dacă ai fost dezamăgit de Traian Băsescu/The country is burning. Give a like if you were disappointed with Băsescu*, *Da, demiterii lui Băsescu!/Yes, for the dismissal of Băsescu*).

During the analyzed period, July 7–9, 2012, the pro-Basescu pages had 59 posts, and the pages against Basescu had 208 pages. Using devices, such as photos, posters, texts, and discursive functions, such as acclaims and attacks, the two implicated groups succeeded in involving their virtual friends in liking, commenting, and sharing the information related to this sensitive political issue in Romania, thus creating real *N-Fluence networks* (Tapscott 2011). However, the most persuasive activity was carried out by the opponents of the president through 124 acclaims and 257 attacks. The supporters of the president used more acclaims, whereas the opponents mainly used attacks. As expected, both groups more frequently focused on Politics (65 %) than on Character (35 %) and had a more intense online activity at the middle and end of the campaign.

Starting from the interactivity displayed on the pages of both groups (supporters and opponents of the president), especially through likes, comments and shares, we may observe a greater involvement of the Romanian internet users in supporting a political cause. This involvement in sharing and commenting the political information in the online environment started with the 2004 "digital guerilla" (Momoc 2010), continued with "the dialogue" on the websites of the presidential candidates in 2009 (Cmeciu and Pătruţ 2012) and was consolidated with the forming of groups and political communities on Facebook. Capitalizing the collaborative ethos of the Net Generation members, social networks may contribute to the consolidation of the deliberative democracy in the online environment. Nevertheless, the greatest challenge of shifting the online democracy into the offline environment still remains.

References

Andrei, C. (2012). *Cele şapte motive ale suspendării preşedintelui Traian Băsescu. Ce conţine documentul USL*. Available at http://www.gandul.info/politica/cele-sapte-motive-ale-suspendarii-presedintelui-traian-basescu-ce-contine-documentul-usl-9813858. Accessed 15 Jan 2013.

Babbie, E. (2010). *Practica cercetării sociale*. Iaşi: Polirom.

Benoit, W. L., Blaney, J. R., & Pier, P. M. (1998). *Campaign '96: A functional analysis of acclaiming, attacking, and defending*. New York: Praeger.

Boşoteanu, I. C. (2011). New media in alegerile prezidenţiale din 2009. *Sfera Politicii, 8*(162), 47–56. Available at http://www.sferapoliticii.ro/sfera/162/art06-Bosoteanu.php. Accessed 7 Jan 2013.

Ciocotişan, F. (2011). *Cine este cel mai tare politician de pe Facebook?* Available at http://impactnews.ro/Politic/Cine-este-cel-mai-tare-politician-de-pe-Facebook-48577. Accessed 15 Jan 2013.

Cmeciu, C. M., & Pătruţ, M. (2012). Visual framing of intertexts in political reversing mirror websites. *Cultural Perspectives—Journal for Literary and British Cultural Studies in Romania, 1*(17), 45–63.

Cozma, R., & Chen, K. J. (2011). *Congressional candidates' use of Twitter during the 2010 Midterm Elections: A wasted opportunity? Lucrare prezentată la.* International Communication Association Annual Conference, Boston. Available at http://www.allacademic.com/meta/p490948_index.html. Accessed 17 Jan 2013.

Dalsgaard, S. (2008). Facework on Facebook. The presentation of self in virtual life and its role in the US elections. *Anthropology Today, 24*(6), 8–12.

Dinu, C. (2012). *Referendum 2012. Rezultate finale Biroul Electoral Central.* Available at http://www.gandul.info/news/referendum-2012-rezultate-finale-bec-prezenta-la-vot-46-24-pentru-demiterea-lui-basescu-au-votat-87-52-iar-impotriva-11-15-9913998. Accessed 20 Jan 2013.

http://www.facebook.com/daJosBasescu

http://www.facebook.com/DEMITEL.PE.BASESCU?ref=ts&fref=ts

http://www.facebook.com/FlacaraDemocratiei2?ref=ts&fref=ts

http://www.facebook.com/groups/flacara.democratiei/?ref=ts&fref=ts

http://www.facebook.com/pages/Demite-lro/293331550765909

http://www.facebook.com/pages/E%C8%99ti-sup%C4%83rat-pe-B%C4%83sescu-De-ce/392726400786616

http://www.facebook.com/PresedinteleTraianBasescu

http://www.facebook.com/TaraArde29

Kushin, M. J., & Yamamoto, M. (2010). Did social media really matter? College students' use of online media and political decision making in the 2008 election. *Mass Communication and Society, 13*(5), 608–630.

Momoc, A. (2010). Online negative campaign in the 2004 Romanian presidential elections. *Styles of Communication, 2*(1), 89–99. Available at http://journals.univ-danubius.ro/index.php/communication/article/view/735/667. Accessed 19 Jan 2013.

Momoc, A. (2011). Candidaţii populişti şi noile tehnologii (Blog, Facebook, YouTube) în alegerile prezidenţiale din 2009. *Sfera Politicii, 8*(162), 39–46. Available at http://www.sferapoliticii.ro/sfera/162/art05-Momoc.php. Accessed 15 January 2013.

O'Neill, N. (2008). *The Facebook election results.* Available at http://allfacebook.com/the-facebook-election-results_b2089. Accessed 20 Jan 2013.

Pătruţ, M. (2013). Pro şi contra suspendării preşedintelui. Referendum pe Facebook. *Sociologia Românească, 1*, 29–39.

Pătruţ, M., & Cmeciu, C. (2010). Dezbaterile electorale—un joc discursiv ritualic. *Sfera politicii, 3* (145), 57–63. Available at http://www.sferapoliticii.ro/sfera/145/art09-patrut_cmeciu.html. Accessed 10 Jan 2013.

Stromer-Galley, J. (2000). On-line interaction and why candidates avoid it. *Journal of Communication, 50*(4), 111–132.

Sweetser, K. D., & Lariscy, R. W. (2008). Candidates make good friends: An analysis candidates' uses of Facebook. *International Journal of Strategic Communication, 2*(3), 175–208.

Tapscott, D. (2011). *Crescuţi digital: Generaţia net îţi schimbă lumea.* Bucureşti: Publica.

Tedesco, J. C. (2007). Examining internet interactivity effects on young adult political information efficacy. *American Behavioral Scientist, 50*(9), 1183–1194.

Toader, F. (2009). Barack Obama—noua „faţă" a politicii americane. In T. Sălcudeanu, P. Aparaschivei, & F. Toader (Eds.), *Bloguri, Facebook şi politică.* Bucureşti: Tritonic.

Vitak, J., Zube, P., Smock, A., Carr, C. T., et al. (2011). It's Complicated: Facebook users' political participation in the 2008 election. *CyberPsychology, Behavior and Social Networking, 14*(3), 107–114.

Westling, M. (2007). *Expanding the public sphere. The impact of Facebook on political communication.* Available at http://www.thenewvernacular.com/projects/facebook_and_political_communication.pdf. Accessed 15 Jan 2011.

Zhang, Y., Tang, L. S., & Leung, L. (2011). Gratifications, collective self-esteem, online emotional openness, and traitlike communication apprehension as predictors of Facebook uses. *Cyberpsychology, Behavior, and Social Networking, 14*(12), 733–739.

Part III
Social Media in Mobilizing People for Riots and Revolutions

Chapter 15
Social Media Censorship vs. State Responsibility for Human Rights Violations

Case Study of the Arab Spring Uprising in Egypt

Joanna Kulesza

Abstract The chapter presents the contemporary international consensus on the limits of the right to free speech online. The author examines state-imposed online filtering in terms of its compliance with international law, especially with human rights treaties granting freedom of expression and access to information. The White House implemented "Internet Freedom" program, whose aim is to introduce software enabling the circumvention of local content control in "filtering countries", is thus subject to thorough analysis. The analysis covers recent (2011) events in Egypt, where the world's first successful attempt at shutting down the Internet within state borders was completed. Although enforced through legitimate state actions this first-ever Internet shutdown was circumvented with technology offered by U.S.-based Google. This technology and its use seemed to meet the goals of the "Internet Freedom" program, introduced by the White House a few months prior to the Egypt events. In the course of the argument, the author discusses international responsibility for the possible breach of their international obligations by both: Egypt and the U.S. She provides for the assessment of the legality of the actions of Egyptian authorities' executing a nationwide ban on Internet that constitutes an infringement of freedom of expression, as well as the responsibility of the United States for their failure to halt a U.S. legal entity enabling users to circumvent Egyptian blocking.

Keywords Internet • Free speech • State responsibility • International law • Internet governance • Sovereignty • Proportionality • Access to information • Human rights • Due diligence

---

J. Kulesza (✉)
Department of International Law and International Relations, University of Lodz, Kopcinskiego 8/12, 90-232 Lodz, Poland
e-mail: joannakulesza@gmail.com

B. Pătruţ and M. Pătruţ (eds.), *Social Media in Politics*, Public Administration and Information Technology 13, DOI 10.1007/978-3-319-04666-2_15,

15.1 Freedom to Access Information as a Human Right

Freedom of speech holds a well-recognized place in the human rights catalogue. The contents of this right have been defined in a series of international law documents, following the blueprint enshrined in Article 19 of the Universal Declaration of Human Rights (UDHR).[1] According to its stipulations, free speech is composed of three complementary rights: the right to hold opinions, the right to seek and receive information and last but not least the freedom to impart one's own views and ideas. Furthermore, according to this document, considered evidence of customary human rights law, freedom of speech may be exercised "through any media and regardless of frontiers". The non-binding 1948 compromise, worded in Article 19 of the UDHR took almost 30 more years to become the binding International Covenant on Civil and Political Rights (ICCPR),[2] which similarly phrases freedom of speech in its corresponding Article 19. It also confirms everyone's right to "hold opinions without interference" (par. 1), seek and receive as well as to impart information (par. 2) of all kinds. All those freedoms are granted to all regardless of national borders and may be exercised in any form: orally, in writing, print or through any other mean of expression. This article is fundamental to any media law regulation, granting all media the right to freely distribute information. Unlike in the UDHR however, which generally refers to any limitation on human rights in its Article 29 par. 2, Article 19 ICCPR directly deems the right to free speech a non-absolute one.[3] In its Article 19 par. 3, ICCPR identifies this particular freedom as inseparable from special duties and responsibilities resting upon each individual. Since the freedom of speech inherently brings the threat of infringing the rights and freedoms of others, be it through defamation or libel, it may be subject to certain restrictions. Any such restriction however ought to be provided for by law and introduced solely when necessary for guaranteeing the respect of the rights or reputation of others or for the protection of national security, public order, public health, or morals. What is more, it must be proportionate: any restriction is subject to case-specific assessment of the degree of interference confronted with the importance of the purpose of such a restriction.[4]

The UN Human Rights Council (HRC) has gone to great lengths to detail what this general limitative clause of Article 19 par. 3 means in practical terms, when providing its Resolution 12/16 on the freedom of opinion and speech.[5] Yet the

---

[1] United Nations 1948. Universal Declaration of Human Rights, further herein: UDHR.

[2] United Nations 1966. International Covenant on Civil and Political Rights, further herein: ICCPR.

[3] According to article 29 par. 2 UDHR everyone shall be subject to limitations determined by law states in the exercise of their rights and freedoms. Such limitations may be introduced only to safeguard "due recognition and respect for the rights and freedoms of others" or in order to meet the requirements of "morality, public order and the general welfare in a democratic society".

[4] See e.g.: Deibert (2008) at 81. In the ICCPR regime, the proportionality principle is derived from the word "necessary" used in Article 19 par. 3 discussing the limitative clauses. See e.g.: Yutaka Arai (2002) at 186.

[5] United Nations 2009.

application of those guidelines remains a challenge.[6] Regardless of the difficulties in defining grounds for limiting free speech, such as reasons of national security or protection of morality, it remains undisputed, that blocking access to all information provided through electronic means is a violation of the right to free speech, when exercised without a legitimate justification, based on an act of law applicable in a particular case. Any general blocking of Internet content, in particular keywords-based Internet filtering of websites or services, resulting in depriving all individuals within state jurisdiction of access to certain categories of information is not a proportionate restriction on the right to free speech, as defined by the international law documents cited above, as it infringes the complimentary freedom to seek and receive information. Yet the very fact of limiting access to certain content does not deem the infraction illegal, since, as already stated above, freedom of speech is not an absolute right. The UDHR in Article 29 par. 2 as well as the ICCPR in Article 19 par. 3 both provide for its limitations, however introducing those may only be case-specific, done solely for the grounds named above and based on a particular act of law. A general state-imposed and nation-wide limitation to seek and access information through a particular media or of a certain character may be considered a violation of the limitative clause enshrined in the ICCPR.[7] In some exceptional cases, however, such a general limitation may be considered justified, as described in the derogative clause of Article 4 ICCPR. Also the European Convention on Human Rights regime, which served as the blueprint for the ICCPR definitions of freedom of speech standards,[8] provides that a state's obligation to guarantee such freedom may be lifted in "time of war or other public emergency threatening the life of the nation".[9] Yet even in such a highly exceptional situation freedom of speech must remain granted to aliens while performing their political activities in all respects of Article 10, therefore includes state obligation to grant them the right to seek and share information through all media available.[10]

[6] See generally e.g.: Sadurski (2002).

[7] See Sect. 15.4 below.

[8] Council of Europe 1950. The Convention for the Protection of Human Rights and Fundamental Freedoms is usually referred to as the European Convention on Human Rights, further herein: ECHR. ECHR foresees for the right to free speech in its Article 10. The European Court of Human Rights' (ECtHR) jurisprudence implies a positive obligation of states to prevent any interference with that right, even when such intrusion comes from private third parties, rather than state authorities. See e.g. European Court of Human Rights (2008). In Khurshid Mustafa and Tarzibachi v. Sweden the Court asserted its jurisdiction in a case relating to national court decisions in a case between private parties, where effectively the national court practice disallowed state residents to enjoy rights guaranteed by the convention. See also: European Court of Human Rights (2001), where in VgT Verein Gegen Tierfabriken v. Switzerland the Court asserted that there is an inherent positive obligation of states to ensure the protection of fundamental rights guaranteed by the convention through their effective implementation in national legal systems.

[9] Article 15 ECHR.

[10] Article 16 ECHR.

OpenNet Initiative—an organization focused on monitoring national filtering practice worldwide[11]—defined four primary reasons states name when imposing limitations on the right to seek and impart information.[12] Among those, the social grounds for filtering, usually based on ethical standards shared by national or regional communities, referring to the protection of morality or religious values are the less controversial ones, while states openly claiming limiting access for the reasons of protecting the governing party or authoritarian state leader meet with strong criticism from NGOs and human rights violations allegations.[13] The criticism is usually aimed at state authorities although it is rarely them directly affecting the blocking. They usually introduce stringent legal regulations within acts of national law obliging Internet Service Providers (ISPs) to enforce a form of private censorship over content defined within such act as harmful or potentially dangerous to state interests.[14] As Internet filtering is no longer the domain of authoritarian states however, some democracies also introduce ISP imposed access limitations, yet usually enforced following a court order in a particular case.[15]

15.2 Technology and Regulation of Online Censorship

"Internet filtering" is a term describing a wide variety of activities.[16] Initially, it was used to refer to the practice of states considered to be authoritarian or undemocratic, such as China or Iran, where ISPs were legally bound to deny users access to certain content, e.g. pornographic or immoral according to national laws and local social

---

[11] The OpenNet Initiative is a collaboration of the Citizen Lab at the Munk School of Global Affairs, University of Toronto, the Berkman Center for Internet & Society at Harvard University, and the SecDev Group seated in Ottawa. See: Open Net Initiatve (2013).

[12] Deibert 2008 at 9. The declared grounds for Internet filtering include: "social" filtering enforced for the protection of morality and other social values, filtering done for political reasons, i.e. preventing criticisms of current political model, filtering done for state security reasons, i.e. aimed at preventing internal unrest, and subsequently limiting access to technical tools enabling circumvention of the blocking being imposed by ISPs.

[13] See e.g.: Noman and York (2011).

[14] See: Deibert (2008) at 32 ff.

[15] See e.g. the Italian court's decision on blocking Access to the Pirate Bay website because of alleged contributory copyright infringement: Doe (2008).

[16] Controlling access to various categories of electronic content may be affected by applying a combination of software and legal methods, but also with the use of extra legal tools and undisclosed methods, including ones outsourced to private parties. Internet filtering is being affected through i.e. hacking or the application of computer viruses, as well as DDoS attacks onto websites containing controversial or illegal content and servers hosting it. See: Deibert et al. (2010) at 6–7. *Distributed Denial of Service Attacks* consists of simultaneous requests for one IP number that is the target of such an attack, sent from various locations and different computers. Consequently, a domain located on a computer with a particular IP number ceases to respond.

standards.[17] That obligation meant that entrepreneurs offering Internet access were legally bound to verify whether online content was intact with national laws and moral norms. Service providers met those requirements in various ways. Initially they were using filtering programs,[18] based on key word searches,[19] also by putting together so-called black lists of prohibited website addresses, offering content deemed illegal within a certain jurisdiction or white lists of websites accessible throughout the country.[20] Some of them would hire administrators and volunteers, following all online content as it was entered online and reporting for takedown whatever part of it they felt was against the law or morality.[21]

Initially, any Internet filtering was considered undemocratic and therefore undesired within democratic states.[22] Individual protesters and NGOs would deem any state censorship contrary to free speech guarantees and the very idea of the World Wide Web, designed for free, global transfer of ideas.[23] Obliging ISPs to distinguish between legal and illegal or moral and immoral content seemed contrary to this basic prerequisite of the web and put them in a very difficult position. Forcing ISPs to verify each and every piece of data through the lens of national laws or morality brought about an undesired chilling effect, raising ISPs to the rank of preventive censors. They would rather disable access to content the legal character of which they found in any way doubtful then face legal charges for hosting it.

Yet, democratic societies were founded on the prohibition of any censorship.[24] Neither in Europe nor in America ISPs were or are obliged to render preventive

---

[17] In China any content that could endanger "national unity" is deemed illegal, in Myanmar, Egypt, or Malaysia any criticism of the governing party is disallowed. Liberia additionally requires the blocking of websites that include "anti-Liberian materials", while Zimbabwe limits access to any sites that could "raise unease or sorrow". See: Privacy International, GreenNet Educational Trust (2003) at 20.

[18] Filtering software often comes from U.S.-based companies. For example, Cisco software was one of the pillars of the Great Firewall of China, including server-operating programs and ones supporting the national educational networks. Cisco was also working on a Chinese "Next-Generation Network", the so-called ChinaNet Next Carrying Network, CN2. Doe 2004b.

[19] If a domain name or the website include any of the designated keywords, such as "sex" in the case of pornographic content or "Falun Gong" in case of politically motivated one, access to such a website was automatically blocked. Users would usually receive a 404 error message. See: Deibert et al. (2010) at 4–5.

[20] See: Deibert et al. (2010) at 529–530.

[21] Deibert et al. (2010) at 552.

[22] See: Doe (2004a) at 8–9. Yet until 2010 and the U.S. Internet Freedom program, discussed herein below, no state authority directly addressed the filtering policies as undemocratic.

[23] Doe 2004a at 8–9.

[24] Council of Europe (2011b): "Action by a state that limits or forbids access to specific Internet content constitutes an interference with freedom of expression and the right to receive and impart information. In Europe, such an interference can only be justified if it fulfills the conditions of Article 10, paragraph 2, of the European Convention on Human Rights and the relevant case law of the European Court of Human Rights." Furthermore, the Committee emphasized that "states should not, through general blocking or filtering measures, exercise prior control of content

censorship over the content they provide access to.[25] With time, states on both sides of the Atlantic found forever more reasons to limit free access to content, be it for the traditional interests of state security or new reasons like intellectual property protection.[26] Currently the majority of European and American states include in their legal systems so-called notice-and-takedown procedures, affecting free speech online. They provide for ISPs obligations to limit access to certain content deemed contrary to national laws following either a court decision or a notice received from individuals or corporations. ISPs themselves may also limit the amount of information they render access to, as defined within their terms of service. Yet, as a general rule neither in Europe nor in America are ISPs obliged to render preventive censorship, i.e. to verify all the content they host or enable access to for its legality.[27] They are rather obliged to act only when they are made aware of the illegal character of certain content that is already published. What follows is an eager debate on the form and contents of information that the ISPs should be in disposition of and the procedure, based upon which certain content is to be made inaccessible.[28] The notice-and-takedown procedure is being criticized as granting ISPs too much freedom in deciding on the legal character of individual content and censoring information based on their own assessment, without a court decision.[29]

Blocking access to certain content within particular jurisdictions remains therefore an eagerly disputed subject. Those opposing this form of online censorship feel that blocking access to certain content generates unreasonably high costs of filtering software deployed, while not solving the true problem behind illegal content available online. Quite the opposite—it adds to the difficulty in identifying and apprehending the culprits.[30] There is also the element of risk brought about by any form of censorship. Legitimizing it brings about the inevitable threat of authorities using such an exception for other purposes than those originally intended. Black lists of inaccessible websites are being kept secret by the ISPs working together with the police, only at times allowing for civil society participation in putting them together, yet making it impossible to verify through traditional democratic tools the information actually being blocked within a jurisdiction. The black lists are set

made available on the Internet unless such measures are taken on the basis of a provisional or final decision on the illegality of such content by the competent national authorities and in full respect for the strict conditions of Article 10, paragraph 2, of the European Convention on Human Rights." Such measures may only be applied towards "clearly identifiable content" and must be proportionate.

[25] See: Deibert (2008) at 120–123.

[26] See: Open Net Initiative 2013, Reporters without Borders (2013).

[27] But see the recent Delfi v. Estonia case where the ECtHR recognized ISP's editorial liability for user content. ECtHR (2013).

[28] See: European Court of Justice (2010). In the case *Scarlet Extended SA v. Société belge des auteurs, compositeurs et éditeurs SCRL (SABAM)* the Court found that a judicial order to enact prior content control of uploaded and downloaded user data, laid upon a Belgian service provider, is against community law.

[29] See e.g.: Chilling Effects Clearinghouse (2013).

[30] See e.g.: (McNamee 2013).

together by ISPs working together with police enforcement agencies, therefore it is difficult to assess what addresses they actually contain and may serve as a pretext for limiting access to information that is politically dangerous to those in power. Only unlimited access to electronic content may prevent a risk of candid state censorship.

Proponents of limiting access to certain detrimental online content claim that even though the filtering technologies are not perfect, they are one of the numerous preventive measures used to limit the harmful effects of illegal materials, such as child pornography. Effective crime enforcement requires the engagement of all tools available, both off- and online, meaning also disabling access for those who wish to access illegal content online.[31] Just because the method does not guarantee a perfect success rate does not mean one should not impose it. Proponents of such filtering policies include state authorities and law enforcement agencies, but also telecommunication companies, who exclude access to illegal content from the scope on their services, introducing filters for any service rendered.[32]

15.3 The Case of Egypt: The First Ever State Sponsored National Internet Blackout

In February 2011, authorities in riot-driven Egypt decided to take the state off the Internet—the last medium still available to their statesmen.[33] The blackout was achieved by applying the never before used practice of ordering all country-based ISPs to halt rendering their services.[34] This was the first ever case for a state to completely take its nation offline. Autocracies such as Cuba or North Korea scrupulously limit individual Internet access, be it through high price policy or formally restricting access to computers with an Internet connection, yet have never before decided to just switch off national critical Internet infrastructure. The reaction of the international community to the Egyptian precedent was also unique. Within a few days of the blackout, Google, a U.S.-based company,[35] offered its users located within Egypt the possibility to overcome the blocking enacted by

[31] See e.g.: Weckert (2000) at 105–111, who justifies the enactment of Internet filtering in Australia with those very arguments.

[32] One of the strongest proponents of Universal Internet filtering has been India, see e.g.: Agence France-Presse (2012).

[33] The same method was very likely used repeatedly a year later in Syria also entangled in internal turmoil. See e.g.: Coldewey (2013).

[34] According to Renesys, a company specializing in analyzing cyber espionage, Egyptian authorities probably ordered individual ISPs to disconnect all international Internet connections. Enforcing that decision did not however impact the international data flow to and from Egypt. Cowie 2011.

[35] Using a technology newly purchased from a start-up company SayNow, working together with Twitter, owned by a U.S.-based company: Obvious.

Egyptian law enforcement.[36] The solution used was a simple one, yet quickly brought about the intended aim: following a decision by the authorities, the ineffective blocking was ceased within 24 hours from introducing the ground-breaking Google service.[37]

This unprecedented incident clearly depicts the core of the problem with Internet filtering. The decision of Egyptian authorities to disallow any Internet access from state territory clearly was an interference with the individual freedom of speech. Google's reaction may be considered a first enactment of the 2010 "Clinton doctrine" for online freedom, aimed at states exercising online censorship as announced by Secretary Clinton in early 2010 during her engaging speech at the Newseum.[38]

This unprecedented practice provokes the question about the international law limits on free speech online, in particular the right to access information. International law's answer to questions on state responsibility for this particular limitations imposed on individual right to free speech are presented below.

15.4 State Immunity, State Sovereignty, and Limits of Individual Right to Free Speech Online

In order to answer the question on state responsibility for the infringement of individual human rights online, with particular attention paid to the right to access and share information, limited in early 2011 by Egyptian authorities a brief reference to the international law doctrine on state immunity ought to be made. This will allow us to classify a nation-wide Internet blackout as either sovereign state competence or a breach of an international obligation by that state bringing about its international responsibility. The contemporary understanding of state immunity reflects the limits of sovereign state power. It includes the distinction between *acta de iure imperii*—a term describing the exclusive, sovereign power of a state[39] and *acta de iure gestionis*—actions taken up by a state yet considered equal to those of private entities or individuals, since not restricted to sovereigns alone.[40] The latter include, for instance, engaging in private enterprises, taking on commercial endeavors, or entering so-called

[36] See e.g.: Doe 2011a, b.

[37] The system was based on using two particular international telephone numbers—information provided to those numbers was automatically, promptly published on Twitter with a keyword #Egypt. According to a Google representative, delivering information in this way did not require their authors to have Internet connectivity. Information so delivered was also available as audio under the very same telephone numbers or by accessing a devoted website: twitter.com/speak2tweet. See: Doe 2011a, b.

[38] Clinton 2010.

[39] Such as, primarily, enforcing legislative, executive or judicial jurisdiction, using treaty powers or the legation right.

[40] Performing, for instance; commercial activity. For the difficulties in assessing that divergence see e.g. the Libyan assets freeze case discussed in Rutzke 1988 at 241–282.

Bilateral Investment Treaties. In such cases, no state immunity is granted and a state may be held liable for any harm arising out of such activity, including civil litigation in foreign courts. On the other hand, the breach of state obligations falling into the *acta de iure imperii* category may lead to international responsibility of a state according to customary international law and the law of treaties, as described by the International Law Commission in its 2001 Draft Articles, yet may not be subject to the assessment of foreign national courts or other state organs.[41]

According to this distinction, the situation in Egypt clearly remains within the exclusive competence of a state, therefore represents an element of exercising state sovereignty. It may therefore be referred to in terms of a possible breach of international obligations laid upon Egypt at the time of the blackout, in particular its human rights obligations. Its legality may not however be assessed by national courts or other organs of another state. According to the UDHR or the ICCPR, state competence undoubtedly includes the right to restrict access to online content within state territory, yet international law introduces certain limitations on how and to what extend those restrictions are to be enforced.[42]

Assessment of the proportionality of that restriction and its compliance with international human rights norms, in particular the permissible limits of the right to access and impart information of Egyptian residents, remains a different issue. As already mentioned, the right to access information may be limited for particular reasons and in specific cases. A general ban on access to information ought to be assessed as the breach of Egypt's international obligations towards human rights protection, in particular those of the ICCPR, that Egypt is a party to. Article 19 ICCPR includes the above-mentioned requirement of proportionality that Egypt failed to meet. The derogative clause named in Article 4 ICCPR allows a state to "take measures derogating from their obligations under the Covenant (...) in time of public emergency which threatens the life of the nation and the existence of which is officially proclaimed". A state "availing itself of the right of derogation shall immediately inform the other States Parties to the present Covenant, through the intermediary of the Secretary-General of the United Nations, of the provisions from which it has derogated and of the reasons by which it was actuated". Egypt never met that requirement, therefore no justification for the restriction according to Article 4 ICCPR may be found. Such interpretation seems confirmed by a recent ECtHR decision in a similar case against Turkey discussed below.

[41] International Law Commission 2001 at 62.

[42] There is no doubt that state authorities were not deprived of their power at the time of the Internet blackout, therefore the fact of effectively disabling Internet access ought to be regarded as an act of legitimate state power being enforced. Separate is the issue of proportionality of the enforced limitation.

15.5 The Yıldırım Case

The assessment of the nation-wide Internet blackout as a breach of international obligation in the case of Egypt might follow the very same line of reasoning, justifying state's responsibility for the breach of its international obligation, as provided for by the ECtHR in the recent Yıldırım case.[43] A brief look at this groundbreaking case on Internet filtering shows a Turkish Internet user, Ahmet Yıldırım, who was deprived by Turkish authorities of the technical capability to share his ideas online through a personal website he had maintained within one of the numerous services offered in Turkey by Google: Google Sites. The restriction of access to all Google sites available in Turkey, including that run by the plaintiff, followed a court decision on content deemed illegal in Turkey, whose author could not be identified nor—consequentially—trialed. The regional court in Denizli issued an order directed at the national office for telecommunication (*Tur.*: Telekomünikasyon İletişim Başkanlığı, further herein: TİB) to disable access to all Google services in Turkey, claiming no other effective method of limiting access to the one website containing incriminating data was at hand. All of the almost 35 million Internet users in Turkey, that is nearly half of the Turkish population, lost access to all Google services offered in that country.[44] Their right to receive and impart information was infringed. This alleged violation of Article 10 ECHR was the basis for a successful claim by Mr. Yıldırım. The ECHR found that disallowing access to millions of websites because one of them contains information deemed illegal is a clear breach of the proportionality requirement included in the delimitative clause of Article 10 par. 2. Mr Yıldırım was awarded 7500 EUR as indemnification and 1000 EUR as costs reimbursement. The ECtHR clearly identified the proportionality prerequisite, present in Article 10 as one requiring a limitation enforced against individual in particular cases, where a nation-wide blocking of particular content did not meet that standard.

Should the same analysis be provided following the ICCPR standards and its fulfillment by Egypt in the case discussed, Egypt would also fail to meet the proportionality requirement as under no circumstances may disabling all Internet access be considered "proportional" or "case-specific" in terms of the HRC guidelines. Yet, one must keep in mind that the ICCPR regime offers no effective regime for enforcing its applicability, unlike the ECHR. While analyzing the international responsibility of Egypt, one must realize that any prosecution of that breach, not to mention enforceable international responsibility of the state is highly unlikely. Despite Egypt's participation in the ICCPR system and its obligation to impose any limitations solely within the rigid framework of HRC comments, the existing human rights violations assessment procedures give little hope for effective enforcement of free speech violations sanctions, even though the abovementioned

[43] European Court of Human Rights. 2012. Yıldırım v. Turkey.

[44] Miniwatts Marketing Group, World Internet Stats, http://www.internetworldstats.com/europa2.htm#tr (accessed Nov. 19, 2013).

UN HRC Resolution 12/16 on freedom of speech clearly disallows state parties to impose any limitations on the right to peaceful assembly and access to ICTs.[45]

All the procedures, the one on individual complaint[46] as well as the special ones created within the UN to protect human rights, are primarily initiated by the HRC, which is currently dominated by African and Muslim states, supported by China and Russia, who all represent a vision of free speech different from the one present in European or American legal systems.[47] The effectiveness of the Council's action has been strongly criticized over the years and even the introduction of a U.S. member, aimed at amending the unsatisfactory current situation proved futile.[48] In this context, chances to find international support and legitimization for sanctions against extensive Internet filtering in Egypt or elsewhere seem weak. Without such international authorization, any action aimed at limiting excessive exercise of state sovereignty over the access to online content remains contrary to the procedures adopted in international law. The controversial concept of humanitarian intervention, which claims legitimate the use of force by one or numerous states in defense of human rights violations victims may not be applied to violations of freedom of speech, freedom to communicate or freedom of assembly, since no peremptory norms safeguard those particular liberties, unlike in the case of e.g. genocide.[49]

The assessment presented above clearly shows that state imposed Internet blackout regarded as a restriction of access to any media may be recognized as a violation of international law, but lacks efficient international tools to counteract. The 2010 proclaimed U.S. Internet Freedom doctrine, aimed at helping victims of free speech violations worldwide, in particular in the Arab Spring entangled states, remains therefore a challenging piece of legal analysis discussed herein below.

15.6 The Clinton Doctrine and State Jurisdiction

On January 21, 2010, U.S. State Secretary Hilary Clinton declared war on Internet censors. Her speech, intentionally held at the free speech museum in Chicago, was acclaimed as the start of the Clinton Doctrine in foreign American politics. A term re-used to denote the relevance of the online human rights policy to President Clinton's commitment, in 1999, to protect ethnical minorities in Kosovo. The U.S. Secretary of State at the time of the Arab Spring proclaimed the White

[45] United Nations 2009.

[46] Egypt is not party to the First Optional Protocol introducing the individual complaint procedure.

[47] Evans 2008.

[48] See e.g.: Robertson (2006) at 1–40.

[49] See: e.g. Newman (2002) at 102–120. Such an intervention might be deemed legal should acts of genocide or war crimes be accompanied by the Internet blackout.

House intended to protect human rights abroad again, yet this time in a different setting and in another environment. The rights to be protected were also different: Clinton claimed U.S. aimed at protecting free speech, right of access to information, freedom of assembly and freedom of religion expressed online.[50] She clearly condemned China, North Korea, Egypt, Vietnam, Tunisia, Uzbekistan, and Saudi Arabia for the limits they impose within their territories on freedom of expression and flow of information online. She identified such practices as a clear violation of those states residents' right to access information. The analysis presented above confirms such assessment.

Clinton went a step further and—regardless of the existing, yet ineffective, UN human rights protection system—announced U.S. help for all residents of the states limiting access to information through Internet filtering in exercising the individual right to access information.[51] She announced U.S. plans to develop and deploy technology allowing to circumvent any state-imposed blocking. Clinton was the first state official to directly speak out against state-imposed Internet censorship. Until then, the tacit consensus among states was that online filtering remained within the exclusive competence of each state. It was a year after her Newseum speech that Clinton introduced the Internet Freedom program, which consisted of specific plans to help individuals deprived of their human right to freely access information.[52] The Internet Freedom program, even before it came to its fruition in Egypt, might have been critically assessed from international law's point of view. On behalf of one of the most powerful states in the world, Clinton announced she intended to support individuals residing in territories of foreign states in their breaching of local laws.

The initial question brought about by Clinton's statement is not new to international law disputes: it is the question of the hierarchy between human rights principles and state sovereignty. All that was new in this case was the fact that the human right in question was to be exercised online. Internet adds to this long-lasting dispute by including the question of limits of state power over critical elements of the network, including root servers or domain registries, the proper functioning of which is the necessary element of enabling free exercise of the right discussed herein. The question on permissible state interference in the daily operation of critical Internet infrastructure, as that operated by Egyptian ISPs, is a direct reflection of the question of limits of state interference with individual rights. The challenge with answering that question relates directly to the transnational character of the non-territorial cyberspace when confronted with the primarily territorial specific of exercising national jurisdiction.[53]

---

[50] Clinton 2010.

[51] For the definition of Internet filtering see e.g. Deibert (2008) at 15.

[52] Clinton 2011.

[53] For critical remarks of the implications of applying territorial jurisdiction over the cyberspace see: Kulesza (2012) at 1–30.

There is no doubt that any state action, which results online, regardless whether aimed at content—blocking access thereto or removing it, or at infrastructure-through a DDoS attack which disables certain hardware, brings about transboundary effects. An e-mail message that fails to reach its recipient (i.e. a U.S. resident) outside the jurisdiction of state where the sender is located (i.e. Egypt) limits the right to exchange information of both parties involved. Similarly, blocking the publication of information on current events in Egypt limits the right to access information of anyone outside Egyptian territory, including those in the U.S. One could raise the argument that such information, particularly if published in English, might have been targeted at those outside Egyptian territory. In this hypothetical situation, the U.S. would have the right or might even be considered obliged[54] to protect the right to access information of its residents, recalling the effective jurisdictional principle, since the harmful effects were present within its territory, where the recipients never gained access to information intended to reach them, or that of passive personal jurisdiction, allowing the state of the victim's nationality to exercise its powers. The U.S. would then be authorized to act in order to safeguard the right to access information of its residents, should that right be endangered following an act of law of a third party.[55] Such an interpretation of jurisdictional principles may bring unaccountable consequences, since any restriction on electronic content accessibility inherently holds unavoidable, global consequences on right to access information. The principles of effective or passive personal jurisdiction must therefore be applied with great caution. Content published online is simultaneously accessible everywhere where the Internet is, and the act of such content being removed deprives potential recipients of information contained therein of their right to access information.

The 2011 case of the U.S. citizen, Joe Gordon, sentenced in Bangkok to two and a half years in prison offers the perfect example of the threat engendered by applying effective jurisdiction to online activities, and in particular to free expression. Gordon posted links to the unauthorized biography of the Thai king while residing in the U.S.[56] and was considered by Thai authorities to have committed a *lese majeste* crime as per the Thai criminal code.[57] Upon his arrival to Bangkok for family holiday, this U.S. citizen was arrested, tried and sentenced to prison for the crime he committed online while in his U.S. home, yet the effects of which were felt in Thailand. The Thai courts applied effective jurisdiction, well recognized in international law. What is more, they have passed a new Computer Crimes Act that explicitly surrenders all insults to the monarchy committed online or through mobile phones to Thai jurisdiction. Its application to online activities creates a new threat to the rule of law. No one publishing online may any longer be certain

---

[54] See: European Court of Human Rights (2008).

[55] See: U.S. District Court for the Eastern District of Virginia, Alexandria Division (2010).

[56] Doe 2011b.

[57] Thai *lese majeste* laws mandate a jail term of 3–15 years for anyone who "defames, insults, or threatens the King, the Queen, the Heir-apparent, or the Regent." Thai National Administrative Reform Council (1956).

whether the content he or she uploads breaches the laws of a state where the Internet is accessible making him or her one of the Joe Gordon's of the Internet age. Applying effective jurisdiction to online activities unavoidably brings about an undesired chilling effect and deprives all authors of online content of any legal security. What is interesting about the original Joe Gordon case is the fact that the U.S., after having proclaimed their Internet freedom doctrine, chose not to intervene in any way in order to protect their citizen and his individual right to free speech online. Commentators justified this lack of reaction with the strong economic and political ties binding the two countries.[58]

As explained above the tacit consent granted by the White House to Google services in Egypt may hardly be justified by the human rights doctrine, yet may be considered contrary to the U.S. obligation to undertake any diligent action to prevent private interference with foreign sovereignty. According to the principle of due diligence, recognized in international law, the U.S. might be held internationally responsible for lack of due diligence of its authorities in preventing Google's interference with foreign states' sovereignty.[59] This aspect of the interrelationship between human rights and state sovereignty is discussed in more detail below.

15.7 "Internet Freedom" vs. State Responsibility

Both Clinton's declarations discussed above are material sources of international law. They constitute unilateral acts of state.[60] It is also clear that such acts have no direct effect on national laws and jurisprudence. They bring no obligation of U.S. individuals or companies to prevent any online censorship. Such an obligation, in order to be effective, would need to be enshrined within a national act of law. It would also be difficult to show that the particular actions taken on by Google in Egypt were the direct result of any U.S. official policy, less the Clinton statements. Neither of those statements includes a direct authorization for any entity to act on behalf of the U.S. and should they even include one, as already mentioned, such declarations are not a source of national U.S. law. The U.S. therefore holds no direct responsibility for the actions of Google in Egypt. Google did not act on behalf of or following an authorization of the U.S. authorities. Yet this does not mean that the U.S. may not be considered liable for the effects of Google's actions.

Legitimate decisions of Egyptian authorities require the respect of other states, which is a direct consequence of the principle of sovereign equality, fundamental to any international law regulation or practice. The principle of state sovereignty and the obligation of other states to respect it is usually derived from Article 2 par. 4 and

[58] Associated Press 2011.

[59] Pisillo-Mazzeschi 1992 at 9–51.

[60] International Law Commission 2006.

confirmed by par. 7 of the very same article in the United Nations Charter (UNC).[61] As rightfully pointed out by R. Vark, the obligation to respect other states' sovereignty includes an obligation to prevent potentially damaging acts originated within state territory. This duty of prevention also includes the obligation to cooperate with potential victim states in any way necessary to eliminate the harmful effects of the interference.[62] This obligation means that even when a state is not able to effectively protect the rightful interests of another sovereign state it may not passively allow for private parties to use its territory or other resources within its jurisdiction to interfere with those interests. This principle of due diligence in preventing the harmful use of state resources has been confirmed by rich jurisprudence, with the leading Teheran hostages case.[63] In its decision, the ICJ confirmed Iran's responsibility for the inaction of its authorities aimed at preventing harm to U.S. interests represented through its diplomatic mission in Teheran, which was raided upon by individual, private Iranians protesting against the U.S. interference in the region. The ICJ confirmed, that even though those actions of the individuals may not be directly attributed to the state, the latter is nevertheless responsible for the lack of preventive actions on the side of its authorities contractually obliged to actively protect the diplomatic mission in Teheran. As the ICJ explained, the fact that the acts of the militants may not be directly attributed to Iranian authorities "does not mean that Iran is, in consequence, free from any responsibility in regard to those attacks, for its own conduct was in conflict with its international obligations. (. . .) Iran was placed under the (. . .) obligations (. . .) to take appropriate steps to ensure protection" of U.S. diplomats and their mission.[64] The ICJ confirmed, that Iran "failed to take appropriate steps" to protect U.S. personnel and that "the total inaction" of Iranian authorities was contrary to its international obligations.[65]

The court identified the duty of a state to act with due diligence when fulfilling its international obligations with the possibility to attribute to it harmful consequences of private individuals' actions, should those follow the lack of due diligence on behalf of state organs.[66] Enabling state territory for individuals or entities attempting to cause harm in other jurisdictions may be identified as an internationally wrongful act and give grounds to state responsibility for the lack of due diligence on behalf of state authorities in preventing such transboundary damage.[67] This conclusion is justified by the contents of Article 14 par. 3 of the 1992 ILC's

---

[61] United Nations 1945.

[62] Vark 2006 at 192.

[63] International Court of Justice 1980 at 3.

[64] International Court of Justice 1980 at 31.

[65] International Court of Justice 1980 at 32.

[66] Bratspies and Miller 2006 at 233, who conclude that the existence of such a preventive obligation allows attributing to the state the very actions of private individuals. The ILC doctrine on transboundary harm emphasizes however that it is the lack of action of state authorities in preventing harmful events rather than the actions themselves which give ground for state responsibility.

[67] International Law Commission 2001 at 62.

Draft Articles on state responsibility, as according to its leading editor, the Committees Special Rapporteur on state responsibility J. Crawford, the rules defined within the draft relate also to "the breach of obligation to prevent a given event".[68] An obligation to prevent a given effect is usually defined as a best efforts obligation, requiring states to undertake any reasonable or necessary means in order to prevent a given effect, however without the guarantee that such an event will not take place. The standard of due diligence in set for each individual case, depending on its circumstances.[69] According to the UN Special Rapporteur on transboundary harm issues, P. S. Rao, "a breach of the due diligence obligation could be presumed" also "when a State had intentionally or negligently caused the event which had to be prevented or had intentionally or negligently not prevented others in its territory from causing that event or had abstained from abating it."[70] A state may therefore be considered responsible for the consequences of not introducing appropriate legislation, not executing national laws, or not preventing illegal activities within its jurisdiction or control.[71] The breach of a due diligence obligation also occurs when state authorities knew or should have known, regarding the circumstances, that a particular activity may result in transboundary harm.[72]

The U.S. government was aware of the action undertaken by Google that was aimed at making ineffective the procedures introduced by the legitimate Egyptian authorities,[73] yet took no action to prevent Google's plans. The due diligence obligation derived from Article 2 par. 4 UNC would require the U.S. authorities to make the company cease rendering the service effectively harmful to Egyptian internal policy. This conclusion, implied by the current international law jurisprudence, seems unsatisfactory to those seeking effective tools for preventing human rights violations online. A more optimistic answer may be proposed when reexamining the notion of state sovereignty, referred to above.

15.8 State Sovereignty in Cyberspace

In so far as extensive content filtering exercised by states like Egypt or China is considered undemocratic in Europe or America, international law foresees for no effective tools to prevent it. What is more, the existing catalogue of peremptory

---

[68] International Law Commission 1992.

[69] Brownlie 1983 at 45 names as criteria for attributing state responsibility the causal link between the negligence of a state authority and a breach of international law.

[70] United Nations 1999 at 8.

[71] United Nations 1999 at 8.

[72] United Nations 1999 at 8 where the issue of responsibility for transboundary damage in international watercourses is discussed.

[73] Google's service was so successful that the very next day after its employment Egypt re-enabled Internet access throughout the country.

norms clearly confirms that any state willingly or even negligently enabling its territory to infringe other state's sovereignty is in breach of its international obligations and may be subject to international responsibility. It requires other states to respect the sovereign decisions of state authorities, unless the UN Security Council finds them contrary to international law and allows for an intervention in the internal affairs of a state.[74]

This state of affairs seems undesired for two reasons named above. Any state activity regarding online content brings instantaneous and unavoidable transboundary effect wherever the Internet is accessible. Regarding the lack of effective international solutions to this undesired transboundary effect, every state whose residents have been harmed by such national decisions limiting access to online content, could individually address the breach based on its effective or passive personal jurisdiction. For this particular reason—the unavoidable interdependence between local and transboundary effect of Internet filtering—the international community is forever more strongly addressing states' obligation to refrain from interference with online content.[75]

Defining the limits of free speech has always been strongly rooted in culture and since its very recognition was identified within states' exclusive competence, unless states were willing to share it within a treaty regime or an international organization based upon such a treaty. The universal character of the global network that allows for instantaneous global communications seems to require a change in this contemporary paradigm. A universal standard for free speech online seems a necessary condition for preserving the unique global information network and saving it from fragmentation. What is being defined as *public service value of the Internet*[76] or the recognition of Internet access as a civil right within national legal regimes[77] justifies such a demand. At the same time, a proposed international obligation to freely provide access to online content is being narrowly defined—it refers solely to the obligation to ensure transboundary data flow.[78]

At a time of ever-growing globalization and when one-third of world's population is online,[79] it is necessary to stimulate the debate on fundamental values that

[74] As already mentioned, the idea of humanitarian intervention remains controversial and therefore still may not be accounted for as one of the universally recognized international law concepts, primarily due to the lacking uniform and universal *opinio iuris*. See supra 45 above.

[75] See e.g.: Council of Europe (2003) or Council of Europe (2011a, b, c).

[76] See e.g.: Council of Europe (2007).

[77] Internet access is recognized as a fundamental right in Finland or Lithuania.

[78] What is meant here would be a situation where blocking the free flow of information online in one state causes significant limitations to Internet access in another jurisdiction, which uses the filtering states' infrastructure. An example of the 2008 conflict between Russia and Georgia may be named. Georgian electronic infrastructure was blocked, which was followed by Armenia losing any Internet connectivity, as it was solely dependent on the Fibre Optical Cable System Trans Asia Europe, running through Georgia. See: Council of Europe (2009) at 22.

[79] According to Miniwatts Marketing Group, specializing in Internet statistics, 34.3 % of world's population had Internet access by the end of 2012; see: http://www.internetworldstats.com/stats.htm. Accessed 23 May 2013.

should be protected online and the ways and means in which to protect them.[80] In the course of that debate, the particular character of the medium discussed must be of major consideration. Regarding the architecture and governance structure of the network it seems a modification of the traditional notion of sovereignty is necessary due to the increasing need for enhanced human rights protection online.[81]

It is for those reasons that some authors propose the idea of *cooperative sovereignty*,[82] derived from the concept of treaty-based shared sovereignty, recognized, for instance, within the European Union, as an alternative to the existing derivative of the Westphalian order, fundamental to the current geopolitics.[83] This proposal seems well fitted with the unique principle of multistakeholderism in Internet governance.[84] According to this principle, Internet governance is executed jointly, although "in their respective roles" by three stakeholder groups and any effective consensus requires their cooperation.[85] Next to states, the stakeholder groups include business and civil society, with the latter covering NGOs, academia and individual users.[86] Following the multistakeholder principle decisions on the accessibility of online content, as any other on the issue of Internet governance, ought to be made by consensus of representatives of the three stakeholder groups. Unlike in international relations known thus far, it is no longer the states that hold the decisive voice in determining the future of this unique medium that is the Internet.

This interesting concept so far remains largely in the dogmatic sphere. It seems yet distant from becoming binding international law, as that would require either its recognition within an international treaty, adopted by states, yet open to other stakeholders[87] or a uniform customary practice of states supported by an *opinio iuris*. Both solutions would require time for their development and do not guarantee the current flexibility of governance, necessary for the quickly evolving nature of the cyberspace as its subject matter. Those shortcomings require for at least a temporary resolution to international soft law mechanisms,[88] yet the cooperative sovereignty proposal is worth remembering. As already mentioned the transboundary character of cyberspace, creating a direct threat to national rule of law and legal security of state nationals calls for the reconsideration of the notion of sovereignty. The *cooperative sovereignty concept* is based on the presumption that

---

[80] See: Council of Europe (2011a, b, c).

[81] See generally: Kreijen (2002).

[82] See e.g.: Weber (2010) at 19, Perrez (2000) at 264 f. proposing the general duty to cooperate as a principle of international law.

[83] See: Krasner (2004) at 19 ff.

[84] Weber 2010 at 14.

[85] See: United Nations (2005) at 4.

[86] See: Kleinwächter (2005) at 79.

[87] See: Kulesza (2012) at 152–155 where the author presents the concept of an Internet framework convention.

[88] See: Council of Europe (2010).

it is possible to identify shared values undermining different interpretations of sovereignty, which will then allow for the identification of universally accepted, fundamental values. Cooperative sovereignty could then stimulate any further discussion on the possible compromise on sharing state powers.[89] Such a compromise would need to envisage the sovereignty-based state prerogatives with obligations laid upon states according to international law, in particular human rights law. Weber suggests that states share a joint, international obligation to create and implement policies focused on human rights protection.[90] Perez identifies the cooperative sovereignty with the international obligation to cooperate as one of the principles of international law.[91] It is in that context that the need to identify and implement a universal standard for protecting free speech online should be understood. Achieving such a compromise seems possible in the light not only of the rapid development of human rights law in the last 60 years, but particularly in the recent U.N. Human Rights Council's First Resolution on Internet Free Speech—a soft law document, symptomatic for the increasing interest of the UN in international Internet law issues.[92] The Council calls upon all States to promote and facilitate access to the Internet and international cooperation aimed at the development of media and information and communications facilities in all countries.[93] A hard-law follow-up remains to be expected.

References

Agence France-Presse. (2012). India defends internet censorship. *The Jakarta Globe*, August 24. http://www.thejakartaglobe.com/archive/india-defends-internet-censorship/. Accessed 23 May 2013.

Associated Press. (2011). American sentenced to prison for Thai royal insult. *3 News*, December 8. http://www.3news.co.nz/American-sentenced-to-prison-for-Thai-royal-insult/tabid/417/articleID/235841/Default.aspx. Accessed 23 May 2013.

Bratspies, R. M., & Miller, R. A. (Eds.). (2006). *Transboundary harm in international law: lessons from the Trail Smelter arbitration*. Cambridge: Cambridge University Press.

Brownlie, I. (1983). *System of the law of nations, part I: State responsibility*. Oxford: Oxford University Press.

Chilling Effects Clearinghouse. (2013). The chilling effects clearinghouse homepage. http://www.chillingeffects.org/

Clinton, H.R. (2010). Remarks on internet freedom. http://www.state.gov/secretary/rm/2010/01/135519.htm. Accessed 23 May 2013.

Clinton, H.R. (2011). Internet rights and wrongs: Choices & challenges in a networked world, remarks. http://www.state.gov/secretary/rm/2011/02/156619.htm. Accessed 23 May 2013.

---

[89] Weber 2010 at 14.

[90] Weber 2010 at 16.

[91] Perrez 2000 at 264 ff.

[92] Human Rights Council 2012. On international Internet law, its genesis and principles see generally: Kulesza (2012), 130 ff.

[93] Human Rights Council 2012 at 2.

Coldewey, D. (2013). Syria goes dark again in widespread Internet blackout. *NBC News*, May 7. http://www.nbcnews.com/technology/syria-goes-dark-again-widespread-internet-blackout-6C9830083. Accessed 23 May 2013.
Council of Europe. (1950). Convention for the protection of human rights and fundamental freedoms as amended by protocols No. 11 and No. 14. Council of Europe Treaty Series No. 194.
Council of Europe. (2003). Declaration of the committee of ministers on freedom of communication on the Internet.
Council of Europe. (2007). Recommendation of the committee of ministers to member states on measures to promote the public service value of the Internet.
Council of Europe. (2009). Internet governance and critical internet resources.
Council of Europe. (2010). International and multi-stakeholder co-operation on cross-border Internet. Interim report of the Ad-hoc Advisory Group on Cross-border Internet to the Steering Committee on the Media and New Communication Services incorporating analysis of proposals for international. http://www.coe.int/t/dghl/standardsetting/media/mc–s–ci/default_EN.asp. Accessed 23 May 2013.
Council of Europe. (2011a). Declaration by the committee of ministers on internet governance principles.
Council of Europe. (2011b). Declaration by the Committee of Ministers on the protection of freedom of expression and information and freedom of assembly and association with regard to Internet domain names and name strings.
Council of Europe. (2011c). Recommendation of the committee of ministers to member states on the protection and promotion of the universality, integrity and openness of the Internet.
Cowie, J. (2011). Egypt leaves the internet. *Rensys*, January 27. http://www.renesys.com/blog/2011/01/egypt–leaves–the–internet.shtml. Accessed 23 May 2013.
Deibert, R. (Ed.). (2008). *Access denied: the practice and policy of global Internet filtering*. Massachusetts: MIT Press.
Deibert, R., Palfrey, J. G., Rohozinski, R., & Zittrain, J. (Eds.). (2010). *Access controlled: The shaping of power, rights, and rule in cyberspace*. Massachusetts: MIT Press.
Doe, J. (2004). A starting point: Legal implications of internet filtering. OpenNet Initiative. https://opennet.net/docs/Legal_Implications.pdf. Accessed 23 May 2013.
Doe, J. (2004). Cisco announces IP next-generation network advancements for service providers. http://newsroom.cisco.com/dlls/2004/prod_120604.html. Accessed 23 May 2013.
Doe, J. (2008). Italy cracks down on Pirate Bay. *New York Times*, August 14. http://www.nytimes.com/2008/08/14/technology/14iht–webpirate.15301147.html. Accessed 23 May 2013.
Doe, J. (2011a). Egypt crisis: Google launches 'speak to tweet' service. *The Telegraph*, February 1. http://www.telegraph.co.uk/news/worldnews/africaandindianocean/egypt/8295219/Egypt-crisis-Google-launches-speak-to-tweet-service.html. Accessed 23 May 2013.
Doe, J. (2011b). Thailand jails US man Joe Gordon for royal insult. *BBC online*, December 8. http://www.bbc.co.uk/news/world-asia-16081337. Accessed 23 May 2013.
European Court of Human Rights. (2001). VgT Verein Gegen Tierfabriken v. Switzerland. Case number 24699/94.
European Court of Human Rights. (2008). Khurshid Mustafa And Tarzibachi v. Sweden. Case number 23883/06.
European Court of Human Rights. (2012). Yıldırım v. Turkey. Case number 3111/10.
European Court of Human Rights. (2013). Delfi v. Estonia. Case number 64569/09.
European Court of Justice. (2010). Scarlet Extended SA v. Société belge des auteurs, compositeurs et éditeurs SCRL (SABAM). Case number C-70/10.
Evans, R. (2008). U.N. chief tells rights body drop rhetoric, blocs. *Reuters*, December 12. http://www.reuters.com/article/2008/12/12/us–un–rights–idUSTRE4BB67820081212. Accessed 23 May 2013.
Human Rights Council. (2012). The promotion, protection and enjoyment of human rights on the Internet. U.N. Doc. A/HRC/20/L.13.

International Court of Justice. (1980). United States Diplomatic and Consular Staff in Tehran.
International Law Commission. (1992). Draft articles on state responsibility: Titles and texts of articles adopted by the drafting committee. U.N. Doc. A/CN.4/L.472.
International Law Commission. (2001). Draft articles on responsibility of states for internationally wrongful acts, with commentaries. U.N. Doc A/56/10.
International Law Commission. (2006). Guiding principles with commentaries applicable to unilateral declarations of states capable of creating legal obligations. U.N. Doc. 61/10.
Kleinwächter, W. (2005). Multistakeholderism and the IGF: Laboratory, clearinghouse, watchdog. In W. J. Drake (Ed.), *Reforming Internet governance: perspectives from the Working Group on Internet Governance (WGIG)* (pp. 535–582). New York, NY: UN Publishing.
Krasner, S. D. (2004). The hole in the whole: Sovereignty, shared sovereignty, and international law. *Michigan Journal of International Law, 25*(4), 1075–1101.
Kreijen, G. (2002). *State, sovereignty, and international governance*. Oxford: Oxford University Press.
Kulesza, J. (2012). *International internet law*. London: Routledge.
McNamee, J. (2013). MEPs propose web blocking yet again, Digital Civil Rights in Europe. *EDRi-gram newsletter*, April 24. http://www.edri.org/edrigram/number11.8/web-blocking-gambling-again. Accessed 23 May 2013.
Newman, E. (2002). Humanitarian intervention, legality and legitimacy. *International Journal of Human Rights, 6*(4), 102–120.
Noman, H., York J.C. (2011). West censoring east: The use of western technologies by middle east censors, OpenNet Inititive. http://opennet.net/west-censoring-east-the-use-western-technologies-middle-east-censors-2010-2011. Accessed 23 May 2013.
Open Net Initiatve. (2013). Open net initiative homepage. https://opennet.net/. Accessed 23 May 2013.
Perrez, F. X. (2000). *Cooperative sovereignty*. The Hague: Kluwer Law International.
Pisillo-Mazzeschi, R. (1992). The due diligence rule and the nature of international responsibility of states. *German Yearbook of International Law, 35*, 9–51.
Privacy International, GreenNet Educational Trust (2003). Silenced, an international report on censorship and control of the internet. http://www.docstoc.com/docs/147504632/Silenced—an-international-report-on-censorship-and-control-of-the-internet. Accessed 23 May 2013.
Reporters Without Borders. (2013). The list of Internet enemies. http://en.rsf.org/internet.html. Accessed 23 May 2013.
Robertson, G. (2006). *Crimes against humanity*. New York, NY: The New Press.
Rutzke, C. R. (1988). The Libyan asset freeze and its application to foreign government deposits in overseas branches of United States banks: Libyan Arab Foreign Bank v Bankers Trust Co. *American University International Law Review, 3*(1), 241–282.
Sadurski, W. (2002). *Freedom of speech and its limits*. Dordrecht: Kluwer Academic Publishers.
Thai National Administrative Reform Council. (1956). Order (No. 41) Full text available in English at: http://thailaws.com/law/t_laws/tlaw50001.pdf. Accessed 23 May 2013.
U.S. District Court for the Eastern District of Virginia, Alexandria Division. (2010). Microsoft Corporation v. John Does 1—27, case number 1_10CV156 (LMBIJFA).
United Nations. (1945). United Nations Charter.
United Nations. (1948). Universal declaration of human rights. U.N. Doc. A/RES/(III).
United Nations. (1966). International covenant on civil and political rights. U.N. Doc. A/6316.
United Nations. (1999). Second report on international liability for injurious consequences arising out of acts not prohibited by international law by Mr. P.S. Rao, Special Rapporteur, U.N. Doc A/CN.4/501.
United Nations. (2005). Report of the Working Group on Internet Governance. www.wgig.org/docs/WGIGREPORT.pdf. Accessed 23 May 2013.
United Nations. (2009). Resolution adopted by the human rights council, freedom of opinion and expression. Un. Doc. A/HRC/RES/12/16.

Vark, R. (2006). State responsibility for private armed groups in the context of terrorism. *Juridica International, 11*, 184–193.
Weber, R. H. (2010). New sovereignty concepts in the age of internet. *Journal of Internet Law, 8*, 12–20.
Weckert, J. (2000). What is so bad about internet content regulation? *Ethics and Information Technology, 2*(2), 105–111.
Yutaka Arai, Y. (2002). *The margin of appreciation doctrine and the principle of proportionality in the jurisprudence of the ECHR*. Antwerp: Intersentia.

Chapter 16
Social Media Effects on the Gezi Park Movement in Turkey: Politics Under Hashtags

Kamil Demirhan

Abstract This study aims at understanding the role of social media in the Gezi Park movement in Turkey. The movement started as a protest of an environmentalist group then it turned into a social-political movement. The protestors were opposed to the project of re-building Gezi Park and Taksim Square that is the public area at the center of Istanbul. Politicians, demonstrators, the public and media have agreed on the fact that social media had a significant role in this movement. Social media, especially Twitter, was regarded as the main reason of this movement. The effect of social media on politics on the development of social movements and political participation is often evaluated as an important topic in current academic studies. This study contributes to this literature by focusing on the role of social media in the Gezi Park movement. The analysis consists of Twitter functions, Twitter actors as users, and the forms of communication on Twitter.

Keywords Social media • Twitter • Political participation • Social movements

16.1 Introduction

Social media channels, such as Facebook, YouTube, and Twitter, are used by different actors in political and social movements all around the world. Social media is regarded as a communication and interaction channel in these movements. Social media were used in the Gezi Park protests, and it had effects on the transition of events from protests of a small group of environmentalist to a social-political movement. Besides all the social media tools, Twitter took a significant role in the protests. Twitter hashtags were used intensely during the protests. Individuals, social groups, civil society organizations, and other democratic actors shared

K. Demirhan (✉)
Department of Political Science and Public Administration, Hacettepe University, Ankara, Turkey
e-mail: demirhankamil@gmail.com; demirhankamil@hacettepe.edu.tr

B. Pătruţ and M. Pătruţ (eds.), *Social Media in Politics*, Public Administration and Information Technology 13, DOI 10.1007/978-3-319-04666-2_16,

their opinions, thoughts, experiences, and demands over Twitter. The various functions of Twitter were used in the protests. Twitter usage in the Gezi Park movement provides examples for the claim that it has additional functions as being effective in social, cultural and political issues.

The data of this study consists of tweets in hashtags related to the movement rather than tweets in the pages of social groups or organizations. The people tweeted mostly in the hashtags related to the protests, and they used Twitter individually during the movement. However, tweets were not only sent by individuals, but also social groups and non-governmental organizations (NGOs). Social media usage rate is high in Turkey but the awareness of its functions is low. Twitter usage on the Gezi Park movement contributed to the increase of awareness of different actors about its effects on social and political processes. Nevertheless, it is clear that political and social actors cannot evaluate its effects comprehensively and critically. One may notice that there is a developing discourse about the effects of social media on social and political movements. Government agencies, people, organizations and protesters idealize the effects of Twitter. Governments, people, and organizations are acknowledging social media channels as the main actor of protests rather than analyzing their functions and effects on the process. In this study, the role of Twitter in the movement is discussed in terms of its functions, actors, and the characteristics of communication among users. It does not focus on the discussion of whether social media is responsible for the entire process or not.

The first part of this study gives information about the Gezi Park protests in terms of its reasons, development, characteristics, and actors. This part also provides opinion about the democratic conditions of Turkey in terms of the reactions of the ruling party during the protests, the effectiveness of civil society, the freedom of the media, the effectiveness of political and social organizations, and the civic culture in Turkey. The second part addresses the role of social media in politics. Specialized literature indicates different functions of social media in social and political movements and they give information about different cases. The third part explains the different examples of Twitter usage in social movements, protests, and political processes. These cases provide information about the functions of Twitter and its role in movements. In addition, they provide methods for analyzing the role of social media in these movements. The fourth part analyses Twitter usage and its effects in the Gezi Park movement. It also explains the method and data of the study. The last part discusses the role of Twitter in the protests and evaluates the results of the study as a conclusion.

16.2 Understanding the Gezi Movement: Content and Development

To understand the role of Twitter in the Gezi Park movement, it is useful to look at the development process of protests, participants' demands, and government responses. The Gezi Park protests were started on May the 28th, 2013 by environmentalists who are currently the members of Survive Gezi Park Association. They came together to protect trees from being cut down in order to realize a government project of re-organizing Taksim Square with the construction of "Taksim Military Barracks" which was designed to be a shopping, residential and historical area. Members of this civil platform demanded the preservation of the park and trees in their current form. They resisted the local authorities' use of police force against the struggle of a small group of environmentalists. This use of force increased the tension between the police and the group members. Disproportionate police force and intolerance of the government authorities on the demonstrators caused the reactions of the people. The protests attracted public interest. The people supported the struggle of the environmentalists for the park and for the protection of their social areas in the city center. People also reacted against the use of violence by the police. People came to Gezi Park spontaneously. Deputies, university students, workers, cultural groups, the fans of football teams, people of various professions such as doctors, academicians, and lawyers, and so many other groups of people were in Gezi Park and they condemned the police intervention. They also criticized the legitimacy of government because some of its decisions were regarded by people as threats for their rights and freedoms.

On May the 29th, the second day of the protests, the Prime Minister of Turkey explained that the construction process will continue on Taksim Square and Gezi Park, and he criticized the demonstrators. The Prime Minister called the demonstrators as "çapulcu" which means "spoiler" in English, (blog.milliyet 2013). These explanations increased the tension. After The Prime Minister's response about the events, the police started to use force to break up the demonstrations using pepper gas and tear gas. Against the police force, people reacted and resisted stronger than before. The Prime Minister was criticized by the public because of ignoring the democratic demands of people. Demonstrators appropriated the "spoiler" label and they used it as nickname in social media profiles. They used it for motivation in comic statements as "We are çapulcu", "I am every day çapulling" etc. Thus, they made the negative connotation of the label of "çapulcu" ineffective. Supporters of the protests used the term of "çapulcu" to give it a positive meaning as "someone sensitive to the ecological problems or someone has political awareness".

Apparently, the Gezi Park movement brought the conflicting parts of society together. They united in Taksim Square to protect Gezi Park. It is known that squares have been important areas for the political movements since Ancient Greece. People come together on the squares of the different cities in the world. It is seen that the demonstrations of Gezi Park were held in the squares of various cities in Turkey such as Taksim in Istanbul, Kızılay in Ankara and Gündoğdu in İzmir. After the beginning of the protests, the demonstrations spread almost all the cities in Turkey. While Gezi Park was the center of the protests, Taksim Square became the symbolic area of the movement. People came together and resisted in Taksim, then they went back to Gezi Park. There was a very famous slogan "Taksim is everywhere, resistance is everywhere." During the protests, authorities claimed it as illegal. Government agencies supported the use of police force against the groups. They accused these groups of being marginal and ideological. Although there were marginal groups and provocative actors among the protestors, most of them did not threat the public order. In the protests, the tension between the police and the demonstrators continued during 4 days. On May 31, 4 days after the beginning of the demonstrations, the District Administrative Court decided the stay of execution about the construction of "Taksim Military Barracks". This decision did not do enough to stop the demonstrations, and it did not influence the government about the project. The Prime Minister criticized the decision. The demonstrations were in all the cities of Turkey apart from a small one called Bayburt.

Twitter was used intensely by different actors during the protests. Mainstream TV channels did not broadcast the protests. For example, "CNNTurk", a prestigious news channel, broadcasted an animal documentary instead of the protests (yurtgazetesi 2013). A limited number of TV channels broadcasted news about the protests. Many people used social media channels to be informed about the events. The influence of Twitter caused increase in the awareness of the communicative power of social media. For example, the Prime Minister claimed that Twitter is a troublemaker (Cihan 2013a). Politicians, organizations, news channels, and people focused on the effects of Twitter. The demonstrators wrote the slogan "revolution will not be televised, it will be tweeted" everywhere. Different actors used Twitter as an alternative communication channel. During the protests, there were many hashtags mocking the government reaction against the protests. However, there was a pressure on Twitter communication. Police organized social media operations. For example, 24 people were arrested in İzmir. They were accused of encouraging the people to rebel (Hürriyet 2013a).

The ongoing unrest in the North African and Middle Eastern countries created worries about the possibility of civil war in Turkey. Observers asked the question "Is Turkey like the other countries in a revolution process?" However, demonstrations in Turkey were different from North African and Middle Eastern countries. Turkey has an important democratic experience. During the protests, civil war did not break out in Turkey. Demonstrators created a collectivity, and they did not use violence against each other. The experience of the Gezi Park movement shows that different groups can develop collective goals, and they can act together in order to realize these goals. For example, in Turkey, the conflict between secularism and anti-secularism was invisible during the protests. Secularist groups protected the anti-secularist groups when they were praying on the public area on the regional day of Muslims. On the other hand, anti-secularist groups took side with secularists in the demonstration. Another example is the collaboration of football fans groups. Beşiktaş, Fenerbahçe, and Galatasaray are competing teams in the Turkish football league, and their fans contend with each other. However, they were altogether during the protests. It decreased the possibility of civil war, in contrast with the political discourses aiming at dividing the society (Hürriyet 2013b). The demonstrations can be characterized as civil disobedience or passive resistance rather than a civil war.

The protests were in many cities in Turkey. There was tension between police and demonstrators in Hatay, near the Syrian border of Turkey. In Hatay, a young man was shot by a policeman, and he died. Another man was killed in Kızılay, in Ankara. After these incidents, the protests continued increasingly day after day. Many people were injured by tear gas and pressurized water. Provocative groups used stones and sticks to attack the police. On June the 15th, the Prime Minister said "I declare it so clear that if Taksim Square will not be given up by demonstrators, the police of this country know how to drive them out of the area" (Cihan 2013b). On June 15, the police removed the people from Taksim Square and Gezi Park. However, this intervention did not end the protests. On June 17, the demonstrators were driven out from Kuğulu Park which is very close to the National Assembly of Turkey. The people lost their confidence in the government and its agencies. The demonstrations were continuing on the twentieth day of the movement. People found new forms of protesting: "standing-man" was one of them. A man started standing in front of Atatürk Cultural Center on Taksim Square (Cihan 2013c). This practice spread out to the country, and people supported the protest of this man standing like him. This indicated that the Gezi Park movement was non-violent, individual, non-ideological, and disorganized.

The authorities of the international institutions such as the European Parliament, the European Commission, and the White House National Security Commission of the U.S. called for the Turkish Government to be tolerant to the demonstrators. The protests influenced the economy of Turkey. On the one hand, the protests affected the political and economic image of Turkey negatively. On the other hand, the democratic character of demonstrations strengthened the image of Turkish civic culture.

According to the data provided by the government, 115 police officers and 58 protestors were injured in the first 7 days of the protests (Memurlar.net 2013). The Turkish Medical Association General Secretary claimed that more than 3,500 people were injured, 3 of them seriously, in the protests within the first 7 days (gundem.milliyet 2013). One of the seriously injured citizen who was 19 years old died after one month. The Turkish Medical Association General Secretary declared that one police officer died because of an accident during the intervention, and three demonstrators died in the events. 7,822 people were injured within 21 days, 59 of them seriously (insanhaber 2013). Thus, it is easy to observe that the police intervention did not end the protests. Furthermore, it caused an increase in the reactions of demonstrators. It is seen that the authorities did not rationally analyze the beginning and development process of this environmental protest. Authorities ignored the demands of people, they disregarded the demonstrators, and politicians excluded the different opinions and the democratic demands of the people. The demonstrations started spontaneously, but it was the police intervention which turned them into a mass reaction. The mass media did not inform the people and did not broadcast the events. This also caused people to react.

The use of social media in the Gezi Park movement can be explained as the awakening of social and political actors in Turkey and their becoming aware of the effects of social media on social and political events. Demonstrators used Twitter as an alternative communication channel. While demonstrators were using social media, the Prime Minister criticized their effects. In connection with this criticism, some policies were determined aiming at cleaning the Internet of "insecure content". Moreover, users were accused of Twitter use to encourage people to "rebel". It can be said that both positive and negative judgments about the effects of Twitter on the process of social and political movements were not carefully evaluated. It is seen that the effects of social media were not systematically analyzed. Interpretations and judgments about the effects of social media are considered beyond the real effects of social media. Therefore there is a need for this kind of movements to be analyzed systematically.

16.3 The Effects of Social Media on Politics: Literature Review

The effects of social media can be discussed in parallel with changes in politics, and information and communication technologies in the process of globalization. In this process, the relationship between social movements and politics has been strengthened. The role of political ideologies and the power of political organizations in the development of political actions has been diminished. Nowadays, the influence of social basis on the social and political movements is stronger than the power of ideologies. The movements are organized more spontaneously, and they address the social problems of people (Çakır and Demirhan 2011). In the action process, social groups or individuals prefer non-organized forms of participation. New information and communication technologies (ICTs) have a significant role in the development of these social and political movements since ICTs provide communication, information, and interaction possibilities to the people, social groups and un-structured organizations (Bennett and Segerberg 2012). After the development of WEB 2.0 technologies, Internet has gained much more power than before. WEB 2.0 technologies make communication more interactive. Thus, Internet users have become political actors affecting the political processes. For example, they can help in the diffusion of information. This is seen as an alternative to the mass media. Internet users share information, create content on the Internet utilizing WEB 2.0 technologies such as forums, chat rooms, wikis. These communication and interaction spaces are mostly open to the public. In this respect, the communicative power of the Internet provides opportunities for citizens to participate in political processes.

Social media potentials are especially underscored to increase political participation. The effects of social media on politics are often discussed in terms of the deliberative and radical democracy. Although these approaches have different views about the effects of social media, they agree upon their positive effects in political participation as alternative spaces (Eriksen 2005; Wright and Street 2007; Hauben and Hauben 1997; Tsagarousianou 1999; Fenton and Downey 2003; Dahlberg 2007).

The literature on social media focuses on the various roles of social media in political participation. Firstly, social media provide a pluralist environment for political discussions and they support free communication (Dahlberg 2001;

Dahlberg and Siapera 2007). According to Macintosh (2004: 1), the Internet provides different communication spaces such as forums, chat rooms, e-mail groups etc. These spaces provide opportunities for citizens to participate the decision making processes. Gimmler (2001: 33) suggests that the Internet provides a deliberative atmosphere to the development of civil society and pluralism. Zheng and Wu (2005: 522) emphasize that the Internet provides free deliberation platforms. Vesnic-Alujevic (2012: 466) explains how the Internet provides free, inclusive and participative discussion platforms: "The Internet is often seen as a new discursive space, which could lead to more inclusion and participation in the public debate for all citizens and not only political elites as it had previously been the case."

Secondly, online journalism is emphasized in terms of the relationship between the Internet and political participation. Information is important in developing political debates and providing political participation. Online journalism creates an opportunity for citizens to produce and disseminate information using online forums, blogs, and microblogs. Thus, citizens are a part of journalism. Online journalism influences the traditional power relations in the media (Woo-Young 2005: 906). Quinn and Lamble (2008: 43) explain the online journalism as "this form of citizen journalism includes things like publication of photographs or video taken by amateurs who happened to be at the right place at the right time as the London bombings in July 2005". Quinn and Lamble (2008: 43) stress that social media users interact with each other by publishing news in their blogs or other spaces in the social media. Such news and information are open to the feedback and responses of the people. They can share their opinions, experiences, or feelings about news. Social media makes journalism more interactive. Online journalism contributes to the citizens' participation. Citizens write blogs, load videos, and share photos on the Internet. This is the agentless type of communication. The effects of social media on journalism decrease the domination of traditional media (Bennett and Entman 2001). Loader and Mercea (2011: 759) claim that social media are a democratic innovation in journalism: "Freed from the necessities of professional media and journalist skills or the centralized control and distribution of industrial mass media organizations, social media are instead seen to be technologically, financially and (generally) legally accessible to most citizens living in advanced societies."

Thirdly, social media help to set a new social environment and social collectivity. They provide communication and interaction networks (Chadwick and May 2003). Vesnic-Alujevic (2012: 466) explains this matter as "the interactivity, as a recurrently used concept in the new media theory, is used as a benchmark for establishing the differences between the so-called old and new media." Social networks are important to develop interaction among people. Social network sites (SNS) have the role to set and develop new networks. Boyd and Ellison (2007) define social network sites as "web-based services that allow individuals to construct a public or semi-public profile within a bounded system, articulate a list of other users with whom they share a connection, and view and traverse their list of connections and those made by others within the system." Social network sites connect people, groups, and organizations. These connections provide new information channels for social media users. Social networks make the dissemination of information easier. Online discussion platforms provide spaces for people to discuss about social and political issues (Kim 2011: 971). The number of actors in an online social network is important for understanding the power of that network. The network power is important in the spreading of information rapidly (Castells 2011). Pluralism in a network is as important as solidarity. Most of the online networks are open to the individual participation of all users. This option contributes to pluralism in a network (Kim 2011: 972). Social network sites are not limited to the local and national borders. This opportunity is important to set communication as local, national, and trans-national. Harlow and Harp (2012: 209) suggest that social network sites like Facebook and Twitter are effective on the development of communication, organization, discussion atmosphere in society. They stress that social network sites provide alternative political spaces to increase citizens' active participation.

Fourthly, social media have a significant role in the new social movements. The concept of the new social movements refers to the movements after the 1970s that had no basis in class conflicts (Wieviorka 2005). Wieviorka (2005: 5) explains the social movements as "... the protest movements in post-industrial societies were no longer the working-class movement, historically on the wane, but the struggles of students, anti-nuclear groups, regionalist groups, women, and so on." The new social movements include various social and political problems. Stalker and Wood (2012: 179) underline its inclusiveness: "These movements seek the full participation of diverse participants as they establish alternative institutions, relationships, and networks". The new social movements may focus on the issues of education, environment, urbanization, economy, health, social justice, equality etc. (Bennett 2003; Stalker and Wood 2012). Individuals, social groups, non-structured organizations and civil platforms are the main actors of the new social movements. Stalker and Wood (2012) explain the new social movements in relation to the protests against the 2010 meetings of G20 summits in Toronto. According to Stalker and Wood (2012), "protesters attempt to challenge and sometimes disrupt the summits, while building temporary alternative institutions such as horizontal decision-making bodies, legal and medical support collectives, care collectives for those with disabilities and childcare programming. Protestors are "environmentalists and socialists, student activists, human rights campaigners, anarchists, feminists and those concerned about global inequalities all see the summits as a target of claims and a site of convergence" (Stalker and Wood 2012: 179). A variety of communication channels were used to organize and mobilize the people. Social media channels such as Facebook, YouTube, and Twitter are used as communication channels in new social movements. Bennett (2003: 143) stresses that "networks of activists demanding greater voice in global economic, social, and environmental policies raise interesting questions about organizing political action across geographical, cultural, ideological, and issue boundaries." The new social movements are the new ways of political participation (Della Porta 2012: 42). Political actors and processes in the new social movements are different from traditional ways of participation. Some of the traditional elements of political participation such as political parties, elections, political leadership, constitutional legitimacy, ideology, consensus, mediated communication, and representation are not adequate to understand the participation in the new social movements. Social media provide communication, interaction, coordination among demonstrators (Stalker and Wood 2012: 181). Stalker and Wood (2012: 192) underline the effects of e-mail groups and social network sites for the organization and mobilization of people during the protests in the G20 summit. In addition, they explain their observations about the advantages of social media in the production and the diffusion of information. Maireder and Schwarzenegger (2012: 172) emphasize the role of social media in participation: "Social media applications, in particular, Twitter and the social network service Facebook, played a remarkable role in the communication and coordination of participants, as well as for the perception of the movement by the general public."

Social media provide channels for the communication, organization, and mobilization of people in political processes. Thus, they diversify the ways of political participation. For example, communication on social media is important in organizing social movements. It is open to individual participation. This kind of participation does not exclude the interests, preferences and demands of individuals or small social groups unlike the ideological one. This way of participation is not limited to the membership of political parties or political organizations (Loader and Mercea 2011: 759). Bennett and Segerberg (2012: 23) explain the ways of individual participation as "sign up for email list, Twitter hash, share this, RSS feed, email a decision maker, blogging account on site, commenting on site, delicious, delicious tag, friend feeder, post photo, post video, post audio, Facebook group, YouTube, Flyers/posters, contact organization, sing a petition, interactive map, calendar, donations". These ways of participation were used in the protests of G20 and Climate summits in 2009 (Bennett and Segerberg 2012: 23).

16.4 Twitter in Social Movements and Protests

Social media include online forums, social networking sites, blogs, and microblogs. Wikipedia, Twitter, Facebook, Google+, LinkedIn, YouTube, Pinterest, Instagram are the most popular social media channels. These channels contain various social, economic, and political activities. Twitter is the most popular micro-blogging site on the Internet. Twitter is defined as an information network (Twitter 2013; Park 2013). The contents in Twitter are open to all users. If someone tweets an opinion in a hashtag, it will be seen by the followers of this hashtag (Park 2013: 1641). In the recent social movements and protests, Twitter has been used by demonstrators, citizens, politicians and other actors (Maireder and Schwarzenegger 2012; Small 2012; Park 2013; Demirhan 2013). Due to the effects of Twitter during the protests in the Middle East, North Africa and the West (Iran, Tunisia, Egypt, Bahrain, Yemen, Syria, the U.S., and the U.K.), it is defined as a powerful political instrument (Maireder and Schwarzenegger 2012; Bennett and Segerberg 2012; Park

2013). Moreover, its role during the revolutions in the North African countries caused them to be labeled as “Twitter revolutions” (Christensen 2011).

The main elements of Twitter are tweets, hashtags, re-tweets, followers, and trending topics. The term “tweet” means the message that is sent by the users, and the term “re-tweet” (RT) means sending the same tweet again by another user. The “follower” means the following activity of users to each other. The term “trending topic” (TT) indicates the popular topics. The numbers of ten popular hashtags or topics are apparent on the list of trends on Twitter. One can see the trending topics of a city, country or the world. The number of followers indicates the popularity of users on Twitter. The term “hashtag” means that a topic is created or labeled by someone. Hashtags are important to organize tweets. In addition, they provide a group of data to the researchers who want to analyze them. Small (2012: 110) explains the term “hashtag”: “A hashtag is what Twitter calls a tag. Designated by a “hash” symbol (#), a hashtag is a keyword assigned to information that describes a tweet and aids in searching. Hashtags are not native to the Twitter platform. Rather they are a community-driven convention, popularized during the San Diego forest fires in 2007.” Hashtags collect the messages and contents about an issue. Small (2012: 110) explains this situation as “hashtags features as organizing the tweets around a single topic; organizing people by interests or events; sharing information; widening the messages to a larger audience than one follower; Hashtags are searchable on Twitter, Google.” Maireder and Schwarzenegger (2012: 174) explain hashtags as “within the Twitter conversations, its hashtag feature—keywords that mark the text messages sent through Twitter as belonging to a specific discourse together with its high communication transparency—enable people to follow all the messages on a specific topic”. One can access data about a social or political issue under a hashtag. The application of trending topics is an important component of the communication on Twitter since hashtags on a TT list inform the people about the issues in the different parts of the world. This is a way to express a social and political movement to the users all around the world. Thus, the labels of hashtags gain importance due to their functions. Therefore, they should be short, clear and expressive.

The studies analyzing the role of Twitter in political processes emphasize some functions of Twitter. Small (2012: 120–122) explains its role in the Canadian federal politics. Small determines that Twitter is used for information sharing, opinion sharing, communicating, and comment sharing in this process. Bennett and Segerberg (2012: 24) state that hashtags were used to support the protests in the G20 summits. Maireder and Schwarzenegger (2012: 172) explain the functions of Twitter during the protests against the education policies of the Austrian government. Maireder and Schwarzenegger (2012: 172) insist that Twitter was used in the process of communication and the coordination of different groups in the protests that they were called as ‘unibrennt’ (‘university is burning’) in Vienna. It was also used for the dissemination of news during the protests. Maireder and Schwarzenegger (2012: 180) emphasize the role of Twitter in political processes, and summarize its functions as “the distribution of news on the movement’s activities,” “the mobilization of human resources,” “the mobilization of material resources and the coordination of things and people". Maireder and Schwarzenegger (2012: 187) state that there were many hashtags about the protests, and Twitter was intensely used during the protests in Vienna.

The number of Twitter users in Turkey is equal to the 16.6 % of all the Internet users (Comscore 2012). Turkey is on the eighth place in the Twitter use world ranking; the Netherlands is on the first place with the rate of 26.8 % (Comscore 2012). Twitter was used during the Gezi Park movement, and it operated as a communication instrument. Hashtags about the movement were listed in the world-wide trends during the protests. Fourteen days after the beginning of the protests, there were nearly 13.5 million tweets about the Gezi Park movement (cnnturk 2013). This number increased during the following days. On June 20, the number of tweets in the hashtags of #DirenGeziParkı and #OccupyGezi was 16,507,328. The number of users was 1,523,933 (socialdigger 2013). These hashtags were popular during the movement. However, there were also other hashtags that were used intensely. One of them was the #duranadam (standingman). The number of tweets in this hashtag was 407,238 within the 3 days after the beginning of the standing man protest (twitturk 2013). When all the tweets are accounted, it is seen that many people used Twitter during the Gezi Park movement.

16.5 Method and Data

Tweets about the Gezi Park movement are the main data of this study. I determined the popular hashtags that were open during the movement and I analyzed the tweets in these hashtags. The analysis of this study focuses on the role of Twitter in social movements and protests. In this context, the tweets are used as data to understand the role of Twitter in social and political movements in terms of its functions, actors and the form of communication. I focused on the profiles of Twitter users and the features of communication on Twitter. Moreover, I figured out some new functions and features of Twitter in the protests. This study is a case study that can be defined as "research [that] investigates a single phenomenon, instance, or example" (Gerring 2004). I used the content analysis to evaluate the tweets. The literature about the role of Twitter in politics has examples of this research technique (Maireder and Schwarzenegger 2012; Small 2012). The contents of tweets are evaluated in terms of the questions "How is Twitter used in political events?" "What functions has it?" "Which were the actors that used this instrument?" and "How did the communication process form on Twitter?" I considered two main points of the use of Twitter in the movement. The first point is about the functions of Twitter in the Gezi Park movement. I applied the investigation functions of Twitter into the Gezi Park movement to test their validity in this case. These functions are coordination among people, the mobilization of people, the mobilization of resources, the cooperation among actors, the dissemination of information, self-organization, creating new communication spaces, and developing public discussion. In addition to this application, I observed the new features of Twitter in this process. The second point is the users, and the features of communication on Twitter. I classified the users, the contents of tweets, and the roles of actors in the movement. It should be noted that I concealed the profiles, names, and accounts of individuals in the examples because of ethical reasons. I also translated the contents of tweets into English. The original tweets can be found in the footnotes.

During the protests, the hashtags of "direngeziparkı,"[1] "direngeziparki," and "occupygezi" were used more actively. This study focused on the tweets in these popular hashtags. The hashtag of *#direngeziparkı* was started on May 30. The total number of tweets in this hashtag is at least 59,878 and the number of retweets is at least 88,518. The hastag of *#direngeziparki* was started on May 31. The total number of tweets in this hashtag is at least 38,443, and the number of retweets is at least 65,369 (ecktr 2013). The hashtag of *#occupygezi* was started on May 28. The total number of tweets in this hashtag is at least 30,628, and the number of retweets is at least 54,993.

16.5.1 Functions

The functions that are coordination among people, the mobilization of people and resources, the cooperation of actors, the dissemination of information, self-organization, creating new spaces to communication, and including many people in the political discussions were used during the Gezi Park Movement. The transnational participation and the building of a new socio-cultural area in Twitter can be added to these functions. How were all these functions used in the Gezi Park movement? In order to answer this question, we need to analyze the usage of Twitter and illustrate it with examples.

16.5.1.1 Reporting News and the Spread of Information

Tweets contain very much information and news about the Gezi Park Movement. Most of the tweets are about the police intervention, the court decisions, the situation of demonstrators, and the administrative decisions. If the tweets had the news and information about the police intervention and the situation of demonstrators, they were re-tweeted by the users more than other tweets. The process of informing the people and reporting the news was not professional. These processes were informal and sensitive. The experiences of the actors were directly reported by themselves without any agent. Therefore, the news was more personal, simple, and private in these tweets. People were informed on Twitter spontaneously. Informal and sensitive information about the movement was effective on the readers of the news. The professional news media and the amateur news channels used Twitter as well as the people. The news reported by these news platforms were re-tweeted

[1] The word of "diren (!)" means in English "resist (!)".

more than the news reported by individuals. The reliability of the news on Twitter is a problem. Twitter users have trusted more the news reported by the news channels. This trust may be explained by the fact that people have been accustomed to being informed by the professional news channels. However, the professional news media suddenly lost this confidence during the Gezi Park movement because professional news media did not broadcast the protests at the time. The amateur news channels were followed by users more than other media. They were also more active on Twitter. The examples of news in Twitter were reported by the different actors of the Gezi Park movement.

The first example explains the user generated information. In this example, a user informs people about the police intervention. This user is a witness of the events and expresses the details of the intervention. These tweets inform the users about the position of demonstrators. The tweet below is not only a piece of news but also a call for help. In this respect, it also makes the readers a part of the protests.

i.... K.... @i....k.... 3 June
We are now exposed to tear gas, we are in the ... hotel, and there are persons who fainted. #direngeziparki (24 RT) [2]

The second example explains the information generated by the news platforms. The news platforms used Twitter during the Gezi Park movement. In the following tweets, the news reported by the platform of *Diren Gezi Parkı* gives information about the protest. The name of this platform shows us that it aims at reporting the events about the movement only. What is different from individually reported information is that it is not the direct expression of the actors in the events.

Diren Gezi Parkı @DirenGeziParki 3 June
22:17 - Police throw gas bomsb in the distinct of Gümüşsuyu! #DirenGeziParki (126 RT)[3]
Diren Gezi Parkı @geziparkibildir 15 June
Police attacked at the ... Hospital with a panzer[4]*: #direngeziparkı* (169 RT)[5]

The third example explains the information reported on Twitter by a professional media channel. This channel is opposed to the government policies and it clearly supported the movements. This channel used more formal statements unlike the informal and sensitive statements generated by individuals.

Ulusal Kanal @ulusalkanal 11 June
Police encircled Gezi Park. This is real war. Police throw gas and stun grenades. Infirmary is discharged. #direngeziparki (250 RT)[6]

---

[2] Cok sert bir gaz bombasi yedik simdi, ... otel'e sigindik, bayilanlar var #direngeziparki (24 RT)

[3] 22:17 - Polis, Gümüşsuyu'nda rastgele gaz bombası sıkıyor! #DirenGeziParki (126 RT)

[4] in fact, it was an armored personnel carrier

[5] Diren Gezi Parkı@geziparkibildir 15 Haziran
Polis, ... Hastanesi'ne TOMA ile su saldırısında bulundu: #direngeziparkı (169 RT)

[6] Ulusal Kanal@ulusalkanal 11 Haziran
Polis Gezi'nin çevresini kuşattı. Resmen bu bir savaş. Gaz ve ses bombaları atılıyor. Revir tahliye ediliyor. #direngeziparki (250 RT)

Information and news on Twitter have spread among the users in a short time. Thus, people accessed the information about the protests. This diffusion of the news expanded the public discussion and more people used this space to express their opinions. People also used this space to communicate with each other. In this communication, people motivated themselves and helped each other. The following examples explain this communication among people. In the first tweet, a witness of the events makes a call to inform the family of a demonstrator about their children being arrested by the police. In the second tweet, the demonstrators call for medical help for themselves.

BB.. @crickettut.... 15 June
E... M... said (her/his) name in the distinct of Altunizade when arrested. Please, spread this tweet till it reaches her/his family. @edih..t #direngezi (872 RT)[7]
Sel... @Se..... 15 June
@edih..t #DİRENGEZİPARKI 2 min. Now we need a doctor at Cihangir Oba street, he/she is injured and (her/his) head is bleeding!!!! RT Emergence Emergence (351 RT)[8]

16.5.1.2 The Confirmation of the News and Information

News on Twitter contains videos and photographs. These visual contents are important to verify news. The reliability of information was an important problem during the Gezi Park movement. Government claimed that the news on Twitter about the events in the movement was false. The demonstrators notified Twitter users to be careful as concerned the spam accounts and fake news that could lead to provocations. Therefore, users checked the information in tweets controlling the different news sources and instruments such as videos and photos of the events. Different instruments were used to access and confirm the information on Twitter during the movement. Videos and photos informed the people about the details of the events. People also determined some rules for the reporting process on Twitter. Due to the problems about the reliability of the news, the users started to add the date, time, and place of an event while reporting it. The following examples explain the use of visual contents in tweets. The Tweet in the first example informs the people about the case that the demonstrators captured a buldozer and drove it into a police APC. This news seemed a joke but the photo of this incident included in the tweet verified it. This photo was presented under the tweet as Fig. 16.1.

---

[7] BB..@crickettut.... 15 Haziran
Altunizade de gözaltına alınırken bağırdı E... M...... Ailesine ulaşana kadar yayalım. @edih..t #direngezi (872 RT)

[8] Sel... @Se..... 15 Haziran
@edih..t #DİRENGEZİPARKI 2 dk Şuanda Cihangir Oba Sokak'a doktor lazım kafasından kan geliyor !!!! RT ACİL ACİLLL (351 RT)

Fig. 16.1 The demonstrators captured a dozer and drove it over a police panzer

On.. Pos. .... @op. .... 2 June

Demonstrators captured a buldozer in Inönü, and drove it towards APCs. RESISTANCE! #occupygezi #direngeziparki[9]

Another example is related to the government authorities' allegation that the demonstrators drank alcohol in a mosque, a religious place in Islam where alcohol consumption is forbidden. After this accusation, people sent tweets containing videos and photos showing the inside of this mosque during the incident. In these videos and photos the demonstrators are shown as injured, they are not drinking alcohol, and the mosque is seen as infirmary. In these images, doctors treat the injured people. Moreover, a video on Twitter presented the statement of the Imam of this mosque. He was declaring that nobody drank alcohol in the mosque and all the people needed help. The photo in the following tweet shows the interior of this mosque. This photo is presented under the tweet as Fig. 16.2.

Se... Er.... @Ser..Er.... 3 June

That is the mosque in the photo, yesterday night the Imam opened the doors. White jacketed persons are doctors, and there are victuals on the floor. #direngeziparki[10]

The last example of the confirmation of the news and information is related to the police intervention. The user informs people about the position of the police sharing a photo. This photo is presented under the tweet as Fig. 16.3.

mer.. y.... @mrv_y.... 15 June

Police use gas continually. And we cannot go on. Nobody moves forward. #direngeziparki #occupygezi[11]

---

[9] On.. Pos. .... @op. .... 2 Haziran
İnönüde dozer ele geçirildi, TOMA'ların üstüne sürülüyor. DİRENİŞ! #occupygezi #direngeziparki

[10] Se... Er.... @Ser..Er.... 3 Haziran
Şu meşhur fotoğrafta ki cami,dün gece İMAM açtı kapılarını.Beyaz gömlekliler doktor,yerde erzak var. #direngeziparki

[11] mer.. y.... @mrv_y.... 15 Haziran
Uzuncayirda polisin gaz mudahalesi devam ilerleyemiyoruZ ama kimse kipirdamiyor. #direngeziparki #occupygezi

Fig. 16.2 Inside of a mosque

Fig. 16.3 The user informs people about the position of the police sharing this photo

All these videos and photos served to verify the news on Twitter. They support the reliability of the news and information. Moreover, it may be said that sometimes they were more impressive than the words.

16.5.1.3 The Function of Inclusion in the Process of Communication

A couple of days after the protests broke out, the mainstream news media channels had to start broadcasting the protests in the important cities of the country such as İstanbul, Ankara, and İzmir. However, protests spread to many districts and local areas during this period. Information about the local protests were reported on Twitter. Communication on Twitter connected center and periphery. The example of three tweets in one hashtag shows this relationship. The first tweet informs the people about the protests in Batıkent, is a district of Ankara. The second tweet informs the people about the protests in Bağdat Avenue—a street of İstanbul. And

Fig. 16.4 The supporters from London

the third tweet informs people about protests in Taksim—the center of İstanbul. Twitter was used by people all over the world to support the protests. Tweets given below show Twitter connecting the different parts of the world. The first tweet contains a photo of the supporters in London. The photo is presented under the tweet as Fig. 16.4.

Hal.. E. @hlte..... *3 June*
Photo: London Trafalgar Square, Support continues to resistance in Turkey #occupygezi...[12]

Another tweet also has a photo presenting the support of villagers in Ayder, where there is a well-known plateau in the city of Rize placed at an altitude of 1,350 m in the region of the Black Sea. The demonstrators are villagers supporting the Gezi Park movement. The photo is presented under the tweet as Fig. 16.5. In this photo, the villagers hold a banner giving the message that "Here is Ayder with you, Taksim!"

Bu.... Uz...... @Bu......U.......... *12 Haziran*
From AYDER #occupygezi #geziparki greetings to Gezi Park![13]

---

[12] Hal.. E. @hlte..... 3 Haziran
Photo: Londra Trafalgar Meydanı'ndan Türkiye'de yaşanan direnişe destek devam ediyor. #occupygezi...

[13] Bu.... Uz...... @Bu......U.......... 12 Haziran
AYDER 'den #occupygezi #geziparki na selam var!

Fig. 16.5 Villagers supporting the Gezi Park movement

16.5.1.4 Coordination, Communication, Information and Organization

Communication on Twitter helped in the organization of the Gezi Park movement. The people in the movement communicated with each other about the meetings, their locations, the atmosphere at the meeting places, the secure routes to reach to the meeting points. The following example explains the communication, coordination, and organization processes in the Gezi Park Movement. The first tweet presents the information concerning the place of the protests. One person is going to the protests in Ankara and calls for other people to go as well.

> *Rob. . ..* @robi. . . *13 June*
> *Does anyone desire to go to Ankara to support the movement? Today, we are going by bus, contact us, we are expecting you to support us (RTplz) #direngeziparki*[14]

The second tweet was tweeted by the platform of "Ayağa Kalk Taksim". This platform announced the addresses of the infirmaries that helped injured people.

> *Ayağa Kalk Taksim* @ayagakalktaksim *3 June*
> *Persons who need it, there is an infirmary in the . . . Hotel, please share this information. #direngeziparki @DirenGeziParki*[15]

The third example is the tweet of the İstanbul Pharmacy Association that presented the list of pharmacies and their addresses that were open during the night.

> *İst. Eczacı Odası* @ist_eczaciodasi *3 June*
> *You can find the contact details of all the night-pharmacies in İstanbul on the link that http://nobetci.ieo.org.tr/ #direnbesiktas #direngeziparki*[16]

---

[14] Rob. . .. @robi. . . 13 Haziran Ankaraya destek için gitmek isteyenler var mı? Bugün araba kaldıracağız. Ulaşın destekleriniz bekliyoruz. (RTplz) #direngeziparki

[15] Ayağa Kalk Taksim @ayagakalktaksim 3 Haziran
İhtiyacı olanlar için . . ... Otel'de revir bulunmakta arkadaşlar, yayalım lütfen. #direngeziparki @DirenGeziParki

[16] İst. Eczacı Odası @ist_eczaciodasi 3 Haziran
İstanbul'daki tüm nöbetçi eczanelerin harita ve iletişim bilgileri http://nobetci.ieo.org.tr/ #direnbesiktas #direngeziparki

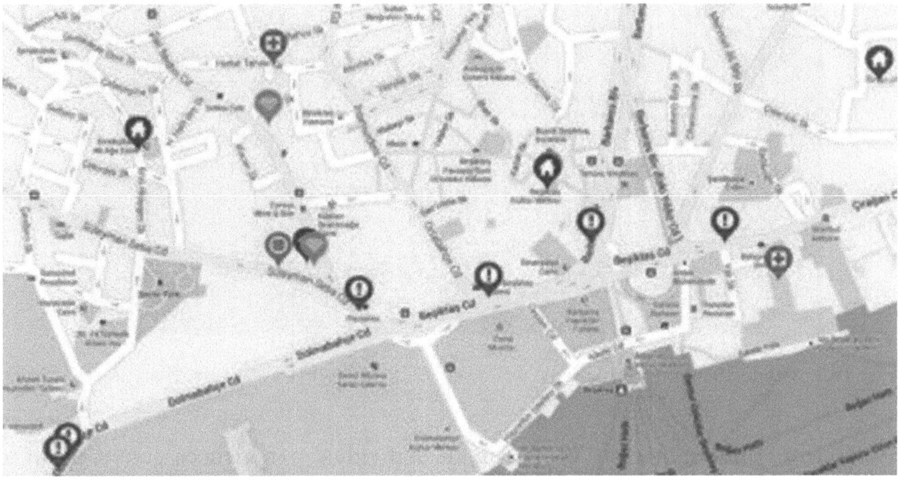

Fig. 16.6 The police points on the Google map

The fourth example is one of the tweets informing people about the dangerous districts where police attacked the demonstrators.

Er.... D.....z @er.........az 3 June
Police throw gas bombs at Dolmabahçe – Kabataş. Be careful and avoid, that is not our place! #DirenGeziParkı #occupygezi[17]

The fifth tweet has an image that indicates the police checkpoints on the Google map. The photo of this image is presented in Fig. 16.6 under the tweet.

Bitti B... @Bitt..... *2 June*
Current situation in Beşiktaş: exclamation marks show the police checkpoints. Time: 2:55 from #occupygezi map pic.twitter.com/ABu702biKk[18]

The eighth tweet informs people what should be done if one is arrested by the police. Contents in the photo of this tweet advise people about legal matters. This photo is presented under the tweet as Fig. 16.7.

Ece Il..... @Ece..... *3 June. Everyone, read, get and share it!! #direngeziparki* [19]

Lawyers informed the people about legal procedures, doctors informed the people about medical issues and advised them about what should be done after tear gas attacks. The demonstrators explained how a gas bomb can be rendered

[17] E... D... @e...d... 3 Haziran
Dolmabahçe - Kabataş'a gaz bombası yağdırıyorlar dikkatli olun ve kaçın oradan, orası yerimiz değil! #DirenGeziParkı #occupygezi

[18] Bitti B...@Bitt... 2 Haziran
Beşiktaş son durum: Ünlem işaretleri polis noktaları.. Saat 2:55 #occupygezi map'ten pic. twitter.com/ABu702biKk

[19] Ece Il... @Ece... 3 Haziran Herkes okusun,bilsin paylasin!! #direngeziparki

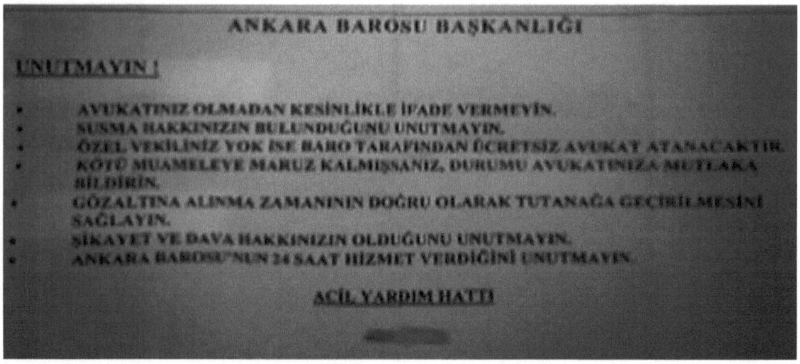

Fig. 16.7 Guide about legal processes

ineffective. Information on Twitter made individual experiences converge on a common platform. It seems that the experiences of people created a sense of collectivity. The people used Twitter to organize the movement, they communicated and collaborated on Twitter. The tweets, giving important information to help people, spread rapidly on Twitter. People were interested in this kind of tweets rather than in the tweets presenting the users' opinions.

16.5.1.5 The Mobilization of Resources

The people organized and mobilized the resources by communicating on Twitter during the movement. The demonstrators tweeted their needs and the people sent medical materials, food, and tents to the demonstrators. The supporters of the protests also provided Internet connection to the demonstrators. This process was not organized by an organization or an agent. The following examples explain the mobilization of various resources during the movement. The Internet users, living near to the districts where the protests took place, shared their Wi-Fi passwords on Twitter. The photo in the first tweet contains Wi-Fi passwords tweeted by the people to provide Internet connection to demonstrators. This photo is presented under the tweet as Fig. 16.8.

Ka.. @Ka..... 15 June Taksim - İstiklal - Beyoğlu Wi-Fi Passwords, Please share it! #direngeziparkı[20]

The second tweet gives the addresses of the logistic areas where food and other materials were gathered. Many people sent food to these areas. Doctors established infirmaries and people sent medicines to these infirmaries. The addresses of infirmaries and the needs were tweeted.

[20] Ka.. @Ka..... 15 Haziran Taksim - İstiklal - Beyoğlu Wi-Fi şifreleri Yayalım lütfen! #direngeziparkı

Fig. 16.8 Wi-Fi passwords tweeted by the people to provide Internet connection to demonstrators

Tar... Flo.... @tar....... 15 June

+++++An infirmary opened in Harbiye on the opposite side of the Military Museum, there is also the infirmary of The Union of Chambers of Turkish Engineers and Architects in İstiklal. #direngeziparkı[21]

The third tweet contains a photo giving the list of needs. This photo is presented under the tweet as Fig. 16.9.

Duy... iron.... @Duy.......... 12 June

Taksim Dayanışması (Solidarity) - Taksim Gezi Park Very Urgent list of requirements #DirenGeziParki[22]

People used Twitter to contact injured demonstrators. In the fourth tweet, a user tries to contact the woman injured by a gas capsule and informs that a plastic surgeon will help this woman. Many users re-tweeted this call for help for the woman.

Bur... T.....@paz...... 12 June

Can anyone connect if he/she knows this friend please? A plastic surgeon will treat her scar. #direngeziparkı[23]

These tweets explain the mobilization of resources and the organization of help to the demonstrators. They also explain a different way of participation by communicating on Twitter. The people provided Wi-Fi passwords, retweeted requirement lists, or order goods from the market to be sent to the demonstrators. All these present examples of participation by using Twitter.

---

[21] Tar... Flo.... @tar....... 15 Haziran
+++++Harbiye'de revir açıldı. Askeri müzenin karşısında, İstiklalde TMMOB reviri de açık. #direngeziparkı

[22] Duy... iron....@Duy.......... 12 June
Taksim Dayanışması - Taksim Gezi Parkı ÇOK ACİL ihtiyaç listesi #DirenGeziParki

[23] Bur... T.....@paz...... 12 Haziran
Bu arkadaşımızı tanıyan lütfen ulaşabilir mi? İz kalmaması için plastik cerrah destek verecek. #direngeziparkı

Fig. 16.9 The list of needs

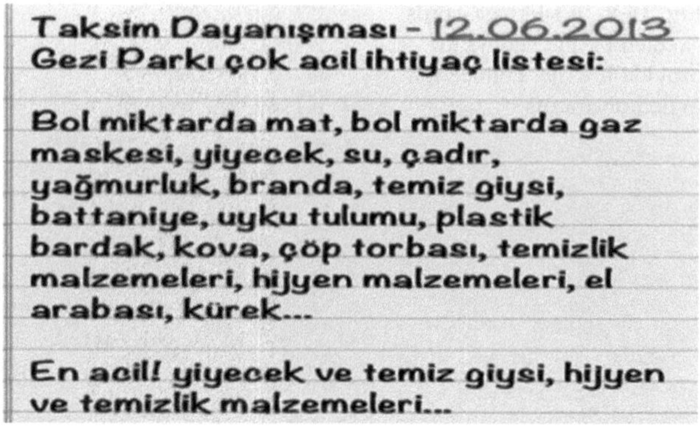

Taksim Dayanışması - 12.06.2013
Gezi Parkı çok acil ihtiyaç listesi:

Bol miktarda mat, bol miktarda gaz maskesi, yiyecek, su, çadır, yağmurluk, branda, temiz giysi, battaniye, uyku tulumu, plastik bardak, kova, çöp torbası, temizlik malzemeleri, hijyen malzemeleri, el arabası, kürek...

En acil! yiyecek ve temiz giysi, hijyen ve temizlik malzemeleri...

16.5.1.6 Self-Organization

The demonstrators took attitudes according to the rules determined by themselves. They criticized some treatments of the demonstrators. For example, police attacks were criticized in the discussions on Twitter. They discussed how demonstrators should behave in the movement. The demonstrators tried to find provocateurs in the movement. They tweeted the photos of provocateurs and warned people against them. It seems that Twitter was an instrument of self-organization in the movements. The users could discuss, communicate and coordinate. Twitter provided opportunities for the verification of information and for sharing experiences on a platform open to the public. The following tweets exemplify communication for self-organization.

gıcıklı tu.... @de....... *3 June*

If there are provocateurs who still throw stones or bottles, and shout offensive slogans, immediately remove them #direngeziparkı[24]

cen.... ş@cen........ *3 June Do not do it; racism, partisanship, fake information, provocation, offensive slogans, damage to property #direngeziparki*[25]

16.5.1.7 New Social and Cultural Spaces

People created many works of art during the Gezi Park movement. They shared the videos of their activities on Twitter. Users watched these videos. Communication on Twitter connected people in Gezi Park and on Twitter. Gezi Park was live on Twitter. People in Gezi Park created a new social and cultural space. People on Twitter were part of a new social and cultural space. Demonstrators in Gezi Park

[24] gıcıklı tu....@de....... 3 Haziran
etrafınızda hala taş atan, şişe savuran, küfürlü slogan atan birileri varsa onları oradan uzaklaştırın hemen #direngeziparkı

[25] cen....@cen........ 3 Haziran BUNLARI SAKIN YAPMAYIN; Irkçı söylem, Parti Yandaşlığı, Yanlış bilgi, Kışkırtma, Provokasyon, Küfürlü slogan, Mülke zarar verme #direngeziparki

composed creative sings and performed plays on the streets. All these works of art contain information about demonstrations, resistance, government and police intervention and expressed people's opinions and emotions. These works of art were shared on Twitter and watched by millions of people.[26] Demonstrations also influenced many artists. Singers composed songs related to the Gezi Park movement. Artists organized painting workshops. People made movies and documentaries. All these art products were shared on Twitter. They created common cultural meanings and symbols in the spaces on Twitter. People were informed about these artefacts when watching the tweets. They also participated in this process of commenting and sharing new contents and they contributed to the process by re-tweeting tweets.

16.5.1.8 Motivation

Tweeted photos and videos motivated people. These images showed the people's resistance to police attacks and their struggle with the police. The following tweets exemplify the diffusion of these images and people's opinions about them. The photo in the first tweet presents police use of pepper gas on a woman dressed in red whose hair is ruffled by the pressure of tear gas. However, she is not running away. The courage of this woman is seen in this image and it certainly motivated people. Moreover, women deputies in Italy supported this woman in red in the Italian parliament. Thus, they protested the police intervention against the movement. The photo of this event is given in the tweet. The photo is presented as Fig. 16.10.

Ba. .... @bag. ... ... 12 June
Today, women deputies in Italy dressed in red to Support "the Woman in Red" #direngeziparki #occupygezi[27]

The photo in the second tweet, a woman faces a police APC. In the tweet, users shared their feelings about this woman. The photo of this woman is presented as Fig. 16.11 under the tweet.

Yeş... @Par. ... ... 3 June
You are looking like Rachel Corrie, you are very beautiful..#occupygezipygezi[28]

The photo in the third tweet shows an ordinary market where the goods do not have price labels. People liked this market, because it illustrated the solidarity of the people. The photo of this market is presented as Fig. 16.12 under the tweet.

---

[26] http://haber.mynet.com/gezi-parki-eyleminin-dillere-dusen-sarkilari-703267-geziparki/

[27] Ba. .... @bag. ... ... 12 Haziran
İtalya'da kadın milletvekilleri 'Kırmızı Elbiseli Kız' için bugün kırmızı giyindiler.. #direngeziparki #occupygezi

[28] Yeş... @Par. ... ... 3 Haziran
Rachel Corrie gibisin yemin ederim, çok güzelsin. #occupygezi

Fig. 16.10 Woman deputies in Italy dressed red clothes to support "Red Dressed Woman"

Fig. 16.11 A woman is against the armoured personnel carrier

Taksim Dayanışması @taksimdayanisma *3 June*

In Taksim there is the best sharing wall in the world, very original and wonderful things are in Gezi #direngeziparki[29]

---

[29] Taksim Dayanışması @taksimdayanisma 3 Haziran

Dunyanin en guzel paylasma duvari Taksim Gezi de cok farkli muhtesem seyler oluyor #direngeziparki

Fig. 16.12 The solidarity of people in a market—no price labels

16.5.1.9 The Mobilization of People

People shared much information about meetings and demonstrations and they were invited to them. People were continually informed about the events during the demonstrations. People accessed information from different sources and they used this information to help the demonstrators. For example, they tried to direct demonstrators to secure areas. The following tweets are examples of tweets trying to direct people to secure areas and to mobilize them to engage in the meetings.

*Ol. .... @*MC_.... *3 June*

Confrontations stopped in Girne. We are moving to Karşıyaka. Support us without provocation RT #direngeziparki[30]

*Zeyn. ..... @*zer. .... *3 June*

Don't go to Akaretler; police wouldn't find any group to attack. Please, let's go to Gezi. The goal is to resist in peace #occupygezi #direngeziparki[31]

Lambdaistanbul@lambda_istanbul 11 June

Tonight at 7 pm we will meet after the call of the platform of Taksim Solidarity on Gezi Park. This is just the beginning, keep on resisting! #occupygezi[32]

---

[30] Ol. .... @MC_.... 3 Haziran

Girnede olaylar durdu karsiyakaya cekiliyoruz provakasyona gelmeden destek verin RT #direngeziparki

[31] Zeyn. ..... @zer. .... 3 Haziran

Akaretler'e kimse gitmesin; catisacak muhatap bulamasinlar. Haydi lütfen Gezi'ye. Amac baris icinde direnmek. #occupygezi #direngeziparki

[32] Lambdaistanbul @lambda_istanbul 11 Haziran

Bu aksam 19:00da Taksim Dayanışması'nin çağrısıyla Gezi Parkında toplaniyoruz. Bu daha başlangıç mücadeleye devam! #occupygezi

16.5.2 The Users as Actors and the Form of Communication

This part of the study answers the questions about the users, and the form of communication on Twitter. Who are Twitter users and what is the content and characteristics of the tweets? What are the roles of actors in the participation process? The answers show that the users are individuals, social groups, NGOs, civil platforms, activist hacker groups, as well as other users such as media channels, political parties, and deputies. These Twitter users used its functions during the movement. They participated in the movement in various ways.

16.5.2.1 Users as Individual Actors and Participators

The majority of Twitter users were individuals during the Gezi Park movement. The users' profiles are important in the identification of their general features. Users that tweeted in the hashtags each have a photo in their Twitter profiles. They used a name and surname that looked like real names. Of course, these profiles could be fake. Users also used nicknames. Some of the nicknames made reference to the word of "çapulcu" (its meaning has already been presented).

The reliability of information was an important problem for individual users, especially if tweets include information about an urgent situation and there is not enough time to confirm it. This problem is also related to the reliability of Twitter accounts. The contents of previous tweets of users can be analyzed to identify users. If an account is active for a long time, this account possibly is one of a real user. However, that is not enough to make a user trustworthy since people can use new Twitter accounts as much as they want.

Some observations about individual users explain the goal, form, and content of communication on Twitter. The users continually shared their opinions and impressions about the Gezi Park movement. They criticized the provocations and the position of government. Some individuals tweeted to organize the movement or mobilize the people. Individuals tweeted or re-tweeted videos and photos expressing their experiences. Individuals discussed on Twitter about the legitimacy of the government. Tweets about individual experiences such as exposure to tear gas or being faced with a police attack were re-tweeted more than other tweets. In addition to these experiences, calling for doctors' assistance for or medicines, information about the police checkpoints and the location of demonstrators were re-tweeted.

Individual users in the hashtags were opponents to the ruler party. They criticized decisions and actions of government agencies. Individual users supported the demonstrators. This indicated that although individuals had particular interests, they were unanimous in supporting the movement. Individuals used informal language and the communication was emotional. Nevertheless, the expressions of individuals were open and intelligent, if tweets contain an important information. Emotional tweets expressed sadness, worry, friendliness, or excitement. Although some tweets contained irony and swearwords about the government and the police, users warned people to be calm and respectful. This attitude can be related to that users regarded the importance of the label and contents of messages under the hashtags. Since they were open to the public and many people watched the process by means of these hashtags. Tweets affected the opinions of people about the movement. Public support was important for the demonstrators.

People used Twitter to connect people and they expressed their feelings. They created a space on Twitter by tweeting their opinions during the Gezi Park protests. Individuals communicated with each other on Twitter and created networks. Twitter provided communication space for individuals to criticize politicians, mainstream media, government authorities, intellectuals, and all the actors who disregarded the movement. Individuals used different tools to express their own opinions. For example, they shared caricatures, songs, videos, and news. Individuals questioned the legitimacy of the policies of the government. In this process, they were not under the influence of any political organization.

A user targeted to the ruler party; the user called the government to account because of the deaths and this user demanded the resignation of the government and considered the government responsible for the events. This user did not use any intermediary such as a political party to express his/her opinions.

sim... öz....... @si......86 3 June
We are not going home before the resignation of those responsible and the withdrawal of the Police, #occupygezi these people did not die for nothing[33]

This demand is clearly political. Firstly, people shared information, experiences and opinions on Twitter during the movement. Hence, it provided a platform for the discussion about the events. Communication about a social issue is the first step towards political participation. Secondly, government officers followed this platform during the protests. It meant that this user's demand probably reached the authorities. In addition to the offices of government, it was of interest for many national and international organizations; social groups, non-governmental organizations, mass media, and international institutions followed the events on Twitter. It operated as the media and the users informed the people about the current debates. Thirdly, legal procedures concerning the tweets were started by lawcourts. They held individuals responsible for the contents of their tweets. Fourthly, tweets in this space were regarded by political elites as a threat for their power. It means that Twitter users were regarded as a power group in politics. This user's demand was directly presented by its owner when he or she tweeted it in the hashtag of #occupygezi and can be defined as a technique of political participation.

[33] sim... öz....... @si......86 3 Haziran
Polis çekilmeden, sorumlular istifa etmeden/görevden alınmadan asıl şimdi #evedönmüyoruz #occupygezi bu insanlar boşuna ölmedi

16.5.2.2 Users as Groups, Platforms, NGOs, and Participation

Different social groups used Twitter during the Gezi Park movement. These groups were environmentalist groups, human rights supporters, civil platforms, associations, civil society organizations, and football fans groups. Social groups used Twitter, but they used their Twitter pages more than the hashtags. The problem of reliability for individuals was not an issue for social groups and civil platforms. People trusted the tweets shared by social groups more than tweets shared by individuals. The groups used their symbols in their profile photos. Social groups tweeted in these hashtags and they used the functions of Twitter. Tweets of these groups are more grammatical, and the language of their tweets more formal than that of individual tweets. They tweeted to support the protests, to invite people to meetings, to create solidarity with different groups, to help people in different legal and technical issues, to lead people, and to inform them.

Social groups, national and international non-governmental organizations, associations and civil platforms participated in the movement using Twitter. Some of these actors were Greenpeace Turkey, Lambda Istanbul, Istanbul LGBTT Solidarity Association, Istanbul Pharmacy Association, Union of the Turkish Bar Associations, Çarşı Beşiktaş fan group. Non-governmental organizations did not use flags in the meetings in the protest areas as they did not want to spoil the spontaneity of the movement. However, they used their flags and symbols on Twitter. The symbols of these groups and organizations had positive effects on the Twitter users to evaluate and rely on the contents of tweets.

Tweets shared by these social groups and organizations show that they were organized around some common goals. These groups assumed roles in the processes of communication, mobilization and organization by means of their tweets. Organizations informed the demonstrators about legal procedures, medical issues and the other issues. Organizational tweets were activity-based rather than discussion-oriented. Moreover, these social groups and organizations established national and international networks. These networks were important to ensure the support of people and organizations in Turkey and abroad. For example, Greenpeace Turkey connected with other agencies in the world and informed them about the events in Turkey. Thus, this organization used its networks to create international awareness about the Gezi Park movement. The following tweets examplify this function of the networks.

Greenpeace Türkiye @Greenpeace_Med 1 June

Support from Greenpeace International Director to Gezi, condemnation of police violence: #occupytaksim #direngeziparkı[34]

Greenpeace UK @GreenpeaceUK 1 June

Friends in @greenpeace are asking for all the help we can give to counter Turkish media blackout on #occupygezi

[34] Greenpeace Türkiye @Greenpeace_Med 1 Haziran Greenpeace Uluslararası Direktörü Gezi'ye destek, polis şiddetine kınama: #occupytaksim #direngeziparkı

Greenpeace Québec @greenpeaceQC 1 June
..@EDa...... With Gezi protestors, to protect the right of passive manifestation[35]

The social groups took part in the political debates and protests. They used Twitter in the processes of communication, information sharing, organization, mobilization, and motivation. However, they did not use Twitter as much as individuals did. They mostly used their Twitter pages. Among these groups, civil platforms tweeted in the hashtags more than other social groups and organizations. For example, the Taksim Solidarity platform tweeted in the hashtags. The Taksim Solidarity platform integrated 118 civil initiatives, and it assumed a role in the process of organizing the groups, explaining the demands of demonstrators and conveying these demands to the authorities. Civil platforms tried to create collective action. They also contributed to the increase of the number of social groups on Twitter communication, and to their participation in the politics.

16.5.2.3 Users as Activist Hacker Groups and Participation

Hacker and activist groups such as Redhack and Anonymous are popular in Turkey; they used Twitter in the Gezi Park movement. They utilized the communication functions of Twitter and used Twitter to guide people and mobilize them. Their tweets had ideological contents which was different from the tweets of other groups. They boycotted the political elites and the ruler party. They tried to mobilize the Twitter users during the Gezi Park protests. They participated in the movement hacking the web sites of government institutions. They did not share too many messages under the analyzed hashtags, but they continually used their own Twitter pages.

16.5.2.4 Other Users and Participation

Some of the media channels, political parties, and deputies used Twitter during the Gezi Park movement. They tweeted under the hashtags, but their usage rate was lower than that of all the other actors was. Opposition media channels used Twitter especially for informing people about the demonstrations. Among the political parties, only the Republican Peoples' Party shared a limited number of tweets in these hashtags.

In general, the analysis shows that users as individuals shared messages intensely in the hashtags. Social groups and civil platforms used Twitter more than h-activist groups and other actors. Twitter provided an alternative communication and discussion space to these actors. Individuals used Twitter spontaneously; there were no leaders to organize their communication on Twitter. Discussions on

[35] Greenpeace Québec @greenpeaceQC 1 June
"@EDa...... avec protestataires Gezi (Istanbul) pr protéger droit à manifester pacifiquement #occupygezi

Twitter were not structured. In these hashtags, people mostly agreed to criticize the violence. It can be said that almost all the actors tweeted in the hashtags were against the decisions and actions of the government authorities. Political opinions, criticism, information and news were shared in the hashtags and were accessible for national and international actors during the movement.

16.6 Discussion

The Gezi Park movement spread out in a very short time and affected all the country. The first discussion point is the characteristic of this movement. People still try to understand the main reason of the Gezi Park movement. It was related to the social and political problems in the last two decades in Turkey. This movement cannot be explained only as an action to protect the environment. In the last 10 years, the changes in the social, political, and economic structures of Turkey have affected people. This is among the reasons why people participated in this protest, and supported the movement. In addition, it is not a social media revolution as too many communication tools were used during the movement. People saw their neighbors in the streets, they watched news on TV, they phoned each other and they used various ways of communication in this process. Young people used social media intensely. It is clear that Twitter was an important part of the process of communication and participation in the movement. Social media are at the forefront among other communication technologies today as they have important, multiple and complex functions on the communication and interaction process.

The second discussion topic is the relationship between social media and individual participation in politics. Social media are seen as tools to personalize politics since they provide options for individual participation. However, social media opportunities are not limited to personal participation. They also provide opportunities for organizations. This study shows that individuals tweeted in the hashtags more than organizations did; the study can be related to the selection of the hashtags. Organizations used their twitter pages intensely; this shows that organizations adapted to opportunities offered by Twitter.

The third discussion topic is whether Twitter is an alternative communication channel in politics. Twitter is seen as an alternative communication channel for the actors in the social movements. Twitter is regarded as a space for free communication and freedom of expression. People broadcasted the events and they informed the public about the developments while the mainstream media did not broadcast the events. While the demonstrators taped videos using their cameras during the protests and shared these on Twitter, the mass media did not do the same thing. In this respect, Twitter provided an alternative area. However, this area has limitations. Firstly, Twitter is open to everyone. State officials or police can watch these tweets on Twitter like other people. Some people were indicted because of their tweets. Secondly, Twitter users can be manipulated and they can be mobilized to hazardous actions. Thirdly, there is a power relation among Twitter users. In addition, Twitter is a company operating in the current economic system. Due to these reasons, Twitter has a limited position as an alternative and free communication channel.

The fourth discussion topic is about the relationship between online and offline spaces. Twitter is not independent from the offline activities of the actors. It cannot lead all the processes by itself. However, these spaces are interrelated to each other. Participation on Twitter is related to the offline participation of actors. Personal experiences in the offline areas are the sources of communication on Twitter. Furthermore, Twitter has effects on the creativity of people in offline spaces since people know that they can share their opinions or artistic products on Twitter. People involved in the movement did not only share their activities. Their activities were also discussed by users on Twitter, and people tweeted their opinions about these activities. When the demonstrators exposed police intervention and gas attacks, they contacted people on Twitter and shared their experiences. Thus, users became the witnesses of these events. Cultural materials about the movement spread among the users. People witnessed the events as they progressed due to the fact that they were constant users of Twitter. For example, if one were not a Twitter user, one would not understand the meanings of some of the activities. People on Twitter and those participating in the movement created a common language among them. These statements show that offline and online communication support each other.

16.7 Conclusion

This study explains the effects and roles of Twitter in the Gezi Park movement. It focuses on the functions and uses of Twitter and the form of communication on Twitter. Its methodology consists of analyzing the contents of tweets and studying the questions in terms of the specific examples of tweets. This study regards the Gezi Park movement from a different perspective. It presents it as a new form and space for politics on Twitter. This study presents that actors used, during the movement, the functions of Twitter, as these functions are presented in the literature. Moreover, additional functions of Twitter in politics are described. The analysis of hashtags indicates that most of the Twitter users were individuals. Nevertheless, other actors too, such as social groups and platforms, or h-activist groups tweeted in these hashtags.

The results of this study support the claim that Twitter provides means of participation for organizations as well as individuals. Organizations generally prefer to use their Twitter pages rather than the hashtags. The results also show that the role of Twitter in political and social movements is related to the other features of the movements such as offline processes and limitations of Twitter. It means that Twitter affected the Gezi Park movement by ensuring political participation of people, but it cannot be said that Twitter started the events or was the main reason of the movement. Twitter was not the only channel of communication and it is not a space without people.

References

Bennett, W. L., & Entman, M. (2001). Mediated politics: An introduction. In W. L. Bennett & M. Entman (Eds.), *Mediated politics*. New York, NY: Cambridge University Press.

Bennett, W. (2003). Communicating global activism. *Information, Communication & Society, 6* (2), 143–168.

Bennett, W. L., & Segerberg, A. (2012). Digital media and the personalization of collective action – social technology and the organization of protests against the global economic crisis. In B. D. Loader & D. Mercea (Eds.), *Social media and democracy*. Oxon: Routledge.

Blog.milliyet (2013). Prime Minister's explanations about the demonstrators. http://blog.milliyet.com.tr/capulcu-modasi/Blog/?BlogNo=418570 Accessed 15 June 2013.

Boyd, D. M., & Ellison, N. B. (2007). Social network sites: Definition, history, and scholarship. *Journal of Computer-Mediated Communication, 13*(1).

Çakır, D., & Demirhan, K. (2011). Political character of the social actions in the process of globalization: A case study. *International Journal of Social Sciences and Humanity Studies, 3*(2), 159–168.

Castells, M. (2011). A network theory of power. *International Journal of Communication, 5*, 773–787.

Chadwick, A., & May, C. (2003). Interaction between states and citizens in the age of the internet: "e-Government" in the United States, Britain, and the European Union. *Governance: An International Journal of Policy, Administration, and Institutions, 16*(2), 271–300.

Christensen, C. (2011). Twitter revolutions? Addressing social media and dissent. *The Communication Review, 14*(3), 155–157.

Cihan. (2013a). Prime Minister's explanations about the rebuilding of Taksim http://www.cihan.com.tr/news/Basbakan-Erdogan-Taksim-e-yapilacak-caminin-yerini-acikladi-CHMTA0NDU4My8x Accessed 06 June 2013.

Cihan. (2013b). Prime Minister's explanations. http://www.cihan.com.tr/news/Basbakan-Erdogan-Gezi-Parki-ndaki-eylemcilere-yarina-kadar-sure-tanidi-CHMTA2MDA1NS8xMDA1 Accessed 06 June 2013.

Cihan. (2013c). The standing-man. http://www.cihan.com.tr/news/-Duran-Adam-a-374-haber-sitesi-5-gazete-yer-verdi-CHMTA2MTU5OC8x Accessed 19 June2013.

Cnnturk. (2013). The number of tweets. http://www.cnnturk.com/2013/bilim.teknoloji/teknoloji/06/15/gezi.parki.tweetlerinin.linguistigi/711774.0/index.html Accessed 16 June 2013.

Comscore. (2012). The Netherlands Ranks #1 Worldwide in Penetration for Twitter and Linkedin. http://www.comscore.com/Press_Events/Press_Releases/2011/4/The_Netherlands_Ranks_number_one_Worldwide_in_Penetration_for_Twitter_and_LinkedIn Accessed 13 Feb 2012.

Dahlberg, L. (2001). The internet and democratic discourse: Exploring the prospects of online deliberative forums extending the public sphere. *Information, Communication & Society, 4*(4), 615–633.

Dahlberg, L. (2007). The internet and discursive exclusion: From deliberative to agonistic public sphere theory. In L. Dahlberg & E. Siapera (Eds.), *Radical democracy and the internet*. New York, NY: Palgrave Macmillan.

Dahlberg, L., & Siapera, E. (2007). Introduction: Tracing radical democracy and the internet. In L. Dahlberg & E. Siapera (Eds.), *Radical democracy and the internet*. New York, NY: Palgrave Macmillan.

Della Porta, D. (2012). Communication in movement - social movements as agents of participatory democracy. In B. D. Loader & D. Mercea (Eds.), *Social media and democracy*. Oxon: Routledge.

Demirhan, K. (2013). Relationship between social media and political parties: The case of Turkey. In A. M. G. Solo (Ed.), *Political campaigning in the information age*. Hershey, PV: IGI Global.

ecktr (2013). The number of tweets in the hashtags. http://ecktr.com/ Accessed 20 June 2013.

Eriksen, E. O. (2005). An emerging European public sphere. *European Journal of Social Theory, 8* (3), 341–363.

Fenton, N., & Downey, J. (2003). Counter public spheres and global modernity. *The Public, 10*(1), 15–32.
Gerring, J. (2004). What is a case study and what is it good for? *American Political Science Review, 98*(2).
Gimmler, A. (2001). Deliberative democracy, the public sphere and the Internet. *Philosophy and Social Criticism, 27*(4), 21–39.
gundem.milliyet (2013). The results of events. http://gundem.milliyet.com.tr/3-u-agir-toplam-3-bin-500-yarali/gundem/detay/1718297/default.htm Accessed 04 June 2013.
Harlow, S., & Harp, D. (2012). Collective action on the web. *Information, Communication & Society, 15*(2), 196–216.
Hauben, M., & Hauben, R. (1997). *Netizens*. London: Wiley/IEEE Computer Society Press.
Hürriyet. (2013a). About the people were arrested by police in İzmir. http://www.hurriyet.com.tr/gundem/23438875.asp. Accessed 06 June 2013.
Hürriyet. (2013b). The explanations of the Prime Minister. http://www.hurriyet.com.tr/gundem/23429709.asp. Accessed 06 June 2013.
Insanhaber. (2013). The results of events. http://www.insanhaber.com/guncel/21-gunun-bilancosu-4-olu-7822-yarali-h16629.html. Accessed 18 June 2013.
Kim, Y. (2011). The contribution of social network sites to exposure to political difference: The relationships among SNSs, online political messaging, and exposure to cross-cutting perspectives. *Computers in Human Behavior, 27*, 971–977.
Loader, B. D., & Mercea, D. (2011). Networking democracy? *Information Communication & Society, 14*(6), 757–769.
Macintosh, A. (2004). Characterizing E-participation in policy-making. Proceedings of the 37th Hawaii International Conference on System Sciences.
Maireder, A., & Schwarzenegger, C. (2012). A movement of connected individuals. *Information, Communication & Society, 15*(2), 171–195.
Memurlar.net (2013). The results of events. http://www.memurlar.net/haber/378927/. Accessed 04 June 2013.
Park, C. S. (2013). Does Twitter motivate involvement in politics? Tweeting, opinion leadership, and political engagement. *Computers in Human Behavior, 29*, 1641–1648.
Wright, S., & Street, J. (2007). Democracy, deliberation and design: The case of online discussion forums. *New Media Society, 9*(5), 849–69.
Small, T. A. (2012). What the Hashtag? A content analysis of Canadian politics on Twitter. In B. D. Loader & D. Mercea (Eds.), *Social media and democracy*. Oxon: Routledge.
Socialdigger. (2013). The number of tweets in the hashtags. http://www.socialdigger.org/geziparki/ Accessed 23 June 2013
Stalker, G. J., & Wood, L. J. (2012). Reaching beyond the net: Political circuits and participation in Toronto's G20 protests. *Social Movement Studies: Journal of Social, Cultural and Political Protest, 12*(2), 178–198.
Quinn, S., & Lamble, S. (2008). *Online newsgathering research and reporting for journalism*. New York: Elsevier.
Tsagarousianou, R. (1999). Electronic democracy: Rhetoric and reality. *Communications, 24*(2), 189–208.
Twitter. (2013). About Twitter. https://twitter.com/about Accessed 04 June
twitturk (2013). The standing man. http://twitturk.com/tweet/search?q=duranadam Accessed 23 June 2013.
Vesnic-Alujevic, L. (2012). Political participation and web 2.0 in Europe: A case study of Facebook. *Public Relations Review, 38*, 466–470.
Wieviorka, M. (2005). After new social movements. *Social Movement Studies: Journal of Social, Cultural and Political Protest, 4*(1), 1–19.
Woo-Young, C. (2005). Online civic participation, and political empowerment: online media and public opinion formation in Korea. *Media Culture Society, 27*, 925.

Zheng, Y., & Wu, G. (2005). Information technology, public space, and collective action in China. *Comparative Political Studies, 38*, 507.

Yurtgazetesi. (2013). About the broadcasting animal documentary on the prestigious news channel "CNNTurk" http://www.yurtgazetesi.com.tr/gundem/cnnturke-sevgiler-h36551.html Accessed 15 June 2013.

Chapter 17
Social Media: The New Protest Drums in Southern Africa?

Admire Mare

Abstract This chapter is an attempt to contribute an African, particularly Southern African, perspective on the role of social media during the Occupy Grahamstown (South Africa), the 20 July 2011 protests (Malawi), the 10 September 2010 food riots (Mozambique), the 1 April 2012 demonstrations in Swaziland, and the flash demonstrations by WOZA and Mthwakazi in Zimbabwe. Using data drawn from 40 in-depth interviews with political activists in five SADC countries, this chapter argues that social media was used differently throughout the four phases (pre-demonstration, ignition, escalation and post-demonstration) of the protests. It demonstrates that in order to fully understand the Southern African protests, we need to look beyond the 'demonstration effect' of the North African revolutions, and focus instead on the demands for political, economic and social rights within each political context and how new media technologies including social media became entangled in these processes. The overriding argument is that the use of social network sites in these protests was far more complicated because of the multi-layered nature of the communication ecologies in each country, which meant that activists creatively appropriate the limited technologies at their disposal. The chapter argues that although Africa is the least connected continent to the Internet, pockets of resistance are beginning to sprout on social media platforms. It demonstrates that in flawed democracies, such as Zimbabwe, Malawi, and Swaziland, social media have become the 'new protest drums', creatively appropriated to convey, not merely warning signals but messages of indignation and discontent. It highlights the increasing interconnected relationship between offline and online activism. It also argues that in times of crisis, social media platforms present

In this study, 'protest drums' are equated to 'talking drums' which are traditional instruments which can be modulated quite closely, their range is limited to a gathering or market-place, and they are primarily used in ceremonial functions such as dance, story-telling, and communication of points to order.

A. Mare (✉)
School of Journalism and Media Studies, Rhodes University, Grahamstown, South Africa
e-mail: admiremare@gmail.com

B. Pătruţ and M. Pătruţ (eds.), *Social Media in Politics*, Public Administration and Information Technology 13, DOI 10.1007/978-3-319-04666-2_17,

activists with an indispensable instrument for early warning, bypassing state media blackouts, disarticulating the official state propaganda, and passing on solidarity messages across space and time.

17.1 Introduction and Background to the Study

Ever since the early 1990s, the use of the Internet in general and new media technologies in particular for political activism has garnered enormous scholarly attention. However, the globalization of protests, which has swept both authoritarian regimes and Western liberal democracies, has spawned serious debate on the relationship between social media and protests, particularly in times of economic hardship. These protests which began with the Spanish *indignados* movement spread to Tunisia (2010–2011), Egypt (2011), Libya (2011–2012), Syria (2011 till present), Occupy Movement in the United States (2011), London riots (2011), Occupy Nigeria (2011) and many others of the Middle East, calling for democratic political change and equitable wealth distribution have highlighted the instrumental role played by new media technologies. There is an emerging body of research particularly focusing on the 'Arab Spring' which shows that social media and other new media technologies were used to both coordinate action by protesters and to report upon the events (Aouragh 2012; Gerbaudo 2012). A key upshot of this emerging research is the creative appropriation of popular social media platforms through the digital sharing of eyewitness accounts of events through interview, reportage, image and video online (Howard and Parks 2012). It is believed that social media have enabled the constitution of alternative public sphere, which allows activists to circulate alternative discourses and share user generated (dis) content. New forms of social media are seen as disrupting constraints placed on traditional sources of information and public debate, whether through state intervention or monopolistic private ownership, and in theory provide platforms for a multiplicity of voices. It is important to point out that social media are not the preserve of progressive social movements, but are also used for counter-revolutionary and anti-democratic purposes by such regimes. It allows these various social groups (progressive, conservative, revolutionary etc.) to lower costs of participation, organisation, recruitment, and training. Rane and Salem (2012: 97) argue that while social media played important facilitation roles during the Arab Spring in terms of inter- and intra-group communication as well as information dissemination, mainstream mass media are still highly relevant to the process. Extending the 'mitigated euphoria' point of view, Aday et al. (2012: 5) reject the sweeping claims about the primary role of the new media technologies ("the Internet causes protest"), arguing rather that "social media allows activists on the ground to disseminate information about protests in real time." They point out that the possible impact of new media on protests can be grouped into five discrete causal pathways: effects on individual attitudes and competencies, effects on social networks and intergroup relations, effects on the organization of protests, and effects on international attention (Aday et al. 2012: 5). For some scholars, new media technologies enable and support the creation of new forms of political organisations, which are thematically oriented, loosely coupled, quickly gathered, and allowing for anonymous affiliation. It is noteworthy to highlight that while social media platforms have inherent strengths they also have weaknesses hence their effectiveness in any given social context depends on how effectively they are deployed and appropriated by ordinary users. The point is that the success or failure of the uprisings largely depends on contextual factors and broader geopolitical contexts (Rane and Salem 2012: 97).

In a wide-ranging scholarly debate on the relationship between social media and political action pitched in hyperbole and hypobole, three camps are identifiable. There are those who celebrate social media's promise for closed societies in ways that resonate with deterministic discourses of the so-called 'information society' (Shirky 2011); those who express pessimism (Gladwell 2010), and those who adopt a more cautious approach (Morozov 2011) that transcends both the cyber-optimist and cyber-pessimist approaches. Social media have been branded the 'new vessel' of cyber-democracy and a 'tool of political freedom', which enable social movements and activist groupings in their quest to reinvigorate democratic processes by cyber-optimists. Clay Shirky, a cyber-optimist, sees new media technologies as having the potential to 'organise, plan, and coordinate direct political actions—elections, demonstrations and insurrections' (2011). This kind of romanticization and objectification of technology propounded by cyber optimists has been critiqued by cyber-pessimists for suffering from the poverty of nuanced analysis. They show that there are some cracks in this wall of the 'social media sublime'. In response, cyber-pessimists like Malcolm Gladwell (2010) dismiss social media activism as based on weak ties and therefore can only demand low-risk participation. Other cyber-pessimists who reincarnate the ghost of Karl Marx's critique of religion as the 'opium of the oppressed' dismiss social media as an 'anti-revolutionary' device that keeps the world quiet and peaceful. Evgeny Morozov (2011) also adds that "Yes, [social media] are affecting the world. But it also looks like the other side—the authoritarian governments—are getting empowered as well". In light of this highly polarised debate, it is important to point out that if we limit our analysis of social media and political action on these two polar extremes, we may miss instances where situated users sabotage, evade, and hack even the most advanced surveillance systems.

While most research on social media and protests has been conducted in the Middle East and North Africa (Rane and Salem 2012; Gerbaudo 2012; Castells 2012), little empirical research has explored the role of social media in the recent protests in Southern Africa. This chapter focuses on Southern Africa, a region that has seen a spike in social protests in recent years starting in Mozambique, Malawi, Zimbabwe, South Africa, and Swaziland. It investigates the role played by social media in the mobilization and coordination of protestors in the five countries. There is a dearth of research on how the social media technologies have changed the ways in which activists in Southern Africa engage in collective action. Although social media have certainly created new spaces for individual self-expression and interest-group mobilization, as broadly indicated in the chapters of this volume, there is need for more empirical, comparative, and cross-disciplinary research to determine whether Southern African netizens are employing these digital technologies in fundamentally different ways from their global counterparts. Rather than focus on whether social media alone can deliver democracy or a political revolution, Aday et al. (2012) advise researchers to explore the variety of ways in which social media might transform the dynamics of political activism. In line with this advice, researchers are exhorted to fill an academic lacuna on how new media technologies may transform (or not) individuals' attitudes and willingness to engage in political action, mitigate or exacerbate group conflict, facilitate collective action, help regimes to better spy on and control their citizens, and garner international attention (Aday et al. 2012: 5). In view of this call, there is need for further research on how social media are impacting on protest campaigns in other regions of the world. It is regrettable that the scholarly focus has been rather on what ICTs *do to* Africans instead of what Africans *do with* ICTs. This has meant that the use of social media by activists that emerge in the context of Western experiences, "are applied out of context, and sometimes awkwardly in Africa" (Ibelema 2008: 36). In view of this, Howard and Parks (2012) also exhort us to continue to gather country-specific cases and conduct comparative work if we are to gain a more complete appreciation of the subtle, often unexpected ways, in which social media and political activism interact.

This chapter therefore investigates the role social media played in the Southern African protests. The main objective of the research is to critically analyze the role played by social media in the mobilizations in the recent protests in Southern Africa. Therefore, the research questions that informed this study were: What role social media have played in the mobilizations in recent protests in these countries? What the similarities and differences there are in social media take up by activists in these countries? What has the 'demonstration effect' of the North African revolutions with their usage of social media been on Southern African protests? In order to answer the above research questions, this chapter draws on a predominantly qualitative research methodology because of its desire to understand events and actions from local perspectives. In line with the research design, the study undertook a critical analysis of academic and newspaper articles on the usage of social media by activists in Southern Africa especially during the pre-demonstration, demonstrations, and post-demonstration periods. This study also relied on key informant interviews with activists who were at the forefront of organizing the demonstrations in the five countries. These semi-structured interviews with activists from the five countries were instrumental in eliciting 'insider perspectives' and 'thick descriptions' on the role played by social media in each social context.

In order to illuminate the role played by social media in the Southern African protests, the study draws on the concept of *alternative public sphere*. As a critique of the Habermasian notion of public sphere, it presupposes the existence of multiple sites of engagement. The Habermasian notion of the public sphere has been criticized for obfuscating the role of other counterpublics that exist parallel to the bourgeois public sphere. These counterpublics allow subordinate groups to find the right voice and words to express their thoughts or articulate and defend their interests in a less threatening public space. This conceptual resource allows us to view social media as 'parallel discursive arenas where marginalized groups in society invent and circulate discourses that relate to their identities, interests, and needs' (Fraser 1992: 123). Thus, scholars operating within the alternative public sphere theory are of the opinion that the popular media [such as corporate social media] outside mainstream journalism may serve to broaden and diversify the existing media landscape and contribute towards voice formation. Popular media such as social media, as Wasserman (2011: 146) observes, "can be seen as not merely technologies transmitting democratic and civic information but also as the location where people are transgressing the hitherto fixed boundaries of what counts as political participation or civic identification". Such a sphere allows for the theorization of the intersections of the popular and the political giving rise to the practices such as of 'everyday forms of resistance'. The next section elaborates upon the research context.

17.2 Context of the Study: Southern Africa

Despite the region's relatively poor transportation and communications infrastructure, Southern Africa is perhaps the best place to investigate the role of social media in the mobilisation of protestors and coordination of collective action. The region has been rocked by a spate of demonstrations since 2010. These pockets of resistance have coincided with the proliferation of new media technologies in people's everyday lives. Compared to North Africa, South Africa still has low Internet penetration, a short history of digital activism and underdeveloped telecommunications infrastructure (limited though rapidly increasing extra-urban mobile access and bandwidth in many areas), it nonetheless provides a good 'testing case' for a close examination of the role of social media in 'choreographing of assembly' (Gerbaudo 2012). This chapter focuses on South Africa, Zimbabwe, Malawi, Mozambique, and Swaziland, which have experienced political and economic crises of different natures and on varying scales (Cammack 2011; Lloyd 2011). In the case of Malawi, Swaziland, and Zimbabwe, protests have often been the result of popular demands for better governance and living conditions and the inability of governments to satisfactorily respond to these demands (Cammack 2011; Makumbe 2009; Daniel 2011). Service delivery protests have become the order of the day in post-apartheid South Africa, leading scholars to euphemistically describe the country as the "capital of social protests in the world" (Alexander 2012). Much of the protest activities during the Mbeki and Zuma eras have emanated from shack settlements and townships rather than the better-resourced suburbs (Alexander 2012), largely because of inadequate service delivery and lack of accountability by local councillors (Booysen 2009).

Although the holding of elections has become commonplace in Southern Africa, not all ballots pass the test of being "free and fair" and many have been charades held by regimes clinging on to power. Out of the five countries studied, only South Africa's elections are judged to be both free and fair. South Africa just falls short of being a full democracy because of weaknesses in political participation and political culture whereas Zimbabwe, Malawi and Swaziland have been characterised as authoritarian regimes while Mozambique has been described as a flawed democracy. Zimbabwe has endured a decade of multilayered and multifaceted politico-economic crises (Makumbe 2009). Disputed elections and economic hardship have spawned running battles between ordinary citizens and political protagonists. There has been a growing discontent over limited political participation, human rights violations, the declining economy, and limited communication platforms (Ndlela 2009: 89). Despite the swearing in of a government of national unity in 2009, Zimbabwe seems to be heading for a prolonged transition, as evidenced by the slow resolution of outstanding issues: while the new government has managed to address issues pertaining to runaway inflation and economic instability, cosmetic political reforms have done little to consolidate or deepen democracy.

Malawi, on the other hand, graced international news headlines for all the wrong reasons, under the tutelage of the late President Bingu waMutharika. The country experienced bad political and economic governance characterised by the narrowing of the democratic space, media repression, and jobless economic growth since 2009 (Cammack 2011). The narrowing of democratic space created new political opportunities structure that gave birth to the civil society grand coalition, which mobilised ordinary citizens around bread and butter issues in July 2011. The government reacted harshly by deploying the military and killing several protestors. Mozambique emerged from years of bitter civil war in 1992 and quickly revoked its Marxist socialist leanings by embracing neoliberal economic policies (Lloyd 2011). The country has won many admirers for its stable political and economic system, yet, on the surface, its superficial stability and prosperity (for a few and for the politically well-connected) has masked widespread social and economic disparities that threaten what passes for peaceful rule (Jacobs and Duarte 2010). This brief hiatus came to an end in September 2010, following a sudden rise in the cost of living, when trade unions and grassroots social movements picketed on bread and butter issues. Yet Swaziland remains the only absolute monarchy on the continent. Often termed as a unique form of 'African' democracy, the Kingdom is governed through the 'tinkhundla' system that was imposed by King Sobhuza II in 1978. This system puts emphasis on the 'word of the King is law' resulting in the suppression of political organisations. In fact, the five countries have been assessed as follows by the Freedom House (2011) (Table 17.1).

17.3 The Media Landscape in Southern Africa

In terms of the media landscape, although all the five countries have constitutions safeguarding freedom of expression, some such as Malawi, Zimbabwe, and Swaziland have toughened their national media statutes in the last couple of years

Table 17.1 Freedom in the world 2011: the authoritarian challenge to democracy (data source: http://www.freedomhouse.org, accessed on May 15, 2013; Freedom House (2011))

Country	Freedom status	Political rights (PR)	Civil liberties (CL)	Trend arrow
Malawi[a]	Partly free	3	4	
Mozambique	Partly free	4	3	
South Africa[a]	Free	2	2	
Swaziland	Not free	7	5	↓
Zimbabwe	Not free	6	6	↓

PR and CL stand for political rights and civil liberties, respectively; 1 represents the most free and 7 the least free rating

Up or down arrow indicates a trend of positive or negative changes that took place but were not sufficient to result in a change in political rights or civil liberties ratings

[a]Indicates a country's status as an electoral democracy

and witnessed cases of arbitrary arrests and intimidation of journalists (Cammack 2011; Moyo 2009; Daniel 2011). Out of the five, South Africa is the only country observing high standards of media freedom. However, the country suffers from a constricted mediated public sphere as a result of increasing levels of media concentration. Media concentration in South Africa has significantly eroded media diversity, thereby alienating the voices of the poor and marginalised groups such as women and youth. In terms of the broadcasting sector, Duncan and Glenn (2010) argue that, far from being a model of how to transform a state broadcaster into a genuine public-service broadcaster, 'South Africa has degenerated into a situation characterised by two distinct centres of power—state interference and over-commercialisation' (Duncan and Glenn 2010). In Swaziland, the state monopoly of both the print and broadcasting sectors continues to militate against the constitution of a healthy public sphere. Delays in finalising key pieces of media-related legislation; intimidation and threats by traditional and state authorities, interference with editorial independence, censorship, physical attacks, and mounting levels of defamation cases have seriously limited the exercise of freedom of expression (Dlamini 2010). Despite many attempts by independent organizations to establish other radio stations, this has been made impossible by the king's refusal to grant them broadcasting licenses. Similarly, Malawi, Zimbabwe, and Mozambique are characterised by state ownership of newspapers and broadcasting stations. Although private media players are there, most of them practice self-censorship because of high levels of state repression, harassment, and physical harm. The five countries under consideration have also experienced massive uptake of internet usage via mobile phones and have literate populations (http://www.internetworldstats.com). The conditions necessary for social media to be a catalyst are present especially in Mozambique, Zimbabwe, and South Africa. Cheap mobile broadband, a proliferation of smartphones and internet-connected hardware means that information can be disseminated quickly and accurately in viral form (Banda 2010). In the five countries studied, social media have proliferated and permeated key facets of social life (Banda 2010). Below are the internet and Facebook usage statistics according to http://www.internetworldstats.com/africa.htm as of 15 May 2013 (Table 17.2).

Table 17.2 The Internet and Facebook usage statistics in Southern Africa, 2013

Country	Internet access rate %	Facebook users
Malawi	716,400 Internet users as of June/2012, 4.5 % of the population, per ITU	203,840 Facebook users on Dec 31/2012.
Mozambique	1,011,185 Internet users as of Dec/12, 4.3 % of the population, per ITU	362,560 Facebook users on Dec 31/12.
South Africa	8,500,000 Internet users Dec/12, 17.4 % of the population, per ITU	6,269,600 Facebook users on Dec 31/12,
Swaziland	251,448 Internet users as of Dec/12, 18.1 % of the population, per ITU.	54,220 Facebook users on Dec 31/11, 4.0 % penetration rate.
Zimbabwe	1,981,277 Internet users as of Dec/11, 15.7 % of the population, per ITU.	Facebook users, data not available.

17.4 Data Presentation and Analysis

17.4.1 It's Complicated: The Role Played by Social Media in Southern African Protests

The findings from this research suggest that the role played by social media in recent Southern African protests was complex. In order to understand the complex nature of the role played by online and offline media in the organization of protest action, it is important to map out each country's communicative ecology. In the context of the Southern African protests, different activists deployed both online and offline repertoires of collective action suitable to their political contexts. Because mainstream media discourses especially state owned newspapers, radio and television stations have tended to delegitimise activists' political demands, the use of new media technologies by activists in Southern Africa reflects an emerging trend of creative appropriation of existing technologies. As already intimated above that the media landscape in Southern Africa is characterised by lack of media freedom and media concentration, activists resorted to alternative spaces or 'parallel market of information' (Moyo 2009) in order inform their target audiences. For instance, given the highly commercialised and concentrated nature of the South African media landscape activists who organised 'Occupy Grahamstown' made use of community newspapers, community radio stations, websites, social media, and community meetings. Even more important was the role played by the 'social layer' (Foth and Hearn 2007) made up of community organizations (such as the Unemployed People's Movement, and Students for Social Justice), rallies and community meetings. These alternative communicative spaces provided useful venues for mobilization, coordination, and organization of the protests.

In contrast, those in Zimbabwe, a country known for draconian media laws and a state media monopoly resorted to accessible diasporic media (such as http://www.new.zimbabwe.com, SW Radio Africa, Radio VOA, and Radio Voice of the People), online newspapers, the private press, Kubatana.net, and social media. The point is that instead of characterising protests in Southern Africa as

'Facebook/Twitter/SMS revolutions' as has been done with North African revolts, there is need to understand the complex nature of existing communication ecologies in each social context—how the 'technological, discursive and social layers' (Foth and Hearn 2007) feed off and into each other—creating a rather multi-layered communication ecosystem. Rather than simply reifying single technologies (such as Facebook and Twitter) at the expense of other equally important offline activities such as militant protest, lobbying of political and economic elites, handing over of petitions and instituting legal actions, there is also need to acknowledge the role played by both mediated and unmediated communication. In social contexts, where the mainstream media is the preserve of political and economic elites, ordinary people tend to create or recreate alternative media platforms to circulate their own discourses. This is clearly seen in Mozambique, where organisers of the September 2010 demonstrations used an everyday technology such as SMSs to mobilize protestors. For instance, in Swaziland, Facebook was useful for scheduling the protests, in Zimbabwe institutional blogs such as Kubatana.net and diasporic media were critical for mobilization and publicizing of flash demonstrations, while in Mozambique, SMSs were used to coordinate and YouTube to broadcast human rights abuses to the world.

The argument of this chapter is that, in Southern Africa, social media did not cause the demonstrations but rather were only implicated as tools and alternative spaces that were creatively appropriated by activists at the point in time. Instead of falling for the cheap behaviouristic model, which says 'social media is the stimulus and critical consciousness and political action as response', as Castells (2012) would like us to believe, I concur with Fuchs (2012) that society's reality is far more complex than that. In the case of Southern African protests, the online media played an active role in publicizing the demonstrations, while traditional (private) media was also instrumental in the mobilisation of protesters. The role of social media before, during, and after the recent spate of protests in Southern Africa can be summed up in three interrelated ways, namely: enabling cyberactivism, which helped to trigger street demonstrations, encouraging civic engagement, through aiding the mobilization and organization of protests, and promoting a new form of citizen journalism, which provided a platform for ordinary citizens to express themselves and document their own versions of reality. Cyberactivism, especially on social network sites such as Facebook and Twitter, was particularly instrumental in South Africa, Swaziland, and Malawi. In South Africa, the Students for Social Justice (SSJ) used its Facebook page to disseminate information and to publicise its demonstration. In the case of Mozambique, journalists and activists such as Erik Charas used YouTube to provide evidence for the demonstrations taking place and exposed police brutality and killings. Facebook allowed information to go from inside Swaziland to outside and from outside back to Swaziland. The role of social media was more pronounced during the actual demonstrations in all the five countries as activists and ordinary citizens updated their statuses and uploaded videos and photos in real time. Cyberactivism as "the act of using the internet to advance a political cause that is difficult to advance offline," adding that "the goal of such activism is often to create intellectually and emotionally compelling digital artefacts that tell stories of injustice, interpret history, and advocate for particular political outcomes" (Howard 2011:145). It differs from mobilization because of the latter's focus on planning, execution, and facilitation of actions. Overall, they are both closely interrelated, since cyberactivism can help to foster and promote civic engagement, which, in turn, gives birth to various forms of mobilization. In the context of Southern African protests, social media provided an alternative public sphere for ordinary people to tell their story and bring the struggles of their everyday life into the semi-public arena. Instead of operating within the structural limitations of state regulated local media, which fosters a particular form of 'institutionalized dissent', organizers in the five countries resorted to alternative spaces or parallel market of information that promoted some form of 'deinstitutionalised dissent'. Other uses of social media were to transmit information on police brutality, blocked roads, telephone numbers of human rights defenders, and safe houses. Social network sites were crucial in supplying the most graphic images of the crackdowns on protesters, but also broadcast messages from battlegrounds, rallying demonstrators, and updating relatives and friends in the diasporas on breaking news.

There is also overwhelming evidence that suggests that traditional media, especially private and community newspapers, played an important information dissemination role in Malawi, South Africa, Mozambique, and Zimbabwe. Each element of the communication ecosystem used during the demonstrations had a particular function. Social media, for instance, were useful for information dissemination, news gathering, and early warning systems, while mobile phones were critical for taking photographs of what was happening and making it available to a wide global audience, and diasporic media weighed in with instant global reporting of events. Interviews with activists revealed that the word of mouth, community meetings, press conferences, and rumours were also important vehicles for mobilizing public support for demonstrations in Southern Africa. Across all the five countries studied here, activists gave vivid accounts of how they used social media and other existing communication tools to mobilize protestors. Some described how they creatively appropriated social media platforms to whip up public opinion, to circumvent media blackout associated with government-owned media and engage in political conversations about the necessity of demonstrations against deteriorating standards of living, political misgovernance, and service delivery challenges. As one activist at Women of Zimbabwe Arise (WOZA) explained: 'For most of our demonstrations, we rely on our website (http://www.wozazimbabwe.org), the private newspapers, 'pirate' radio stations, online newspapers and social media to mobilise demonstrators. We also use flyers, newsletters and word of mouth to spread the message. We are also active on Twitter @wozazimbabwe. Facebook in particular gives us a platform to post news about all our activities, to stir up debates through commentary and whip up public emotion on issues on common concern". Another activist who has worked with Women of Zimbabwe Arise (WOZA) added: 'Indeed, social media has added an interesting dynamic to our fight for a new Zimbabwe. Thanks to new media technologies, we are able to share our strategies with like-minded people via institutional blogs like Kubatana.net, online newspapers such as NewZimbabwe.com and Facebook. We have witnessed a mushrooming of Facebook groups such as Baba Jukwa, Amai Jukwa, Free and Fair Elections, Youthdecidezw and Mthwakazi Liberation Front (MLF) in recent years". As Mare (2009) argues, Facebook has become the most popular space for ordinary citizens to disarticulate hegemonic discourses and to reach to Zimbabweans dotted around the world. Besides using Facebook to reconnect with family members and relatives in the Diaspora, "Zimbabweans have become active 'Facebookers' of the Zimbabwean crisis through posting and reposting of eye-witness accounts, digitally organising events and advancing political and social causes" (Mare 2009). Another noteworthy example is the Mthwakazi Liberation Front (MLF), which advocates for the total independence of the former Kingdom of Matebeleland from present day Zimbabwe. In an effort to mobilise public opinion amongst the Ndebele people in the country and in the Diaspora, the group has developed a sophisticated social media campaign. In an interview, with one of the activists, social media were hailed for facilitating online activism, providing a space to discuss marginality in Zimbabwe's body politic, allowing them to schedule public meetings and fostering networking across national borders.

In Mozambique, organisers of the protests used SMS messaging to mobilise demonstrators. Residents who took to the streets of Maputo were prompted by Short Message Service (SMS) messages that told them to "enjoy the great day of the strike" and to "protest the increase in energy, water, mini-bus taxi, and bread prices." Expressing a similar view, Erik Charas explained that: "Many citizens had advance warning that something was going to happen on 1 September through SMS text messages circulated via mobile phones from unnamed sources, notwithstanding police statements to the contrary. It also became obvious on the day that the level of coordination achieved among many different sites must also have been relying on mobile phones. There was no sign of public mobilisation via Internet or Facebook, which is not surprising given that the demonstrators clearly came from the poorer residential areas, where internet access and internet-enabled phones are still rare". The creative appropriation of the mobile phone explains why SMS has become a key feature of Africa's communication ecosystem—it is cheaper than making an actual call (Banda 2010). During the actual demonstrations, social media platforms were abuzz with up-to-date information on police brutality and running battles between the police and protesters. Another activist based in Maputo pointed out that: "In addition to the text messages that were flying around the city between families and friends swapping updates and advice, the Internet came into its own as a place for sharing information, aggregating and re-disseminating news, and promoting comment and discussion. Social media simply became an outlet through which information was relayed between the technologically connected and to the rest of the world". The argument here is that although social media were implicated in the Mozambican protests, they only came into the scene during the actual demonstrations. As one activist based in Maputo aptly avers: "Being a Mozambican living in Maputo, I would also like to add a comment about Facebook. Facebook played a very important role in disseminating accurate information about the riots that started on September 1 in Maputo. While I was watching what was happening in two local TV broadcasters, through Facebook I was being updated virtually by the second by people who were located in various parts of town. At the same time, I knew exactly what was going on in 7 or 8 streets of Maputo. Journalists could not do this especially in Mozambique. People turned to Facebook to know which road they should use to pick up their kids from school when the riots started, or to return home safely. Some used it to assess whether or not it was safe to go to work on the second day of social unrest in Maputo". In short, in times of information blackout, parallel spaces of communication emerge and as Nyamnjoh (2005:216) observes, 'rumour is mostly likely to become an alternative source of information during a crisis, when there is a heightened need for information in the public. This is especially likely when the conventional media, for whatever reason, lack credibility'.

Similarly, the details of the 20 July 2011 demonstrations in Malawi were circulated via social media (especially Facebook and Twitter), mass emailing, online newspapers (such as Face of Malawi and Nyasa Times), press releases sent out to private radio station (Zodiak Broadcasting Services (ZBS)), and private newspapers. Days prior to the demonstration, Twitter was abuzz with hashtags such as #july20 and #redarmy. While #July 20 referred to the scheduled day for the demonstrations, #redarmy stood for the red shirts protestors wore. The tweet by @DutchessCarol soon after the demonstrations explained the symbolism of #redarmy: "Everyone who was in the streets was to wear red as a symbol of solidarity. Red stands for flames, which is the English name for Malawi". Social media tools facilitated the sharing of experiences, photos, and videos in real time. According to one of the organisers, Billy Mayaya, "If there was no media then our demonstration wouldn't have generated mass appeal. We used mobile phones, SMS, Facebook and emails to liaise and exchange notes with fellow activists throughout Malawi'. We also used traditional media especially newspapers, community and private radio stations to communicate our key messages. We placed advertisements with our key messages 2 weeks before the 20 July on Zodiak Broadcasting Service. The advert had information on the time of the demonstration, conduct during the demonstrations, dress code, and places of picketing throughout the country". The usage of radio in Malawi by organisers to convey the mass demonstration message confirms its 'tag of 'Africa's medium' due to its reach and social embedding in ordinary people's everyday lives' (Moyo 2009). Further explaining the centrality of social media during the protests in Malawi, Mabvuto Banda commented as follows: "Unlike in the Arab springs where organisers used social media to inform the people the impending demonstrations i.e. we are all Khalid Said in Egypt. In Malawi, Facebook, Twitter, and other social media tools were used to show the whole world the brutal nature of Bingu waMutharika's police and youth brigade. People upload content on Facebook, YouTube, and Twitter in real-time". Through status updates, people were able to call others to act, disseminate information, and express their sentiments on the issues at hand.

In South Africa, during the Occupy Grahamstown demonstrations activists resorted to *The Dispatch* and *Grocotts Mail* (a century-old private newspaper in the area) which are sympathetic to the causes of Unemployed People's Movement (UPM), and SSJ for mobilisation of protesters. They also used SSJ's Facebook page, posted a press statement on Abahlali base Mjondolo's website and organised community meetings to rally support. In short, it was a combination of traditional and social media that allowed organisers to reach out to protesters from the eastern and western parts of Grahamstown. As one activist explained: "During our demonstrations, fellow comrades from SSJ deployed social media platforms like Facebook and Twitter in order to keep everyone in the loop". On the other hand, activists in Swaziland relied on foreign newspapers such as the *Mail* and *Guardian*, satellite broadcasts by DSTV, and social media to recruit demonstrators. Given the repressive attitude towards media freedom in Swaziland, the organisers launched a Facebook page called: 'April 12 Swazi Uprising', months ahead of the demonstration in a bid to mobilize public opinion. It called upon 'a hundred thousand men to march into the country's city centres to declare a 2011 democratic Swaziland free of all royal dominance'. The initiators of the group described themselves as 'not affiliated to any political party, union or similar political formations but rather a voice of the people on the streets who are sick and tired of the misrule by the Swazi regime'. Bloggers using pseudonyms also made use of Word Press to publicize the uprisings. As Moyo (2009) observes, the blog or web log has become one of the key tools for alternative communication in the emerging media ecology. Lucky Lukhele, the spokesperson of the Swaziland Solidarity Network aptly explained how activists used different media tools:

> "In the run up to the April demonstrations, we used a wide array of social media tools such as the SSN Blog, Facebook, Twitter, and online newspapers to spread the word of change and democracy in Swaziland. We coordinated the demonstrations mostly online as most of our cadres are based in South Africa. Facebook, in particular, was equally important, as it is the leading source of information to Swazis due to its popularity particularly amongst the youth. It is relatively cheap which makes it accessible to everyone who has internet. The overwhelming majority of Facebook access is via mobile phones. The MTN network was very helpful in this regard because of its Zero Facebook, which allowed ordinary citizens with smart phones to access Facebook free of charge. Social media was critical for us to reach the ordinary people in Swaziland because of government censorship of local media".

From the above, it is clear that instead of hailing social media as the game changers in political activism, we need to view them as 'an 'amplifier,' that contributes to politics in ways more subtle and multi-dimensional than was recognised by the utopian doctrines expounded during the 1990s (Wasserman 2011). Thus, instead of being trapped within the ambit of the 'social media sublime', we need to look at how the usage of new media technologies tilts the balance of power between activists and governments. Such an approach goes beyond technological determinism by foregrounding the importance of the social and cultural shaping of technologies. The point is that the preferred functions of social media (chatting, posting, commenting, messaging, liking and uploading photos), are not fixed in the technology itself, rather they are a site of interpretive work that is entrenched in the complexities of the social interactions associated with the appropriation of the technology. As shown above, different political contexts call for locally-specific technologies that reach the targeted audience. Social media are not magic bullets or liberation technologies but vehicles through which chit-chat (personal communication), political communication, and other texts are disseminated. Instead of hailing social media as 'networks of outrage and hope' (Castells 2012), we need to appreciate the Janus-faced nature of these technologies. As Morozov aptly observes, these technologies of freedom are also surveillance tools for authoritarian regimes. In addition, Fuchs (2012: 780) reminds us that "social media in a contradictory society (made up of class conflicts and other conflicts between dominant and dominated groups) are likely to have a contradictory character: they do not necessarily and automatically support/amplify or dampen/limit rebellions, but rather pose contradictory potentials that stand in contradictions with influences by the state, ideology and capitalism".

17.4.2 Similarities and Differences in Social Media Take Up by Southern African Activists

The findings from this research suggest that there are similarities and differences in social media take up by Southern African activists. Most of the differences relates to whether social media usage by activists was done before, during or after the demonstrations. Unlike in North African revolutions, where social media are believed to have been used to coordinate and execute demonstrations, in Southern Africa, with the exception of Swaziland, most activists made use of traditional (private and community) media for mobilization and only roped in social media platforms to publicise human rights violations. While social media usage in North African revolutions has resemblances to the Southern African situation, they nonetheless differ in that the former has a long history of digital activism and social media was instrumental throughout the protest cycle. Individual countries studied manifested similarities and differences in terms of the use of social media by activists throughout the protest cycles. The differences in the social media take up in the recent Southern African protests were influenced by the prevailing media legislation, affordability of internet charges, political dynamics, social movements' media strategies, and the target audience of the organisers. In fact, low internet penetration rates, low Facebook usage rates, and unaffordable Internet charges militated against the heavy usage of social media platforms during the demonstrations. For instance, in countries experiencing serious democratic regression such as Zimbabwe, Swaziland, and Malawi, activists resorted to social media platforms, institutional blogs, pirate radio stations, and online newspapers to drum up support for the planned demonstrations. In these countries, the state-media were banned from covering press conferences and demonstrations organised by activists derogatively known as 'regime change agents' and 'puppets of the West'. Unlike any other social network site, Facebook was described as the most used platform by activists in Southern Africa because of its social and technical affordances.

In the case of Mozambique, state media blackout forced ordinary citizens to flock to social media to get up-to-date information and disseminate information. As

Jorge Barata observed and twittered, only a few local broadcasters were relaying information: "Demonstrations in Maputo. Radio Mozambique is just playing music, TV airing a math class. News is just on RTP Africa and STV." In Malawi, the only state broadcasting television, Malawi Broadcasting Corporation was barred from covering the demonstrations. As one Malawian activist pointed out: "As you may be aware prior to the 20th July demonstrations, the mainstream media was banned by the Malawi Communication Regulatory Authority (MACRA) from covering the demonstrations; this meant that demonstrators had to resort to alternative media to air out their grievances". Besides simply cutting and pasting social media strategies used in North Africa, activists in Swaziland resorted to these platforms because most of the organisers are banned from living and operating from their country. In the case of Malawi and Zimbabwe and authoritarian media policy regimes and state media blackout on activists played an important role in forcing organisers of the recent protests to work with 'diaspora media'. 'Diasporic media', which refers to the 'mediated public spheres of the diaspora' consisting of radio stations based outside the borders of these countries, online news sites, and activist websites which carry news and advocacy material' (Kupe 2005) played an important role in mobilizing public opinion before, during and after the demonstrations. For instance, clandestine radio stations in Zimbabwe such as *Radio Voice of the People*, *SW Radio Africa* and *Studio 7* provided news and information that the state-controlled media is deemed to suppress; they provided a platform for Zimbabwean activists to debate and discuss the crisis and what needs to be done and to mobilize for democracy. Radio messages, in addition to breaking the barrier of illiteracy through the use of local languages in their simplest forms, also reach different people without discrimination, and the receivers or listeners require less intellectual exertion to understand the message. In Malawi, the role played by diasporic journalism especially *NyasaTimes.com* and the *Face of Malawi* was immense as captured by the following interview extract: "Just before and during the actual demonstrations of July 20, 2011, online newspapers such as *Nyasa Times.com* and *Face of Malawi* were abuzz with news about the impending demonstration. Most of their underground reporters who have sources in high government offices reported and uploaded content in real time. Activists in Swaziland also relied on foreign broadcasting stations such as *SABC* and *DSTV* and independent newspaper *The Times of Swaziland* to mobilize for the April 12, 2011 demonstrations because the state media were gagged from reporting on the event. In Mozambique, a free community newspaper, *@Verdade*, filled the information vacuum by distributing its copies in high-density suburbs in Maputo.

It seems that activists in Southern Africa borrowed mobilisation strategies from a number of countries that have creatively appropriated new media technologies. They used both new media technologies and mainstream media throughout the protest cycles. Borrowed electronic repertoires of collective action were localised to speak to local conditions, for instance, organisers in Maputo seem to have been inspired by the 'power of the mobile many' (Rheingold 2003) which toppled Joseph Estrada in the Philippines. Like in the Philippines, most Mozambicans residing in Maputo received forwarded text messages a day before the demonstrations. This contrasts significantly with what happened in Zimbabwe, South Africa, Malawi, and Swaziland. In the context of Zimbabwe, where spontaneous mass rallies are outlawed through the Public Order and Security Act (POSA), Facebook, Whatsapp, and SMS messages have become spaces for everyday protest, which is articulated through jokes, cartoons, spoofs, and rumours. The use of popular culture is meant to divert attention from state surveillance. This in part confirms Moyo (2009) assertion that 'the SMS remains a powerful tool for mobilizing citizens into action'. It is clear from the foregoing that the similarities and differences in social media take up by Southern African activists adopted a pragmatic approach to the media ecosystem—'you go where the rest of the people go and where it is possible to get your message across'. Other factors at play, which account for the differences in social media take up, relate to the material conditions in which the activists operate and the dynamics of the wider body politic.

17.4.3 The 'Demonstration Effect' of the North African Revolutions on Southern African Protests

The 'demonstration effect' of the North African revolutions has inspired similar uprisings such as the Occupy Movement in the United States of America, London riots, and Occupy Nigeria. The Occupy Movement later spread offline to hundreds of locations around the globe. Of particular importance about these protests has been the usage of social media to link potential supporters and distribute information. While it is tempting to characterize the Southern African protests as 'off shoots' from the Arab Spring, it is crucial to note that "contagion on its own does not explain how protests and demonstrations are effectuated in different social contexts" (Fuchs 2012). The argument here is that the factors that can influence the emergence and development of protests are far more complex than merely labelling them as 'mimicry'. Protest is a complex societal phenomenon, whose emergence and outcome cannot be predicted based on a theoretical model. So, whether protest emerges or not is shaped by multiple factors that are so complex that it cannot be calculated or forecast if protest will emerge as result of a certain crisis or not. Once protests have emerged, media, politics, and culture continue to have permanent contradictory influences on them and it is undetermined if these factors have rather neutral, amplifying or dampening effects on protest As Fuchs (2012) aptly avers, "The emergence of a social movement presupposes societal problems as a material base. Protest is a negation of existing structures that result in frictions and problems and a political struggle that aims at the transformation of certain aspects of society or of society as a whole. Neither the aggravation of problems nor the structural opening of new political opportunities or the increase of resources for protest movements results automatically in protest". His point is that protest appears only "if societal problems are perceived as problems and if this perception guides practices" (Fuchs 2012). In short, political consciousness is a necessary ingredient of any protest action.

In-depth interviews with 40 activists in the five countries under study revealed that the 'demonstration effect' of the North African revolutions only inspired protesters in Malawi (20 July 2011), Swaziland (12 April 2011), and South Africa (October 2011). As for activists in Zimbabwe and Mozambique (September 2010), endogenous factors served as drivers of mass demonstrations. This is not to say demonstrations that occurred in Malawi, Swaziland, and South Africa were not also fuelled by endogenous factors. The point is that both exogenous and endogenous factors coalesced together creating a cocktail of societal problems, which served as a spark plug. Besides learning about the creative appropriation of social media, South African activists were inspired to unite, rise up, and demand accountability from the rulers. Activists especially in Malawi and Swaziland were able to exorcise the ghost of fear, which had militated against the organization of successful protest actions. Whereas in Zimbabwe, protesters were calling for the ouster of President Robert Mugabe and better service delivery, in South Africa, the organizers of Occupy Grahamstown demanded better services and higher levels of political accountability. Pro-democracy demonstrations in Swaziland in April 2011 were called over the lack of freedoms and the increasing dire economic crisis in the country. In Mozambique, the demonstrations which took place in over-crowded suburbs in Maputo were largely fuelled by the skyrocketing prices of fuel and food.

The 'demonstration effect' of the North African revolts on the organization of the 'Occupy Grahamstown' is captured in the following extract gleaned from the press statement posted on Abahlali base Mjondolo's website: "We have been inspired by this global rebellion because the comrades in Tahrir Square showed the world the strength of a united and determined people. We have been inspired by this rebellion because it has clearly told the bankers that their time of ruling the world is over. We have been inspired by this rebellion because it has clearly told the politicians that from Cairo to New York people are determined to rule themselves and to build their own power from the ground up. We will occupy Grahamstown in the name of freedom. We insist that all people have the right to organise themselves according to their own free choices. We denounce the ANC for the murder of Andries Tatane and all the others". One of the organisers of the Occupy Grahamstown acknowledged drawing a lot of inspiration from the North African revolutions and similar uprisings throughout the globe: "Revolutions in North Africa have set the wheel in motion. We are seeing people who have liberated themselves from fear—attained mental and psychological liberation. We have seen this in Tahrir Square, once people have liberated from the concept of fear, no matter how many surveillance tools you can install, it is clear that people will emerge as victors. You can pass as many bills as you want".

One of the organisers of the 20 July 2011 demonstrations in Malawi lucidly explained the 'demonstration effect' of the North African revolutions on their protest action: "There are commonalities in the sense that, in the Arab region and Malawi, citizens are trying to consolidate democracy in their countries. Democratic deepening served as an impetus for us to protest against the government of Bingu wa Mutharika. We were demanding accountability just like the people of Tunisia and Egypt. In fact, when people are fed up with dictatorship, then fear becomes a secondary issue. In the end, the government was forced to open lines of engagement with civil society organisations under the UN facilitation. Although the usage of social media was minimal as compared to North African revolts, a mix of media technologies was used to recruit protesters across the country's three regions" (Billy Mayaya, personal interview, 17 January, 2012). Another activist in Malawi added: "People in Malawi have come to realize that there are other alternatives and effective ways of fighting repressive government. From the comments that one reads on peoples statuses, especially when the trial of Hosni Mubarak is broadcast, it is clear that people believe what happened in Egypt can as well happen in Malawi. Malawians have come to understand there is power in social mobilization and that it doesn't always take a gun, tanks, and armed personnel to bring down a government". In the case of Swaziland, activists were also inspired by the successful use of social media in Tunisia and Egypt: "Social media usage by fellow comrades in North Africa has inspired us to mobilise and demand democratic governance in Swaziland. Yes, Social Media has and continues to force fence sitter into the revolutionary dance floor. It is therefore important for all pro democracy forces and particularly the global digital citizens of Swazi origin to join forces through cyberspace to promote democracy particularly freedom of association and information" (Lucky Lukhele). Even the protest call posted on 'The April 12 Swazi Uprising' Facebook page underscored the role played by North African revolutions: "Inspired by the North African uprisings and the fact that the Swazi economy is now on its knees , the Swazi people will on the 12th of April fill the streets of the two cities in demonstration and they will not leave until the King of Swaziland steps down and hands power to a transition government that will then prepare for the country's first free and fair elections under a multi-party government since 1973".

17.5 Conclusion

This chapter has demonstrated that Southern African netizens, far from being mired in 'backwardness' or passively awaiting external salvation, in regard to attempts to use social media, are creatively moulding these tools to suit their specific needs and devising ingenious technical solutions to overcome the idiosyncrasies of their situations. Despite structural limitations such as poor telecommunication infrastructure, high Internet charges, and underdeveloped mobile telephony services in Southern Africa, the main argument of this paper is that activists and ordinary citizens in Southern Africa creatively appropriated social media platforms to disseminate information, pass on solidarity messages, and exchange mobilisation tactics across space and time. It has shown that the use of social media as new protest drums in Southern Africa is far more complex. This is because social media operates within an already existing multi-layered communication ecology made up of other socially embedded media technologies. Therefore, instead of falling into the trap of the dominant 'social media sublime' and 'techno-dystopian' viewpoints, it is important to acknowledge the creativity of situated political activists who made use of technological tools at their disposal to advance their political goals within the constraints of the wider social context. It has argued that in media-poor societies, traditional repertoires of collection action such as rumour, world of mouth, community meetings, rallies, flyers, and brochures remain indispensable tools of mass mobilization. Instead of supplanting existing repertoires of collective action, social media are implicated as 'an amplifier' rather than 'magic bullets' of protest action. It is clear from the foregoing that political activists no longer rely on town halls and marketplaces to mobilize people for public demonstrations.

Although activists in Southern Africa exhibit similarities in their social media take up with those in North Africa, there are also marked differences. As pointed out, social media were used differently throughout the protest cycles. Whereas in North Africa social media were used to choreograph activists to assemble at Tahrir Square, in Southern Africa, it was instrumental as a platform of citizen journalism. In some cases, activists resorted to diasporic media, word of mouth, SMS messages, community radios, and meetings. It was a whole mix of communication technologies that made it possible for organisers of demonstrations in Southern Africa to reach out to potential demonstrators. Furthermore, instead of glorifying the 'demonstration effect' of the North African revolts, this chapter has argued that protests are manifestations of material societal problems. Thus, in the countries studied here, adverse social, economic and political conditions were central to the emergence of collective action calling for political reform and regime change. While the 'demonstration effect' of the North African revolts inspired activists in Swaziland, South Africa, and Malawi, it is clear from the foregoing that the results and organizational strategies were quite different. More research is therefore required in order to map out online activism practices by activists in Southern Africa and also to examine the link between online and offline activism in individual Southern African countries.

Acknowledgments This study was made possible by generous funding from the Open Society Initiative of Southern Africa (OSISA) and the Highway Africa Chair of Media and Information society, Rhodes University. While their support is gratefully acknowledged, the views reflected in this chapter are of those of the author and not the funders.

References

Aday, S., Farrell, H., Lynch, M., Sides, J., & Freelon, D. (2012). *New media and conflict after the Arab spring: Blogs and bullets ii*. Washington: United States Institute of Peace.

Alexander, P. (2012) A massive rebellion of the poor. Mail & Guardian, 13 April, 34.

Aouragh, M. (2012). Social media, mediation and the Arab revolutions. *Triple C, 10*(2), 518–536.

Banda, F. (2010). *Citizen journalism and democracy in Africa–an exploratory study*. Highway Africa: Grahamstown.

Booysen, S. (2009). Public participation in democratic South Africa: From popular mobilization to structured co-optation and protest. *Politeria, 28*(1), 1–27.
Cammack, D. (2011). Malawi's political settlement in crisis, 2011. Background Paper 4. London: The Africa Power and Politics Programme (APPP) and Overseas Development Institute.
Castells, M. (2012). *Networks of outrage and hope. Social movements in the Internet age*. Cambridge: Polity Press.
Daniel, J. (2011). *Countries at the crossroads 2011: Swaziland*. New York, NY: Freedom House.
Dlamini, L. (2010). *Swaziland: National overview*. Windhoek: MISA.
Duncan, J., & Glenn, I. (2010). Television policy and practice in South Africa. In D. Moyo & W. Chuma (Eds.), *Media policy in a changing Southern Africa: Critical reflections on media reforms in the global age* (pp. 21–40). Pretoria: Unisa Press.
Foth, M., & Hearn, G. (2007). Networked individualism of urban residents: discovering the communicative ecology in inner-city apartment buildings. *Information, Communication & Society, 10*(5), 749–772.
Fraser, N. (1992). Rethinking the public sphere: A contribution to the critique of actually existing democracy. In C. Calhoun (Ed.), *Habermas and the public sphere* (pp. 109–142). Cambridge, MA: MIT Press.
Freedom House. (2011). *The authoritarian challenge to democracy: Selected data from FreedomHouse's annual survey of political rights and civil liberties*. New York, NY: Freedom House.
Fuchs, C. (2012). Some reflections on Manuel Castells' book 'networks of outrage and hope. Social movements in the internet age'. *Triple C, 10*(2), 775–797.
Gerbaudo, P. (2012). *Tweets and the streets: Social media and contemporary activism*. London: Pluto Press.
Gladwell, M. (2010, October 4). Small change: Why the revolution will not be tweeted. The New Yorker. Downloaded from http://www.newyorker.com/reporting/2010/10/04/101004fa_fact_gladwell.Retrieved on 23 November 2012.
Howard, P. N. (2011). *The digital origins of dictatorship and democracy: Information technology and political Islam*. Oxford: Oxford University Press.
Howard, P. N., & Parks, M. R. (2012). Social media and political change: Capacity, constraint, and consequence. *Journal of Communication, 62*(2), 359–62.
Ibelema, M. (2008). *The African press, civic cynicism, and democracy*. New York, NY: Palgrave McMillan.
Jacobs, S., and Duarte, D. (2010). Protest in Mozambique: The power of SMS. Afronline. Retrieved from http://www.afronline.org/?p=8680
Kupe, T. (2005). Diasporic Journalism. *Rhodes Journalism Review, 25*, 14–26.
Lloyd, R. (2011). *Countries at the crossroads 2011: Mozambique*. New York, NY: Freedom House.
Makumbe, J. M. (2009). *Zimbabwe survival of a nation*. Addis Ababa: Ossrea Publications.
Mare, A. (2009). Facebooking the Zimbabwean crisis: Reclaiming or reinventing the public sphere: The case of Zimbabweans living in the Diaspora. A paper presented at the SACOMM Conference. Communication and Media: Past, Present and Future. 26–29 September, North West University, Potchefstroom.
Morozov, E. (2011). *The net delusion: The dark side of internet freedom*. New York: Public Affairs.
Moyo, D. (2009). Citizen journalism and the parallel market of information in Zimbabwe's 2008 election. *Journalism Studies, 10*(4), 551–567.
Ndlela, M. N. (2009). Alternative media and the political public sphere in Zimbabwe. In K. Howley (Ed.), *Understanding community media*. London: Sage Publications.
Nyamnjoh, F. B. (2005). *Africa's media: Democracy and the politics of belonging*. London: Zed Books.

Rane, H., & Salem, S. (2012). Social media, social movements and the diffusion of ideas in the Arab uprisings. *Journal of International Communication, 18*(1), 97–111.
Rheingold, H. (2003). *Smart mobs: The next social revolution*. Cambridge: Basic Books.
Shirky, C. (2011). The political power of social media: Technology, the public sphere, and political change. *Foreign Affairs*. Retrieved April 15, 2011, from http://www.foreignaffairs.com/articles/67038/clay-shirky/the-political-power-of-social-media
Wasserman, H. (2011). Mobile phones, popular media, and everyday African democracy: Transmissions and transgressions. *Popular Communication, 9*, 146–158.

Chapter 18
Information? Conversation? Action?

Gabriel Tarde's Model and Online Protest in the Eyes of Jewish: Israeli Teenage Girls

David Levin and Sigal Barak-Brandes

Abstract The issue of the Facebook social network and its contribution to political and civil action has been discussed in many academic works over the last few years. We seek to contribute our share to this discussion in two ways: (a) by employing the public opinion formation model suggested by Gabriel as a tool to examine the role of the Facebook social network in widening the participation circle of social protests and (b) by giving evidence as to how Facebook functioned in the public atmosphere of protest (the summer protests in Israel 2011–2012)—among Israeli Jewish teenage girls of no political-civil action background. During those years and over long weeks, the streets of Israel were teeming with demonstrators, while mass media raised the protest issue to the top of public agenda, branding the social networks, and specially Facebook, as the ultimate platform for social change. Gabriel Tarde observed that "information", "conversation" and "opinion" were milestones, partaking in the shaping and burgeoning process of public opinion. This model allows posing three questions pertaining to the internet function: (a) is the information streamed through it conducive to political and civil activism?; (b) What is the political role of the online conversation?; (c) Does online activism prompt to action on the streets? The conversations with the teenage girls (aged 12–18) about this topic are part of a wider project that looked into the Facebook social network from different perspectives of identity politics: gender, nationality and age. Indeed, the Zionist mythology ties the inception of the Jewish state with political and civil action by young people, yet surveys performed in Israel reveal that Israeli youth is not inclined to take civil action. The prolific use of the social network by this youth, in general, and by the teenage girls interviewed, in particular, as well as the public atmosphere at the time of the study, inspired a revisit of this virtual platform; we wanted to look into its abilities to empower and change participation patterns among this sector of population, prompting it into political and civil activism.

D. Levin (✉) • S. Barak-Brandes
Academic Studies Division, Media School, The College of Management, Rishon Lezion, Israel
e-mail: ddnsle@gmail.com

B. Pătruţ and M. Pătruţ (eds.), *Social Media in Politics*, Public Administration and Information Technology 13, DOI 10.1007/978-3-319-04666-2_18,

18.1 The Case Study

The summer months of 2011 saw a surge of social protests breaking out around Israel, sparked by the cost of living and housing shortage. These events were central to the agenda of the Jewish majority in the country during those weeks. They garnered intensive, sympathetic media coverage, which highlighted the protesters' young age and attributed a major role to the Facebook social network, pronounced by the media as the driving force behind the protest (Levin 2012). It was under such circumstances that we held the conversations with the eight focus groups of teenage girls—the axis of analysis in this study.

It is for a good reason that age was highlighted as a key feature of protesters. Young people play a major role in the Zionist cosmology. The call out issued by the movement's leaders for diaspora Jews to return to the land of Israel, by the end of the nineteenth century, was linked to the creation of a new pioneer prototype, fashioned in the spirit of Zionism—a rebellious young man, despising the establishment and striving against it (Gluzman 2007). The ethos of ground-breaking, rebellious young people resonates in Israel to this day, despite statistics suggesting the opposite, especially when teenagers are concerned. Israeli surveys show that the Jewish Israeli youth, though very much familiar with current affairs around them, through intensive usage of the internet and Facebook social network, among other outlets, do not tend to engage in political civil action. A comprehensive survey performed recently has shown that 63 % of teenagers in Israel never engage in any kind of social activity.

The society where this youth is brought up is unmistakably Anglo-American by inclination. Most Jewish citizens of the state wish the Israeli culture to resemble that of the USA or England (Hass 1999). Even the role models that prompted the Israeli civil protest were derived from this cultural world.

Since early 2011, Israeli media has been busily engaged with the Arab spring. TV news stories ran on broadcast prime time, offering the media framing of "internet freedom" (Loudon and Mazumdar 2013). These stories attributed the internet the power to bestow a veritable omnipotence on whomever seeking it to distribute information, talk with other people, plan and carry out protests and change the reality they lived in. The democratic, individualistic and western nature of this protest was cultivated with the portrayal of Wael Ghonim-Egyptian Google senior staff—as its icon. The latter was happy to give interviews on Israeli TV as such, declaring his commitment to symbols of individualism, democracy and peace.

Jewish Israel, as a democratic society, is untroubled by government tyranny, yet citizens are still concerned with issues of widening social gaps due to economics, the rising cost of living and above all, the housing prices, which soared by dozens of percents over the first decade of the twenty-first century.

The influences of the Arab states' revolutions (or rather, their coverage) on the Israeli public are evident in the Cottage Boycott, which broke out in June 2011. By the mid of said month, a Facebook group was started, numbering five members, who called the public to boycott products in general, but, first and foremost, cottage cheese, so as to pressurize dairies to lower their prices. The group declared it was not "taking it to the streets", but rather constituting an online coordination of both the boycott and the offline action of every citizen standing in front of the supermarket shelves.

A chance virtual encounter of the group members with a reporter at the popular news website Ynet resulted in the massive publicity of the boycott protest, placing it high on the Israeli public's agenda. It was defined as the "Israeli Tahrir Square protests". Its results, i.e., temporary reduction in prices of cheese as well as other dairy products, a step seemingly meaningless in retrospect, were portrayed by the media as a major victory for a non-politically oriented public employing the virtual social network. This event facilitated both a climate of protest and the glorification of the internet and its uses.[1]

Roughly two weeks after the Cottage Boycott inception, the housing prices protests commenced, also known as the "Tent Protest". It was played out by a demonstrative tent-lodging in the business and luxury properties area of downtown Tel-Aviv, Israel's largest city. This was accompanied by weekly Saturday mass demonstrations, featuring leading performing artists. The media coverage reserved for the Cottage Boycott was applied for this demonstration as well: it revolved around the protest of individuals with neither organizational resources nor political orientation, who carried out successful civil-political moves, again, with the constitutive power of the Facebook social network. Attesting to it is one of the protest slogans, a line from a song by a popular Israeli musician (Shlomo Artzi), who joined the protesters' effort: "One fine morning a man gets up, feeling he is as mighty as a nation and starting to walk".

The girls we met inhabit a "climate of protest", in a western-oriented society that aggrandizes both the individual's power to change his/her world and technology's supremacy. The teenage girls' gender identity constituted a key aspect of the research project that features the following conversations. We wanted to address teenage girls that feminist literature refers to as excluded from the public sphere, lumping them into the private "bedroom culture" (Kearney 2007; McRobbie and Garber 1976). Among other things, we wanted to examine their engagement in the public sphere, which was so stormy at the time.[2] The key role of the "online discourse" during the social protest brings us to the theoretical discussion about its powers. This discussion, as aforesaid, is grounded in the teachings of Gabriel Tarde.

---

[1] Even today (when the prices of all products have risen back up and then some), Jewish and Arab Israelis alike believe in the power of the internet. Data from an Israeli Democracy Institute's survey performed in 2013 reveal that roughly 79.9% of subjects from the Israeli society at large believe that the online protest can have some effect on the government's policy, while 49.6% believe this protest to carry a significant or great weight.

[2] We can also note that among the protest's instigators, two young women were marked as leaders—Daphni Leef and Stav Shafir.

18.2 Gabrial Tarde's Model and the Internet

Gabriel Tarde, a nineteenth century nobleman, is the man behind one of the earliest models that tried to outline how individual opinion might become an influential public one. This model is based on four linearly-organized elements (each stipulated by its subsequent in line). 1. Information (mainly derived from the press). 2. Conversation—held by individuals gathering in public places. 3. Opinion formed and amplified in the shift between conversation contexts. 4. Action—a public manifestation (as in vote or petition)—this, in turn, is transformed into a recurring information that fuels the process. Here, in short, are the key arguments that this model revolves around and the discourse on them in the context of the digital age.

18.2.1 Information

As aforesaid, Tarde, similarly to thinkers of modern mass society such as John Dewey and Alexis de Tocqueville, attributed an important role to the press' distribution power, as an institution that publicly voiced the personal letter and conversation, and charged as it was with "the fusion of personal opinions into local opinions, and this into national and world opinion" (Tarde 1969 p. 318). The press' ability to pass knowledge breeds a huge power—resulting, in turn, in the fact that "One should thus not be surprised to see our contemporaries so pliant before the wind of passing opinion" (p. 318).

Tarde, whose view on the impact of technology, as suggested by this quote and by his general attitude that calls to mind technological determinism (Katz 2006), would have perceived the internet as a means that further increases the power of distributing and sharing "opinions" with people; it removes any financial obstacles in the way of producing knowledge (and by implication, power) and thus offers immeasurably lower costs (Benkler 2006). Anyone in the digital age can see "perfect copies" of the same text, talk to others in the same language (Lessig 2009) and be exposed to considerable amounts of civil-political information, even of the kind that circumvents the state censorship mechanisms. With those benefits, anyone can become a part of a radical public sphere (Dahlberg 2007).

Detractors, on the other hand, will argue that information distributed online is an unnecessary, nay, even harmful, addition to a world already saturated with data. The accessible profusion disperses the topics of discussion across the globe, scattering the options of civic engagement over many fields (Bimber 2000). Thus the internet minimizes the crowd's impact power. Furthermore, citizens ditch the scene of national-oriented civil action, complicated in itself, in favour of the international arena, where citizens' ability to effectively interfere and act is all the more complex (Fraser 2007).

All these are compounded by the increasing, empirical difficulty of taking in, processing and conceptualizing current information, as emerging from the knowledge gap theory (Tichenor et al. 1970) as well as from empiric data that demonstrate the limited capacity of media audiences to process current affairs information (Graber 2004). In addition, human nature, which has never been marked by an avid interest in politics and public action (Peters 1999), is not designed for multiple information. Even without the internet, only few can truly be referred to as "informed citizens" in the traditional sense of the word, i.e., demonstrating interest and active engagement on all levels (Schudson 1999). Therefore, online information actually compounds people's tendency to keep superficially informed on most issues, further exploring only that which is close to their hearts.

18.2.2 Conversation

A conversation between people as defined by Tarde is an event crucial to the formation of public opinion. At that moment, one's thoughts cease to be one's own, becoming public. Gabriel Tarde further clarifies that ideally, in order to have a meaningful conversation, people lay aside the social identities that cast their thought along with the feigned grounded in their social status and channel all their focus into one another's words. "Never, except in a duel, does one observe an individual with all the force of one's attention unless one is talking with him" (Tarde 1969, p. 308).

Tarde further describes conversation as being self-serving, that is, designed for the sheer pleasure thereof and with no intention of achieving premeditated influence. On this aspect, he met disagreement by his followers, such as Jürgen Habermas, who, in true Socratic traditional form, stressed the need to challenge others in order to persuade them (Habermas 1989). Yet, even the man who conceived the social sphere concept conceded that lending an ear to the words themselves and to rational arguments made by others, while being willing to change one's own opinion, were key principles in the process of forming public opinion.

The internet was indeed defined as "the new public sphere" (Dahlgren and Sparks 1997), a zone that not only accumulates information, but also allows to maintain a conversation where, similarly to the Habermassian concept as well as to Lazarsfeld and Katz' two-step flow of communication model, mass media contents are discussed and opinion is formed (Shirky 2010). Technological utopians have even argued that the online conversation has the upper hand over its offline counterpart. As unconstrained by the common presence in the same space, one can focus on the arguments, unfettered by manners and the need to accommodate social statuses. The online anonymity can result in a situation where different people feel mutually equal, which may prompt them into a joint action. In other words, the internet's nature allows to fulfill its democratic potential (Akdeniz 2002; Baek et al. 2012).

Other thinkers and researchers, on the other hand, argue that being as individuals do not share a physical space, their responsibility to pay attention to one another, as well as their ability to have faith in the steadfastness and words of whoever is in front of them, are limited (Shoham and Pinchevski 2001; Dreyfus 2009). It is agreed by all that trust among participants is key to bringing about ongoing, joint social action, online as well as offline (Harlow 2012). And, indeed, some studies show that people who spend a lot of time online, generally, as well as in contexts ideal for conversation (such as online forums), do not tend to put their trust in others (Uslaner 2004). It was recently suggested that another type of online conversation, developed largely in the age of social networks, should be examined; a context wherein the information flow rate is increased and incessant, while the overwhelming majority of communication takes place among people that know each other. It has been argued that communication in networks such as Facebook, Twitter and WhatsApp is marked by terse verbal exchanges, devoid of any substantive content (i.e., short messages, "liking" and chats), that fulfill first and foremost the phatic function of making and maintaining contacts. Some writers appreciate the democratic value of this poor conversation, which can entrench the sense of "connectedness" and community among internet users. On the other hand, it has been argued that the synoptic, non-dialogical nature of this brand of conversation breeds shallowness and superficiality, in both its contents and the social relations it constructs among the conversing parties (Miller 2008).

18.2.3 Opinion and Action

Gabriel Tarde placed the concepts of opinion and action at the bottom of his linear model. He viewed action as the public manifestation of opinion, be it in the form of a vote, comment articles, petitions or any other way of getting public opinion across to governments. We bore the Dreyfus affair in mind. Being a supporter of the French officer accused of treason, he believed that it was the very act of publishing the opinion letter "J'accuse" over the French and global press, as public expression of public opinion, that prompted the French government to re-think its actions.

Tarde followers sought to categorize the public manifestation of opinion expression. Accordingly, Lazarsfeld and Merton (1971) argued that an undesirable confusion persisted between living room conversations and taking to the streets to partake in assemblies. This confusion, they further argued, bred "narcotizing"—a false sense of political participation which is actually detrimental to the latter's purpose. The internet supposedly solves this problem. It allows introducing opinions into the public domain, including those whose holders fear the regime or social sanction (Lynch 2011). It allows both joining online activities and signing online petitions and facilitates inter-web activities—raiding and crashing websites or inundating them with protests or spam (Vegh quoted in Harlow 2012; Wheeler 2003). Nevertheless, many still argue that the internet undermines civil political action, as it does not prompt people into taking to the streets—the only place where the true power of public opinion can be realized (Ganz and Kohn 2010, quoted in Sivitanides and Shah 2011). The web might even prevent such a step. These arguments rely on the massive decrease in street demonstrator numbers as opposed to the surge in people that voice their opinions online, to say nothing of those whose political activity amounts to hitting the Facebook "Like" button.

The social networks, argues Evgeny Morozov, create a half-hearted, meaningless activism, or "slacktivism" (Morozov 2011). This sense, in turn, foils a more meaningful action, as it is enough to inspire a good feeling of involvement that entails neither time nor physical effort. In this spirit, Michah White suggested the term of "clicktivism" by arguing that online petition signing undercut the value of social movements just as McDonald's undercut that of slow-cooking (White 2011).[3]

18.3 Methodology

The analysis offered is based on comments made in eight focus groups that comprised 35 Israeli Jewish teenage girls, aged 12–18, most of which can be categorized as upper middle class. Familiarity with Facebook was a necessary condition to their participation in the interview. We used a snowball-type sampling: when a girl of the right age group was tracked, expressing willingness to partake in this study, she was asked to assemble a group of girl friends or acquaintances together, for the purpose of holding a focus group. Every interview took place in the home of one of the participants, usually the girl who had put the group together, and lasted an hour and a half on average. Every group comprised 4–5 participants. Researchers conditioned focus group participation by an informed consent form signed by the girls' parents. Participating girls were rewarded a token gift by the end of the conversation. Conversations, as aforesaid, revolved around many issues: Facebook friendships, usage levels and parents' involvement, to cite but a few. The analysis offered here has its main focus on the girls' insights into the wider circles of their social reality at the time.

18.3.1 Information

The daily routine of the teenage girls whom we met constituted a constant juggling of the time they could afford to spend on Facebook and an endless list of tasks to be performed at the site. Some of the tasks were pre-planned (writing a birthday card to a girlfriend, liking a commercial company for coupons and updating statuses, to name but a few), while others were occasional (random conversations and browsing through profiles).

---

[3] http://www.guardian.co.uk/commentisfree/2010/aug/12/clicktivism-ruining-leftist-activism.

The girls used the network while on vacation and stayed up, especially in the course of summer holidays, updating and keeping updated online throughout the mornings, after school and even during recess. Nevertheless, the massive amounts of information only kept piling up, requiring swift browsing through and selection. While online, they frequently came across political and civil information, which, as aforesaid, was very prevalent in the Israeli discourse during those months. They were also approached with offers to join activities and sign petitions. We have found that they were exposed to the abundant information about the miracle-working powers of the internet in anything to do with social initiatives (in one of the groups, one girl enthusiastically told us about the online mobilization to save the life of a tiger in a Chicago zoo), and in the same context, to the media framing of "internet freedom"—viewing the web as a revolution-constitutive element.

A. (15): The social protest started on Facebook.
AM. (15): They wouldn't have gone like, 'Let's do it with two kids' if no one had joined in on Facebook.
A. (15): The revolution in Libya and Egypt was started on Facebook as well.
G. (15): Plus, many organisations today operate on Facebook. Greenpeace, for example, operate on Facebook and so do many organisations that in this way can promote demonstrations and agree on the date, time and place, and it's not like making phone calls and worrying about it. If you're doing it on the phone, you get fewer participants than you initially wanted. On Facebook it it's much more massive.
AM. (15): It can make a difference, but only if there's a really big mass of people.

Exposure and public atmosphere inspired the girls' first interest in this kind of information. Girls from all groups reported that they had joined Facebook groups that upheld a social-economic message. These included Israeli groups such as Social equity (the housing protest group) and the Cottage Boycott; local-youth groups—petitions against McDonald's prices and the movement to reduce cinema popcorn prices and global groups, such as Anonymous and Greenpeace. In the context of protest, they also cited friendships in fan communities that petitioned to bring one artist or another to Israel, and every so often, in mock-protest groups, such as "Restore Kinder Egg to its Original Shape". The latter group introduced the sense that signing various protest petitions had become not only a popular fashion, but also a banal, derided undertaking.

When further asking about protest-related information, we found out that: (1) Girls from all groups were exposed to information distributed by protest groups with a fluttering glance, while quickly browsing through pages. It may be that this form of reading resulted in their finding it difficult to understand the background of some of the protests. (2) They preferred to keep updated and even act as part of some protest groups associated with "youth" or the "global village", as opposed to those that tackled the Israeli reality.

Browsing through webpages, as described by the girls, was more akin to TV channel zapping than to reading a book, watching a movie or having a conversation out on the street. The last three options mean choice, as engagement therewith entails time or money resources. Choosing a TV channel to watch, on the other hand, is casual, entailing neither commitment, identity-wise, nor extra fees (Meyrowitz 1985). The glance involved in watching TV is a fluttering, unfocused one, unlike the in-depth, focused gaze, typical of movie-watching, for example (Ellis 1982). In true "televisional" spirit, we found that the girls we were talking to thought nothing of skipping and "consuming" information about all manner of protests.

N. (13): I joined both the popcorn and cottage protests, plus the McDonald's boycott.
D. (13): I joined the Bruno Mars thing.
D. (13): I joined the Justin Bieber thing... (Talking on top of each other).
D. (13): I also did the Katy Perry thing. Katy Perry and Bruno Mars" (petitions to bring artists to Israel, D.L, S. B).

The swift reading and the glance fluttering over the profusion of information also bred an inability or unwillingness to explore seemingly complex details. This was one girl's impression of a protest she had taken care to be updated with and even link other people to:

A.(15): Greenpeace actually argue that Google somehow use green energy, I don't know, they don't pollute with their factories, not sure how it works, and Facebook do pollute with their factories. So Greenpeace's purpose is to make Facebook use green energy, to stop their pollution.

On another level of discussion, we argue that the bundling together of Greenpeace, Google, Facebook, Justin Bieber and Katy Perry was not accidental. The girls preferred to draw away from their surrounding "here" and "now". It was only when explicitly asked that interviewees mentioned the Israeli protests. The arguments behind this priorities list were often unambiguously provided:

A.(17): For us Facebook does not serve to express our political view and stuff, our social view, economical view and what not. Not at all. So, in a way, that's why we don't get into this or that. There's nothing in it for us and we don't care.

M. (13): I join everything that I think is right. It's like, I don't care about the cottage stuff, it's not like it's me that's paying for it.

The girls cited the functional logic as the driving force of deciding "which information to focus on" (in other words, what is it that I find important at this stage of my life). Nevertheless, reading between their lines and factoring in the great significance they attributed to how they presented themselves on the Facebook social network, a link emerges between their choice of "protests" and the wish to publicly express their affiliation to the youth community, with its mythological, "nationless" nature. This comes at the expense of "here and now"—perceived as the preserve of the adult world. A.'s citing of the adolescent "us" was, therefore, meant to signal the connection she shared with a socially-constructed concept, cultivated by the culture industry and referencing a mythological similarity between youth at all far ends of the globes; a similarity greater than the one they share with their parents (Carey 1967).

M's words compound this notion by clarifying another aspect that distinguishes adolescents from their parents, a distinction that prevents them from sympathizing with the latter—i.e., their lack of economic obligation.

The self-enforced affiliation with youth led them to focus not only on global issues, but also on protests concerning local affairs that revolve around consumerism, a trend that is age-distinctive in itself. This may serve to explain the avid interest taken by girls of all groups in a sub-protest of the greater housing protest; an endeavor perceived by adults as marginal, nay, amusing, and attracting little media coverage—the protest against popcorn prices in movie theatres' canteens:

N. (13): The popcorn thing is really annoying! Especially if I get pocket money and I have to give it all, like, from my money…

In other words, the girls gave the protest climate their own interpretation—using it to express their wish to lay down the rules of the game and navigate sites where they are not expelled for loitering (Boyd 2008); adult-free zones. Their attitude to information about protests echoed their attitude on the adult world in other contexts. Not only did they prevent unfamiliar adults from entering their online list of friends, they also tended to block their parents and adult family members from reading their Facebook pages and again, avoided any risk of being associated with "adult issues".

Analysis of the conversations with the girls shows that the link between the amount of information on the one hand and democratization on the other, as perceived by Tarde, as well as by technological utopians, does not necessarily exist. Even if a consciousness of change is indeed at play, the straddling of so many issues, across the globe, and the walls erected between age groups clearly compromise the ability of social protests to be effective. To project from Tarde's words, in a world saturated with information, public opinion is not a breeze that accumulates force, but rather a series of little wind outbursts that blow in every direction, often, as we are about to see, not in the face of social order, but rather at its tail.

18.3.2 Conversation

As mentioned before, girls not only read information, but also talked. In their wanderings around the Facebook social network they found themselves associated with two contexts of conversation with other users. The first context is multiple-participant group conversation: the Facebook group, among other things, discusses a social issue then plans actions. The other context is private conversations with friends. For us, observing how girls placed themselves in these two kinds of conversation further structures the social network's role and status as a site to establish public opinion. We found that the first kind of participation in conversation, involving mute presence or the odd contribution of a word or a Like to the online discussion, gave girls a sense of partaking in a political community.

SHI. (15): It's like I'm a part of something bigger, that I've actually done something that can contribute to the community. Yes, you feel good with yourself. It's nice. It's a good feeling.

SH. (17): Yeah, I have often been sent event information you must join. I've never really joined these events, but I've seen many people commenting, liking it, many people supporting and liking to express the other opinion, like...

The girls describe the phatic communion—viewing the "Thin relations" sense (Margalit 2002 cited in Frosh 2011) between participants as a means to define them as a "community". This concept, originating in the study of the binding role of greetings and casual conversations in tribal societies, ended up in the twenty-first century, in the study of technology audiences and their attribution to TV watching (Frosh 2011) or to minimal participation in discussions or online conversations. Indeed, reading the girls demonstrates the effectiveness of this brand of communication. Girls had a sense of belonging while half talking, half standing by, even though conversation was held by the one who was truly active. The concept of protest and protest groups, therefore, gained a palpable significance in their imagination, thanks to Facebook.

Yet, beyond this faint sense of connection, commitment and association, the girls have shown us that, in their daily routine, the social network was not a place where they held in-depth, meaningful conversations, with neither stranger nor familiar people. The choice of who to talk to, from the tens and sometimes hundreds of people whom they have confirmed as friends, was described as random and perfunctory.

Z. (18): Sometimes at one o'clock at night on Facebook, this guy is online, this girl is online, I'm online, so it's 'Hi, what's up?' And it kills another hour in a boring night.

Such conversations had a time cap to them. Just as girls demonstrated impatience towards information that required time to internalise, so were they petulant to individuals who elaborated their conversations, an attitude summed up by the expression, "digger" (in Hebrew, short for "brain digger", that is, being verbose in a way that appears to be an incessant repetition of the same sentence).

A. (15): ...someone you don't really like or talk to and don't really feel like answering and they start telling you the sagas of their lives-that's called digging.

The feeble nature of conversation probably also had to do with the amount of work the girls felt required to "cover" online, coupled with using norms. As mentioned before, girls knew they must keep browsing fast and meet all their "obligations", not to mention the constant flow of news. Swiftly leaving a conversation with the pretext of "someone's calling me", at times even ignoring present parties, was perceived by them as a moral, nay, polite step, in the name of equal distribution of time and attention.

Moreover, due to the long hours they spent online, they found no fault in the fact that using Facebook coincided with other activities that demanded at least some of their attention. Their PC screens, with no exception, had a news website or a YouTube window open simultaneously, with a TV set on at the background and their homework spread on the table.

G. (14): When you're on Facebook, having a heart-to-heart with someone, you can do many other things while having this 'heart-to-heart'.

SH. (14): That's right; I listen to music.

HG. (14): While at it.

Furthermore, the girls experienced no pangs of conscience because they assumed their partners in conversation to know they were not free to "really" talk.

On another aspect, the conversation described by the girls brings to mind the proceedings of the ideal conversation as described by Gabriel Tarde: commitment-free and carried out aimlessly. On the other hand, in reference to another aspect suggested by Tarde, that is, the similarity between conversation and duel as two situations where people concentrate on each other heart and soul, the gap between the two "conversations" seems huge.

No wonder, therefore, that in all age groups girls declared that, when it came to crucial conversations, they turned to the phone or arranged to meet face-to-face. Most of them mentioned this was their custom in personal conversations, while a minority declared it was their habit for mundane conversations as well.

Z. (18): If it's an important discussion I want, I don't do it on Facebook... I want to see, I want to deal with the person I'm discussing a subject with... which is like really important, a cornerstone of Israeli society. I want to deal with the person I'm talking to... to ask a question and then another and another one, and then maybe they can get your point.

As an alternative, the same interviewee addresses another online zone where discussions take place and which, in her opinion, are more focused and require further commitment:

> "...I wanted to make a film about religious homosexuals, so I logged on to their forum to do research. Over there, some really important things are discussed, but I don't think there's a Facebook forum. Is there a Facebook forum?"

The flimsiness of conversation as a convention is therefore coupled with the inundation of information and both serve as good arguments for those who do not believe the internet to be a start-up site for civil political activity. We shall now turn to examine the significance of using the social network for the expected outcome of this move-opinion.

18.3.3 Opinion and Action

According to Tarde's linear model, the success of the public opinion move is measured by how much the action forces regimes to change their ways. Tarde and his followers alike defined this stage in terms of public voicing of opinions. The internet no doubt excels in it. Nevertheless, and as they noted, some questions remain unanswered: How many mental resources does one invest in distributing one's opinion? How much is one prepared to invest in distributing it offline? Does the internet in itself possess the constitutive power to spur a public into action? As it appears at this point, from the girls' point of view, online activity produces not only a sense of conversation, but also a sense of action, yet it seems the power that generates devotion to protest activities is human, rather than technological.

When observing the three kinds of actions allowed by the internet, that is, keeping updated and joining offline activities, signing a petition and partaking in digital warfare, there is no doubt that the girls preferred the latter two. They joined protest groups and were happy to sign petitions, whatever their causes. Some of them viewed it as an expression of political efficacy, the ability to make a difference.

Y. (15): Because it's got many people. When I publish something in this group, many people see it and so many people join in and it can, like, really make some kind of difference.

Some girls experienced this feeling through their membership in fan communities working to bring one artist or another to Israel. Some groups mentioned joining the global campaign of the Twilight saga fan community against the series' producers.

A. (14): We went on and on, like every day, on their wall. They just blocked us three times a day. They like blocked us, but after a couple of hours the blocking is cancelled, so you resume working their ears off. We've already had emails sent to our Facebook account, like, "Stop it!" and we like didn't stop and went...

This interviewee then exposed the powers behind the interest and investment. The consumerist action is associated not only with the sense of phatic affiliation we have discussed above, with the remote the global youth community, but also with a real sense of connection that takes place offline as well.

"It's just that there are groups... They just say, 'Start working this magazine's ear off, start writing and asking them to do what we want'. We uploaded pictures and had all these petitions and groups going and friendships were starting to form for real! It's like, I even met girls I see like quite often. We have fan get-togethers, and every time, we get kicked out from another place, because we make such a racket."Nevertheless, this brand of activism loses much of its lustre when the driving forces behind it are revealed. We found that the adolescent need to experience togetherness and a sense of efficacy in regards to youth culture products was often exploited by elements from the culture industry. Such corporations inundated the girls we have talked to, as well as (so we assume) good many others, with information about ways to supposedly protest against them, so as to make corporations change, demanding that they offered an entertaining media product suitable for the girls. In the same spirit, the managers of Taylor Swift called her Israeli fans to act in order to bring her for a concert in Israel:

SH. (14): And so far, if I'm not mistaken, thousand plus people have signed and it's got to make it to something like 3,000.

These entrepreneurs joined tens of other commercial elements that exploited the "protest spirit" to prompt the girls into "pseudo-activism", thus promoting commercial campaigns. Accordingly, one girl told of a furniture manufacturer that encouraged internet users to "Like" its ads, promising the girls a contribution to a planned trip to the Nazi concentration camps in Poland.[4] When asked about the

[4] The trip to Poland is a familiar practice of Israeli youth. High school teenage girls and boys are invited to join the groups that visit Nazi extermination camps in Poland so as to grasp the horrors of the European Jews holocaust.

prospect of changing reality through the internet, one girl referred us to the website of a commercial bank that encouraged users "to change reality" and sway its marketing directions with their input.

The girls' enthusiasm at the prospect of an offline meeting led us to conclude that the key to activism indeed lay outside the bedroom, away from the keyboard. We went on to sieve through the girls' words for clues to show that deep, ongoing involvement in public-social activity is associated with connections made offline with esteemed people and institutes. Accordingly, in one group, a 15-year-old reminisced about her first meeting with representatives of "Anonymous for Animal Rights", which took place within her school and ended with a link to the organization's Facebook page. Having logged in, she came across the subscription option, received a "friend" status in the group and joined the mailing list of event invitations. "Whenever something new happens, they alert you on Facebook that something's up. Then you can reply or sign, you can do many things."

Even in the context of the housing protest, girls attributed power to the organizational capacity of a familiar, official body, which they found legitimate. Many of the girls were members of youth movements and, indeed, the siding of such bodies with protesters (an action somewhat kept in the dark by the media, as compared to the great weight placed on the "internet freedom") prompted the girls to take to the streets. This is how one of them described the online and offline combination offered by her movement:

Y.: They informed on Facebook from two places. Via the movement itself and also, like, there's the Bnei Moshavim movement,[5] where they publish stuff, and they also opened a group of all the kids going with the Bnei Moshavim to the bigger demonstration near the Azrieli mall (Tel Aviv), and like, according to this, they went to organise buses on Facebook.

The girls' serious approach to social activities linked to by their school or youth movement, which have lent these undertakings prestige and legitimization, is all the more evident when compared with other girls' dismissive attitude to online message distribution by unfamiliar elements that ask them to act. Such was the approach taken by the girls (all of whom members of the housing protest Facebook group) to an unknown source's call to lock out high schools in sympathy with the housing protest causes:

A.(15): I despise the 4/9 move to study in a protest tent.
David: OK. Is there such a group? What is it about?
A (15): Just a bunch of morons writing. They like found this excuse not to go to school.

The anchor of interpersonal communication proved therefore to have a significant weight. It had the power to reinforce the act of joining one of the hundreds of "protests" emerging online, converting it to an actual offline action. Unexpectedly, alongside the school and youth movements, parents too materialized as an

[5] Youth movement designed for residents of Jewish agricultural settlements in Israel.

initiating, prompting factor. This was the case, for example, for the 13-year-old that recalled how she and her mother "made a sign together and screamed" during a protest against the rising public broadcasting tax. Others consciously joined the Cottage Boycott

Following Parents' Explanation

A. (15): We boycott Tnuva (the big milk and dairy corporation).[6] My mom doesn't buy Tnuva stuff.

P. (13): OK, I joined it because my mom explained it to me and eight NIS for cottage is way too much.

D. (13): I joined in too.

The meaningful action, therefore, is added to the meaningful conversation. Even girls that spend the majority of their time online undergo deep experiences in what little time they have left to live offline.

18.4 Summary

As you might recall, the purpose of this work was to examine the extent to which the intensive use of the Facebook social network, especially in a particular public atmosphere, prompted girls that were not necessarily active to participate in the social protests of 2011. We did so in light of Gabriel Tarde's linear model, wondering whether the network had informed girls about the protest and made them participate in conversations about it, as well as in online or offline activities endorsing it.

Figuratively speaking, it can be said that girls sensed the protest spirit and conceived the network as its champion, yet the same spirit blew their thoughts elsewhere.

The public climate led girls to take interest in the "protest", yet the urge to encompass the massive online abundance, as well as manipulative actions by elements with economic interests combined with predominant images adopted by the girls—appropriate interests for adolescents—prevented them from concentrating on "local" issues. This abundance also compromised their ability to look deeply into certain issues.

The phatic nature of their online behavior was enough to make them feel part of a protesting community, yet, at the same time, prevented them from developing their own discussions with their friends. We found that time pressure, a typical feature of Facebook usage, its no-strings-attached context and the norms that forbid the act of so-called "digging" sabotage any chance of developing a conversation.

The many options of acting without getting out of the house tipped the scales in favor of virtual protest activities. These actions, convinced though the girls were in

[6] http://en.wikipedia.org/wiki/Tnuva

their power, do not usually signal willingness to invest time resources and mental strength in political social activity.

Nevertheless and maybe so as not to indulge nostalgic musings, two bright sides can be found when exploring the impact of the "protest spirit" and the internet function on the political conduct of girls we talked to, along with many others:

The importance of interpersonal communication—we found that the teenage girls, despite their many online hours, were interested in conversation and social action when taking place, whether in their peer company or sponsored by youth movement leaders or parents (as long as they did not peep in their Facebook profiles). We have seen that even school can encourage political social activity, assisted by the internet. The combination of relationships based on interpersonal communication on the one hand and online information on the other seems to be a good one.

Training ground—in recent years, several researchers have pointed to the political potential of processes typical of fan communities. It was argued that processes such as starting communities, forming inter-community coalitions and organising protests in the service of an artist or a show constituted a "training ground" for young people, in preparation for future political participation (Van Zoonen 2004; Kraidy 2007). We can therefore wonder whether the activity of fan communities joined by the girls functions in this spirit. Naturally, the synchronic nature of our study cannot provide us with information about the future, yet there is no doubt that it was also activities such as this that fuelled the protest spirit and the faith in the power to change reality among these teenage girls, during the summer of 2011. Such questions merit further exploration in future studies.

Acknowledgments The authors wish to express their gratitude to the Research Authority of the College of Management Academic Studies, Rishon LeZion, Israel, for their financial support of this research.

References

Akdeniz, Y. (2002). Anonymity, democracy, and cyberspace. *Social Research, 69*(1), 223–237.

Baek, Y. M., Wojcieszak, M., & Carpini, M. X. D. (2012). Online versus face-to-face deliberation. Who? Why? What? With what effects? *New Media & Society, 14*(3), 363–383.

Benkler, Y. (2006). *The wealth of networks: How social production transforms markets and freedom (1st ed.)*. New Haven, CO: Yale University Press.

Bimber, B. (2000). The study of information technology and civic engagement. *Political Communication, 17*(4), 329–333.

Boyd, D. (2008). Can social network sites enable political action? *International Journal of Media & Cultural Politics, 4*(2), 241–244.

Carey, J. (1967). Harold Adams Innis and Marshall McLuhan. *The Antioch Review, 27*(1), 5–39.

Dahlberg, L. (2007). The Internet, deliberative democracy, and power: Radicalizing the public sphere. *International Journal of Media & Cultural Politics, 3*(1), 47–64.

Dahlgren, P., & Sparks, C. (Eds.). (1997). *Communication and citizenship: Journalism and the public sphere in the new media age*. London: Routledge.

Dreyfus, H. L. (2009). *On the internet*. New York, NY: Taylor & Francis.

Ellis, J. (1982). *Visible fictions: Cinema, television, video*. London: Routledge & Kegan Paul.

Fraser, N. (2007). Transnationalizing the public sphere. *Theory, Culture & Society, 24*, 7–3.

Frosh, P. (2011). Phatic morality: Television and proper distance. *International Journal of Cultural Studies, 14*(4), 383–400.

Gluzman, M. (2007). *The Zionist body: Nationality gender and sexuality in modern Hebrew literature*. Hakibbutz Hameuchad (Hebrew): Tel Aviv.
Graber, D. (2004). Mediated politics and citizenship in the twenty-first century. *Annual Review of Psychology, 55*, 547–571.
Habermas, J. (1989). *The Structural transformation of the public sphere: An inquiry into a category of bourgeois society*. Cambridge, MA: MIT Press.
Harlow, S. (2012). Social media and social movements: Facebook and an online Guatemalan justice movement that moved offline. *New Media & Society, 14*(2), 225–243.
Hass, H. (1999). Leisure culture in Israel- 1998. *Phanim, 10*, 107–139. Hebrew.
Katz, E. (2006). Rediscovering Gabriel Tarde. *Political Communication, 23*(3), 263–270.
Kearney, M. C. (2007). Productive spaces: Girls' bedrooms as sites of cultural production. *Journal of Children and Media, 1*(2), 126–141.
Kraidy, M. M. (2007). Saudi Arabia, Lebanon and the changing Arab information order. *International Journal of Communication, 1*(1), 139–156.
Lazarsfeld, P. F., & Merton, R. K. (1971). Mass communication, popular taste and organized social action. Media studies: A reader, 2nd edn. (Edinburgh: Edinburgh University Press, 1999), pp. 18–30.
Lessig, L. (2009). Against transparency. *The New Republic*. October, http://www.tnr.com/article/books-and
Levin, D. (2012). The cottage ban: The conjunction between news construction and facebook's social protest. *JOMEC, 1*, 2–15.
Loudon, M., & Mazumdar, B. T. (2013). Media representations of technology in Egypt's 2011 pro-democracy protests. *Ecquid Novi: African Journalism Studies, 34*(1), 50–67.
Lynch, M. (2011). After Egypt: The limits and promise of online challenges to the authoritarian Arab state. *Perspectives on Politics, 9*(02), 301–310.
McRobbie, A., & Garber, J. (1976). Girls and subculture. In S. Hall & T. Jefferson (Eds.), *Resistance through rituals* (pp. 209–221). London: Hutchinson.
Meyrowitz, J. (1985). *No sense of place*. New York, NY: Oxford University Press.
Miller, V. (2008). New media, networking and phatic culture. *Convergence: The International Journal of Research into New Media Technologies, 14*(4), 387.
Morozov, E. (2011). *The net delusion: The dark side of internet freedom*. Philadelphia: Perseus.
Peters, J. D. (1999). Public journalism and democratic theory: Four challenges. In T. L. Glasser (Ed.), *The idea of public journalism* (pp. 99–117). New York, NY: The Guilford Press.
Schudson, M. (1999). What public journalism knows about journalism but doesn't know about "public". In T. L. Glasser (Ed.), *The idea of public journalism* (pp. 118–133). New York, NY: The Guilford Press.
Shirky, C. (2010). "The political power of social media." Foreign Affairs. N.p., 20 Dec. 2010. Web. 31 May 2013. http://www.foreignaffairs.com/articles/67038/clay-shirky/the-political-power-of-social-media
Shoham, S. G., & Pinchevski, A. (2001). The medium is the barrier. *Anthropological Linguistics, 27*, 149–167.
Sivitanides, M., & Shah, V. (2011). The era of digital activism. http://proc.conisar.org/2011/pdf/1842.pdf
Tarde, G. (1969). Opinion and conversation. In T. N. Clark (Ed.), *On communication and social influence: Selected papers* (pp. 297–319). Chicago: University of Chicago Press.
Tichenor, P. A., Donohue, G. A., & Olien, C. N. (1970). Mass media flow and differential growth in knowledge. *Public Opinion Quarterly, 34*(2), 159–170.
Uslaner, E. M. (2004). Trust, civic engagement, and the Internet. *Political Communication, 21*(2), 223–242.
Van Zoonen, L. (2004). Imagining the fan democracy. *European Journal of Communication, 19* (1), 39–52.
Wheeler, D. (2003). The internet and youth subculture in Kuwait. *Journal of Computer-Mediated Communication 8*(2). (http://jcmc.indiana.edu/vol8/)

Chapter 19
The Role of Social Media in Mobilizing People for Riots and Revolutions

Four Case Studies in India

Swati Bute

Abstract India, the second most populous country in the world, is also a country with a very high percentage of youngsters. Social media are popular amongst Indian youngsters. People of the 15–35 age groups use them in a higher percentage especially in urban areas. Social network websites, YouTube, Facebook and Twitter are the most popular, but some young people also write on blogs. Initially used for making online friendship, developing relationships, business contacts and interacting with global masses, social media have recently been used for mobilizing youngsters for revolutions and riots. India has witnessed different agitations and road protests in cities like New Delhi, Mumbai and Bangalore in 2011–2012 and 2013. During the Anti Corruption Movement and Mass Agitation against Delhi Gang rape, social media were fully exploited to mobilize people, to gather them and to raise voice against injustice and the faulty system responsible for high-level corruption and poor law and order situation in cities. But, in some other cases, they also served for spreading rumors, misinformation and creating panic and chaos amongst common people, specifically during the Ethnic Conflicts in Assam in 2012 and, recently, in 2013, during the communal riots in Muzaffarnagar. Domestic and cross-border anti-elements, non-state actors misused social media to disturb law and order by spreading rumors and uploading false content and images on the internet. In this chapter, the author has tried to understand the nature of these four events, the role of social media in positive and negative message creation and circulation, the patterns of information flow on social media and the impact of social media messages.

S. Bute (✉)
AMITY School of Communication, AMITY University, Noida, India
e-mail: swatibute11@gmail.com

B. Pătruţ and M. Pătruţ (eds.), *Social Media in Politics*, Public Administration and Information Technology 13, DOI 10.1007/978-3-319-04666-2_19,

19.1 Introduction

Social media is the medium of new age. It is bringing changes at individual level and in social life. New media refers to on-demand access of content anytime, anywhere"[1]. If we can compare globally, the overall Internet penetration in India is lower than in the rest of the world. India has the third largest Internet population in the world after China and the US"[2]. However, in terms of national coverage, "only 150 million Indians have Internet access in a country of 1.2 billion. That is significantly lower than other emerging markets"[3]. People living in far-flung villages and towns are still not connected to the Internet. In India, people belonging to the age group of 15–35 years, who live in metropolitan cities and have proper Internet access use social media. According to a recent report by the Internet and Mobile Association of India, Facebook is the leading website, accessed by 97 % of all social media users in India"[4]. With so much of growth still left to come, the influence of social media is only bound to grow"[5].

Social media connects people and keeps them updated "after Arab Spring citizens of different nations are more empowered than ever before"[6]. Like other countries, India has also have witnessed a series of protests and movements. Social media played a central role in mobilizing people and coordinating protests and in some instances also played a negative role in spreading rumors and creating chaos and panic amongst the social media users and common people. "As compared to other aspects of social movements, New Media is becoming a more significant and instant way of disseminating information globally, the virtual world is gradually finding its social relevance and people not withstanding their geographical location are able to view/review/analyze events across the world"[7]. Social media is an open platform; people use it for both right and wrong purposes. In the UK riots in August

[1] Anna Hazare's "India against Corruption: Role of New Media in Mass Movement," http://sciencesblog.org/management/anna-hazares-india-against-corruption-role-of-new-media-in-mass-movement/, Accessed on May 8, 2013.

[2] 2013 India Internet outlook, http://techcircle.vccircle.com/2013/02/01/2013-india-internet-outlook/, Sandeep Aggarwal, February 1, 2013, Accessed on May 14, 2013.

[3] Why only 3 % of India has home internet access, http://qz.com/66146/why-only-3-of-india-has-home-internet-access/, Tim Fernholz, March 22, 2013, Accessed on May 14, 2013.

[4] Study says social media revolution set to get bigger, http://www.thehindu.com/sci-tech/technology/internet/study-says-social-media-revolution-set-to-get-bigger/article4516369.ece, Ramya Kannan, March19, 2013, Accessed on May 8, 2013.

[5] Welcome to the social media revolution, http://www.bbc.co.uk/news/business-18013662, May 10, 2012, Accessed on May 8, 2013.

[6] Delhi gang rape: Social media exposes governments manhandling of truth, http://janamejayan.wordpress.com/2012/12/30/delhi-gang-rape-social-media-exposes-govts-manhandling-of-truth/, posted on December 30, 2012, Accessed on May 15, 2013.

[7] Anna Hazare's "India against Corruption: Role of New Media in Mass Movement," http://sciencesblog.org/management/anna-hazares-india-against-corruption-role-of-new-media-in-mass-movement/, Accessed on May 8, 2013.

2011, social media was wrongly used: "Social media, particularly BlackBerry messenger, helped to ignite and organize rioters in Britain, but experts say such tools are now a fact of life and simply alternative forms of communication—for good or evil"[8]. Year 2011 was rightfully called a year of social activism in India. "With Anna Hazare stealing much of the media limelight, social activists mounted a determined offensive over issues ranging from corruption and black money to tribal rights. Anna Hazare fasted in Delhi thrice during the year forcing the government to take steps to unveil an independent body with powers to investigate and prosecute corrupt officials"[9], and then the world had seen public outrage on Delhi Gang rape in 2012, which was again mobilized by social media. In the series of incidents, different actors again used social media during ethnic conflicts in Assam and communal riots in Muzaffarpur city of Uttarpradesh but for different purposes. Primary investigations say that domestic and cross-border antinational elements were involved in spreading the doctored and threatening messages during the ethnic conflict in Assam, while the regional political rivalry played important role in the Muzzafarnagar incident in which social media was used for spreading rumors and tension.

This chapter discusses four different situations in which social media were actively used in India to mobilize and influence people for riots, conflicts, revolutions and movements.

19.2 Case One: Social Media and the Anti Corruption Movement

In 2010, Anna Hazare, a social activist started a movement against corruption following major corruption scandals in the Commonwealth game and telecommunication industry in India. Initially, people, media and politicians did not take it seriously. As a first action in this movement, the Indian government drafted a version of anti graft ombudsman known as the *Lokpal* bill. "Many citizens and social activists considered the proposed measure weak, as it did not cover the prime minister, members of Parliament, and cabinet ministers under the law. Dissatisfaction gave rise to a national protest in 2011"[10]. This time, different strata of the

[8] U.K. riots reveal social media double standard, http://www.cbc.ca/news/world/story/2011/08/10/social-media-riots.html, Prithi Yelaja, August 10, 2011, Accessed on May 14, 2013.

[9] A year of social activism in India, http://www.indiatribune.com/index.php?option=com_content&view=article&id=7599:a-year-of-social-activism-in-india&catid=107:coverpage&Itemid=471, Accessed on May 20, 2013.

[10] Analyzing Social Media Momentum, India's 2011–2012 Anticorruption Movement, U.S. Government Office of South Asia Policy, Sasha Bong, Kenneth Chung, Karen Parkinson, Andrew Peppard, Justin Rabbach, Nicole Thiher, Workshop in International Public Affairs, University of Wisconsin System, Spring 2012, updated on page 4 on January 3, 2013, Accessed on May 20, 2013.

society came together and Anna Hazare was the face of the movement, as she started a public hunger strike to put pressure on Prime Minister Manmohan Singh Government. He took the country by storm, in demanding that the Jan Lokpal Bill drafted by Anna Team be passed"[11]. Anna Hazare managed to inspire and mobilize even the ultra-modern Indians—"Indians for whom the word "social" only means having a profile on social networking sites"[12]. "Anna Hazare fast" was the first real "social networking movement" in India. Internet & Social Media sites have been abuzz with articles/messages showing support for Anna Hazare's fight against corruption and his plea to pass Jan Lokpal Bill"[13].

It was the relentless coverage by Indian News Channels as well as by Twitter and Facebook that helped the movement to flourish. Social media was an important substance of the show and played a crucial role in promoting the movement. The government claimed that the Facebook and Twitter generation drives the protest and no one will come on the street to take part in the movement started by Anna Team. But against all these calculations, people reached out from every corner of the country to stand up against corruption, the movement categorized by many as the second struggle for independence"[14]. The Internet and mobile phone have become the tool of the new wave of social activism"[15]. People from different parts of the country gave their support to Anna Hazare. No political party was involved in this movement and that was the greatest merit of the movement that he had started. The fast ended on a very positive note, when the Government of India accepted the idea of Jan Lokpal Bill. As for Jan Lokpal Bill, "there will be a separate body to investigate and curb the corruption"[16].

19.2.1 The Role of Social Media

Indian people are social in nature, Indian culture gives a feeling of bondage; that is why, even after the popularity of the Internet and mobile phones, a high percentage of people do not use social media and mostly believe in information which comes

[11] Anti-Corruption Movement: Part 1, http://alteranation.com/topic-details.aspx?topicid=7, February 28, 2013, Accessed on May 8, 2013.

[12] Anna Hazare's "India against Corruption: Role of New Media in Mass Movement," http://sciencesblog.org/management/anna-hazares-india-against-corruption-role-of-new-media-in-mass-movement/, Accessed on May 8, 2013.

[13] Anna Hazare, http://timesofindia.indiatimes.com/topic/Anna-Hazare, Accessed on May 8, 2013.

[14] Anna Hazare's "August Kranti" on Facebook—a Case Study, http://www.indiadigitalreview.com/article/anna-hazares-august-kranti-facebook-%E2%80%93-case-study, Sandeep Amar, Head - Marketing and Audience, Indiatimes, Accessed on May 8, 2013.

[15] The impact of Social Media, http://www.thesundayindian.com/en/story/the-impact-of-social-media-/31/27616/ , January 8, 2012, Accessed on May 8, 2013.

[16] http://www.civilserviceindia.com/subject/Essay/anna-hazare-movement-against-corruption%20.html, Accessed on May 20, 2013.

from traditional media: Government sponsored media, authorized organizations/ people, friends or relatives. The majority of people have the perception that social media is a pastime tool and not a serious mode of communication or information sharing. In general, the majority of the people do not speak openly on issues related to Governance, politics and corruption, though corruption is a serious problem in India for a long time. People have accepted corruption as a normal thing. So, when Anna Hazare started his movement, many shared the opinion that this movement will not go long and will not be very effective. The movement was not supported by any political party, but had received a lot of support from people from different social strata such as intellectuals, media people, retired bureaucrats, Government officers, corporates and representatives of civil society. In some context, it was influenced by the Arab spring and other revolutions in which social media played an important role in mobilizing people for social causes. Since its inception, the entire movement was well-organized and coordinated. The team involved in this movement used social media in a very positive and productive way and were able to get maximum public attention and support. At the beginning, traditional media ignored and did not give much coverage to news and developments of this movement, but later it was difficult for them to ignore mass attention which this movement was getting on social media and micro blogging sites. Social media, specifically Facebook and Twitter played a very important role in information sharing and content generation related to the movement. Before this movement, it was considered that social media is a status symbol for college students and people who afford the Internet, a computer and a laptop only use these media. During the 2008 Mumbai flood, when people used social media and Twitter to inform each other, it was reported that only a group of people having all these luxuries used it. But during Anna Hazare's movement, the picture was totally different and contrary to all myths people used these media for information creation and sharing and took part in the movement on a large scale.

But on the other hand, the Government did not succeed in using social media in expressing its stand on this issue and highlighting some of the unconstitutional demands raised by Anna Team for which it was pressurizing the Government. After one year and a half since the movement, Anna Team ceased to function and the members involved in this movement are now working separately for different causes, some members have created political parties and are busy in the preparation of the upcoming elections in 2014. They are raising funds for election through social media and getting people's views on issues that are important to people, and on which they will work if they come to power.

19.3 Case Two: The Mass Agitation Against Delhi Gang Rape

On 16th December 2012, a 23 year-old female student was gang raped in a public transport bus in New Delhi, the capital of India. She was traveling with her friend. She died on December 28, 2012. An agitated mob, specifically youngsters came on roads for protests against the failure of the system in providing security to the citizens. Millions of people used Twitter and Facebook to organize protests "demanding action against the people involved in gruesome gang rape"[17]. Netizens across India started expressing their anger and sorrow over the death of the Delhi gang rape victim. People active on social media had given new names to the victim as "Damini" (Thunder) and "Nirbhaya" (Fearless). Thousands of people, specifically students from colleges, representatives of opposition political parties, social workers from different national and international NGOs took part in the street protest to make strong laws against the culprits and give security to women, immediate action against the culprits and resignation of the police Chief Commissioner for some acts committed by the police against the protesters. "The Black Dot of Shame" campaign gained momentum on social media. On the other hand, people from other parts of the country expressed their views on social media on the same demands, which local people were demanding. The agitation over online social media platforms intensified greatly after the Delhi Police isolated key areas like India Gate in a bid to prevent protesters from gathering and voicing their anger"[18]. Under the public agitation, the government drafted a new bill on violence against women which the parliament passed, all the culprits were arrested and the legal procedure went on in the court for final verdict.

19.3.1 The Role of Social Media

The entire agitation was emotional and mostly students were involved in this movement. This movement again was mobilized through social media. In some sense, it was a reflection of frustration of Indian youth against the faulty system. Different NGOs and opposition political parties also took part in the agitation. Students and NGOs used social media for coordination and information sharing.

[17] Are we ready for a social revolution, http://www.indiaonward.com/inclusive-society/are-we-ready-for-a-social-revolution/, Virginia Sharma, accessed on May 8, 2013.

[18] Protest against Delhi Gang Rape intensifies on Social Media, http://efytimes.com/e1/fullnews.asp?edid=97483, EFYtimes News, Accessed on May 15, 2013.

19.4 Case Three: The 2012 Ethnic Conflicts in Assam

Bodo is the main tribe of Assam, the North East State of India. People belonging to Bodo tribal community are not happy with Muslim migrants of Bangladesh, the neighbouring country of India. In July 2012, the murder of 3 Bodos by Muslims was the cause of conflicts in which 70 people died and around 4,85,000, people displaced and had taken shelter in the official camps. In the riots people from both the communities killed each other to take revenge. Muslims living in other parts of the country showed anger on the killing of Muslims in Assam and organized several street protests in different parts of the country. In India, diversity exists at many levels such as geographical, linguistic, cultural, socio-economic and educational. India has 35 States including 7 union territories. Multilevel diversity is a cause of internal conflicts. Assam is one of the N–E States of India. The northeast region of India consists of seven States—Assam, Nagaland, Manipur, Arunachal Pradesh, Mizoram and Tripura. In comparison to other N–E States, Assam is situated in the plain area and is in the centre of other N–E States. Other N–E States touch borders with some of the East Asian and South East Asian countries. The N–E region of India is full of natural resources and one of the most ethnically diverse areas of Asia. More than 200 ethnic tribal groups live in North East India.

The geographical positioning of the northeast region is the reason behind its slow progress and development. People are mostly dependent on natural resources and agriculture. Due to fewer opportunities, a struggle for survival can easily be seen in day-to-day activities, which many times comes out as a frustration and takes a form of internal conflicts between different groups living in this region. For a long time, this area is under insurgency, which is another reason for its slow growth. Illegal migration from neighbouring countries has increased the pressure on livelihood resources. Competition in getting natural resources and land has widened the differences among natives and migrants from other countries.

19.4.1 The Role of Social Media

After the July 2012 incident with its post riots and protests, a series of misleading text messages and doctored images started coming on mobile phones. The pictures showed people from a particular community fighting the Muslims. After this, Assamies people living in other cities of India started getting death threatening messages on their phones. In messages, they received a warning to leave particular cities and go back to their home State (Assam) before *Id*, a holy festival of Muslims which comes on completion of the month of Ramzan (a month in which Muslims fast). In the messages, they were given death threats that Muslims would attack northeastern students and migrants if they did not go back to their home state. "Tens of thousands of people hurriedly boarded overcrowded trains to the northeast"[19]. Provocative and offensive content was uploaded on the Internet and social media websites—Facebook, Twitter and YouTube—to frighten northeastern people living in different parts of India. Threats and counter-threats spread through digital media. Thousands of northeastern people started going back to Assam, the trains were filled and people were waiting on railway stations to get a train. "Taken aback by the mass exodus, the government says the unity and integrity of the country is at stake"[20]. Indian Government claims that "elements based in Pakistan had orchestrated a fear-mongering misinformation campaign using text messages and social media that helped set off nationwide panic among migrants from India's isolated northeastern states"[21]. Indian authorities blamed Pakistan; Government of India had submitted a report, based on the investigation, showed Pakistan's involvement in creating the chaos. On the other hand, "several reputed international news sites have highlighted that it is India's internal element that is involved in spreading hate messages and not the Pakistan"[22]. The Government blocked around 300 websites and banned bulky SMSs for 20 days to stop panic and chaos. Social media analyzers said that "government's recent crackdown on hundreds of websites is warranted, but says it needs to be more sophisticated and aggressive in handling threats and rumors emanating from the internet"[23].

19.5 Case Four: The Muzzafarpur Riots

Around 43 people were killed, 93 injured and 50,000 were relocated in a communal dispute Hindu and Muslim community people Muzzafarnagar in Indian State Uttar Pradesh on 27th August 2013. Communal tension continued till 17 September 2013. The cause of the most communal violence was an accident and eye teasing. Motorcycles of Hindu and Muslim boys collided and gave birth to the dispute while eye teasing by an Muslim boy provoked the brothers of the girl to a fight, followed by the killing of the Muslim boy and than the murder of the two Hindu boys by the

[19] India Asks Pakistan to Investigate Root of Panic, http://www.nytimes.com/2012/08/20/world/asia/india-asks-pakistan-to-help-investigate-root-of-panic.html, Jim Yardley, August 19, 2012, Accessed on May 20, 2013.

[20] India Debates Misuse of Social Media, Anjana Pasricha, August 21, 2012, http://www.voanews.com/content/india-debates-misues-of-social-media/1492129.html, Voice of America, Accessed on February 20, 2013.

[21] See footnote 1.

[22] India blames Pakistani social media activists for causing Assam unrest, http://www.moremag.pk/2012/08/23/india-blames-pakistani-social-media-activists-for-causing-assam-unrest, Mudassir Jehangir, August 23, 2012, Accessed on March 19, 2013.

[23] India Debates Misuse of Social Media, http://www.voanews.com/content/india-debates-misues-of-social-media/1492129.html, Anjana Pasricha, August 21, 2012, Accessed on February 20, 2013.

boys of another community—all this being a serious reason of the conflict. On 31st August, people from the Hindu community organized a meeting to revenge the death of the two Hindu boys. In the first week of September, clashes and disputes erupted between two communities. Violence turned ugly after the death of a media person. Army enforced curfew in the affected areas.

19.5.1 The Role of Social Media

Chief Minister of Uttar Pradesh, Mr. Akhilesh Yadav, blamed social media, specifically YouTube, Facebook and Twitter for intensifying the riots and tension. A video circulated through social media was posted on the mobile phones of the villagers and fuelled the tension, later proven to have been a fake, an old video which was shot in Pakistan's Sialkot districts. The State Government blamed and charged Bhartiya Janata Party (BJP) leader with circulating this fake video, even though BJP denied these charges.

19.6 Patterns of Information Flow on Social Media

Social network sites allow to create personal news and to include sources of information from where you are getting news or information. By doing so, the user can customize the flow of information. The user can also choose how and when the information can be delivered. In the conversations of social media, two methods are popular: the first is to collect as much information as possible and the second to set parameters to collect only selected information. It is up to the users what method they use. Social media also allows users to contribute in information flow. Users collect news information, which is more important to them, and remove information, which is less important to them; they get information from multiple sources and select the news according to their needs and preferences. Social media contributes to liberalization in creation and distribution of news and information on the Internet and digital media. When we say that social media liberalizes the flow of information, then it is necessary to look and analyze if the concept of free flow of information really exists on the Internet and social media or it is also influenced by some actors who know the psychology of social media users living in different parts of the world and direct the activities on social media according to their set agendas and try to influence users; in some cases, situation and circumstances they use social media as a medium to misguide users on certain issues and as a source of propaganda. Therefore, not all information that flows on from social media is valid and true, nor the thoughts and views are always a representation of mass users. Making fake profiles and hiding individual identity is the common trend in social media communication; the creation of multiple profiles by a single individual is another common habit of Internet users and that is why more academic researches are required in this field to understand usage, content generation and information sharing on the Internet and social media.

If we can see the pattern of information flow in the four incidents of India in which social media played important role, we find that, in the first two, namely—Anna Hazare's movement and the Delhi gang rape, the people involved in information and content generation and sharing were urban and educated people, mostly college students, retired and working officers, educated professionals, corporate representatives of civil society and even media people. They were aware what information is right or wrong, which are the right sources to get right information, what information to read and circulate and what content to be generated, they were not influenced by any third party to take any action or believe what was coming from social media, while in the case of the ethnic riots in Assam and the communal dispute in Muzafarnagar, the receivers were passive users of intentionally and purposefully generated messages. In both cases, they used the same strategy by posting doctored images to hurt the feelings of people and to create a panic and fear amongst them.

In last few years, the number of Internet and mobile phone users has increased very fast, but this number covers diverse populations consisting of different socio-cultural, economic and education groups. It has been said that users are active Internet contributors and are empowered by technological developments and are participating in online content generation and want to test and experience the value of their opinions, views and thoughts. But, in some of the social media communication studies, it has been found that not all the users are active contributors, but divided into certain groups such as followers, critics, passive observers or spectators. Same things apply for the Indian Internet users, if we can analyze the pattern of their engagement, we find that most of them come under the category of followers and critics. They do not show much contribution in authentic and quality content creation, but generally follow the trends from western countries. Their comments come in positive/negative or black and white manner, we generally do not find rational thoughts or comments that show their deep knowledge of the subject, rather their comments show very superficial knowledge about the subject/topic or issue. Sometimes, we also find a sense of frustration in their comments and it is very easy to provoke or influence such a mob by circulating any comment/picture or video to fuel them. It is easy to influence and divert online discussions by circulating any comment, which can trigger them. Though Internet users participate in information and content creation, their participation is not active, a big percentage of social media users are passive recipients of a group of active users.

It is being observed that Indian social media users are highly influenced by western social media users in their engagement with all Internet activities and patterns of sending comments and content on the Internet. By doing this, they try to create a virtual personality that is entirely different from their real personality and not a actual representation of what they are and think; actually, they try to create a persona which is more similar to Global mass in behavior, language, by using certain words, making comments and by uploading pictures and videos.

19.7 The Impact of Social Media Messages

Anything that is new catches people's attention and anything that is communicated by or communicated in a group gets more attention, appreciation and recognition. Social media is a new media and, at this stage, people are thrilled to use and experience what this media provides and what is available on the Internet and social media. They are also more enthusiastic to test different applications provided by advanced technology. Since lot of excitement is related to the use of social media, people generally believe what comes from this media. Social media has given lot of freedom to individuals, not only in getting connected with global masses, building relationships, creating business contacts, expressing thoughts, views, but also in depicting an entirely different personality on the Internet and in directly taking part in information or content generation.

This entire experience is new for the users. It has been observed that a high percentage of users are literate and educated, but the conversations on the Internet show little knowledge of the subjects/topics and issues on which they comment online. Under such circumstances, they are more dependent on others to get valid and authentic information, but it is not necessary that the people on whom they are dependent for information to be experts of the subject and know it fully, in such cases, half-cooked information travels on Internet. Instead of creating valid and authentic information, people start commenting on whatever comes online, without understating the validity, authenticity and seriousness of the information.

New media gives a sense of individuality and privacy. It is also available on mobile phones; therefore, users constantly remain in touch with all happenings, which gives them a sense of proximity with social media and messages. They find it more reliable than other media or information sources, specifically at times of emergency or crisis and start believing on whatever comes from social media and the Internet; therefore, they have a strong impact on them. Social media is still in its inception period and not much work has been done to assess the content trends and the habits of social media uses. Social media users are involved at multiple levels and to understand and assess these multiple roles requires multilevel research approaches and methodologies.

19.8 Conclusion

India is witnessing a significant technological revolution and is using it to get connected with diverse range of people, who are feeling empowered by all this exposure and are showing more openness in expressing their views online. However, not all users are active users of social media, a big percentage of them are passive in nature and easily get influenced and affected by what others inform them.

It has been observed globally that different people take part in information generation at different times, having different constructive and destructive purposes, intentions and objectives to get different types of responses and reactions from users. Such trends, patterns and habits definitely affect global communities, active on the Internet and social media websites as well as local societies if used for long time. Users' feedback, response and reactions on constructive and destructive messages differ according to their different geographical, educational, cultural, political and economic backgrounds. But it is also true that, when information flows on a global platform, it directly or indirectly affects all those who get access to information in both constructive and destructive ways.

Chapter 20
Cyber Tools and Virtual Weapons

Social Media in Politics

David Mathew

Consider the Following Situation, If You Will

A secret committee has been formed in order to ensure the continuation of a particular movement. This movement is led by a man whose name and ideas are well known, although many do not agree with what he professes. The committee has been set up by one of this controversial speaker's most loyal supporters, a man whose ambition was to form a Praetorian guard around the Well-Known Man and to monitor the behaviour of a younger member who is suspected of harbouring opinions contradictory to those of the Well-Known Man. The other aim of the committee is to preserve the purity of the group's central tenets, as decided by the Well-Known Man.

Perhaps this sounds like the inner workings of a cult (and perhaps you will still believe this to be true, even when you know the identities of the key players). As it happens, the Well-Known Man was Sigmund Freud, the originator of psychoanalysis. His loyal supporter was Ernest Jones, and the man under scrutiny was none other than Carl Jung. The year was 1912. In an atmosphere of cronyism, idolatry and suspicion, Freud enthusiastically embraced the very notion of secrecy, and membership was tightly controlled: indeed, hagiographic agreement with Freud's ideas seems to have been the only ticket accepted for admission into the society. Rejection of his theses was tantamount to betrayal; and a perceived personal rejection of Freud was sufficient to have someone branded as an enemy.

If such a set-up already bears the markings of a form of conditioning, and if the clear inference is that this was bound to end badly, then the demise of this secret committee also wears a certain badge of irony. For all of its shady machinations and pseudo-aggressive inclusivity, the committee imploded because—and this is the ironic touch—the members did not actually like each other very much. In the words

D. Mathew (✉)
Centre for Learning Excellence, University of Bedfordshire, Bedfordshire, UK
e-mail: david.mathew@beds.ac.uk

B. Pătruţ and M. Pătruţ (eds.), *Social Media in Politics*, Public Administration and Information Technology 13, DOI 10.1007/978-3-319-04666-2_20,

of Phyllis Grosskurth (1991: 195), ‘fantasy had been dissolved by the harsh reality of human beings unable to get along together.’

One hundred years before the advent of what we now call social media, the anecdote of Freud’s Inner Circle gives an example of what we now take for granted, from a contemporary point of view. The scurrility, the changing of political affections, the fluctuations and oscillations of comradeship, the bullying: all of these, surely, represent social media’s potential at its dangerous worst. In one way, therefore, we might even argue that the principles behind social media (good and bad) are in fact nothing new. Granted, the tools have been updated but the resentments and cooling affiliations are as old as the human story itself.

Alternatively, Consider a Separate Scenario

The date is 2002, the place Baltimore, U.S.A. The American crime show The Wire premiered on 2 June of that year, and it was set in the Maryland city. In addition to its interweaving plot-lines about drugs and politics, brutality and betrayal, it’s intermingling of dense and slangy Baltimore Police speech and felon argot, and its blurring of professional boundaries, one of its main stories concerned the telephone tapping of a network of payphones used by criminals going about their narcotic business. By listening in to the heavily encoded conversations, the police are able to make connections and arrests: the Wire of the title can mean many things in different contexts.

Watching this series now (and please bear in mind that we are only discussing a passing of time of little more than a decade), it is obvious that this is a crime drama that was born before social media had made much noise or had gathered much attention to itself. How much easier to catch those dealers would have been if they had only had Facebook to use instead of payphones!

Or perhaps the best illustration is one in which the author relays his own reflections on a news story that seems, even now, 2 years on (at time of writing) scarcely believable. I refer to the United Kingdom riots of 2011, news of which certainly made an appearance on Italian TV, where I happened to be at a conference at the time. And as we began this observation of several vignettes with a reference to Sigmund Freud, I would like to show the riots through the lens of one of his most famous theories, if I may: the theory outlined in *Group Psychology and the Analysis of the Ego* (Freud 1921).

This was Freud’s second essay (after *Totem and Taboo* in 1913) on the subject of collective psychology. He submitted that individual and social psychology are more or less identical, and he asked us to question the emotional bonds that hold collective entities together. ‘The impulses which a group obeys may according to circumstances be generous or cruel, heroic or cowardly,’ he argues, ‘but they are always so imperious that no personal interest, not even that of self-preservation, can make itself felt.’ In other words, the group ideal is what we sacrifice our individuality to, on occasion.

Nowadays—in the west at least—in the absence of public executions, freak shows, or the exhibition of beheaded traitors (with their hair combed nicely and their faces washed for easier audience recognition, as a warning), it is perhaps to the world of crime in general that we might turn for a clear example of Freud's theories on group psychology in action. More specifically, we might turn to the phenomenon of the riot. In the summer of 2011, England saw a series of city riots that re-confirmed much of what Freud taught us in *Group Psychology and the Analysis of the Ego*, and was all the more surprising for its intensity and faux-sporadic nature. What happened? Aside from the customary pollutants, what was in the English urban air during those weeks? That technology was used, both to coordinate and choreograph events (using mobile phones, networking sites, Twitter), and to stay one step ahead of the police, is now established; but how did the riots grip the public's imagination so powerfully, to such an extent that among the rioters were practitioners of professions such as teaching?

As an Englishman, I have long since become used to the violent behaviour of my countrymen. I have witnessed, via the television, mob aggression sparked (say) by an unsuccessful football match result, especially abroad; I have witnessed racist scraps, student protests, political skirmishes. This felt different. It was the inclusivity of the recent riots that made the United Kingdom (and Europe) sit up and think: it was not so much every man for himself, as: every man join the hive mind. The rioters were not of one race, one class, or one political party; nor were they of one age group, one gender, or one ideological opinion. In fact, one of the defining features of this particular string of riots was its lack of defining features. Come one, come all, was the unspoken battle cry; and England rallied to the call as if it was what it had been waiting for, all of its life. The city streets did not know what had hit them.

Social media-augmented political action was what had hit them (or so it was claimed); and the self-justification of political intent, however retrospectively it is made, is a frequent companion of those who would organise such attacks. (These attacks, let us remember, were not only on the forces of law and order, but were also on bystanders and innocent shop-owners.) And while we might argue that the British riot is not exactly new, we can balance this by saying that it is at least fairly uncommon, and that social media had aided the orchestration and execution. However, it is not true to claim that violence is impossible without social media. Of course not: in the past, riots managed perfectly well without social media to help them along. But via the use of cyber tools and virtual weapons, we can look again at the two component words of social media and remember that while media remains 'a means of communication', the original definition of social has corrupted over centuries. Where once, in the early sixteenth century for example, it was defined as 'characterized by friendliness or geniality' (from the Middle French social (14c.) and from the Latin *socialis*, 'united, living with others'), social also means grouped by means of antagonism or anxiety. Or in other words, what Freud surmised in *Group Psychology and the Analysis of the Ego* (and what he failed to predict in the example of the secret committee) was that an individual's awareness of, and adherence to, the unconscious wishes of the group cannot last forever. Sooner or later, an individual's sense of anxiety is impossible to ignore.

For the moment, however, let us stay in the hive mind. As a result of the summer of 2011, opinions on the subject of rioting seem to have been altered, however temporarily. This is because, for the vast majority of people in England, home is (was?) a safe place to live, and outbursts of such violence had been shocking, newsworthy, but rare—largely the work of *homo urbanis* of a lower social order. This can no longer be the case. Suddenly, in the space of days, this view had to be challenged and qualified: London had 'erupted', and other cities followed suit: other cities wanted a piece of the action. Why might this have been the case? Bearing in mind the presence of social media as a means of translating solitary thought into something that the Group Mind will understand and allow one to 'think'; and bearing in mind the political structures—perceived repression, for example—that could have led to bad feelings in the first place, structured chaos and unstructured violence had become a social adhesive.

'A group is extraordinarily credulous and open to influence,' Freud tells us in *Group Psychology*, 'it has no critical faculty, and the improbable does not exist for it. It thinks in images, which call one another up by association... The feelings of a group are always very simple and very exaggerated. So that a group knows neither doubt nor uncertainty' (Freud 1921: 78). If we take Freud at his word on this point (and nothing among the news coverage would seem to contradict him), then we might view the violent group mind as something of a paradox. It is undeniably violent in order to achieve its group-goals, but we might also argue that its basic simplicity of mission is also self-protective. The crowd threatens before it has a chance to be threatened... even if there is no counterweighted force levelled against it. This is politics in action.

As Freud continues: 'It respects force and can only be slightly influenced by kindness, which it regards merely as a form of weakness. What it demands of its heroes is strength, or even violence. It wants to be ruled and oppressed and to fear its masters' (ibid). Or as Will Self (Self 2011) would have it: 'The dominant trait of the crowd is to reduce its myriad individuals to a single, dysfunctional persona. The crowd is stupider than the averaging of its component minds.' Parenthetically we might add that the groups followed (unconsciously, of course) some of Freud's reasoning in *Civilization and Its Discontents* (1930), especially with reference to not loving one's neighbour in the group... or even trusting him!

More and more, the effects of psychoanalysis and the more insidious traits of social media sound similar. Even the vigorous expansion of the former discipline in Freud's own lifetime (as it spread within medicine, especially in the United States, and to other forms of therapy, to literature, art, popular culture and the social sciences,) and the rash-like multiplication of social media in our own times are broadly analogous. Furthermore, the robust and belligerent criticisms aimed at both—by their more splenetic detractors—can be viewed as similar. And why did psychoanalysis attract such waves of bad feeling? Why do some people view social media as a pervasive threat? Arguably, because we are hardwired to be anxious of change. Anxiety is a sensation of unease that is caused by a prediction (often made on an unconscious level) of something bad that is about to happen; and it is plain to see why it has been a subject much covered in psychoanalysis. For some users, the Internet itself is overwhelming—a vast, amorphous entity, filled with stressors and unseen menace that recalls the Big Other of one of Freud's followers, Jacques Lacan. In the words of Dylan Evans (in turn, one of Lacan's followers):

> The big Other designates radical alterity, an other-ness which transcends the illusory otherness of the imaginary because it cannot be assimilated through identification. Lacan equates this radical alterity with language and the law, and hence the big Other is inscribed in the order of the symbolic. Indeed, the big Other is the symbolic insofar as it is particularized for each subject. The Other is thus both another subject, in his radical alterity and unassimilable uniqueness, and also the symbolic order which mediates the relationship with that other subject.' (Evans 1996: 133).

The Other is watching us while we work; again on an unconscious level, the Other is Facebook, the Other is the very technology that we use and in which we swim or flail (depending on one's point of view). If it is true that it is natural to feel anxious about change, then it is also fair to feel anxious about the fact that we cannot see the end of the changes that have been imposed upon us.

But what of social media's more positive aspects? If an impression has been formed that the implications of the rapid swelling of social media are entirely negative (socially, personally, epiphenomenalistically or politically negative), let us look at some different anecdotal evidence. After all, we might well agree that the Internet is rather like a river: it is impossible to step into it twice and to find it exactly the same on both occasions. Surely, the same can be said of social media itself: that it will change; that it can be used as a force for societal good. Not only are the tools used for social media constantly developing, social media itself—as a political space, a learning space, perhaps—is also developing and thereby affecting the way that it is used. To risk over-straining my own metaphor, we have crossed the river several times now, and the previously unexplored country on the other side is more familiar to us with every visit. We have started to draw our maps. We have started to lay our cables and light our fires. And every time we make the crossing, we can fill in more and more of the map. It does not matter at first that we do not understand all of the wildlife—any more than we need to know what is happening, specifically, in the social media industry—it is more important to know approximately where we are going in our new environment. Using instinct as our tool, we venture forth; and organisations that refuse to adapt and to move with our times risk eventual alienation. As several headlines have proclaimed in recent years, 'The Revolution Will Not be Televised... But It Will Be Tweeted.'

Once again, of course, this brings us to politics. 'The Revolution Will Not Be Televised' is a song by Gil Scott-Heron; it was first recorded it for his 1970 album *Small Talk at 125th and Lenox*. The song's message is obvious from its title; perhaps a more interestingly observation is the aforementioned proliferation of its title in recent headlines (it has been used and re-used like an example of Open Educational Resources). The headline has been used to cover events as diverse as U.S. midterm elections, regime change in the Middle East, and the London riots mentioned earlier. In fact, the headline itself is interesting at face value. Televised politics (one inference might be) are redundant politics: the authentic voice of the people will be heard (*is* heard?) via the channels of Facebook, Twitter and Tumblr. For every negative application of a micro-blogging site (a real-time invitation to riot, for example), there is a positive application that might be used in the moral counter-balance. Social media allows us both to gauge and to proffer opinion, in a manner that is never meant to be anything but ephemeral: it is the equivalent of a thermometer, reading the political temperature *of the moment*. Who would have thought that we might ever be able to be 'friends' with our local, regional or national political representative?

'The Revolution Will Not Be Televised... But It Will Be Tweeted' provides a clear and ongoing message with regards to the interdependence—we might even say symbiosis—between social media and politics. After all, at first glance, democracy and social media would appear to be easy bedfellows: indeed, in these days of boasted transparency, a direct communications channel between the governed and the government would seem like perfect sense. But to what end? The logical follow-through is a journey towards an interconnected, symbiotic body politic (perhaps a good idea?), or a maelstrom of unmanageable political din, what with our age of mass loquacity showing no sign of taking a pause for breath. Now that the social web, in many cases, is the default place where people spend time on discussions of issues that are important to them, there is little chance of the current situation changing any time soon. The users of social media, we might say, have responded to and made a political decision that affects us all, in one way or another.

References

Evans, D. (1996). *An introductory dictionary of Lacanian psychoanalysis*. London: Routledge.

Freud, S. (1913). *Totem and taboo. Standard edition of the complete psychological works, volume 13* (pp. 1–161). London: Hogarth Press.

Freud, S. (1921). *Group psychology and analysis of the ego. Standard edition of the complete psychological works, volume 18* (pp. 65–143). London: Hogarth Press.

Freud, S. (1930). *Civilization and its discontents. Standard edition of the complete psychological works, volume 21*. London: Hogarth Press.

Grosskurth, P. (1991). *The secret ring: Freud's Inner circle and the politics of psychoanalysis*. Boston: Addison-Wesley Publication.

Self, W. (2011) The only verdict: get him to the asylum. New Statesman 08 August 2011. http://www.newstatesman.com/culture/2011/08/crowd-humanity-society. Accessed 14 May 2013.

List of Contributors

Nyarwi Ahmad is Ph.D. Candidate at Politics and Media Research Group, The Media School, Bournemouth University, UK and Lecturer in the Department of Communication Sciences, the Faculty of Social and Political Sciences, University of Gadjah Mada (UGM), Yogyakarta, Indonesia. He graduated from the Undergraduate program (BA Hons/By Research), Department of Communication Sciences, UGM, Yogyakarta, Indonesia (May, 2005), and the Graduate Program of Master in Management of Political Communication, the University of Indonesia, Jakarta (July, 2008). He was researcher associate of the Indonesian Circle Survey Group (Lingkaran Survei Indonesia Grup/LSI Grup-Jakarta) (2006–2008), expert staff of the Indonesian Broadcasting Commission (Komisi Penyiaran Indonesia) (2007–2008), and consultant of public campaign programs of the new Higher Education Regulation (the World Bank, Jakarta and the Directorate of the Higher Education, The Ministry of Education and Culture, Republic of Indonesia) (2011–2012). E-mail: gloryasia2008@gmail.com.

Theresia Anderson received her B.A. in Psychology and African-American studies from California State University, Northridge in 2012. She plans to pursue a career in the area of multicultural research with a focus on ethnic and cultural hybridity, geriatrics, and social psychology—dealing primarily with the Black global populations. At Cal State Northridge, she worked closely with Dr. Theresa White as a research assistant and Associate Student Director of the DuBois Hamer Institute. She continues to work with Dr. White as a research assistant and with Dr. Brad Silverman as a consultant while, preparing to return to graduate school in the fall of 2014. E-mail: ms.theresialynn@gmail.com.

Aslı Telli Aydemir received her B.A. degree in Political Science and international relations; then, she studied feature writing and freelance journalism. She focused on social anthropology and critical studies at M.A. level at Paris 8—St. Denis and on media & communication sciences at Ph.D. level at the European Graduate School. Her research areas of interest and publications in scholarly journals gravitate around social and civic impact of trans- and/or polymedia, new media literacy, cybercultures, social media facilitated activism practices, and networked society

B. Pătruţ and M. Pătruţ (eds.), *Social Media in Politics*, Public Administration and Information Technology 13, DOI 10.1007/978-3-319-04666-2,

informatics. Dr. Ademir worked as a researcher for a multi-partner FP6 project, entitled "Civicweb: Internet, young people and participation" in 2006–2009. She has been working as an assistant professor in the College of Communication and Cultural Studies MA Program of Istanbul Sehir University since 2010.

Sigal Barak-Brandes is a lecturer at The School of Media Studies, College of Management Academic Studies, Israel. Her research interests include gender representations, media portrayal of wife abuse, women and girls' audiences, and media images of girlhood and of motherhood. Her recent publications include "Taming the shame: Policing excretions and body fluids in advertisements for hygiene products" (European Journal of Cultural Studies); "'I'm not influenced by ads, but not everyone's like me': The Third Person Effect in Israeli women's attitude to TV commercials and their images" (The Communication Review); "A beautiful campaign? Analysis of public discourses in Israel surrounding the Dove Campaign for Real Beauty" (Feminist Media Studies). E-mail: brandes1@zahav.net.il.

Günseli Bayraktutan currently works as an associate professor in the Faculty of Communication at Başkent University, Turkey. She has got her B.Sc. degree (1997) in Political Science and Public Administration from Middle East Technical University. She obtained her M.Sc. (2004) and Ph.D. (2010) from the Department of Journalism, Graduate School of Social Sciences, at Ankara University. Her M.Sc. dissertation is about political economy of academical databases and her Ph.D. thesis is on the Turkish blogosphere and the academic intellectuals within this sphere. Her academic interests are research methods, new media, political communication and ethics.

Mutlu Binark (*1968) has been Professor at the Department of Radio, Television and Cinema, Faculty of Communication, Baskent University (TR), since 2005. She teaches media sociology, media theories, and new media culture. She is currently working on new media literacy. She has successfully completed the research projects on "Digital Game Culture and Internet Cafe Usage Patterns of Young People in Turkey." and "New Media and Ethical Issues". Her recent publications are: a book chapter as coauthor in Information and Media Literacy: Criticism, Literacies, and Policies (2009) (ed. M. Leaning); a book chapter in Digital Technologies of the Self, Cambridge Scholars Publishing (2009) (coauthor); a book chapter in *Broadband Society and Generational Changes*, Volume 5 (2011) (coauthor), Peter Lang, and a another book chapter in *Computer Games and New Media Cultures: Handbook Digital Game Studies* (2012) (coauthor) from Springer. E-mail: binark@baskent.edu.tr. For more information, see http://www.yenimedya.wordpress.com and http://www.dijitaloyunkulturu.wordpress.com.

Porismita Borah (Ph.D., 2010, University of Wisconsin-Madison) is an Assistant Professor of Communication in the Edward R. Murrow College of Communication. Ms. Borah's main areas of research interests are political communication, emerging technology, campaigns and international communication. Her most recent research focuses on emerging technologies and particularly explores the influence of the contemporary media environment on traditional news media content as well as its influence on communication theory. Her research interests also include political and health campaigns. These projects have specifically examined the influence of social media in various campaigns. Ms. Borah's research has been published in many prestigious journals including *Journal of Communication and Communication Research*. To learn more about Ms. Borah's work, visit her website at http:// porismitaborah.com/; E-mail: porismita@gmail.com.

Swati Bute is Assistant Professor at AMITY School of Communication, AMITY University Noida, India. She holds a Ph.D. in Communication and Journalism from the University of Pune, India (2008). She was associated with the Institute for Defense Studies and Analysis, New Delhi as a Visiting Fellow (2013). She did her Master's degree in Science and Technology Communication at Devi Ahilaya University, Indore, India (1999). She has been an academic for 5 years. Her areas of interest are Communication Studies and Methods, Social Media Communication, Media and Conflicts, Interpersonal Communication, Communication and Culture, New (Changing) Information Needs, Audience Behaviour and Viewing Habits, Science Communication including Health Communication, Behaviour Change Communication and Radio Production and Journalism. E-mail: drswatibute11@gmail.com, swatibute2@gmail.com.

Andrea Calderaro is a researcher at the Centre for Media Pluralism and Media Freedom at the European University Institute, wherefrom he also received his M. Phil. Ph.D. and in Social and Political Sciences. His research focuses on the Internet an International Politics. He is also an Associate of the "Internet Policy Observatory" at the Center for Global Communications Studies (CGCS)—Annenberg Centre/University of Pennsylvania, he serves as Chair of the ECPR Internet and Politics standing group, a member of the CSISAC board at the OECD, and he is an Executive Member of the International Communication Section of the International Studies Association. Previously, he was Project Director of the "ICTs for the Global Governance of Peace and Security" Project at the University of Oslo (2012), Adjunct Professor at the University La Sapienza of Rome in "ICTs and International Relations", Visiting Fellow at the California Institute of Technology, and he has been consultant for the European Commission, European Parliament, Tactical Technology Collective. His publications include the guest-editing of 'Policy and Internet' special issue on "Online Collective Action and Policy Chance" (2013), and the inaugural issue of the International Journal of E-Politics, IJEP—"E-Politics in a Global Context" (2010). E-mail: Andrea.Calderaro@EUI.eu.

Tuğrul Çomu is a research assistant at Ankara University. He graduated from Istanbul University, Vocational School of Technical Sciences, Radio—TV Broadcasting Program, and Ankara University, Faculty of Communication, Department of Journalism. He received his Master's degree in Gender Studies at Ankara University. His master dissertation is about user-generated content production on video sharing sites. Currently he is a Ph.D. student in the Department of Journalism at Ankara University. His academic interests include new media, new media literacy, new media related participatory culture and visual culture.

Evelien D'heer is a Ph.D. candidate who has been working at the research group for Media and ICT (iMinds-MICT) at Ghent University (Belgium) since 2011. She studied television consumption in a multi-screen living room as well as citizen involvement in the production of hyperlocal news. Since 2013, she has been investigating the role of social media in the public debate during elections. The Ph.D. project is entitled 'Agenda setting in a networked public sphere' and builds upon the agenda-setting framework to understand how social media influence traditional media and vice versa. E-mail: Evelien.Dheer@UGent.be.

Kamil Demirhan is a Ph.D. candidate and research assistant at the Department of Political Science and Public Administration, Hacettepe University, Turkey. His research interests include political participation, civil society, social media and politics, new social movements and globalization. He has publications on ICTs and political participation, social capital and political participation, and politics in the process of globalization. He has taken part in several projects on social media, political participation, and civil society. He is a member of Political Studies Association, and Informatics Association of Turkey. E-mail: demirhankamil@-hacettepe.edu.tr; demirhankamil@gmail.com.

Tomaž Deželan, Ph.D., is Assistant Professor of Political Science at the Faculty of Social Sciences at the University of Ljubljana in Slovenia, and a researcher at the Centre for Political Science Research at the same faculty. He is an associate researcher at the University of Edinburgh, School of Law, where he acts as a country expert for citizenship. His research interests include citizenship concepts, debates and regimes, new modes of governance, parliamentary cohesion, electoral studies, political marketing, youth, gender and civil society. He has authored or co-authored more than 20 peer-reviewed articles in international journals and scientific volumes and 7 scientific monographs. Past projects he worked on or coordinated were funded by the Slovenian research agency, the European Union's FP framework, European Science Foundation of the European Union, European Education, Audiovisual and Culture Executive Agency and various other national agencies. E-mail: Tomaz.Dezelan@fdv.uni-lj.si.

Burak Doğu received his Bachelor's degree from the Journalism Department of Ankara University in 2003. He has completed his Master's degree in Journalism at Ege University in İzmir, where he studied Ludology and Lifestyles in computer games. He has undertaken research for his Ph.D. at Ege University on alternative media studies and has been a research fellow at Università degli Studi di Torino and Università degli Studi del Piemonte Orientale as a part of his doctoral research. While studying for his Master's degree, he joined Izmir University of Economics as a research assistant and was promoted as a full-time instructor in 2008. He coordinates senior-year projects and news studio courses along with several theoretical courses on communication and journalism. He has been invited to lecture at sectoral workshops and has also acted as an organization commitee member in multimedia journalism seminars. His research interests include ludology, digital media, and alternative journalism.

Guido di Fraia is Associate Professor at IULM University (Milan) and Coordinator of the Board of Professors for the Doctoral Course in Communication and New Technologies. He is Scientific Director of the IULM Master in Social Media Marketing and Web Communication. His research interests include: Web 2.0 and Corporate Communication; Political Communication; media narratives; innovative methods in social and market research. He has a degree in Political Sciences at the University of Milan. As a Fulbrighter, he studied Social Psychology and Methodology of Social Research in a Ph.D. Program at UCLA University of Los Angeles.

Leocadia Díaz Romero holds a degree in Law and studied Politics and International Relations with Diplomat Juan José Rubio de Urquía. She completed a Master's degree on Legal Issues and practiced Law. In 2000, she started her academic career. Since then, she has written and defended her European Ph.D., has been teaching a wide range of courses, done teaching and research in Europe and the USA, and participated in conferences and projects. She is an expert on EU Constitutional Law, Global Governance, Comparative Politics, International Relations and Political Communication. Currently, Prof. Díaz is devoted to the research of democracy and social movements in digital societies. Prof. Díaz obtained in January 2011 her Accreditation under the Spanish Quality Agency for Education as "Profesora Contratada Doctora". E-mail: leocadia.diaz@um.es.

Marta Fialová is a Ph.D. candidate at the Department of Sociology, Masaryk University in Brno, the Czech Republic. She is editor-in-chief of the *Czech Journal of Media Studies* and member of the Interdisciplinary Research Team on Internet & Society at Faculty of Social Studies, Masaryk University. Her research interests include audience research, media impact, political communication and new media. E-mail: martafialova@email.cz.

Gözde İslamoğlu graduated from the Radio, Television, and Cinema Department of Ankara University as an honors student in 2009. She continued her studies in critical pedagogy and received a Master's degree from Ankara University, the Graduate School of Educational Sciences in 2010. She is currently doing her master in Radio, Television and Cinema at Gazi University. She is a member of Kocaeli University, Faculty of Communication. Her academic interests are critical media literacy and the new communication technologies/new media.

Joanna Kulesza, Ph.D., is assistant professor at the Department of International Law and International Relations, Faculty of Law and Administration, University of Łodz, Poland. She was a visiting lecturer with the Oxford Internet Institute, the Norwegian Research Center for Computers and Law, Westfälische Wilhelms Universität Münster, and Justus-Liebig-Universität Gießen. She was a post-doctoral researcher at the University of Cambridge and Ludwig Maximilians University Munich. She worked for the European Parliament, the Polish Ministry of Foreign Affairs, and the Council of Europe. She is the author of four monographs on international and Internet law and over 30 peer-reviewed papers. Kulesza has just concluded her work on a monograph on the due diligence principle in international law. E-mail: joannakulesza@gmail.com.

David Levin is a lecturer in The School of Media Studies, College of Management Academic Studies, Israel. He focuses on the conjunctions between the possibilities and limitations of various media, cultural models, and the implications of special contexts of use. His publications include '"Because it's not really me": Student Films and Their Potential as Alternative Media' (International Perspectives on Youth Media: Cultures of Production and Education); The Cottage Cheese Boycott: The Conjunction between News Construction and Social Protest on Facebook (JOMEC Journal); 'Breaking the Spell: How the cell phone transforms time out', (The International Journal of Cultural Studies). E-mail: ddnsle@gmail.com.

Alena Macková is Junior Researcher at the Institute for Research on Children, Youth and Family, as well as at the International Institute of Political Science at Masaryk University. She is a Ph.D. student of political science at the Faculty of Social Studies, Masaryk University, dealing with new media and politics, focusing on political communication and cyberactivism. E-mail: aja.mackova@gmail.com.

Alem Maksuti is a Ph.D. candidate at the Faculty of Social Sciences, University of Ljubljana. His thesis examines the idiosyncrasies of Slovenian election campaigns during the democratic post-communist period. His current areas of interest concentrate on the impact of Internet technologies on the transformation of Slovenian political actors' political communication practices. His broader research interests focus on the areas of political communication, political participation, political culture, and election campaigns. He has authored/co-authored one monograph, several scientific papers, articles published in indexed journals, as well as chapters on elections and political communication in Slovenia.

Admire Mare is a Ph.D. candidate researching on youth, social media, and political activism, at the School of Journalism and Media Studies, Rhodes University, Grahamstown, South Africa. He holds a Diploma in Mass Communication (Harare Polytechnic), B.Sc. Honours degree in Sociology (University of Zimbabwe), an M.Sc. in Sociology and Social Anthropology (University of Zimbabwe), an MA in Journalism and Media Studies (Rhodes University). He lectured at the Harare Polytechnic and Great Zimbabwe University and also worked as a Communication Coordinator at the Foundation for Contemporary Research. His research interests include social media and activism, media and democracy, tabloid journalism, and social media and citizen journalism. E-mail: admiremare@gmail.com.

David Mathew works at the Centre for Learning Excellence at the University of Bedfordshire, UK, and as an independent researcher and writer. His wide areas of interest include psychoanalysis, linguistics, distance learning, prisons, and online anxiety. With approximately 600 published pieces to his name, including a novel based on his time working in the education department of a maximum-security prison (O My Days), he has published widely in academic, journalistic and fiction outlets. In addition to his writing, he co-edits The Journal of Pedagogic Development, teaches academic writing, and he particularly enjoys lecturing in foreign countries and learning about wine. He is a member of the Tavistock Society of Psychotherapists and Allied Professionals, Evidence Informed Policy and Practice in Education in Europe (EIPPEE), and the European Association for the Teaching of Academic Writing. He was also a member of The Health Technology Assessment programme (http://www.hta.ac.uk), as part of the NIHR Evaluation, Trials, and Studies Coordinating Centre at the University of Southampton (2009–2013). E-mail: David.Mathew@beds.ac.uk.

Maria Carlotta Missaglia is a Ph.D. candidate in Communication and New Technologies at IULM University in Milan. She has a Bachelor degree in Drama, Art and Music Study (University of Padua) and a Master degree in Television, Cinema and New Media (IULM University). Her research interests include sociology, communication, and new media. She is particularly interested in political communication and in its relationship with social media and web 2.0. She is working on a research about political participation and the new trends developed by the relationship between social media use and political communication. She is also working with the Professor Guido Di Fraia's research team for the Social Media Ability Observatory as Junior Researcher. E-mail: carlotta.missaglia@gmail.com.

Francesca Musiani (Ph.D., socio-economics of innovation) is a post-doctoral researcher at the Centre for the Sociology of Innovation of MINES ParisTech/CNRS, France. Recently, she was the 2012–2013 *Yahoo!* Fellow in Residence at the Institute for the Study of Diplomacy, Georgetown University (Washington, DC), where she taught in the Master of Science in Foreign Service, and an affiliate of the Berkman Center for Internet and Society at Harvard University (Cambridge, MA). She is the author of *Nains sans géants. Architecture décentralisée et services Internet* (Paris: Presses des Mines). Francesca serves as Co-Chair of the Emerging Scholars Network of the International Association for Media and Communication Research (IAMCR), and as outreach officer for the Global Internet Governance Academic Network (GigaNet). She is a regular author for the Internet Policy Review, a publication of the Humboldt Institute for Internet and Society based in Berlin, Germany. E-mail: francesca.musiani@mines-paristech.fr.

Bogdan Pătruţ is associate professor in computer science at "Vasile Alecsandri" University of Bacău, Romania. He is interested in various fields of research, including social media, computer science applied to social and political sciences, multi-agent systems applied in accounting education, natural language processing, and applied mathematics. He is also interested in social media challenges of the new political environment. He teaches courses on visual programming, programming techniques, algorithms and data structures etc. He published or edited more than 25 books on programming, algorithms, artificial intelligence, interactive education, and social media. He published papers in academic journals (*LNCS*, *IJCCC*, IJNLC etc.) He also presented papers in international conferences (NLDB 2008; BIR 2008; ICCGI 2008; MedDecSup 2011 etc.). He has recently edited So*cial Media and the New Academic Environment: Pedagogical Challenges* (IGI Global 2013) and he organized *SMART 2013—Social Media in Academia: Research and Teaching* (international conference). Dr. Pătruţ is editor-in-chief of the international journals *BRAIN: Broad Research in Artificial Intelligence and Neuroscience* and *BRAND: Broad Research in Accounting and Negotiation*. He is also a software developer at EduSoft Ltd., where he developed *Political Analyst*—software for analyzing political speeches using graph theory. E-mail: bogdan@edusoft.ro, Web: http://www.edusoft.ro/bogdan.

Monica Pătruţ is senior lecturer in political science at "Vasile Alecsandri" University of Bacău, Romania. Her domains of research are political communication, sociology of education, public relations, and social media. She published several papers in international journals such as *Public Relations Review, Journal of Media Research, Sfera Politicii*. She also presented papers in conferences on political communication and published them. Dr. Pătruţ is editor of *Social Media in Higher Education* (IGI Global 2013) and reviewer for the journal *BRAND: Broad Research in Accounting and Negotiation*. She is member of *ECREA (European Communication Research and Education Association)* and member *of* Romanian Sociological Society. She teaches courses on political communication, research methods in public relations, and corporate social responsibility. Currently, Dr. Pătruţ is interested in the use of Facebook in Romanian political life. E-mail: monicapatrut@yahoo.com.

Ioan-Lucian Popa is Associate Professor, Ph.D., at Vasile Alecsandri University of Bacau, Romania; his main interests are English language and linguistics (English phonetics and phonology, translation studies, the English verb phrase, international varieties of English) and has published numerous papers in specialized journals and about a number of specialized books and bilingual dictionaries (*Modal Verbs and Modality in English, An Introduction to Translation Studies, Dicţionar român-englez de proverbe, Dicţionar de afaceri englez-român, Dictionar de afaceri român-englez/englez-român*, etc.). He was editor-in-chief of LiBRI http://www.libri.broadresearch.org. He has recently developed an intense interest in the potential of social media networks and that of ICTs in education and was co-editor for *Contemporary Issues in Education and Social Communication. Challenges for Education, Social Work, and Organizational Communication*, Akademische Verlagsgemeinschaft, München. Web: http://ub-ro.academia.edu/IoanLucianPopa. E-mail: i.l.popa@hotmail.co.

Amaro la Rosa is a psychology graduate a journalist who attended specialization courses at Centro Internacional de Estudios Superiores de Comunicación para América Latina (CIESPAL) and Centro de Análisis de Políticas Públicas (Universidad de Chile). La Rosa is author of 13 books published in Peru, between them we can mention: *Psychology of Communication, Media Psychology, Social Psychology, Communication Theory, People and their Devices: Life stories about Mobile Phones and Media* and *Audience in the Global Society* (in Spanish). Author of 14 articles in books published in Peru, Germany, Ecuador, and the United States. He is Professor and Researcher in the Universidad Femenina del Sagrado Corazón in Lima. Peru. Interest areas: Social media, Mobile phones and Media Psychology.

Sónia Pedro Sebastião is an Assistant Professor at the Institute of Social and Political Science (ISCSP—ULisboa) who has been teaching Cultural Studies, Media Studies and Public Relations courses since 2001. She has published in Portugal her master dissertation about the Swiss Political System (2005), her Ph. D. thesis about the Portuguese identity and mythology (2012), a textbook of Public Relations theory and practice (Comunicação Estratégica—As Relações Públicas—2009), and a book about Contemporary Culture, contributes to cultural, media and digital studies (2012). Her main interests are related with cultural identities and the influence of culture in political constructions and speeches, intercultural business practices and the relation between tradition and technology in Politics, Pedagogy and Public Relations. She is developing a study about Digital Citizenship in Portugal (Digitania©), focusing on political participation via web-based social networks. She is a senior research fellow of the Portuguese centre of investigation: CAPP—Centre for Public Administration and Policies [http://capp.iscsp.ulisboa.pt/], accredited by the Portuguese Foundation for Science and Technology as Excellent. She is also an associated member of ESA (European Sociological Association) where she presents papers in the field of Sociology of Culture (RN07) and Media and Communication Research (RN18), ECREA, EUPRERA (European Public Relations Education and Research Association), and SOPCOM (Portuguese Association of Communication Sciences). E-mail: ssebastiao@iscsp.ulisboa.pt.

Václav Štětka is Senior Researcher and Leader of the PolCoRe research group at the Institute of Communication Studies, Charles University in Prague. Between 2009 and 2013 he was Senior Research Fellow at the Department of Politics and International Relations, University of Oxford, where he worked on a project Media and Democracy in Central and Eastern Europe. His research interests encompass political communication and the role of new media, transformation and democratization of media systems, media ownership and globalization. E-mail: stetka@fsv.cuni.cz.

Pieter Verdegem is an Assistant Professor (Tenure Track) in New Media and Information and Communication Technologies in the Department of Communication Sciences at Ghent University (Belgium). In 2009, Dr. Verdegem obtained his Ph.D. on government strategies in the information society, with a specific focus on e-government and e-inclusion. In 2011, he was a postdoctoral researcher in Uppsala's Department of Informatics and Media. His main research interests are ICT and society, social media, new media, and ICT policies and governance. He has published widely on these topics in scholarly journals. Dr. Verdegem is teaching in the New Media and Society MA programme. He is responsible for the course New Media Studies. He also teaches Media Structures and Media Policy to students in the third year of the BA study programme Communication Sciences. Dr. Verdegem is actively involved in several international networks; among them, the Management Committee of the COST Action IS0906 Transforming Audiences, Transforming Societies. E-mail: Pieter.Verdegem@UGent.be.

Igor Vobič, Ph.D., is Assistant Professor of Journalism Studies at the Faculty of Social Sciences at the University of Ljubljana in Slovenia, and a researcher at the Social Communication Research Centre at the same faculty. His research interests include societal roles of journalism in the contemporary media environment, articulations between journalism and new media, journalists' labor relations and transformations of radio journalism in the digital age. He has recently published in journals Journalism Studies, Journalism Practice, Journalism, Convergence and Javnost/The Public.

Theresa White is an Associate Professor in the Pan African Studies (PAS) Department at California State University, Northridge, having received her Ph.D. and M.A. from the University of California, Los Angeles (UCLA). She is a creative scholar, whose interests include Film Criticism; Feminist Theory; Cultural Studies; Visual Culture; Documentary Film Production; Media Representations; Critical Media Literacy; Sexuality; Masculinity and Health Disparities for Minority Populations. Having taught for more than 10 years, she has been a teaching fellow at the University of California, Los Angeles (UCLA) and a lecturer at Loyola Marymount University in Los Angeles. Dr. White is the Director and Producer of several educational documentary films that offer narratives from marginalized groups—one on globalization, self-esteem, self-image and female empowerment (*Battling Beauty: Re-Presenting Global REELatiies in the Search for Self);* one on Black Masculinity and Manhood in America (*From Buckism to Barackism: Re-Imagining Black Masculinity and Manhood*); and another on *Developing Media Savvy Adolescent Girls in the Fight Against Childhood Obesity* (M.I.S.S.). Her research has appeared in: *Journal of Black Studies* (JBS), *Journal of International Women's Studies* (JIWS), *Interactions: Studies of Communication and Culture, Journal of Visual Literacy* (JVL) and IGI Global International Publishers.

MIX
Papier aus verantwortungsvollen Quellen
Paper from responsible sources
FSC® C105338

If you have any concerns about our products,
you can contact us on
ProductSafety@springernature.com

In case Publisher is established outside the EU,
the EU authorized representative is:
Springer Nature Customer Service Center GmbH
Europaplatz 3, 69115 Heidelberg, Germany

Printed by Libri Plureos GmbH
in Hamburg, Germany